D1548039

# DISPATCHES FROM THE MEXICAN WAR

# DISPATCHES FROM THE MEXICAN WAR

By George Wilkins Kendall

*Edited and with an Introduction by*
Lawrence Delbert Cress

UNIVERSITY OF OKLAHOMA PRESS : NORMAN

By Lawrence Delbert Cress

*Citizens in Arms: The Army and Militia in American Society to the War of 1812* (Chapel Hill, N.C., 1982)

This book is published with the generous assistance of The McCasland Foundation, Duncan, Oklahoma.

Library of Congress Cataloging-in-Publication Data

Kendall, Geo. Wilkins (George Wilkins), 1809–1867.
    Dispatches from the Mexican War / by George Wilkins Kendall ; edited with an introduction by Lawrence Delbert Cress.
        p.    cm.
    Includes index.
    ISBN 0-8061-3121-7 (cloth : alk. paper)
    1. Mexican War, 1846–1848–Personal narratives.   2. Kendall, Geo. Wilkins (George Wilkins), 1809–1867.   3. Journalists–United States–Biography.   I. Cress, Lawrence Delbert.   II. Title.
E411.K32   1999
973.6'2'092–dc21                                                           98-31236
                                                                                    CIP

The paper in this book meets the guidelines for permanence and durability of the Committee on Production Guidelines for Book Longevity of the Council on Library Resources, Inc. ∞

1   2   3   4   5   6   7   8   9   10

In Memory of

Peter J. Ristuben

and

Richard L. Northcutt

and for

Meghan Carol Cress

# CONTENTS

# ILLUSTRATIONS

# ACKNOWLEDGMENTS

THE IDEA FOR THIS BOOK began when members of the staff of the Thomas A. Gilcrease Museum in Tulsa, Oklahoma, showed me a rare edition of George Kendall's *The War Between the United States and Mexico Illustrated* (New York: D. Appleton, 1851). John Drayton encouraged me to stay with the project when distractions mounted. So did my colleagues at the University of Tulsa, Joseph Bradley, Kermit Hall, and Paul Rahe, and at Willamette University, Jerry Hudson, Barbara Mahoney, and Robert Hawkinson. The work for this book was done with the support of the Jay P. Walker Chair in American History and Government at the University of Tulsa and the Dwight and Margaret Lear Chair in American History at Willamette University. Melinda Lee provided important assistance when the project began and coordinated much of the proofreading of the manuscript. Alana Hughes, Sandy Booth, and Robert Minato came to my rescue when my computer failed me. Sarah Jennings helped put the manuscript into final form, and Bill Nelson drew the maps. Joyce Tracy at the American Antiquarian Society in Worcester, Massachusetts, and Marcella Hull at the University of Texas at Arlington rendered valuable assistance.

This book is dedicated to two important friends from my past and to a friend for whom the future holds much. I am, as always, indebted most to my best friend, Linda, for her continuing support and encouragement and for one final round of proofreading.

LAWRENCE DELBERT CRESS

# DISPATCHES FROM THE MEXICAN WAR

# INTRODUCTION

## The Mexican War, Foreign Correspondents, and George Wilkins Kendall

### AMERICAN DIPLOMACY AND MEXICAN POLITICS

THE UNITED STATES DECLARED WAR on Mexico in May 1846 after a year of clumsy diplomatic and military maneuvering in both countries. Diplomatic ties had been broken fourteen months earlier when President John Tyler signed a joint congressional resolution (on March 1, 1845) inviting Texas to join the Union, and Mexico recalled its minister, Juan N. Almonte. Mexico considered the subsequent annexation—a process that culminated when Texas formally joined the Union on December 29, 1845—an act of war. Still, the Mexico government, led by the moderate and reform-minded José J. Herrera, maneuvered to find a negotiated settlement that would preserve national pride and open the way for reforms at home. Herrera's government was willing to accept the annexation, but the claim by Texas that its southwestern boundary was the Rio Grande posed a major problem.

Mexico considered the Nueces River to be its boundary with Texas. Spanish maps of colonial Mexico and the Spanish government's 1816 designation of the Nueces as the boundary between Texas and New Spain bore out that claim; so did maps prepared in 1829 and 1836 by Stephen Austin, founder of the American settlements in Texas. With independence, however, the Republic of Texas had extended its southern and western frontier to the banks of the Rio Grande, asserting an old American claim based in Thomas Jefferson's view of the extent of the Louisiana Purchase. The mouth of the Rio Grande was only 125 miles south of the Nueces. Most of the disputed territory involved the vast region north and west of San Antonio; the Arkansas River marked its northern border, and the Rio Grande, which reaches into the Rocky Mountains above Santa Fe, defined its western limits. The United States, which had supported the Texan claim during the preceding decade, now insisted that that claim be recognized in any annexation settlement with Mexico.

The territorial claims of Texas represented only a part of the expansionist ambitions of the United States. President James K. Polk was eager to add the territory between the headwaters of the Rio Grande and the Pacific Ocean to the United States, as well. Thus, when President Herrera sought to open low-level negotiations over Texas annexation in early November 1845, Polk sent John Slidell to Mexico City with instructions to offer $30 million in exchange for both the recognition of the Texan claims and the cession of the western intermountain region and California. Unfortunately, Slidell also bore diplomatic credentials that assumed the reestablishment of normal relations between the two countries.

His power already diminished by domestic political intrigue and rumors of American troop movements along the Rio Grande, Herrera now found himself in an untenable position. He had not expected diplomatic relations to be reestablished until after the Texas question had been resolved. Moreover, persuading the fractious Mexican Congress to accept the loss of Texas was a formidable challenge; no Mexican government could cede more territory, even in exchange for much-needed financial relief. Ultimately, Herrera refused to receive Slidell. By then, Herrera's administration was under attack by both democratic and conservative foes, and he was forced to resign. On January 2, 1846, General Mariano Paredes y Arrillaga—who only a year before had been Herrera's ally in the unseating of Antonio López de Santa Anna—assumed the presidency. Paredes pledged to defend Mexican territory all the way to the Sabine, the river that marked the eastern boundary of Texas.

Meanwhile, news of the diplomatic impasse facing Slidell arrived in Washington just as Texas formally entered the Union at the end of 1845. President Polk had ordered General Zachary Taylor's Army of Occupation to Corpus Christi and the western bank of the Nueces in June 1845, in anticipation of the Texas Convention's acceptance of annexation and amidst rumors that Mexican forces were gathering on the Rio Grande. Now he ordered the restless general to take up defensive positions on the northern bank of the Rio Grande near the Gulf of Mexico. Polk had no interest in the dry and largely unsettled territory immediately to the south of the Nueces, but he was anxious to pressure Mexico into negotiating the sale of California and the Southwest. Congress would leave the capital in early summer of 1846, not to return until after midterm elections in December, and Polk hoped to secure passage of legislation allowing the purchase before adjournment. Moreover, Taylor's troops had suffered from disease and desertion since arriving in Texas the summer before, and the president no doubt feared that further inaction might render the American army incapable of taking the field.

While Taylor readied his army, Slidell waited in hopes that Paredes's government might open negotiations. Those hopes ended on April 7, when word arrived in Washington that Slidell would not be received until the issues surrounding the annexation of Texas were resolved. Ten days later, Polk ordered Slidell to return home. The failure of Slidell's mission was shaped by a variety of factors, not the least of which was Polk's decision to send him to Mexico with full diplomatic credentials. The American diplomat had also found himself stymied by the tangle of Mexican politics.

For two decades, the Mexican people had struggled against deep-seated regionalism, chronic political discord, frequent military rebellions, and class division to create a nation from the northernmost remnant of the Spanish empire. The status of Texas, independent after 1836, also shaped Mexican politics. The Herrera administration had represented moderate forces committed to an amicable resolution of the Texas question. *Moderados* advocated democratic reform of the centralist constitution enacted in 1843 and supported efforts to gradually reduce the influence of the Catholic Church and the army in the affairs of state. They were suspicious of the democratic leanings of republican reformers, however, and aimed to limit participation in political affairs to Mexico's property-owning citizens.

Conservatives, with whom Paredes was allied, found in the failures of the federalist constitution of 1824 and the centralist efforts of 1843 reason to create a monarchy. They looked to the army and Catholic Church as the institutions upon which to build a strongly centralized state. Conservatives opposed concessions to the United States that would deprive Mexico of its eastern province, Texas.

The *puros* stood at the opposite extreme of the political spectrum from the conservatives. Ardent federalists, they advocated a return to the constitution of 1824, an end to the army's influence in political affairs, and the curtailment of the church's economic and political privileges. For them, federalism was a route to republican government and a means to restore Mexican control over Texas.

Opportunism played an important role in Mexican politics. Throughout the decade prior to the Mexican War, unlikely divisions and improbable alliances had rendered unpredictable both the direction of political affairs and the composition of the nation's leadership. Perhaps only the chameleonlike Santa Anna regularly and successfully negotiated the crosscurrents of Mexican politics through the 1820s and 1830s. Late in 1844, he was deposed by a coalition of *moderados* and *puros* who were disillusioned by his arbitrary dictatorial policies. A year later, Valentín Gómez Farías, long identified with *puro* causes and an ardent defender of the territorial integrity of Mexico, joined with Paredes and his conservative followers to unseat Herrera's moderate government. Indecision on the diplomatic front (Slidell remained in the Mexican capital in part because the new government vacillated on the desirability of a negotiated settlement) and military defeat along the Rio Grande in May 1846 foiled Paredes's monarchist ambitions, however. By early summer the alliance that had brought him to power collapsed. In its place stood a coalition of *puro* and *moderado* statesmen linked by the belief that the return of the former dictator Santa Anna offered the best opportunity for defeating the invading Americans.

Santa Anna returned from exile in Havana in August 1846 with the good wishes of the U.S. government. He replaced Paredes as president, resurrected the federalist constitution of 1824, and, at least for the moment, drew into a single government leaders from the *puro* and *moderado* factions. He next took to the field, challenging first Zachary Taylor on the Rio Grande and then Winfield Scott on the National Road from Vera Cruz. While political alliances in the capital continued to shift, the enterprising Santa Anna was the only constant force in an always-tumultuous political environment. Only the conquest of Mexico City would remove him from the scene and open the way for a peace with the United States under the direction of *moderado* leadership.

## THE MEXICAN WAR

On February 3, 1846, General Taylor received orders to move his Army of Occupation to the Rio Grande. On March 8, after six weeks' preparation, he marched approximately 3,500 men, with some three hundred oxcarts and mule-drawn wagons, overland from Corpus Christi. (The artillery train traveled by naval transport.) The army met only token Mexican resistance and arrived near the Rio Grande on March 24.

Taylor set up a small base camp at Point Isabel, near the mouth of the Rio Grande, and on March 28 garrisoned the main body of his army some thirty miles to the southwest, opposite Matamoros. This site became known as Fort Brown. The general immediately armed the fort with eighteen-pound guns capable of shelling the local ferry and the town square in Matamoros. Two weeks later, when reinforcements began to move into Matamoros in response to rumors that General Mariano Arista would soon take command of Mexican forces along the river, Mexican authorities demanded that Taylor's force withdraw to the region north of the Nueces. Taylor declined to move, citing the absence of orders; then, apparently without instructions from Washington, he ordered the Rio Grande closed to Mexican commerce.

Tensions rose quickly in the weeks that followed. On April 24, Arista took command of the Mexican army on the Rio Grande and informed Taylor that hostilities had commenced. Hours later he sent a large cavalry force across the river to disrupt American supply routes to Point Isabel. The next day, some of these troops ambushed a small force of American dragoons about twenty miles upriver from Fort Brown, at Rancho de Carricitos. Eleven men of the eighty-man American detachment were killed, and most of the rest were captured. Taylor received confirmation of the attack on April 26 and immediately sent the news on to Washington, along with a call for reinforcements and the observation that "hostilities may now be considered as commenced." On May 1, after reinforcing the small garrison opposite Matamoros, he withdrew his command to Point Isabel to secure his source of resupply.

The Polk administration meanwhile drifted toward war, increasingly agitated over Mexico's refusal to negotiate with Slidell but only vaguely aware of the mounting tensions on the Rio Grande. Slidell delivered his personal appraisal of affairs in Mexico to President Polk on May 8, and on May 9 the cabinet agreed that the diplomatic impasse could be resolved only by war. Later on the ninth, Taylor's report of the initiation of hostilities arrived, removing from the minds of the cabinet any lingering doubts about the appropriateness of a declaration of war. On May 11, Polk informed Congress that Mexico had "invaded our territory, and shed American blood on American soil." The message included no mention of the attempt by the United States to acquire the Southwest and California, the most important reason that a diplomatic solution had proved impossible. Taylor's report of hostilities swept away, or at least silenced, significant Whig opposition to war, and two days later, on May 13, 1846, Polk signed the congressional declaration of war against Mexico.

Almost immediately Polk sent Colonel Stephen Kearny and a troop of infantry and cavalry units west from Fort Leavenworth along the Santa Fe Trail, with instructions to occupy New Mexico and claim California for the United States. Kearny captured Santa Fe on August 19; by the end of September he was moving with one hundred dragoons westward across uncharted deserts. By that time, the U.S. Navy, with the aid of local American settlers, had taken control of California. Several minor engagements early in January 1847 broke local Mexican resistance and confirmed American authority in the region.

In the meantime, Polk sought to force Mexican authorities to cede the Southwest and California. He sent General Taylor up the Rio Grande valley toward Monterey, and General John Wool and Colonel Alexander Doniphan into Chihuahua from San Antonio and El Paso. Then, during the late summer and early autumn, recognizing that the American army could not be supported in the Mexican interior, the Polk administration shifted its strategic planning southward. In November, the president named General Scott to command an amphibious landing at Vera Cruz. Polk's instructions, which did not mention the capture of Mexico City, called upon Scott to determine the military operations necessary to achieve the administration's diplomatic goals.

Scott took Vera Cruz in late March 1847. Six months later his army stood inside the gates of Mexico City. Santa Anna's army was in disarray and the Mexican government was in turmoil, but peace was still far from at hand.

## NEWSPAPER COVERAGE OF THE WAR

During the two years in which Mexico and the United States were at war, more than a dozen American journalists reported on Zachary Taylor's military maneuvers in northern Mexico and Winfield Scott's march from Vera Cruz to the halls of the Montezumas. Many more "occasional correspondents" and countless letter writers provided news from the front, as well. Together this legion of writers gave American citizens their first-ever independent news coverage of warfare at home or abroad.

The best-known correspondent of the Mexican War was George Wilkins Kendall of the New Orleans *Picayune*, who earned acclaim as America's "eyes and ears" in Mexico. His more than two hundred dispatches, written under the headline "Special Editorial Correspondence" and signed G. W. K., appeared in the *Picayune* and dozens of other newspapers in the United States and Mexico from April 1846 through November 1847. Kendall was not the *Picayune*'s first war correspondent. Christopher Mason Haile earned that distinction with his arrival on the Rio Grande in the last week of May 1846. Haile's early dispatches contain news of the opening battles at Palo Alto and Resaca de la Palma as well as descriptions of life in the American army camps. Kendall joined him on June 6, 1846.

The *Picayune*'s reporters worked in a highly competitive environment. The *Daily Delta* and the *Crescent* had been founded by former *Picayune* employees and were the most prominent of a group of New Orleans papers that also brought news of the Mexican War to the United States. These two

George W. Kendall, ca. 1848. From a daguerreotype, courtesy Special Collections Division, The University of Texas at Arlington Libraries, Arlington, Texas.

papers created alliances with eastern newspapers, as had the *Picayune.* Their correspondents in Mexico became familiar to newspaper readers throughout the country. John N. Peoples, known to his readers as "Chaparral," wrote for both the *Delta* and the *Crescent.* J. G. H. Tobin, the only regular newspaper correspondent to see the battle of Buena Vista, sent the *Delta* "Notes from my Knapsack" which were regarded by some as among the best writing to come from the war. James L. Freaner, perhaps the first newspaperman to reach the Rio Grande in May 1846, covered Taylor's troops for the *Delta* early in the war. He and Peoples also covered the landing at Vera Cruz as well as Scott's march inland to Mexico City. Before the war was over, Freaner, known to his readers as "Mustang," was as famous as Kendall in the United States.

The *Commercial Times* and the *Tropic* (later called the *National*) also were important news sources, although they had no regular foreign correspondents. With some five hundred "printers"—as newspapermen were often called—under arms in Mexico, newsrooms were hardly dependent on full-time correspondents. Those that lacked them relied on ingenuity, the news copy of their competitors, and the frequent "specials" sent from the front by soldiers and civilians to provide news of the war to readers in New Orleans and around the country. The *Evening Mercury* employed no regular reporters in Mexico, but it remained competitive in the New Orleans market by using its afternoon publication schedule to scoop morning papers such as the *Picayune* and the *Delta*. Its agents gathered news from ships entering the mouth of the Mississippi and sent it by express couriers some sixty miles to New Orleans in time to meet afternoon press deadlines. The local Spanish-language press offered competition, as well. *La Patria* provided often-controversial pro-Mexican coverage and employed Spanish-language correspondents in Mexico, Havana, and other Latin American cities. Like many other newspapers, *La Patria* established regular correspondents in Tampico after its fall late in 1846, and in Vera Cruz after the capture of that city in March 1847.

Kendall and his colleagues in Mexico could trace their craft to its origins in the efforts of London newspapers during the 1790s to gather news of the events surrounding the French Revolution and the rise and fall of Napoleon. The *Times* of London, frustrated by its lack of access to official news sources and suspicious of government efforts to limit its coverage of events abroad, led a group of newspapers in establishing networks of correspondents capable of providing quick and reliable news from the Continent. Coverage through the Napoleonic era and after was sporadic at best, however. Henry Crabb Robinson, the first reporter sent abroad by a major newspaper, provided the increasingly independent *Times* with hard-to-get news from Hamburg and Madrid during two assignments between January 1807 and early 1809. Because Robinson had a propensity for literary rather than political news and an informal approach to his duties, he kept his readers waiting for his reports of Napoleon's victory over the

Russians at Friedland in June 1807 and the British defeat on the Spanish Peninsula at Corunna in January 1809. Unhappy with the attention Napoleon's victories got in the independent press, the Duke of Wellington and other British commanders greatly restricted press coverage in the last years of the war with France. No British journalists were even near the armies during the later Peninsula campaign or at Waterloo.

Peace brought the return of independent British correspondents to Europe, now in search of political and financial news. By the 1830s, London's newspapers, the *Times* foremost among them, had correspondents in the capitals of western Europe as well as in Constantinople, New York, and Washington.

Until the 1830s, American newspapers maintained no foreign correspondents, but they were filled with foreign news. The enterprising Charleston *Courier* gathered news from ships calling en route from Havana to Spain and gave its readers the country's first accounts of the political revolutions that rocked Latin America in the 1820s. With the advent of the steamship and the mass-circulation penny press in the mid-1830s, foreign correspondents became a part of American journalism. Although William Howard Russell of the *Times* of London is often called "the world's first war correspondent" for his dispatches from the Crimean War, Russell appeared on the scene nearly a decade after American reporters filled the penny press in the United States with dispatches from the war with Mexico.

James Gordon Bennett, the Scottish-born founder of the New York *Morning Herald*, began his newspaper career translating news of political rebellion in Latin America for the Charleston *Courier*. In the late 1830s, the *Herald* employed correspondents in London, Glasgow, Paris, Brussels, Berlin, and Rome. Bennett then quickly extended his network of sources of "specials" to Mexico, Canada, and the Republic of Texas. By the eve of the Mexican War, Bennett had made the *Herald* the best-known paper in the United States by distributing the reports of his foreign correspondents, without charge, to smaller newspapers outside the New York area. Until telegraph service revolutionized the communication of news in 1847, Bennett and his competitors used courier pigeons and pony express riders to speed the news from steamships arriving off the Atlantic coast and from remote inland locations to the waiting presses.

The *Picayune*, New Orleans's leading newspaper by the mid-1840s, had also established itself as an important source of the news on the national scene. It used trains, stagecoaches, horseback riders, and steamboats to bring news from the nation's major eastern cities twenty-four to seventy-two hours ahead of the public mail service. With typesetters on board the steamers that carried the news from Mobile to New Orleans, press-ready forms could then be delivered directly to the newspaper's office.

The *Picayune*'s ability to send news in the opposite direction provided the basis for Kendall's preeminence as a correspondent before and during the war with Mexico. The towns and cities along the Mississippi and Ohio Rivers and along the eastern seaboard from Charleston to Boston were eager for news from Mexico. The U.S. government and the independent press used steamboats and sailing ships to take the news from the Southwest to New Orleans and beyond. Supported by free postal service for the exchange of newspapers, editors around the country had an ample supply of copy.

Speed was everything in the competitive news business. Private efforts to construct a telegraph line from Washington to New Orleans got under way in November 1846, after Congress refused to finance the project, but by war's end telegraph service had reached only as far as Petersburg, Virginia. In the absence of a complete telegraph system, alliances among newspapers to expedite the movement of news were common. The *Picayune* joined with the Baltimore *Sun*, the Charleston *Courier*, and other newspapers to share news through an express system that depended upon a private pony express—a common but actually illegal practice—to cover the breaks in steam and wire services. Such cooperative systems were effective. Much to the chagrin of U.S. mail officials, President Polk got the news of the American amphibious landing at Vera Cruz from a telegraph message sent to him by the Baltimore *Sun*.

When war broke out in May 1846, it took nineteen days to get news from the Rio Grande to Washington. By September, Kendall had organized a team of mounted couriers to move the news of the battle of Monterey overland from the interior to Point Isabel, where it was taken by waiting steamers on to New Orleans—all in just eight days' time. On the other hand, rumors circulated for a month before official word arrived describing the bloody battle at Buena Vista in February 1847. Dispatches from the camps around Vera Cruz moved quickly, taking advantage of the regular steamer traffic to New Orleans and Mobile. But when the army moved inland, abandoning its lines of communication to the coast, news slowed to a trickle. The American press reported rumors of Scott's mid-September conquest of Mexico City within ten days, but a month passed before word arrived from the newspaper correspondents who were on the scene. Military and bandit activity on the road between the capital and the coast hindered the movement of news during the winter months. Yet, in general, public and private news service improved as the war continued. By the summer of 1848, news regularly traveled from Mexico City to Washington in just seventeen days.

## GEORGE WILKINS KENDALL

George Kendall was both a product and a creator of the innovative and competitive newspaper environment of the 1840s. He was born to Thaddeus Kendall and Abigail Wilkins on August 22, 1809, in Mont Vernon, New Hampshire, near the Vermont border. He spent his early childhood on the move through Vermont and southeastern Canada with his father, a rambling shopkeeper. At the age of seven, George left his wandering family in Montreal and joined the household of his grandfather Samuel Wilkins, a prominent figure in local political, church, and military affairs in Amherst, New Hampshire. There he received a rudimentary education, ample exposure to public affairs, and an introduction to the newspaper world.

In 1825, the young man was apprenticed as a printer in the shop of the Amherst *Herald*, a newspaper launched by one of the Kendalls' cousins to promote the Universalist movement. The newspaper did not last the year, but George Kendall's newspaper career had begun. He spent a year with the Boston *Statesman*, during which time he began to nurture what would be a lifelong interest in theatre. Then he was off to New York City, but the lack of printing work sent him north to Albany and west along the Erie Canal into Ohio and Indiana. Kendall paused in Detroit in 1829 to gain a journeyman printer's training before heading off through the Old Northwest, down the Mississippi to New Orleans, and across the Deep South to Mobile, through Georgia, and on to Charleston. He stopped in North Carolina for a time to run a stage line, gaining experience that would serve him well in Mexico. Kendall arrived back in New York City in 1832. He was twenty-three years old, well traveled, and a master of his trade.

A cholera epidemic in New York City and the lure of the Southwest soon had Kendall on the move again. By 1835, he was back in New Orleans. Two years later, he founded the *Picayune* with Francis A. Lumsden, his friend since 1834, when they had worked together at the *National Intelligencer* in Washington. They named the paper for a Spanish silver piece valued at one-sixteenth of a dollar, the smallest coin in circulation in New Orleans at the time. Published on cheap paper, supported by aggressive reporting, and filled with news and features that poked fun at local affairs as well as reports reprinted from newspapers around the country, the *Picayune* was the South's first penny press.

The founding of the *Picayune* marked the beginning of a long and successful partnership characterized by Kendall's frequent travels in search of news and Lumsden's steady service in the newspaper's editorial office. In its first year, the newspaper survived a national economic collapse and a yellow fever epidemic in New Orleans. In 1838, the publishers launched a weekly edition and extended circulation into the newspaper-scarce Republic of Texas. In the same year, they established a private pony express service linking the *Picayune* to the newspapers on the eastern seaboard. But it was to the west that Kendall and the *Picayune* were drawn most strongly. The newspaper provided extensive coverage of affairs in the new republic and quickly earned a reputation as an advocate of expansionism, Texas annexation, and, if necessary, war with Mexico. Lumsden traveled to Texas in 1838 and 1839, seeking news and opportunities to expand the *Picayune*'s circulation. By 1840, the newspaper's circulation in the republic stood at about 2,000.

Kendall went to Texas for the first time in May 1841. He had been looking for an opportunity to explore the western interior. He made plans to join Colonel Pierce M. Butler, a federal Indian agent and former governor of South Carolina, on an expedition from the Red River to Santa Fe, but the trip failed to materialize. Not long afterward, the news reached New Orleans that Texas governor Mirabeau Lamar was mounting an expedition to Santa Fe with the aim of cementing the republic's claims to the vast northwestern region that extended to the headwaters of the Rio Grande, in what is now south central Colorado. Texas officials sought more than territorial aggrandizement. They hoped that the Santa Fe expedition could redirect the rich trade of the upper Rio Grande, then linked to St. Louis over the Santa Fe Trail, south across the plains and into the commerce-starved ports of the Texas gulf coast.

Kendall decided to go along on Lamar's expedition. He supported the republic's territorial and commercial aspirations, and he was drawn by a journalist's curiosity. He obtained a passport from the Mexican vice-consul in New Orleans so that he could leave the expedition before it reached Santa Fe and travel south through central Mexico, all the way to the capital. He also planned to send reports of his travels back to the *Picayune*, a habit he had developed during his trips along the eastern seaboard in search of supplies and equipment for the newspaper.

Kendall traveled by boat to Houston and then overland to Austin to meet his fellow adventurers. A delay in the expedition's departure gave him time for a hurried trip eighty miles south to San Antonio, in which he traversed the Texas hill country that would eventually become his home.

Back in the Texas capital, Kendall found a spot in one of the expedition's wagons, as he had broken his right ankle on the eve of departure. The group left Austin on June 18, 1841.

The Santa Fe expedition turned into a disaster, and through it Kendall established his reputation as a courageous adventurer, a keen observer, and a well-informed commentator on the affairs of Texas and Mexico. His *Narrative of the Texan Santa Fe Expedition,* published in New York in 1844, recounts the ill-planned and hazardous trip west, the group's capture by Mexican officials near Santa Fe, the execution of three of their leaders, the long and torturous march to Mexico City, and the imprisonment that followed. Kendall and a small band of Texans were captured near Santa Fe on September 16, having gone ahead of the main party to make contact with Mexican authorities. A month later Kendall was sent south to Mexico City with 180 other prisoners, a journey that brought him to the outskirts of the capital early in 1842.

The prisoners were the objects of bellicose comments in the American press and in Congress over the next few months, as British and American diplomats negotiated with Santa Anna's government for their release. Kendall suffered from smallpox while imprisoned and spent two months incarcerated among lepers before being held in chains with a contingent of survivors from the Santa Fe expedition. He finally gained his freedom in April 1842. Traversing the route he would see again with Scott's army, he returned home to New Orleans through Vera Cruz. He immediately began to provide the *Picayune*'s readers with reports of his experiences as well as insights into Mexican affairs.

During Kendall's year-long absence, the *Picayune* had established a reputation as an authority on the Southwest. Correspondents along the eastern seaboard and in Texas and Mexico had kept its columns filled with news of Kendall's plight and other developments in the region. When Mexican forces attacked San Antonio in March and again in September 1842, the *Picayune* provided news to the nation. When Great Britain extended diplomatic recognition to Texas later the same year, the newspaper closely followed efforts to prevent the annexation of the republic. Reports filed from Texas and Mexico described the efforts of British chargé d'affaires Charles Elliot and his French counterpart, Alphonse de Saligny, to arrange Mexican recognition and favorable trade concessions for Texas.

In April 1845, Kendall traveled to Texas to report on the diplomatic intrigue and to encourage supporters of annexation. While he was there, a *Picayune* reporter in Vera Cruz spotted the British chargé d'affaires returning from a secret mission to Mexico City. Weeks later, word swirled through the

country that the Mexican Congress had agreed to accept Texas independence in exchange for the republic's renunciation of annexation to the
United States. Through his dispatches published in the *Picayune*, Kendall
contributed to the popular uproar that followed, and he added to the
widespread rejoicing when the Texas Congress rejected the Mexican offer
and embraced annexation in late June 1845. Through all of this, *Picayune*
reports and editorials, often bearing George Kendall's byline, could be
found in newspapers around the nation. Indeed, on the eve of the war with
Mexico, no other newspaper rivaled the *Picayune* as a source of news
about Texas and Mexico.

## REPORTING FROM THE FRONT

Kendall left New Orleans for Texas late in March 1846 to cover the treaty
negotiations being conducted by the U.S. government with the Comanches
north of Austin. Perhaps he had not anticipated the outbreak of the war; or
he may have left New Orleans in order to position himself closer to the
Texas-Mexico frontier. In the months before Kendall's departure, the pages
of the *Picayune* were filled with news of the Slidell mission and troop movements along the Rio Grande frontier. In any event, when news of hostilities
reached Kendall, he immediately struck out across the open country of
south-central Texas, arriving at Point Isabel, nearly four hundred miles
away, in early June, already having sent a dozen dispatches. With C. M.
Haile covering events at the army's headquarters for the *Picayune*, Kendall
joined a company of Texas Rangers scouting the road to Monterey. In the
weeks that followed, he regularly traveled with Benjamin McCulloch's Texas
cavalry while organizing a system of mounted couriers and steamboats to
send news back to New Orleans. That system served the *Picayune* well in
September, when American and Mexican forces clashed south of the Rio
Grande at the Mexican town of Monterey.

The battle of Monterey was the first major engagement covered by
regular correspondents. Private couriers carried the news of the army's
exploits back to New Orleans in eight days, beating the government agents
who bore the official news. The *Picayune* published scanty details on
October 3, following with Haile's full account the next day. (The *Delta's*
James Freaner also witnessed the battle, but his reports never reached the
eager hands of typesetters in New Orleans.) Kendall sent only sketchy
reports before leaving northern Mexico late in October.

After arriving in New Orleans on November 13, he wasted no time filing
a lengthy account of the battle in an extra, published on November 19.

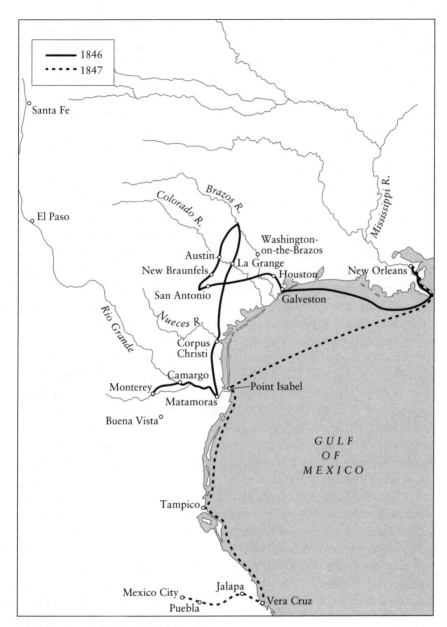

Kendall's travels during the Mexican War.

Until this point, most of the reports in the *Picayune*, and therefore much of the nation's coverage, had been from Haile. When the war moved south to Vera Cruz early in 1847, Kendall emerged as the *Picayune*'s foremost correspondent. He led a band of journalists covering what was perhaps the war's most reported event, the landing at Vera Cruz. He broke the news of the American victory at Cerro Gordo and kept readers informed of the rumors of peace and the machinations of Mexican politics through the slow news summer of 1847. His reports of the American victories at Contreras and Churubusco were the first to be published in the United States. Kendall shared with Freaner the honor of sending to New Orleans the first full account of Scott's capture of Mexico City in September 1847.

After the center of military activity had moved south to Vera Cruz and inland after April 1847, most newspapers, including the *Picayune*, had begun to maintain correspondents in Vera Cruz to gather news. D. Sully handled the *Picayune*'s affairs there, with important assistance from Francis M. Dimond, a customs agent and former American consul in the city. After Cerro Gordo, General Scott abandoned regular communications with the coast, leaving correspondents the option of either waiting for the occasional military train on its way to the coast or hiring couriers to make their way through the bands of guerrillas and robbers that frequently disrupted travel. Kendall and Freaner, among others, depended on private express riders until the army established reliable mail service from Mexico City to Vera Cruz in March 1848. Kendall kept four to six riders in hire, frequently sending out duplicate copies of dispatches at intervals of several hours. For the couriers, such travel was dangerous. As many as twenty-five couriers serving American correspondents were captured or killed during the summer and fall of 1847.

Whereas war correspondents in Europe had found access to battlefields difficult, Kendall and his colleagues in the press generally enjoyed close ties with army commanders and regularly used military transport and personnel to move information to New Orleans. Haile, whose past military experience probably opened many doors, joined General William J. Worth's staff as a volunteer aide during the battle for Monterey and was with the army when it broke through the west side of the city on September 23. Kendall saw combat on September 22 while riding with a company of Texas Rangers that served as Worth's scouts. He then served as General Worth's messenger during the heavy house-to-house fighting on September 23. Afterward, Kendall was never far from Worth's headquarters, a circumstance that inevitably shaped his coverage of hostilities. His dispatches from Monterey, for example, said little about the exploits of the troops commanded by

General David E. Twiggs. As Kendall noted, with the army "operating in different places at the same time, it is impossible to get hold of everything." He also missed General Taylor's victory at Buena Vista in mid-February, having made his way, with virtually all of the other correspondents, to Tampico to cover Scott's attack on Vera Cruz.

Moreover, when Worth's forces were engaged, Kendall often became as much a soldier as a journalist. After seeing action at Monterey, he observed the battle of Cerro Gordo from the rear with those of Worth's troops who were being held in reserve. At Contreras, Churubusco, and the gates of Mexico City, Worth's division was again heavily committed and so was Kendall. At Churubusco, General Gideon Pillow praised Kendall for "promptly bearing and delivering orders." In Worth's official account of the battle of Molino del Rey, he cited Kendall as being among several civilians who "came upon the field, volunteered their acceptable services, and conducted themselves, in the transmission of orders, with conspicuous gallantry." Although Kendall never mentioned it, Worth reported that the correspondent had been wounded while carrying orders during the fighting at Chapultepec. The *Delta*'s Freaner reported the incident, and the *Picayune* then advised its readers that its lead correspondent had been hit by a musket ball, suffering a slight wound to the knee.

Not all the correspondents' military duty was at the front. While the army was in Tampico preparing to move on Vera Cruz, Kendall and Lumsden apparently served as judges in a court that tried soldiers for civil crimes.

## KENDALL'S WAR

Kendall's close ties with the military did not mean that he was uncritical. On the Rio Grande, at Vera Cruz, and during the march to Mexico City, he frequently criticized the government's failure to adequately supply the army. He voiced his dissatisfaction over the lenient terms Taylor had granted the Mexican army at Monterey, wrongly blaming the Polk administration more than the army for allowing less than a total surrender. He defended Scott's decision to lay siege at Vera Cruz rather than storm the city's defenses, arguing that the strategy had saved both American and Mexican lives, and he defended the reallocation of military resources from the Rio Grande to Vera Cruz early in 1847. Throughout the war, he never missed a chance to complain about what he considered to be the Polk administration's misguided efforts to secure a negotiated settlement with Santa Anna. When Scott agreed to an armistice after the victories at Contreras and Churubusco, Kendall was particularly critical, expressing the view that Mexico City could have been taken with ease. That criticism sparked a lively debate in the Washington *Union* and other Democratic Party newspapers. The papers charged the war's most prominent correspondent with unfair attacks on administration policy and with inadequately covering the exploits of Democratic generals such as Franklin Pierce and James Shields.

Kendall had a keen eye, a good ear, and a sharp wit. He was intrigued with the lives and customs of the ordinary people he met. Crossing the Brazos River early in May 1846, he described a band of Comanches, noting in particular the camp activities of the women and children. The customs and conditions of the German settlers in the Texas hill country caught his eye, too, as did the efforts of Mexican peasants to deal with the spring floods along the Rio Grande.

Caught up in the spirit of Manifest Destiny, Kendall reflects in his writing an expansionist vision of America and condescension toward all things Mexican. At Matamoros, he reported the transformation of that small town into "an American city," noting later that the American occupation of northern Mexico represented "a long step toward civilization." "The Mexicans," he continued, "would never have made anything out of the country." At Tampico early in March 1847, he celebrated what he called "the go-aheadity of the Anglo-Saxon race." Throughout the war, he took great delight in reporting the arrival at the army's encampments of theatre troupes, hostelries, food vendors, newspapers, and other evidence of the American culture.

The rugged Mexican landscape attracted Kendall, even as he described the clash of armies. Contempt for Mexico's civilian and military leadership pervades his coverage of the last six months of the war. When the press of events allowed, he frequently wrote reflective pieces, news analysis of a sort, that explored topics as wide-ranging as Santa Anna's intrigues, the goals of the Polk administration, life in the army camps, and the terrors of Mexico City earthquakes.

Kendall saw and described the costs of war. While the popular prints that circulated during and after the war tended to ignore its horror, Kendall and his colleagues did not. Their graphic accounts provided images of war at a time when newspapers still lacked the technology for mass printing that would make the lithograph a central feature of news coverage during the American Civil War. Kendall's description of an exhausted Mississippi soldier trying to sleep with all his "clothes on, belted round with two pistols, and a Bowie, boots on, and spurs to boot, out doors on the ground in a single blanket, and raining at that," left little doubt about the conditions of military service. Of the much-covered amphibious landing at Vera Cruz, he wrote a short and vivid account of the first wave of "no less than seventy heavy surf boats, containing nearly 4000 [American] regulars," every man anxious to be first to plunge into the waist-deep water as the boats neared the shore, and of the soldiers' subsequent march without drinking water, "under a broiling sun."

Kendall mixed reports of troop movements, artillery exchanges, and infantry encounters with often graphic descriptions of the dead and dying. At Monterey, he provided a first-hand account of street fighting that caught an American unit in a "deluge of musket balls and grape." Near Vera Cruz, he described the death of a young captain when a "cannon ball carried away almost his entire head, took off the arm of a drummer boy and wounded a corporal besides." He worried aloud about the tremendous losses sustained by Worth's division during the strategically pointless victory at Molino del Rey, and described in unflinching terms the assault at Chapultepec. Recalling the entry into Mexico City, Kendall recounted heavy street fighting. "Orders were given," he wrote, "to shoot every man in all the houses from which the firing came while the guns of the different light artillery batteries swept the streets in all directions." Finally, Kendall reported with clear pleasure the execution of fifty deserters outside Mexico City. The last thirty, he told his readers, "were compelled to stand upon the gallows until the flag they had deserted was flying from Chapultepec, and were then all swung off at the same time."

Writing two and sometimes three or more times a day, pausing in the midst of front-line confusion, sorting through rumors and incomplete reports, Kendall conveyed to readers across the United States not only the excitement of soldiers engaged in combat but the tragedy of civilians swept up in the forces of war. He reported the plight of civilians caught in the street fighting in Monterey, and described the conditions of those trapped inside the besieged city of Vera Cruz. In May 1847, he sent to the United States accounts of starvation in Mexico City: "Gaunt distress stalks through every street and thoroughfare, and even the better disposed are compelled to steal or call upon charity to save them from starvation."

His dispatches, especially those penned during the rush of battle, had the urgency and immediacy of modern journalism. Pausing for a moment to send off a dispatch during the battle at Cerro Gordo, Kendall told his readers: "I write this amid confusion of all kinds, and with no other table than knees. A hundred Mexican officers are around me, making out their paroles, while our own dead are being carried by and consigned their long resting-place by the road-side." Welcomed by readers at home, such accounts, together with detailed casualty lists, occasionally drew the ire of American military and civilian leaders.

Kendall filed his last Mexican War dispatch on October 29, 1847, giving no particular indication that he was soon to return to New Orleans. (He rarely used his column to discuss his own activities.) On November 1, he left Mexico City with the first military train to depart for the coast after Scott's capture of the city. His departure was no secret, however. The *American Star's* October 28, 1847, edition noted that Kendall "returns home with the train that leaves during the week." The *American Star* continued: "He is no stranger in Mexico, and his letters, both from this and Gen. Taylor's column of the army, have been copied into almost every journal in the Union. We observe that his name is honorably mentioned in Gen. Pillow's report of the battles of Contreras and Churubusco, as also in that of Gen. Worth of the storming of the Chapultepec and the garitas. He is at present in Mexico as an individual in civil life only, but he has lost no opportunity of taking part in the great battles before the city." *Picayune* readers learned of his pending return on November 6, 1847, when the paper printed, along with the *American Star's* report, the following brief notice: "We learn with mingled feelings of pleasure and regret that our associate now in Mexico is ere this upon his journey home."

## DIPLOMATIC RESOLUTION

Scott's army occupied Mexico City and Kendall was on his way home, but the war was far from over. The diplomatic issues that had led to war remained unresolved. Moreover, Polk and his advisors had become convinced that military conquest alone could not end hostilities. Since Slidell's recall in April 1846, the Polk administration had combined military pressure with diplomatic initiatives in an effort to satisfy American territorial ambitions. Peace "feelers" extended concurrently with Taylor's campaigning in northern Mexico during the summer of 1846 produced no results; neither did secret communications with the Mexican government during the following winter. Military successes at Buena Vista and Vera Cruz in February and March 1847 raised hopes once more that a diplomatic settlement might be obtained. The realization by Americans that a peace treaty would have to be negotiated before diplomatic relations could be resumed increased the prospects for peace.

In April, the Polk administration sent Nicholas P. Trist, chief clerk of the State Department, to Mexico with instructions to offer up to $30 million for Texas and the disputed territory west and north of the Nueces River,

New Mexico, and upper and lower California. The United States also hoped to secure the right of transit across the Isthmus of Tehuantepec. The mission was intended to be secret—Polk hoped to avoid the criticism of Mexicans and Americans who opposed a peaceful settlement—but news of Trist's arrival in Mexico appeared in Kendall's dispatches and elsewhere by mid-May.

Tensions between the diplomat and General Scott derailed initial efforts to open diplomatic discussions, but by June Trist had enlisted the good offices of the British minister in Mexico, Charles Bankhead, to deliver the American proposal to Mexican authorities. July saw a flurry of activity at Scott's headquarters in Puebla and Mexico City, but no diplomatic resolution. With Scott's army threatening to take Mexico City, negotiations were opened again at the end of August.

The Polk administration, however, knew little or nothing of Trist's efforts after early June. Word trickled into Washington of Scott's military successes in August and the armistice that followed, but the administration still had no understanding of the diplomatic situation. Indeed, Polk thought that Scott and Trist had been duped by Santa Anna, a view informed in part by Kendall's highly critical assessment of the August armistice that appeared in the *Picayune*. Believing that Scott had sought the armistice and that Mexican authorities had rejected the terms included in Trist's instructions, and unaware of the capture of the capital and the fall of Santa Anna, Polk ordered the diplomat's recall on October 5. He had no immediate plans to send a new emissary. If Mexico wanted peace, it should surrender to General Scott.

Trist did not receive word of his recall until November 16. He had spent the past two months awaiting new instructions from Washington and observing the chaotic political situation in Mexico. He was shocked when he received Polk's directions, conveyed through Secretary of State James Buchanan, and considered them misinformed, ill-conceived, and poorly timed. That the president knew nothing of the events of mid-September was understandable; more troubling was Polk's apparent sympathy with the sentiment of some in the United States that peace should be linked to the annexation of all of Mexico. Only days before, debate in the Mexican Congress had taken a moderate turn that held out real prospects for peace. Fearful that failure to negotiate with Mexico's newly named peace commissioners would lead to the renewal of hostilities, and convinced that territorial acquisition south of the Rio Grande would threaten the political stability of the United States, Trist decided to remain in Mexico. He made this decision in consultation with his close friend James L. Freaner, the

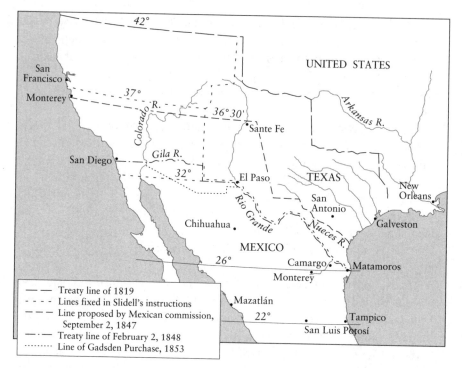

Boundaries proposed for the Southwest.

*Delta* correspondent and Kendall's rival. In early December, Trist advised Buchanan that he intended to negotiate a treaty based on the instructions sent with him in April.

   The negotiations that led to the signing of the Treaty of Guadalupe Hidalgo began on January 2, 1848, and proceeded quickly. Any lingering hopes that British pressure on the United States might produce more favorable results for Mexico disappeared by mid-December, when news arrived that Great Britain had no plans to intervene. About the same time, General Scott, who supported Trist's plan, issued a general order proclaiming an intention to expand the American occupation. Moreover, President Polk had earlier severely reprimanded Trist for even suggesting a compromise involving the Nueces. All those involved recognized that the acceptance of the Rio Grande as the Texas-Mexico border was a necessary starting point for any successful treaty. In this environment, the commissioners quickly established the southwestern boundary of Texas at the Rio Grande. Discussions over the boundary that stretched from the Rio Grande at El Paso to the Gila River and on to the Pacific Ocean just south of San Diego took longer to conclude—in part because accurate information about the geography of the region was hard to obtain—but the basis for an agreement was in place by January 9. Trist committed the United States to pay $15 million for the territory.

Negotiations then turned to an assortment of nonterritorial issues. Trist agreed to commit the United States to pay more than $3 million to satisfy Americans' claims against the Mexican government, and to accept responsibility for maintaining order among the American Indians residing in the ceded territories. American aspirations to secure transit rights across the Isthmus of Tehuantepec generated no serious discussion. The British merchant house Manning and Mackintosh had acquired that concession the year before—one of many ties between British consul Ewen C. Mackintosh and the Santa Anna government—and British officials in Mexico were insistent that it not be traded away.

Meanwhile, Trist labored under the fear that new orders would arrive from Washington that would force him to end negotiations. He also worried that Scott would succumb to pressures from Washington to actually expand the area of the army's occupation—an act that might derail negotiations entirely. When Mexican officials hesitated to allow their commissioners to sign the negotiated treaty—since they sought financial pledges to assure them of the government's viability and of the immediate withdrawal of American forces—Trist and Scott maneuvered to pressure the Mexican government to sign. Through Percy W. Doyle, the ranking British official in the capital, they informed the Mexican commissioners that Scott would occupy the temporary capital of Querétaro if the delays continued. Doyle also reported that private sources were prepared to loan up to $300,000 to the Mexican government until the United States paid some of the funds agreed to in the treaty.

This maneuvering, coupled with mounting pressures on the government from Mexican proponents of annexation with the United States, brought an end to the stalemate. On January 31, Manuel de la Peña y Peña, Mexico's provisional president, ordered that the treaty be signed. Two days later, Trist and the Mexican commissioners met a few miles north of the capital at the shrine of Mexico's patron, Our Lady of Guadalupe Hidalgo, to formally conclude their negotiations.

On February 3, Freaner left Mexico City for Vera Cruz and Washington carrying a copy of Trist's treaty and dispatches from Scott concerning the military situation around the Mexican capital. He traveled in the service of the U.S. government and not his newspaper, the *Delta*. Close behind him followed a courier in the employ of the *Picayune*. The two men reached the coast at about the same time. Freaner departed immediately for Mobile aboard the USS *Iris*. The *Picayune*'s courier was delayed in Vera Cruz, because Scott had directed the port closed for two days to ensure that the official news reached Washington ahead of newspaper accounts. However, the *New Orleans*, which carried the *Picayune*'s courier, outsailed the *Iris*, and the two steamers reached their destinations on the American Gulf Coast near the same time. The *Picayune* sold a special edition on the streets of New Orleans on February 13 and immediately sent the news east through its system of express riders. Aided by telegraph service from Petersburg to Washington, the *Picayune* delivered news of the treaty to the newspaper offices of Washington on the afternoon of February 19; Freaner arrived at Secretary Buchanan's door later that evening. Before the week was out, Kendall's well-oiled courier system had spread the news all the way to New England.

President Polk convened the cabinet on February 20 to discuss whether the results of Trist's unauthorized negotiations should be submitted to the Senate. His advisors were split, but Polk forwarded the treaty, asking only for the rejection of a provision recognizing the legitimacy of Mexican land grants in Texas. Polk might well have refused to submit the treaty, since it had been negotiated against his direct order. But the president faced an increasingly unpredictable political situation. The new Whig majority in the House of Representatives had opened the new year with a resolution condemning the war and demanding that peace come without territorial gains for the United States. Similar sentiment existed in the Senate, but so did the view that Scott's campaign into central Mexico had earned the United States territorial concessions far south of the Rio Grande. Polk had little choice but to push for ratification before the varying sentiments about the territorial provisions of a peace settlement combined to deny him his territorial ambitions.

The Senate debate, conducted in secret through the last week of February, confirmed Polk's fears and forced him to send a second message urging ratification. He warned the Senate that failure to ratify might mean the indefinite continuation of the war at a great expense of lives and treasure. Meanwhile, popular sentiment, fanned by the *Picayune*'s account of the treaty, clearly supported peace. Finally, on March 10, 1847, the Senate narrowly approved Trist's treaty ending the war. The Mexican Congress, as reluctant to act as some in the U.S. Senate, ratified the treaty late in May. President Polk received the officially ratified document on July 4, 1848.

The American occupation had all but ended by July. The evacuation of the American army had begun in mid-May, as word of the impending ratification circulated around the Mexican capital. In the last weeks of May, preparations at Vera Cruz for the disembarkation of the army began with the collection of transports and the assignment of General Persifor F. Smith to oversee activities there. The garrisons at outlying posts around Mexico City were abandoned. American troops began to leave the Mexican capital on May 27; the last contingent of General Worth's Second Division left the city on June 12 and was en route from Vera Cruz to New Orleans by the middle of July. The occupation officially ended early in August, when the First Artillery, a company of dragoons, and a contingent from the quarter-masters' corps charged with the removal of the last of the army's supplies departed the coastal city.

### KENDALL'S POSTWAR CAREER

During his last days in Mexico City, Kendall collaborated with Carl Nebel, a German artist already well known for his depictions of the Mexico landscape, on an account of the Mexican War illustrated with a set of lavish and authoritative lithographs. While Nebel remained behind to complete sketches and paintings of the battlefield sites in the area surrounding Mexico City, Kendall returned briefly to New Orleans, then toured the major cities of the east coast. He departed New York City for Europe the day after the U.S. Senate completed its work on the Treaty of Guadalupe Hidalgo. In London and Paris, Kendall worked on his book and arranged for its publication.

*The War Between the United States and Mexico Illustrated*, a portfolio-size text with twelve hand-colored lithographs depicting the major battles of the war, received high praise when it appeared; one reviewer noted that "the work itself bears witness, that the truly graphic description could only have been accomplished by an observer, and that, an acute, accurate, and impartial one." Kendall had visited every battle site depicted save Buena Vista. The Boston *Sentinel* considered the volume's stunning color lithographs and battle accounts "valuable to the historian, invaluable to the military man . . . and a beautiful specimen of art."

Years later Kendall wrote, but never published, an extended history of the Mexican War. His plans to write while in Paris were set aside when the Revolution of 1848 swept the city; he had arrived in Europe only weeks after the abdication of Louis Philippe and the establishment of the Third Republic. He was in the streets of Paris during the unsuccessful June Days workers' uprising and, during the summer and fall, watched the machinations of the General Assembly that led to the installation of Louis Napoleon as president in December. He found himself supplying the *Picayune's* readers with a steady stream of news and analysis describing the tumultuous events that overwhelmed Europe at mid-century.

Kendall had little confidence in the liberal reformers in France or elsewhere. His travels to the capitals of Europe—including Berlin, where he witnessed great political demonstrations—only confirmed his general view that Europe was ill-prepared for democratic liberalism. The tide of reform waned in the new decade, but Kendall continued to inform the *Picayune's* readers of events in Europe periodically until he permanently departed the Continent for Texas in 1856.

Kendall's days in Europe were interrupted by frequent trips to the United States. In 1850, he was in New York to sign a contract with D. Appleton and Company for his illustrated history of the war. He visited New Orleans, then traveled to Texas, where he began a search for land on which to settle. Back in the United States the next year, he visited New York and New Orleans and prepared to join an expedition heading west from St. Louis for Fort Laramie. Treaty negotiations were scheduled with the American Indian nations of the front range of the Rockies, and Kendall planned to report on the proceedings for the *Picayune*. He failed to reach Fort Kearny (in what is today south-central Nebraska) in time to join the main expedition, however, and was forced to limit his reporting to a smaller council held in neighboring Pawnee County.

This was Kendall's last venture into the west in search of news, but he was in Texas again looking for land before 1852 came to a close. This time he was successful. Wandering through the open country between the Nueces and Brazos Rivers, Kendall returned to the Texas hill country around New Braunfels—a town he had visited en route to the Rio Grande in 1846—and there purchased an expanse of land upon which he would establish a successful sheep ranch. Although he would make regular trips to his thriving homestead, nearly four years would pass before he moved his growing family from Paris to Texas.

In 1849 Kendall had married Adeline de Valcourt, the eighteen-year-old daughter of a French military officer and a member of an aristocratic family of declining means. The marriage was little known in the United States, although speculation about the forty-year-old Kendall's marital designs were not uncommon in the American press. Fearing that his mother would not approve of Adeline's Catholic faith, Kendall insisted that news of his marriage not cross the Atlantic while the older woman lived. Rather amazingly, he and his wife managed a trip to the United States in 1851 without divulging their secret. The couple had four children while they lived in Paris.

In 1856, Kendall moved his family to Texas, along with a French Rambouillet Merino flock that became the foundation for sheep ranching in the state. In the hill country that as a county would bear his name, he spent his remaining years raising sheep, working on his history of the Mexican War, and writing occasionally for the *Picayune*. His final years were difficult. The Civil War disrupted Kendall's access to the wool markets in Atlanta and cut off the income he had come to expect from the *Picayune*. Bad weather, inflated Confederate currency, reluctant slaves, Indian unrest, and an unreliable free labor market made life precarious as well. Peace reopened the market for wool and saw Kendall, after a brief trip to Paris in 1866, take an active role as the editor of the *Picayune*. Seeking to avoid the tumultuous political environment that engulfed postwar New Orleans, he set a firm editorial policy promoting agricultural and industrial progress as the key to southern reconstruction. His health deteriorated steadily, though. A life of adventure on the frontier was taking its toll. Burdened by personal debt long obscured by poor accounting and an easy line of credit from the *Picayune*, and exhausted by dysentery, constant colds, failing eyesight, and the morphine used to treat his ills, he returned to Texas in the spring of 1867 only to find his ranch home and his flocks in disarray. A difficult summer of hard labor followed before he died on October 21, 1867, at his Post Oak Spring ranch near Boerne, Texas. His wife, who would live another fifty-seven years, attributed the cause to "congestion of the lungs." He lies today on the property he once owned, under a tombstone that describes him as a poet, journalist, author, and farmer, "eminent in all."

### BIBLIOGRAPHICAL NOTE

Fayette Copeland used George Kendall's personal papers to write *Kendall of the Picayune: Being His Adventures in New Orleans, on the Texas Santa Fe Expedition, in the Mexican War, and in the Colonization of the Texas Frontier* (Norman, 1943), but the papers were scattered among family members soon after and were not available to scholars until the Amon Carter Museum arranged to use them during the preparation of the important *Eyewitness to War: Prints and Daguerreotypes of the Mexican War, 1846–1848*, edited by Martha A. Sandweiss, Rick Stewart, and Ben Huseman (Fort Worth, 1989). The papers, which include very little material on the Mexican War period, are now in the Special Collections Division of the University of Texas at Arlington. Thomas W. Reilly's "American Reporters and the Mexican War, 1846–1848" (Ph.D. dissertation, University of

Minnesota, 1975) is indispensable for understanding Kendall's work as a journalist during the Mexican War. Lauriston F. Bullard's *Famous War Correspondents* (New York, 1914) includes a brief sketch of Kendall's activities. John Hohenberg's *Foreign Correspondence: The Great Reporters and Their Times* (New York, 1964) mentions Kendall, in an interesting account of the early history of foreign correspondence.

The Mexican War was quickly obscured in the American memory by the long shadows cast by the Civil War. Nevertheless, historians have written a number of important studies of the Mexican War. K. Jack Bauer's *The Mexican War, 1846–1848* (New York, 1974) is a standard military history concerned primarily with tactics and strategy and is written from a distinctly American perspective. John S. D. Eisenhower's more recent *So Far from God: The U.S. War with Mexico, 1846–1848* (New York, 1989) reflects the influence of military historians interested in the lives of ordinary soldiers and the conditions they endured as well as the design and execution of military strategy and maneuvers. Eisenhower's book also provides a greater sense than others do of the war's impact on the Mexican domestic front. Justin H. Smith's two-volume history titled *The War with Mexico* (New York, 1919) is indispensable for its thoroughness and use of primary materials in Mexico and the United States, although it is dated in its interpretation of the war.

More narrowly focused studies have also added much to the literature of the Mexican War. James M. McCaffery's *Army of Manifest Destiny: The American Soldiers in the Mexican War, 1846–1848* (New York, 1992) reviews the experience of the American common soldier during the war. Valuable for understanding naval affairs is K. Jack Bauer's *Surfboats and Horse Marines: U.S. Naval Operations in the Mexican War, 1846–48* (Annapolis, 1969). The most thorough account of the diplomatic maneuverings surrounding the war is David M. Pletcher's *The Diplomacy of Annexation, Texas, Oregon, and the Mexican War* (Columbia, 1973). Dean B. Mahin's recent *Olive Branch and Sword: The United States and Mexico, 1845–1848* (Jefferson, N.C., 1997) sheds new light on Nicholas Trist's diplomatic efforts and is a useful history of political and diplomatic developments during the war years. Robert W. Johannsen's *To the Halls of the Montezumas: The Mexican War in the American Imagination* (New York, 1985) explores the cultural context into which Kendall's dispatches flowed. Cecil Robinson's introduction to *The View from Chapultepec: Mexican Writers on the Mexican-American War* (Tucson, 1989) provides a useful review of the historiography, both Mexican and American, of the war.

Enrique Krause's *Mexico: Biography of Power: A History of Modern Mexico, 1810–1996* (New York, 1997) provides a starting point for understanding Mexican politics in the first half of the nineteenth century. Pedro Santoni's *Mexicans at Arms: Puro Federalists and the Politics of War, 1845–1848* (Fort Worth, 1996) offers a useful account of the complex political maneuvering that characterized Mexican politics in the war years.

A number of published journals and letter collections complement Kendall's account of the war with Mexico. Among them are *Monterrey Is Ours! The Mexican War Letters of Lieutenant Dana, 1845–1847*, edited by Robert H. Ferrell (Lexington, 1990); *Volunteers: The Mexican War Journals of Private Richard Coulter and Sergeant Thomas Barclay, Company E, Second Pennsylvania Infantry*, edited by Allan Peskin (Kent, Ohio, 1991); and *The Mexican War Journal and Letters of Ralph W. Kirkham*, edited by Robert R. Miller (College Station, Texas, 1991).

The most comprehensive collection of documents relating to the Mexican War can be found in *House Executive Document 60, 30th Congress, 1st Session*, of the Congressional Serial Set. Francis B. Heitman's *Historical Register and Dictionary of the United States Army, from Its Organization, September 29, 1789, to March 2, 1903* (Washington, D.C., 1909), and the appendix of Cadmus M. Wilcox's *History of the Mexican War*, edited by Mary R. Wilcox (Washington, D.C., 1892), were used in the preparation of this study. The latter volume, which includes rosters of the regular and volunteer officers who served in Mexico, was used extensively to identify the many officers who served in the war. Norman E. Tutorow's *The Mexican-American War: An Annotated Bibliography* (New York, 1981), remains the most comprehensive bibliography available. Mary-Jo Kline's *A Guide to Documentary Editing* (Baltimore, 1987) directed the preparation of the documents in this edition.

## EDITORIAL NOTES

The *Picayune* published 214 dispatches written by George W. Kendall, including a lengthy account of the battle of Monterey written in New Orleans from notes taken at the scene. Most of the dispatches appeared in the *Daily Picayune*, which appeared Tuesday through Sunday. Many also appeared in the *Weekly Picayune*, published on Mondays, and a few appeared only in the weekly edition of the paper. The latter group is indicated in the text, along with the date each appeared in the *Weekly Picayune*. All other dispatches bear the dates on which they were published in the paper's daily edition. On a few occasions, the *Picayune* published extracts of Kendall's reports; those occasions are noted. Otherwise, the dispatches appear in their entirety.

Kendall's handwritten dispatches do not survive. The text used for the preparation of this edition is the microfilm edition of the New Orleans *Daily Picayune* distributed by University Microfilms International. The copy is generally of good quality; where the newspaper copy was illegible, the text was checked against original newspapers at the American Antiquarian Society. The *Weekly Picayune* is not available on microfilm and was consulted at the American Antiquarian Society.

The dispatches are arranged by the dates on which they were authored. Only in September 1847, does the order in which Kendall wrote them differ significantly from the order of publication. The rearrangement occurred when the *Picayune* delayed until after the surrender of Mexico City the publication of a series of dispatches filed just before the renewal of hostilities.

Original spelling and punctuation have been retained, with some exceptions. Datelines have been standardized, with the month and place fully spelled out and any italics eliminated. Obvious printer errors have been silently corrected and odd spacing in the typeset text has been conventionalized. The hyphens used in "today," "tomorrow," and "tonight" by the *Picayune*'s printers have been removed. An "e" has been inserted to correctly spell "aides"; "dispatch" has been spelled with an "i" instead of an "e"; and the extra consonants in words such as "travelled" have been eliminated. Otherwise, the quirks of nineteenth-century spelling have generally been retained. Italicized type, although used inconsistently, has been retained, in part to illustrate the newness of Spanish words that are now familiar to English speakers. Finally, the brackets [ ] Kendall used to set off text have been changed to parentheses ( ). New editorial additions in the text are enclosed in brackets [ ]. The manuscript has been proofread by reading new copy aloud against the original newspaper text.

Place names are true to Kendall's rendering except in a few instances where printer errors appear to have created inconsistencies. Kendall spelled Monterey with one "r," as did most writers in the nineteenth century, and he rendered Vera Cruz as two words. In a few cases, Kendall or his printers confused the spelling of a person's name or misstated an initial. Albert Sidney Johnston's last name, for example, was consistently misspelled in the original text; so was the name of Michael Chevallie, an officer serving with the Texas volunteers. Both of these names and a few others have been silently corrected to ensure identification throughout.

Chapter headnotes and footnotes have been used to provide a brief history of the Mexican War and to clarify issues raised in Kendall's dispatches. Kendall's footnotes are identified as his. Only when the information provided cannot be found in the standard histories of the war are further references provided. Kendall mentioned more than five hundred individuals—American and Mexican officers as well as civilians—in dispatches, usually referring to them by title and last name only. Whenever possible, a full name and (when necessary) military unit have been provided in a footnote where the individual is initially mentioned. Additional biographical information has been provided only for individuals who played a prominent role in Kendall's dispatches or in the history of the Mexican War.

# CHAPTER ONE

# WITH THE ARMY ON THE RIO GRANDE
## APRIL 2 - AUGUST 5, 1846

GENERAL ZACHARY TAYLOR ESTABLISHED his Army of Occupation along the Rio Grande opposite the Mexican town of Matamoros on March 28, 1846. At about the same time, George Kendall set out from New Orleans for Texas to report on negotiations with the Comanches in northern Texas and perhaps also to be near the Mexican frontier in the event that hostilities erupted. On May 8, from high on the Brazos River, Kendall reported having received word of the commencement of hostilities with Mexico and announced his plans to leave immediately for Matamoros. Taylor had already forwarded to Washington word of the deaths of his quartermaster, Colonel Trueman Cross, and Lieutenant Theodoric H. Porter at the hands of guerrilla forces and of the capture of eighty American dragoons by 1,600 Mexican cavalry. On the day Kendall wrote, Taylor's troops engaged a Mexican force that was positioned at Palo Alto to prevent the resupply of the Americans under siege at Fort Brown. The Mexican Army of the North, under the command of General Mariano Arista, suffered heavy losses and fell back to Resaca de la Palma. The next day Taylor drove Arista's army across the Rio Grande. The declaration of war against Mexico followed on May 13.

As Kendall passed through Legrange on the Colorado River on his way to Corpus Christi, American forces were preparing to occupy the evacuated city of Matamoros on May 18. On June 10, Kendall had just reached Point Isabel when Taylor, in what was the army's first move toward Monterey, sent a unit of the First Infantry upriver to Reynosa. The remainder of the army—with Kendall in tow—soon followed, while Taylor considered whether to march inland toward Linares or move farther upriver. With word that water was in short supply in the region around Linares, Taylor moved the army to Camargo, at the confluence of the Rio Grande and the San Juan River, beginning July 6 and on to Mier early in August. After considering a route through China and Caldereyta, Taylor elected to approach Monterey through Mier and Cerralvo in order to avoid numerous and difficult crossings of the San Juan.

Galveston, April 2, 1846

Notwithstanding the heavy rain and pitchy darkness of Monday night last, which detained us in the Mississippi several hours, the *Alabama* arrived here last evening easy enough, the latter part of the trip being pleasant to a degree. It was a little rough and shaky when we first came over the bar at the mouth of the Mississippi, causing the total loss of several very valuable breakfasts, but it was not long before the Gulf was as smooth as a mill-pond asleep. I have a good story to tell about a sea-sick Hoosier on board the *Alabama*—a chap with hickory-bark trowsers and a pepper-and-salt coat, who came down the Mississippi captain of a Wabash flatboat—but the joke will keep and perhaps improve.

You will see accounts of the recent election in Texas, held for members of Congress, in the papers. If the extreme bad weather continues as far as San Antonio and Austin, it is thought that Williams is elected, he leaving Houston with such a send-off in the way of a majority. If the heavy rains reached the West, the friends of Col. Cooke, and some of the other candidates, could not turn out, if they would. Williams's majority was enormous here—449 votes out of 541 cast.[1]

The[re] is no late news from the "Army of Occupation" that I can learn. Rumors are afloat that skirmishes have taken place; but they are doubtless without foundation. One thing I learn here, which gives me a better opinion than ever of Gen. Taylor. He gave strict orders that no gamblers nor liquor sellers should follow him from Corpus Christi, or approach within seven miles of the line; but some whiskey dealers being found close in, their jugs and demijohns were smashed, and they themselves sent back in irons.

Seymore[2] is still doing a heavier business here at the Tremont than ever, and has emphatically made it the crack house of Texas. The captain is a first-rate A1 clever fellow, and was formerly "one of the boys" in New York.

We are off for Houston immediately—the party all well.

G. W. K.

*Daily Picayune*, April 7, 1846

1. The first congressional elections in Texas were held on March 30, 1846. The Trinity River east of Houston divided the two Texas districts. Samuel May Williams, a banker and merchant from Galveston, and William G. Cooke, the state adjutant general and a veteran Texas politician and military leader, were among a field of six seeking to represent the western district. Kendall and Cooke had both been on the ill-fated Texas expedition to Santa Fe in 1841.

2. Seymore is not identifiable beyond having set up business at Galveston's Tremont Hotel, but Kendall seems to have known him from his days as a young newspaperman in New York City.

Houston, Texas, April 4, 1846

An express came in last evening from Torrey's Trading House, high up on the Brazos, with news that Gov. Butler and party, accompanied by Pahayucah's band of Comanches, would arrive at that station in a day or two, and that a numerous party of the Rocky Mountain Indians, who have recently joined the prairie tribes, are with them.[3] This news is to the 25th ult. from the trading house, and I learn farther that the great treaty with the different bands of Indians is to be held on the 25th inst., the United States Commissioners anticipating little difficulty in coming to terms with a majority of them. The grand council was to have been held at the Comanche Peak, but the Indians thought that was a point rather too far within their lines. The rascally Wacoes, fearing that a treaty might interfere with their thieving propensities, may not come in—the other tribes are said to be anxious to come to an amicable understanding with the United States. Torrey's Trading House is but a short distance above the buffalo grounds, and I shall not fail to be there by the 25th inst., if there is any kind of a chance. There will be an immense number of the prairie warriors on the ground—some say as high as 25,000—but this is probably overrated.

"Speaking of guns always puts one in mind," &c. I saw a magnificent present of Indian "fixins" being made up for my friend Porter, of the "Spirit,"[4] yesterday. A bear skin, large enough to cover the hide of a buffalo bull, is one of the trinkets, while Comanche bows, arrows, tomahawks, and what not, fill out the collection. I would like to see "York's Tall Son" rigged out in all this prairie finery. He would be "Big Indian, heap" arrayed in toggery so decidedly savage.

I am told, but I know not with what truth, that Rice Garland, the runaway judge of our Supreme Court, was seen here a day or two since, traveling under the assumed name of Col. Tallifer. Rumor had him at Havana a month or two since.

---

3. Formerly governor of South Carolina, Pierce M. Butler was the U.S. agent to the Cherokees at Fort Gibson, Indian Territory. He and M. G. Lewis served as Indian commissioners during treaty negotiations with the Comanches, Wacoes, Keechies, Tonkaways, Wichetas, and Tawa-karroes concerning trading rights and criminal activity. Negotiations took place at Council Springs near the Brazos River in Robinson County, Texas. The commissioners considered the extended negotiations, which continued through the winter and spring of 1845 and 1846, to have prevented "the outbreak of savage violence" on the Texas frontier as tensions mounted between the United States and Mexico. "A Report of Messrs. Butler and Lewis relative to the Indians of Texas and the Southwestern Prairies," 29th Cong., 2d sess., House of Representatives Doc. No. 76 (Serial 500), 1–9. These negotiations were the first conducted by federal authorities in the newly annexed state of Texas. Butler was killed on August 20, 1847, while commanding South Carolina's Palmetto Regiment at the battle of Churubusco.

4. William Trotter Porter, editor of the New York *Spirit of the Times.*

The badness of the roads has prevented the returns of the recent election for members of Congress from coming in as fast as they might, but it is thought here that Pilsbury stands a good chance of being elected, notwithstanding the heavy majority Williams received in Galveston. A few days will tell the story.[5]

We start for San Antonio immediately after breakfast, and on as fine a set of horses as you could pick out of the general run of stables. You shall hear from me again at San Felipe or Gonzalez. Party all well.

G. W. K.

*Daily Picayune,* April 9, 1846

Columbus, Texas, April 9, 1846

Who says it never rains in Texas! I asked this question last year about this time, and not fifty miles from this place.[6] It had then rained some ten days steadily—it has not rained quite as long, perhaps, this time, but such a shower as fell last Saturday at Houston, just as we were getting ready to start on our journey, beat anything I have ever seen. We saddled up and left after it had subsided, but found the prairie between Houston and Piney Point a perfect sheet of water, and before we reached our destination for the night, after the sun was down, another deluge was pouring upon us, while the darkness was made even more intense by the vivid flashes of lightning. For an instant the prairie would be lit up, as if with a brilliant display of pyrotechny; but the next instant, and for almost minutes, the darkness was as a wall of the blackest gloom: at one time I thought my eye-sight had entirely left me. But this interests you but little—we reached our lodging-house, soaked through and through, and although we were obliged to sleep upon the floor, in a small room with about fifteen persons of all nations and languages, contrived to get through the night comfort-

5. Timothy Pilsbury, a Democrat from Brazoria County and a veteran of the Texas House and Senate, defeated Williams. As a member of the Texas congressional delegation, he joined David S. Kaufman in the House and Sam Houston, the former president of the Republic of Texas, and Thomas Rush in the Senate.

6. Kendall had traveled to Texas in the early spring of 1845, after Congress voted to annex Texas, to encourage popular support for annexation and to report for the *Picayune* on British efforts to maintain the republic's independence. Both houses of the Texas Congress voted for annexation in June; a popular convention meeting in Austin approved annexation on July 4, 1845; and a popular referendum approved the measure by a lopsided margin on October 13, 1845. Texas officially became a state on December 29, 1845, when President James Polk signed congressional legislation accepting the new state's constitution. For Kendall's activities, see Fayette Copeland, *Kendall of the Picayune: Being his Adventures in New Orleans, on the Texas Santa Fe Expedition, in the Mexican War, and in the Colonization of the Texas Frontier* (Norman, 1943), 131–39.

ably enough. I learned one thing by this night's operations; three Germans can talk more and smoke more, in any length of time you may specify, than thirty Americans and three hundred Englishmen—if I was crowded I would throw in a "smart chance" of Frenchmen. We parted our German friends the next night—got two of them in a room by themselves, and one of them in a bed in our room—when what did the latter do but fall to smoking and talking to himself! Loquacious people are these Germans—but to our journey.

The next day we made thirty miles, after "cooning" our saddles across a log and swimming our horses over Buffalo Bayou—now so swollen by the previous deluge that it looked like a young Mississippi. Our *compagnon du voyage*, Count Holynski, who hates water like a cat, got a distinct glimpse of "the elephant" at this crossing—he has "seen the animal" a dozen times since then.[7] We should have had much difficulty in getting over this bayou had it not been for another companion, young B., who swims like an otter and is not afraid of the rheumatism. He swam one of the horses over, and after this we got the rest of the *caballada*[8] across without difficulty.

We had another delightful time in rafting and swimming across a creek six miles from the Brazos, on the opposite side of that stream from this place, and when we finally reached the ferry at San Felipe, just at dark, we found the river up, full of drift, and that it was utterly impossible to get our horses over. Obliged to leave the poor animals in the midst of a heavy rain, we made out to cross ourselves in a log dug-out, and finally effected a lodging under shelter. I have never seen "elephants" so thick in Texas as they are this season. The next day we spent in studying the theory of driftwood, and watching the rise and fall of the Brazos, more particularly the rise—and yesterday we made out to reach this place with little difficulty, crossing the San Bernard without wetting our saddle-skirts, and getting over the Colorado without trouble. We are now about starting for Gonzalez and San Antonio, and with every prospect of good weather and roads.

G. W. K.

*Daily Picayune*, April 30, 1846

---

7. Alexander John Joachim Holynski, a veteran of the Polish uprising against the Russians in 1830–1831, traveled extensively in the United States and South America during the 1840s. The expression "to see the elephant" apparently originated in the Southwest and referred to disappointment in the face of high expectations. Kendall himself offered one of the earliest definitions of the expression in his *Narrative of the Texas Santa Fe Expedition* (New York, 1844), I, 108–110. Robert W. Johannsen, *To the Halls of the Montezumas: The Mexican War in the American Imagination* (New York, 1985), 87–90.

8. A group of horses.

San Antonio, April 15, 1846

One does not feel, after riding thirty or thirty-five miles, altogether so much like writing as he might, and this I must offer as an excuse for not sending you a letter from Gonzalez or Seguin. I say thirty or thirty-five miles—we traveled more on account of losing our road on several occasions; and here I would offer my humble petition to Congress, praying that that truly enlightened and partially dignified body may make an extensive appropriation for furnishing any quantity of guide-boards for Texas. We made a most excellent bargain when we got this new State, and I believe that Captain Elliot[9] himself, if he could have effected the same arrangement for her Britannic Majesty, would have stipulated to stick up a finger-post at every fork and cross-road in the country. So many out-of-the-way miles have we traveled, or rather have our jaded nags traveled with us, that they fervently join in this our petition.

We arrived at Seguin in the midst of a most disagreeable norther, and it being late, and one of our horses needing a shoe, we stopped all night at Johnson's instead of crossing over and remaining on this side the Guadalupe, at Flore's Rancho, as we had contemplated. Johnson's is a most excellent place, however, and on the particular night we were there we were indulged and edified by a lecture upon phrenology and physiognomy, more particularly phrenology. Who says that science is not marching westward with rapid strides, and who says that the Rev. Levi Chace, of Fall River, Massachusetts, is not helping it along "all he knows"? The Rev. Levi Chace was the name of the lecturer, a clergyman of the Universalist persuasion,[10] I believe, and if he was not so very instructing, he was most essentially amusing. He has a Yankee twang that would all but be the death of Pardon Jones or Sam Slick,[11] and when he obtained the services of a tall Texan as

9. Charles Elliot, Royal Navy, was the British chargé d'affaires to the Republic of Texas from 1842 to 1845.

10. Universalism came to the United States during the American Revolution. In 1779, John Murray established the first Universalist church, preaching the movement's doctrine of universal salvation through divine grace.

11. Pardon Jones was a fictional character in the regional literature of the southwestern border in the 1840s. He was the creation of Kendall's fellow *Picayune* correspondent, C. M. Haile, and from September 10, 1845, to November 11, 1846, was a vehicle for humorous commentary on Mexican affairs and on the war. Regional vernacular, exaggeration, and slapstick characterized the Pardon Jones material. Thomas W. Reilly, "American Reporters and the Mexican War, 1846–1848" (Ph.D. dissertation, University of Minnesota, 1975), 121–24. Sam Slick was the creation of the Canadian humorist Thomas Chandler Haliburton. Slick first appeared in the pages of the Halifax *Novascotian* in 1835. A prototypical Yankee entrepreneur, he was the vehicle through which Haliburton introduced such maxims as "It's raining cats and dogs," "The early bird gets the worm," and "Don't take any wooden nickels."

a sitter—a man with a shocking head of hair, long enough and thick enough to conceal woodchucks as well as organs of combativeness, destructiveness, philoprogenitiveness and what not—when, I say, he got hold of this customer and began to give us his character, I, for one, wanted to go out and "holler." "This," said the learned lumpologist,[12] laying his open hand upon the top of the Texan's head—"this is the organ of 'hope.' When this organ is small, or but slightly developed, the individeral is alwers a borryin' trouble; but, on the contrary, when it is large, the possessor has a full sheer of confidence in anything he undertakes." I might go on and give further extracts from the lecture of the Rev. Levi Chace, of Fall River, Massachusetts, but this must suffice. I presume he is a worthy man, and he must pardon me for saying that he is a full-blooded Yankee.

I find this place, San Antonio, much improved since last year. Everything—business, fandangoes, &c.—appears lively and stirring, and there has been a great influx of strangers and a rise in rents and real estate. The appearance of Col. Harney and the U. S. Dragoons, with the aid rendered by Major Hays and the daring Rangers under him, has inspired confidence in every quarter.[13] Let but a line of military posts be established from here to the Rio Grande—it must be done—and this portion of Western Texas will flourish to a degree unknown even in the annals of America. For richness of soil and salubrity of climate I hardly know of any part of the United States that can compare with it.

They have no news here from the Rio Grande, and the movements of Gen. Taylor are unknown, except from rumor. They talk here as though the Mexicans would certainly fight, but of this you obtain more correct information direct at New Orleans.

We start tomorrow for Austin, by way of the great German settlement of New Braunfels.[14] From the former place we shall proceed to the Indian treaty at Torrey's station, where I hope to see something worthy of relating.

G. W. K.

*Daily Picayune*, May 1, 1846

12. Phrenologist. Phrenology linked the shape of the skull to character traits and mental capacity and was a popular pseudoscience in mid-nineteenth-century America.

13. William S. Harney, Second Dragoons, was a veteran cavalry officer with a reputation for cruelty that he had earned fighting American Indians in Florida and Wisconsin. John (Jack) Coffee Hays commanded a mounted regiment of Texas volunteers. Since Texas independence, many of these veteran soldiers had served in the frontier warfare against American Indians and Mexicans.

14. New Braunfels was founded in 1845 by Prince Carl zu Solms-Braunfels. Commissioner general for the Adelsverein, a society of German noblemen from Mainz, he sought to recreate in Texas the feudal social order that was destroyed in Europe by the Napoleonic wars. Copeland, *Kendall of the Picayune*, 259.

New Braunfels, Texas, April 17, 1846

Leaving San Antonio yesterday, after an early dinner, we jogged on to this place at a rapid rate. The distance is thirty-three miles good, although some call it only thirty; yet we got in just after dark. As we neared the new German settlement we saw numbers of fires burning, and as we entered the outskirts a strong stench of burning feathers, partially ameliorated or softened by tobacco smoke, was wafted directly in our faces. The latter we could account for—it's a way the Germans have, this of smoking—but the burnt feathers rather staggered us. One of our party suggested that there might be now and then a flea in the colony, as it is termed, and that it was one way the inhabitants had of ridding themselves of customers so troublesome. He was right—there are fleas at New Braunfels, *some*—and several of our party slept out in the open air, to keep out of their way. But fleas are not confined to this place alone—they may be met with any where at this time of the year. The Germans this season are planting to some considerable extent in the neighborhood, the town looks thrifty and busy, and in a year or two New Braunfels will be a place of importance.

On our way here we met a company of U. S. Dragoons, under Capt. Blake,[15] with several Shawnee and Delaware Indians as guides, on their way to San Antonio from a short excursion to the region watered by the Perdenales. The men looked well and healthy. On this stream, or near it, the Germans are about to plant another colony, and when this is established, another is to be planted still farther northwest, on the San Saba. Of course these new emigrants lack that practical knowledge which is necessary to ensure immediate success in a country like this, but their proverbial industry and economy will doubtless carry them triumphantly through. Large numbers of them are now on the way; they have chosen positions highly advantageous, both as regards fertility of soil and salubrity of climate, and in the course of but few years theirs will be numbered among the most flourishing settlements in all Texas.

The night before we left San Antonio a young Frenchman or Creole from Louisiana was robbed of near $3000 at a fandango, as was supposed by some American or English pick-pocket. There were four $500 bills in the amount, all on New Orleans banks. I was at the fandango, and it was certainly crowded enough—Mexicans, Lippans,[16] Americans, and what not

15. George A. H. Blake, Second Dragoons.
16. The Lippans, a small band of Apaches numbering around five hundred, lived near San Antonio.

being present—to give the most bungling operator in the pocket-picking line a glorious chance for a harvest.

We are about leaving for Austin, and directly in the face of a storm which looks as though it might turn out one of unusual length and violence. If we can cross the Blanco, Onion Creek, and some other streams before they are swimming, we shall be lucky. I like water well enough, but this thing of crossing deep and swift-running streams on horseback is a species of navigation I do not affect to any remarkable extent.

G. W. K.

*Daily Picayune*, May 3, 1846

Austin, Texas, April 20, 1846

The rain, which threatened us with a thorough soaking and wet bed at the New Braunfels, passed off by the time we had reached the beautiful St. Marks, and early in the evening we stripped our horses at the Manchac Spring, a noted camping-ground between this and San Antonio. The next morning we saddled up, and a few hours' ride brought us here, hungry as hunters—for we had had little or nothing to eat for the previous twenty-four hours.

The establishment of the seat of Government here has completely "resurrected" the place.[17] Last year at this time the only denizens of the houses were hogs and fleas—now every one is filled, and they are even building more. So far as regards news, I have not a word to give, other than what you will find in the papers. I have been told, since my arrival here, that the public debt of Texas, which does not amount to more than $8,000,000, will be repudiated—one person tells me that they will not give even a league of land to cancel it.[18]

We are off this afternoon for the scene of the treaty which Gov. Butler is endeavoring to form with the Indians of Texas, and are told that the buffalo are to be found in immense herds between here and that place.

G. W. K.

*Daily Picayune*, May 1, 1846

Camp of the Indian Commissioners, Brazos River, May 8, 1846

I anticipated remaining here until the great Indian treaty came off, which will take place, probably, next week, but an express has come in

17. Washington-on-the-Brazos had been the capital of Texas during the interim from 1842 to 1845.

18. The United States would assume the Texas debt of approximately $10 million as a part of the Compromise of 1850. In exchange, Texas would concede its claim to the territory of New Mexico east of the Rio Grande.

from Austin with the exciting intelligence of the murder of Col. Cross[19] on the Rio Grande and the commencement of hostilities with the Mexicans, and I am off tomorrow in the direction of Matamoros. The news has created the greatest interest here, and all are anxious to have the treaty over as soon as possible.[20]

There is now good reason to believe that the Comanches will be well represented at the great council. Buffalo Hump, with one or two of his captains, arrived here the latter part of last week, and today Jack Hany, a noted interpreter and runner of the Delaware tribe, came in with a large body of the Comanches, headed by old Mopechocopee, a celebrated civil chief, besides Yellow Wolf, Bear Tail, Santa Anna, and other war chiefs of distinction. This latter chief is a fine, portly looking fellow, weighing over two hundred pounds, and with a countenance expressive of both good humor and good nature. They say, however, that he is one of their fiercest and most relentless warriors. They all came in, Mopechocopee taking the lead, in regular order, followed by a raft of women and children all mounted, and I would not have missed the spectacle on any account. The women sat their horses fearlessly, and astride after the manner of their lords and masters, while the children were clinging on anywhere and everywhere; and as well might one undertake to shake a squirrel from a limb as one of these small specimens of the genus Comanche from their horses. The women at once struck the camp, arranged all the buffalo skin wigwams, brought water from a delicious spring hard by, built fires, and in half an hour's time all were feasting themselves upon buffalo meat, the lean part boiled while the fat they swallowed raw as we would bread. I have never before seen these wild people while quietly encamped, and watched their little household and domestic manners with much interest.

Many of the more noted chiefs paid an early visit to the quarters of Gov. Butler, who has been very unwell for several weeks but is now slowly recovering. While there they had a smoke and a short talk, appeared friendly enough, and after the visit was over stalked quietly off to their quarters. I noticed that the plainest dressed man among all the Comanches was old Mopechocopee himself, for he had nothing on but a coarse tow shirt; the younger chiefs were rigged out in all sorts of finery and painted in colors the most fanciful. There was a wonderful lack of substantial dress, however, and I could not help thinking of the summer costume of the Georgian, who arrayed himself simply in a shirt collar and pair of spurs,

19. Trueman Cross, General Taylor's quartermaster, disappeared while riding near camp on April 10, 1846. He was found dead on April 21.
20. Treaty negotiations with the Comanches were concluded on May 15, 1846.

and also of the Indian high up on the Mississippi during the intense heat of the last summer, who scorned any other garment than a piece of rope.

Gov. Butler and Col. Lewis are now expecting old Pahayucah in daily, with a numerous retinue of distinguished chiefs and braves from the more important bands of the upper Comanches. At about the same time it is thought the Wacoes and Keechies will be in their full strength, when the council will at once be held and the best possible terms made with all the different tribes. The question of the right of soil in Texas, so far as the Comanches are concerned, will not be touched if I understand the matter right; but then a line will be resolved upon and run as soon as circumstances will admit, regular traders of good reputation appointed to reside among them, and the Comanche made to obligate themselves not to cross the borders unless by special permit. Grounds will also be allotted to the smaller tribes, all of whom dread and fear the Comanches, and probably with good reason. The commissioners have certainly used every exertion to make an effective treaty with the wild prairie tribes, have encountered difficulties innumerable, and delays which have taxed their patience to a degree; yet I now believe that they will be enabled to make a treaty which will be of incalculable importance, more especially to the border settlers.

I have picked up many items and incidents, which I can work up in readable form, but for which I have no room now. The wild night dances of the Tonkaways and Lippans, carried on for twelve, sixteen or twenty hours at a time without cessation, would excite most especial wonder in those who had never seen them before.

I have been promised the final result of the treaty, which I trust you will receive in good time. Tomorrow I start towards Corpus Christi, but you shall hear from me on the road.

G. W. K.

*Daily Picayune*, May 22, 1846

La Grange, Texas, May 16, 1846

In a former letter I said that they stood in great need of guide-boards or finger posts in Texas: they stand in need of post offices as well. From Bucksnort to this place, by the route I traveled, there is not a single post office, and loud are the complaints of the settlers in consequence. This section of the country, however—over one hundred miles in length—is sparsely populated, and the roads I have found in most wretched condition. I have got so used now to swimming or rafting one or two streams a day, that it seems as though something was wanting if I miss the amusement in a twenty-four hours' travel.

Up to our arrival here the people have appeared quiet in relation to the Mexican war, apprehending, perhaps, that their services might be needed nearer home to check any Indian outbreak that might occur; but here the inhabitants are all up in arms. Perhaps I should say off in arms, for a large company of mounted riflemen, under Capt. Tom Green, started yesterday for the rendezvous at Corpus Christi. This command we shall overtake before it reaches that place. On Tuesday last I learn that Capt. Ben McCulloch left Gonzalez with a large company of experienced rangers, and on picked horses.[21] Capt. McC. is an old hand at fighting both Mexicans and Indians, brave and at the same time cautious, and will doubtless render a good account of himself. While I am writing, a company of mounted riflemen is entering the place from Washington County; so we shall find the road full of volunteers on the way to the frontier.

As regards news from Matamoros, of course you get it much earlier direct than they can obtain it here. A person might almost as well have inquired about Gen. Taylor's movements among the Sikhs on the Sutlej[22] as where I have been. There are any quantity of rumors of wars and fighting here, however, and the Colorado boys, as they have ever been in times past, are eager to reach the scene of action.

We start for Corpus Christi this evening, and shall travel much by night owing to the heat of the noon-day and the swarms of prairie flies that annoy our horses.

G. W. K.
*Daily Picayune*, June 3, 1846

Corpus Christi, May 25, 1846

A gentleman leaving tomorrow morning for St. Joseph's Island[23] gives me an opportunity I might not otherwise have had to send you a few lines. I had no chance to write from Goliad or San Patricio, the only towns through which I passed on the long and tiresome route from La Grange to this place, and it may be that even this letter will see the Rio Grande before it is really on the way to New Orleans. Before this reaches you, the news will doubtless be in the Crescent City that Gen. Taylor has taken Matamoros, and I now learn that he has sent to St. Joseph for all the camp women and other supernumeraries of the army.

21. Thomas Green, First Regiment Texas Mounted Volunteers, and Benjamin McCulloch, Independent Texas Mounted Volunteers.

22. The Sutlej River flows from Tibet through northern India and eastern Pakistan.

23. St. Joseph Island, near Corpus Christi, served as a temporary home for many of the men and supplies that Taylor eventually moved to the Rio Grande.

You may think it strange that I have no intelligence of import to communicate, but just reflect for one moment where I have been the while since this Mexican war broke out. From the Indian Treaty ground to Matamoros—the way we have been compelled to travel and it has been the shortest—the distance is in the neighborhood of five hundred miles, and the longest kind of English miles at that you may rest assured. We have now accomplished some three hundred and fifty miles of this, and horse flesh, nor mule flesh could do no more in the same space of time. In the early part of the journey we had nothing but mud and water through which to swim and flounder; after crossing the Yegus, and entering the Labadie prairie, our poor animals were set upon by swarms of flies, more numerous than the locusts of Egypt, if I have any idea of mathematics. In the daytime our horses could not feed if we encamped, so busy were they fighting these ravenous insects; and as we were obliged to make much of the journey in the night, you may well judge that they were completely travel-worn and jaded down on our arrival here. They are to have but one day's rest, however, as we are off in the morning for the Rio Grande.

I learn that half New Orleans has volunteered for this Mexican war, and that the printers of the city are strongly represented.[24] The more the better. I humbly trust and hope that Gen. Taylor's instructions may be such that he can push ahead and settle our affairs with Mexico at once. Follow up his past successes with vigor, and the gasconading braggarts will be yelping like hounds before winter sets in.

Major Hays is now here at Corpus as they call it, but starts with us in the morning. Our party will be at least one hundred and fifty strong, Capt. Green's company from Lafayette numbering fully eighty men, while Capt. Early's from Washington[25] is full and every way effective. We passed the latter company at Goliad, and gained one day on the road here, owing to a stampede among their horses caused by Indians in the night. Why the prowling rascals did not pick us up, for there were only two of us, is a little singular.

24. The *Picayune* estimated that approximately five hundred "printers" had volunteered for service in Mexico—enough, its editors feared, to hinder the publication of newspapers in New Orleans and elsewhere. For example, Francis Lumsden, the cofounder of the *Picayune*, led the Gaines Rangers, a company of Georgia volunteers, to Mexico in June 1846. Soon after the unit arrived in Matamoros, however, its enlistment period ended. Lumsden stayed on with the army, filing some dispatches of his own from the Rio Grande before returning to New Orleans in early September. Copeland, *Kendall of the Picayune*, 165.

25. Frank S. Early, First Regiment Texas Mounted Volunteers, brought troops from Washington County, Texas.

The officers in command of the men here talk of starting for Matamoros by the inland route, and some of them anticipate a brush with the Mexicans before reaching the Rio Grande, as it is said that Canales[26] has a strong force of rancheros and regular soldiers on this side of the river in the chaparral. Better mounted men or better armed men, or more resolute men than these Texas volunteers, it would be hard to drum up, and they will give a good account of themselves.

G. W. K.

*Daily Picayune,* June 5, 1846


Camp on La Grulla, June 2, 1846

I write you a hasty scratch, on a sheet of paper crumpled out of all shape. We have just crossed La Grulla, (the Crane,) a horrible arroyo having an outlet into Laguna del Madre. For more than a mile we were obliged to lead our poor horses through a boggy, muddy, miry, and most slippery flat, where the salt water comes up at high tides, and where we found just enough of the briny element to conceal the treacherous footing underneath. Immediately on reaching a muskeet thicket on this side, finding fresh water in abundance, we encamped. A Mexican guide, who has piloted us thus far by a shorter route than that taken by Gen. Taylor, returns tomorrow morning to Corpus Christi, and by him I send this scrawl.

Since my last letter we have been joined by a company of well mounted men from Montgomery county, besides several small parties, and we now muster in the neighborhood of three hundred. Gen. Sidney Johnston, Col. Reuben Brown, Capt. Scarritt, and several other gentlemen came into camp last evening while we were on the Agua Dulce, and go on with us. As yet Gov. Henderson has not come up, but it is thought he will overtake us in a day or two. In addition to Gen. Lamar, I am told that Col. W. G. Cooke and Gen. Burleson accompany Gov. H.[27]

The morning after we left Corpus Christi, Major Jack Hays was chosen by acclamation to command the volunteers as far as the Rio Grande. It is

26. Notorious among Texans along the Rio Grande frontier, General Antonio Canales had built a powerful political base in northern Mexico around powerful federalist sympathies and a determination to retain Texas. His aspirations included the creation of an independent Republic of the Rio Grande that would unite the northern tier of Mexican states. He commanded a single renegade regiment that was suspected to have been involved in the death of Col. Cross.

27. James Pickney Henderson, governor of Texas, left his post temporarily to command the division of Texas volunteers with the rank of major general. Mirabeau B. Lamar served as his division inspector, and Edward Burleson, formerly vice president of the Republic of Texas, was his aide-de-camp. Mentioned are Albert Sidney Johnston, Texas Rifle Volunteers, and Jeremiah M. Scarritt, Engineers.

still said that Canales is in the neighborhood of Arroyo Colorado in considerable force. We shall reach that stream in two or three days, and in the meantime Capt. Chevallie[28] has been sent ahead with a company of spies to keep a bright look out.

The weather is dreadfully hot and extremely hard upon our horses.

G. W. K.

*Daily Picayune*, June 14, 1846

Camp on Arroyo Colorado, June 5, 1846

I write this from a beautiful Camp-ground, two miles this side the Arroyo Colorado. We passed that stream, barely saving our horses from swimming by taking advantage of the tides. Not the least fresh sign of Mexicans was discovered, although the spies ranged the Chaparral both above and below the ford. The evidences of what they have done, however, were plainly enough visible in the vicinity, for we saw the remains of no less than seven of the unfortunate Rogers party, so cruelly murdered here a few weeks since. Five skeletons, one of them apparently female, were lying upon the banks, where they drifted after their throats had been cut; two others were discovered near the wagons. The wolves and buzzards had done their work upon all, and many a deep threat of vengeance was uttered by the Texan Volunteers as they looked upon the remains of their countrymen. The story of their barbarous murder has already been told—I will not repeat it.

Col. Kinney, who has just arrived in Camp from Corpus Christi,[29] informs us that Gov. Henderson's party are this side of that place, and within fifty miles of us. Another company from Montgomery County is also *en route*. These Mounted Riflemen are rather a rough-looking set of customers just now, but they will be found hard to deal with.

We shall reach Point Isabel tomorrow, from whence I will send you a line.

G. W. K.

*Daily Picayune*, June 14, 1846

Point Isabel, June 7, 1846

We got in safe yesterday, although a few of the men had to foot it on account of broken down horses. A small sample of a *stampede* in camp night before last caused a bit of excitement, and a rainy norther towards

---

28. Michael H. Chevallie, First Regiment Texas Mounted Rifle Volunteers.
29. Henry L. Kinney had founded the trading post that became Corpus Christi.

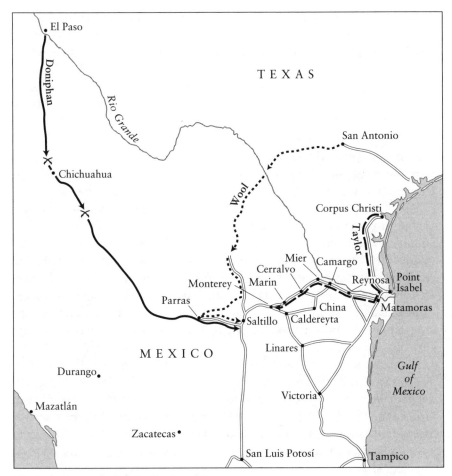

Northern theater during the Mexican War.

morning gave us a thorough soaking and any quantity of discomfort; but these things, however disagreeable, we are used to. To say we don't mind them would be stretching the matter a shade too far.

The Texan volunteers are in good health, with one or two exceptions, notwithstanding their food has been scarce and indifferent and much of the water on the route horribly bad. The wild bulls in the neighborhood of the Colorado suffered to some extent, a great many having been killed by the men for their meat. It was tough as wagon tire, however, and required a bark mill to grind and digest it. One of the volunteers said that he intended to rig a small one in his stomach if ever fate compelled him to travel the road again.

Our regular correspondent[30] here has furnished you with all the army news stirring. I shall push on for Matamoros this evening or tomorrow morning, and there join some of the companies advancing into the interior of Mexico.

G. W. K.

*Daily Picayune*, June 14, 1846

Matamoros, June 12, 1846

A more hybrid city at this present time, than this same Matamoros, does not exist, for it is completely overrun with a little of everything—regular and volunteer officers, regular and volunteer soldiers, speculators, sutlers,[31] camp followers, Texas rangers, loafers, gamblers, and what not of the Anglo-Saxon stock, besides a goodly portion of the Mexican population. The latter have got the first scare over in a measure, and many of those who fled at the outset of active hostilities are gradually creeping back to their old homes and repairing damages. They find some of their houses better ventilated than when they left them; for your cannon ball walks in without knocking, and enters without so much as desiring you to open a door—cutting a road through roof or wall as may best suit its convenience.

What a convenient thing it would be, could a man recollect all the anecdotes—and their name is legion—of the two great battles which opened the door for the entrance of the American troops into Mexico—a man does not like to carry about a note book and pencil to clap down every story he listens to. Martin Scott[32]—Capt. Martin Scott—you have not forgotten him, have you? If you have, the coons have not: well, they tell a story of him,

---

30. The *Picayune's* "regular correspondent" was Christopher Mason Haile. He was hired to cover the war on the Rio Grande in mid-May 1846, becoming one of the war's first full-time newspaper correspondents. He arrived at Point Isabel on May 25, and his first dispatch appeared in the *Picayune* on May 29, 1846. He was in Mexico with many fellow West Pointers, having been a member, although not a graduate, of the class of 1840 at the United States Military Academy. He returned to the army in April 1847, after covering the landing at Vera Cruz, and served under Scott in Mexico City until December 1847. He left the service in July 1848 and become the editor of the Plaquemine, Louisiana, *Sentinel*. On September 10, 1849, Haile died of yellow fever that he had contracted while at Vera Cruz. Usually referred to as C. M. Haile, he signed his dispatches "H." Reilly, "American Reporters and the Mexican War," 109–36.

31. Sutlers were civilian contractors who purchased food and supplies and sold them to soldiers.

32. Martin Scott, Fifth Infantry, had already earned a reputation for bravery by his exploits at Palo Alto and Resaca de la Palma. He was a great hunter, always traveling with a pack of hounds, and was an excellent marksman. He was killed at Molino del Rey, outside Mexico City, on September 8, 1847.

which perchance you have heard before, to the effect that during one of the recent battles he found leisure, besides bringing his command regularly into action, to indulge a little in his favorite pastime of target shooting, discharging a well-known gun of his no less than eight times at the Mexicans. If he did so, it is safe to presume that no less than eight of the *Greasers*—the Texans have given the Mexicans the cognomen of *Greasers*—are not at the present time numbered among the living. The captain has probably wasted as little ammunition as any man alive—never throws away a shot.

I hear some talk of opening the theatre here with an American company. A well organized corps of players could do a thriving business just now, but how long it would last I cannot say. Whenever the army moves, there must still be a considerable force left behind to garrison Matamoros; so that a company might continue to do a good business. An excellent band from one of the regular regiments was playing for hours last night in the *Plaza Principal*; and drew quite a crowd of the Mexican population.

I saw a little Mexican lieutenant—a sinister looking scoundrel with an extremely bad face—sent off to Point Isabel yesterday as a prisoner. He was caught beating and otherwise maltreating one of his wounded countrymen, and endeavoring to force him off to join the forces of Arista.[33] The fellow was frightened half out of his wits, yet I had no pity for him.

A Mexican captain of artillery, a prisoner in the camp, tells a good story of Canales and his great haste to get upon the Mexican side of the Rio Grande after the last great battle. He had reached the stream, had thrown himself into a boat, and was about pushing off, when a burly padre, one Father Leary as he was called, came rushing up to the bank and prayed lustily for a passage over. The boatman hesitated about pushing off, while the padre was making for the craft, up to his knees in mud. "Shove her off!" shouted the frightened Canales, as some of the American mounted men appeared in sight. "One moment, for the love of God!" ejaculated the priest, with outstretched arms. "Let go that rope, there!" again shouted Canales. "I shall sink," responded the priest, in doleful accents, and still floundering onwards towards the canoe. "He will drown, General," said one of the oarsmen, struck aghast at the idea of seeing a holy man thus perish. "Let him drown, then, d—n his soul; don't you see the cursed

33. Arista was in Linares, where he had retreated after the defeats along the Rio Grande, with a thousand infantry and a few squadrons of cavalry.

Americans are close upon our heels," shouted Canales, as he himself cut
the rope and shoved the boat into the stream. Father Leary was drowned,
sure enough.

G. W. K.

*Daily Picayune*, June 27, 1846

Matamoros, June 13, 1846

Rare wags[34] may be found among the Texas Volunteers, yet the funniest
fellow of all is a happy-go-lucky chap named Bill Dean, one of Chevallie's
spy company, and said to be one of the best "seven-up" players in all
Texas. While in Corpus Christi, a lot of us were sitting out in the stoop of
the Kinney House, early one morning, when along came Bill Dean. He did
not know a single soul in the crowd, although he knew we were all bound
for the Rio Grande; yet the fact that the regular formalities of an
introduction had not been gone through with, did not prevent his stopping
short in his walk and accosting us. His speech, or harangue, or whatever it
may be termed, will lose much in the telling, yet I will endeavor to put it
upon paper in as good shape as possible.

"Oh yes," said he, with a knowing leer of the eye, "oh, yes; all goin'
down among the robbers on the Rio Grande, are you? Fine times you'll
have, over the left. I've been there, myself, and done what a good many
of you won't do—I come back: but if I didn't see nateral h–ll—in August
at that—I am a teapot. Lived eight days on one poor hawk and three
blackberries—couldn't kill a prairie rat on the whole route to save us
from starvation. The ninth day come, and we struck a small streak of
good luck—a horse give out and broke down, plumb out in the centre of
an open prairie—not a stick in sight big enough to tickle a rattlesnake
with, let alone killing him. Just had time to save the critter by shootin'
him, and that was all, for in three minutes longer he'd have died a
nateral death. It didn't take us long to butcher him, nor long to cut off
some chunks of meat and stick'em on our ram-rods; but the cookin' was
another matter. I piled up a heap of prairie grass, for it was high and dry,
and set it on fire; but it flashed up like powder and went out as quick.
But—"

"But," put in one of his hearers, "but how did you cook your horse meat
after that?"

"How?"

---

34. The *Daily Picayune*, June 26, 1846, printed this dispatch with the opening phrase "Race
nags"; the *Weekly Picayune*, June 29, 1846, reads "Rare wags."

"Yes, how?"

"Why, the fire caught the high grass close by, and the wind carried the flames streakin' across the prairie. I followed up the fire, holding my chunk of meat directly over the hottest part of the blaze, and the way we went it was a caution to anything short of locomotive doins. Once in a while a little flurry of wind would come along, and the fire would get a few yards the start; but I'd brush upon her, lap her with my chunk, and then we'd have it again, nip and tuck. You never seed such a tight race—it was beautiful."

"Very, we've no doubt," ejaculated one of the listeners, interrupting the mad wag just in season to give him a little breath: "but did you cook your meat in the end?"

"Not bad I didn't. I chased that d—d fire a mile and a half, the almightiest hardest race you ever heer'd tell on, and never gave it up until I run her right plumb into a wet marsh: there the fire and chunk of horse meat came out even—a dead heat, especially the meat."

"But wasn't it cooked?" put in another of the listeners.

"Cooked! no!—just crusted over a little. You don't cook broken-down horse flesh very easily, no how; but when it comes to chasing up a prairie fire with a chunk of it, I don't know which is toughest, the meat or the job. You'd have laughed to split yourself to have seen me in that race—to see the fire leave me at times, and then to see me a brushin' up on her again, humpin' and movin' myself as though I was a runnin' agin some of those big ten mile an hour Gildersleeves in the old States. But I am a goin' over to Jack Haynes's to get a cocktail and some breakfast—I'll see you all down among the robbers on the Rio Grande."

And so saying Bill Dean stalked off. I saw the chap this morning in front of a Mexican fonda, trying to talk Spanish with a *Greaser* and endeavoring to convince him he was a "d—d robber." Such is one of Bill Dean's stories—if I could only make it as effective on paper as he did in the telling, it would draw a laugh from those fond of the ludicrous.

G. W. K.

*Daily Picayune*, June 26, 1846

Matamoros, June 14, 1846

There is little news stirring in camp. Capt. Ogden, one of Gen. Smith's aides, who came in yesterday from Reynosa, where Col. Wilson is encamped with 300 U. S. troops, reports that Canales had been in and endeavored to make some kind of terms—a bargain, probably, to sell himself to the Americans for a compensation.[35] The scoundrel is up to any kind of a game to make money, and would sell his own grandmother if he could pass her off for an Egyptian mummy or any kind of a curiosity by which money could be made.

Capt. Banigan, a Mexican officer wounded at the battle of Resaca de la Palma, died this morning of lock-jaw. He was a brave little fellow, spoke English well, and if I mistake not, was a friend of the Texan prisoners while in the city of Mexico.[36] I called to see him yesterday, to ask him some questions, but found him in no condition to converse. Today I learn with regret that he is dead. It has been the good or ill fortune of nearly all the best of the Mexican officers to be either killed, wounded, or taken prisoners.

From this out, Matamoros is to be decidedly an American city. Let things turn as they will—no matter when peace comes or upon what terms it comes—the Americans have got in here, now, have opened stores, coffee-houses, restaurants, billiard-rooms, hotels, and the like, have introduced ice and mint-juleps—a long step toward civilization—and their back tracks will never be discovered. Well, it's all for the best. The Mexicans would never have made anything out of the country in the neighborhood more than a living.

You have perhaps heard the report, ere this, that Generals Ampudia and Arista have gone to the city of Mexico to prefer charges of cowardice and the like against each other.[37] As to Ampudia a pretty plain case can be made out: Arista, so they all say, stood his ground to the last; but this thing of endeavoring to stay the go-aheadity of the American soldiers is beyond the power of the Mexicans, let them be commanded ever so well. I have ridden over both the great battlefields, and little as I know about military affairs I can see that nothing but the fact that Gen. Taylor's men stood up to their work and went ahead gave them the victory.

35. Persifor F. Smith, Second Brigade, had been active in legal and militia affairs in Louisiana before the war. He was a veteran of the Seminole Wars and was commissioned a colonel in the regular army when the war with Mexico began. He received a brevet promotion to brigadier general in September 1846. Also mentioned are John B. Ogden and Henry Wilson, First Infantry.

36. The members of the 1841 Texas expedition to Santa Fe had been imprisoned in Mexico City.

37. The Mexican government sent General Pedro de Ampudia to Matamoros in response to the American advance to the Rio Grande in the spring of 1846. The Cuban-born general was known for his cruelty and was unwelcome among the people of Matamoros. At the request of local citizens, he was soon replaced by Mariano Arista, although he stayed on as a subordinate. After Arista's court-martial and dismissal from the army in July 1846, Ampudia was named general-in-chief and given command of the Army of the North. Arista, who spoke English and had lived for a time in Cincinnati before the war, served as president of Mexico from 1851 to 1853.

You would think, were you in the streets of Matamoros at this time, that New Orleans had been moved. I see old and familiar faces at every turn, and I am glad to learn that nearly all the Louisiana volunteers are enjoying good health.

G. W. K.

*Daily Picayune*, June 24, 1846

Matamoros, June 15, 1846

Take it all through, the Louisiana delegation must have been highly gratified with the reception they met with from the different U. S. officers here, and at Capt. May's[38] camp, midway between this and Point Isabel, where they were again feted in style most magnificent. An account of the dinner in this city has probably ere this reached you.

It would seem that Gen. Taylor, who has now over 10,000 regulars and volunteers under his command here, is only waiting supplies and transports from New Orleans to march onwards towards the mountains. He certainly has a force amply sufficient to cope with anything at present this side of San Luis.

Capt. Ben McCulloch, who commands a company of Rangers, is off immediately on a scout into the interior, and I have joined his party.[39]

G. W. K.

*Daily Picayune*, June 24, 1846

Reynosa, Mexico, June 21, 1846

After a hurried eight days' reconnaissance on horseback into the interior of Mexico, during which time we have traveled over two hundred miles, the Texan Rangers have just reached Reynosa, Gen. Taylor's instructions recommending our commander, Capt. McCulloch, to come in at this place after scouring the country as far as possible in the direction of Linares. We reached El Mesepate, a point within two days' travel of that place, in four days, and Capt. McC. would have proceeded farther had there been a possibility of procuring corn for his horses; but finding that he was already over one hundred miles in the heart as it were of the enemy's country, that the next water was thirty-six miles distant and reported brackish, and that

38. Charles A. May, Second Dragoons, was celebrated in song, poetry, and paintings for his heroic actions at Resaca de la Palma.

39. On June 12, Taylor ordered McCulloch to explore the region around Linares as an alternative route to Monterey. Learning that the route had insufficient water to support a large troop movement, Taylor proceeded with plans to move the army to Monterey via Camargo, where forage and water were in greater supply.

there was no possibility of obtaining forage for the horses other than a scanty supply of grass, our commander wisely determined upon leaving this route to Monterey, and striking into the upper road, in a northerly direction, at a point near the large rancho of La Coma. While at El Ebonillo he learned that Canales, with sixty men only and near six hundred fresh horses, was but one day's march ahead of him and traveling towards La Coma or El Coronel, and with the hope of overtaking him a forced march was made; but on striking the road near the former place, Capt. McC. was told that the noted ranchero chief had four hundred men with him close by, and had taken good care to send his extra horses to a place of safety. To proceed farther into the interior with thirty-five men only, encumbered with eight pack mules, was deemed not only inexpedient but imprudent; so our horses' heads were turned towards this place, where we have arrived all safe.

On starting from Matamoros the party numbered forty as well mounted and well appointed men as ever started upon a scout. To throw any Mexicans upon a wrong scent who might be watching him, our commander took the direct road to Reynosa, and encamped the first night near the Rancho de Guadalupe. The next morning, after leaving the rancho a short distance in the rear, the course was altered to the south, and before night, after a thorough soaking from a shower, we were in the main road to Linares, and in the same path taken by Arista's army in its flight. The horse of one of the men becoming lame during the day, Capt. McC. reluctantly ordered him to make the best way he could into Matamoros.

On the third morning a young man was badly wounded by a fall from his horse while endeavoring to overtake a small party of armed Mexicans. His injuries were so severe that it was found necessary to send him, too, back to Matamoros; and as several ranchos had already been passed, it was deemed prudent to send three men with him. This reduced the party to thirty-five, all told. Of the party pursued, one escaped by reaching a mesquit thicket; the others left their horses so hotly were they pressed, threw away their *escopetas* or carbines, cartridge boxes, coats, and even their spurs, and succeeded in eluding pursuit owing to the thickness of the chaparral. If they get over the scare as easily as they got away, I am much mistaken. Of all the different parties encountered on the road, this was the only one that escaped. The leader of it drew his *escopeta* upon Capt. McC., who was in advance when they first came up, but thought it more discreet to run than to fire.

It would be difficult to picture the astonishment and alarm at the different ranchos as the Rangers entered them, or the consternation of those upon whom we came suddenly upon the road. By forced night marches our commander frequently got upon the other side of some of the settlements, and rode into them as though direct from Monterey or Linares, and going toward Matamoros. By doubling and twisting about they were thrown completely off the scent, and were willing to answer any questions with a readiness that showed they thought life or death depended upon their alacrity. At El Ebonillo a supply of corn sufficient for two days was procured for our horses, their own prices being paid for every kernel; this, with the exception of a small quantity obtained from the carts of a traveling merchant on the upper road, was all that could be procured.

The result of the information picked up by the reconnaissance, in a few words, amounts to this: that two days before we reached El Mesepate there was a body of 1000 Mexican infantry at Linares, and that a force of cavalry, the precise number of which could not be ascertained, was stationed at different ranchos in the vicinity; that Arista had recently sent down commissioners in the neighborhood of El Ebonillo, who had purchased five hundred fresh horses to remount some of his cavalry at Monterey; that many of his troops, especially such rancheros as had been pressed, were daily deserting him; that the men of Canales, too, or many of them, were leaving his fortunes in disgust, those sticking by him only doing it from a hope of plunder, or from having no other means of gaining food. That he was aware of Capt. McC's being in his neighborhood there is little doubt; but whether he was unable to catch up with the hurried, and complicated movements of the Texans, or fearful of giving them battle, is more than this deponent can say. I say hurried and complicated movements of the Texans; why, from the time of our leaving Matamoros to our reaching this place the men neither took off coats, boots, nor spurs; not an extra or second shirt was carried by one of them; and although the weather was rainy much of the time, and two heavy northers visited us while encamped, there was not a minute at any time when any man's pistol or rifle would have missed fire, or he would not have been up and ready for an attack. I have seen a goodly number of volunteers in my time, but Capt. Ben McCulloch's men are choice specimens.

The 1st U. S. Infantry, under command of Lieut. Col. Wilson, are stationed here, and both officers and men are generally in good health. The entrances to the Plaza Principal, where the soldiers are quartered, are filled with loose stones in such a way as to resist an attack from cavalry, and no fears of the Mexicans endeavoring to retake the place, at least with success, are entertained.

A steamboat is now in sight, and the wondering inhabitants are flocking down to the river's bank in throngs, to see her come in. "Mira! mira! la steamboat!" is on every tongue as they hie onward. In Stephen Austin's time, before the Texan revolution, he made one trip as high as this in a small craft propelled by steam, and prayed for permission to use his vessel in the navigation of the river; but as the *arrieros* or muleteers thought it would interfere with their calling, the authorities would not grant his request. Not all the muleteers in Mexico, backed by all the authorities, can prevent steamboats from running on the Rio Grande from this, henceforth and forever.

A fellow has just brought a verbal message to Col. Wilson, from a female who requests that her name may never be mentioned to the effect that Col. Juan Seguin is to attack the place tonight with a numerous force, and that he will be assisted by a large number of the inhabitants. Seguin is a Texan, of San Antonio de Bexar, and although always well treated by that Government, turned traitor.[40] The woman says that he will certainly attack the place, and perhaps has some reason; yet few believe he will make the attempt, and none fear the result.

G. W. K.

*Daily Picayune*, July 7, 1846

Reynosa, Mexico, June 22, 1846

In my last I mentioned the story of the woman to Col. Wilson, to the effect that this place was to be attacked during the night by Seguin. Well, the night has passed and Reynosa is still safe in the hands of the Americans. A woman would hardly make up such a tale unless she had some grounds to work upon, much as the Mexicans delight to deal in falsehood and the marvelous. Seguin would no doubt like to attack the place if he had the least prospect of success, and his emissaries, very likely, have been tampering with the inhabitants, and endeavoring to obtain their assistance; that he will have the temerity to come in at any time, day or night, is not believed, although every precaution has always been taken by Col. Wilson to guard against an assault. Seguin joined the Texans in their

---

40. Juan Seguin was born in Texas and served with Sam Houston at the battle of San Jacinto. He represented Bexar County in the Texas Senate for two terms before being elected mayor of San Antonio in January 1841. When the Mexican General Rafael Vasquez raided Texas and occupied San Antonio early in 1842, Seguin found himself caught between Mexican officials eager to undercut his influence in Texas and political rivals in Bexar County who questioned his loyalty to the Republic. In April 1842, he resigned as mayor of San Antonio and sought asylum in Mexico. J. Milton Nance, *Attack and Counter Attack: The Texas-Mexican Frontier, 1842* (Austin, 1964), 9–54.

Revolution, commanded a company under Houston at the battle of San Jacinto, and was always esteemed to be a brave officer and loyal citizen; but he turned traitor in one of the darkest hours of Texas, and lost all—character, and I believe fortune.

But if Reynosa was not beleaguered by armed men, and if no villainous saltpetre was burnt, nor lead thrown, we passed anything but a comfortable night of it. The early part was most disagreeably hot and sultry—enough of itself to prevent sleep although we were encamped out of doors and on the hard ground: but to add to this, every dog in the town kept up a most incessant barking, and each separate whelp seemed engaged in an attempt to out-bark and out-howl his neighbor. How many dogs there are in Reynosa, I have no means of ascertaining, there being no tax upon the curs, nor any statistics from which correct information can be obtained; yet as the number of inhabitants is put down at 3000, I should think that by multiplying them by seven hundred and fifty—judging from the noise they make altogether—you might get somewhere in the neighborhood of the number of dogs. When we have no positive data to go upon we are obliged to resort to guess work. Well, these rascally whelps barked away the hours until a rain-storm came up, and then we had a thunder gust for an accompaniment. Pleasant country this! but rather hard on that portion of the American people this side the Rio Grande. Do you know that I sometimes think of the St. Charles, the Verandah, and of Hewlett's[41]—their sumptuous dinners and comfortable beds?

Yet, with all the drawbacks above enumerated, we still made out to nap it awhile towards morning. I could not help laughing at a young Ranger whose blanket was within good hearing distance of mine. "Well," said he, "if I'd been told when I left Mississippi, a year ago last spring, by any one of my particular friends, that I could ever sleep in this way—that I could ever catch a wink with all my clothes on, belted round with two pistols and a Bowie, boots on, and spurs to boot, out doors on the ground in a single blanket, and raining at that, I'd a told him that he lied, sure." It's pretty much so.

The steamboat in sight, when I wrote you yesterday, was the *Aid*, all the way from New Orleans, Capt. John E. Hyde. The populace, male and female, flocked down to see her, and gazed with open-mouthed wonder as she let off steam. The younger brood of Mexicans had never seen anything of the kind before, and perhaps some of them had never even "heern tell" of a steamboat. The *Aid* brought up a heavy freight of Army

41. Hotels in New Orleans.

stores for the troops here, and starts back for Matamoros again this afternoon. As the roads are in a miserable condition, a party of us, including
Capt. McCulloch, go down in her.

G. W. K.
*Daily Picayune*, July 7, 1846

Matamoros, June 28, 1846

The steamboat *Neva*, the same we met while on the way from Reynosa
to this place, was to have started last evening on another trip up with a
detachment of the 7th U. S. Infantry; but a couple of engineers having
pronounced her boilers defective and unsafe, she has been laid up for the
present. The soldiers were ordered up to reinforce the command of Colonel
Wilson at Reynosa, previous to a move upon Camargo. The weather has
been so bad, and the roads are in such a horrible condition, that the
infantry will hardly be able to march for a week or so.

Matamoros is certainly going ahead. I see that the Washington Ball-
Room is to be opened this evening for the first time under that title, with a
grand Mexican fandango—admittance 50 cents. And then gambling rooms
are opened in every street, bar rooms at every turn, and eating rooms stare
the hungry in the face on all sides. An inundation has been poured in
upon Matamoros that she will not get rid of easily.

Gen. Taylor is now worse cramped and hampered for want of transportation than ever, and the Quarter Master General's Department "catches it"
on all sides and from all quarters. There are volunteers and regulars
enough to march at any time, and to any point—there are more volunteers
already here than are wanted, idle and uneasy at the inactivity—yet the
commander general cannot move for want of transports. With six small
steamers, at the present stage of water, healthy and commanding points
could easily be reached on the Rio Grande; but they are not here, and the
arms of one of the largest armies ever brought into the field by the United
States are tied for want of proper management at home. There is something wrong, too, still in the post office department, and loud are the
complaints in every quarter.

I have not a line of news to communicate—we are all in the dark and in
the mud. Capt. McCulloch is still here, although a part of the company
remains at Reynosa. He will probably move up his entire command as
soon as the weather will permit.

G. W. K.
*Daily Picayune*, July 7, 1846

Matamoros, Mexico, June 30, 1846

General Taylor's camp on this side of the Rio Grande is yet above water in spots, although the chances of being driven or drowned out still look about even. I sat upon the banks of the river this morning with my feet paddling in the water; so you may learn how near we are to an inundation. I wish that some of those members of Congress, who are pleased to designate the officers of our army as "epauletted loafers," and "wasp-waisted vampires hanging about high places," could get a glimpse of them now—in fact, could share their privations and discomforts with them. They would forever after hold their tongues. The poor devils—although they laugh at and make light of the annoyances which beset them—appear in plight most pitiful, many of them really not having had a dry rag to their backs or a dry blanket to sleep in for near a fortnight. "Hanging about high places"! Why, they have been wading about low places, half way up to their knees in mud and water—Gen. Taylor and Col. Twiggs among the rest—and nothing but an absolute fear of being drowned out has driven any from their position. The two regiments of Louisiana Volunteers—Marks's and Walton's—on the opposite bank of the river, occupy higher ground; yet they are bad enough off in all conscience.[42] All are still enjoying a better degree of health than one could suppose they would, but I am fearful, if they remain here too long, that some epidemic may make its appearance among them.

Volunteers are still arriving by regiments, and still Gen. Taylor is without transportation or any means of moving them. Where are the steamers ordered to be purchased long since for the use of the army? Here is a stage of water high enough to reach Reynosa and Camargo with ease and safety, yet there is not a safe conveyance even across the river. I cannot conceive a situation more trying to the patience and more mortifying to the feelings of the commander-in-chief than the one he is now placed in. With men enough to march to any quarter he has not the means to move them an inch.

From the interior the news is various and contradictory. It is said that a portion of the Mexican infantry has left Linares for some point near Tampico, and very likely such is the case. For some time the inhabitants of Matamoros believed that the troops would return and retake the place—

42. David E. Twiggs received one of the two regular army brigadier general commissions created by Congress with the outbreak of the Mexican War. Mentioned are Samuel F. Marks, Third Regiment Smith's Brigade of Louisiana Volunteers, and James B. Walton, First Regiment.

could not for one moment suppose that the Americans would be allowed to hold quiet possession of the city. I believe that they have now given up all hopes. The number of Mexican soldiers at Monterey is known to be small. Arista, whose course has been sustained by the Government, is at his hacienda near that city with a few men only. The number of infantry at Linares is at present only 800, with a small force of cavalry in the neighborhood. Gen. Paredes[43] is said to be en route for Monterey with 6000 men—some say as large a number as 8000. Scouting parties of Texans will probably be sent out as soon as the roads are in traveling condition; and then it will be difficult to ascertain the full force and intentions of the enemy.

The fourth of July will soon be upon us, and I learn that extensive preparations are being made to celebrate it with all honor.

What a rare chance does this place now present for a theatrical or some speculation of the kind, although I do not know how long it would last. At present, the gambling rooms, bar rooms, restaurants, &c., are picking up all the surplus change. I saw a small troupe of Mexican tumblers or circus riders parading the streets yesterday, mounted on miserable horses. The leader was bespattering the North Americans with praise while his horse was bespattering them with mud. I could not learn whether he collected much of an audience.

G. W. K.

*Daily Picayune*, July 8, 1846

Matamoros, Mexico, July 3, 1846

Did I or did I not, in one of my former letters, say there were no mosquitoes in Matamoros? If I asserted there were none I was entirely and most distinctly in the wrong, for within a night or two they have made their appearance in myriads, adding another item to the catalogue of discomforts attendant upon life hereaway. The camp on both sides the river, after two or three fair days, has dried up, however, so that all can get about without incurring the annoyance and danger of being stalled or drowned in the mud. The river is within a few inches of coming over the banks, yet it is nearly at a stand and the hopes now are that there will be no overflow.

---

43. Mariano Paredes had become president in January 1846 after the fall of José Joaquín Herrera's moderate government. Opposed to any concessions to the United States, he pledged to defend Mexico's territorial integrity all the way to the Sabine. In July, with his control of the government rapidly slipping away, he announced his intention to take command of the Mexican forces fighting on the Rio Grande. He was deposed when Santa Anna returned to Mexico in August, and spent a brief time in prison before being exiled.

Salutes will be fired tomorrow, the anniversary of our independence, and the glorious 4th will doubtless be celebrated in becoming style. A strange story has got abroad among the Mexican residents, and is firmly believed by many, to the effect that the city is to be given up by Gen. Taylor to be sacked as a part of the celebration, that the women are to be violated, and the children carried off as slaves. How such a tale could get wind and obtain credence I know not, but that there will be hiding and skulking away during tomorrow is as certain as the day comes.

Independent of the news published in the Matamoros *Reveille*[44] of this morning, we have any quantity of rumors from the interior of Mexico. A majority of them are probably entirely destitute of foundation, yet it may not be amiss to give them a place in print. One account has it that Herrera is again at the head of the Government, while Paredes continues in command of the army. Another report is to the effect that in the west of Mexico there has been a *pronunciamento*[45] in favor of Santa Anna, calling for the immediate return of the tyrant to the country, while there is still another announcing that the inhabitants of Zacatecas, heretofore the fiercest and hottest-headed of all in favor of war with the United States—have now risen in favor of immediate peace. Such are some of the rumors. I might give you a hundred afloat here. You, in New Orleans, have perhaps a better opportunity of ascertaining the truth or falsity of the reports than we have.

The steamer *Aid*, the pioneer steamer to points above this, has just appeared in sight from Brazos Santiago, and the *Cincinnati* is shortly expected. When they arrive, it is said that a detachment of four companies of U. S. Infantry, with provisions and baggage, will go on board destined for the occupation of Camargo. Capt. McCulloch's Rangers, and probably some of Walker's[46] old men, will operate with the regulars, but will take the land route on horseback. The position of Canales and Seguin is not known; but I am thinking they will be heard of in the neighborhood of Camargo.

Let me revert once more to the great want of transportation felt here. Had Gen. Taylor received the number of volunteers he called for in the first instance, with a sufficiency of steamers with which to move them and their

44. Founded by Samuel Bangs and Gideon Lewis, the four-page *Reveille* included one page of news in Spanish. The paper was closed down briefly when the anti-American tone of its Spanish-language page provoked the ire of General Taylor's command. The *Reveille* was one of several newspapers published by Americans in Mexico during the War. Copeland, *Kendall of the Picayune*, 162. Reilly, "American Reporters and the Mexican War, 1846–1848," 149–51.

45. An insurrection or uprising.

46. Captain Samuel H. Walker, a member of the ill-fated Mier expedition of 1842 (see note 71 below), later served with the U.S. Mounted Rifles. He was killed at Huamantla on October 9, 1847, in one of the last significant engagements of the war.

subsistence, it is thought by those best informed, that the 4th of July would have been celebrated tomorrow in Monterey instead of Matamoros. The Mexicans certainly could not have recovered from the panic with which they started from Resaca de la Palma in season to make a formidable stand this side the mountains, so that Monterey could have been taken almost without firing a gun. It is too late now. A tardiness in forwarding steamers has deprived the commanding General of a most glorious opportunity of occupying one of the strongest holds of the enemy.

A good story is told of the manner in which Arista's officers were treated after their hurried return to Monterey. A ball was given to a large party of officers who had just arrived from San Luis, or some point in that direction, and at this ball Arista's defeated and disgraced underlings appeared, in uniforms fresh brushed and with all their appointments scoured up to the brightest. The orchestra struck up, and among the first to pay their respects to the ladies and ask their hands for the waltz or cotillion, were the fellows who had danced so nimbly to a different tune at the Resaca. The answer of the ladies was noble, and at the same time cutting to a degree: "We do not dance with our own sex!"

There has been some dissatisfaction in the Andrew Jackson Regiment of Louisiana Volunteers, and thinking that a false coloring may be given to the movements of the officers I will relate the circumstances so far as I have been able to learn them, believing that in the main I am correct. It seems that a large portion of the officers, learning that there was a strong probability that the six months' men would be disbanded, and deeming that there would be little or no fighting done nor any call made upon them for active service during that period, sent a letter to Gen. Taylor requesting information, and asking permission to return home rather than remain idle pensioners upon the Government. In all this they were very right. Gen. T., I believe, has referred the matter to Gen. Smith, and this popular officer will doubtless settle the affair satisfactorily to all. The situation of the volunteers has been gloomy enough—remaining for weeks inactive in camp, the weather bad enough to make the Grand Turk himself curse his prophet, and with but poor prospects of a change of situation or circumstances: yet it is now an understood thing that the Louisiana Volunteers will have the first opportunity of signalizing themselves if any farther demonstration is to be made into the enemy's country; and this, when it comes to be known generally, will quiet any uneasiness that has been felt.[47]

---

47. One thousand Louisiana volunteers arrived at Point Isabel in mid-May. Restless for want of action and unwilling to extend their service to a full year, virtually all started home by August 1.

Our dates from New Orleans—of letters only—are to the 26th ult., a heavy newspaper mail being still behind. When the roads are in such condition that the wagon train can recommence travel between this and Point Isabel, they will come tumbling in by the cart load.

The health of the volunteer camp is but indifferent, although bowel complaints are almost the only diseases prevalent, and they are generally of a mild type. In Col. Marks's Regiment the measles have made their appearance, several men being now down with the complaint. I trust it will not spread.

They are to have quite a celebration tomorrow in the volunteer camp, when a speech is to be made by Captain Ogden,[48] of Rapides. Company D of the Andrew Jackson regiment is also to give a grand dinner, to which a large portion of the principal officers, both Texan and American, if I can now make such a distinction, have been invited. The company is in the main composed of printers, and they will carry the thing out in capital style.

G. W. K.

P. S. It is said that several Mexicans were killed in rows last night—some say five or six—by drunken brawlers who hang about the camp of the Texans. There were several disgraceful scenes enacted during the night, but I do not believe so many were killed as is stated. The misfortune is, that a large portion of the Texans are obliged to suffer for the faults of a few.

*Daily Picayune*, July 17, 1846

Matamoros, Mexico, July 4, 1846

There was no such thing as sleeping this morning, after sunrise, except in cases where the burning of powder in 6, 12 and 18-pounders might operate as an opiate. Never has the glorious Fourth been ushered in with such a shower of salutes as resounded in camp this morning. I could distinctly hear Forno cracking and banging away on the other side the river, while Ridgeley's, Bragg's, and other batteries kept up the din on this.[49] The beauty of it is that these salutes were fired with Mexican powder—some that was captured.

No general celebration of the day has been settled upon, but different parties are keeping it up in different ways. I have had half a dozen invitations, but have been so busy in making preparations for a trip to Camargo

---

48. George P. Ogden, Louisiana Mounted Volunteers.

49. Henry Forno, Louisiana Volunteer Artillery, and Randolph Ridgely and Braxton Bragg, both of the Third Artillery.

with Captain McCulloch, that I could not attend. The printers over in the Andrew Jackson regiment will probably go ahead of all in their banquet— they know how to do it.

Matamoros looks more and more like a branch or faubourg of New Orleans. In the streets I have seen the old and well-known faces of Judge Woodroof and Capt. Tufts. Young Hagan from Mobile, with his little party of mounted men, has just arrived. He is to join one of the Texas spy companies—I hope McCulloch's.

G. W. K.
*Daily Picayune*, July 17, 1846

Matamoros, July 5, 1846

Yesterday passed off without any accident that I can hear of, which is a piece of decidedly good fortune when it is taken into consideration that so many men were engaged in its celebration here. It is a day fruitful of disaster all over the Union, and I was fearful that many lives might be lost here.

I spoke a few days since of a company of Mexican tumblers who were parading the streets drumming up an audience. Here is a bill of their performance for today, copied verbatim:

FOURTH OF JULY
SPLENDID ENTERTAINMENT!

The company of Rope Dancers that now reside in the Republic of Rio Grande, have much pleasure in announcing to the public that upon the Fourth of July, in commemoration of the glorious Independence of the United States, they will bring forward one of their most brilliant exhibitions so well calculated to please, at which time the principal Actress will appear upon the tight rope, giving one of her most happy presentations.

N. B.—Pay for entrance at the door. Seat, Fifty Cents.
*Long live the United States of America!*

Don't it strike you, after reading this, that the Mexicans have a slight insight into a system known as the gag? They have their "show" in the open air. I visited them in the afternoon. It was distressing to see a poor devil dancing upon the tight rope directly in the face of a scorching sun. One word of the orchestra: it was composed of a bass drum, a tenor drum—both of primitive appearance and construction—four bass wood clarionets, dug out fresh, and a huge tin instrument the name of which I could not understand. It appeared to be a cross of the bugle and ophiclyde, with a small sprinkling of the hautboy.[50] I have not got over that instrument yet, after a good night's sleep. The audience was respectable as regards numbers—the performance wretched.

I must be in a hurry to get this off before the mail closes.

G. W. K.

*Daily Picayune*, July 18, 1846

July 5, 1846 [An extract.]

McCulloch's Rangers are off immediately after breakfast—this is early in the day you must understand—on another trip up the country, and I am hurrying myself to accompany them. The streamer *Aid* is not off yet, but is to leave immediately, so I learn, with the detachment of the 4th U. S. Infantry destined for Camargo. You shall hear from me from the first point whence I can send a letter in that direction.

[G. W. K.]

*Daily Picayune*, July 17, 1846

Reynosa, Mexico, July 8, 1846

McCulloch's Rangers, which corps I have again joined, arrived here yesterday from Matamoros, after a trip which was hard enough both upon American men and American horses. The road is crooked enough at the best of times; but now that the Rio Grande is over its banks, we were obliged to turn out into the high and dry chaparral a dozen times, and had to wade, dig and flounder through water, mud and mire until the patience of the men and strength of the poor horses was entirely exhausted. And then the weather down in this Southern latitude—a hot sun overhead and not a breath of air stirring in the thick and matted chaparral—verily, this thing of scouting through Mexico may be exciting enough, but is far from being agreeable any way it can be fixed. Not a sign of a tent do we take along, while shade and shelter are matters not pertaining to the country. You can form some idea of campaigning among the "greasers" and then weep.

The steamer *Aid*, Capt. Hyde, has just arrived with three companies of the 7th U. S. Infantry, under Capts. Holmes, Whiting and Paul, on board. The rest of the regiment, all under Capt. Miles, will be here in a day or two, either by land or water, when a move will be made towards Camargo.[51] We

50. The ophiclyde was a valved brass instrument; the hautboy was an oboe.

51. The move to Camargo began late on July 6 when elements of the Seventh Infantry, commanded by Dixon S. Miles, left Matamoros for Camargo on board the steamer *Enterprise*. With Miles were Theophilus Holmes, Gabriel Paul, and Henry Whiting, Taylor's staff quartermaster. Mechanical difficulties delayed their arrival until July 14.

learn here that that city has suffered much from the overflow of the river, different accounts giving the number of houses washed away or destroyed as being between one and five hundred. That the place has suffered much there can be no doubt, but the full extent cannot be known until we reach the place.

The high water has been of incredible injury to the crops on the Rio Grande, some asserting that even three-fourths of the cotton and corn in the bottoms have been destroyed. It will not only go hard with these "from hand-to-mouth" people, whose only thought is of the day, but I am fearful that it may occasion difficulty in giving Gen. Taylor the means of subsisting his troops to the extent he anticipated from the appearance of the crops a short while since. Three weeks ago, when I went down on the *Aid* to Matamoros, there never was as good a promise of an abundant harvest, and all were cheerful; now the poor Mexicans are stalking about waist deep in the corn fields, the families have been driven off to the high grounds, and every face is shrouded in gloom. The war has been of service, real service to the inhabitants on the Rio Grande, but the freshet has ruined them.

You have seen drift on the Mississippi in high water times; drift is a different thing here. To be sure you see a few small trees and a heap of light brush floating along at intervals; but the principal drift, if I can believe the words of one who I am half inclined to believe is a bit of a wag, is watermelons and dead horses. A strange combination, but I have seen both coming down together.

They have been expecting an attack from Canales again here, and the *Plaza* has been placed in a stronger state than ever, but no Canales has appeared. Report had it that he was coming in last night, with fire and sword, but the different watches passed off quietly. He is not coming into this place.

G. W. K.
*Daily Picayune*, July 14, 1846

Camargo, Mexico, July 16, 1846

The city of Camargo—or what is left of it—stands on the south side of the river San Juan, and three miles only from the Rio Grande. Its population has been as high as 6000; but previous to *la creciénte*,[52] as the people call the recent dreadful flood, it has fallen to 5000, and is now much less than that number. Many of the inhabitants, who have lost all,

---

52. A freshet or flood.

will never return, choosing higher ground in the vicinity on which to rebuild their *jacales*, as their houses or tenements are termed.

The extent of the freshet, or the rapidity with which the waters of the San Juan rose, have not been exaggerated. In this place alone no less than eight hundred and sixty houses—among them some of the best houses— were either much injured or totally destroyed, the frightened inhabitants flocking to the hills in crowds when they saw that the place must inevitably be inundated. The houses immediately around the Plaza, including the church and the dwellings of the priest and alcalde, were injured but little, although the waters gave even these a thorough soaking. To compute the entire loss sustained by Camargo were impossible; it would not amount to as much as many might suppose, for hundreds of the houses were of little value; yet the amount of suffering, as most of the people have lost their all, has been frightful.

Many amusing stories are told of the means resorted to by the superstitious old women to stay the progress of the dreaded flood. One old crone, when the waters lacked by but a few inches of running over the banks, rushed to the river with a small image of our Savior and the Holy Virgin, and loudly implored them to stay the progress of *la creciénte*. An American near told her to quit this flummery, go to her house, and save as much of her property as possible. She beckoned him away, and called more loudly than ever on the mute images in her hands to arrest the flood. Again she was told to leave, but not until a heavy surge of water reached her, accompanied by a crumbling in of the banks, did she receive sufficient admonishment that her prayers were of no avail. Then she turned and ran as fast as she could; and well was it for her that she did so, for in ten minutes more the water reached her house. The only persons who remained in the place were the few American residents, who lived in canoes while the city was under water. Nearly opposite where I am now writing is a large mesquit tree, in the top of which they built a roost which still remains.

The weather here is insupportably hot during the middle of the day, with little air stirring as was the case at Reynosa. On the march from that place to this the Infantry suffered dreadfully, especially this side of *Laguna del Pajaritas*, or Lake of the Little Birds, there being no water on the road and the sun pouring his hottest rays directly upon their backs. Several fell to the ground exhausted by the heat, while others were so much overcome that it was necessary to give them places in the forage wagons. McCulloch's Rangers did not suffer to the same extent, being all well mounted; but this thing of campaigning in a southern latitude during mid-summer is not so particularly pleasant under any circumstances. To be sure, by sounding the reveille at half-past 2 o'clock in the morning and starting at 3, much of the march is through with before the sun is yet up; but starting off at such an unseasonable hour and being obliged to lay about during the heat of the day without shade, for we have no tents, comes rather hard on the American people—on a portion of them at least. Bivouacking and all that sort of thing may sound very well in ballads, but when it comes down to the stern reality of the thing it is distinctly a different matter.

There is no news stirring—no intelligence as yet of the movements or whereabouts of Canales and Carabajal.[53] So soon as I can get the names of the different officers of the American force here, which composes the advance guard of the army of invasion, I will give you the list.

G. W. K.

*Daily Picayune*, August 1, 1846

Camargo, Mexico, July 17, 1846

The *Enterprise* steamboat is off in an hour, but before she leaves I wish to give you, for the information of their friends in the U. States, a list of the officers now at this place, which is as follows:[54]

Capt. D. S. Miles, 7th Infantry, Command'g.
Lieut. F. N. Page, Adjutant.
Lieut. F. Britton, Commissary and Quartermaster.
B. M. Byrne, and G. M. Prevost, Assistant Surgeons.
Lieut. T. J. Wood, Topographical Engineer.
Lieuts. Thomas and Johnston, Light Artillery.
Capts. Holmes, Ross, Whiting, Gatlin and Paul, 7th Infantry.
Lieuts. Hopson, Hanson, Little, Humber, Gantt, McLaws, Van Dorn, Gardner, Potter, Strong and Clitz, 7th Infantry.

---

53. José María J. Carabajal (or Carvajal) was a political and military ally of Antonio Canales. Born and educated in Texas, he was a delegate to the convention that wrote the constitution for the Texas Republic. He moved his family to Tamaulipas after Texas secured its independence. He continued his separatist activities in northern Mexico into the 1850s. J. Milton Nance, *After San Jacinto: The Texas-Mexican Frontier, 1836–1841* (Austin, 1963), 145–47.

54. Those mentioned here and not previously identified are Francis N. Page, Seventh Infantry; Forbes Britton, who would later settle with Kendall near New Braunfels; Barnard M. Byrne; Grayson M. Prevost; Thomas J. Wood; Francis J. Thomas and Richard W. Johnston, Third Artillery; Richard H. Ross; Richard C. Gatlin; Nevil Hopson; Charles Hanson; Lewis H. Little; Charles Humber; Levi Gantt; Lafayette McLaws; Earl Van Dorn; Franklin Gardner; Joseph H. Potter; Erastus B. Strong; and Henry B. Clitz.

The companies of the 7th Infantry now here are "E," "C," "D," "K," "F," and "J." The entire force of regulars composing the advanced guard of the army this side of Reynosa, is between 250 and 300, but to this force must be added McCulloch's Rangers, upwards of 70, making a force of between 3 and 400 in all. The regulars are encamped in the houses around the Plaza; the Rangers under the falling roofs of some deserted jacales higher up the river. The Mexicans here are much more friendly than those at Reynosa, and more reconciled to the appearance of the Americans among them.

They are hourly expecting more steamboats at this place, with additional provisions, forage, and military stores. The army, or at least one division of it, will move from this point towards Monterey, distant 150 miles. In the meantime it is thought that scouting parties of Rangers may be sent up in the neighborhood of Mier, and other towns on the river, and if they do I will give you full particulars of their adventures.

G. W. K.

P. S. I heard it stated a day or two since that Gen. Arista had sent in a courier to Gen. Taylor, requesting that a force might be sent on to his hacienda near Monterey, to take him prisoner. According to the story, Gen. A. is under strict watch and cannot move without having the eyes of some of the Government emissaries upon him. I give this story precisely as I heard it.

G. W. K.

*Daily Picayune*, August 1, 1846

Camargo, Mexico, July 21, 1846

A report came in this morning that Gillespie's[55] company of Mounted Rangers from San Antonio, Hays's old men, was seen yesterday afternoon on the banks of the Rio Grande, opposite Mier. They have probably come in direct from Bexar, and it is thought will be down this afternoon. I cannot hear of a circumstance other than the above which can be worked up into an item of intelligence, and in the absence of all news allow me to give a few speculations as to the intentions and movements of some of the Mexican leaders of note this side of Sierra Madre.

It was for a long time a favorite scheme of Arista's to bring about a union between Texas and the States of the lower Rio Grande. The people of Nueva Leon, Coahuila and Tamaulipas, ground down by the taxes imposed upon them by the Central Government, and not receiving either benefit or

55. Robert A. Gillespie, First Regiment Texas Mounted Rifle Volunteers.

protection therefrom, have always been ripe for revolt; and perhaps the only reason why they have not before this raised the *grito*[56] of revolution has been because they had not the means within themselves to cope successfully with the Centralist forces, coupled with the fact that they have never had a leader on whom they could depend. Canales, when in 1839 he pronounced in favor of the Constitution of 1824, and crossed the Rio Grande with Jordan's men, might have succeeded in everything he undertook had he been honest, or had a brother-in-law of his, Col. Molano, been faithful to the cause; but it is a well known fact that immediately after Jordan had won his great victory near Saltillo, and the Federalists were everywhere in the ascendant, that the money of the Central Government effected what its arms could not. The brave Jordan was sold, although he succeeded in getting safely out of the country, while the exertions of Fisher, Wells, Ross, and other American officers, in favor of Federalism, all went for nothing. A good round sum was the price of the treachery of the Mexican leaders, and Canales, either directly or indirectly, doubtless came in for a full share.[57] I cannot learn that Carvajal, (usually, but erroneously spelled Carabajal) who was educated in the United States, and speaks and writes English well, had any hand in the bargain and sale.

With all this corruption Arista had nothing to do. He was a Central leader at the time, and it was not until the annexation of Texas to the United States came to be seriously agitated that he began to entertain hopes of overturning the Central power in the departments this side of the Sierra Madre, and by a union with Texas forming a strong middle Republic.

---

56. A cry or scream.

57. In 1839, Reuben Ross had obtained permission from the Texas government to organize a volunteer company to protect the region south and west of Houston. Hearing that a force of Mexicans and Indians, encouraged by Mexican authorities, were gathering between the Nueces and the Rio Grande, Ross joined forces with Antonio Canales. Canales was one of a group of political-military leaders in northern Mexico who were pledged to the federalist structure embodied in the Mexican Constitution of 1824 and were in open rebellion against Santa Anna's centralist government in Mexico City. Samuel W. Jordan, captain of a company in the Texas service charged with protecting the frontier near San Antonio, and other Texas officers contributed men to the company, which was organized in August 1839. Originally expecting to serve in a separate command under the Texas flag, this force served under Canales during 1839 and 1840. Col. William S. Fisher, an officer in the First Texas Infantry, added three more companies to the force in August 1840. Joe Wells also served with Canales along the Rio Grande in 1840, commanding a force of about one hundred Texans. In September 1840, Jordan and about 120 Texans joined a small federalist force under the command of Juan Nepomuceno Molano on a march deep into the Mexican interior. When Morales surrendered his force to Mariano Arista in Victoria in October, Jordan and his men were left to fight their way back to Texas. Canales abandoned his Texas allies and accepted an armistice offered by Arista in November 1840. Nance, *After San Jacinto*, 209–16, 331–63.

Without the co-operation of the then "Lone Star Republic" he could do nothing, and to effect this he opened a correspondence with several influential men at Corpus Christi and other points. Even if he effected his object of bringing about the union, he had the sagacity to foresee and to foretell that in a very few years the Anglo-Saxons would have a preponderance in the new Republic that would take from him his influence and authority; yet this he was willing to overlook, as he said for the good of his countrymen. There are no men in the world who have the welfare of the people so much at heart as the Mexican leaders, although they all have a most singular way of showing it.

The final annexation of Texas to the United States completely frustrated Arista's plans, upset his hopes, and in a great measure embittered him against the Americans, from whom he had expected so much assistance: yet not so with Carvajal, Canales, and some of the other Mexican revolutionary leaders. These latter still hoped that the appearance of the American army at Corpus Christi might be turned to their advantage in some way, and with these hopes a correspondence was opened with some of the officers stationed there, and the camp was also visited by one of the master spirits, Carvajal. The full nature of the communications he made I am not acquainted with, but that he in some way expected aid in the scheme of separating the departments this side the Sierra Madre from the Central Government there is not a question.[58] To patch out the new Republic it is probable that he was desirous of holding all the country this side the Nueces and was equally desirous that the American force should not advance a step farther in the direction of the Rio Grande. He knew, too, that the Government of Mexico would oppose, to the utmost of its abilities, the progress of the American arms, would throw a large force into Matamoros, and that thus the expectations of the revolutionists, of a speedy release from Central bondage, would be retarded or completely frustrated.

Whatever Carvajal might have thought, or whatever he might have advised, Gen. Taylor was ordered to take up ground opposite Matamoros and marched his army from Corpus Christi with that intention. When Canales and Carvajal saw the immense preparations made to oppose him,

58. In February 1846, Canales and Carvajal proposed to General Taylor that an independent Republic of the Rio Grande be established in northern Mexico under the protection of the United States in exchange for an agreement by Taylor not to cross the Nueces River. Taylor refused to halt his advance but did agree to pass these communications on to Washington. Nothing came of the matter. K. Jack Bauer, *Zachary Taylor: Soldier, Planter, Statesman of the Old Southwest* (Baton Rouge, 1985), 123–24.

and saw that Arista had taken the command against the Americans, they, too, joined the army with a large body of rancheros. They could not well do otherwise, with all their talk of a separation from the central power and their great hatred of central tyranny, for the success of the Mexican arms was looked upon as certain; and where would they have been with the American prisoners in Matamoros and they standing aloof and taking no hand in the matter? The result of the grand battles of Palo Alto and Resaca de la Palma, the occupation of Matamoros by Gen. Taylor, the flight of Arista with the remnant of his army, and the dispersing of the rancheros, are matters well known, and it now remains to be seen what scheme, if any, the revolutionary leaders will next hit upon.

Carvajal is very sore upon the subject of the defeat of all his hopes, and blames the American Government for treating his propositions with silent contempt. His family is now in this place, but he himself, although within a few hours' ride, does not feel disposed, either from fear of personal harm or a desire not to commit himself with his countrymen, to come in. Whatever may be his motives or his designs, he has the reputation, with the Americans as well as the Mexicans, of being a brave and intelligent man, and more honest even than many of his neighbors. I might give you the rumors of the whereabouts of Canales, of Seguin, of Antonio Perez, and of some of the other partisan officers, but it would all amount to mere speculation.

G. W. K.

P. S. Gillespie's company has just come in from Mier. The Captain reports that Canales left that place a short time previous to his arrival. He had but a small force, and went off, as was supposed, in the direction of Monterey. I do not believe he is far off. Antonio Perez went through Loredo a few days since with a large *caballada* of horses and mules.

*Daily Picayune*, August 11, 1846

Camargo, Mexico, July 23, 1846

Affairs begin to look a little more lively in this particular section. The steamer *Big Hatchee* came up this evening with Major Staniford[59] and the rest of the 5th U. S. Infantry on board, so that we have two regiments of regulars, the 5th and 7th, already quartered here. To this force must be added the section of Bragg's Artillery and the two companies of Dean Rangers under McCulloch and Gillespie, forming quite an army when all are paraded. A portion of the 8th U. S. Infantry is en route, and some of

---

59. Thomas Staniford.

the Louisiana Volunteers are also said to be on the way to Reynosa. To feed all this force, every steamer comes loaded down with salt meat, hard bread, coffee, sugar, and other articles, and Lieut. Britton, who has been acting here as Commissary and Quartermaster, has had his hands full to find places to store everything since *la creciénte* carried away so many houses.[60] The Mexicans, who have never seen such an immense amount of subsistence before, and probably did not think there was as much in the world, look on with perfect astonishment as they behold barrels rolling in all directions, and one old woman innocently asked yesterday if all the Americans alive were coming to Camargo?

In the meantime, we have intelligence from the interior which looks as though it might be in part authentic, although it is difficult to place reliance on Mexican statements of any kind. As the story goes, they commenced fortifying Monterey on the 20th of last month, (June,) and at the very latest date they had ten heavy cannon in position; and further, that the State of Nueva Leon, of which Monterey is the capital, has been peremptorily called upon to furnish 7000 men for the army, but that not a soul had stepped forward to join; still further, that there is a force of 3000 in the neighborhood of Linares, while to sum up, it is asserted that Paredes has reached San Luis Potosí with a force of 8000 men, on his way to Monterey. A part of this intelligence is doubtless entitled to some belief—another portion is entirely destitute of foundation—and it is difficult to separate the true from the false. One thing may be put down as certain: the inhabitants of Nueva Leon have been called upon to turn out and volunteer for the common defence of the country, and the inhabitants of Nueva Leon will not move an inch in the matter. The defeat of the Mexican army opposite Matamoros broke down whatever spirit they may have possessed, and under any circumstances, I believe they prefer independence and a separation from the Central Government, to clinging longer to its tottering fortunes. Nothing probably restrains them from coming out openly and declaring themselves, except fear—a fear that possibly the Americans may not be successful in the end, and that in such case Paredes, or whoever might be in power, would visit them with a heavy hand.

The Mexicans in this section are certainly placed in a most awkward situation, and many of them know not how to act nor what to do. They have been threatened with punishment the most severe if they show favor or render assistance to the invading army, and with these threats hanging

60. Taylor used seven steamers to move troops and supplies to Camargo. The baggage train and artillery moved overland under infantry escort.

over them, along comes Gen. Taylor promising them protection, and at the same time offering to pay the highest price for any subsistence they may be called upon to dispose of, or any assistance they may be able to furnish in the way of transportation—far better treatment and better protection than they have ever received from their own Government. To leave their homes and fly to the interior, in obedience to the mandates of Paredes, would be to sacrifice almost everything; to remain and show favor to the Americans, with the threats of future punishment and confiscation of property staring them in the face, places them rather between hawk and buzzard, as the saying is—in a dilemma from which they find it difficult to extricate themselves. Efforts are being made by the United States agents to procure transportation for provisions and stores into the interior. As soon as I can ascertain the result I will write.

One word about Canales's men. It is said that many of those who have left him are now cutting cord wood on the river bank for the steamboats, and are making money by it.

G. W. K.

*Daily Picayune*, August 9, 1846

Camargo, July 24, 1846

The steamer *Brownsville* came up last evening with two companies on board, one of the 8th U. S. Infantry and the other of the 3d U. S. Artillery, and the report now is that Gen. Worth[61] is on the way and will be here in a day or two. Army stores are tumbling in by wholesale, every boat bringing as much as she can stow, while preparations are rapidly going on to start much of it towards Monterey. I learn that one man—an Irishman living here—has contracted to furnish no less than one thousand pack mules for the use of the army.

The alcalde of Camargo—a specious fellow not over burthened with honesty or love of *los Americanos*—has been trying, it is thought, to throw some obstacles in the way of the Quartermasters—tampering with the inhabitants, and secretly advising them not to hire out their mules for the use of the army. Some say that he is a heavy proprietor in the town of New Camargo—a place building up three miles above this on the San

61. William Jenkins Worth, a veteran of the War of 1812 and the Seminole War in 1838, commanded the Second Division. Involved in a dispute over rank, Worth resigned his commission in early May after President Polk rejected his claim to be second in command. He withdrew his resignation when hostilities appeared eminent but still missed the battles at Palo Alto and Resaca de la Palma. He took up his command at Matamoros late in May. Worth joined Winfield Scott's army when the war moved south to Vera Cruz in March 1847. An ambitious and controversial figure throughout the war, Worth died of cholera while serving in Texas in 1849.

Juan—and wants all the force he can raise to open roads and otherwise help his own interest along. A little plain talk has opened his eyes if not his heart, and he will probably not be much in the way hereafter. Take them as a body, the biggest rascals in rascally Mexico are the alcaldes. Alike destitute of moral honesty or love of the people, they are generally and universally despised. The poor man stands no chance of obtaining justice at their hands, the rich man's extra dollar always turning the scales in his favor, and I believe that Gen. Taylor would adopt no better way of conciliating the majority than by ringing the bells of every place he enters, collecting all the people, and then bringing the alcalde into the centre of the Plaza and giving him a sound thrashing. Not a blow would be lost, for nine out of ten of them deserve punishment any day of the year; and then it would be such rare fun for the people. I do not exactly recommend the commanding general to adopt this novel plan of conciliation—I simply give my opinion as to the effects it would have.

The 8th Infantry has a full and well ordered band, and last evening the ears of the people of Camargo were greeted for the first time with "Hail Columbia" and "Yankee Doodle," to say nothing of "Lucy Neal," "Dance de Boatman, Dance," and other airs of kindred nature. It carried the feelings of the Americans home again to hear these strains in such an out-of-the-way place.

I learn that a small party of Rangers are to leave today for Mier, and that in three or four days another party is to reconnoitre the road as far as China, in the direction of Monterey. If they meet with any adventures you shall be informed.

The *Brownsville*, by which I send this letter, is probably the fastest boat that has yet visited Camargo. She made her last trip down and back in a little over four days. Now that wood depots have been established at different points on the Rio Grande all the boats—and there are some ten or fifteen of them—will meet with far greater dispatch. The wood used is almost entirely mesquit, and the Mexicans are glad to furnish it at $2.50 per cord.

Nothing new from the interior, and everything quiet in this neighborhood.

G. W. K.
*Daily Picayune*, August 9, 1846

Camargo, July 27, 1846

To break the dull monotony of camp life we had another Indian alarm yesterday morning. The alcalde came in great haste and trepidation to the commanding officer of the troops here, stating that the Comanches were laying waste the ranches on the other side of the river above the mouth of the San Juan, murdering the inhabitants and carrying off captive the children. McCulloch's Rangers were at once detailed to cross the Rio Grande, and were all in the saddle in almost no time.

To my thinking, these Indian disturbances will be fruitful of much trouble. If I am not much mistaken, at the great treaty recently held by Gov. Butler and Maj. Lewis, high up on the Brazos, it was understood that the Indians were not to be molested in any war they might be engaged in with Mexico. It might not have been "so stipulated in the bond," yet the commissioners in the then existing state of affairs between the United States and Mexico were not in a situation to say to the different tribes that they must war no more with a country that was then a common enemy. That they might and did say to them, that they were at liberty to wage hostilities conformably with the usages of civilized nations, there can be little doubt: but that they told them not to approach the Mexican frontier, would have been a piece of absurdity, not to say stupidity, they were not the men to be guilty of.[62] Following the final ratification of the treaty, the provisions of which have not yet been published, came Gen. Taylor's successes at Palo Alto and the Resaca de la Palma and the taking of Matamoros; after which an entirely new face appears to have been put upon the nature of the operations this side the Rio Grande. The conciliatory system had not then been adopted, nor were the people promised protection, nor had proclamations appeared indirectly calling upon the inhabitants this side the Sierra Madre to throw off the oppressive yoke of the Central Government.

In the meantime, some of the wild tribes have organized their bands, and are now carrying on destruction and death upon the frontier. It is the bounden duty of the United States, as I look upon the matter, to afford protection to the inhabitants upon the east bank of the Rio Grande; but to what extent the Indians can be legitimately interfered with on this side the river is another matter. The result of all this is now looked for here with much interest, and the adventures of McCulloch's men with the Indians shall be detailed to you at the earliest opportunity.

62. The treaty concluded by Butler and Lewis did not specifically address the future of relations between Mexico and the signatory American Indian nations. The terms of the treaty were controversial in Congress, however, because Texas retained control of all public lands, making problematic the national government's ability to provide "protection" for the native tribes and to claim "the sole and exclusive right of regulating trade and intercourse." "Treaty with the Comanches and Other Tribes," *Indian Affairs: Laws and Treaties*, comp. by Charles J. Kappler (Washington, 1904), 554–56. Robert A. Trennert, Jr., *Alternative to Extinction: Federal Indian Policy and the Beginnings of the Reservation System, 1846–1851* (Philadelphia, 1975), 63–67.

I can give you, perhaps, the first "steamboat accident" which has occurred on the Rio Grande. The *Neva* struck a snag yesterday, about nine miles below this, and is said to be a total loss. She had two companies of troops on board—the men losing a large portion of their effects, while Uncle Sam[63] is also a loser to the extent of no small amount of army stores. It is singular no other accidents have occurred.

The *Aid*, Capt. Hyde, came in yesterday morning, and the *Mercer* arrived in the afternoon with General Worth on board. The town is now fairly overrun with troops, and a move toward Monterey with a portion of them is talked of.

A soldier belonging to the 5th U. S. Infantry was shot directly through the head yesterday, by one of Gillespie's volunteers; yet the man is still alive and likely to live. Cause, liquor—not of his living, but of his being wounded.

G. W. K.<br>
*Daily Picayune*, August 6, 1846

Camargo, July 28, 1846

The talk is still of Indians and Indian outrages. Day before yesterday the Comanches attacked a rancho between this and Mier, killed nine Mexicans and took off no less than fourteen women and children prisoners. Last night, so rumor has it, they stole upwards of twenty horses from Gillespie's men, while they were encamped near the house of an American living four miles below this on the opposite side of the Rio Grande, besides taking off all the animals belonging to the rancho. I can hardly credit this; but should it prove true it will go hard with the Comanches. Capt. Gillespie's command is composed principally of Jack Hays's old men, and they will not give up the chase after their horses in a hurry.

We have another report to the effect that six Americans, while driving in beef cattle from Loredo to San Antonio, were set upon by the Comanches and all killed, together with fourteen Mexicans who were in company. I still contend that the Indians have the right to carry on war on this side the Rio Grande with the Mexicans, but this thing of murdering Americans upon the high road in Texas puts a different face entirely upon the matter, and the treacherous savages should be pursued and severely punished at once. They should be told, too, that all the inhabitants on the east bank of the Rio Grande are under our protection, and threatened with war to extermination if they molest a single person.

---

63. The U.S. government. The origin of the term is obscure, but it may derive from the nickname used by Samuel Wilson, an inspector of army supplies during the War of 1812.

While upon this subject, I would mention one little circumstance I witnessed yesterday—a circumstance, the like of which has not often occurred since the creation. Four or five Mexicans, armed with swords and carbines, came riding into the Plaza praying for aid against the Comanches! Now here are a people, with whom we are at war, entering one of our camps with arms in their hands, and praying one enemy to protect them and theirs against another enemy. I suppose it is all right, as the man says in the play, when told that his wife has run off; it merely looks strange, that's all.

I learn that the steamer *Aid* starts with a detachment of troops tomorrow for Mier, to take possession of that place. I shall go up in her if I can get oȗ. In the meantime Gen. Worth is hunting a camp for the troops at a point higher up on the San Juan, and parties will soon be thrown forward in the direction of Monterey. Pack mules for the transportation of army stores, are being collected every day, while all the men are anxious to be on the move towards the mountains.

I regret to learn that the Louisiana Regiments have been disbanded, but still cannot blame the men for refusing to enlist for twelve months.[64]

I send this letter down by the *Mercer*, which starts immediately. The *Panola*, *Exchange* and other boats are on their way up.

G. W. K.

*Daily Picayune*, August 6, 1846

Camargo, July 29, 1846

The loss by the sinking of the steamer *Neva*, a day or two since, appears to be greater than was at first anticipated. The officers and soldiers were compelled to leave much of their baggage, with such rapidity did she go down; the United States is a heavy loser in the way of army stores; and the 8th Infantry, Gen. Worth's regiment, lost its band, or rather the band of the 8th lost all their instruments. Take it all round this appears to be a bad country on bands. The chest containing the instruments of the band of the 7th Infantry, at the bombardment of Fort Brown,[65] was burst all to flinters by a shell which entered it—bugles and trombones being knocked into a discordant smash by the bomb. Here again is another set of instruments put out of tune by being drowned in the Rio Grande past recovery, while it is but a short time since that Gen. Woll had half the members of a band

64. Short of transportation and supplies, Taylor found the some 5,000 short-term volunteers a liability, and in late July he sent home those who refused to enlist for a full year.

65. Fort Brown, located on the Texas side of the Rio Grande across from Matamoros, was bombarded by General Arista early in May, on the eve of the battles of Palo Alto and Resaca de la Palma.

shot down by the Texans in a night attack upon San Antonio de Bexar.[66] This makes three destroyed one way and another in this meridian and to this should be added the band of the redoubtable Micheltorena, the members of which wore out an entire set of brass instruments in their extraordinary zeal to march on and drive Com. Jones out of Monterey, on the Pacific, after that officer had evacuated the place to their certain knowledge.[67] The loss of this latter band caused a good deal of noise and merriment at the time, I well recollect, and was charged to the account of the United States, to be by that Government paid for. I believe it was never fully settled whether the bursting of the instruments was caused by excess of valor or wind—probably an extra amount of both. I again say that this is a bad country on bands, and that the climate is very destructive of harmony.

But to mix in a little of the serious. Camargo is as busy a place, just now, as you could well find in twelve months' travel. Steamboat after steamboat is arriving and departing, barrels, boxes and bales are seen rolling in all directions, drumming and fifing is heard in all quarters, soldiers are marching and counter marching, and one can hardly move about without breaking his neck over some of the "pomp, or pride, or circumstance" of Mexican war, especially the circumstance, for under that head I suppose we must class the pork, beans, sacks of corn, and other Government stores with which the streets and river banks are covered. The Mexicans look on with perfect astonishment, and in their stupidity and ignorance probably wonder that there is so much subsistence for man and beast in the world.

I now learn that but six of Gillespie's horses were taken night before last, and that there is reason to believe the thieves were Mexicans. I would not care so much about being caught in the shoes of those who have taken them if they are found, be they Mexicans or Indians. A part of McCulloch's command is still out on the opposite bank of the river—the remainder are lying encamped here.

As for amusements here, we have nothing of the kind. Many of the youngsters, when not on guard duty, spend the morning and evening on the river banks, eyeing the señoritas as they come down with their jars for water, and watching their antics while bathing, for they all dip themselves

---

66. General Adrian Woll, a one-time Napoleonic officer, had led a raid against San Antonio in September 1842 as part of Santa Anna's continuing efforts to disrupt life in Texas.

67. Commander Thomas apCatesby Jones had occupied Monterey, California, briefly in October 1842, based on the mistaken belief that the United States and Mexico had gone to war. General Manuel Micheltorena was named governor of California in the aftermath of that incident.

in the San Juan regularly. Women are graceful at almost anything they undertake, but there are four things at which they cut but a sorry and awkward figure: chopping wood, throwing brick-bats, chasing turkeys through high grass, and swimming. I beg pardon of one and all, but the truth must be spoken.

The *Exchange* and *Panola*, steamers new in this trade, came up yesterday afternoon and are off this morning, back to Matamoros. If anything turns up on the trip to Mier, or at the town, you shall hear of it all in good season. The *Aid* starts in a few minutes with company B of the 3d. Artillery on board, destined to occupy that place.

G. W. K.

*Daily Picayune*, August 16, 1846

On Board Steamer *Aid*, Foot of a Reef on the Rio Grande, July 29, 1846

I commence this letter at the foot of a reef or *chute* in the Rio Grande, about one mile above the mouth of the San Juan, and at a place where we are likely to be detained some time if we get through at all. There is no great amusement, that I can see at least, in watching the operations of a yawl's crew as they are feeling about in the river ahead with a long pole, hunting for deep water and snags, so I will set down and attempt to picture the scene immediately on board and alongside the steamer.

There is a rancho close by—a large one I should suppose—and every man, woman and child has flocked down to the river's side to see the steamboat. With wonder and with fear—more especially with fear—do the natives gaze at our craft, the women hugging their little ones closer as the engineer lets off a little phizz—don't you call it *phizz*?—of extra steam. An old American pilot we have on board—one who has seen three steamboats before in his life and is not afraid—is endeavoring to persuade some of the señoritas to come on board, while a rascally-looking ranchero is telling them not to stir a step, as *los Americanos* want to tie them and carry them off. The individual has been told, by an American who speaks the language, that he is an infamous old liar, and that he must shut up. He has shut up, and two or three middle-aged women, with no particular fear of being carried off, have ventured up the planks and are slowly edging along towards the cabin stairs. The prettier samples, meanwhile, have betaken themselves to the upper bank of the river, and many of them doubtless think they are looking their last at their older and more venturous aunts and mothers. One sinister-looking scoundrel is eyeing us from the shore, a cast of whose face in sand I should like to possess. A mold from it, in which to run brass door-knockers, would be a treasure—it would grin the face off a hyena, located upon a door upon the opposite side of the street, completely out of countenance. The fellow was so ugly I could not take my eyes off him—I fairly liked his looks. The first bevy of females, after examining the boat in all its parts, are wending their way ashore, while a younger brood, who have mustered up courage, are advancing to gratify their curiosity. The yellow, pink and blue paper, with which the ceiling of the boat is decorated, Chinese fashion, appears to take the eye of the girls, for expressions of *muy bonita*—very pretty—are on every lip. They see the ornamental fast enough, but the really useful escapes their observation. Greedy boys, anxious to be the possessors of bits and picayunes, have brought *duraznos* and *sandias*—peaches and watermelons—on board, and find a ready market, while venders of chickens and other notions are also reaping for them a rich harvest. Naked boys and half naked girls are clustered about, with no definite object, and the whole scene is one of strange wildness to those unaccustomed to such things. The steamboat bell has just rung, an examination of the channel has commenced, the captain thinks it would be imprudent and dangerous to go ahead, the *Mexicanos* are scampering ashore, and our bows are rounding to in the direction of Camargo. Thus has ended the second Mier expedition.[68] The company on board, which is commanded by Capt. Vinton,[69] will now probably go up by land, taking pack mules to carry their baggage, while a smaller boat than the *Aid* may be sent up light to examine the river.

Before I forget it, I want to ask you one question: Do you know anything about the "Rose of Alabama" in New Orleans? Here, among regulars and volunteers, they appear to think, and especially to sing, about nothing else save the "Rose of Alabama." Who is the "Rose of Alabama"? Is she a relation of "Lucy Neal," who was born in Alabama and whose master's name was Beal? One of the waiters of the boat, as he is washing his dishes near me, is singing all about the virtues and the beauties of the "Rose of Alabama," a person of no note whatever when I left the States. One of the firemen, as he chucks his sticks of wood into the furnace, with four horse-power is singing the praises of the "Rose of Alabama." Is D. Tucker, Esq., dead, and have the Misses Long and Neal been forgotten? Is a dandy from one of the Carolinas, whose first name was James, sunk into obscurity? I will give a premium of a splendidly bound edition of the "Western Songster" to anyone who will give reliable information as to the birth, parentage, education and present condition of the "Rose of Alabama." Seriously,

68. See note 71 below.
69. John Rogers Vinton, Third Artillery.

the song is in everyone's mouth in the army, and I suppose is some new Ethiopian refrain which has obtained a name and popularity at home— deservedly, too, for the air is taking and of no inconsiderable neatness. Who is the "Rose of Alabama"?[70]

G. W. K.

P. S. *Camargo, 12 o'clock.*—We have got back here, safe and sound, and I now learn that the troops will start early tomorrow morning for Mier on foot. No intelligence has as yet come in from the Rangers who are out after Indians. Some of them will probably be in tonight. This is the second letter I have written today, but there is not a line of important news in either.

G. W. K.<br>*Daily Picayune*, August 16, 1846

Mier, Mexico, July 31, 1846

Capt. Vinton's command entered this place this morning without the least show of opposition, the inhabitants thronging to the Plaza in crowds as the troops filed into it and stacked their arms in front of the house of the alcalde. It seemed to me as though there were men enough in the square to have beaten us off with nothing else save the loose rocks lying about; yet not a hand was raised.

Mier is by far the most pleasant, cleanly and well regulated place we have yet seen in this part of Mexico. It is built on a hill overlooking a clear running stream of the same name, three miles from the Rio Grande, and is said to contain 6000 inhabitants, although I do not know where they stow them all. You may well recollect that it was in this place that the Texans under Col. Fisher were compelled to surrender, after they had killed twice their own number of Mexicans.[71] The houses occupied by the Texans during the battle were pointed out, and still bear the marks of the desperate conflict.

70. Alexander Beaufort Meek, Alabama jurist, journalist, poet, educator, and songwriter, wrote "Rose of Alabama." Johannsen, *To the Halls of the Montezumas*, 239.

71. After Adrian Woll captured San Antonio in September 1842—the second conquest of the city that year—Texas president Sam Houston ordered General Alexander Somervell to pursue the retreating Mexican army to the Rio Grande and into the Mexico mountains if conditions warranted. Somervell's men captured the Rio Grande towns of Lando and Guerro before their commander ordered an end to the expedition. Nevertheless, about three hundred men under the leadership of William S. Fisher set out to invade Mexico. Overwhelmed by a superior Mexican force commanded by Pedro de Ampudia, the Texans surrendered by Mier on December 26, 1842. Joseph D. McCuthchan, *The Mier Expedition Diary: A Texan Prisoner's Account*, edited by J. Milton Nance (Austin, 1978), xvii–xix.

I have stated that the number of the inhabitants is put down at 6000; admitting that it is 4000, it was still entered and taken possession of by 93 men only—85 regulars and 8 of McCulloch's Rangers, acting as a mounted guard. You could not serve any town in the United States in that way, and this place is a perfect fortification from its position and the strength of the houses, which are of stone. Capt. Vinton's command occupies a large school-house in one corner of the Plaza, near the church—strong, and at the same time commodious and comfortable quarters. It is Company B, of the 3d Artillery, or "Red-legged Infantry," as it is now called from the fact that the men are at this time serving as infantry, while they wear the red or artillery stripe down their pantaloons. I give you a list of the officers, who are all in good health: Capt. J. R. Vinton, Asst. Surgeon Prevost, Lieuts. S. Van Vliet[72] and F. J. Thomas.

The Comanches, who have committed many ravages in this vicinity of late, are said to have left for the mountains of Texas with their prisoners and plunder. Many of the women and children from the adjoining ranches, driven in by the Indians, are still here.

I return to Camargo in the morning with the Rangers. If I could have my own way I should remain here, for it is worth forty of Camargo.

G. W. K.
*Daily Picayune,* August 15, 1846

Camargo, August 2, 1846

A few hours after we left Mier yesterday, the Comanches killed and scalped the alcalde within a few hundred yards of the outskirts of the place. He was returning from his rancho in the neighborhood at the time, and was shot from a fence or some other cover. To show the impudence of the Comanches, and the great contempt in which they hold their Mexican enemies, I will relate one little incident—one farce, if I may so call it, of their production. The day before the Americans took possession of the place—this I was told by one who saw the whole proceeding—a small party of Comanches appeared on the opposite bank of the river, and within three hundred yards of the town. One of the Indians had not a rag upon him save a green Mexican uniform coat, faced with red and trimmed with yellow, and was armed with nothing save a Mexican bugle or trumpet. This he held to his mouth and sounded to the full strength of his lungs. Up and down the river bank he blew and blasted away upon this instrument, regardless of tune, but anxious to make all the noise he could in that part

---

72. Stewart Van Vliet, Third Artillery.

of the world situated immediately opposite Mier. The cry of "*los Indios*" was raised, the women and children scampered, while the men rode furiously up and down the streets out of reach of balls and arrows, and signed papers and swore that they would do great things, besides dying in defence of the town. It is said they completely broke down their horses in parading and dashing about, and were not ready to start after the Indians until they saw and knew that the Indians had had their fun out and were completely out of reach.

There is no mistake that a large force of Comanches is on this side the Rio Grande, committing depredations and murdering the inhabitants with impunity. Parties of them have appeared at Guerrero, a city some thirty miles above Mier, have stolen a great many horses and mules, and have killed several of the principal citizens, among them one of the town council. The authorities of the place have sent in their submission to the officer in command of the United States troops here, and would doubtless be delighted to see an American force in the Plaza. You may ask, why do not the Mexicans turn out in force—outnumbering, as they do the Indians, ten to one—give them a sound drubbing, and drive them out of the country. It is because they are too lazy in the first place, and too timid in the second. So far as I can see, the men here spend one-third of the day in sleeping, one-third in bathing, and the other third in doing nothing—not a very profitable employment of time they would say away "Down East."

Camargo is now overrun with troops, the white tents of the soldiers covering acres and acres. The Rangers start out tomorrow on a scout in the direction of Monterey, and bodies of regulars with army stores will probably soon follow. Everyone is anxious to get away from this place, to move anywhere. You may think in New Orleans that you know something about hot weather and mosquitoes. You "don't know nothing."[73]

Some fuss has been raised about the pack mules employed to transport Government supplies, but as a large number of wagons have reached this place, all difficulties will doubtless be obviated.

G. W. K.

*Daily Picayune*, August 15, 1846

---

73. Disease decimated the approximately 12,000 troops jammed into Camargo. Regarded by local residents as particularly unhealthful, Camargo was a hot, insect-ridden, dusty town with water available only from the polluted San Juan River. One in eight men encamped there—approximately 1,500—died. Volunteer forces suffered particularly high losses.

Camargo, August 3, 1846

I have just seen a letter, dated yesterday at Reynosa, the writer of which calls for a detachment of mounted men to guard a large drove of pack mules to this place. He has reliable information, so he says, that a gang of brigands has been organized in the neighborhood of Reynosa to cut up any and every small party they may meet upon the road, and he further states that some of the principal men of that place are engaged in this scheme of pillage and murder. I trust the scoundrels may be found out. The conciliatory system has been lost upon them, and some other should be tried. We are treating thousands of individuals here with consideration and respect who would turn round and cut our throats the first opportunity that occurred, and *con mucho gusto*, to use one of their favorite expressions.

Troops still continue to pour in, several companies having arrived, since I wrote yesterday, on the steamers *Roberts* and *Big Hatchee*. Gen. Worth has moved the camp to high and dry ground on the San Juan, a mile below Camargo, where the soldiers are far more comfortable. How Napoleon used to dispose of his tremendous armies is a mystery to me. Huddled as close or closer than comfort will allow, even eight or ten thousand men here take up a wilderness of space.

Capt. Gillespie's Rangers remain in camp here, while McCulloch's are off this morning in the direction, as is supposed, of Monterey, scouring the country as far at least as China, and possibly farther. Reports that large parties of armed men have been seen in that direction, among other companies that of Seguin, have reached this place. The Rangers will find them if they are to be found.

We have no farther accounts of the ravages of the Comanches in the neighborhood of Mier or Guerrero. No American troops have started for the latter place, and I do not know that it is the intention of the commanding officer to dispatch any; but he has authorized the authorities to enlist an armed company of mounted men for home protection.

Should any opportunity occur, I will send you a letter from the interior, but I am fearful there will be no chance until the company returns to this place.

G. W. K.

P. S. An express has just come in from Mier. The rider contradicts the report that the alcalde had been killed, but says there are a good many Indians lurking about.

G. W. K.

*Daily Picayune*, August 15, 1846

China, Mexico, August 5, 1846

China is in the hands of the Americans—not the great and celestial Empire, with its Bangs and Whangs, its Tings and Lings—but the little pueblo or town in Mexico of the same name, situated on the Rio San Juan some sixty-five or seventy miles above Camargo. Ben McCulloch, with fifty-five of his men, arrived in sight of the place about 1 o'clock this morning, after a forced march of over fifty miles. At the Rancho de Sacate he learned, from a Mexican who had just arrived, that Col. Seguin was in China with upwards of one hundred mounted men, and at once formed a plan for his capture. This was yesterday afternoon about 2 o'clock. Hiring the same Mexican who brought the intelligence, for a guide, our captain started off at a rapid pace, only halting a short time towards sundown to cool the horses' backs and make a "hasty bowl" of coffee. Before reaching the large rancho or hacienda of El Toro, within three leagues of China, the horse of the guide gave out, broke down completely, and it was found necessary to leave him. This did not in the least alter McCulloch's plans, for he kept on at the same rapid pace. The hacienda of El Toro extends for a full half mile along the river, and the wondering inhabitants were all out in front of their huts as we passed. Not a word was exchanged, the Rangers riding single file and in silence through the place. A little after midnight the white belfry of the church at China was seen some half mile distant, the bright moonbeams bringing it out in bold relief. A little farther on a halt was called, twenty men were left as a rear guard, and with the rest of the company our captain moved on, circling the town and making towards the main Monterey road to cut off any force that might endeavor to retreat. We had just reached the opposite side of the town, and had arrived at a large road, when the sharp crack of a rifle was heard from the rear guard, now near a mile off. A halt was called, strict silence kept, and every ear was ready to catch the reports of other shots, for it was at first surmised that the Mexicans had attacked our comrades; but not another gun was discharged and no sounds reached us save the barking of innumerable dogs, every cur in the town having been alarmed. The order had been given for both parties to enter the place at daybreak, and as it still lacked an hour or two of dawn, we were halted in the road and told not to take either saddles or bridles from our horses. No further alarm save from the opposite side, and hard as was the road, and without blankets, many of the men were soon asleep while holding their animals—the long hard ride having brought on a fatigue and drowsiness that could not be overcome.

With the first ray of the morning we were again in the saddle. A delay of half an hour, chasing a couple of Mexicans seen leaving the town, made it broad day before we entered the plaza, and when there we found the rear guard already in quiet and peaceable possession. They had had all the fun and excitement on their side, for it seemed that they had taken one prisoner, who was caught endeavoring to spy out their position, and the rifle had been discharged at two others—fellows on horseback—who were evidently reconnoitering, and who put spurs to their horses when ordered to halt. During the evening following the report of the rifle, the prisoner escaped from the person guarding him. Thus ended the conquest of China[74] by the Americans.

Upon inquiry, it was now found that McCulloch was within an ace, as the saying is, of catching Seguin, and had not some of his scouts or friends given him notice of the approach of the Rangers, he would have fallen into their hands. It was only at dark that he received intelligence of our approach, when seventy-five of his men at once broke and run for the chaparral. At 10 o'clock—some two hours before our captain reached the outskirts of the town—twenty-five more were in the saddle and off, and it is said that Seguin himself was only two hundred yards distant when the rifle was discharged at one of his spies; and further that he, too, made at once for the chaparral as fast as his horse would carry him.

The Rangers followed on the trail of the runaways until a point was reached where they were scattered. Scouts of the enemy were seen on the distant hilltops watching our advance, but as it was deemed useless to pursue the fugitives farther on tired horses, and they knowing every foot of the country, we were ordered back to town, and are now occupying the very quarters recently filled by Seguin's men. History mentions but few instances where a handful of men have driven double their number from a strong position, for such this really is, without some show of resistance.

In haste,

G. W. K.
*Daily Picayune,* August 25, 1846

74. This place is pronounced *Cheena*, as I have mentioned, I believe, in a former letter. It is spelled, however, as I have written it. —*Kendall.*

# CHAPTER TWO

# THE BATTLE OF MONTEREY
## AUGUST 9 – NOVEMBER 19, 1846

ANTONIO LÓPEZ DE SANTA ANNA returned to Mexico from Havana through the port of Vera Cruz on August 16, 1846, with American acquiescence. The former Mexican dictator had lived in Havana since his overthrow and exile in early 1845. His return complicated the already chaotic political situation in Mexico; it also contributed to the decision of the Mexican army to defend Monterey. Santa Anna opposed a pitched battle with the invading American army unless victory was certain. Pedro de Ampudia was now in command of the Mexican army in the north and was eager to establish his own military reputation before Santa Anna exerted control. He pressed to defend Monterey with the approximately 7,000 regulars and 3,000 rancheros at his disposal. Indeed, only reluctantly did he abandon his plans to attack Zachary Taylor's army in the open countryside around Marin.

Led by William Worth's Second Division, Taylor's force, including 3,200 regulars and some 3,000 volunteers, left the Rio Grande in mid-August and on August 19 began the sixty-mile march from Camargo to Cerralvo. The advance forces left Cerralvo on September 12, and the army regrouped in Marín on September 15 before marching on to the outskirts of the well-fortified city of Monterey on September 18. Taylor divided his command on September 20, ordering Worth west to cut off the road to Saltillo and attack the fortification at that end of the city. The main body of the army, under the command of William O. Butler and John Garland and temporarily in command of David Twiggs' division, attacked from the east.

The battle raged for three days, with the troops under Butler and Garland making little headway while Worth's forces, which included George Kendall, overran the Mexican defenses from the west to reach the heart of the city. Ampudia surrendered on September 25, but Taylor's victory was costly. With 120 men killed and over four hundred wounded or missing, casualties totaled about 8.5 percent of the 6,220 men engaged. The larger Mexican army suffered casualties of about 5 percent.

Taylor allowed the Mexican army to evacuate Monterey, taking along one battery of field artillery and ammunition, their officers' side arms, and their cavalry horses; he also agreed to an eight-week truce. Both decisions earned him the wrath of officials in the Polk administration who believed he should have demanded a complete surrender and immediately pushed farther into the interior. When the news of the terms of the surrender reached Secretary of War William L. Marcy early in October, he ordered an immediate end to the armistice.

In the meantime, Ampudia retreated to San Luis Potosí, about three hundred miles south of Monterey, where Santa Anna was building an army to stop the American advance. Taylor's army moved in mid-November to Saltillo, about seventy-five miles southwest of Monterey, where Worth directed preparations for the expected appearance of Santa Anna. Kendall returned to New Orleans in October to await the beginning of the spring campaign.

Camargo, August 9, 1846

I wrote you a hurried scratch from China, giving an account of our trip to that place and of the flight of Seguin and his men. McCulloch remained there but one day, occupying Seguin's quarters the while. We started on the 6th inst. for this place, and arrived safe and sound yesterday morning without meeting with any resistance. It was thought the Mexicans might rally, upon ascertaining the small force of the Rangers, and attempt to cut them off at the Paso de Sacate; but not an armed man was seen as we entered the place.

Previous to our leaving China our captain told the alcalde to give his best compliments to Col. Seguin on his return, and further to inform him that he had called at his room on a visit, had remained there twenty-four hours, and regretted that he was compelled to depart without seeing him. In a few days, possibly he might return, when he hoped he might find him at home! Seguin will not like that, for he is a proud and sensitive fellow.

China is but a small place, numbering not more than 5 or 700 inhabitants. The principal part of the men, so far as I was able to judge, are gamblers, robbers and smugglers, and all looked surly and cross—not appearing to like the idea of a handful of Rangers taking their town without a struggle. From the high lands in the neighborhood we could distinctly see the high, blue mountains a short distance this side of Monterey, their summits looming far above us and seeming to pierce the very heavens. I would give a good deal to catch a mouthful of the fresh air that is circling about their tops, and imagine we shall all be climbing them in the course of a few weeks—no one cares how quick.

The steamer *Hatchee Eagle* arrived here last evening, Gen. Taylor and his staff coming up on her. The talk now is of an immediate movement towards Monterey, making a depot for provisions at some point on the route. Whether the army is to move by way of China, or is to cross the San Juan at this place and march on the other side of the river, has not yet been settled upon, I believe. There are now near 3000 men, all regulars, encamped here, and hosts of volunteers are *en route* and shortly expected—some of them this afternoon.

The general impression among the best informed, as regards the chances of the Mexicans giving another battle, is that Gen. Taylor will have an opportunity of gaining fresh laurels at Monterey or near that place. On the river the inhabitants appear friendly enough, but in the interior the case is different. Accompanying McCulloch on his different scouts I have had a good opportunity of judging, and the general bearing and tone of the principal men has been as much as to say, "You are having your way now, and we must grin and bear it; in a short time you will be hurrying out of the country at double-quick time, with the Mexican soldiers in the ascendant— then we shall have our day." I do not believe, for one moment, that the conciliatory system can make friends of these people. They despise and hate us, and nothing but their fear induces them to conceal their real feelings.

I might here mention that Col. Balie Peyton[1] came up with Gen. Taylor. I believe that he is to accompany the army in all its movements.

G. W. K.

*Daily Picayune*, August 25, 1846

Camargo, August 10, 1846

By a boat about leaving I send you a line, although I have not an item of news to communicate.

There was a grand parade of all the regular troops last evening, and a magnificent show they made. Gen. Taylor and staff passed the different regiments as they were extended in line, and expressed himself highly gratified with their appearance. Gen. Worth is drilling the men constantly, and the masterly style in which they perform their evolutions beats anything your humble servant has ever seen in the way of military tactics.

---

1. Balie Peyton, whose first name is spelled in a variety of ways, was a prominent Whig attorney from New Orleans who became an aide and political ally of William Worth. President Taylor later appointed him minister to Chile.

The *Whiteville*, Capt. Dunn, by which boat I send this, came up last night with a detachment of Gen. Sydney Johnston's Texas Infantry on board. This part of the regiment is commanded by Maj. Wells, Gen. J. himself being on the way by land.[2] McCulloch's Rangers are to be disbanded tomorrow, their term of service being out. He will have another company of mounted men immediately in service, Gen. Taylor having given him permission to enlist for three months only. None but those having crack horses will be allowed to join, as the company is to scour the country towards Monterey a long distance in advance of the army, and may be obliged to retreat whenever it comes across a superior force.

G. W. K.

*Daily Picayune*, August 25, 1846

Camargo, Mexico, August 11, 1846

One step towards Monterey is to be taken tomorrow. Capt. Duncan's[3] battery, accompanied by a small portion of McCulloch's men, leaves this place in the direction of the mountains, and by some road on the opposite side of the river. It may be looked upon only as a reconnaissance, although an artillery force is with it. Of whatever befalls them on the road you shall be made acquainted all in good time. If the command does not take Mier in the route it will go close to that place.

News has reached here this morning to the effect that the city of Guerrero has pronounced in favor of the United States Government. The people of that place have all along been friendly towards the Americans, or have so seemed; but whether from any love they might bear them, or from fear of the encroachments of the Comanches, is a matter I am not able to determine at this present writing. I believe, honestly, that the people of Guerrero have some intelligence and are better disposed than those of any place on the river.

By way of a letter from Mier, it would seem that McCulloch came even nearer having a brush with Seguin's men, at China, than was at first supposed. When the rifle was discharged at one of his spies his main command was not a mile off, and a general scamper at once followed. Had

2. Albert Sidney Johnston commanded this group of approximately 150 men who remained after a dispute over the terms of enlistment caused most the regiment of Texas Riflemen to leave the army on the eve of the Monterey campaign. Johnston became inspector general of Major General William O. Butler's division of volunteers. James Mayo Wells, Texas Volunteers, later served with the Twelfth U.S. Infantry.

3. James Duncan, Second Artillery, was involved in the political infighting that divided Winfield Scott's command in the months after the fall of Mexico City.

there been daylight at the time, although it is now said they numbered over 200 strong, they would not have got off so easily.

The crack steamer *Brownsville*, by which I send this, brought up two companies of the advance of the Baltimore troops last evening, the rest coming on by land. They are a hard-looking set of "b-hoys" to all appearance, but I have no doubt will do good service. Capt. Blanchard's company of twelve-months Louisiana volunteers, recruited from the regiments recently disbanded, entered camp this forenoon.[4] They look fierce yet weather-beaten, and ready for any kind of a scrape. The last I saw of them they were hunting shade, with a vertical sun pouring his hottest rays upon them. There is no use talking about hot places so long as Camargo stands where it now does. Whew!

I will write again before leaving here, if anything of importance turns up.

G. W. K.

*Daily Picayune*, August 25, 1846

Camargo, August 17, 1846

Capt. Duncan, with a small party of Texan Rangers, recently sent out on a reconnaissance into the interior, got back this morning, after having scoured the country on the other side of the San Juan as far as Cerralvo, a pleasant town half way to Monterey. On the second day Capt. McCulloch was sent into Mier very much indisposed. The night before, he shot a Mexican, who was caught on an American horse and who attempted to escape by running. The fellow broke through the chaparral, and made a good race for his life; but McC. was too fast for him.

On the second night, after a forced march of great length, Capt. Duncan threw his men at different points around the town of Punta Aguda, having learned that a Mexican officer named Ramirez was in the place with a detachment of recruits for Canales.[5] So complete was the surprise that Capt. D. was enabled to reach a ball room in the centre of the town, where a grand fandango was then in full blast, without a soul suspecting his approach. His object was to take any Mexican officers prisoners that might be then stationed in the place, and supposing that they might be at the

---

4. Of the volunteers recruited in Louisiana, only Captain Albert C. Blanchard's "Phoenix Company" remained after Taylor tried unsuccessfully to persuade them to extend their initial three-month enlistment to twelve months.

5. Canales's troops served under the command of Francisco Mejía, formerly the commander of Mexican forces at Matamoros. Mejía headed the army in northern Mexico briefly between Arista's court-martial and Ampudia's elevation to commander. Punta Aguda was reputedly Canales's headquarters.

fandango, he ordered all within the room not to move, after telling them, in the first place, that every avenue to the town was guarded by the Rangers. Notwithstanding this order, some of those inside the room went covertly out and endeavored to leave the town; but one of them was shot dead in the attempt, and another had his arm shattered by a rifle ball from one of the Texans. The latter was brought back to the fandango room, where his wound was dressed in one corner, the dance going on the while at the request of Capt. D., although with not as much spirit as it might. Finding that he could get hold of no prisoners of importance, the commander of the party continued his march to Cerralvo, arrived there without hindrance or molestation, and after an examination of the place, returned in safety by way of Agua Leguas and Mier.

Cerralvo, it is thought, will be made a depot, offering every facility in the shape of good water and a commanding position. The road on the other side the San Juan will also be chosen as the best by which to move the army, although a portion may march by way of China. The news from Monterey leads everyone to suppose that the Mexicans intend making a bold stand there, and offering every resistance to Gen. Taylor in their power. Recruits and regulars are concentrating at that point, the fortifications are being strengthened, and the greatest activity prevails. A force of 1000 well appointed cavalry arrived at Saltillo a few days since, and report now has it that Torrejón[6] has been sent down with a large party of mounted men to cut off Col. Hays. I hope he may find Hays, for that officer will be glad to see him.

Gen. Persifor F. Smith arrived this morning. He is to take command of the 2d brigade, composed of the 5th and 7th regiments of U. S. Infantry. Our regular correspondent H. will probably be able to give you a full account of the organization of the army about to move toward Monterey.

G. W. K.

*Daily Picayune*, August 28, 1846

Mier, Mexico, August 30, 1846

I came up to this place last evening, in company with four or five of McCulloch's men, and an express going in to Camargo gives me an opportunity of sending you a line.

There are no troops here, Capt. Vinton's company having been sent on towards Cerralvo; but there are some twenty or thirty stray Texans in the

---

6. Anastasio Torrejón, the principal cavalry officer in northern Mexico, first saw action against the United States in command of a 1,600-man cavalry that killed or captured eighty American dragoons on April 25, 1846. The incident played a central role in Polk's decision to call for a declaration of war.

place, and the inhabitants, although they number five or six thousand, are entirely civil. There has been hard fighting here in times past, and the people probably do not care about a repetition.

From Cerralvo, for which place we start today, I hear that all is quiet. Gen. Worth is encamped there, and in the course of ten or twelve days the whole army will reach the place. All accounts go to show that it is a delightful town, the water clear and plentiful, and the climate healthy and most salubrious. This is a great deal more than can be said of Camargo, for there there is much sickness. The place is to be garrisoned by volunteers, and it is feared, should the weather continue hot and sultry as at present, that not a little disease will prevail.

You may hear further from me at Punta Aguda or Cerralvo.

G. W. K.

*Daily Picayune*, September 12, 1846

Punta Aguda, August 31, 1846

I have this moment arrived at this place, and am off in a few moments for Cerralvo; but an opportunity of sending down by Capt. Sibley[7] induces me to give you a line.

Gen. Smith is encamped here, on high and beautiful ground and with a clear stream of water running directly past. The health of the command—at present some seven or eight hundred—is excellent, and from the position of the camp it must continue so. Capt. Blanchard, of the Louisiana company, tells me that he has not a man who is really sick.

A gentleman just in from Cerralvo informs me that the impression there was, that the Mexicans would make a bold stand at Monterey. One thing is certain, all the ranchero leaders have drawn off their forces in that direction. There are several organized bands of robbers on the roads in this neighborhood, but as yet they have not had the temerity to attack anyone.

My companions—there are only three of them—are Col. Fitzpatrick, young Musson, of New Orleans, and a gentleman by the name of Thomas, from Maryland.[8] They all have joined McCulloch, who is expected up at Cerralvo in three or four days.

G. W. K.

*Daily Picayune*, September 12, 1846

7. Ebenezer S. Sibley, quartermaster.

8. Mentioned are Eugene Musson, a Louisiana volunteer and aide-de-camp to General P. F. Smith, and Herman B. Thomas, who was later killed at Monterey. Colonel Fitzpatrick is not identifiable.

Cerralvo, September 2, 1846

This is decidedly the pleasantest and most salubrious place the American troops have yet found in Mexico, and that portion of Gen. Worth's command stationed here are reveling in a climate of delicious temperature. Autumn has now arrived, although the weather is still warm; yet cool airs from the mountains close by temper the heat, while bubbling and swift-running brooks, clear and limpid, are met with at almost every turn and afford the finest opportunities for bathing. Heavy showers, to be sure, fall daily; but the ground never becomes muddy, and the rains only serve to clear and render more pure the air—a compensation exceeding any discomfort they may produce. And then the view from the town is one of rare and beauteous grandeur. Rising high above, their blue peaks piercing heaven's vault, stand the mountains between this and Monterey. It is not their height that gives them their magnificence; but they stand out in a boldness of outline seldom seen in any land, with naught intervening to destroy the view. In a clear day I am told they can be seen seventy miles—in Texas a long way the other side of the Rio Grande. So much for Cerralvo, its climate and situation: now for such news as I am able to gather.

In a hasty scratch from Punta Aguda, written two days since, I stated that the common talk in Gen. Smith's camp was that the Mexicans would make a bold stand at Monterey: such, too, is the talk here. It is impossible to get hold of positive intelligence, yet such information as can be obtained that can be relied upon would make it appear that there are at this time 4000 regulars in Monterey and vicinity, besides a large force of raw militia—the latter recruited any and every way, but principally by force. In an open field these men would be of no value whatever—behind breastworks they may be of some service. The Bishop's Palace and the Cathedral have been fortified, while redoubts have been thrown up at different commanding points. The number of guns the Mexicans have is not exactly known, but they are doubtless well supplied, especially with heavy artillery. The Bishop's Palace and Cathedral, already mentioned, are a short distance outside the town and occupy commanding positions. The entire force is under the command of Gen. Mejía for the present, but it is thought that he will soon be superseded by some other officer of more experience; in fact, it is currently reported here and believed that Ampudia has already arrived, with three fresh brigades, and assumed entire control. A short while since and the citizens of both Monterey and Saltillo were dispirited and disposed to give up without a struggle: the recent movements at the City of Mexico, the reported union of all parties for common defence, and the advance of fresh troops to their aid, have given them new zeal, and they now talk bravely of chastising the robbing and perfidious Americans to their heart's content. Such are the commonly received reports, at this time, of the situation of affairs at Monterey, the force there, and the feeling of the inhabitants.

In the meantime, Gen. Taylor is to advance upon the place with a force numbering about 7000, of whom nearly one half are as well-drilled regulars as any in the world. Gen. Smith, at Punta Aguda, is constantly drilling his men—the 5th and 7th U. S. Infantry and the company of Louisiana volunteers—and they will be sure to give a good account of themselves if called upon. The same may be said of that portion of Gen. Worth's command now here—composed of the 8th U. S. Infantry, Col. Childs's[9] artillery battalion and Capt. Duncan's battery—for this force is in as fine condition as any it has ever been my lot to witness. I am fearful that Gen. Taylor has chosen too small a number of men with which to advance, taking into consideration the liability to sickness on the march and the detachments which must be left behind; yet he knows best, and as for failing that is out of the question. If the American troops should meet with all the force that Mexico can muster there is to be no defeat—it is to be victory or a grave in the mountains.

G. W. K.

*Daily Picayune*, September 22, 1846

Cerralvo, September 3, 1846

Three men were picked up last night by Gen. Worth's picket guard, coming in from the Monterey side, who appear to be suspicious characters. They represent themselves as rancheros belonging to this section, and as having fled from the mountains in order to avoid being pressed into service; but as they were armed, and had twenty odd rounds of Government cartridges each, and besides told different stories, they have been detained and are in prison. It is thought they are spies and belong to Canales's party.

Ampudia is really at Monterey, and in command of the army there. I have just seen a proclamation of his, dated on the 31st ult.—four days since—in which he goes on in the usual bombastic style of his gasconading countrymen. He begins by saying that "the hour has finally arrived for taking prompt and energetic measures to protect the Departments of the East from the rapacious Anglo-Americans, and declares that all who aid them in any way are traitors and spies and if caught shall suffer death without benefit of clergy." He next goes on to speak of the "torrent of evils

---

9. Thomas Childs, First Artillery.

that has been brought upon the sacred (!) territory of Mexico by the contraband trade that has been carried on by the usurpers," and then, using the faculties in him vested, he declares:

1st. All natives and strangers, who directly or indirectly give aid to our enemies of their own will, shall be shot.

2d. Those who, after the publication of this decree, shall continue the odious contraband traffic with our enemies, shall suffer the same penalty mentioned in the preceding article.

Then follow two other articles, calling upon all the authorities to use every care and exertion strictly to carry out the demands of the General, and also commanding every private citizen—as he has the power—to aid in bringing the criminals to justice. The whole thing has been gotten up by Ampudia for effect: he knows that his countrymen are assisting the Americans in procuring transportation and furnishing supplies, and thinks by threats to put a stop to it. His proclamation will have little effect, although it places the inhabitants in this section in a still more awkward situation than ever. Called upon by the American Generals to furnish supplies at the highest prices, their cupidity cannot withstand such appeals; threatened with death by their own Generals, their fears are again worked upon in a way anything but agreeable. As I said in a former letter, the people here are really "between hawk and buzzard."

The rumors current at Monterey, four days since, were, that Santa Anna[10] would come on himself and take command of the army in person. Arista is in the City of Mexico, it is said, on trial charged with cowardice and traitorous designs—all a ruse to cover the disgrace and defeat which the great and truly magnanimous Mexican nation received at Palo Alto and the Resaca.

There are those here who think that the Mexicans will not make any resistance at Monterey, but will fall back upon San Luis or some other

10. Antonio López de Santa Anna dominated Mexican politics during the second quarter of the nineteenth century. He first appeared on the scene in the early 1820s, as a supporter of Agustín de Iturbide, and later led the revolt that deposed him. Over the next decade, Santa Anna successfully turned back a Spanish invasion at Tampico, conspired to promote and depose several presidents, found a home at different intervals in both the federalist and centralist political camps, and was chosen president in his own right. He dissolved the republic in 1835 and declared himself dictator in time to lead the unsuccessful fight against Texas independence. He was back in Mexico in 1838 to rebuff the French invasion at Vera Cruz, a feat that cost him a leg but reestablished his political base. He returned to the presidency in the early 1840s and ruled as a dictator until early 1845, when he was overthrown and exiled. He returned in 1846 with the acquiescence of the United States and the support of *puro* and *moderado* politicians seeking a means to secure a military victory over the Americans. He lived in exile from the war's end until 1853, when he returned for a brief and unsuccessful stint as dictator. He died in 1876.

strong place on the advance of Gen. Taylor, and all for the purpose of concentrating a larger force. Gen. T. will probably be within cannon shot of Monterey by the 18th of this month, or 20th at farthest, and then the story will be told. If Ampudia makes one of his stands there it is not a "*quien sabe case*"[11] to tell how the thing will result.

G. W. K.

P. S. Since writing the above, I learn that 2000 troops of the line arrived at Monterey on Monday last, the 31st ult., with four pieces of field artillery. It is also said that ten guns had been placed in position, and every effort was being made to mount some old guns previously laid aside. There is no cavalry force at Monterey, but it is thought that at Caldereyta, this side, there is a considerable number of mounted men. Canales is at Marin, also this side of Monterey, with 600 rancheros, and it is thought that Carvajal is with him. These people are determined to fight somewhere.

G. W. K.

*Daily Picayune*, September 22, 1846

Cerralvo, September 6, 1846

The two companies of Texas Rangers, under Capts. McCulloch and Gillespie, returned last evening from a scouting tour in the direction of Monterey, and brought back more full information of the enemy than had been heretofore received. Capt. Meade,[12] of the Topographical Engineers, accompanied the Rangers, having been sent out by Gen. Worth to examine the roads.

The party started from here on Friday afternoon, without pack mules or baggage of any kind, and with only three days' provisions. Before sundown, and at the foot of the mountains, a suspicious looking Mexican was caught. He endeavored to escape by running, but on finding that his horse was unable to carry him off safely he turned at some cattle he saw by the roadside and pretended that he was a *vacara*, or cow driver, and hunting an estray. This ruse, however, did not get him off, and a great deal of information was finally extorted from him by threats. He stated that Canales was near Papa Gallos in considerable force, and that there was also a body of regular cavalry under Col. Carrasco[13] in the neighborhood. As Papa Gallos was a place they had been ordered to examine, the party hurried onward. The road was exceedingly rough, full of loose rocks, and extremely hard upon the horses; yet this did not in the least check the advance.

11. An idiomatic phrase meaning something like "It's anyone's guess."
12. George G. Meade would later command the Union army at Gettysburg.
13. José María Carrasco.

The small rancho of Papa Gallos, about thirty miles from this, was passed without an accident, but an old fellow at one of the *jacales* stated that two couriers or express riders, carrying news of the advance of the Texans undoubtedly, had passed a short time previous, going ahead in hot haste. A little farther on, about 1 o'clock in the morning, the advance guard of the Rangers came suddenly upon the pickets of the enemy, and although they gave them a hard chase the fellows succeeded in getting off by taking to the chaparral. In the pursuit, however, one of them dropped his lance—a regular cavalry—which was picked up and brought in.

It was now ascertained that the Rangers were within but a short distance of the camp of the Mexicans, and that the latter had chosen a strong position—in an *arroyo* or a dry gully—from which to defend themselves. They outnumbered the Texans, too, in the ratio of nearly eight to one, having 500 rancheros at least under Canales, and from 2 to 300 regular cavalry under Col. Carrasco; and under these circumstances there was no other alternative left than to retire. The Texans went about two or three miles on the back track, where on finding a strong natural position they encamped for a few hours to rest their jaded horses. An attack was certainly anticipated, for the Mexican leaders must have known the force of the Rangers; yet the morning hours wore away and the sun rose without alarm.

On first ascertaining the force of the Mexicans, from the prisoner who had been taken, McCulloch sent back a note to Gen. Worth. This officer immediately dispatched six companies of regular artillery and infantry on the road, to sustain the Rangers in case they were beaten back. They were met on the return, three or four leagues from here, and all came in together.

The route taken by this scouting party was the right hand one to Monterey, passing Marin. The left hand road, which goes through Caldereyta, is thought to be the worst of the two over the mountains, and the other will probably be the one taken by the army. Whether there are any more troops on the route than those encountered near Papa Gallos is not known, but the appearance of these would indicate that Ampudia is keeping a bright look out for the advance of the American army, and perhaps with the intention of opposing its progress before it reaches Monterey.

Gen. Smith's brigade came up this morning from Punta Aguda, so that Gen. Worth now has something like 1700 men under his command. The residents here have been expecting an attack from their own leaders nightly, and hundreds have left the town for the ranchos in the neighborhood.

This place, or the name of it, has all along been spelled Seralvo. A Mexican says it is Cerralvo, and signifies a white or early morning light upon the mountains. The appearance of the neighboring mountains, between daylight and sunrise, is exceedingly magnificent.

G. W. K.
*Weekly Picayune*, September 28, 1846

Cerralvo, September 7, 1846

From what I can gather, a plan is on foot to surprise Canales and Carrasco in their strong hold near Passa Gallos. It will be a difficult matter, so wide awake and cautious are these fellows, but no harm can be done if it fails.

The prisoner taken the other night by McCulloch turns out to be a shrewd chap and of no inconsiderable importance. He admits that he was sent ahead to better himself in the way of swapping horses—that is, by leaving his own and stealing one of ours—and also to collect information in relation to the strength and position of Gen. Worth's camp. Canales will probably wait some time for his return, for he is fast enough here.

There is a rumor here—nothing but a rumor, mind you—that Santa Anna is advancing upon Monterey with 40,000 men. I might give you a column of other reports in circulation, but they are all of little moment and come from most unreliable sources—Mexican mouths.

I am fearful, after this, that the chances of sending letters to New Orleans will be few and far between. I shall snap at every opportunity, however.

G. W. K.
*Weekly Picayune*, September 28, 1846

Marin, Mexico, September 15, 1846

This place was entered by the first division of our troops this forenoon, and, contrary to the expectation of many, without a gun being fired. Early in the morning, at Ramos, Gen. Taylor dispatched McCulloch's Rangers to reconnoitre, and on reaching a hill overlooking the town, eight hundred or a thousand yards distant, we came in plain sight of a large body of the enemy's cavalry, ranged in the principal street, and evidently much flurried by our appearance. They were armed with new escopetas and lances, and among the uniforms were many of bright scarlet.[14]

With a force entirely too small to approach nearer having only 25 men with him, McCulloch ordered a halt. The plaza was concealed from sight by the church and the adjoining buildings, making it impossible to tell

---

14. Ampudia sent a force of 1,000 cavalry under Torrejón to harass the advancing American forces. McCulloch's men met about two hundred of them at Ramos on September 14.

whether there were any infantry or artillery in the town or not. The place offered every opportunity for concealing an enemy of thousands and as our commander was not so particularly certain that the Mexicans might not send an 18-pound shot, or some missile of the kind, up our way on a flying visit, we were ordered to scatter a little along the brow of the hill. Scouts in the meantime were sent out to prevent a party from getting in our rear, as the advance of Gen. Taylor was still several miles off.

For an hour we sat watching the hurried movements of the cavalry in the town, unable to make out their intentions. Horsemen were plainly seen dashing and cavorting about, while men on foot were jumping to get out of their way. Several generals—Mexicans of the lower orders dressed in greasy buckskin—were taken in the chaparral close by us, or voluntarily came up, who stated that the party below us was commanded by Gen. Torrejón, who had driven them out of the place and had threatened to destroy their houses by fire before *los Americans* should gain possession. They pointed out their *jacale* and *casas* to us, and implored our assistance in saving them! Singular war this and more singular the people!

In about an hour the cavalry began to move off in order, taking the route towards Monterey, now indistinctly seen lying at the foot of a large mountain ten or eleven leagues off. Their rear had not yet left the place before McCulloch, accompanied only by Col. Peyton of our city, was dogging after them, intent on watching their movements. In half an hour's time our captain appeared near the main street and beckoned us down, and in five minutes more we were all in the plaza. Nearly every house was closed, and the few men we met—for the women had all been taken off—greeted us as *amigos*, or friends, with their hats in their hands. One old fellow, living in a large house next door to the church, said he had been beaten—severely beaten—after we appeared in the night, by some of Torrejón's officers, to induce him to leave; but regardless of blows he had determined to stick by his premises and property. All the inhabitants had been shamefully abused, their property taken from them, and they were then driven into the chaparral; and we were told that in an hour's time more, had our company not appeared in sight, they would have set fire to the place.

Such is the policy which has been adopted and such the course pursued by Torrejón at every rancho and town since the Army left Cerralvo. To drive off the inhabitants and destroy all the supplies on the road is the game they are now playing, certainly determining to harass Gen. Taylor if they do not intend to fight him. The Mexicans all along on the road spoke confidently that Gen. T. would meet with stout resistance at this place, but the force we met only amounted to some 800 or 1000 cavalry, and they started off without firing a gun, as I have stated above.

The army remains here tomorrow to await the arrival of Gen. Worth's division. It is said we do not move towards Monterey before the day after tomorrow.

G. W. K.

*Daily Picayune*, October 6, 1846

Camp near Marin, September 16, 1846

Gen. Taylor has moved his camp a league this side of Marin, the inhabitants of which are returning to their homes in squads. It contains, I should think, 3000 souls, and is well built and delightfully situated. Below lies a wide and apparently fertile valley, encircled by lofty mountains, and than the appearance of the latter, especially at sunrise, nothing can be more magnificent. I might preach about them for hours, but must let our correspondent "H" walk into the descriptive, as he has more leisure than your humble servant.

Gen. Worth's division came in this morning in good order, and I am pleased to learn that there are but few men on the sick list in any of the regiments. Gen. Smith is with Gen. W., as you already know, and it is said the Louisiana company, attached to his brigade, is one of the best and most orderly in the Army.

Gen. Butler[15] will be up tomorrow, with the rear, and then the entire Army will move towards Monterey. What is to be done there no one can conjecture, farther than it is an understood thing that Gen. Taylor is to march into the city come what may. I am told that he says if there are 2000 men there he will fight them, and if there are 50,000 he will fight them: he has been ordered to Monterey by his Government, and there he is going. No matter what the force that may oppose, no one thinks of anything but victory, cost what it may. By next Sunday the story will probably be told.

We had a funny scene in our company this afternoon. Two or three of the men, while out on picket, found a mule load of baggage belonging to a Mexican officer. The animal had probably *stampeded* during the retreat of the day before, and Torrejón's men were in too great a hurry to hunt up runaway mules. The letters found would show that the owner was Don Ignacio something or other, captain of the 3d company of Guanajuato

---

15. President Polk named William O. Butler, a veteran of the War of 1812 and a successful Kentucky lawyer and politician, to command the First Division of Volunteers, composed of soldiers from Kentucky, Ohio, and Indiana. Butler joined Scott in the Mexico City campaign and in February 1847 succeeded him in command of the army in Mexico.

cavalry, and to set forth that Don Ignacio was a man of some consequence: he had a scarlet coat of the finest broadcloth, covered with pure silver buttons, ornamented with rich silver embroidery, and upon the breast of which was an order. His cap was of blue velvet, richly ornamented with silver band and tassels, while his cavalry pantaloons, of blue broadcloth foxed with morocco, had a wide stripe of red down their outer seams. Among the baggage was also mattress, several pillows the cases of which were elaborately worked, and other fine bed furniture, and in addition to all this, as if this were not enough, there were some half a dozen red, green and figured petticoats, a dozen pair of beautiful little pink, blue and white satin slippers, to say nothing of a dozen neatly wrought linen camisas—all the wardrobe of some pretty *Poblana*[16] girl, who had doubtless followed Don Ignacio to the wars.

After all this "large and elegant assortment" had been opened, our orderly sergeant—the son of a member of Congress from Tennessee—rigged himself out in the showy uniform of the Mexican officer, and strutted forth to detail a picket guard, decidedly the best dressed man in the invading Army from Gen. Taylor down. In the meantime there were others who girt the Poblana's petticoats about them, and then executed divers Cracoviennes and Cachuchas,[17] to the great amusement of the bystanders and to the great danger of stampeding all our horses. Altogether the scene was extremely diverting, and I put it down as a little episode in the life we have led of late.

The letters found were principally from the family of the officer, but there was one from Gen. Cortazar, dated at Celaya about the latter part of August, in which that general warmly hopes that Don Ignacio may be successful in assisting to drive the perfidious invaders of Texas from the country. So far, to say the least of it, Don Ignacio has not realized Gen. Cortazar's hopes to any considerable extent, although there is no telling what he may do yet. All joking aside, the Guanajuato officers are among the most intelligent and gentlemanly in the Mexican Army. A detachment of them had charge of the Texan Santa Fe prisoners in the city of Mexico, four or five years since, and from them they always received the best treatment to my certain knowledge.[18] It has been said by the Mexicans here, that the officer who lost his baggage was the last to leave Marin, and that he did all in his power to protect the inhabitants from abuse. I have

16. A female resident of Puebla. The city, later occupied by the Americans, is midway between Vera Cruz and Mexico City.

17. Dances.

18. Kendall had been imprisoned in Mexico City for four months as a member of the ill-fated 1841 Santa Fe expedition.

spoken of the Poblanas above: if you wish to read a graphic account of them get hold of Madame Calderón's work on Mexico.[19]

McCulloch is resting his animals today, but will probably be off on a scout tomorrow or next day. Two New Orleans gentlemen came up and joined his company this evening—Messrs. Foucher and Lewis—and I have heard it stated that Gens. Lamar and Burleson will join shortly.

Should anything turn up before we go out I will drop you a line. At present we have not a word of news of the enemy.

G. W. K.

*Daily Picayune,* October 6, 1846

Camp near Marin, September 17, 1846

We are still here, although it is probable we may be ordered out tonight or early tomorrow morning. Gen. Butler's division came up this morning, so that the force here is now between five and six thousand. With this the commander moves upon Monterey. The news from that city is still indefinite and unsatisfactory. A fellow was picked up this morning who says that he has been employed upon the ditches and fortifications there, and further that he made his escape two days since with others. His story is, that the women have all been sent off, that Ampudia's force is in the neighborhood of 8000, and that he is determined to hold out. I simply give this as his story. He has certainly described the different works and fortifications in the neighborhood with great accuracy.

The fellow farther says, that Gen. Torrejón is a few leagues in advance of this, destroying everything in his way and driving off the inhabitants. This looks reasonable, for it is in keeping with his movements of the past few days.

Gov. Henderson has not yet come up, but it is thought will be along tonight with the mounted Texas men.

A mail or express rider is just on the eve of starting by who I send this. It will probably be the last chance I shall have to write until the Army reaches Monterey.

G. W. K.

*Daily Picayune,* October 6, 1846

Camp near Marin, Afternoon of September 17, 1846

Just as the mail was closing the following proclamation of Ampudia was handed to me. You will see that it is dated day before yesterday. A

19. Fanny Calderón de la Barca, *Life in Mexico* (Boston, 1843).

great many of the precious documents were found in the mud near our camp, doubtless dropped by some of Ampudia's agents to draw off the affections of the regular soldiers. It is the "weakest invention of the enemy" I have ever seen, and it is unnecessary to say will have no more effect than the falling of a leaf among them. Copy it entire, give it his own spelling and punctuation, and pray have some charity for Ampudia's English:

> Army of the North
> General in Chief. Head Quarters, Monterey,
> September 15, 1846

It is well known that the war carried on in the Republic of Mexico by the Government of the United States of America is unjust, illegal, and anti-Christian for which reason no one ought to contribute to it.

The Federal Government having been happily reestablished, a large number of Battalions of the National Guard in the States of Coahuila, St. Luis Potosí, Guanajuato, Zacatecas, Querétaro and others are ready to be on the field and fight for our independence.

Acting according with the dictates of honour and in compliance with what my country requires from me in the name of my Government I offer to all individuals that will lay down their arms and separate themselves from the American Army, seeking protection, they will be well received and treated in all the Plantations, Farms or Towns, where they will first arrive and asisted for their march to the Interior of the Republic by all the Authorities on the road, as has been done with all those that have passed over to us.

To all those that wish to serve in the Mexican Army their offices will be conserved and guaranteed.

> Pedro de Ampudia

I have no time for comment, as the express rider's bag is closing, but you ought to hear the laughing this proclamation has excited in camp.[20]

> G. W. K.

P. S.–Here is "the last brickbat" from Ampudia. It is in Spanish, has some connection with his English proclamation, and perhaps you had better translate it.

20. Kendall's confidence in the commitment of American soldiers did not coincide with reality. Desertion during the Mexican War was higher than in any other American foreign war, totaling more than 8 percent of the regular and volunteer enlistees. Approximately 9,000 American soldiers deserted during the Mexican War; 4,000 of those left while the army was in Mexico. The rate among the regulars, many of whom were foreign-born, was approximately 13 percent. Robert R. Miller, *Shamrock and Sword: The Saint Patrick's Battalion in the U.S.-Mexican War* (Norman, 1989), 23–24.

(Translation of the "Circular.")

Headquarters of the Army of the North,

September 15, 1846.

The object of the circular which is annexed in English is to make known to individuals among the troops of the United States who, I am informed desire to abandon that flag—the kind disposition with which they will be welcomed and protected under the flag of Mexico, whose only device is to resist the unjust aggression of the neighboring Republic and to open wide the arms of the Republic to those who seek the shelter of her flag with friendly purpose. Therefore, I now direct you that such soldiers as may present themselves from the enemy's ranks with friendly purposes unequivocally evinced, be assisted and conducted to the interior of the Republic by the most convenient points and roads. But those who present themselves in a hostile attitude, or who under friendly appearances conceal sinister designs against the sacred rights of the Republic—against these you are directed to make war in every mode. And in case the conduct of those who present themselves should be doubtful, and it be difficult to determine whether their purposes be friendly or hostile, you will send them under a secure guard to headquarters; and if this be not possible, from circumstances which may occur during the war, you will have them march to some point in the interior beyond the reach of the enemy's advanced parties. I make this communication to you for your punctual and exact compliance therewith, holding you responsible for the slightest omission in regard to any point contained in this order, the high importance of which is well known. God and Liberty.

A messenger from the Spanish Consul at Monterey has this moment arrived. He desires Gen. Taylor to give him and the other foreigners in that city the usual protection, &c. If the mail would only stop an hour I might say more.

G. W. K.

*Daily Picayune*, October 6, 1846

San Francisco, September 18, 1846

The Army is now encamped at this place, within twelve miles of Monterey, and the probabilities grow stronger and stronger that tomorrow forenoon active hostilities will be commenced on the part of the enemy. Yet never have I seen men in such excellent spirits. One feeling animates every man, and many a soldier will be disappointed if tomorrow's sun goes down without at last a chance of feeling the batteries the Mexicans have erected around the city.

Our company has had quite an excursion today. News came to Gen. Taylor early in the morning that Torrejón's cavalry were encamped near Pescaria Chica, a small rancho to the left of the main road towards Monterey and in the direction of Caldereyta. He at once ordered Col. May, with a squadron of dragoons and McCulloch's and Gillespie's companies, to make a dashing march in that direction, and if possible disperse the party. It had been said that Torrejón had planted himself in this position with the intention of attacking the baggage and pack mules in our rear.

Pescaria Chica was reached without seeing anything of the enemy other than look-outs or scouts on the distant hills, but abundance of "sign" was visible showing that Torrejón had been in the neighborhood. His instructions not permitting him to move farther, Col. May, after procuring a guide from the alcalde, struck up the Aqua Fria towards the Monterey road. The people at the different ranchos we passed were frightened out of the little sense God has vouchsafed them, and at the crossing of the stream a Mexican was seen galloping off at a rapid rate. On being told to halt, and on seeing a dozen guns aimed at him, the fellow halted, and was compelled to guide the party into the main road. Thus ended a well-laid plan to catch the noted Torrejón. He was a little too smart to be entrapped.

Gov. Henderson, with the two regiments of mounted men under Cols. Hays and Wood,[21] have just come. They are to form the advance guard tomorrow, so it is said. The order of march is as follows: The first division, under Gen. Twiggs, follows Gov. H.; the second division, under Gen. Worth, comes immediately after; while Gen. Butler brings up the rear. Close order will be kept, and a strong picket thrown out to watch the enemy.

I don't know when I shall have an opportunity to send this letter—I write it so that you can be enabled to "keep the run of the game," as the saying is.

G. W. K.

*Daily Picayune*, October 6, 1846

Camp near Monterey, September 19, 1846, 12 o'clock, M.

A fire has been opened this morning from the batteries of the enemy. About 8 o'clock, Gen. Taylor being in advance with the two Texas regiments, the Bishop's Palace appeared in sight. It is on a commanding eminence, about a mile and a quarter or a mile and a half from the city, and is strongly fortified with a new-made ditch around it plainly visible to the naked eye at the distance even of two miles.

---

21. George T. Wood, Texas Volunteers.

A heavy fog hung like a mantle over the city as we neared it, concealing everything from sight; but when within a mile and a half the fog slowly lifted, and now could plainly be seen the forts and batteries of the Mexicans. The tri-colored flag was waving over the main fort, but no other banner could be seen.

Gen. Taylor kept steadily on, in the advance, until within some fifteen hundred yards of the city, when suddenly a dense smoke from one of the batteries, followed by the loud boom of a twelve pounder, caused a sudden halt. I should have previously said that before the city appeared in sight a sharp rattling of musketry announced that our pickets had come in collision with the outposts of the Mexicans. The latter fired a heavy volley at our men, but fortunately no one was killed or wounded.

The first ball from the batteries fell short, striking the ground before reaching the point where we had been halted, tearing up the ground, and then ricocheting along through the chaparral; the next three or four were directed with better aim, one ball going over the heads of Gen. Taylor and staff and so close that it was at once evident that the Mexican gunners had got the range. The party now moved off, Maj. Mansfield and some of the engineer department dispersing themselves singly in the chaparral and approaching close to examine the works of the enemy.[22]

The firing from the fort continued until the Mexicans had wasted six or eight 9 or 12-pound shots; the Texan regiments being now ordered to retire out of reach of the batteries and for the purpose of giving their horses water. They did not leave, however, until they gave shouts of exultation and defiance that might have been heard in the city.

In an hour's time we were again within sight of their batteries, which they opened once more with their heaviest guns; yet not a man or horse was struck. A 9-pound shot, as it came bouncing along through the bush close by us, stampeded a pack animal to the great danger and disarrangement of the baggage—this was all the loss so far. In ten minutes more, and while their batteries were still at work upon us, we were ordered to retire upon Gen. Taylor, who had encamped the entire Army at some cool and delicious springs of water in a pecan grove about three miles from the city.[23]

22. Joseph F. K. Mansfield's reconnaissance affirmed Taylor's plan to send Worth's division to the west to attack the strategically important fortifications on Federation Hill and Independence Hill. This allowed the Americans to cut off Ampudia's supply line to Saltillo while the main body of the army attacked from the east.

23. While the advance party tested the Mexican defenses, Taylor ordered the army to camp in a spring-rich grove of oak and pecan trees about three miles from Monterey, known as Bosque de San Domingo. Americans called the area Walnut Springs.

Half-past 2 o'clock, afternoon.—Capt. Pike Graham, with a squadron of dragoons, and Capt. Gillespie's company of Texan rangers, is now out with Major Mansfield and Capt. Sanders[24] and Scarritt, of the Engineer Department, on a reconnaissance—the dragoons and rangers being sent to support and cover them. It is thought the Mexicans have at least fifty cannons in position.

Three o'clock.—A heavy firing of artillery, now distinctly heard in camp, would denote that Major Mansfield has been disturbed in the reconnaissance. He will go to the Bishop's Palace, however, and into the very city, if the service demands. Gen. Taylor with all his staff and other officers, are going out in an hour to survey the grounds between this and the city.

Half-past 5 o'clock.—I have just returned from a visit to the works of the enemy, a party of us going almost right within point blank range of their guns, but scattering about so that they never could get more than a single man to fire at. They have given Graham's and Gillespie's companies at least a dozen rounds, but without injuring a man. A heavy ball passed within a foot of one of the latter's men, and so close to the horse that he shrunk almost to the earth. We thought at first that both man and horse were stricken to the ground, but it was only the windage of the ball that frightened the latter. My old friend, Tom Hancock,[25] of Santa Fe memory, remarked, that "the Greasers shot uncommonly well for them," and he has had as much experience in this way as any man living. Capt. Ridgely and Col. Peyton, while approaching to examine a battery at the edge of the town on the Caldereyta road, were fired upon by a party of lancers stationed close by—neither injured, although the "scopet balls," as the boys call them, flew all about them. Major Mansfield has now gone in the direction of the Bishop's Palace, for the purpose of examining the works in the neighborhood.

Ten o'clock, night.—The engineers, with Graham and Gillespie, have just come in safe after proceeding even as far as the Saltillo road on the other side of the Bishop's Palace. Major Mansfield reports that there are several commanding positions that can be stormed and taken—one a battery of five guns. The intentions of Gen. Taylor will be known tomorrow, but I do not think that anything will be done before Monday.

G. W. K.

*Daily Picayune*, October 6, 1846

24. John Sanders, Engineers.

25. Kendall had hired Tom Hancock, an experienced frontiersman, to go along with him on the 1841 Santa Fe expedition. Copeland, *Kendall of the Picayune*, 166.

Camp opposite Monterey, September 20, 1846, 8 o'clock, morning

By a Mexican now waiting to start for Camargo, I send this with other letters. There is no certainty that they will go through, but with the chances that they might I pack them off.

It is now raining; but as my weatherwise knowledge does not cover this section, I cannot tell with what prospect of continuance.

It is thought that one of the enemy's batteries will be stormed tomorrow morning. As it looks now, the infantry will have the hottest part of the work.

There are some who still think the enemy will leave without a strong resistance—a majority, however, think they will hold out to the last. Every officer and every soldier in the Army is in excellent spirits and confident of victory. In great haste,

G. W. K.
*Daily Picayune*, October 6, 1846

Monterey, September 29, 1846

I should have written you before this late hour; but I knew, all the while, that our regular correspondent "H" was keeping you well acquainted with the stirring events of the past week, and little time had I, even could I have put hands upon writing materials, to give you an account of the doings of the 2d division of the Army. From the time the Mexican Lancers commenced the attack upon our advance, late on the afternoon of the 20th inst., up to the final capitulation on the afternoon of the 24th, there was literally no rest to the soles of the feet of any man in Gen. Worth's command. The rain on the nights of the 20th and 21st, combined with the constant expectation of an attack from the enemy, were causes sufficient to drive away sleep; but to these should be added hunger and that excess of fatigue which drives off slumber, as well as the circumstance that many of us had wounded comrades demanding attention; with this combination of drawbacks you can easily conceive that one had little time or inclination for writing.

Speaking of wounded comrades reminds me of poor Thomas. He was one of the most daring spirits in McCulloch's company, and had his horse wounded in the charge the enemy's lancers made upon us on the morning of the 21st. On the following morning, while storming the battery on the height overlooking the Bishop's Palace, he was mortally wounded, and after suffering incredibly died on the morning of the 24th. A musket ball shattered his hip joint, at the same time that the brave Capt. Gillespie was shot through, and the two are now quietly resting side by side on the

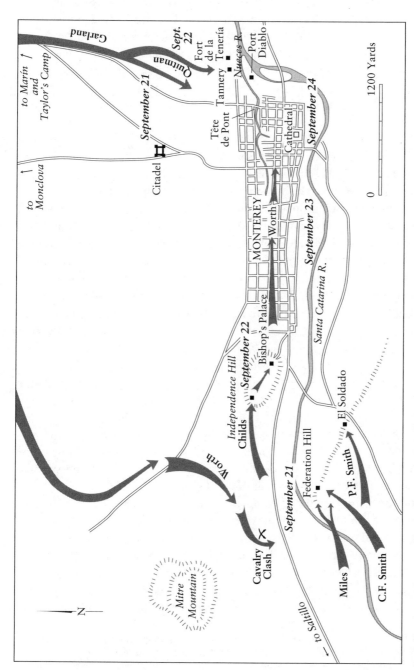

The battle at Monterey, September 21–24, 1846.

height where they received their death wounds—Mount Gillespie as it has been appropriately named by Gen. Worth. The friends of Thomas are among the most respectable in Maryland; he was in the same mess with myself, and it may afford his acquaintances some consolation to know that every attention was paid him, during his last hours, that circumstances would admit.

Of the thousands of Mexican soldiers that occupied this Gibraltar of a town a few days since, not as many hundreds now remain. At one time, so confident were Ampudia and his generals of success, they sent Romano[26] with fifteen hundred or two thousand cavalry in the rear of Gen. Taylor, to cut off his retreat. The "redeeming" game of the Texans and regulars on the afternoon of the 23d—digging through and under houses, taking inch by inch, but never giving one—and then the close proximity of the 24-pound mortar so successfully worked by Maj. Munroe and Lieut. Lovell[27]—all combined to intimidate the Mexicans to a degree that induced them to sue for terms. Shells from the mortar fell and exploded all around the great Cathedral: had one entered that establishment, filled as it was with ammunition, every house on the main Plaza would have been riven to fragments, and the loss of life would have been fearful. To spare the shedding of so much blood, and so terrible an injury of property, were some of the main causes that induced Gen. Taylor to offer the Mexican commander the terms he did.

I saw Ampudia as he left town for Saltillo on the morning of the 26th—rode along in his escort for a mile or two. The base and lying wretch—for every page in his black history proves him such—looked crest-fallen, nervous, and timid to a degree. He was fearful lest some of the Texan rangers, many of whom had deep wrongs still to avenge, might shoot him from the way-side; and as he rode through their encampment, situated directly on his route, he could not conceal his fears. They allowed him to pass, however, without even a cry or shout of exultation.[28]

Opinions are various in camp as to whether the Mexicans will now offer peace, or make a stout resistance at Saltillo, a larger portion I believe inclining to the latter opinion. A Mexican who arrived from that place yesterday reports that they have already commenced fortifying it on an extensive scale; but this should be taken merely as a rumor or story of a Mexican—the most unreliable information conceivable. Again, a great many are discontented at the terms given the Mexicans, and think that

26. Romano is probably Manuel Romero, commander of a Mexican cavalry brigade at Monterey.
27. John Munroe, Second Artillery, and Mansfield Lovell, Fourth Artillery.
28. Ampudia had defeated the Texans at Mier in 1842 and had a well-deserved reputation for cruelty along the Mexican frontier in the last years of the Texas Republic.

they now will certainly fight again after being let off so easily. Had the battle continued on the 24th three hours longer the Mexicans would undoubtedly have been on their knees crying and begging for their lives. A terrible carnage would have ensued had not Ampudia sent in proposals for a surrender of the town, for his forces were huddled, if I can use such a term; and all this Gen. Taylor well knew. To carry out the known conciliatory policy of our Government, however, appears to have been his aim—to spare life and property, in accordance with his instructions, his object—and this should relieve him from all censure in the matter. For myself, having some slight knowledge of Mexican character, I believe the whole policy of our Government is, and has been wrong for years. Shower any quantity of magnanimity upon this people and it is entirely thrown away—they neither feel nor appreciate it. An inherent pride, which grows upon them with every step in downward and disgraceful career, causes them to look with a pretended scorn upon every offer of generous for-bearance in their adversity, and as well might Van Amburg[29] attempt to conciliate his tigers and hyenas by choice bits of meat and love pats on the head as these people by acts of kindness. The policy has been tried all summer, and the effects of its workings has been shown by rascally extor-tions on the part of those of whom our Government has attempted to purchase provisions, and by every exertion on the part of the military to cut our Army in pieces when it beleaguered this place about. But enough of this for the present—a word or two of news, such as I have to offer.

The two Texan regiments, under Cols. Hays and Wood, will probably return home in the course of a week, and should hostilities recommence fresh regiments, mounted on the best horses that can be procured, will at once be raised.

An express has come in, stating that Gen. Wool, with 3500 men, was to leave San Antonio yesterday for Chihuahua. What in the name of all that is reasonable, so large a force is going in that direction for, is more than I can make out. That whole section is now in the hands of the Comanches, as it were, and the difficulty of moving so large a number of men, when one quarter of the force is more than is necessary to subjugate any army now there or that can be sent, looks to me as almost insurmountable. With not double the number, Gen. Taylor has marched upon one of the strong-holds of the country and driven off an army complete in all its appoint-ments—if Gen. Wool goes to Chihuahua with the number stated, it seems to me that he will have no other enemies to contend with than the worst

29. The reference is probably to Isaac A. Van Amburgh. With various partners, he operated circuses throughout the United States from 1821 to 1865.

of all—hunger and suffering. I hope that he will march this way, where his services may really be needed.[30]

Gen. Taylor is still encamped at the old ground, three miles from here—Gens. Worth and Smith are in town. The main part of the wounded officers are doing well. Gen. Butler is recovering, while Cols. McClung and Mitchell[31] are also in a fair way.

G. W. K.

*Daily Picayune*, October 21, 1846

Monterey, September 29, 1846, 5 o'clock afternoon

An express rider has this moment arrived from Salinas, which place he left this morning. It is only a day's ride this side of Saltillo, and he states, on the authority of a Mexican, that Santa Anna arrived at that city yesterday morning or the evening previous, and at once commenced fortifying the place with vigor. He had no less than 13,000 with him, which, added to those which left here under Ampudia, will swell his army to over 20,000 men. Report farther has it, that he is to erect works and batteries close by the Rinconada—the limits of our lines by the sixty days' truce.[32] If all this should prove true, the army may have bloodier work to do than ever. One thing is certain—Santa Anna was hourly expected here when Gen. Taylor arrived, and many think that Ampudia's reasons for wishing to retire was the fact that he found himself to a degree surrounded after the successes of the 2d division, and was anxious to form a junction with his master on the best terms he could make. We shall know more about this matter in a day or two.

Lieut. Dilworth, of the 1st U. S. Infantry, died this forenoon of his wounds. Capt. R. H. Graham, who was badly shot, it is thought is mending. He belongs to the 4th U. S. Infantry.[33]

30. General John E. Wool, the third-ranking officer in the army, left San Antonio for Chihuahua on September 23, 1846, with a command of more than 1,400 men. His army grew to nearly 3,400 soldiers, of which only six hundred were regulars. After crossing into Mexico in mid-October, Wool's army occupied Monclova early in November amidst growing friction between regulars and volunteers. With water in short supply along the route, and with the arrival of word that the Mexican forces in Chihuahua had moved south to join Santa Anna's army at San Luis Potosí, Wool abandoned his march to Chihuahua and moved to Parras, then in late December on to Saltillo, where General Worth was preparing for the expected appearance of Santa Anna's army.

31. Alexander K. McClung, First Mississippi Rifles, and Alexander M. Mitchell, First Ohio Volunteers.

32. Santa Anna was actually on his way to San Luis Potosí, about three hundred miles south of Monterey. He ordered Ampudia to move the remnants of his army from Saltillo to San Luis Potosí. Santa Anna arrived there on October 8 and began to plan for operations against the American army. In the months that followed, he built an army of about 25,000 men.

33. Rankin Dilworth and Richard H. Graham.

I shall write by the first opportunity, and if I can collect all the information I want, will give you a full description of Gen. Worth's division.[34] Operating in different places at the same time, it is impossible to get hold of everything in a day.

The mail is just closing, so in haste,

G. W. K.

*Daily Picayune*, October 21, 1846

Galveston, October 27, 1846

The *Palmetto* going out towards New Orleans this evening gives me a chance of sending you a line, although I have little in the way of news to communicate.

The *McKim* and *Florida*, propellers, are both in port here from Brazos Island. The former came in, with her machinery out of order, three days since, and having been repaired will sail tomorrow: the *Florida* experienced head weather, and was obliged to put in for water. She, as well as the *McKim*, was crowded with sick and discharged volunteers, several dying on the passage up. If anything is needed it is a comfortable Government transport on which to send home the sick and disabled soldiers.

From Monterey to Matamoros, among both Americans and Mexicans, a great deal of sickness prevails—chills and fevers and intermitting fevers. I have come in for more than a full share of both, but am now on the mend. I regret to state that two able officers died here last night and are to be buried this afternoon—Col. William S. Fisher, who commanded the noted Mier expedition, and Capt. Francis S. Early, who commanded the Washington company of Texas Rangers at the battles of Monterey. The former had just married a young and accomplished wife; the latter was hourly expecting his family to meet him at this place.

The U.S. steamer *Spitfire*, Capt. Tattnall,[35] arrived at Brazos Island on the 19th inst. from Chagres.[36] She had on board Capt. Wm. C. Nicholson, Lieut. Leigh and Passed Midshipman Duer, U. S. N., who had all been sent down to Chagres with dispatches for the Pacific squadron. They are now on their way to New Orleans on the *McKim*. The news from California,

---

34. Kendall's account of the battle appeared in the *Picayune* on November 19, 1846, upon his return to New Orleans.

35. Josiah Tattnall.

36. Chagres was on the eastern coast of the Isthmus of Panama, near what became the eastern terminus of the Panama Canal.

brought by these gentlemen, has doubtless been anticipated by the arrival of Com. Sloat.[37]

I am glad to see that at length our Government is to prosecute the war against Mexico with some show of reason and vigor. Recall Gen. Wool from his nonsensical and Quixotic expedition to Chihuahua, order him to join Gen. Taylor and help out in the operations against Saltillo and San Luis, and the eyes of the Mexican rulers will soon be opened. All that will be wanting will be the subjugation of Tampico, and the establishment of depots of provisions on the road between that and San Luis, to throw all of Northern Mexico completely into our power.

G. W. K.

P. S. The *Florida* sails tonight for New Orleans—the *McKim* early tomorrow morning.

*Daily Picayune*, October 30, 1846

New Orleans, November 19, 1846[38]

Before commencing a detailed account of the part taken by the 2d division of Gen. Taylor's army, under Gen. Worth, in the capture of Monterey, it may be necessary to carry the reader back to the events of the four or five days preceding the combined attack upon the city.

The two slight skirmishes between McCulloch's Rangers and Torrejón's Lancers, which occurred on the 14th September, opened the eyes of many of those who had all along held firmly the belief that the Mexicans would not make a stand at Monterey. One of the skirmishes above mentioned, which occurred midway between the miserable rancho of Papa Gallos and Ramos, resulted without loss to McCulloch's men, although two or three of the Mexicans were badly wounded and one of their horses was killed. The Texan commander had but 35 men in all, while the Mexicans numbered at least 300; yet the latter, fearful as they afterwards said of being drawn into an ambuscade, retreated precipitately to Ramos, dropping several lances and escopetas in their flight.

It was during this affair that McCulloch, who, with one man only, was watching the motions of the Mexicans from a hill overlooking their posi-

37. Fearing British interference in California and on hearing word that the Bear Flag Republic had been declared, Commodore John D. Sloat landed 250 sailors and marines without resistance at Monterey, California, in July 1846. He declared the United States in possession of upper California before yielding his command to the newly arrived Commodore Robert F. Stockton.

38. This dispatch was written after Kendall's return to New Orleans, "from hasty notes taken at the time and recollections of the varied scenes." It was widely reprinted in newspapers around the country and was his only extensive report on the battle of Monterey.

tion, rescued, by a ruse, a member of his company from a situation perilous in the extreme, and in which his own impetuosity had placed him. Anxious to obtain a shot at one of the pickets of the enemy, he had pursued two or three lancers until he was directly upon the main camp, and where his destruction was inevitable. At this moment McCulloch saw him, and with lightning thought hit upon a trick to save this too venturesome ranger. Drawing his sword and flourishing it over his head, and at the same time telling the comrade who was with him to beckon with his hand as though calling upon a force secreted in his rear, the two dashed towards the Mexicans at top speed. The ruse worked—the affrighted lancers, probably thinking that a host of the dreaded *Tejanos* were upon them, scampered as fast as their horses would let them, and never checked their flight until they had crossed the beautiful stream which skirts the borders of Ramos.

At this point they halted and formed; but McCulloch was not yet done with them. Leaving 15 men three quarters of a mile in the rear in a strong position, and ordering 5 more to display themselves upon a hill close by, with 15 men only he advanced directly up within two or three hundred yards of the Mexicans. They were drawn up in regular battle array, as if anticipating a charge—three hundred men pitting themselves fiercely against fifteen—and apparently determined to make a desperate stand. McCulloch now fired an escopeta at them—one of their own which they had dropped in their previous flight. So heavily was it loaded—for the Mexicans are not niggardly in the use of powder—it nearly kicked our commander from his horse. A heavy volley from the lancers was the answer made to this single shot—a volley by which not a man was touched and only one horse wounded among the Texans. A loud yell of defiance from the latter, unaccompanied by a single shot, was followed by a precipitate retreat of the Mexicans, a heavy dust as they passed through the main street denoting their route. McCulloch was close upon their heels, and made a hasty examination of the place; but seeing that they had formed upon a hill beyond the town, in the direction of Marin, our commander ordered his men to retire slowly and fall back upon Gen. Taylor. Thus ended the events of the 14th September—events trifling enough, but yet showing that the Mexicans were not altogether so friendly as many supposed them to be.

Early on the following morning, the 15th, McCulloch was ordered to march in advance and reconnoitre the large town of Marin. He was accompanied by Captain Williams,[39] of the topographical engineers, and Col.

---

39. William G. Williams, Topographical Engineers.

Peyton of this city—the latter going out as an amateur. On reaching a hill overlooking the town, seven hundred or a thousand yards distant, the lancers of Torrejón could plainly be seen in the principal street. They saw the Texans, too, and for the space of an hour dashed and cavorted about as though meditating an overwhelming charge upon the little party which was quietly watching them; yet they finally rode off at an opposite quarter of the town, and as they marched out on one side of the Plaza, McCulloch's men were in at the other. It was thought by many that the Mexicans would give Gen. Taylor battle at this place, but such never seems to have been their intention.

Choosing a pleasant encampment three miles on the other side of Marin, Gen. T. remained there during the 16th and 17th, to allow the rear to come up with the provisions and baggage, and give the men a little rest from the fatigues of the previous marches. On the 18th Sept. the army crossed the Agua Fria without hindrance, and that night bivouacked at San Francisco, twelve miles only from Monterey. In the morning Gen. Taylor dispatched Col. May, with a squadron of dragoons and McCulloch's and Gillespie's Rangers, with the hope that the officer might cut off Torrejón near a rancho called Pescarin Chica; but the wily Mexican had left and made good his way to Monterey.

At an early hour on the morning of the 19th, and in full order of battle, the army took up its march, the route lying through cultivated fields and past small clusters of *jacales*, or thatched houses, many of which had evidently just been deserted by the terrified inhabitants. Ahead of the advancing columns, in fact on either side, rose high and precipitous mountains—a huge frame, as it were, to the quiet and lovely valley which they encircled. Many of the higher summits were capped by a dense fog; yet enough of their steep and craggy sides was still visible to give the whole scene an appearance of rare sublimity and grandeur. A little distance beyond the beautiful grove of San Domingo, and just as the white tents of the enemy upon the height overlooking the noted Bishop's Palace appeared in sight, a short halt was called for the purpose of consultation: and here it may be proper to remark that Gen. Taylor himself, accompanied by his staff and several officers besides, was in advance, followed by McCulloch's and Gillespie's Texan Rangers, which had that day joined Col. Hays's regiment for the first time. On detached service during almost the entire summer, many of the men had not seen their comrades from the new State since the time they left them in Matamoros in June. The night previous Gov. Henderson had arrived with the two Texas regiments, under Hays and Wood, and they were now placed in advance,[40] Gen. Twiggs following with the 1st Division of the Army, Gen. Worth with the 2d, and Gen. Butler bringing up the rear.

A small scouting party of Texans were in advance of all, some half mile ahead, and scarcely had Gen. Taylor recommenced the march ere a rattling fire of small arms announced that they had come upon the enemy's pickets. A busy hum ran through the ranks as this prelude to the grand work of the glorious three days reached the ears of the men, yet the march was still onward and in order. When upon a slight swell of ground overlooking the city, now but little more than a mile distant, a heavy fog hung like a mantle over all—cathedral and barricade, fort and outer work alike concealed—but soon the fleecy covering was lifted by the sun, and now could plainly be seen the citadel, forts, and other defences which guarded every approach to the noted capital of Nueva Leon—the stronghold of Northern Mexico. The tri-colored flag was floating lazily over the citadel, but no other banner could be seen. Not a soul was discovered moving in any direction—all was still as the grave itself—and it seemed, after the affair with the picket guard, as though the army was advancing upon a deserted city, until suddenly a dense smoke was seen issuing from one of the bastions of the citadel, followed by the loud boom of a cannon and the swift flight of a 12 pound shot as it sped past the column and mowed down the matted chaparral in its distant flight. Another belching forth of smoke and another report followed, succeeded by a third, and as one of the balls struck a few yards in advance of Gen. Taylor, and then ricocheted over the heads of the advance without doing injury, a cry of exultation rose on the still morning air, which, as it ran along the columns in the rear, swelled into a perfect shout of defiance. The line extended miles and miles along the road, and now every man pressed eagerly onward, every eye brightened, and a feeling of enthusiasm was seen and felt which cannot be described.

The firing from the citadel continued until the Mexicans had wasted six or eight shots, when Gen. Taylor ordered the Texan regiments to retire to an irrigating ditch close by to water their horses, while he himself slowly fell back to the springs of San Domingo. In an hour's time we were again within sight and reach of their main batteries, and were again greeted by round shot from their heaviest guns, yet not a man was injured. A 12 pound shot, as it ploughed along through the chaparral, stampeded a pack animal close by the Texan column, causing him to run off with all his

40. Kendall, riding with McCulloch's company, accompanied the Texas regiments.

baggage; but this was all the loss sustained so far. An order now coming for all the troops to retire, the Texans fell back upon the main camp in the beautiful walnut grove around the springs of San Domingo.

During the afternoon a party was sent out to make as thorough a reconnaissance as possible. It consisted of Major Mansfield, Capt. Sanders, and Lieut. Scarritt, of the engineer department, and Lieut. Meade of the topographical engineers. To cover this party, Capt. Pike Graham was dispatched with a squadron of dragoons, and Capt. R. A. Gillespie's Texan Rangers. They were repeatedly fired at from the batteries of the enemy, pursuing their reconnaissance until nightfall within range of their guns. After dark a hurried detour was made in the direction of the road leading from Monterey to Saltillo. The works on the height overlooking the Bishop's Palace were examined, as well as the approaches on the western side of the city, and at 10 o'clock the party returned to safety to Gen. Taylor's camp without the loss of a man.

The morning of Sunday, the 20th September, opened with a drizzly rain, but as the sun rose above the mountain tops all was bright again. Deeming the possession of the heights in the rear of the city and the command of the Saltillo road of the greatest importance, both to prevent the arrival of reinforcements and to cut off the retreat of Ampudia, Gen. Taylor at once ordered Gen. Worth's division upon this enterprise. The verbal orders to Gen. Worth were to occupy, at all hazards and sacrifices, the Bishop's Palace with the strong height above it and any other points that might command the Saltillo road. At the time it was currently reported that Santa Anna was advancing, with a powerful and well-appointed force, to the relief of the beleaguered city; so that the importance of occupying the above named positions will at once be seen.

About noon the division, nearly 2,000 in number, took up its line of march, and a better drilled or more perfect body of men, perhaps never set out upon perilous emprise. One word as to its composition: the 5th regiment U. S. Infantry under Major Martin Scott, the 7th under Capt. Miles, and Blanchard's company of Louisiana twelve months volunteers, composed one brigade under Gen. P. F. Smith; the other brigade, under Col. Staniford, consisted of Col. Childs's Artillery Battalion—companies from the different regiments of artillery now acting as infantry—Duncan's battery of horse artillery, the 8th U. S. Infantry under Capt. Screven, and Mackall's battery of horse artillery.[41] This force, so far, was entirely composed of regulars except Blanchard's company, and numbered about 1750; and to this should

---

41. Richard B. Screven, Eighth Infantry, and William W. Mackall, First Artillery.

be added the choice of Col. Hays's regiment of mounted Texas Rangers, swelling the number, as we have already stated, to about 2000 effective men. The Texans were alike unencumbered, either by blankets or baggage, food or cooking utensils, while the regulars had but scanty supplies of provisions for four days only.

A company of pioneers, under Lt. McCown,[42] was sent ahead to clear a road, through the cornfields and chaparral, for the artillery and provision train. The route lay out of range of the guns of the citadel, yet the movements of the division could plainly be seen from the height above the Bishop's Palace. The road leading to Monclova was passed without difficulty, and in a short time afterwards the advance reached the Pescaria Grand road. Here a small branch road, but little traveled, however, was found leading towards the great Saltillo thoroughfare, and this was at once taken. A little farther on, the division was halted in order that the men might fill their canteens, a small cluster of *jacales* affording the opportunity; and in the meanwhile Gen. Worth, accompanied by Gen. Smith and a few other officers, commenced ascending the hill on the right of the road in order to examine more closely the defences on the crest overlooking the Obispado, or Bishop's Palace, and the best point whence to assail that important position. It was while our commander was thus engaged, and while the men were drawing water from the wells on the left of the road, that Gen. Burleson, who had been in advance with a small scouting party, rode hurriedly in with the startling information that a large body of the enemy, both cavalry and infantry, had appeared beyond the point of a hill a short distance in advance, and were forming evidently with the intention of opposing the farther advance of the division. It might assist the reader perhaps here to state, that to the right of the road rose a succession of hills and mountains, in many places forming abrupt declivities, while to the left lay a succession of cultivated fields, cut up by irrigating ditches, and stretching half a mile or more to the foot of Independence Hill—*Loma de Independencia* as the Mexicans term it—on which the tents and breastworks of the enemy were plainly visible.

Gen. Worth, on learning the intentions of the Mexicans, at once dispatched a small reconnoitering party of McCulloch's men in advance, with the rest of the Texans and a body of infantry to support them. On reaching a point in the road about one thousand yards farther on, the advance were told, by several Texans who had clambered up a hill to the right, that a small body of Mexican cavalry had dismounted at the edge of a cornfield,

42. John P. McCown, Fourth Artillery.

about seventy yards from the road on the left, and had sought a cover evidently with the intention of firing upon the rangers or any other body that might appear. The next moment a rattling fire of escopetas was opened upon the scouts, followed by a discharge of round shot and shell from the battery on Independence Hill. One of the latter fell in the field directly between the Texans and Mexicans, doing no other injury when it burst than damaging the corn immediately around it. There were many men in the advance whose acquaintance with this peculiar species of warlike missile was very limited—one, in particular, the writer knows full well, who had never ever seen one before.

Finding that the fire of the enemy could not be returned, and it being now near sundown, the Texans were ordered to retire to some small jacales by the road-side, and there bivouack for the night. Before a picket guard was detailed—before we had even time to unsaddle our horses—a sharp fire was opened upon us in the yard from three or four hundred of the Mexican cavalry—a detachment which had evidently dogged the Texans when they retired, and had now taken ground on the point of a hill overlooking their position, and from which they intended to annoy them. Col. Hays promptly ordered out Acklen's[43] company, to take the chaparral on foot as skirmishers, while the rest of the Texans were told to cover themselves as well as possible by means of the fence and hold themselves in readiness to repulse a charge. This was between sundown and dark, and a misty rain was just setting in. After pouring in shower after shower of balls into the yard, the most of which went over the heads of the assailed, the Mexicans retired towards the Saltillo road. Of the Texans but three were wounded, although several horses, tied in the back part of the yard, were struck. But few shots were returned at the assailants, as they were concealed by the chaparral; yet the dead body of one lancer was found the next morning, and it was thought that others were wounded.

Within the yard of the small cluster of jacales—wet, uncomfortable, with little or nothing to eat, and in constant expectation of an attack—the advance of the Texans passed the night, the entire division encamped by the roadside in the rear. The horses fared far better than the men, for in one of the houses a large supply of dry corn was found, belonging probably to the Mexican Government, which was used without stint. Several pigs, kids, and chickens were killed in the yard by the men; but to kindle fires would show the enemy our exact position, so that there was little chance to cook. The yard was within range of the batteries on Independence Hill; yet as the

---

43. Christopher B. Acklen, First Regiment Texas Mounted Rifles.

Mexicans probably could not see the exact position of the division, they did not fire a gun after night.

At daylight on the morning of the 21st September every man was upon his feet—wet and without coffee or breakfast the Texans were soon in the saddle and the whole line in motion. To gain the Saltillo road was now Gen. Worth's main object. At 9 o'clock on the previous night, by a dim light and in the rain, he had written to Gen. Taylor a hurried account of the events of the afternoon, and at the same time intimated his belief that the enemy would oppose his entering the Saltillo road if possible. The sequel will show that he was right.

In close order of battle, the division moved onward, the Texans under Hays and Walker in the advance, infantry skirmishers under Capts. C. F. Smith and J. B. Scott close up; while one of Duncan's 6 pounders, under Lt. Hays, was ready to unlimber at any moment.[44] The batteries from Independence Hill immediately opened upon the column, and especially upon the baggage train, but did little execution. The Mexicans afterwards said that they fired at the train supposing the covered wagons were filled with our soldiers.

The head of the columns had now advanced about a mile and a half, and had approached within some three hundred yards of the Saltillo road, when suddenly, as the point of a hill was turned, a large force of the enemy, both cavalry and infantry, was discovered ahead, a body of the former thrown across the road, while in the direction of the Bishop's Palace the avenue appeared to be filled with both lancers and foot soldiers. The green and red pennons of the former, as seen above the corn, gave them a daring and dashing appearance. McCulloch's and Acklen's companies, being in the advance, were at once thrown into the chaparral to the right of the road, and the men were ordered to dismount in a kind of ditch or gully which would partially protect them in case the lancers made a charge. The latter were near two hundred yards distant and a straggling fire from the rifles of the Texans was at once opened upon them, yet finding the firing ineffectual the rangers were ordered to remount, advance upon the enemy, and when within good rifle shot turn their horses into a cornfield on the left and take to the fence by the road side. This movement, although executed in plain view of the Mexicans does not appear to have been understood by them, for they charged furiously upon McCulloch's company, which by some accident had not received the order to seek the cover of the fence. They first opened with

---

44. John B. Scott, Fourth Artillery, and Charles F. Smith and William Hays, Second Artillery.

regular volleys from their escopetas, and then gallantly dashed their horses at the single company of Texans who were still mounted, and who really should have retired to the rear at the onset; but as the lancers came down the road and hillsides a galling fire was opened upon them by the Texans at the fence, while McCulloch's men at the same time poured in a perfect storm of lead from their rifles, double-barreled guns, and pistols. The lancers tumbled from their saddles by dozens; yet with uncommon daring the survivors dashed onward, engaging, hand to hand, with the rangers still mounted. The regular skirmishers, under Capts. Smith and Scott, now opened upon the lancers over our heads, firing at those higher up the hill, while the 6 pounder of Lieut. Hays was also brought to bear upon the squadron upon the summit. Parties of regulars were also dashing into the cornfields and opening upon such of the enemy as were in the road leading towards the town—sharpshooters were seeking every cover whence to assail their tottering and bewildered ranks—the dismounted Texans were creeping up and giving them a murderous fire at every point—and in far less time than it takes to record it the discomfited Mexicans were routed and flying in every direction. That portion of the squadron of lancers which charged so fiercely upon McCulloch were nearly all killed before his men were ordered to retire, and had every ranger in the company been in possession of one of Colt's repeating pistols—a most efficient weapon in the hands of mounted men—not a Mexican would have escaped.

Thus ended the lancer charge, as it is called, on the morning of the 21st—a charge in which the Mexicans behaved with unwonted gallantry. By their own admission their loss in this brilliant affair was 150 in killed and wounded. Among the former was Lieut. Col. Juan N. Najera and Capt. Gutierrez,[45] two of their best officers. Thirty-two of their killed were buried the next morning in one pit on the immediate scene of conflict, while many others, who were able to drag themselves a short distance to die, were afterwards found in the neighborhood. A great number of their horses were also killed in the charge, no less than nine white ones being found immediately on the ground. On our side, strange as it may appear, the loss was trifling. Several of McCulloch's men received severe wounds in the charge, and many horses—among others that of Col. Walker—were wounded. But one man, a Texan, was killed, and he unfortunately came to his death at the hands of one of the regular skirmishers. Why more were not killed may certainly be put down as a miracle, for at one time two

45. José Gutierrez de Villanueva.

Heights of Monterey, from the Saltillo Road, looking toward the city from the west. Toned lithograph (hand-colored), 1847, by Frederick Swinton, after Daniel Powers Whiting, © Amon Carter Museum, Fort Worth, Texas (1974.2.3). Kendall described the event on November 19, 1846.

distinct currents of balls, from both Mexicans and our own skirmishers, were flying over the heads of a portion of the Texans.

Before the smoke of this fierce conflict had yet died away, Gen. Worth ordered the columns to advance, and a few moments found the main part of the division in the Saltillo road. A few scattered jacales were found at the junction of the roads, built at the edge of the cornfields which extended towards the Rio San Juan de Monterey, and hardly had our light batteries taken a position, and commenced firing upon the sand-bag breastwork upon the crest of Independence Hill, before a battery of two heavy guns, which had previously been concealed, was opened on our column with round shot from the height to the right known as Loma de Federacion, or Federation Hill—a high summit immediately overlooking Gen. Worth's position. It was a plunging fire, the balls striking directly among our men; and with such precision did the Mexicans serve their guns that the commanding general at once advanced the main part of his division to a sugar house in the direction of Saltillo, and completely out of reach of the enemy's cannon. Major Martin Scott, with the 5th U. S. Infantry, was left near the junction of the roads, to protect and cover the baggage train, then passing slowly along over the scene of the recent conflict with the lancers. As we said before, the rear of the division received a continued fire of round shot and shell from the battery on Independence Hill; yet suffered no other loss than the wounding of one or two men, and the killing or maiming of some of the horses.

It was while the main part of the division was moving towards the sugar house that Capt. McKavett,[46] of the 8th U. S. Infantry, was struck in the hip by a round shot and instantly killed. A sergeant in the same regiment was wounded, and a horse in Col. Duncan's battery killed about the same time; but otherwise the column sustained no loss. Capt. McK. was a brave and most meritorious officer, and died much regretted by all who knew him.

It was now about 11 o'clock, and the firing from the battery on the right—Federation Hill—still continued with unabated ardor. In a small jacal on the southern side of the road near two hundred baskets of Saltillo apples were discovered, which an old Mexican freely retailed at the rate of one dollar per hundred. He was the only male present; but in the same building were several women, who, regardless of the round shot and grape which were continually falling about them, busily employed themselves in cooking and making *tortillas* for our hungry soldiers, the latter paying,

---

46. Henry McKavett, Eighth Infantry.

scrupulously for everything they purchased. It was a singular scene—Mexican females cooking for the enemies of their country, while very likely their husbands or brothers were busy on the height above pouring death and destruction into their very midst.

About this time Major Scott, learning that the Mexican Lancers were forming in the vicinity of the Bishop's Palace with the intention of charging upon his position at the junction of the two roads, dispatched three of the Texans in that direction to obtain full information. The lancers, but two short hours previous, had retreated hurriedly by this very road, dead horses, and trails of blood from the wounded, being seen at every step of their disordered flight. The party now sent towards the Palace were greeted by repeated showers of grape and musket balls, but returned in safety with the information that the Mexican cavalry were nowhere in sight. At every interval between the discharges of the cannon on Federation Hill a heavy firing was now heard on the other side of the town, three miles distant, plainly denoting that our friends were in hard and active conflict with the enemy in that quarter.

At 12 o'clock, noon, finding that the battery of Federation Hill must be silenced, Gen. Worth resolved upon the daring plan of carrying it by storm. The position or even the existence of this stronghold was unknown when the division left Gen. Taylor's encampment on the previous day; yet as its subjugation was necessary before any other movement could be made, Gen. W. promptly dispatched a party of regulars under Capt. C. F. Smith, aided by a body of Texans under Major Chevallie, to carry the position at any sacrifice. The latter force consisted of detachments of the companies of McCulloch, Tom Green, R. A. Gillespie, Chandler, McCown, and Ballowe,[47] while Capt. Smith, accompanied by Lieut. Ed. Deas and Gibson, had four companies of regulars—one his own, and the others commanded by Lieuts. Shackleford, Van Vliet, and Phelps.[48] There were 250 regulars in all, while Texans swelled the force to near 100. It is needless to say that a better or braver body of men was never sent upon undertaking so full of peril, or that the movements of the little band were watched with breathless anxiety by the entire division.

In marching towards the point of the hill which appeared the most accessible, Capt. Smith struck off through a cornfield with the hope of concealing his march from the enemy. Arrived at the river, which he was com-

47. Eli Chandler, Fourth Independent Mounted Company, Texas Volunteers, and Jerome B. McCown and Samuel L. S. Ballowe, First Regiment Texas Mounted Rifles.

48. Edward Deas and John W. Phelps, Fourth Artillery; Horatio G. Gibson, Third Artillery; and Muscoe L. Shackleford, Second Artillery.

pelled to cross, it was found impossible to ford it owing to the steepness of the banks; but a distance of three or four hundred yards up the stream brought the party to a good ford not more than waist deep, and into the swift current they at once dashed. A heavy fire from the Mexican battery was at once opened upon them, showing that they had been discovered; yet the river was passed without the loss of a man, and in three minutes afterwards the party was moving swiftly onwards through the chaparral towards the base of the hill.

At a quarter to 1 o'clock, Gen. Worth deeming it prudent to support Capt. Smith, dispatched the 7th U. S. Infantry, under Capt. Miles, to his aid.[49] Fortunately this officer struck off more to the left, found a good ford lower down the river, and was enabled to reach a position at the foot of the hill before Capt. Smith, and with far less fatigue to his men. A heavy fire of grape was immediately poured into the 7th, and from the crest of the hill companies of the sharpshooters of the enemy were at once seen scrambling down the precipitous sides and opening at the same time a continuous and rattling fire of musketry. Several of his men fell wounded around him, yet Capt. Miles held firm to his position—he had been ordered to support Capt. Smith, and consequently would not advance until that officer had arrived with his men. To divert the attention of the Mexicans from that officer, however, Capt. M. dispatched a small party, under Lieuts. Gantt, Gardner and Little, to skirmish with the enemy above, and it was while thus engaged that his men were wounded.

So far, the movements of the enemy only could be discovered from Gen. Worth's position, the dense chaparral around the base of the height completely concealing his own men. It was a trying moment for all; for an incessant firing, of both grape and musketry, was pouring upon the storming parties, while not a solitary shot was returned. In this state of things the commanding general dispatched, Gen. P. F. Smith, with the 5th U. S. Infantry under Major Scott and Blanchard's Louisiana Volunteers, with the orders to support and sustain the attack—Gen. S. to take command of the entire movement on reaching the ground. That officer crossed the river immediately in front of Gen. W.'s position, and on reaching the base of the hill found Capt. Smith's command ascending with as much rapidity as the ground—steep, craggy, and covered with thick and matted chaparral—would admit. Regulars and Rangers, under a galling fire, were scrambling up and eagerly pressed forward; yet not until they were within good rifle distance, and the enemy was in plain sight did they open upon

49. There were seven companies of the 7th Infantry in all, commanded by Capts. Holmes, Gatlin, Ross, Paul, Whiting, and Lt. Humber. The adjunct was Lt. Page. —*Kendall.*

their adversaries: then, with shouts and volleys, they pressed eagerly up the steep and ragged cliffs. The enemy made a desperate struggle to maintain their position by a heavier discharge of musketry than ever, for the height was now so nearly perpendicular that they could not depress their cannon; yet they could not bear up against the terrible shock of their Anglo-Saxon foes. The dreaded Texans, who had unnumbered wrongs to avenge, were picking off each his victim at every shot—from every cover issued a leaden messenger of death—while the more open and more regular discharges of the well directed infantry were telling with an effect that staggered the Mexicans in their very stronghold. Onward, still onward, pressed the stormers—louder and louder grew their shouts as the front ranks of the enemy recoiled. The vantage ground of the latter was as nothing—the onslaught was too violent for them to withstand. The victors dashed furiously into their very works, the enemy fled affrighted, and even before they were yet out of range Lt. Deas had one of their own cannon turned upon the retreating foe. As the flag of the victors was displayed upon the crest a shout, louder than any which had preceded it, rose upon the air, while a response from their companions in the valley below told how well they appreciated the valor by which the heights had been won.

While this brilliant action was going on Gen. Smith, with the 5th and Blanchard's volunteers, now joined by the 7th, was rapidly marching along the southern side of the hill. He had discovered, about a quarter of a mile below the battery, just taken, a regular fortification of the Mexicans which had not previously been seen and at once determined upon its capture. Shouting at the top of his voice, "Take that other fort!" he advanced at a rapid step towards the work, many of those on the height also rushing at once to take a part in this new adventure. Again the Mexicans opened upon them with a heavy and continuous fire, not only of grape and round shot but of musketry; but to check the onward course of our men was impossible. With shouts and volleys they marched to the onslaught. The Mexicans skirmishers were driven in, the very breastworks of the fortification were clambered over by the victors, the Mexicans retreated from the work in disorder, and as they fled down the road leading towards the river, again was one of their own guns turned upon them, for in their hot haste they had no time either to discharge or spike it. Even the standard of the enemy was left flying, and as it was torn down, and the banner of the 5th and 7th rose triumphantly in its stead, a shout of exultation went up that must have been heard by Ampudia in the very heart of the city.

Until the flying Mexicans had reached the Bishop's Palace did their own cannon continue to annoy them, and even after they were within its walls and outer works they found little respite. A plunging fire was kept up until dark, which was returned from the Palace with shells and round shot, and perhaps the history of war affords few instances so full of grandeur and sublimity as this. Every discharge of cannon seemed to have its thousand echoes in the otherwise quiet and secluded valley. Hemmed in by the huge mountains of the Sierra Madre, the reverberations would crash and re-echo across the valley; and as the latter narrowed in width towards the gorges of Santa Catarina and the noted Rinconada, the reports would follow each other in such rapid succession that it seemed as though a thousand cannon were engaged in man's destruction instead of the half dozen so vigorously plied. The events of the afternoon of the 21st September will not soon be forgotten by those who participated in them.

The Mexican loss upon the heights was severe, many being found dead at the points where the different conflicts occurred. On our side some fifteen only were killed and wounded, strange as it may appear considering that the advantages of ground and breastwork were all on the side of the enemy. Among our wounded were Lieuts. Rossell[50] and Potter—the former of the 5th and the latter of the 7th Infantry. It should here be stated that Cols. Hays and Walker, with a small detachment of their men, were dispatched by Gen. Worth in season to take part in the storming of the second work, *El Soldado* as the Mexicans called it, and that many of Major Chevallie's party, not content with being in at the taking of the crest, were also among the first to subdue the battery below it.

At a quarter to 4 in the afternoon, after Gen. Worth had dispatched a party to the heights to bring down the wounded, he sent off a messenger to Gen. Taylor with a hurried report of his success thus far in storming the works of the enemy—at 8 in the morning he had dispatched a note with the result of the engagement with the lancers. To keep possession of the heights taken it was necessary that a strong force should be retained there, and Capt. C. F. Smith was accordingly ordered to pass the night with his regulars on the first height taken, Capt. Miles to remain at the fort of El Soldado with the 7th, while Major Scott was thrown farther down the ridge of hills with the 5th, to a commanding point nearly abreast of the city. As the sun went down a heavy rain set in; yet at three exposed points, without shelter, without blankets, without food—the different parties remained all night, and without a murmur. The Texans, who had left their horses saddled and tied to fences in the vicinity of the sugar-house, were ordered down to look after their animals. They had nothing to eat—were wet, fatigued, worn

50. Nathan B. Rossell.

out as it were—yet were still eager and willing to take part in the stirring scenes of the morrow, let the morrow bring forth what it might.

To gain possession of the height on the left as the reader looks towards Monterey—Independence Hill—was now Gen. Worth's object, and to obtain it he resolved upon storming the rugged and precipitous cliff. Again it may be well to observe that this point is on the highest part of the hill, and is 350 or 400 yards, by a gradual ascent, from the Bishop's Palace, which it commands and overlooks. The crest of the height, in order to make it more secure against the attack of a storming party, had a breastwork of sand-bags high enough to protect the enemy's artillery and infantry, while to add to the strength of the place the last twenty yards on the ascent was almost perpendicular—so steep that the only way to gain the breastworks was by climbing up by means of the projecting crags and fissures in the rocks, or by clinging to the stunted growth of thorny bushes which had found root among them.

At 3 o'clock on the morning of the 22d September the storming party, guided by Capt. Sanders and Lt. Meade, left Gen. Worth's main camp, now near the junction of the roads where the Mexican lancers made their charge on the previous morning. The command was given to Col. Childs and con-sisted nearly as follows: three companies of the Artillery Battalion under Capt. Vinton, and three of the 8th Infantry under Capt. Screven, while 200 Texas Rangers, under Cols. Hays and Walker, were also detailed as sharp-shooters. Lt. Benjamin was the acting adjutant, while the officers were Capt. J. B. Scott, Lieuts. Lovell, Gill, Bradford, Farry, Ayers, Longstreet, Wain-wright, Holloway, Merchant, and Montgomery of the regulars,[51] and Capts. R. A. Gillespie, Ben McCulloch, Tom Green, Acklen, Jas. Gillespie, Herbert[52] and Ballowe of the rangers. A larger force of the Texas Rangers would have been detailed for this hazardous service, had not a portion of them been on picket guard in the direction of the mill of Santa Catarine.

The morning was dark, damp and drizzly, while the height itself was cloaked and completely hid by a dense fog. Silently the party moved on-ward, the base of the hill being gained while the Mexicans were still igno-rant of its approach. The men had even got some distance up the ascent before the enemy were aware of it, the first intimation they received being the rattling of the tin canteens of the regulars. No sooner did the officer in

51. Regular officers not previously identified are Calvin Benjamin, Samuel Gill, and Edmund Bradford, Fourth Artillery; Joseph F. Farry and George W. Ayers, Third Artillery; and James Longstreet, George Wainwright, Edmund B. Holloway, and William R. Montgomery, Eighth Infantry. Merchant is not identifiable.

52. Claiborne C. Herbert, First Regiment Texas Mounted Rifles.

command of the breastwork above learn that our force was upon him than he at once poured his skirmishers down the descent, and opened an incessant fire of musketry—at random for the day had hardly yet dawned—upon the advancing columns. Not a man drew back or faltered—every regular and ranger pressed eagerly upwards, in the face of death itself, to be the first to reach the stronghold of the enemy. So soon as the latter could be seen they were greeted with loud cries and a heavy discharge of musketry and rifles, were driven back to their breastworks by the impetuosity of the charge, and after a short but hard struggle were finally routed from their strong position and the next moment were running in disorder down the declivity towards the Bishop's Palace. A loud shout of exultation from our troops announced the possession of the crest, for it was not yet open day, and the colors of the victors were soon waving over the scene. Some ten or twelve of the enemy were killed in the charge, and many were wounded: had not our men been exhausted and out of breath on reaching the height the loss of the Mexicans would have been much more severe. The loss on our side was trifling as regards numbers but irreparable in another sense; for it was while storming this height that Capt. R. A. Gillespie and young Thomas, who were in the very advance, received their death wounds. More gentle or more daring spirits never lived, and side by side they are now resting within the breastworks they were the first to reach.

The orders given to Col. Childs were to gain possession of the crest at any hazard or sacrifice, but to risk nothing in an attempt on the Palace until he received farther instructions from Gen. Worth. Capt. J. B. Scott, however, acting for the time as Major of the right, was sent down the hill with a party of regulars and rangers to reconnoitre. The Mexicans charged them near the Palace with no inconsiderable bravery; but they were repulsed and driven back with loss, and Capt. S. maintained his position until relieved by Capt. Vinton.

At 8 o'clock Col. Childs was reinforced by three companies of the 8th Infantry under Col. Staniford, the 5th under Major Scott, and Blanchard's volunteers, who had passed the night on the heights on the opposite side of the river. All were wet, tired and hungry, yet not dispirited: since the morning of the 20th no one had had opportunity to cook a morsel, and the regulars, meanwhile, had shared the scanty supply of hard biscuit in their haversacks with the rangers who had no provisions whatever; yet not a murmur was heard. One of the sweetest morsels the writer of this recollects ever to have eaten was a small piece of biscuit and a thin slice of cold pork, given him by a regular, an Irishman—but to return to the active scenes in the drama.

Throughout the morning the enemy, from the loop-holes, windows and parapets of the Palace, continued to pour an incessant fire of musketry upon our men, besides round shot and grape from the cannon. Those near the crest were protected by the sand bag breastworks, while the Louisianians under Blanchard, the Texans under Walker, and the companies of regulars under Capts. Merrill, Chapman, and Bombard,[53] and Lieuts. Ayers and Bradford, who had been thrown forward near the Palace under Capt. Vinton, were partially covered by the chaparral and the nature of the ground. This force met with some loss, but considering the number of balls thrown it may be put down as trifling.

About 10 o'clock, Gen. Worth ordered Lieut. Roland,[54] of Col. Duncan's battery, to proceed to the crest of the hill with a 12 pound howitzer. After incredible exertion the piece was dragged and lifted up the jagged and precipitous cliff, placed in position about half-past 12, and at once opened a brisk fire of shell and schrappnall upon the Bishop's Palace. The effects of the howitzer, which had been covered by an epaulement of the captured battery, were at once visible: with remarkable accuracy the shells were thrown directly into the windows and other openings of the enemy's works, the Mexicans were driven from every loop-hole and parapet, and as a last resort attempted a heavy charge, with both cavalry and infantry, upon our advanced posts. The cavalry were received with a galling fire when within thirty steps of the front ranks of Louisianians, regulars and rangers, turned their horses at once, and fled with all speed; the infantry broke in confusion; or men pressed eagerly after them, and so close that they had not time to rally even at the Palace gates; a short struggle ensued with those still inside the walls, and in a few seconds more the noted work was in the hands of the Anglo-Saxons. The Mexican flag was at once torn from the castle by Lieut. Ayers and the stars and stripes ran up, while Col. Walker and one of McCulloch's men cut the blue and yellow signal flags from the cross in front of the works. Quicker than thought the cannon of the enemy were turned and opened upon them, Duncan's horse battery was in an incredibly short time in position in front of the Palace and pouring in a shower of iron hail, the Mexicans fled in their terror even past Arista's garden and the Campo Santo, and the victors were shouting over their new success. Thus, by a series of brilliant, and well-planned, and successful movements, in the very face of obstacles which appeared almost insurmountable, Gen. Worth found himself in full possession of three of the

---

53. Moses E. Merrill and William Chapman, Fifth Infantry, and James V. Bombard, Eighth Infantry.

54. John F. Roland, Second Artillery.

enemy's batteries, the stronghold known as the Bishop's Palace, seven pieces of artillery and a large quantity of ammunition and entrenching tools, two of their standards, and what was of still greater importance, the entire occupation of the Saltillo road and a complete command of all the Western portion of the city of Monterey.

At half-past 8 o'clock in the morning, Gen. Worth had dispatched a courier to Gen. Taylor, announcing the capture of the hill over the Palace, and at the same time wishing to know whether it would not be advisable to send his wounded to the main camp at San Domingo, as they embarrassed his movements. At 8 o'clock in the evening Gen. W. sent off another courier, announcing his continued successes, and at the same stating his intention, as the enemy might possibly attempt to retreat in the night, to send a detachment to the jacales a mile in the rear to burn them and throw up signal rockets should they really undertake a movement toward Saltillo. It was necessary to dispatch this information so that the general in chief might understand the cause and nature of the conflagration should it occur. The night passed off, however, without an alarm, or movement of any kind among the Mexicans, if we except the occasional flight of rockets in different parts of the city, signals which were understood only by the Mexicans themselves.

At an early hour on the morning of the 23d September, orders were given to bring all the wounded, from the jacales to which they had at first been carried, up to quarters which had been provided for them at the Bishop's Palace. About the same time Major Brown,[55] with a detachment of regular troops, was sent to occupy the mill of Santa Catarina, it being reported that heavy reinforcements were on the march from Saltillo to join Ampudia if possible. It was afterwards learned that no less than seven hundred pack mules, loaded with flour and *bizcochos*[56] for the beleaguered army, had approached within a short distance of the mill under a small escort; but seeing the American banners floating from the different heights, the officer in charge at once retraced his steps towards Saltillo.

As the morning advanced towards midday we could plainly see, from the Palace front, that the other divisions of the army were in hard conflict with the enemy on the Eastern side of the city. From the barricades and other works of the Mexicans the loud booming of cannon thundered upon the ear, while rattling peals of musketry from every house top told that the contest was a close and a severe one. Gen. Worth had no positive orders from Gen. Taylor to make an attack upon the Western side of the city, yet

55. Harvey Brown, Fourth Artillery.
56. Mexican hard biscuits. —*Kendall.*

deeming the movement of dire importance he wisely determined upon approaching with his whole force towards the Cathedral. With this intention he called in all his troops from the neighboring heights, and at the same time dispatched orders to Col. Hays to hold his entire regiment in readiness to enter the city on foot as sharpshooters. At 2 o'clock, Col. Childs was ordered to advance to the attack with two columns: the left composed of four companies of the 8th Infantry, under Capt. Screven, and two 6 pounders belonging to Lieut. Mackall's battery; the right consisted of four companies of the 7th Infantry, under Capt. Holmes, with a 12 pound howitzer of Mackall's battery, while four companies of the Artillery Battalion, under Capt. Vinton, followed at the proper distance as a reserve. The advance column, under Col. Childs, passed the *Plaza de la Capilla* without difficulty and entered the *Plazuela de Carne*, without losing a man; in crossing the latter a heavy fire of musketry was opened upon him from the house tops, which continued until he had reached a house in the southeastern corner of the square. Capt. Sanders accompanied his party, with a small detachment carrying pick-axes, ladders, crowbars and battering machines, and broke into every place along the street which might afford a cover for the troops.

In the meanwhile the right column advanced up a street nearer the river, and reached a deserted barricade, about four squares from the Cathedral, without loss; but now a tremendous firing was opened by the enemy, from loop-holes, parapets, and cross batteries, rendering the farther advance through the street impossible. The men were ordered to cover themselves by means of the barricades and houses, and in the midst of a deluge of musket balls and grape Gen. Worth and his staff rode up.[57] To form a full plan of attack was the work of but a few moments. Gen. P. F. Smith was ordered to take the immediate command. Col. Duncan's battery was at once ordered up to act as circumstances would warrant, one half the Texans, under Col. Hays, were sent to the right with instructions to make the best way they could towards the Grand Plaza by digging through the houses, while the other half of the rangers, under Col. Walker, were dispatched to the left to assist Col. Childs in his approaches in that quarter. This disposition of his forces was made by Gen. Worth under a galling fire from the enemy, yet fortunately not a man was seriously injured.

While these plans were maturing in almost the heart of the city, Major Scott, of the 5th Infantry, who had been all the morning pouring a plung-

57. The officers with him at the time, if we recollect aright, were his aides, Lieuts. Wood and Pemberton, Gen. Smith and his aides, Lieuts. Van Dorn and Hanson and one or two others. — *Kendall.*

ing fire of round shot at the Cathedral and other works from the height on
the Southern side of the river, was now in full march towards the centre of
active operations. Major Munroe, too, who had arrived from the other side
of town with a 10 1/2 inch mortar, was at once busily employed in planting
a bed for it in the Campo Santo, the intention being to open upon the
Cathedral with shells as soon as it became dark. But few men had been left
to guard the Palace, with the prisoners who had been taken; yet as every
cannon and musket had been loaded, and as guns and captured lances had
been placed in the hands of the cooks, colored servants, and other supernumeraries, the place was deemed perfectly safe against any attack the
Mexicans might make.

Between 3 and 4 o'clock the battle in the city became general. An
incessant rattling of small arms, and a heavy firing of cannon from the
barricades of the enemy, was kept up from the first; yet above even these the
sounds of the pick-axe, the crow-bar and the battering ram could be heard
as the assailants were slowly but surely working their way towards the heart
of the enemy's works. Inch after inch was taken, but not an inch was given.
As the regulars or rangers reached the top of some new house a fresh shout
of exultations would rise, striking terror into the hearts of the assailed. If the
head of a Mexican appeared above a parapet some rifle ball would instantly
pierce it—if but a hand was shown at a loop-hole, the owner of it was at
once a cripple. In the meantime the batteries of Duncan and Mackall were
not idle: grape and round shot—direct firing and horizontal ricochets—every
plan was adopted to annoy the enemy.[58] The flag of the Spanish Consul,
flying in Morelos street near the post office, was pierced in a hundred
places—the iron bow windows of the houses, which projected but a few
inches into the streets, were torn and rent asunder by round shot. The city
had been partially deserted by the inhabitants: still many women were seen
in the doorways and in the streets, and even where the battle was raging,
freely offering our men oranges and other fruits. Frightened out of their
senses, they yet seemed impressed with the belief that we were to conquer,
and thus attempted to propitiate our protection and good will. Many ladies,
too, of the better class—the wives and daughters of civil functionaries and
merchants as well as officers of the army—remained in their houses,
determined to abide the issue of the siege. In one room in particular, into
which our men had picked an entrance through a wall of massive thickness,

58. The officers of the light artillery were Lieuts. Roland, Hays, Irons, Clark, and Curd. —
*Kendall.*

Joseph F. Irons, First Artillery; Henry F. Clark, Second Artillery; and Thomas J Curd, Fourth
Artillery.

a large number of females were found. They were alarmed to a degree that was painful, filled as their ears had been with lying stories of the brutality of the Americans of the North as our people are called by the Mexicans, and it was with the greatest difficulty that they could be assured of their safety.

It was not until the sun was down, and darkness had covered the scene, that the battle ceased—not until it was impossible to distinguish friend from foe that the conflict in the least abated. Gen. Smith now sent a communication to Gen. Worth to the effect that he could hold all his positions during the night, and it was immediately determined upon to withdraw none of the troops save such as the Texans as were with Hays on the river side of the town. Even these would not have been called back had not their horses needed attention, and had not some of them been required for picket guards and other duty in the rear.

But although the active conflict had ceased, the troops in the city did not rest from their labors. A bakery—*El Panderia del Gallo*—which was located immediately at Gen. Smith's position and under fire of the enemy, was set in active operation by Lt. Hanson, one of his aides, and furnished batch after batch of bread during the night for the half-famished men. Many were detailed for guard duty on the house tops and other conspicuous points, others were employed in carrying the wounded into the Bishop's Palace,[59] while in front the work of digging and undermining still went on. A 12-pound howitzer was fairly lifted into the second story of a house in the Plazuela de Carne, and thus placed in a position where it could rake the house tops in the direction of the Grand Plaza, and even the Cathedral itself. The mortar in the Campo Santo, under direction of Major Munroe and Lieut. Lovell, commenced throwing shell at the latter at 8 o'clock in the evening, and continued during a portion of the night with an effect that is said to have frightened the cowardly Ampudia to a degree. Had one of the shells bursted in the Cathedral, so filled was that immense building with ammunition, the explosion would have been most disastrous to the property as well as lives of the Mexicans. The latter, from the citadel outside the town, opened their mortars at once upon Major Munroe's position, yet did little or no execution.

Gen. Worth's intentions were to renew the conflict with redoubled vigor at daylight the next morning, and to carry out his determination extra

---

59. Capt. Gatlin, of the 7th Infantry, was wounded during the afternoon. The number killed and wounded on our side was inconsiderable when we reflect upon the immense number of balls, grape and round shot thrown by the enemy. Several horses in the batteries of Duncan and Mackall were killed, yet few of their men were injured. The loss of the Mexicans was far greater than ours, owing to the close shooting of our men. —*Kendall.*

pick-axes and crowbars were sent forward, barrels of powder procured with which to blow up the larger buildings around the Grand Plaza if deemed necessary, and other measures devised to attack the Mexicans in their very strongholds. The night passed without any incident worth recording, but with the first streak of daylight the Texans, who had dug and picked their way to the post office, opened a murderous fire upon the enemy, who were upon house-tops not twenty steps distance: The rangers occupied the Governor's house as well as the post office, the latter but little over two squares from the Grand Plaza, while the Eastern Texas regiment under Col. Wood, which had been operating with Gens. Taylor and Twiggs, had the evening previous reached points as near on the other side of the Cathedral, thus huddling the enemy if we can use such a term and leaving them but one road by which to retreat towards Saltillo, and that a by path through the mountains. With 2000 additional men Gen. Taylor could have hemmed the Mexicans completely.

We have said that the battle was renewed at early daylight on the morning of the 24th September. It was commenced by Walker's men, from their advanced position near the post office, and with disastrous effect to the enemy. Two or three of the Texans had crossed the street during the latter part of the night, and picked a hole through the solid wall of a house on the opposite corner. As the last stroke of the pick-axe went through the heavy masonry a company of Mexican infantry, stationed inside, attempted to escape by the door in front. One half of the company were shot dead before they crossed the street, so murderous was the fire of the Texans from the post office, and at the same time a new line of operations was opened by the assailants.

About sunrise, and while the advanced parties of the combatants on either side were yet engaged in active conflict, a white flag was seen advancing from Ampudia's quarters in the Plaza. The din of the battle now ceased, and as our readers know not to be renewed. We might go on and give many incidents which occurred during the 24th September, and up to the time when the terms of capitulation were finally signed; we might also recount many interesting events which occurred before the Mexicans finally evacuated the city; but this account, which was only designed to give a plain statement of Gen. Worth's operations in the capture of Monterey, has already been spun out to double the length originally intended, and we are admonished that it is time to draw towards a close. Before laying down the pen, however, we cannot but call the reader's attention to the events of the four days preceding the capitulation, and to the gallant spirits who, amid fatigue, hunger and suffering, achieved deeds which will always fill one of the brightest pages of our nation's history. The repulse of the lancers; the storming, in open day, of the rugged crest of Federation Hill, and the carrying of the fortification of El Soldado by assault; the storming, again, of the breastworks of Independence Hill amid the darkness of night; the capture of the noted Bishop's Palace; the advance into the heart of the city while a tornado of grape and canister was sweeping from every embrasure and battery, and while every loop-hole, parapet, and house-top was sending forth hurricanes of musket and escopet balls;—these are but part of the achievements performed by men who toiled incessantly, day after day and amid storm and rain, without sleep, without food, *and without murmuring.* The country cannot be too grateful to the head that conceived and the hands that carried out a succession of gallant exploits which so materially aided in the great crowning triumph—the capture of Monterey.

[G. W. K.]

*Daily Picayune,* November 19, 1846

# CHAPTER THREE

# VICTORY AT VERA CRUZ
## FEBRUARY 25 – APRIL 13, 1847

BY THE END OF OCTOBER 1846, the Polk administration, seeking to force Mexico to sue for peace, had determined that an attack deeper into northern Mexico was logistically insupportable and without clear strategic advantage. Plans were laid to seize Vera Cruz as the first step toward a possible assault on Mexico City. President James Polk reluctantly chose General Winfield Scott to lead the campaign after failing to find a way to appoint his personal choice, Senator Thomas Hart Benton. In the meantime, Commodore David Conner occupied Tampico without a struggle on November 14, 1846, after Santa Anna withdrew the Mexican garrison there to strengthen his forces at San Luis Potosí. (Conner had supported the army's operations in Mexico since General Zachary Taylor moved the American army in Texas from Corpus Christi to Point Isabel.)

Scott left Washington for the Rio Grande late in November, planning to begin the campaign against Vera Cruz by February 1, before the expected springtime onslaught of yellow fever along the coast. He collected his invading army at Lobos Island, sixty-five miles southeast of Tampico, with troops coming from the United States and from Taylor's command in northern Mexico, including General William Worth's forces. Numerous delays, however, prevented Scott from moving the assembled 12,000-man army the two hundred miles south to the staging area at Anton Lizardo (some twelve miles beyond Vera Cruz) until early March. Word of the clash of American and Mexican forces at the battle of Buena Vista on February 22 and 23 reached the Gulf Coast as Scott's forces sailed south. After marshaling his army at San Luis Potosí, Santa Anna had marched it northward late in January, looking for a military victory that might slow Scott's preparations to attack Vera Cruz and compel peace overtures from Washington. Taylor met him in mountainous terrain south of Saltillo and scored a hard-won victory that forced Santa Anna to retreat southward. Taylor had fought his last major battle against the Mexicans; antiguerrilla campaigning preoccupied his command for the remainder of the war.

Meanwhile, Scott, with George Kendall observing from on board ship, launched an amphibious assault on an undefended beach south of Vera Cruz on March 9. Sandy terrain, violent storms, and tropical insects made the establishment of American lines around Vera Cruz difficult, but Scott accomplished the task with the assistance of his naval counterparts, Commanders Conner and Matthew Perry. The city fell on March 27, 1847, after four days of heavy bombardment from army and naval batteries. Almost immediately, preparations began to move the army inland and away from the threat of yellow fever.

Steamship *New Orleans*, Off Brazos Island, February 25, 1847

We have just arrived here, after a pleasant run of three days from New Orleans. As yet I have been unable to go ashore, and am therefore unable to give you all the news; but from several lighters[1] which have passed us we learn that Gen. Scott has already gone towards Tampico, and that Gen. Worth is on board the steamer *Edith* lying near us, and shortly to proceed by the same destination. His entire command is probably on shipboard, and a large portion of it has very likely sailed ere this for Tampico or the rendezvous at Lobos.[2]

The larger part of our passengers have left us this morning, on their way to join Gen. Taylor at Monterey.[3] Among them are Cols. Weller and Mitchell, Dr. Chamberlin, and several other officers of the Ohio volunteers. Gen. Jesup has gone to see Gen. Worth, but will probably continue on this boat to Tampico.[4]

Some twenty sail of square-rigged vessels are now lying here, many of them, I am told, with water on board for the use of the troops. Others are doubtless discharging stores for the troops in the direction of Monterey.

---

1. Large flat-bottomed barges used to unload or deliver goods from larger ships.

2. Scott left Brazos Island for Tampico on board the army steamer *Massachusetts* on February 15. After arriving at Tampico on February 18, he reached the forces gathering on Lobos Island on February 21, 1847.

3. Taylor's command was actually in Saltillo, some sixty-five miles south of Monterey. After receiving, on November 2, the administration's directive to end the armistice signed after the battle of Monterey, Taylor moved immediately to extend the region under American control. Saltillo was undefended and offered a strategic position from which to guard the southern approaches to Monterey. Neither Taylor nor the Polk administration believed an advance on Santa Anna's army at San Luis Potosí, three hundred miles to the south, was logistically possible or strategically necessary.

4. Not previously identified are John B. Weller and E. K. Chamberlin, First Ohio Volunteers. Weller was formerly a congressman from Ohio and would later become a U.S. Senator from California. Quartermaster General Thomas S. Jesup was responsible for gathering the equipment and supplies necessary for the landing and siege at Vera Cruz.

The *New Orleans* was too heavily loaded to run fast, but has proved herself certainly a very comfortable sea boat. Out of the large number of horses on board—her decks being crowded fore and aft—only one has been lost on the trip down.

I am in hopes to be able to go ashore before starting for Tampico, in which case I shall have an opportunity of sending you all the news stirring. At present I can only say that matters look lively enough here. Steam lighters are continually passing in and out, small boats are communicating constantly between the different vessels, and everything appears on the move.

Yo..rs, &c.,

G. W. K.

*Daily Picayune*, March 12, 1847

Steamship *New Orleans*, Off Brazos Island, February 26, 1847

I wrote you a hurried scrawl yesterday, which I sent ashore by a boat which came alongside last evening. This morning I intended making a landing myself, but toward the latter watches of the night one of the dreaded northers so common on this shore sprang up, and by breakfast time it was blowing so hard that no boat could live a moment on the reef, or among the breakers which we can plainly see dashing over it. Pleasant, this! being confined on ship-board during a gale, in open sight of land, and no earthly means of reaching it except at great risk of being drowned! There is some amusement, however, in watching the different vessels lying anchored in our vicinity, to see them "rarin' and pitchin'," as Sam Slick would say, in calculating how far, per hour, they will drag their anchors, and the probabilities of their being compelled to hoist sail and put out into

"The wide and open sea,"

for a refuge they cannot find near the land.

The *Edith* sailed last evening for Tampico, with Gen. Worth, his staff, and several officers on board. I could see many familiar faces on the quarterdeck, but had no opportunity of speaking with them. The *Edith* was compelled to sail without the mail for Gen. Scott which was brought by the *New Orleans*. The mail was sent from this place up to Point Isabel, instead of being opened here, and hence this vexatious delay. Here the mail is first received, and here the officers with whom I have conversed say that the mail should be first opened.

Gen. Jesup, with Capt. Grayson[5] and other officers, are on shore, but there is no chance of them getting off to us tonight.

Saturday Forenoon, February 27.—The sea wrought and was tempestuous all night, our vessel rolled and pitched as though she would break from her fastenings, and this morning it is blowing harder than ever. An old salt prophesied as much last night when the sun went down, for he said his face was uncommonly red and angry. The barometer says "change." I wish it would change, for heartily sick am I of this. The poor horses, too, look as if they were anxious for a change, for their eyes are dull and their ears hang drooping and listless as they sway backwards and forwards with every motion of the vessel. The top-gallant masts of all the ships in our vicinity have been sent down, and there they are, with their teeth up in the very face of the gale, tossing and pitching like mad— now their bowsprits pointing high in the air, as some huge wave lifts the vessel, and anon diving apparently into the depths of the sea as the water recedes. The winds and the troubled surges are in the meantime howling anything but an agreeable accompaniment, the noisy gulls are screaming around us, and as if in mockery of all this a young midshipman, on his way down to join the squadron off San Juan de Ulúa,[6] is singing such a fadge as

> "A life on the ocean wave
> A home on the rolling deep,"

and other absurd nonsense of a kindred nature, including an earnest desire on his part to spend his days where

> "The winds their revels keep"

Out upon all such revelries say I. If the winds are disposed to hold revels, I prefer being inside some good thick wall of brick and mortar while they are at it, and not out upon the treacherous waves of a treacherous coast. A landsman, however, as an offset to the midshipman, has struck up with

> "Cease rude Boreas, blustering railer!"

---

5. John B. Grayson, commissary.

6. The fortress of San Juan de Ulúa, commonly called "the castle," stood on a coral reef three-quarters of a mile off the coast and directly opposite Vera Cruz.

I like that chap. There is some sense in him, for he chants like a rational being. I wish that "rude Boreas" would hearken to his plaint.

Afternoon.–The gale has in a measure subsided, and the waves are becoming more quiet. We can see the make of two or three lighters inside, raising steam probably, and they may very likely come out over the bar this afternoon with Gen. Jesup. Then, ho! for Tampico, is the earnest wish of all, for all those who are not actually sea sick are really sick of the sea.

I have written this short letter, not for any news it contains but to show you why I have not been able to get hold of any news. Should one of the steamers firing up come alongside us before night she will not remain long enough for me to add anything, so I must fain fold this up and send it off with the hope of furnishing you something more interesting next time.

Yours, &c.,

G. W. K.
*Daily Picayune*, March 12, 1847

Brazos Island, February 28, 1847 [An extract.]

I made out to get on shore last evening from the *New Orleans* and this morning hastened to give you such intelligence as I can gather.

The news from the direction of Monterey, or rather the rumors and reports from that quarter, are important. An express arrived at Matamoros on the 26th inst., Friday, from Col. Curtis at Camargo. That officer states that an express left Cerralvo on the evening of the 23d from Col. Morgan, with an injunction to him to stop all trains between Camargo and Monterey. Col. Morgan's regiment was to leave Cerralvo at daylight on the morning of the 24th, but its destination was unknown. The enemy was reported as advancing in great force, but from what point is not designated. Col. Morgan received his orders direct from Gen. Taylor.[7]

This is the substance of the intelligence brought by the express. Verbally I hear it rumored that Gen. Mejía has thrown a large force into Linares, where he commands in person, and it is thought by some that he intends attacking Matamoros and perhaps the depots at this place, at

7. On February 22, a unit of Mexican mounted lancers had joined with a guerrilla force to ambush an American supply train of more than one hundred wagons, traveling from Camargo. The incident, which took place the same day that Santa Anna's army engaged the American force at Buena Vista, cut Taylor's ties to his supply base on the Rio Grande. Mentioned are Samuel D. Curtis and George W. Morgan.

Brazos Santiago, and at Point Isabel.[8] This is however mere surmise. The present almost defenceless positions of these posts would favor such a move on the part of the enemy, but whether he will have the courage to attempt it is another matter.

In a letter I wrote on board the *New Orleans* I stated that many of the vessels lying off this place had water on board. For the most part they are taken up to transport the 2d dragoons under Col. Harney, their horses and equipments, and Col. Duncan's battery of light artillery and horses. The greater part of them are already on board, and with good weather it is thought that all will be off in two or three days. Gen. Jesup is here on shore, pushing matters with the greatest vigor.

Last accounts placed Gen. Taylor at Agua Nueva, twenty miles on the other side of Saltillo, with the most of his force.[9] All the reports would go to confirm that Santa Anna has a large body of men in his neighborhood, but whether with the intention of attacking Gen. T., or passing him and falling upon the American posts and depots on the Rio Grande, no one knows. Everyone says that a good general would have adopted the latter plan long since, as the withdrawal of nearly all the forces from the river would have almost insured the success of a descent.

G. W. K.

*Daily Picayune*, March 12, 1847

Brazos Island, February 28, 1847

I wrote you a letter this morning—it is now afternoon—in which I gave you the current rumors here. Nothing new has since transpired, although I have heard additional reports in relation to the movements and operations of the enemy, both this side the mountains and on the other side of Saltillo.

There are those who *think*—of course no one *knows* anything positively—that Santa Anna intends making a feint with a considerable force in the neighborhood of Gen. Taylor, with the intention of diverting the attention of that officer, and when this is effected to pass him with a large body of

8. Mejía was with Santa Anna's forces south of Monterey. No organized Mexican units were in a position to take the American outposts along the Rio Grande, although guerrilla activity in the region was significant.

9. Taylor's army, an inexperienced force of about 4,700 troops, moved out of Saltillo in mid-February, taking up positions seventeen miles to the south at Agua Nueva before withdrawing to more defensible positions at Buena Vista with the approach of the Mexican army. Santa Anna had marched an army of about 21,000 men from San Luis Potosí toward Saltillo beginning on January 27, 1847, but only 15,000 were available for action on the eve of the battle of Buena Vista.

light troops and make an attack upon Camargo, Matamoros, or some of the depots in this vicinity. Nothing could be easier at this time, drawn away as the force along the river now is;[10] but still I doubt whether Santa Anna has the nerve to make such a demonstration. A few days or weeks will tell the story.

The ship *Prentice* is now lying off this place with three companies of the Mississippi volunteers on board—those of Capts. Clarke, McWillie and Daniel, all under Major Price.[11] They have lost nine men since they left New Orleans from sickness, and are still said to be suffering. I believe they are to be landed here.

All here anticipate that stirring news will soon reach them from Gen. Taylor's camp. Ben McCulloch has passed on with a small but well mounted company.[12] The necessity for a larger force of this description in the field, to act as scouts and to traverse the roads between Camargo and Monterey, is becoming more manifest every day, and our Government should at once accept the services of all that offer on their own terms—for a year, for six months or even for three.

The alcalde of Matamoros, on the pretence that the land was owned by a citizen of that place, has issued an order prohibiting all Americans from chopping wood for the steamboats opposite that city, and all the way down to the mouth of the river. What a pity it is that an alcalde could not occasionally be hung. They nearly all deserve it, and matters would go on much more smoothly.

I have just been talking with a gentleman, who thinks that Santa Anna is making a feint in the neighborhood of Saltillo with the intention of withdrawing attention from San Luis while he is sending off a large force to Vera Cruz. There may be something in this.

It is now thought that the commands of Cols. Harney and Duncan—dragoons and light artillery—will all be on shipboard and off tomorrow or next day. The *New Orleans* will not sail for Tampico until tomorrow, and

10. The buildup of forces to support the invasion at Vera Cruz had significantly reduced the force available to Taylor. Scott had requested that the 4,000 regulars under Worth's command, five hundred dragoons, five hundred volunteer cavalry, and as many volunteer infantry as could be spared be sent to the mouth of the Rio Grande by the middle of January. When Taylor was slow to respond, Scott ordered Worth's command to the coast early in January 1847.

11. Mentioned are William J. Daniel and Ezra Price, both of the Second Mississippi Volunteers. McWillie and Clarke are not listed among the officers who served with the Mississippi volunteers, although Charles Clarke served as colonel of the Second Regiment.

12. McCulloch's Texans scouted Santa Anna's advancing force at Encarnación, providing Taylor with accurate information on Santa Anna's strength as late as February 21.

in the meantime I will write again in case anything turns up. I send this in care of Col. J. B. Walton.[13]

Yours, &tc.,

G. W. K.
*Daily Picayune*, March 12, 1847

Brazos Island, March 1, 1847

We have no farther information from the direction of Camargo or Monterey. The fact that Gen. Taylor has ordered all the trains to cease running between the two places would show that he had good reasons to believe there was a large force of the enemy in the vicinity, bent upon making an attack upon any defenceless point.

The ship *Mayflower* has arrived here with three additional companies of the Mississippi volunteers on board under Lieut. Col. Kilpatrick. He has lost seven men of his command since he left New Orleans, while the vessel on which the command of Col. Davis was placed has lost about as many. The sea voyage has finally been of advantage, as there are now but few sick in the regiment. The men are all to be landed here and probably will move toward Monterey. The entire loss of the regiment since leaving New Orleans has been twenty-three.[14]

They are still getting the dragoon horses and equipments on board the vessels outside, although the wind is fresh and the water rough. Whether the *New Orleans* will sail for Tampico today is a matter of doubt.

Gen. Scott is said to be encamped at or near Lobos with 4000 men, and on beautiful ground. You probably have later intelligence from him, however, than we have here.

I am in hopes that we shall receive later intelligence from Gen. Taylor before sailing. All are sanguine in the belief that there soon will be stirring times in the direction of Monterey.

Yours, &tc.,

G. W. K.
*Daily Picayune*, March 14, 1847

Brazos Island, March 1, 1847, Afternoon

The lighters which went out this morning with dragoon horses have been compelled to return without effecting a shipment of the animals. The

---

13. James B. Walton, First Regiment, Smith's Brigade of Louisiana Volunteers.

14. Kendall is probably referring to the units of the Second Mississippi Volunteers commanded by Joseph H. Kilpatrick and Reuben Davis. The First Regiment of Mississippi Rifles, under the command of Jefferson Davis, was also with Taylor's army at Buena Vista.

sea was altogether too rough, and to have attempted to get them on board would have endangered half their lives. This is one of the vexatious causes of delay which have kept back the movements of the army from this place. Out of sixteen successive days in the month of January there were only two on which the vessels outside the bar could be reached, and it has been nearly as bad through February. It is still hoped that Col. Harney's command may get off tomorrow.

Matamoros, I learn, or at least the Plaza, is strongly fortified. In the meantime the inhabitants, induced by the reports of an attack upon the place, are rapidly moving out. This thing of endeavoring to frighten off the inhabitants from the river towns is a game which has long been played by the Mexican rulers. There may or may not be truth in the present reports.

I believe that the *New Orleans* will sail this evening. If she does, you will next hear from me at Tampico or Lobos.

G. W. K.

*Daily Picayune*, March 14, 1847

Tampico, Mexico, March 4, 1847

We arrived off this place yesterday, and as the *New Orleans* was unable to get over the bar, a portion of the passengers, myself among the number, came up to the city in a small steamer. During the night a norther sprang up, driving the vessel outside to sea; but the gale was of short duration, and now at 12 o'clock the *New Orleans* is back again and anchored near the bar. She will come up this evening if there is water enough on the bar, at least so I learn.

New Orleans papers of the 25th ult. came up last evening in the brig *Perfect*. I see by the *Picayune* of that date that Mr. Haile had anticipated a portion of the intelligence contained in the letters I wrote from the Brazos.[15] Here they will have it that Gen. Taylor has defeated the advance of Santa Anna, killing upwards of four hundred of the enemy.[16] I might give you the story as it came to me, but I suppose that Mr. Lumsden,[17] who is still here, has sent you on a full account.

---

15. Haile had been reporting from the mouth of the Rio Grande, covering the preparations by Worth's Second Division for its move to Vera Cruz. Reilly, "American Reporters and the Mexican War," 193–94, 234–37.

16. This is the first of a series of rumors Kendall reported concerning the battle of Buena Vista, which occurred on February 22 and 23, 1847. General Taylor's forces sustained heavy losses: 665 killed, wounded, or missing, or about 14 percent of those engaged. Mexican casualties totaled 2,100 troops, with 1,800 killed and 300 wounded.

17. Francis Lumsden returned to Mexico in mid-February to cover the siege of Vera Cruz, traveling from Tampico with General James Shields, who commanded the recently raised Illinois

The reports in relation to the movements of Gen. Scott are contradictory. Almost all agree, however, that a portion of his force is already off Anton Lizardo, where it is said the Mexicans have thrown up batteries to prevent our landing, and there are many who think that the battle of Vera Cruz, if battle it is to be, is about to be or already has been fought. —The brigades of Gens. Quitman and Shields[18] are still here, as also a number of officers who came down on the *New Orleans*. They are all anxious to see the fandango at Vera Cruz, and it will be altogether too good a joke if they are disappointed.

Everything in and about this place would go to prove the go-aheadity of the Anglo-Saxon race, and that everything is fast Americanizing. Here we have an American newspaper, the American theatre, the United States Hotel, the Union Restaurant, and an American court of justice. Someone remarking that the judges of the latter know but little of the law, not having been bred to the profession, an old citizen within hearing exclaimed: "Confound the law—we have had enough of that here—what we want is justice, and we are getting that now."[19]

Speaking of the theatre, the managers, Hart & Wells, appear to be doing a thriving business. Leonard, the Irish comedian, is now playing an engagement, and is crowding the theatre with delighted audiences. Should the Americans obtain possession of Vera Cruz, and I suppose no one doubts it, the company will probably proceed to that place. Theatres generally do not have their signs out, but "American Theatre" stares you here over the establishment in the biggest kind of capitals.

The Louisiana regiment and the Baltimore battalion I believe are to be left to garrison this place. The officers, as a matter of course, do not like this inactivity when a stirring battle is about to take place; but they are obliged to put up with it. Somebody must be left behind, yet I am sorry the lot has fallen upon our Louisianians. They may still have plenty of fighting, however.

---

volunteers. His reports were highly jingoistic and not particularly reliable. Shortly after the siege, he returned to New Orleans to stay, having broken a leg while on a scouting mission with a company of dragoons. Reilly, "American Reporters and the Mexican War," 193–94.

18. John A. Quitman and James Shields were among six brigadier generals appointed to command the volunteer brigades raised for the Mexican War. Quitman, a respected militia leader in Mississippi, proved one of the best civilian generals. He later served as military governor of Mexico City. Shields led the Illinois volunteers and, while suffering a nearly fatal wound at Cerro Gordo, earned a reputation as an outstanding officer.

19. While the army was in Tampico, Kendall and Lumsden served as judges on a court that tried soldiers for civil crimes. Copeland, *Kendall of the Picayune,* 187.

It was Gen. Miñon who is said to have commanded the Mexicans in the night attack upon Gen. Taylor.[20] The report comes from the Mexicans— nothing positive has been received.[21]

If the *New Orleans* comes over the bar this afternoon, she will probably sail for Gen. Scott's headquarters tomorrow.

Yours,

G. W. K.
*Daily Picayune*, March 19, 1847

Tampico, March 5, 1847

Not a line of anything new stirring. The *New Orleans* is still outside the bar, but an endeavor will be made to bring her over this afternoon. It is said the horses now on board are to be landed here, the stalls broken up, and some 500 men belonging to the brigades of Gens. Shields and Quitman, with those officers and staffs accompanying them, will be placed on board, and then the steamer will proceed with all speed to Anton Lizardo. Such at least is now the talk here.

It is said that a schooner, with ninety volunteers on board and no fresh water, was blown off in the last norther, and has not yet returned. I hope it is not so.

The *Home* is about hoisting sail, so I must close.

Yours,

G. W. K.
*Daily Picayune*, March 19, 1847

20. José Vicente Miñon was actually near Saltillo and was not involved in the main fighting at Buena Vista.

21. News was slow to reach the coast because most of the correspondents, including Kendall, had chosen to cover Scott's preparations for the landing at Vera Cruz. Haile had traveled to Monterey in early January to cover the regulars under Worth's command in the expected battle with Santa Anna. But, learning of the Second Division's orders to join Scott, he too returned to the coast. The *Delta*'s J. G. H. Tobin participated in the battle and prepared detailed accounts, but most of them never reached New Orleans. Moreover, Taylor, distracted by the need to care for his weakened command, did not rush to prepare an official account. In addition, communication was difficult with Mexican guerrilla forces regularly disrupting travel on the roads that stretched from the rear of the American lines to the Rio Grande. As a result, Taylor's official reports were still in Monterey as late as March 2. While rumors were common throughout the month, the first reliable account of events at Buena Vista appeared in New Orleans in an extra published by the *Picayune* on March 21, 1847. The newspaper's agent reached New Orleans by steamship two days before government officials brought the news to the Crescent City. Copeland, *Kendall of the Picayune*, 186–87. Reilly, "American Reporters and the Mexican War," 206–26.

Tampico, March 6, 1847

Rumor follows rumor here in such quick succession, that before we have time to digest one another crowds it aside and both prove eventually untrue. Yesterday the city was agog with the startling intelligence that Santa Anna had attacked and defeated Gen. Taylor at Agua Nueva, and even the names of some of the officers killed were given. I don't believe a word of it, although that we may soon expect to hear of battles in that section is reasonable. Santa Anna really intends either to hazard an action at Agua Nueva or near that place, or else in making a feint with a large force to distract attention from certain designs of his upon other points.

I enclose the Tampico *Sentinel*[22] of today, in which you will see all the news as well as rumors.

In haste,

G. W. K.
*Daily Picayune*, March 19, 1847

Tampico, March 6, 1847–10 o'clock A.M.

I wrote you a few lines in haste this morning, enclosing a number of the Tampico *Sentinel* of today.

I heard it stated this moment that the English steam packet, for the safety of which fears have been entertained, is known to have left Havana on the 9th of February, and had not arrived at Vera Cruz on the 20th. You probably know more about her than we do. There is a rumor here to the effect that she has positively been lost on the coast.

There are those here, well posted up in Mexican affairs, who think the report of Gen. Taylor's defeat by Santa Anna has been got up to cover a complete victory over the forces of the latter by the Americans near Agua Nueva. There is no coming at the truth of anything at present, but a few days will tell the story.

Yours, &c., &c.,

G. W. K.
*Daily Picayune*, March 19, 1847

Tampico, March 6, 1847–4 o'clock P.M.

I don't know whether I shall be able to get this letter off by the schooner

22. Founded by two New Orleans printers, J. R. Barnard and William Jewell, the *Sentinel* began publishing in Tampico on February 6, 1847, and moved on to Vera Cruz with the army in March. The *Picayune*'s Francis Lumsden may have served as the paper's editor for a short time. Reilly, "American Reporters and the Mexican War," 201.

*Home* or not; but I wish to give you one more rumor and the last, and if I get it off it is all well and good.

It is said that a report reached here this morning from the city of Mexico to the effect that a pronunciamento or revolution headed by the clergy had occurred, that Gómez Farías, the Vice President, had been deposed; that an editor of one of the papers had been placed in his stead, and that the objects of the revolution had been carried out in every particular. Considering the power of the clergy, and their well-known hostility to Gómez Farías, there is some reason in this.[23]

The Mexican army is reported to be suffering to an incredible extent not only for clothing but for the absolute necessities of life. In the meantime agents are riding through the country, exacting contributions in every town. In Altamira, only a few days since, $300 were raised in this way.

By the looks and actions of the Mexican population I know that there can be no truth in the report that Santa Anna has beaten Gen. Taylor in a pitched battle; on the contrary, their whole appearance would, if anything, indicate the reverse. Good news shows too plainly in the faces of these people to be mistaken.

The *New Orleans* will not get off until tomorrow morning. In addition to Gen. Jesup, Surgeon Gen. Lawson,[24] Capt. Grayson, and others of the regular army, she takes down to Vera Cruz Gens. Quitman and Shields, with a portion of their brigades. Col. H. L. Kinney accompanies Gen. Jesup. There will be 650 troops in all on board, composed principally of Alabamians and Georgians.

I am fearful that this letter, along with two others I wrote this morning, must find some other conveyance besides the *Home.* She has now gone down to the bar, and if she has been able to get outside I shall leave the letters to go by some other vessel.

Yours, &tc., &tc.,

G. W. K.

---

23. Since the 1830s, Valentín Gómez Farías had pushed reforms designed to reduce the privileges enjoyed by the Catholic Church in Mexico. He had recently pushed through Congress legislation extracting significant revenues from the church. Kendall was wrong about Gómez Farías's overthrow. Gómez Farías withstood efforts by *moderado* politicians and church leaders to remove him from office, including an armed revolt in late February 1847, led by Matías de la Peña y Barragán, known as the "revolt of the *polkas*." Gómez Farías remained in power until Santa Anna returned to Mexico City to take up the powers of the presidency on March 23, 1847.

24. Thomas Lawson.

P. S.–March 7.–The report of the revolution in Mexico is correct–the National Guards joined the clergy. Salas is President. Santa Anna at the head of the army. Papers by next vessel.[25]

Gen. Taylor has had no fight, but has fallen back upon Saltillo and Monterey.

G. W. K.

*Daily Picayune*, March 19, 1847

Tampico, March 7, 1847–10 o'clock Forenoon

In haste I would inform you that I have this moment received Mexican papers of later date and with highly important intelligence. I send them down to the bar by a messenger on horseback, and in case the *Home* has not gone out you will receive them by that vessel. If she has left I shall leave them to be forwarded by the *Apalachicola* or some other vessel.

In haste,

G. W. K.

*Daily Picayune*, March 19, 1847

Tampico, March 7, 1847

I sent off a package of letters and papers by the *Home*; but as some other vessel may arrive in New Orleans ahead of her, I give the sum and substance of the news.

There has been another *pronunciamento* at the city of Mexico, headed by the clergy, as is said, and in which they were joined by the national guard. Gen. Barragán appears to have been the principal mover, and Gómez Farías has been put down. One account has it that Gen. Salas is now President, and that Santa Anna retains command of the army. This new revolution has been entirely bloodless.

There is no mistake that Gen. Taylor has retired from Agua Nueva, and has fallen back towards Monterey. *El Republicano*[26] of the 25th ult. says

25. General José Mariano Salas served as acting president of Mexico when Santa Anna marched north to San Luis Potosí late in September 1846. In December, the Mexican senate narrowly elected Santa Anna to the presidency. A political opponent and rival of Salas, Gómez Farías was elected vice president and assumed the duties of acting president when Santa Anna joined the army in the north in January 1847. Meanwhile, Salas took up command of the national guard's Hidalgo Battalion, which was involved in the unsuccessful revolt of the *polkas* against Gómez Farías in the last days of February.

26. *El Republicano* was a voice of *moderado* political sentiment and was often critical of Gómez Farías. The *Picayune*, in its March 21, 1847, edition, described *El Republicano* as the "best index to the state of feelings in Mexico." By the time this dispatch was published on March 23, the *Picayune* had already published accurate accounts of the battle of Buena Vista.

that Santa Anna was making forced marches after him, and that he had thrown Miñon and Torrejón, with a heavy force, between Gen. T. and Monterey, with the intention of cutting him off and annihilating his army—rather a difficult job to undertake.[27] All accounts agree that both armies have suffered greatly from excessive cold weather and the heavy snows which have fallen.

The wound received by Capt. Hunt, in the duel with Col. De Russey, was very slight, hardly taking him from his duty.[28] All rank was waived, and the parties appeared on the ground as private citizens. Under the circumstances, there was no way to avoid the hostile meeting.

Yours, &c.,

G. W. K.
*Daily Picayune*, March 23, 1847

Camp near Vera Cruz, March 11, 1847

The work of investing the city of Vera Cruz is going rapidly on, and by tomorrow morning it will probably be complete.[29] A fire from the batteries on the land side of the city has been kept up, with short intervals, during the day, yet few of our men have been killed. The army has to mourn the loss of Capt. Alburtis, of the 2d Infantry, who was killed by an 18-pound shot. During a short action this morning, with the cavalry of the enemy, Lieut. Col. Dickenson, of the South Carolina volunteers, was seriously although not dangerously wounded[30]—five men besides of this regiment were wounded.

Shells of the heaviest kind have been thrown today within Gen. Worth's lines, but fortunately no one in this division has been killed so far. The fighting as yet, at least so far as our men have been engaged, has been with parties of infantry and cavalry, thrown out to annoy our columns as they advanced.

Tonight I learn that some of the tanks supplying the city with water will be cut off. The entire army, although suffering much from marching over the sand hills in the hot sun and from want of water, is in excellent spirits.

---

27. Santa Anna's army actually returned to San Luis Potosí, arriving there on March 9, 1847, the same day that Scott landed at Vera Cruz. Suffering from cold weather and a shortage of food and water, the Mexican army sustained greater losses on the march than it did on the battlefield at Buena Vista. More than half of the soldiers who marched north from San Luis Potosí did not return.

28. Copeland S. Hunt, Third Regiment Smith's Brigade Louisiana Volunteers, and Lewis G. De Russey, Louisiana Volunteers.

29. Scott's army landed at Vera Cruz on March 9. Bad weather, sandy terrain, and skirmishes with Mexican cavalry units delayed the encirclement of the city until March 13.

30. William Alburtis and James P. Dickenson.

Tomorrow it is probable that some of our own mortars will be in position, and then the game will commence in real earnest.[31]

I write this in great haste, learning that a vessel is about leaving for New Orleans.

G. W. K.

*Daily Picayune*, March 26, 1847

Camp near Vera Cruz, March 12, 1847—Morning

I wrote you a hasty letter last evening, with a short account of the movements of the day. After it was closed the Rifles under Col. Smith had a brisk action with the enemy, in which the latter, after a partial success at the outset, were finally driven back with considerable loss. This morning the line of investment—some five or six miles in extent—will probably be complete.

I do not think, from all that I can see and learn, that Gen. Scott will be able to plant his batteries for several days to come; and until he can make a good show he will not open upon the town at all. When the bombardment does commence it will be in earnest.

On the body of a Mexican officer who was killed last evening in the engagement with the Rifles, a letter was found which he had just written to one of his friends. It appears to have been closed after the affair of the morning, as he alludes to it. After a few lines in relation to some money matters, and an allusion to some business with Santa Anna whose principal hacienda lies near Vera Cruz, the writer goes on to say:

"I much regret that Concha, (the name of a girl), was so timorous that they had to send her to the rancho. According to my mode of thinking there is yet no great occasion for such fears. From what I hear, the Americans, to the number of 7 or 8000, have disembarked near Vera Cruz, and have occupied Casa Mata, which was abandoned. The light troops at the Cemetery, with some other column, are skirmishing with the enemy on the sand bank of the Encanto, in front of the Little Wells. Our troops are very enthusiastic, and it is said that on account of the expected arrival of 600 men from Alvarado, the Colonel of Puebla has offered to march out of the city with his men and some others, and give the enemy a little battle. (This may have been the action in which the writer of the letter was killed.) Until now, the Americans have attempted nothing worthy of attention. This morning four wounded men belonging to our squadron were brought in, which is all up to the present time. It appears that the Americans have had more killed and wounded than

31. Scott's artillery was not ready to fire until March 21.

we have, as it has been ascertained that some of our cannon at the barricades have been aimed with fatal effect. It is said at your house that the Americans are in the neighborhood of the Perritos, and in all probability will arrive today or tomorrow as far as Bergarra."

This letter was signed M. Muntada, and was found, along with some cigars, in his pockets. The information that reinforcements were expected from Alvarado induced our commander to throw out a strong picket in the direction of the Alvarado road.

Capt. Vinton of the artillery has been ordered to take up a position at a lime kiln close in to the walls of the city, and this he has effected without loss. Anticipating an attack upon this point last night, Gen. Worth went out, after dark, with two companies, to support Capt. V.; but nothing occurred. There was some little skirmishing at the different pickets during the night, but otherwise all was quiet.

Col. Harney's dragoons have not as yet arrived, yet their services are greatly needed. It is said that a large train of pack mules, which went out of the city yesterday, took a heavy amount of specie as well as valuables. All this property might probably have been captured had Gen. Scott had a cavalry force. It was also reported last evening that something like 1000 Mexicans were seen coming in towards sundown, by the main road from Mexico, with a large drove of cattle for the beleaguered city; but as the investment was not then complete, and as we had no cavalry, they could not be taken. I learn, however, that Gen. Twiggs, who commands on the northern side of the city, succeeded during the day in capturing quite a number of cattle. A norther is now blowing, which it is hoped will bring in the 2d Dragoons.

At the magazine, which was captured day before yesterday, a considerable quantity of ammunition was taken. It was evidently of English or American make, as it was labeled "short range," "long range," &c. &c., in good vernacular. The Mexicans managed to get off safely the larger portion of their ammunition, and it is now carefully stowed away inside the city walls.

Capt. Alburtis, who was killed yesterday, was sitting at the foot of a tree at the time he was struck. The ball carried away almost his entire head, took off the arm of a drummer boy and wounded a corporal besides. It had gone entirely over one of the Pennsylvania regiments before it reached the spot where the brave but unfortunate captain was sitting.

It would take a page of our paper to give full effect to a description of the first landing of our troops on the afternoon of the 9th—a more stirring spectacle has probably never been witnessed in America. In the first line there was no less than seventy heavy surf boats, containing nearly 4000 regulars, and all of them expected to meet an enemy before they struck the shore. Notwithstanding this, every man was anxious to be first—they plunged into the water waist deep as they reached the shore—the "stars and stripes" were instantly floating—a rush was made for the sand hills, and amid loud shouts they pressed onward. Three long and loud cheers arose from their comrades still on board, awaiting to be embarked, and meanwhile the tops and every portion of the foreign vessels were crowded with spectators of the scene. Not one who witnessed it will ever forget the landing.[32] Why the Mexicans did not oppose us is a greater mystery than ever, considering their great advantages at the time and that they have since opposed every step of our advance.

The troops, both regulars and volunteers, have suffered incredibly since the landing—marching over the heavy sand hills, without water, under a broiling sun during the day, and sleeping out without tents or bedding during the heavy dews which have fallen at night—exposed, too, to a continual fire from the batteries from the enemy; yet not a murmur has been heard. Anything can be effected with such troops.

Yours, &c.,

G. W. K.

*Daily Picayune*, March 26, 1847[33]

U. S. Sloop of War *Albany*, Sacrificios, March 12, 1847—Afternoon

I came on board Capt. Breese's vessel[34] this morning, to finish a letter I had commenced on shore; yet ere it was completed a fierce norther sprung

32. Scott and Conner selected a smooth section of beach in Mocambo Bay, called Collado, as the site for the invasion. About three miles southeast of Vera Cruz, it was sheltered somewhat from the northers and could be protected by the fleet's heavy guns. The American force sailed from Anton Lizardo to a staging area at Sacrificios Island, just offshore from the landing site, in time to begin the landing late in the day. Just before sundown, General Worth led ashore the initial wave of 5,500 men, in surfboats rowed by sailors and protected by fire from naval gunboats directed toward shore. The invaders met no resistance. Before the evening ended, 8,600 men were ashore. Approximately 12,600 soldiers landed over the next two weeks. Kendall's brief account of the landing fails to capture the historical significance many Americans attached to the event. The fact that Cortes had landed at the same spot, and likewise on Good Friday, evoked romantic images of conquest from the pens of many writers. Military leaders saw evidence of American military prowess in the event, which was larger and more successful than the English amphibious landing in Egypt in 1801 and the French landing in Algiers in 1830. Johannsen, *To the Halls of the Montezumas*, 100.

33. This dispatch appeared first on March 25, lacking the third, fourth, and fifth paragraphs included here.

34. Samuel Breese's ship provided a base from which Kendall and other correspondents worked before Vera Cruz surrendered.

up, and there is now no communication with the shore. There has been no appearance of active operations on land, however, although there may have been some slight skirmishing with the column under Gen. Twiggs.

There is a camp rumor—the camp is always full of rumors—to the effect that Gen. Scott does not intend to accept the surrender of the city unless the castle is included in the capitulation. I trust it may be so.

The *McKim*, crowded with troops, came in today during the norther, and is now anchored near us. Two or three brigs and schooners also made their way inside of Anton Lizardo. It is hoped that the present wind will bring in Col. Harney's command, as well as the vessels laden with ordnance, wagons, mules, and other important means and munitions for carrying on the siege with vigor.

Col. Totten,[35] with other engineer officers, were out on foot yesterday among the sand hills, making a reconnaissance. Although fired upon by the batteries, not one of the party was injured. Today they were to continue their reconnaissance, and by this time have probably selected the different points at which to place their batteries.

A strange story is in circulation in relation to the last revolution, which has been termed the *pronunciamento de los Mugeres*, (Declaration of the Women.) As the tale runs, it is said that the priests have enjoined upon all married women to forsake their husbands for a space—to deny them all marital privileges until they would promise to join the church party and use their influence in opposing the obnoxious laws sequestrating or hypothecating the property of the clergy.[36] This story is told with all seriousness, and may be true. The holy padres certainly deserve credit for their originality, if they have thus attempted to work upon the men through their wives.

I have not seen a paper in relation to the last revolution, but am told that all was anarchy and confusion at the city of Mexico at last dates. Our only sources of information are the officers of the foreign vessels on this station, and this source we have been nearly deprived of for the last three days.

The norther—(it is now 9 o'clock, night)—is fast dying away, and a week of good weather will probably ensue in which to get ashore such of the siege guns and mortars as have arrived. Most nobly has the navy acted from the first, and gallantly have the officers been ready to undertake any and every exertion toward the operations of the army.

G. W. K.
*Daily Picayune*, March 26, 1847

35. Joseph G. Totten served as General Scott's chief of engineers.
36. Gómez Farías's removal from power led quickly to the repeal of the *puro*-sponsored legislation that confiscated church property for the support of the war effort.

U.S. Sloop of War, *Albany*, Sacrificios, March 13, 1847—Morning

The *Portia*, so it is said, is to sail immediately, and by her I send you a few lines more. The norther has completely blown itself out, so that by breakfast time the surf boats will again be enabled to reach the shore.

At half-past 3 o'clock this morning the enemy opened with round shot and shell, not only from the batteries around the town but from the castle. Rockets were also thrown, and the sky at times was completely lit up by them; yet a large portion of them fell far short. In the meantime, our own men are compelled to remain quiet and take this fire—the hardest duty a soldier has to perform. All are anxious to strike back, and they will be gratified in the course of a few days.

In haste,

G. W. K.

*Daily Picayune*, March 25, 1847


Camp near Vera Cruz, March 13, 1847—Afternoon

There was some slight skirmishing yesterday afternoon and last evening, and before daylight this morning a general alarm in camp as the Mexicans opened their different batteries and commenced throwing shells from the castle: yet it all amounted to but little. The enemy evidently expected a general attack, as they threw up rockets, fire balls, &c., completely lighting up the sand hills and chaparral around the walls.

During the night a reinforcement of 800 Mexicans passed into the city, taking the beach north of Gen. Twiggs's command, which had not at that time fully completed the investment. Their safe arrival within the walls was announced by loud shouts, the ringing of bells, and other rejoicings. In a few hours longer they would not have got in so easy.

The wound of Lieut. Col. Dickenson, of the South Carolina regiments, is improving. No other officers than those already mentioned have been killed or wounded so far.

A fire, of both round shot and shell, has been kept up on the command of Capt. Vinton, stationed at the lime kiln near the southeastern walls of the city, but as yet with little effect. It is estimated that one of our mortar batteries will be placed at this point.

Two or three persons, supposed to be spies, have been captured. One of them pretends to be a Frenchman, and is very anxious to be released, as he says his wife is about to be confined. Another favors one of Queen Victoria's gracious subjects, although he pretends not to understand a word of our vernacular. In addition, a well-dressed female has been captured, who has been caught outside the works under suspicious circumstances. A

Mexican has also been captured, who says he is a gardener; yet he was detected last night showing lights near Gen. Patterson's[37] lines, and as is supposed to direct the fire of the enemy. He will not go back to Vera Cruz in a hurry.

We are yet without any definite news in relation to the battle between Gen. Taylor and Santa Anna, yet the better informed think that the latter has met with a signal defeat. There are those in camp, however, who deem Gen. T.'s situation as still critical, and who believe that he is surrounded if not beaten. I do not believe it, although a paper found on the body of a Mexican officer killed yesterday would go to show that our army has been completely surrounded, if not cut to pieces.

They are now, 3 o'clock, landing mortars from the ship *Tamaroo*. The other vessels with the siege train have not yet arrived, although several sail are in the offing.

I sent you a number of letters this morning by the *Portia*, together with a topographical sketch of Vera Cruz and the line of investment. Enclosed I send you another sketch.

Reconnoitering parties are going out this evening towards the town, and smart skirmishing is anticipated. You shall have a full account of all that occurs. There are rumors in camp—only camp rumors, mind you—to the effect that on account of the non-arrival of the ordnance vessels an assault upon the city is to be attempted. Were I to give you every report that is current I should have my hands and you the paper full.

I send this by the cutter *Ewing.* If before she sails I have the opportunity to write another letter I shall improve it.

Yours, &c., &c.,

G. W. K.

P. S.—I have just got hold of a report, direct from Vera Cruz by one of the foreign vessels, which I believe. It is said that the revolution against Gómez Farías in the city of Mexico is making head-way, and it is thought he will be put down. The coalition now is, "Santa Anna, the clergy," and it is reported that the priests have already sent him on $200,000 as an earnest of their determination to support him.

The report that a reinforcement of 800 got within the walls of Vera Cruz last night is confirmed, and great was the rejoicing in consequence. This morning the inhabitants were in high spirits, and expressed themselves as fully able to defeat Gen. Scott.

---

37. Robert Patterson, a Pennsylvanian with Democratic political ties, commanded the Second Division of Volunteers, consisting of troops from Illinois, Tennessee, Georgia, Alabama, and Mississippi.

A letter from Mr. Bankhead, the British Minister,[38] confirms the report of the defeat of Santa Anna by Gen. Taylor. This is the amount of the news from the city of Vera Cruz this morning.

G. W. K.

*Daily Picayune*, March 30, 1847

Camp near Vera Cruz, March 14, 1847—Afternoon

The norther which commenced at sundown yesterday still continues, completely cutting off all communication with the vessels lying off or under Sacrificios. Shells are occasionally sent towards Gen. Worth's lines from the castle, but in the main they have fallen short. Capt. Vinton continues at his position near the lime kiln.

Day before yesterday Gen. Scott received notes from the French and Spanish consuls in Vera Cruz, or rather they were dated on that day and came to hand last night. The writers ask his protection for the subjects of their respective Governments, and this morning he sent two officers of his staff, Capts. Lee and Scott,[39] under a white flag to the city, with answers to these notes. Whether these officers will be permitted to enter the city is questionable. Gen. Scott sends a safeguard to the consuls, and promises that the property of their citizens shall be protected as far as possible; yet this will afford them little safety from a bombardment of the city. The safeguards will protect them in case the place is taken by storm or assault, as the penalty of forcing them is death.

At this time, half-past 3 o'clock, they are throwing 13-inch shells from the castle of San Juan de Ulúa, and one of them has just bursted a short distance from where I am writing, yet without doing any harm. I wish you could hear one of these huge projectiles in the air as they are coming, and see the scattering they make. The roar they make may be compared to that of a tornado, and every man within a quarter of a mile of the spot where they strike thinks they are about to fall on his individual head. The consequence is, that there is a general scampering to and fro—I mean when the men are lying idly about camp—and so deceptive is the sound that one is just as apt to run directly towards as from them. It takes two men to pack the mere shell itself, yet I intend sending one of them to New Orleans if possible as a sample.

38. Charles Bankhead, seriously ill during the months before the fall of Mexico City, played only a minor role in the diplomatic maneuvering that preceded the city's capture.

39. Robert E. Lee, Engineers, and Henry L. Scott, Fourth Infantry. Both men served on Scott's general staff. Lee, of course, became a Confederate war hero; Henry Scott married Winfield Scott's daughter.

A large number of vessels have come in within the last twenty-four hours, some of them doubtless laden with ordnance and ordnance stores. So soon as the norther blows over they will be landed and placed in position, and then we shall be able to talk back at the Mexicans. So far, they have had the argument entirely on their own side, if I may except the skirmishing with light arms, of which there has been far from inconsiderable.

Neither the *Portia* nor the *Ewing* can get out. By one of them I shall send this.

Yours, &c.,

G. W. K.

P. S.—Capts. Lee and Scott, who went out with the white flag with notes to the consuls, have returned. As was supposed, they were not allowed to enter the city, but were detained some three or four hundred yards outside the walls. Three officers came out to meet them, one of whom took the notes and afterwards brought a receipt that they had been delivered. Many of the inhabitants—ladies among them—were seen upon the walls and adjoining houses.

The line of investment is now complete and all communication with the city landward cut off. Two French vessels have succeeded in eluding the blockade favored by the wind, and have doubtless taken in "aid and comfort" to the enemy. The firing from the castle, and also from the batteries, continues.

G. W. K.

*Daily Picayune*, March 30, 1847

Camp near Vera Cruz, March 15, 1847—Morning

Another night has passed off quietly, no alarm of consequence disturbing the lines. The enemy is occasionally throwing round shot and shell, yet with little effect. One of the latter, and of the heaviest size, struck directly in the midst of the 8th Infantry last night, but did not injure a man.

There is a prospect of some little close fighting today, as our outposts are to be thrown in nearer the city walls. Some of our riflemen and sharpshooters are already in motion, and if the Mexicans will allow them to come near enough they will render a good account of themselves.

The norther has ceased—it is now near 9 o'clock, A.M.—yet communication with the vessels is still difficult on account of the heavy surf. Last night there was a report that the ship *Louisville*, with Col. Duncan's battery on board, had gone ashore at Anton Lizardo, and Maj. Graham, with a detachment of the 4th Infantry, was sent down by Gen. Worth to afford any assistance. The report is not confirmed this morning.

Yours, &c.,

G. W. K.

*Daily Picayune*, March 30, 1847

Camp near Vera Cruz, March 15, 1847, 10 o'clock A.M.

A schooner has just come in from the Brazos, with Gen. Taylor's official dispatches of his recent great battle with Santa Anna. All painful rumors are now at an end, and while the army here are rejoicing at the brilliant results of this battle, the rejoicings are mingled with deep regrets at the loss of the many brave officers who have fallen.

Gen. Scott, with his staff, has just started out on a visit to the entire line of investment. He will return to his headquarters this evening. There is some talk that the heavy guns of the squadron will be brought ashore and used in battering the town and castle. I sincerely trust the gallant officers of the navy may have a hand in the coming bombardment.[40]

A Mexican bearer of dispatches was caught last night while endeavoring to pass our lines. He was shot at and wounded by one of Capt. Magruder's[41] men, yet made his escape with the loss of his bag of papers. Among his documents was an address to the Governor of Jalapa, praying for reinforcements and provisions, and setting forth that Vera Cruz had been deserted by the Supreme Government. A lot of proclamations were also found, a copy of which I enclose for publication. It is about as weak an invention of the enemy as could well be imagined, and pray give the Mexicans the full benefit of their spelling and punctuation of the English language. A true bill for the murder of our vernacular, in the highest degree, could be found against them—but read for yourselves:

*Vera Cruz to the honest men in the enemy's camp.*

You are brought here to make us an unjust war, and have come deceived, for the people you have to contend with, is not that you are told it is, in the United-States.

We are strong and desirous to measure our arms with yours. Come, do come near us and you will have a doubtless proof. You can't expect other

40. Scott, lacking the heavy artillery needed to breach the walls of Vera Cruz, reluctantly accepted naval assistance, first from Commodore David Conner and then from Commodore Matthew C. Perry; he borrowed three 32-pounders and three 8-inch shell guns from the fleet. The so-called Seaman's Battery, manned by naval gunners and commanded by Captain John H. Aulick, commander of the frigate *Potomac* and second in command of the Home Squadron, opened fire on March 22, 1846. The U.S. Army artillery arsenal included guns, which fire a flat trajectory; howitzers, smaller pieces that use a reduced charge and an elevated muzzle to deliver shot of the same size; and mortars, heavy pieces that fire at a steep angle. The six-pounder gun, with a range of 1,500 yards and a weight of 880 pounds, was the army's standard field piece. The twelve-pounder howitzer was also commonly used in the field. Siege operations required heavier pieces; the big naval guns used at Vera Cruz weighed in excess of 5,000 pounds. John S. Eisenhower, *So Far from God: The U.S. War with Mexico, 1846–1848* (New York, 1989), 379–80.

41. John B. Magruder, First Artillery.

results of your imprudent enterprise than to perish under the severe influence of the climate. Yellow fevor which has already begun, one after one will cary away all of you very soon without a comfort, having for a grave the ardorous sand now under your feet.

But we have our arms open to receive all of you as friends, for we know that many honest people, is amongst you no matter the religious cread, we all are christian, we are all brothers, and we are all the creatures of the same heavenly Father. Come to us as friends, and you will see, and you will know by glad experience, that the mexicans are not at all the half savages, half barbarous, that you were told in the United-States. You will find frankness and true generosity, and true happiness living with us, you will find plenty and productive work, and a delicious climate not farther than twenty leagues. You may enjoy there an everlasting spring, a constant beautifull greens and abundant means of subsistenca in very productive lands, which we will give you as your property. You will also have complete fredom of conscience and liberty to adore the creator of the world in the way you please. Do exchange your arms of an enemy, for the embrace of a friend— grant God that it be so for your felicity.

These precious documents were intended for circulation in our camp, but would not have half as much effect upon the men as the "ardorous sand" which is blowing about their eyes and ears.

The reported loss of the ship *Louisville* I believe to be untrue.

The wind continues out of the north, but not with half the violence. I doubt, however, whether anything can be landed from the vessels today.

Yours, &c.,

G. W. K.

P.S.—11 o'clock. —They are at this moment rattling away with the heaviest kind of shells from the castle, and two of them have just struck within a few yards of one of the tents of the quartermaster where I am writing this. It would be amusing—in fact laughable—to see the scattering they make, were there not some little danger mingled with the performances. We are almost out of their reach, however, few of the shells coming this far before they burst or fall short.

G. W. K.
*Weekly Picayune*, April 5, 1847

Camp near Vera Cruz, March 17, 1847

I have just returned from an unsuccessful chase after the cutter *Ewing*, with two or three letters in my pocket I was very desirous to get on board.

The unusual and most unreasonable weather of the last two days, a fierce norther blowing the while, has prevented all communication with the vessels under Sacrificios.

Since my last letter, which enclosed a proclamation to the "honest" men of our army to desert, the "greasers" inside the city walls and in the castle have been amusing themselves by making targets of our men, and blazing and banging away, with round shot and shell, at anything and almost everything that appears in sight. This morning, at daylight, there was a general rattling of small arms at the outposts, the Mexicans having thrown out pickets outside the walls. I cannot understand that anyone was injured.

Our correspondent H has probably made you acquainted with the fact that dispatches have been intercepted concealed in a block of wood. It was really an ingenious device of the enemy.

A sailor was found this morning, just back of the lines, with his throat cut. Straggling parties of sailors and soldiers have visited Madellin and the mouth of the river, and committed many atrocities. Several of them have been arrested, and I trust may be severely punished.

From appearances now the surf boats will be busily engaged today in getting ashore mortars, ammunition, and such stores as are needed. The officers of the navy continue to work, and with zeal in furthering the advance of the army.

Yours, &c.,

G. W. K.
*Daily Picayune*, March 31, 1847

Camp before Vera Cruz, March 18, 1847

I rode over to the extreme left of Gen. Patterson's line yesterday, to Gen. Quitman's headquarters—about four miles over the road, but fully ten through the sand hills. The volunteers attached to this division appear to be in good spirits enough, although a little impatient at the delay in attacking the city. For want of quoits[42] they are pitching the 18-pound shot which was kindly (?) pitched within their lines by the Mexicans, or in other camp amusements.

But ten mortars have been landed so far, out of the great number ordered, and so far as I can learn no others have arrived. A heavy responsibility rests upon the War Department in not having the ordnance here in due season, for here are some 12 to 15,000 men completely paralyzed as it were for their essential arm in the attack upon Vera Cruz. They may come

42. Flat iron rings pitched at a stake in a game of the same name.

in by the time those already landed are in position, or they may not—such is the position in which Gen. Scott now finds himself.[43]

Col. Harney has arrived with his dragoons, but has lost more than half of his horses—here is another great drawback to the immediate attack upon the place.

Several vessels are leaving this morning to land supplies on the other side of the town, at the camp of Gen. Twiggs. This will save a great deal of heavy hauling through the sand hills.

There was more skirmishing this morning with the pickets of the enemy, but it amounted to but little. The Mexicans only venture out in small parties to reconnoitre our advanced works. All this time (6 o'clock A.M.) they are throwing shells upon the line of investment. Our men have become used to this amusement.

Com. Conner fired a salute yesterday in honor of Gen. Taylor's victory. I wonder what the Mexicans in the castle and town thought of it.

G. W. K.

*Daily Picayune,* March 31, 1847

Camp before Vera Cruz, March 18, 1847—Afternoon

I sent a number of letters this morning to the ship *Oswego,* learning that she was to sail this evening or early tomorrow morning for New Orleans. I now hear that the bark *Dudley* is also to sail tomorrow, and write a few lines to send by her.

The Mexicans in the city have been remarkably quiet today, wasting less ammunition than any day since the investment of the place. They did throw a few shell this morning, it is true; but not enough to hurt, and it may now be said that we are in quiet possession of the cemetery and lime-kiln, and without loss.

Of the siege ordnance now landed I can enumerate four long 24-pounders, two 8-inch howitzers, and ten 10-inch mortars. There is a report—merely a camp rumor—that with this small train Gen. Scott is to open upon the city on Saturday—the day after tomorrow. What a pity, what a sin, nay, what a shame it is that all the ordnance called for is not now here, ready to be placed at once in position. Men, means of every kind—enough to beleaguer the strongest place in Christendom—are here, *save the great essential ordnance,* without which the army is as nothing. The Mexicans, in the meantime, are

---

43. This observation, as well as other criticisms of the War Department, evinced complaints from the Polk administration and Democratic Party newspapers, such as the Washington *Union,* about the fairness of the *Picayune*'s coverage. Reilly, "American Reporters and the Mexican War," 255–56.

fairly laughing at us, as their papers would indicate, and accuse us of playing a sneaking and cowardly game instead of boldly coming forward to give them battle. I trust that this conceit may be driven out of them; yet the delay, as regards both the health and temper of our men, is to be dreaded.

The *Yazoo* is a total wreck, and a large portion of Col. Harney's horses have been lost. He will still be able to mount 300 men, and with these may do essential service.

Parties of mounted Mexicans have annoyed Gen. Twiggs's rear, driving in his pickets, &c., yet nothing farther. They are evidently trying to get into the city, but are completely shut out.

Half-past 4 o'clock, P. M.–The enemy have again opened a fire upon our lines, yet with little effect that I can learn. This thing of lying day after day under a fire, without the opportunity of returning it, is anything but amusing–rather trying upon the patience than otherwise.

Yours, &c.,

G. W. K.

P. S.–I learned, just as I was folding this letter, that the firing I mentioned above was from the water battery of the castle, and that the guns were aimed at the steamer *Eudora* while she was taking provisions round to Gen. Twiggs's brigade, on the other side the town. The Mexicans blaze and bang away at anything that comes in sight, to say nothing of range. There is now some appearance of another gale, but I trust that the signs may prove deceptive.

*Daily Picayune*, April 3, 1847


Camp before Vera Cruz, March 19, 1847–Forenoon

The *Oswego* and *Dudley*, by both of which I send letters, sailed this morning for New Orleans–this I shall forward by the next vessel.

Everything has been quiet since yesterday at this time. Last evening the Mexicans amused our men by throwing shells and Paixhans shot for an hour or so, and since then have not deigned to greet us with a single gun.[44] Some of our men consider themselves slighted in not being fired upon this morning.

Last night a large party of our men under cover of the darkness, selected the ground and made all the excavations and preparations for planting batteries within five or six hundred yards of the enemy's works.

---

44. Paixhans artillery guns fired conical projectiles rather than spherical balls. They were designed by the Frenchman Henri Joseph Paixhans for naval use and were introduced in 1824.

Capt. Talcott's[45] howitzer battery went out to support the party, in case of an attack; but they either were not discovered or else the Mexicans did not deem it prudent or meet to disturb them.

Tonight it is thought some of our batteries will be placed in position, and by Sunday at farthest it is expected the fire of the enemy may be returned. The vessels with the ordnance have not yet arrived, and expressions of regret and annoyance to see the army thus crippled are on every tongue. In the perplexing dilemma Gen. Scott must do the best he can.

Yours, &c.,

G. W. K.
*Daily Picayune*, April 2, 1847

Camp Effort before Vera Cruz, March 19, 1847—Afternoon

After I had closed my letter this forenoon the enemy opened, with round shot and shell, from all his batteries, directing his fire at different points of our lines, but mainly at the points near the cemetery—the calm of the morning only foreboded a storm. I cannot learn, however, that the firing had any other effect than amusing or exasperating our men by turn, although missiles flew all round them.

It is now certain that a portion of our heavy guns and mortars will be placed in position tonight, and all will be in readiness to commence operations on the town by the day after tomorrow. It is thought probable that Gen. Morales,[46] the commandant, will be first summoned to surrender, and on his refusal the bombardment will at once commence. Gen. Scott has a sufficiency of heavy ordnance to destroy the city, no doubt of that; yet the *morale* upon the castle, were all the mortars he required last fall now here, would be far greater. The city might have been taken by assault any night since the investment was complete; but it would have cost five or seven hundred men, and no good commensurate with the outlay of human life would have grown out of it. In this position matters now stand.

The sun is out, the weather extremely hot, and the only bright spot in the picture is a fresh sea breeze. Were it not for this the men at work on the beach would drop down from exhaustion.

Three or four vessels, it is said, are to sail for New Orleans tomorrow, by one of which I shall send this. In the course of two or three days we shall

---

45. George H. Talcott, Voltigeurs and Ordnance.
46. Juan Morales had responsibility for the defense of the city and the castle.

be enabled to give you intelligence of more interest than we have yet been enabled to send off.

Yours, &c.,

G. W. K.
*Daily Picayune*, April 2, 1847

Camp before Vera Cruz, March 19, 1847—5 o'clock P.M.

Our news from the city of Mexico, received in a roundabout way, would prove that a most sanguinary revolution—or rather a series of revolutions—is raging in that city, the different parties being all by the ears, and fighting each other with unwonted ferocity.

It is said that even the British minister, Mr. Bankhead, at last dates hardly dared venture into the streets for fear of being shot by some one of the different contending factions. Gómez Farías has his party, and the priests have their party, those in favor of peace have a party, and then there are the men of war, the Santa Anna men, the Almonte men, and what not. All was "confusion worse confounded," and I can neither make head nor tail of the different rumors.[47]

The Mexicans have been firing since noon today, and from most of their batteries, and the roar of round shot and shells has been constantly dinning in the ears of our men. Strange that they do not effect more. They must think they are destroying the Yankees, as they now term all of us, by dozens, else they would not keep up such incessant firing.

The weather continues fine for landing, and munitions and supplies are rapidly accumulating at the depots. The officers of the navy continue to use their best efforts.

---

47. The situation in Mexico City was indeed chaotic. After initially supporting Gómez Farías against the *polkas* rebels, Santa Anna shifted position in mid-March. By the time he had returned to the capital from San Luis Potosí, he had distanced himself from the *puros* while making peace with the church and strengthening ties with the *moderado* leadership. The invasion at Vera Cruz forced Santa Anna to leave Mexico City immediately, however, making it necessary to prevent Gómez Farías from once more assuming the interim presidency. *Moderado* and *santanista* politicians thus conspired to replace the vice presidency with a substitute president. The Mexican Congress followed their lead, abolishing the vice presidency and electing the *moderado* candidate, Pedro María Anaya, to the office of substitute president. Juan N. Almonte, who served as minister to the United States until diplomatic relations were broken in March 1845, was the *puro* candidate for the substitute presidency. The *moderado-santanista* coalition grew increasingly sympathetic to a negotiated settlement in the months that followed; the *puros*, seeking to regain their lost influence in national affairs, assumed an increasingly strident prowar posture. Pedro Santoni, *Mexicans at Arms: Puro Federalists and the Politics of War, 1845–1848* (Fort Worth, 1996), 190–97.

By the next day after tomorrow I am in hopes of being able to send you off an account of some of Gen. Scott's doings.

Yours, &c.,

G. W. K.

*Daily Picayune*, March 31, 1847

Camp before Vera Cruz, March 23, 1847—1 o'clock, P.M.

The bombardment of the city has been incessant all the forenoon, the enemy returning the fire at intervals from the castle as well as the batteries of the place.[48] A vessel with thirteen additional mortars has at last come in, so it is confidently stated, and with these, and the guns from the navy, Vera Cruz will be an uncommonly hot place in the course of a day or two.

A prisoner brought in this morning—a fellow who pretends that he has a family outside the walls—says that our shells did immense damage during the night. An officer of distinction, according to his story, was badly wounded, and he further states that a bomb entered the house of the American consul, Mr. Hargous,[49] and, besides doing great damage, injured severely a female who either had charge, or else had taken refuge in the building. Of course all the houses in the city must fare alike during the siege, those of the foreigners as well as the natives; yet I trust the latter part of the fellow's story is incorrect in the present instance.

2 o'clock. —Another rascally norther, which no one thought of or expected, has just burst upon us with force, and again all communication with the vessels is cut off. Some one says that the Orizaba,[50] the highest mountain peak in Mexico, looked angry and frowning this morning; but in watching the bombardment I did not notice it. The white top of Orizaba is always plainly visible just before a norther.

I learn that the little "Mosquito Fleet," as the small flotilla which came up and fired upon the town last evening and this morning is called, sustained some damage from the shells of the castle.[51] When they hauled off they were certainly in the hottest kind of a place.

---

48. Army and navy artillery opened fire on Vera Cruz on the afternoon of March 22, after General Morales rejected Scott's call to surrender.

49. An army agent and important news source for Kendall, Louis Hargous had been U.S. consul in Vera Cruz. Hargous had come to Kendall's aid during the latter's imprisonment in Mexico City in 1842. Copeland, *Kendall of the Picayune*, 197. After the war, Hargous and his brother Peter purchased the transit rights across the Isthmus of Tehuantepec from the British merchant house Manning and Mackintosh.

50. Mount Orizaba is over three miles high and clearly visible well out to sea.

51. The Mosquito Fleet consisted of two steamers, *Spitfire* and *Vixen*, and four gunboats, *Bonita*, *Petrel*, *Falcon*, and *Tampico*.

The untimely death of Capt. Vinton, one of the most finished and meritorious officers in the army, is deeply regretted by all. Brave to a fault, of a mind highly cultivated, of a disposition most amiable, and at the same time of a piety which never obtruded, he has been cut off in the prime and vigor of life. No officer in the army stood higher with his fellows—no one could be more sincerely mourned.

The norther still continues, and a tremendous surf is again rising. I trust the gale will be of short duration.

Yours, &c.,

G. W. K.

*Daily Picayune*, April 4, 1847

Camp before Vera Cruz, March 23, 1847—9 o'clock, Night

We have just had a regular alarm and men out in camp, all owing to a report that 2000 Mexican cavalry were on their way to attack us in rear, and force their way through the lines of the city. The scene at the quartermaster's department was exciting and most ludicrous. Seven full companies of the odds and ends of camp—wagoners, hostlers,[52] cooks, boatmen, clerks, servants generally, and what not—were collected and armed, and every preparation made to annihilate the 2000 cavalry aforesaid; but not an enemy appeared, and the whole affair ended in less than smoke.

Another excitement, which had some foundation came from the direction of the city. In some way a number of small thatched buildings, near the city walls, caught fire about an hour since; and what with the dryness of the materials of which they were constructed, and the violence of the wind, an immense sheet of bright flame rose high in the heavens. The lurid glare lit up every domo and turret within the walls, and for a space the scene was one of inconceivable grandeur. Some of the ignorant thought the citizens were going to make a second Moscow of Vera Cruz;[53] some thought one thing, some another—the real cause of the conflagration is yet a mystery. All is now dark and gloomy in the direction of the city save when the fuse of some shell, in its curvated flight, is seen by the watchful looker.

52. Hostlers tended to the needs of horses.
53. The reference is to the burning of Moscow by the Russians during Napoleon's occupation in 1812.

The officers of the navy are busy dragging their heavy pieces up to the battery prepared for them, working by night as well as day. I trust they will be ready to open tomorrow.

Yours, &c.,

G. W. K.
*Daily Picayune*, April 4, 1847

Camp before Vera Cruz, March 24, 1847—8 o'clock A.M.

The night has passed at comparative quiet, an occasional cannonading being kept up on either side as if to keep one another awake. This morning the firing from our mortar batteries has almost entirely died away, and it is thought it will not recommence until we have a far greater number of guns in position. The bombardment was certainly commenced too soon.

There are those who think the fire of last night destroyed the roofs of a number of the largest stores in Vera Cruz. The conflagration was certainly the most grand I have ever witnessed.

The norther has partially subsided, and they will be able to land munitions from the vessels in the course of a few hours probably. Shells are now wanted, more than anything else.

Yours, &c.,

G. W. K.
*Daily Picayune*, April 4, 1847

Camp before Vera Cruz, March 24, 1847—10 o'clock A.M.

The din of the bombardment has somewhat slackened, it being found that the wagons cannot carry ammunition to the batteries during the day sufficient to keep all the guns at work; still our mortars continue to throw shell into the city at intervals, and every one must take effect somewhere. Under cover of the darkness tonight every means of transportation at the command of the quartermaster will be brought into requisition to carry up powder and shells, and in addition the battery of twenty-four pounders and 8-inch howitzers is to be placed in position. It is impossible to judge accurately of the effect of the 68-pound Paixhans shot from the navy battery, although they are seen striking the walls and houses of the city.

Half-past 11 o'clock A. M.—A shell from one of our mortar batteries has just struck within the city, and has set fire to a building which must be a depot for ship stores, as a dense black smoke is rising. The forts and batteries of the enemy are returning our fire at intervals, both with round shot and shells. In the battery where the navy guns are placed, called the Malibran battery, four sailors have been killed this morning by the round

Bombardment of Vera Cruz. Toned lithograph (hand-colored), 1851, by Adolphe-Jean-Jean-Baptiste Bayot, after Carl Nebel; reproduced from George Wilkins Kendall, *The War between the United States and Mexico Illustrated* (New York: D. Appleton and Company, 1851), plate 4; © Amon Carter Museum, Fort Worth, Texas (1972.186.4).

shot of the Mexicans. —Lieut. Baldwin[54] has also been slightly wounded, and two sailors seriously.

Afternoon, 2 o'clock. A shell from one of the enemy's guns has dismounted one of our mortars, wounding three or four who are serving it. Lieut. Arnold,[55] who had command of the gun met with a very narrow escape. A large train of wagons, on the way to the batteries with ammunition, has been obliged to return on account of being too much exposed to the shells of the enemy. The bursting of a single bomb near the mules must inevitably frighten the entire train.

9 o'clock. Night.—The enemy, after opening from all his batteries towards sundown, has now slackened his fire. Our mortars still keep up the game at intervals. Large trains of ammunition are now on their way out to supply the different batteries.

March 25—8 o'clock A.M.—Every gun and mortar on both sides apparently, have been hard at work ever since sunrise this morning—the roar of the heavy ordnance is tremendous. There was another conflagration last night illuminating the entire city; but it is said the fire only amounted to the burning of some small jacales near the city walls. During the night Capt. Talcott, with his rocket and howitzer men, took up a position near the Fort of Santiago and threw rockets at that work.[56]

I learn that the steam frigate *Princeton,* with Com. Conner on board, sails this morning for Philadelphia.[57] Her boilers are so near burnt out that she is now of little use here.

10 o'clock, A.M.—Every one of our guns are now keeping up an incessant firing upon the city. The enemy directs the most of his guns at the Malibran battery. I hear that two or three deserters came in during the night from the city, who describe the effect of our shell as tremendous.

Capt. Plummer, of the ship *Talbot,* is about sailing for New Orleans. The wind is fair and he cannot wait longer.

In haste,

G. W. K.
*Daily Picayune,* April 4, 1847

54. Charles H. Baldwin, passed midshipman.

55. Lewis G. Arnold, Second Artillery.

56. Major George Talcott's battery fired forty Cosgreve and ten Hale rockets on March 24 and 25, 1847.

57. Matthew Perry relieved Conner in the midst of the siege on March 20, 1847. Conner's tour as commander of the Home Squadron had been extended to late March when it was thought that the siege of Vera Cruz would take place in February.

Camp before Vera Cruz, March 25, 1847—Forenoon

I sent off a package of letters a few minutes since by the ship *Talbot*, but learning that the bark *Carolina* is also about to sail, I send off a hasty sketch by her.

Every gun in every one of Gen. Scott's batteries is now at work upon the city, and nothing but a continuous roar of artillery can be heard. The entire strength of our batteries at this time is as follows: ten 10-inch mortars, four long 24-pounders, three 68-pound Paixhans guns, three long 32-pounders, two 3-inch howitzers, besides a number of cohorns—not more than one-third the number that should have been here at work, according to the original programme of the attack on Vera Cruz, but still enough to keep up an incessant din upon the works of the enemy. In the meantime the enemy is busy with his heavy guns from San Juan de Ulúa, from Santiago, and from all the forts and batteries around the city, and above the roar of the cannon a dense smoke is rising, plainly pointing out the scene of the conflict.[58] For close work, for hand-to-hand combat, Monterey was far ahead of this; but for grandeur and sublimity this far exceeds any attempt that has ever yet been made by the American arms.

I learn that last evening four foreigners came in from the city to Gen. Scott, stating that the effect of his shells upon the place was very destructive, both to property and life—especially upon harmless citizens and women and children—and praying that the bombardment might cease, so that neutrals and non-combatants might be permitted to leave. This petition was signed by four of the foreign consuls, but I believe came entirely too late. Gen. Scott's answer, if it has not already been made, I learn will be to the effect that the inhabitants, both native and foreign, had timely warning of his arrival and intentions; that they saw his approaches and were well aware of his determination to capture or destroy the city; that the foreigners were all presented with safeguards in due season, and the citizens were given full permission to retire; that the city was duly and formally summoned to surrender, and that now all who are in it are compelled to take the consequences. Such, I imagine, will be the sum and substance of his answer, although I am not certain that I am right in every particular. Gen. Scott will certainly be right not to listen to anything of the kind, and the whole responsibility must rest on the Mexican commander, Gen. Morales.

---

58. The main army batteries were positioned opposite Vera Cruz's southeastern wall. The naval battery was positioned about 750 yards to the north, across a road and rail line leading to the south and opposite the southwestern corner of the city wall. Fort Santiago was located on Vera Cruz's southeastern corner, along the shore opposite San Juan de Ulúa. Fort Concepcion, the city's other major fortress, stood at the northern extent of the city's eastern wall.

There are those who think that the city cannot hold out twenty-four hours longer, but of this I am unable to judge. So far the enemy has fired at least five times to our one, although the effect from our batteries is doubtless infinitely greater.

G. W. K.

*Daily Picayune*, April 6, 1847

Camp before Vera Cruz, March 27, 1847–9 o'clock A.M.

Not knowing what vessel is to sail first, I have written duplicates of this letter to send off by any and every conveyance. It contains a hurried statement of the events of the past three days.

On the 25th inst. a portion of Col. Harney's dragoons, with two pieces of artillery under Lieut. Judd and small detachments of the 1st and 2d Tennessee volunteers under Cols. Campbell and Haskell, had a sharp engagement with a strong force of the enemy at a fortified bridge a short distance this side of Madellin. The barricade at that bridge was carried by assault, and the Mexicans were afterwards entirely cut to pieces and dispersed by the mounted dragoons. They lost 49 or 50 men in killed, besides many wounded; on our side the loss was 3 killed, and 6 or 7 wounded—among the latter Lieut. Neill of the dragoons, severely but not dangerously injured by a lance.[59]

Yesterday morning, the 26th, before daylight, a severe norther sprang up. At sunrise, a white flag came in from the Mexicans, and under cover of a truce for the benefit of foreign families were overtures for a surrender. The batteries of the enemy had been mostly silent the night previous. Gen. Scott appointed a commission, consisting of Gens. Worth and Pillow[60] and Col. Totten, to confer with the officers selected by the Mexican Gen. Landero,[61] it being stated that Gen. Morales was sick. The members of our commission, if I am rightly informed, were instructed to insist upon the unconditional surrender of Vera Cruz and the castle of San Juan de Ulúa. Gen. Morales having designated himself as commander of both, with all the arms and ammunition—the prisoners to be sent to the United States if Gen. Scott deemed it expedient. Gen. Worth and the other commissioners went out in the afternoon, when the Mexican officers requested until 9 or 10 o'clock this morning to give their answer.

59. Henry B. Judd, Third Artillery; William B. Campbell, First Tennessee Volunteers; William Haskell, Second Tennessee Volunteers; and Lewis Neill, Second Dragoons.

60. Along with John A. Quitman and James Shields, Gideon Pillow took up his command having come directly from civilian life. A friend and law partner of President Polk, he proved to be the weakest of the six new brigadier generals appointed for the war with Mexico.

61. José Juan Landero was second-in-command at Vera Cruz.

Yesterday afternoon a deputation of five citizens of Madellin came up and requested Gen. Scott to send down a regular armed force to occupy that town and protect their property.

Some twenty odd sail of vessels, mostly schooners and hermaphrodite brigs, have been driven ashore by the violence of the norther, and several square-rigged vessels have been dismasted under Sacrificios. The gale has been one of uncommon fury. It has abated this morning, and I see several small boats filled with French and probably other families, between the castle and Sacrificios. They have been stopped by Com. Perry and not allowed to proceed toward the fleet. With the timely warning they all had, they should have left the city before they did. Gen. Scott told them plainly what he intended to do, and it is their own fault if they did not believe him.

March 27−10 o'clock, A. M.−Gen. Worth and the other officers of the commission have just started for the lime-kiln, which is little over a quarter of a mile from Fort Santiago, to hold a last talk with the Mexicans. I have learned, since I commenced this letter, that Gen. Scott will permit the Mexican soldiers, after laying down their arms, to go free to their homes on parole.[62] An hour or two will probably tell the story, and I shall keep this letter open until the result is known. If the Mexicans do not come to terms, there will be a din of round shot and shell about their ears such as they have not as yet been accustomed to—our batteries are increased and in the best condition.

Half-past 1 o'clock, P. M.−The commission has not yet returned from the lime-kiln, so we are yet ignorant of the result of the deliberations. An hour or two since a messenger came down to Gen. Scott from the lime-kiln, probably for fresh instructions on some debated point. The Mexicans will palaver until the vomito[63] or millennium comes, if they are permitted, which I trust and feel assured will not be the case. Their commander at first asked for the same terms granted the Mexicans at Monterey—to march out with colors flying, drums beating, trumpets blowing, and their arms at their sides—but of course Gen. Scott will accede to no such terms. The two cases are by no means parallel. At Monterey Ampudia had two roads open by which to retreat—here the Mexicans are completely hemmed in on all sides, by land as well as water, and entirely without the chance of escape.

---

62. Besides demanding the surrender of Ulúa along with Vera Cruz and the forfeiture of all war materiel, Scott initially insisted that only officers and local national guard forces be paroled, while the men of the regular army would be imprisoned in the United States. The terms agreed to on March 27, 1847, included the surrender of the castle and the city as well as war materiel, but allowed for officers to keep their arms and horses and for the parole of the entire Mexican army.

63. Yellow fever.

Quarter past 3 o'clock, P. M.–From a messenger who has just arrived from the lime-kiln, where the joint commission is sitting, it is understood that the Mexicans have accepted Gen. Scott's terms, and it is expected that the treaty of capitulation will be signed in the course of an hour or two by the commanders on either side. Rumor has it that two-thirds of Vera Cruz is in ruins–the effects of our Paixhans shot and shells. Never has so strong a place been taken with so little loss.[64] I shall probably send this letter, or a duplicate, by the *Princeton*, as I am told that she is to touch at the Balize,[65] at Mobile or Pensacola. To return to the present state of affairs: fearing that the Mexicans may not come to terms, Gen. Scott is sending up additional mortars to the batteries. If the capitulation is not signed, the destruction and carnage will be terrible.

7 o'clock, P. M.–The news now is, that all the articles of capitulation have been accepted by the Mexican officers, and that the papers have gone to the castle, as well as to the city, for the signatures of the respective commanders; after this, the documents will be signed by Gen. Scott, and then the stronghold of Mexico will be in the hands of the American troops. It is asserted that many of the Mexican officers will refuse to accept their paroles, in which case they will probably be sent to New Orleans. In front of some of our batteries a number of volunteers have already approached to the city walls, and it is even asserted that the Mexicans have come out and sold them liquor. I am told that a guard has been sent out to bring in all stragglers.

11 o'clock, P. M.–The thing is all settled. The commission has returned, the capitulation has been signed by all parties, and day after tomorrow, at 10 o'clock, the Mexicans are to march out of their "heroic" city, which they were to defend until not a man was left, stack their arms in presence of our whole army, and then set out on their parole as the cheapest way of getting rid of them.

Thus has fallen Vera Cruz, and along with it the famous castle of San Juan de Ulúa. If so much has been effected with the limited means in the hands of the engineers, what would have been done with the entire amount of ordnance called for, including Alger's big gun, which has arrived at last? Why, Vera Cruz would have been a heap of shapeless, sightless ruins in twenty-four hours after the bombardment commenced, while the *morale* upon the entire Mexican nation would have been immense. And then, again, it might have been an agreeable and a pleasant sight to the officers of the

64. American losses were thirteen killed and fifty-five wounded.

65. Balize was a pilot site used for navigation about fifty miles southeast of New Orleans. It eroded away about 1900.

foreign vessels, lying under Sacrificios and watching all of Gen. Scott's movements, to have seen any of our mortars at work instead of ten—to say nothing of the useful lesson they would have been taught. The actions of some of the foreigners, in not wishing to leave the city until their own dwellings were trembling about their ears, would indicate a doubt in their minds of the ability of the Americans to capture the place. They have found themselves mistaken, many of them when it was too late for either their safety or comfort: and hereafter the opinion will probably obtain, that when an American army sets itself down before a Mexican city, it is going into it most distinctly.

I shall probably send this letter by the *Princeton*, and a duplicate by some other vessel. If possible I shall get the terms of capitulation to send on.

Yours, &c., &c.,

G. W. K.
*Daily Picayune*, April 4, 1847

Camp before Vera Cruz, March 28, 1847—11 o'clock, A. M.

This is the first quiet day we have had in the last twenty, and words cannot picture the inconveniences, the annoyances, and the sufferings the army, both regular and volunteer, has experienced during this period. One half the time the sun has been fairly broiling the men in the valleys and upon the sand hills—the other half, with scanty rations and without tents, a large portion of the men have been exposed to the rude, cold northers, and to clouds of sand that fairly blinded the eyes already inflamed by the fierce rays of the sun. The water, too, has been indifferent, and in many cases scarce, thousands of ticks and other insects have covered the men, and the labor has been incessant in the trenches, both by day and by night: yet all has been borne without murmuring. To be sure, there has been some repining at the fact that the grand programme of the performances before Vera Cruz, in so far as regards the non-arrival of all the heavy ordnance advertised in the bids of the day as intended to open the ball with, has not been carried out to the full extent hoped for and anticipated; still, all have gone to work cheerfully with the limited means at hand, and the result of the siege must forever remain a monument in their praise. The head of the army and the heads of brigades, the chiefs of ordnance, of the engineers, and of the artillery departments, not forgetting the gallant spirits of the navy, have all been indefatigable and untiring in their efforts; the quartermaster's department has been zealous in giving its quota of aid; the chiefs of the commissariat have done all in their power to furnish supplies for the troops with alacrity—in short, all has been done that could be done to gain possession of a position that the enemy fondly deemed impregnable. To specify each officer who has signalized himself by name would occupy too much time and space at this writing—to say less than I have done would be put down to my credit as a flagrant neglect.

Gen. Worth has now gone out to choose a ground on which the enemy are to lay down their arms tomorrow morning. The ceremony is one that every person is anxious to witness, and I shall endeavor to obtain a front seat at the show. It is thought that the stars and stripes will be waving over the city and castle shortly after 10 o'clock, and I am told that the man-of-war steamer *Princeton* will delay her departure until after the event.

From the city of Mexico, through the foreign fleet, I have later intelligence to communicate. On the 19th inst. it is reported that Santa Anna was in the capital, that he had joined the clergy, had put down the revolution of Gómez Farías and Salas, and that with his new associates he is now anxious for peace. This news comes from a source that appears to me reliable, and I give it believing it to be in the main correct. It is further reported that Santa Anna is at the head of 1000 regular troops, and that, aided by the church party, is able to make headway against any opposition.[66] In this distracted country, and among this uncertain population, it is hard to tell or even surmise what a day may bring forth: yet with the powerful aid of the clergy Santa Anna may be enabled to keep the reins of power in his hands for a space, and make peace or continue the war as may best suit his purposes—I am disposed to think, since his meeting with Gen. Taylor,[67] that he has become heartily disgusted with the war.

Mr. Dimond,[68] our former consul at Vera Cruz, and who was wrecked on board the British steamer the *Alicranes*, is now here in good health. Knowing Mexico and its population thoroughly, he may be useful in a thousand ways to Gen. Scott. Speaking of wrecks puts me in mind of the recent disasters here. There are near thirty wrecks in all within a mile of where I am writing,

66. Santa Anna returned to Mexico City on March 21, 1847, bringing an end to the fighting between the factions led by Gómez Farías and Barragán. With Pedro María Anaya installed as substitute president and the clergy mollified with the repeal of the anticlerical legislation passed under Gómez Farías, Santa Anna left the capital on April 2, marching an army of 7,000 men east along the National Road to seize the National Bridge, a critical point on the highway between Vera Cruz and Cerro Gordo.

67. The reference is to the battle of Buena Vista.

68. Francis M. Dimond served as an important source of information about Mexican affairs during 1845. When the Polk administration began to consider an invasion at Vera Cruz in October 1846, he was called to Washington from his retirement in Rhode Island for advice. He later traveled to Havana at the behest of General Scott to recruit agents to operate inside Mexico. K. Jack Bauer, *The Mexican War, 1846–1848* (New York, 1963), 22, 66, 233–34, 237.

and I have sent a man to gain all the information in relation to them in his power.

I will endeavor to write a description of the evacuation tomorrow. The number of Mexican officers captured is nearly as follows: 5 generals, 18 colonels, 37 lieutenant colonels, 5 majors, 90 captains, and 180 lieutenants. There are those already who think that a full and most unconditional surrender should have been insisted upon—that we had every means to enforce it—but I shall say nothing until I have read all the articles.

I have just seen the New Orleans *Jeffersonian* of the 17th inst., in which the sailing of bomb vessels for Vera Cruz is announced. There is no use in being in any hurry about it—three years from next December will do just as well.

Yours, &c.,

G. W. K.
*Daily Picayune*, April 4, 1847

Camp before Vera Cruz, March 29, 1847

Since writing yesterday I have been able to gather the full sum and substance of the terms of surrender, and under the circumstances I do not see how it can be complained of by the most exacting. The Mexican members of the commission were Col. Gutierrez de Villanueva, Lieut. Col. Manuel Robles and Col. Pedro M. Herrera—courteous men, all of them, as I learn by those who were present. I have been unable to procure a copy of the terms of capitulation, but it amounts to the following.

The garrisons in the castle and different forts are to march out and lay down their arms at 1 o'clock on the 29th of March, (today,) the officers to preserve their side arms, horses, saddles, and bridles. At the time the arms are given over the Mexican flags are to be saluted by their own batteries and immediately struck, after which the city, the Castle of San Juan de Ulúa, and the Forts Concepcion and Santiago are to be occupied by the division of Gen. Worth. The Mexican officers are to give parole that their men do not again take up arms until exchanged. In the meantime, all the arms, munitions of war and public stores, in the castle and in the different forts and batteries, are to be turned over to the American army—the armament to be considered as liable to be restored at the termination of the war by a definite treaty of peace with Mexico, which means, if I understand it, provided Uncle Sam pleases. The sick and wounded Mexicans are to be permitted to remain in the city, under their own surgeons, the private property of all is to be protected and the religion of the people respected.

Such, if I understand the thing rightly, is the amount of the different articles of the capitulation. It might be well here to state that Capts. Mackenzie[69] and Aulick, of the navy, were added to our commission as advisers towards the close of the convention. I presume that Gen. Scott would have placed an officer of the navy regularly on the commission had it been possible to reach the fleet at the time that body was formed.

It is bruited about that Com. Perry with the smaller vessels of the navy, is to sail down to Alvarado this afternoon, and that Gen. Quitman's brigade is to start tomorrow by land for the same destination.[70] The object is, if the place makes the least resistance, to attack it by land and water.

Let me give you a rumor current in camp, but not one word of which do I believe. As report has it, Gen. La Vega[71] is at Jalapa, or between this and that city, with 9000 men, ready to oppose Gen. Scott's advance. After the recent severe reverses of the Mexicans it would be hard to concentrate that force. I send this, along with other letters, by the *Princeton*, and the boat of that steamer is now waiting.

In haste,

G. W. K.
*Daily Picayune*, April 4, 1847


Vera Cruz, March 30, 1847

Formal possession was taken yesterday of the "heroic" city of Vera Cruz, by Gen. Worth, different portions of his division occupying the national palace, the castle of San Juan de Ulúa and the forts of Santiago and Concepcion, as well as the batteries and works of all kinds. The whole ceremony was grand and imposing beyond anything it has ever been my lot to witness. At 10 o'clock the different Mexican regiments marched out and laid down their arms, in presence of a large portion of our army; yet very properly not one murmur of exultation rose upon the air. The Mexicans piled their arms in good temper, mortifying as it must have been to them, and marched off, with their women, without saying a word. As

---

69. Alexander Slidell Mackenzie served as the Polk administration's emissary to Santa Anna in Havana during the summer of 1846. He was the younger brother of John Slidell, having taken the name of his mother's family.

70. Scott hoped that at Alvarado, a major ranching center, Quitman could capture the horses, mules, and cattle needed to support the army's move inland. Perry's mission was to capture what remained of the Mexican Navy. Neither mission was successful.

71. Rómulo Díaz de la Vega was captured and then exchanged at Resaca de la Palma. He was later named chief of the Army of the East and was captured once more at Cerro Gordo.

the "stars and stripes"[72] were run up at the different works, salute after salute resounded from our different batteries as well as from the navy, and by 1 o'clock in the afternoon all was order and quiet. Gen. Worth, who yesterday received his brevet of major general, was by a singular coincidence also appointed Governor of the city of Vera Cruz and the castle. He marches, however, with the army, yet will remain here long enough to regulate, thoroughly, the municipal regulations of the place. I might here state, that Mr. Dimond, our former consul here, has been appointed collector of the port.

The city, or at least the northern portion of it, has been torn all to pieces—the destruction is dreadful. The other parts of the place would have suffered in the same way had the bombardment of the place continued another day.

There is a report today that Alvarado will give up without a fight. I shall learn more of the truth of this rumor before night. In the meantime Gen. Quitman's brigade is to march down to that place.

[G. W. K.][73]
*Daily Picayune,* April 9, 1847

Vera Cruz, March 30, 1847

I gave you a hurried scrawl this morning, thinking the *Alabama* was to sail immediately. I now learn that she is not to leave until tomorrow for New Orleans. Gen. Jesup goes home in her, and I am told that a Mexican officer is also to take passage. Were it not that I desire to see a little more of this place, and perhaps take a trip down to Alvarado, I should be wending my way homeward.

It is impossible to get at the loss of the Mexicans by the bombardment, yet it is certain that women, children and non-combatants have suffered the most. Some say that 150 have been killed, some more and some less: as regards the destruction of property, that shows for itself.[74] Hardly a building south of the Plaza Grande but is either burnt, torn in pieces, or much injured, and the streets are filled with rubbish and fragments. The National

72. The Mexican War was the first in which Americans fought under an official national banner. As of 1834, army regulations had described and designated the familiar American flag as the official banner of the armed forces. Before that date, soldiers had fought under regimental or unit flags. Johannsen, *To the Halls of the Montezumas,* 52.

73. No initials end this dispatch, but an editorial note reads "We subjoin such of Mr. Kendall's letters as have not been anticipated altogether."

74. Mexican officials estimated that four hundred to five hundred civilians and six hundred soldiers were killed; a British officer on the scene estimated one hundred civilians and eighty soldiers killed. American forces fired 6,700 artillery shells into Vera Cruz during the siege.

Palace, which is on the Plaza and near the outer range of our mortars, had five shells bursted within it, one of which killed a woman and two children lying asleep in the kitchen. The Cathedral, on an opposite side of the Plaza, was also somewhat injured, but the churches south of it, and nearer our mortars, suffered the most. I write this letter in a house which must have been hot enough during the bombardment, for the signs of shell are all around me. The residence of our former consul Mr. Hargous, was struck twice. One of the shells came through the roof, lodged at the foot of a bed which a gentleman had just left, and completely demolished everything in the room, and the furniture was of the most costly description. One of the inmates describes the explosion as tremendous—the house shook in all its parts as with an earthquake, and his first impression was that everything in it had been rended into fragments. Months, probably years will elapse before Vera Cruz is in the situation where the siege found it.

Many of the foreigners here are raving, perfectly outrageous, at the method taken by Gen. Scott to reduce the place—they would have had him attack it by storm, and thus destroying life instead of property! They blame him, too, for not allowing some of the foreign families, after they came to their senses and found that the city was really to be destroyed, to leave the place and take refuge on board vessels which were out of harm's way. A pretty time, truly, after all the solemn warnings they received, to accuse Gen. Scott of want of humanity. They were told, plainly and positively, that the town would be taken, either by regular siege or by storm, and yet it would seem that they did not believe it; and when the truth did finally break in upon them, and they discovered their error, they must needs pester Gen. Scott with requests for a cessation of hostilities until they could move out, and thus deprive him of all the advantages an incessant bombardment gave him. Our commanding general properly referred them to Gen. Morales as the appropriate person to call upon in their great emergency. He had probably advised them to remain, and now he must aid them in their extremity of peril. Find fault with the bombardment, forsooth!

The Mexican bulletins, too, some of which I send you, find fault with the mode of attack. They say it was barbarous and cowardly, and ask why the city was not boldly assaulted? Strange that they should have forgotten to attack the American army on its landing, as any other people most certainly would; to assault our men while commencing the work of entrenchment; in short, to annoy us in fifty different ways, all which they might have done. But no, they are annoyed to think that Gen. Scott did not fall into their strongest snare, and are exasperated because he saw fit to save the lives of his own men, at the expense of their property and of their utter discomfiture. The city would have been assaulted and stormed in another twenty-four hours, or as soon as a breach was made, and a horrible night it would have been for all within the walls. Not one half the men who laid down their arms yesterday would have survived—innocent blood, besides, would have flowed without measure—scenes would have been enacted at which humanity would have wept.

It would seem that we cannot please the Mexicans and foreigners by any system of fighting we may adopt. Monterey was taken by assault, and they complained and said that it should have been reduced by regular approaches, Vera Cruz has been captured by regular approaches, and they are fierce in their denunciations that it was not stormed. I presume that in neither case the American commanders endeavored to please their enemies, and that they will not lose a wink of sleep in consequence of their animadversions.

I shall endeavor to write you another letter before the *Alabama* sails, giving you such news as is stirring. The army will probably move towards Jalapa in a day or two.

Yours, &c.,

G. W. K.
*Daily Picayune*, April 9, 1847

Vera Cruz, March 31, 1847

Gen. Quitman's brigade set out on the march for Alvarado last evening. The place is distant some thirty or forty miles south, and they will probably reach it by tomorrow night. I presume that some of the smaller vessels of the navy, under Com. Perry, will go down to take part in case the Mexicans see fit to defend it. The impression, however, is, that they will leave it without a struggle.

From the direction of the city of Mexico we can gain no intelligence. There appears to be no doubt, however, that Santa Anna arrived there on the 20th or 21st inst. and at once took sides with the clergy against Gómez Farías. Nothing farther has been learned in relation to the report that there was a large force of Mexicans, under La Vega, at or near Jalapa. The army will proceed in that direction in the course of a few days, and then we shall know all about it.

I was witness to a singular scene yesterday. A large concourse of Mexicans—old men, women and young girls—were gathered around the door of one of our commissaries, and each struggling, as you have frequently seen people at the ticket office of a theatre on a crowded night, to be first in. On enquiring, I found that rations of food were being distributed to the hungry and half-starved throng, and their greedy looks plainly showed to what extremity of hunger they had been driven. I cannot learn that there was much suffering for want of food in Vera Cruz during the bombardment, but there is always a large population in every Mexican city—from "hand-to-mouth" people—who know not today where they will obtain their dinners on the morrow.

Since writing the above I learn that a Frenchman has just arrived from the city of Mexico who reports that there are not one thousand armed men, all told, on the road from this to the capital. He says there were nine guns in position at Puente Nacional, but only sixty men to serve them. It would seem perfect madness for the Mexicans to continue the war, yet I suppose they will hold on a while longer.

The amount of spoils of war taken by the capture of Vera Cruz is immense. Over 4000 muskets were laid down on the ground, and it is known that a great number were left secreted in the city by men who went out in citizens' clothes instead of their uniforms. The number of cannon and mortars, in the town and castle, is not as yet known, but it is already ascertained that there are over 300! To this should be added an immense amount of powder, ball, shells, Paixhans shot, &c., &c., enough to conquer the country all the way to Acapulco. Quite a speculation for Uncle Sam. Two flags are flying from San Juan de Ulúa, one belonging to the army and the other to the navy.

The Frenchman who brought the report from the city of Mexico says that he met the unarmed Mexicans, who laid down their arms on the 29th inst., scattered along the road between this and Mango de Cluvo. Some of them had hardly advanced three leagues, and were already suffering for want of food!

Gen. Quitman takes down to Alvarado the South Carolina, Georgia, and Alabama regiments. He also has an artillery force with him, Capt. Steptoe's[75] battery, I am informed. One object of the expedition is to open a road from whence mules, horses, and supplies for the army may be procured. The country down that way is said to abound with them. I am fearful you will find our letters reach you in a jumbled and confused manner—the fault lies with the winds and waves, for frequently we could not reach a single vessel for three days at a time.

It is said that the *Alabama* will positively sail this morning for New Orleans. If she does not, I will write again.

Yours, &c., &c.,

G. W. K.
*Daily Picayune*, April 9, 1947

---

75. Edward J. Steptoe, Third Artillery.

Vera Cruz, April 1, 1847

Although the result is not yet known it is generally conceded that the expedition to Alvarado will not meet with any enemy. Agents have arrived here from that place, this is most certain; and they say that the armed force there all fled on the capture of Vera Cruz being known. I started for Alvarado, intending to see the show there whatever it might be; but the vessel on which I was to go got off before I could reach her.

From the direction of the city of Mexico we have variety of rumors. All agree that Santa Anna has reached the capital, but the accounts conflict as to his present position and prospects. One report has it, that with a miserable remnant of his army he has joined the clergy, and is making headway against the stubborn Gómez Farías. Another and late report, is to the effect that Santa Anna, finding the clergy determined upon holding on to their rich property entire and of making overtures of peace to the United States, at once joined Farías, and was now bent upon seizing every penny belonging to the priesthood to carry on the war against the "usurping barbarians of the North." One thing is certain—all was anarchy and confusion at the city of Mexico five days since, and guns and bloodshed were the order of both day and night. Party was arrayed against party, faction against faction—all were by the ear, and there was neither head, tail nor body to the Government. The entire population, like the Ishmaelites, those "greasers" of old, were fighting and quarreling—each man's hand was turned against his neighbor. It is impossible to divine what all this will end in, unless it be in a state of affairs worse confounded than the present, if such a state can be.

There is of course a strong party—at its head the commissioned officers of the country—opposed to peace; for with that would go all their hopes of preferment, and, what is of more consequence to them now, bread. So long as the war continues, they are sure of a place in the army, and with it a chance to rob out of every dollar raised and extorted to carry it on. More unprincipled men have never existed; for, too cowardly to fight and win booty of their enemies, they content themselves with plundering their own people. Not one in ten of them has a spark of that patriotism which seeketh its country's good, all their vaunting to the contrary, and this extensive faction, the friends of peace have to contend with. The latter party is composed of the clergy, anxious to preserve the immense wealth and influence they have accumulated by fraud and humbug; the property holders, who fret at seeing their estates despoiled, and who are anxious to collect their rents; to these must be added a few honest, well informed men, conscious of their utter inability to contend with the American arms, and desirous of seeing an end put to a war which brings nothing to their country but additional disgrace. Which of these parties is to succeed in the end remains to be seen.[76]

We hear dreadful tales of the atrocities committed by the prisoners who laid down their arms outside the city on the 29th ult. and who were then turned loose upon the country on their parole. It is said they scattered in every direction, and are plundering the poor and defenceless inhabitants of the interior without hindrance and without remorse. The officers lay hands upon every horse and every mule, without money and without price, and the unfortunate devil thus despoiled is kicked if he utters the most feeble demurrer. The house as well as the garden of the poor laborer is entered by gangs of unorganized soldiers, his family insulted and his substance carried off. If he utters one word of complaint—his treatment is still worse, and he is fain to call upon his God for that protection his country and its laws are unable to afford him. Such is the present state of affairs throughout the country between Vera Cruz and the cities of Jalapa and Orizaba, for the former garrison has taken the different roads to those places, and words but feebly express and picture forth the desolation which is everywhere seen.

We have reliable intelligence from Puente Nacional up to yesterday afternoon. At that time, Gen. La Vega was there in command of 1000 men. They were deserting daily in squads, and he was shooting all he caught to prevent those who remained from running away. Many of the Mexican prisoners who left here had passed the bridge, and what tales they told of the strength and prowess of the American army! They will have it that our shells are filled with horrible combustible instead of powder, and cite the dreadful destruction they occasioned in the city in proof. Canalizo,[77] but without any force, had come down as far as the bridge, but immediately returned to Mexico. Gens. Morales and Landero had passed through La Vega's quarters, along with many other officers. They would prefer going to the United States as prisoners to accepting their parole, yet I believe they have given up the idea altogether. Col. Gutierrez even went so far as to ask a passage on the *Alabama*, and every arrangement was made for his departure; but a letter from his wife at Puebla, who was in great distress,

---

76. Kendall's characterization of Mexican politics was only vaguely accurate. In the spring of 1847, both *moderado* and church leaders, like their *puro* rivals, supported the war effort. By August, *moderados* and *santanistas* were looking for a negotiated settlement while *puros* clamored for the continuation of hostilities as a means to reestablish their political influence and to preserve Mexican national honor. Military leaders could be found in both camps.

77. Valentín Canalizo, commander of the Army of the East after Vera Cruz and a Santa Anna loyalist, directed the defense of Cerro Gordo before Santa Anna arrived.

induced him to change his course. In the meantime, so straitened are many of the Mexican officers, that they are fairly begging money of the Americans to get out of the city.

Gen. Worth, the new Governor of Vera Cruz, adopted most stringent and at the same time most appropriate police regulations. A large number of the Americans are already at work tearing down the barricades and opening the walls of the city—the latter for the purpose of letting fresh air into the streets. They say that several cases of the *vomito*, or yellow fever of the country, have already appeared; but I shall inquire farther before I give credit to the story.

Yours, &c.,

G. W. K.

*Daily Picayune*, April 10, 1847

Vera Cruz, April 2, 1847

We have not as yet heard from Alvarado, although there is no doubt the place is by this time in quiet possession of the American arms. This morning a detachment, composed in part of the 2d Dragoons, under Col. Harney, started for Antigua, an old town north of this, to take possession, and from this point reconnaissance will probably be made towards Puente Nacional and Jalapa.

From appearances, I do not think that Gen. Scott will march with the main army into the interior for some days to come. He is straitened to a degree for want of transportation, and it would be but bad policy to move until everything is in readiness. The lateral movements—those by way of Antigua and Alvarado—will have the effect of bringing all the horses, mules and subsistence in on both sides the main road to Mexico into the American camp.

In a letter I wrote yesterday I gave the rumor from the city of Mexico, brought by gentlemen direct from that place. I have also received a copy of the *Diario del Gobierno*,[78] of the 24th ult., which has been sent to you. The news from the city is various and contradictory, and I doubt whether the inhabitants themselves know what they are about, what they are contending and fighting for, or how all is to end. Heretofore the game has been more easily understood—there has been only one *pronunciamento* at a time: now there appears to be some four or five under full headway, and each new arrival gives a new phase to affairs in Mexico. The old man's explanation to his little son, of the power which set the steamboat in

78. Published in Mexico City, *Diario del Gobierno de la República Mexicana* had monarchist leanings.

motion, applies to all attempts to give a true picture of the present political state of Mexico. "Pa," said the juvenile, "Pa, what is it makes the steamboat go along?" The old man straightened himself, "My son," said he, pointing to the piston rod, "do you see that thing there going so?" and with his arm he worked an imaginary piston rod. "Yes, Pa, I see it." "Well," continued the old man, pointing to the shaft, "do you see that thing there a going round?" and with his arm he again made revolutions and worked an imaginary shaft. "Yes, Pa, I see that, too." "Then, again," resumed the anxious parent, "don't you see all them things a going criss-cross, and around, and whirling about?" "Yes," resumed the boy, "I see them too." "Well," continued the old man drawing in a long breath and attempting to look sagacious, "my son, those things all get mixed up and cranky, and the boat shoots ahead!" So it is with the political affairs, of Mexico—things here got "mixed up and cranky," and the revolutions go ahead. That is about all that can be said at present, from the light before us, of the condition of this distracted country.

Among others who have arrived here within the week are two or three gentlemen from Mazatlan. They say that both Upper and Lower California are in peaceable possession of the Americans.[79] They say nothing of the arrival of Gen. Kearny in California; but he might have reached Monterey, on the Pacific without their knowing it.[80] They speak of a boat belonging to one of our men of war having been upset, and that all on board perished. I shall endeavor to obtain further particulars.

The weather is excessively hot here in Vera Cruz, especially in the early morning, but about 10 o'clock a fresh sea breeze springs up, partially tempering the fierce rays of the sun. At night come myriads of mosquitoes, to say nothing of fleas, and except during the northers, I believe we were about as comfortable while out among the sand hills. As an accompaniment to the mosquitoes, as if they were not enough to drive sleep from any reasonable set of men, there is a rascally Mexican watch-

79. California south to Los Angeles was in American hands by mid-August 1846. An American-supported revolt against Mexican authority along the Sacramento River in June led to the creation of the Bear Flag Republic. The insurgents, under the command of John Charles Frémont, quickly extended their control into the San Francisco Bay area. Commander John Sloat occupied Monterey Bay in early July. Commander Robert Stockton, Sloat's successor, sent a contingent of marines and Frémont's volunteers south to occupy Los Angeles soon afterwards. They took the city, which had been abandoned by Mexican authorities, on August 12. Stockton then claimed California for the United States and named Frémont governor.

80. Having captured Santa Fe for the United States, Stephen W. Kearny left for California on September 25, 1846. He reached California early in December with a force of about one hundred dragoons. See Chapter Four, footnote 40, for Kearny's role in ending Californian resistance to American authority.

man immediately under our windows, who every half hour sings out in most doleful cadence, "Ave Maria purisima! las dos y sereno o unblado": "Hail, Mary most pure! it is 2 o'clock and the night is clear or cloudy," as the case may be. Now, this is all very well for a person who happens to wake up at 2 o'clock, or any other hour of the night, and is anxious to know the hour and state of the weather and does not care about rising to strike a light or poke his nose out of doors; but to one who does not care what o'clock it is, or whether it rains, blows, or what not, all this information is excessively ill-timed. From certain demonstrations I have seen made it is not very probable we shall be disturbed much longer by this particular fellow. All are willing to compromise with him—to let him off provided he will go off out of hearing—and the hints he has received already will have a tendency to induce him to change his beat.

Rations continue to be served out by our commissaries, to the suffering poor. They would else starve, and what the unfortunates would have done, had it not been for our timely arrival and succor, it is hard to tell. In the meantime, hundreds of Mexicans have been employed at $1.50 per day; yet few of them cared about going to work until they had received papers showing that they were *forced* into the service. They are fearful that when the Mexican authorities are reinstated they will be punished for aiding the enemy.

I doubt whether Vera Cruz was ever as quiet and peaceable as at present—it certainly was never as well governed. Gen. Worth has adopted a series of municipal laws and regulations, which are enforced to the letter, and I believe all are satisfied. Goods are coming in under the new tariff, the mole is a scene of great activity, and all is bustle.

I send you a copy of Gen. Scott's orders, as also other public documents. It will be seen that over four hundred cannon have been captured. Some of those in the castle of San Juan de Ulúa are magnificent pieces.[81] As for ammunition, all the magazines are full of it.

The ships *Arkansas* and *Louisville*, both of them reputed fast sailors, start this evening or tomorrow for New Orleans. I shall send letters and packages by each of them.

Yours, &c.,

G. W. K.
*Daily Picayune*, April 10, 1847

81. Some of the guns captured in the castle were Spanish pieces dating to the early eighteenth century.

Vera Cruz, April 2, 1847

I sent off a package of letters, papers, and documents by the ship *Arkansas*, and now write you a hasty sketch by the *Louisville*, thinking she may possibly arrive at New Orleans first.

All is quiet here. Gen. Worth, in addition to his commercial rules and regulations, has overhauled the police department of Vera Cruz, and everything goes on like a clock work. I doubt whether this city, from the days of the early viceroys down, has ever had as good a code of laws or as good a Governor.

In my letters by the *Arkansas* I neglected to mention the arrival of the British steamer *Tay*. She came in sight yesterday, and after backing and filling about for an hour or two, not exactly understanding the appearance of things about the place, finally came in. The captain was doubtless astonished to see the "stars and stripes" flying from the old castle of San Juan de Ulúa. This morning she started for Tampico.

A detachment, composed in part of Col. Harney's 2d Dragoons, marched this morning to take possession of Antigua, an old place some eight miles north of this. Gen. Scott will not march with the main command for Puente Nacional for some days to come, not having sufficient transportation to warrant an immediate movement; but he will take, or rather has taken, possession of the roads both right and left, in order to obtain supplies of all kinds from the country of the enemy.

Nothing has as yet been heard of the expedition to Alvarado, or at least nothing positive. There is a report that Gen. Quitman met with some resistance on the road, but not the least credit is given to the story.

Yours, &c., &c.,

G. W. K.
*Weekly Picayune*, April 19, 1847

Vera Cruz, April 4, 1847

The expedition to Antigua, under Col. Harney, returned yesterday, completely successful in every way. This side of the place, which is nearly eighteen miles distant by the route they were obliged to take, they found heavy trees across the road, and other obstruction thrown in the way; but the dragoons found a way through all, dashed into Antigua, and succeeded in capturing all the lancers then at the barracks. The main body of them were out reconnoitering, a lieutenant and some eight or ten men being all that were left. These were brought in by Col. H., together with a quantity of lances, escopetas, ammunition, horses, &c.

Those of the enemy who were out at the time evidently got wind of the approach of the dragoons, and succeeded in making their escape towards Jalapa.

Two of Col. Kinney's men came in this morning from Santa Anna's estate, Mango de Clavo, whither they had gone in search of cattle, &c. They found the hacienda, which is described as a rich and most beautiful place, entirely deserted—the doors all open, probably to prevent their being broken in, and the furniture and every valuable removed. The administrator of the hacienda they found concealed at a house two or three miles distant; and to this place he had taken many of the valuables of his master, to prevent their falling into the hands of the Mexican as well as American soldiers. From the information given by this man there can be no doubt that Santa Anna has thousands and thousands of cattle between this place and Jalapa, all of which can be driven in and sold to our army for a fair price. Strange state of affairs, this—Santa Anna making money out of the United States by providing its army with provisions, yet so it is. The "Napoleon of the South" is ever ready to make an honest (!) penny, and I have little doubt has all along considered that Gen. Scott's camp would make a most excellent market for his cattle, and what is more, has connived at their sale.

The accounts brought by Col. Kinney's men would go to show that La Vega had deserted Puente Nacional entirely, and has taken up and is fortifying a strong position at Cerro Gordo, this side of Jalapa. Here, notwithstanding the Mexicans are dispirited and deserting in consequence of the fall of Vera Cruz, La Vega was expecting reinforcements and aid from the city of Mexico and other parts of the interior. The party who bring this information, as they started last night from Mango de Clavo, were passed by some 300 lancers. The latter riding with all speed, scattering lances, escopetas and even their caps on the road. They had evidently but just ascertained that Antigua and some of their friends had been taken, and rode on in the direction of Jalapa as though they fancied Gen. Scott's entire force was after them. It is said that a son of Santa Anna is an active cavalry officer, and has been indefatigable from the first in raising men and taking measures to annoy our army.

Dates from the city of Mexico have been received a little later, but as yet I have been unable to get hold of a paper. From private accounts, notwithstanding their dissensions among themselves, all classes would appear to unite in denouncing every idea of a peace with the United States—the majority of them will not even listen to overtures until every hostile foot is removed from the sacred soil of Mexico. The mission of Atocha is scouted at.[82] Santa Anna, notwithstanding his disastrous defeat at Buena Vista, speaks with confidence of being able to raise an army every way strong enough to resist the advance of Gen. Scott upon the capital. They now talk boldly of bleeding, dying and being buried amid the ruins of the city of Mexico rather than have its streets and gorgeous palaces polluted by "los Yankees;" but as they were going to do the same thing at Matamoros, again at Monterey, and more recently here at Vera Cruz, and changed their minds when it came to the pinch, it is barely possible that some few of them may be left alive to tell of the surrender of the great city. It would be far better for the country if its officers would talk less and die more.

I wish to mention one fact that rather astonished me. I was passing a house in the ruined part of the city last evening, when a good-looking but scantily dressed woman accosted me for *limosnas* or alms, all to celebrate a grand *funcion* in the cathedral. Beckoning me to enter her house, she handed me a paper to read and pointed to a large plate of silver—half dollars, quarters, and dimes, for the most part American—which was lying on the table. The paper went to show that there was to be a solemn *funcion* or observance in the church, all to return thanks that the city had been surrendered to the Americans before the entire population was killed and the place entirely destroyed by the shells of the enemy;—and to raise money for this purpose they were calling upon the Americans! I helped to swell the fund to the extent of a dollar, and intend to have a sight at the performance as the worth of my money. The Mexican officers borrow money of the Americans, the hungry Mexican population clamor about

82. Spanish-born, naturalized American citizen Alejandro José Atocha met secretly with President Polk even before hostilities broke out, to promote the exiled Santa Anna as the person most likely to negotiate a resolution of the issues that had pushed Mexican-American relations to the crisis level. In January 1847, he returned to Washington with word that Santa Anna was prepared to discuss an end to hostilities and that California might be purchased for $15 million to $20 million. Atocha urged the Polk administration to send negotiators to Havana to meet with Mexican officials. Polk refused to take the initiative, his previous diplomatic initiatives having been rebuffed. Nevertheless, understanding the need to negotiate before the resumption of full diplomatic relations, Polk agreed to appoint peace commissioners once Mexico signaled its intention to do the same. Atocha carried that message with him when he arrived in Vera Cruz on a U.S. Navy revenue cutter. In Mexico City, he discovered that Santa Anna was in the north, preparing for battle with Taylor, and found acting president Gómez Farías struggling to retain political power. In an effort to gain political advantage, Gómez Farías, a longtime opponent of territorial concession to the United States, published an exaggerated account of the American demands and jailed Santa Anna's apparent emissary. Atocha returned to Washington in March with word that Mexico would send commissioners only after the United States had raised the blockade and removed its armies from Mexican soil. David M. Pletcher, *The Diplomacy of Annexation: Texas, Oregon, and the Mexican War* (Columbia, 1973), 477–81.

our commissaries' depots for bread, and now they ask us to defray the expenses of one of their observances or celebrations—I hardly know what they will want next.

I have said but little about the evacuation of this place by the Mexicans, on the 29th ult., because I have had little time. It reminded me more of the "Departure of the Ishmaelites" than aught else I can compare it to—the long procession of soldiers, national militia, and people of all classes and sexes as they poured out of the walls of the city set off as this is with huge, antique-looking domes, and other architectural ornaments. As at Monterey, there was the same throng of camp women, carrying every conceivable implement of ornament and use, especially of the former, to say nothing of innumerable parrots, poodle dogs, and other absurdities of a kindred nature. It is a singular fact that the poorer people in every country, the greater number of dogs they must have about them; but in no nation does the half-starved population affect the animal to the same extent as in this. There was one fellow in the procession that marched out of Vera Cruz that I particularly noticed. He certainly looked like a priest, both in garb and mien: but then as he had a fiddle in one hand and a fighting chicken in the other, it may be unfair to class him among the holy brotherhood. I shall not soon forget the man and his baggage at all events. The weather continues hot—insupportably hot in the middle of the day—but all my inquiries would induce me to believe that as yet there is little sickness among the troops. The report that the dreaded *vomito* had broken out was certainly premature. All think, however, that the sickness must appear in the course of a week or two, but probably not until Gen. Scott has moved onward with the main portion of the army.[83] If all Santa Anna's cattle are brought in, or only a portion of his immense herds, it will accelerate movements greatly. It is said that the *Edith*, or some other steamer, will leave for the United States tomorrow. You shall have another letter by her.

Yours, &c., &c.,

G. W. K.

P. S. I have just conversed with a very intelligent man—one who should know Mexico well. He says that the inhabitants in the interior, with the exception of a few of the clergy and proprietors of houses and lands, are farther from wishing a peace with the United States than ever. *Quien sabe?*[84] But I more than half believe him.

*Daily Picayune*, April 14, 1847

83. Scott had planned the attack on Vera Cruz recognizing that the army would have to be moved to higher ground before the yellow fever season began.

84. "Who knows?"

Vera Cruz, April 5, 1847

Alvarado, as everyone anticipated, was taken without firing a gun, and the squadron has returned to this place. Capt. Mayo has been left as Governor of the town with a small force, while Capt. Tattnall, in the *Spitfire*, has gone farther up the river to look in at the different towns. I learn that Gen. Quitman's brigade returns tomorrow, and I further hear that Lieut. Hunter, of the *Scourge*–the first vessel in at Alvarado–has been arrested by Com. Perry for going ahead of his instructions, or on some charge of the kind. Better be accused of going too fast than too slow, and I hope that in the present instance Lieut. H. can explain everything satisfactorily.[85] A great number of cannon and other military stores were captured at Alvarado, for there were no less than seven forts and batteries on the water side. It is said that Com. Perry has brought off everything of value, and I trust the report may be true. To my thinking all the more valuable spoils taken from the Mexicans should be carried to Washington City, or some other place in the United States where everybody can see them. There they can always remain as trophies of the American arms, and one of the most pleasant hours I have ever spent was in reading the inscriptions on the old Spanish guns we have captured from Mexicans, and which the latter have treasured as among the most brilliant results of their wars with the mother country. They are covered with figures and devices of most finished and elaborate workmanship, although some of them are more than two hundred years old.

I have been looking, among the lists of appointments for the ten new regiments,[86] for the name of Gen. A. S. Johnston of Texas. As yet I have not seen it, but I hope that so finished an officer, and one that fought so gallantly at Monterey as a volunteer, has not been overlooked. I know full well that long and distinguished services, gallant actions, meritorious conduct, thorough knowledge, and great experience in all military matters are considered by our Government as no claims to reward or promotion; but Gen. Johnston was not in the regular army, and as there was great need of his experience in putting the recruits into some kind of shape, I am really sorry that he was not given some command commensurate with

85. Charles Hunter pointlessly fired a few rounds at Alvarado on March 30, warning the inhabitants of the impending American attack from land and sea. The defenders destroyed their military stores and warships before evacuating the town and taking with them most of the area's livestock. Commodore Perry banished Hunter from the Home Squadron for his actions.

86. In December 1846, the Polk administration asked Congress to create ten new regiments of regulars. Delayed in Congress by partisan disputes, the legislation passed on February 10, 1847. The first recruits raised as a result of this legislation did not reach Scott until midsummer.

his great worth. A colonelcy would have suited him, and his regiment would have been the pride of the new levies—not an officer in the army who knows a musket from a mortar but will tell you that—but the appointment of such men must not be.

We are constantly in receipt of rumors from the city of Mexico—every man who arrives has some new tale to relate. The general impression is, that Santa Anna has succeeded in putting down Gómez Farías, after a great deal of fighting but little bloodshed. What his next movement is to be one cannot tell, yet there are many who think that he is disposed to carry on the war with the United States to the last. That Santa Anna and the leading minds of the country, especially among the higher classes of the clergy, know full well the utter folly of the contest, is certain; but that they can make headway against the swarms of hungry officers and malcontents, who only live by war and convulsions, is problematical.

It is now thought that the army will move forward in the course of a week at farthest, although without a sufficiency of transportation to take along many of what may almost be deemed the indispensables of a march. The great gales of the winter, the immense number of wrecks, and the losses of mules and wagons attendant, have crippled the resources of the Quartermaster's Department to a most annoying extent.[87]

Yours, &c.,

G. W. K.
*Daily Picayune,* April 15, 1847

Vera Cruz, April 6, 1847

Cols. Kinney and Banks, with Capt. Merrill's[88] company of 2d Dragoons, returned last evening from a scout in the neighborhood of Mango de Clavo. The country is full of cattle; but they are described as extremely wild, and difficult either to catch or drive. Some plan will be contrived to bring them over.

I have another report in relation to Santa Anna. I heard it stated confidently this morning that he had advanced as far as Puebla this way; that

87. Quartermaster General Jesup estimated that more than 9,000 wagons and 17,000 mules would be necessary to carry the nearly 3 million pounds of supplies that would be required by the army during the march from the coast to Mexico City. With the failure of the expeditions to Alvarado and Antigua, which were designed to provide mules from the Mexican countryside, Scott had only about a quarter of the 8,000 animals he deemed necessary to move his army inland.

88. Hamilton W. Merrill. Colonel Banks is not identifiable.

he was positively coming on to Jalapa; and that he would raise as many volunteers as he pleased. What he intended to do at Jalapa—whether to fight or to attempt to negotiate a peace—is not stated.[89] I give this as the last rumor up to this moment—8 o'clock, A.M.—before I close this letter another may reach. I saw Señor Arrangoiz,[90] the former Mexican consul at New Orleans, a night or two since. He had just arrived from Havana and had received a permit to proceed towards Mexico. He frankly told me he did not think his countrymen in the least inclined to make peace with the United States.

You may possibly receive rumors—for they are plenty here—to the effect that Capt. Thornton's[91] company of 2d Dragoons has been attacked and cut to pieces by the Mexican rancheros, and other stories of similar import in relation to the different parties that are scouting through the country. There is not a word of truth in any of these tales. Since the rout of the Mexican leaders near Madellin the dragoons have not been able to bring them to action. Young Santa Anna was near Santa Fé day before yesterday, but did not remain in the neighborhood long.

The "show folk" have arrived here. Hart and Wells, the theatrical managers, came in yesterday in the *New Orleans* from Tampico, and I presume will open tonight. The theatre here is a very neat and commodious looking building, with an ornamented front. One or two of our heaviest shells burst inside of it during the bombardment, shifting the scenery and decorations somewhat; but it is said that all can be repaired in a short time.

I read in the papers sad news from Santa Fé—the murder of Gov. Charles Bent and other Americans.[92] I have been anticipating some such outrage on the part of the rascally population of New Mexico for some time, although I thought that Bent knew enough of them, and would take all precautionary means to guard against a surprise.

The Government of Jalapa, it is said, has resolved not to make any resistance at their city whatever. The fate of Vera Cruz is before them—they

89. Santa Anna passed through Jalapa and arrived at his 88,000-acre hacienda at Encero on April 5. Hoping to prevent the American army from moving into the mountains and away from the threat of yellow fever, he selected Cerro Gordo as the place to block the route to the interior.

90. Francisco de Paula Arrangoiz y Berzábal.

91. Seth B. Thornton commanded the dragoons that were overrun by the Mexican Cavalry at Rancho de Carricitos in April 1846.

92. Appointed territorial governor of New Mexico in September 1846, Charles Bent was killed in Taos on January 19, 1847, during a rebellion challenging American rule along the northern Rio Grande.

know that the Americans will enter their beautiful place—and do not wish to see it destroyed. Sensible people, those of Jalapa.

Yours, &c.,

G. W. K.

*Daily Picayune*, April 15, 1847

Vera Cruz, Mexico, April 6, 1847—10 o'clock, A.M.

I have just seen a man who left the city of Mexico ten days since, coming by the way of Orizaba. He gives a most ludicrous description of the fighting at the capital. The Polka or Priest party have been in possession of the Alameida and other portions of the outskirts of the city, while the adherents of the Government have been quartered at the Palace. At 10 o'clock each morning the firing would commence, either party going up to their sand-bag barricades and banging and blazing away, promiscuously and miscellaneously, at anything, everything, and nothing—more especially nothing. The result of one month's hard fighting has been that one poor German watchmaker and a few innocent women and children have been killed or crippled—the belligerents have deemed it either imprudent or inexpedient to come in sight of each other. A more perfect farce has never been enacted.

My informant says that there are some twenty American deserters at the city of Mexico. They rendezvous at the ten-pin alley of a man named Hawkins and are in a most pitiful condition. There are also near one hundred American prisoners in and about the city—perhaps Major Borland's party.[93] It would seem as though there might have been some provision made these men after the battles of Buena Vista and Vera Cruz; but I do not learn that they have been thought of. (Mr. Kendall could not have known at the time he wrote, that Gen. Taylor did think of them after the battle of Buena Vista and that he made arrangements for their exchange and release. It was expected that they would have been delivered up at Vera Cruz before this time. —*Ed.*)

A body of 1000 men, horse and foot, left Puebla a week ago today, in the direction of Jalapa. They all talked right valiantly of driving the perfidious Yankees from their soil, but will think better of it when they meet with a few samples.

My informant met with many of the disarmed garrison of this place between here and Orizaba. They were telling wonderful stories of the size

93. Major Solon Borland, Arkansas Mounted Volunteers, surrendered approximately seventy men (mainly Arkansas volunteers) on January 23, 1847, at Encarnación, south of Buena Vista and about thirty miles from Saltillo. He and his men had been on a scouting mission intended to assess the strength of the army Santa Anna was moving into the area.

of our horses and the terrible effect of our shells. Little confidence will they inspire wherever they go.

It is thought the Mexicans intend making one of their bold stands this side of Jalapa. A few days will tell the story.

In haste,

G. W. K.

P. S.—I send you a copy of the *American Eagle*[94] of this morning. It contains a list of the killed and wounded during the siege, as also many other documents of interest. I have just learned that Santa Anna has reached Jalapa, but know not what credit to place in the report.

*Daily Picayune*, April 15, 1847

Vera Cruz, April 7, 1847

From Gen. Scott's order of yesterday, which I inclose, you will see that Gen. Twiggs's division of the army marches tomorrow morning.[95]

The entire force which garrisoned the different forts and batteries of Vera Cruz, with the castle of San Juan de Ulúa, was a fraction less than 6000 although under 5000 marched out and laid down their arms. As soon as it became known that the place was to be given up, more than a thousand of the regular soldiers are known to have dispersed themselves through the city, and after changing their clothes, marched out as citizens, or else are now living here.

In the meantime, those who scattered through the country, as I said in a letter written yesterday, are telling the most extravagant tales of the strength, size and prowess of "los Yankees." To justify their own defeat they spread the story through the country that our horses are four times the size of theirs, run twice as fast, and are not only savage in their nature, but are trained to run down, tread under foot, and completely annihilate their enemies. Our 10-inch shells they describe as being as large as hogsheads, filled with all manner of diabolical combustibles, make a noise in the air like the howling of a norther, and when they burst destroy and demolish everything around them. The effect of turning all these people loose upon the country, so long as they will continue to circulate such extravagant tales, must be advantageous. If they see fit, in order to hide

94. Founded by John Peoples, the *American Eagle* was the semiofficial organ of the U.S. Army. Peoples established like papers in Jalapa, Puebla, and Mexico City as the army moved inland, through arrangements with General Scott's command. Copeland, *Kendall of the Picayune*, 189.

95. This decision drew protests from General Worth, who thought his experience had earned him the right to lead the army inland.

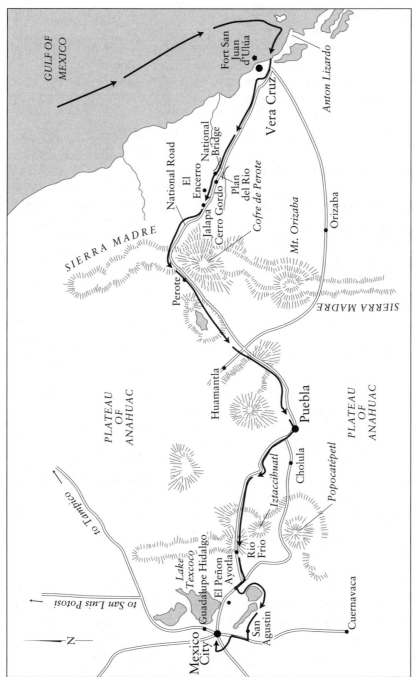

Scott's campaign from Vera Cruz to Mexico City.

the disgrace of their own defeat, to say that they have been contending with giants, centaurs, and the like, so much the better.

You must have noticed in the Mexican papers of late that the editors have ceased to term the Americans barbarians, infamous usurpers, and land robbers, and other complimentary names of kindred nature, and have settled down upon the epithet of *Yankees* as the most opprobrious of all. This is funny enough.

I said yesterday, in a letter sent by the *Edith*, that Com. Perry intended to capture every place on the coast of Mexico. The first move is to Tuspan. The fleet intended to operate against that place sail this afternoon or tomorrow morning. The next point will be Tabasco. I hear a report, but as to its truth I cannot certify, that the Governor of the latter place has sent a letter to Com. P., inviting the latter to pay him another visit! The commodore will be down upon him sooner than he anticipates, perhaps.

The capture of Alvarado by Lieut. Hunter, as well as the other points higher up the river, was a most laughable thing from first to last—a perfect farce in every respect. I may send you a description of it.

Yours, &c.,

G. W. K.

*Daily Picayune*, April 21, 1847

Vera Cruz, April 8, 1847

Not a line of news to communicate in addition to what I wrote you yesterday. Gen. Twiggs's division takes up the line of march for Mexico this morning, and the other divisions will follow immediately. We shall soon know whether the Mexicans are to fight this side of Jalapa.

The weather continues most uncomfortably hot—hot enough to suffocate one after the day breeze which comes from the sea goes down at night. As yet, however, there is no sickness of consequence among the troops.

In my next letter I am in hopes of being able to have some news of interest to communicate.

Yours, &c.,

G. W. K.

P. S.—Since writing the above, I learn that Santa Anna, on the 1st inst., either wrote a letter or issued an order breathing nothing but war to the death with the United States. This has been told me by an intelligent German gentleman. He says that there is a small party in favor of peace, but it is a mere fraction. I give this report as it was given me.

*Daily Picayune*, April 21, 1847

Vera Cruz, April 13, 1847

So many vessels are leaving almost every day that it is hard keeping the run of them. I send a line by every one I hear of.

A German gentleman has just told me—it is now 10 o'clock, A.M.—that Santa Anna was at his old hacienda of Encero day before yesterday. This place is close by Jalapa. Canalizo and La Vega are at Cerro Gordo, where no less than three heights have been fortified. Gen. Scott went out last night; Gen. Worth, with his division, marched this morning, and will bivouack tonight at San Juan, on the other side of Santa Fé. Gen. Twiggs is at Plan del Rio, close by the Mexicans, and there are those who think it more than probable that he has already had a brush with them. It is thought the position at Cerro Gordo can be turned, and in case La Vega and Canalizo make good their retreat that they will make another stand at Los Dios. Time will show.

The hospitals are full, and the sickness is said to be on the increase. I still cannot learn that there has been any well authenticated case of vomito, although many have died of fever. I am off today for the headquarters of the army.

Yours, &c.,

G. W. K.
*Daily Picayune*, April 23, 1847

# CHAPTER FOUR

# CERRO GORDO
## APRIL 14 – MAY 7, 1847

YELLOW FEVER SHAPED STRATEGY in both the Mexican and American camps after the fall of Vera Cruz. While Winfield Scott was anxious to move his army into the Sierra Madre before the dreaded *vomito* season began, Santa Anna hoped to keep his invading adversary boxed up in the low tropical coastal region. Scott set his sights on Jalapa, located some seventy-five miles inland on the great National Road that linked Mexico City to Vera Cruz. The city was 4,600 feet above the coastal plain and in a region reputedly friendly to the Americans. Santa Anna recognized the strategic importance of Jalapa, too. He ordered the newly formed Army of the East to block the route to the interior and the upland fever-free zone to the west. Reaching his hacienda at Encero east of Jalapa on April 5, Santa Anna selected the pass at Cerro Gordo to make his stand—a location he thought would be easily defended and one, if held, that would leave the American army exposed to yellow fever.

Scott's advance units, under the command of David Twiggs, reached Plan del Rio below Cerro Gordo on April 11, 1847, and began probing the Mexican emplacements in the well-fortified pass. As Scott and the rest of the army arrived and as plans for a frontal assault were abandoned, reconnaissance conducted by two young engineer officers, Pierre G. T. Beauregard and Robert E. Lee, revealed that the Mexican positions were vulnerable to an attack sweeping to the left of the defenders' batteries.

On April 17, George Kendall watched from a distance as troops under the command of Colonel William Harney took La Atalya, a strategically important summit on the Mexican left flank; the next day Harney pressed forward to take the summit of El Telégrafo near the Mexican base camp while units under the command of General James Shields and Colonel Bennet Riley skirted the mountain, flanking the Mexican camp and cutting the road to Jalapa. General Gideon J. Pillow's poorly led troops simultaneously attacked the artillery batteries that guarded the National Road, sustaining heavy losses even as the Mexican commanders surrendered when the road behind them was cut. The day ended with Santa Anna in retreat and his army in disarray.

Scott immediately pressed forward to Jalapa despite inadequate transport and uncertain supplies. Santa Anna, meanwhile, regrouped at Orizaba to the south while statements of determined resistance emanated from the Mexican capital. Scott immediately sent William Worth forward to occupy the city of Perote, notorious as the site where the Texans captured at Mier in 1842 had been imprisoned. The advance was intended to reduce the pressures for supplies around Jalapa and to increase the possibility of a rapid advance to Mexico City. Scott, however, finding that a third of his soldiers expected to return home when their enlistments ended in June, settled back into Jalapa and ordered more than 3,000 one-year volunteers to Vera Cruz early in May to ensure their departure before yellow fever swept the coast.

Camp at San Juan, April 14, 1847

I arrived in this camp at 11 o'clock last night, the road from Vera Cruz running for the most part through heavy sand. The division of Gen. Worth, from the excessive heat and wearisome road, suffered incredibly.

The news in camp is stirring. An express has come down from Gen. Twiggs to the effect that Santa Anna was before him, at Cerro Gordo, with 15,000 men, as near as could be judged from reconnaissance made by Capt. Hardee and other officers of dragoons. Lieut. Col. J. E. Johnston has been severely but not mortally wounded while examining Santa Anna's works, which appear to be a succession of breastworks on the eminences in the vicinity of Cerro Gordo.[1] Everything would now go to show that Santa Anna is determined to make a bold stand.

A dragoon, who had been sent down express by Gen. Twiggs, was yesterday found shot by the roadside just beyond this. His papers had not been touched. The Mexicans are playing a bloody and at the same time bolder game than is usual for them, as it is thought they have killed no less than fifty of our men within the last three days on the road.

---

1. Advance elements of Gen. David E. Twiggs's division arrived at Plan del Rio on April 11, 1847. Mentioned are William J. Hardee, Second Dragoons, and Joseph E. Johnston, Topographical Engineers.

Gen. Scott stopped last night nine miles from this—tonight he will reach Gen. Twiggs's position. If Santa Anna is as strong as he is represented, he probably will not be attacked for two or three days.[2]

I write in a great haste.

G. W. K.

*Daily Picayune*, April 23, 1847

Plan del Rio, Mexico, April 16, 1847—Evening[3]

Meeting Lieut. McLane of the navy this afternoon, at Puente Nacional and on his way here, I joined his party and rode over. Major Beall, with a small squad of dragoons, was also along with us. On the road, some six miles back, we came up with a forage party of the 2d Dragoons under Lieut. Anderson, and also Capt. Caswell's company of Tennessee volunteers which had been out after beef.[4] The latter had had a brisk skirmish with a party of rancheros, in which Capt. C. had two men wounded, one of them, a young man of great promise, named J. L. Roberson, badly. His thigh bone was completely shattered, and the poor fellow's sufferings were most acute as they bore him along in a wagon over the rough road. The Mexicans stood their ground in the chaparral with some little bravery at first, but were finally routed in every direction.

I find all excitement and bustle here. The Mexicans, under Santa Anna, are occupying a chain of works along the road, the nearest of which is about a mile and a quarter from Gen. Scott's headquarters in a direct line. The road this side is cut up and barricaded, and every possible means of defence and annoyance has been resorted to. Beyond the first work there are three or four others, completely commanding the gorge through which the road to Jalapa runs—these fortifications on hills, and rising so as to defend one another. It is thought that Santa Anna has 20,000 men with him—the lowest

2. Santa Anna arrived near Cerro Gordo on April 7 and took command of a fresh but inexperienced army he reported to number 12,000 men. Scott arrived there on the fourteenth, having left Vera Cruz after receiving reports from his commanders at the front that Santa Anna planned to defend Cerro Gordo. Worth's division advanced at the same time, after being delayed by the lack of transport.

3. This and the following dispatches from Plan del Rio were carried by Charles Bugbee, an express rider Kendall had brought with him from Vera Cruz. On April 19, Bugbee traveled by steamer and horseback, evading guerrilla bands during the six-hour, fifty-mile trip, to break the news of Cerro Gordo to New Orleans and the rest of the United States on May 1, 1847. Reilly, "American Reporters and the Mexican War," 277–80. Ralph Kirkham, an American officer newly arrived in Vera Cruz, noted that the news of Cerro Gordo arrived "by Kendall's Express, which is ahead of the government one." *The Mexican War: Journal and Letters of Ralph W. Kirkham*, edited by Robert R. Miller (College Station, Texas, 1991), 4.

4. Benjamin L. Beall, First Dragoons; Richard H. Anderson, Second Dragoons; and William R. Caswell, Tennessee Mounted Volunteers.

estimate gives him 15,000—and with these he has 24 pieces of field artillery, besides some 14 heavy cannon in position. Some of the prisoners and deserters from the enemy's camp even place higher estimates, both as to the number of men and guns.

To turn these different works a road has been partially cut through the rough ground and chaparral to the right; and although the reconnaissance is as yet imperfect, it is still thought that a point near the enemy's farthest work can be reached.[5] Gen. Twiggs, with his division, is to march at 8 o'clock tomorrow morning by the new road, and on the following morning it is thought the attack will commence on the works on this side. If Gen. Twiggs succeeds in reaching the rear of Santa Anna, and he will use every exertion, I do not see what is to save him. He is generally fox enough to have plenty of holes out of which to escape, however, and from the great difficulty of reconnoitering his position fully he may have some means of escape here. The general impression now in camp is that this is to be the great battle of the war; and the immense natural strength of Santa Anna's works would justify the belief.[6]

The Mexicans are more on the alert than they have ever been before, and more bold in throwing out their pickets. Not a party can go near their works without being fired upon, and yesterday a soldier of the 7th Infantry fell with no less than seven bullets in his body. It is said that Almonte is with Santa Anna, as also all the principal generals of the country.

Gen. Worth left Puente Nacional this afternoon with his division, and will be up during tonight. He started a little after 1 o'clock this morning, with near 2000 picked men, determined to make a forced march through; but learning on the road that the attack upon the Mexican works was not to commence as soon as anticipated, he returned to Puente Nacional after marching a mile and a half. Capt. Pemberton, one of his aides, rode over here last evening after dark, and returned with the information that the attack had been postponed.

The wounds of Capt. Johnston are doing well. I regret to state that Gen. P. F. Smith is confined to his bed—utterly unable either to ride or walk. He has a violent inflammation of the right ankle and knee, resembling erysipelas,[7]

5. Robert E. Lee discovered this route while on reconnaissance on April 15. The next day, engineers widened the path to enable Twiggs to deploy infantry and artillery forces on the seventeenth.

6. Kendall attended the April 16 meeting at which Scott laid out his plan of attack. Copeland, *Kendall of the Picayune*, 191.

7. Erysipelas, also known as Saint Anthony's fire, is characterized by fever and inflammation of the skin.

which from neglecting several days when he should have remained in his cot, has finally compelled him to lay up. I will write again tomorrow.

Yours, etc.,

G. W. K.
*Daily Picayune*, May 1, 1847

Plan del Rio, Mexico, April 17, 1847—8 o'clock, A.M.

Gen. Worth's division came up during last night and this morning, ready for anything that turns up. A section of the siege train, comprising two 24-pounders and an 8-inch howitzer will be along this afternoon. A subsistence train is also close by, and is very much needed as the army is nearly out of provisions.

Gen. Twiggs's division will march by 9 o'clock. The 1st Brigade, composed of the 1st Artillery, 2d Dragoons and Capt. Kinney's company of the 1st and the 7th Infantry, is under command of Col. Harney during the illness of Gen. Smith; the 2d Brigade consists of the 4th Artillery and 2d and 3d Infantry, under Col. Riley; and to these must be added Taylor's[8] battery and Talcott's mountain howitzer and rocket men, acting under the immediate orders of Gen. Twiggs. The latter company will probably have plenty of work on their hands, and this is just the country for their operations.

I have written this off so as to be able to send you an account of the operations thus far in case anyone is going to Vera Cruz. The road is now so much infested by small parties of the enemy that it is deemed imprudent for a single man to start, let him be ever so well mounted. If I have another chance to write today I shall improve it.

G. W. K.
*Daily Picayune*, May 1, 1847

Plan del Rio, April 17, 1847—11 A.M.

The division of Gen. Twiggs started two hours since, and a heavy cannonade has already commenced upon his line from the furthest of the Mexican works. At intervals, too, the rattling of small arms can be heard distinctly from the dragoon camp where I am writing this. I am going out, with Cols. Duncan and Bohlan[9] and Capt. Pemberton, to the seat of action, and will return here at night to report the progress of the fight. It was not intended, I believe, that Gen. Twiggs should open the fight today, at least

8. Francis Taylor, First Artillery.

9. Colonel Bohlan, who is not otherwise identifiable, may be Colonel Francis S. Belton, Third Artillery.

to bring on a general action, and it is therefore presumable the Mexicans have commenced upon him.[10] I write in great haste.

G. W. K.

5 P. M.—I have just returned from the scene of conflict, and a bloody one it has been, considering the number engaged. A hill this side of the furthest Mexican work, and on which there was no one seen last evening, was found occupied by the enemy's light troops this morning, and to force it was at once deemed indispensable. For this purpose the Rifles under Major Sumner, besides detachments of artillery and infantry, were ordered to charge up the rugged ascent. This they did in gallant style, driving the Mexicans, after a resistance which may be put down as most obstinate. Great numbers of the enemy were killed, while on our side the loss was also severe. Major Sumner was shot in the head by a musket ball—severely but not mortally: Lieuts. Maury and Gibbs, of the Rifles, were also wounded, but not severely, as was also Lieut. Jarvis of the 2d Infantry. I could not learn that any of our officers were killed. The entire loss on our side, in killed and wounded, is estimated at about one hundred; but from the nature of the ground—broken, covered with brush and thick chaparral, and extremely uneven—it is impossible to tell with accuracy. Nor can I, at this time, give even the names of the officers who were immediately engaged.[11]

About 3 o'clock the enemy made a demonstration from the fort on the neighboring height to the one our men had captured, as if with the intention of retaking it; but it all ended in marching down the hill, blowing a most terrific charge on their trumpets, firing a few shots, and then retiring. Their appearance, as they came down the slope, was certainly most imposing. The cannon on the height meanwhile kept up a continuous fire upon Gen. Twiggs's lines, yet doing little execution other than cutting down the trees and brush. As we returned to camp, the fire still continued—the enemy had evidently ascertained the position of the road, which had just been cut, with accuracy, but their balls principally went over.

Gen. Shields, at 3 o'clock, was ordered out to support Gen. Twiggs, with three regiments of volunteers—two from Illinois under Cols. Baker and

10. Twiggs's advance was not intended to provoke a major engagement with Santa Anna's forces. He had been ordered to occupy the summit of La Atalaya on the Mexican left and then wait for the rest of the American army to get into position.

11. Twiggs's troops took La Atalaya, meeting only modest resistance, then rushed down its far side and engaged the well-positioned Mexican forces on El Telégrafo. Most of the losses occurred as the Americans struggled to regain their defensible position on La Atalaya. Mentioned here are Edwin V. Sumner, Second Dragoons; Dabney H. Maury; Alfred Gibbs; and Charles E. Jarvis.

Barnett.[12] They will have warm work tomorrow, if the Mexicans stand up as they did today.

There has been not a little skirmishing today between the forage and beef parties, sent out in the rear, and the rancheros. One Illinois man was killed, and one of the same regiment and a Tennesseean wounded. I could not learn their names.

Tomorrow the grand attack, both upon the front and rear of the enemy, is to be made. Gen. Worth is to move at sunrise, and little peace will the Mexicans have for one twenty-four hours at least.

If possible I shall report and send off the progress of the conflict, although one has little time or convenience in the chaparral for writing.

G. W. K.

*Daily Picayune*, May 1, 1847

Camp near Plan del Rio, April 18, 1847—4 o'clock P.M.[13]

The American arms have achieved another glorious and most brilliant victory. Outnumbering Gen. Scott's force materially, and occupying positions which looked impregnable as Gibraltar, one after another of their works have been taken today, five generals, colonels enough to command ten such armies as ours, and other officers innumerable, have been taken prisoners, together with 6000 men, and the rest of their army driven and routed with the loss of everything, ammunition, cannon, baggage train, *all*.[14] Nothing but the impossibility of finding a road for the dragoons to the rear of the enemy's works saved any part of Santa Anna's grand army, including his own illustrious person.

Among the prisoners is our old friend La Vega, who fought with his accustomed gallantry. The other generals are José Maria Jarero, Luis

---

12. Shields took up positions on La Atalaya too late in the day to engage the Mexican forces. Among the units under his command were Illinois's Third and Fourth Regiments and New York's Second Regiment. Edward D. Baker commanded the Fourth Illinois, while Col. Ferris Foreman commanded the Third. No one named Barnett seems to have served in either regiment, although a William Barrett did serve as a first lieutenant in the Illinois Fourth. Kendall was probably referring to Colonel Ward B. Burnett, commander of New York's Second Regiment, a unit that also saw action at Cerro Gordo.

13. This dispatch was printed in the May 1, 1847, *Daily Picayune* as having been written at 1 p.m. The May 2, 1847, *Daily Picayune* reprinted the dispatch with the dateline April 13, 1847, 4 p.m. The actual date of the battle, April 18, and Kendall's comments about events occurring at 1 p.m. confirm the dateline provided here.

14. The complete rout of the Mexican army left, by official U.S. count, 199 officers and 2,837 men prisoners. Another 1,000 Mexican soldiers probably slipped away before they could be processed. American losses were relatively light: of approximately 8,500 men engaged, sixty-three were killed and 367 wounded.

Pinzon, Manuel Noriega, and José Obando. The names of the colonels I have not been able to gather. Nothing saved Santa Anna but the want of dragoons on the other side of their lines. As it is, his traveling coach, together with all his papers, valuables, and even his *wooden-leg*, have fallen into our hands, together with all the money of his army.[15] No one anticipated, when they arose from their hard bivouack this morning, such a complete victory.

The loss on both sides has been heavy—how could it have been otherwise? The rough and rocky road, cut through rugged defiles and dense chaparral by our troops, is now lined with our wounded. The Rifles, Col. Haskell's Tennessee volunteers, the 1st Artillery, the 7th Infantry, and Capt. Williams's company of Kentucky volunteers, have perhaps suffered most. Gen. Shields was severely, and I am fearful, mortally wounded, while gallantly leading his brigade to storm one of the enemy's farthest works.[16] Gen. Pillow was also wounded, although slightly, while storming a fortification on this side commanded by La Vega. All the field officers of Col. Haskell's regiment were wounded at the same time, save himself. Of the Rifles, Capt. Mason has lost a leg, Lieut. Ewell has been badly wounded, Lieut. McLane slightly.[17] I have already mentioned the gallant Maj. Sumner and other officers wounded yesterday.

I have specified some regiments above which signalized themselves: it happened to be their fortune, in the disposition of the battle, to fall upon what all good soldiers may term pleasant places—the most difficult works to storm—and bravely and without faltering did they execute the perilous

15. The Fourth Illinois seized Santa Anna's carriage and carried his spare cork leg back to Illinois as a war trophy. Santa Anna had lost his left leg after the defense of Vera Cruz against French invaders in December 1838. The fighting was part of the so-called Pastry War (*Guerra de los pasteles*), in which the French navy blockaded the port of Vera Cruz in an effort to force the Mexican government to pay claims owed French nationals. The conflict originated with the claims of a French pastry cook whose shop was destroyed by Mexican soldiers in 1828. Many, including Santa Anna, considered the effort to force the payment of claims to be a pretext for establishing the French monarchy in Mexico. The amputation of Santa Anna's leg had been particularly inept; two inches of bone protruded past the end of the stump. Oakah L. Jones, Jr., *Santa Anna* (New York, 1968), 76–79.

16. Shields, after leading his men around El Telégrafo, surprised the Mexicans at their base camp. He was shot through the lung during the assault. Colonel Edward D. Baker of the Fourth Illinois assumed command when Shields fell. He led the charge through the Mexican camp that cut the road to Jalapa.

17. Pillow mishandled preparations for his brigade's assault on the three batteries that guarded the right side of the Mexican line, causing heavy casualties among his forces. William Haskell's Second Tennessee Regiment lost nearly eighty men—the greatest number lost by an American regiment at Cerro Gordo. Mentioned here are Sherrod Williams, Third Tennessee Volunteers; Steven T. Mason; Thomas Ewell; and George McLane.

duties assigned them. At 1 o'clock this afternoon Gen. Twiggs, whose division has been in the hardest of it, was pursing the flying enemy towards Jalapa. Pinzon, who commanded the forts nearest Plan del Rio, asked of Gen. Worth time to consider before he capitulated. Desirous to come to terms, Gen. Worth gave him *fifteen minutes*, and he surrendered unconditionally! Had he not done so the slaughter would have been terrible.

I write in great haste, and have no time for particulars. The names of the killed and wounded I will ascertain as soon as possible.[18] I think that five hundred will cover our entire loss. Had it not been for the positive cowardice of Santa Anna and Canalizo, who ran, before the battle—at least in brave men's hands—was half lost, it would have been far greater. No one, at present, can estimate the loss of the Mexicans—they are scattered on the hills, in the roads, everywhere.

What disposition Gen. Scott is to make of the prisoners is yet unknown. He may set them all at liberty on their paroles, from the difficulty of feeding them, and to accelerate his own advance movements. We shall hear by tomorrow. I wish he could send the officers at least to the United States, for there is a fine string of them.

It is now impossible to name officers who have distinguished themselves. I cannot however omit to mention Cols. Harney, Riley and Childs, of the regulars; Cols. Baker, Foreman and Haskell, of the volunteers, as everyone is talking of them.

I write this in great haste, and with noise, confusion and everything else around me. You cannot appreciate the victory. To describe the ground and fortifications of the enemy, the difficulty of turning their outer works, and the toil and peril undergone by the troops were impossible.

No time to say another word. I send this off by an express. It is Gen. Scott's intention, I know, to push on towards the city of Mexico with all haste. Tomorrow I will write more fully, and send by Gen. Scott's express.

Yours,

G. W. K.
*Daily Picayune*, May 1, 1847

Camp at Plan del Rio, April 19, 1847—Forenoon

The rout of the Mexicans last evening was total—complete. They were pursued within four miles of Jalapa by Gen. Twiggs, at which point there

---

18. C. M. Haile accepted a first lieutenant's commission in April, leaving Kendall to take up Haile's practice of reporting casualties in detail. The lists prepared by Haile and Kendall, first published after the battle at Monterey, drew praise from the public. Government officials were more critical, fearing that casualty reports would dampen support for the war.

were none to follow. Santa Anna himself, instead of entombing himself as he threatened, escaped by cutting the saddle mule of his team from the harness of his magnificent evach,[19] mounting him, and then taking to the chaparral. His service of massive silver, nearly all his papers, his money—everything in his carriage, even to his dinner, was captured. I have a capital story to tell about this dinner when I have a moment to spare.

The Mexican loss upon the heights was awful—the ground in places is covered with the dead! Among the bodies found was that of Gen. Vasquez,[20] and near him was Col. Palacio, mortally wounded. Their loss in the retreat was terribly severe—every by-path is strewn with the dead. Had our dragoons been enabled to reach them in season, all would have been killed or captured—Santa Anna among them. Canalizo, with his noted lancers, had the prudence to *vamos* early.

Even up to this time it is impossible to give anything like a full or correct list of our wounded officers—it is surprising that many of them were not killed. Lieut. Derby, a gallant young officer of the Topographical Engineers, was badly but not mortally wounded while storming one of the heights. Lieut. Ewell, of the Rifles, is supposed to be mortally wounded. This regiment has suffered terribly. Lieut. Dana, of the 7th Infantry, was badly wounded; Capt. Patten, of the 2d, slightly. Lieut. Davis, of the Rifles, was very badly wounded in the hip.[21] Major Sumner, of the 2d Dragoons, but commanding Rifles is improving.

The list of killed and wounded officers in Col. Haskell's command yesterday I have been able to obtain. It should here be stated that Capt. Williams's company of Kentucky and Capt. Charles Naylor's company of Pennsylvania volunteers were attached temporarily to this regiment. Here is the list:

Killed—1st Lieut. Fred. B. Nelson, commanding company; 2d Lieut. C. G. Gill, Company E. Both these officers were from Memphis.

Wounded—Lieut. Colonel D. H. Cumming, slightly; Major Robert Farquharson, (of the 1st Texas volunteers, assigned to this regiment for the day) severely; 1st Lieut. Wiley P. Hale, adjutant, severely; 1st Lieut. Wm. Yearwood, mortally; 2d Lieut. James Forrest, slightly; Capt. H. F. Murray, severely; 2d Lieut. George T. Sutherland, Kentucky volunteers, severely. The regiment, when in action, numbered less than 400 men, and its loss was 79 in killed and wounded.

19. Kendall (or his printer) probably meant *vache*. It is a French word for the lid of a trunk that was part of a stagecoach.

20. Ciriaco Vasquez's command defended the summit of El Telégrafo.

21. Not previously identified are George W. Derby, Napoleon J. T. Dana, George W. Patten, and Thomas Davis.

La Vega was in command of the Cerro Gordo on the first day of the fight, but a deserter from our dragoons, a German, going into their camp at night, and informing them that the main attack was to be on the right of their line—the work so fiercely attacked by Gen. Pillow, he changed places with Gen. Vasquez. The latter, as I have already stated, was killed—La Vega defended his post until the lines of the enemy were completely turned. Several Mexican colonels have been killed, but their names I have been unable to learn. A brother of Gen. La Vega, a colonel of artillery, was severely, and, as is supposed, mortally wounded.

Hundreds of cases of individual gallantry, in storming the different heights, are mentioned. Col. Childs led on his command on the first day until he had only some forty or fifty men with him. It is also said that Capt. Magruder followed up a charge until he had but nine soldiers left. I cannot now recollect one-tenth part of the instances of almost reckless daring displayed, but shall endeavor to pick them up. I shall also send you on a full return of the killed and wounded if I can obtain it, but at present it is almost impossible to get hold of anything. The wounded are still along the roads for miles, although they are bringing them in as fast as possible.

The army is to advance towards Mexico immediately. Gen. Worth's division marched this morning—Gen. Scott is to march at noon. Santa Anna's coach is to be harnessed up for the purpose of carrying on Major Sumner—better use than it was ever put to before.

The officers and men of the Mexican army—I mean such as are prisoners—are to be turned loose on their parole not again to take up arms during the war. Perhaps it is the best disposition that could be made of them, as any other course would delay Gen. Scott's forward movement. Fifteen of their officers have refused to sign, but have given their parole of honor to report themselves, without delay, to Col. Wilson at Vera Cruz, as prisoners of war. Among these are Gens. La Vega and Jarero, the latter Governor of Perote during the time the Texan prisoners were there, and I believe distinguished for his good treatment of them. These officers will either be kept in the castle of San Juan de Ulúa, or else proceed to the United States.

Gen. Shields is still alive, but it is considered impossible for him to survive. The ball went through his lungs as he was leading his men to storm the farthest work of the enemy.

I write this amid confusion of all kinds, and with no other table than knees. A hundred Mexican officers are around me, making out their paroles, while our own dead are being carried by and consigned their long resting-place by the road-side.

I shall start on for Jalapa this afternoon, and will write by every opportunity. I send you some Mexican papers, as also Santa Anna's last proclamation. It is rich.

G. W. K.

P. S.–I have just learned that there is some hope for Gen. Shields. God
grant he may live.

Col. Baker, who charged on last fort, lost forty-five men in killed and
wounded out of only a portion of his regiment. Lieut. Cowardan, killed;
Lieut. Murphy supposed to be mortally wounded; Lieut. Johnson wounded
in three places, and thigh amputated; Lieuts. Scott, Froman and Maltby,
wounded.[22]

G. W. K.
*Daily Picayune,* May 1, 1847

Camp at Plan del Rio, [ca. April 20, 1847][23]

The storming and capture of the strong works on Cerro Gordo, by the
brigade under Col. Harney, may be looked upon as one of the most brilliant
achievements of the Mexican war–the fate of the battle turned upon it, and
here the enemy had placed an overwhelming force of his best troops. The
hill was steep and naturally difficult of ascent; but independent of this the
ground was covered with loose, craggy rocks, an undergrowth of tangled
chaparral, besides many small trees, the tops of which were cut off some
four or five feet from the ground, and turned down the hill to impede the
progress of the stormers. To climb the height at all, even without arms of
any kind, would be an undertaking that few would care about essaying:
what then must it have been to men encumbered with muskets and cartridge
boxes, and obliged to dispute every step of the precipitous and rugged
ascent? Murderous showers of grape and canister greeted our men at the
onset, and as they toiled unfaltering through a tempest of iron hail a heavy
fire of musketry opened upon them. Not a man quailed–with loud shouts
they still pressed upward and onward. At every step our ranks were thinned;
but forward went the survivors. When within good musket range, but not
until then, was the fire of the enemy returned, and then commenced the
dreadful carnage of the strife. The Mexicans held to their guns with more
than their usual bravery, but nothing could resist the fierce onset of the

22. George W. Cowardan, Richard Murphy, Sheldon I. Johnson, Robert C. Scott, Anderson
Froman, and Charles Maltby, all of the Fourth Illinois Volunteers.

23. This undated and unsigned dispatch is introduced as follows: "Mr. Kendall in one of his
letters gives the following account of the storming of Cerro Gordo." The dispatch focuses on the
events at El Telégrafo.

stormers. Over the breastworks with which the Mexicans had surrounded the crest of the hill they charged, and shouting attacked the enemy in his very stronghold. The latter now fled panic stricken, but still they were pursued: and it was not until the affrighted fugitives had reached a point with out the extreme range of their own cannon, which had been turned upon them at the onset, that they ceased in their flight. The national colors of our country now supplanted the banner of the enemy, the different regimental flags were also planted on the crest, and shouts louder than ever from the victors rose upon the air, struck terror into the very hearts of the enemy in the works still untaken, for they knew that their strong positions had been turned and that they were at the mercy of the men they had scoffed at in the morning. Never was victory more complete, although purchased with the blood of some of our best men. Lieut. Ewell, of the rifles, was among the first within the enemy's breastworks, and it was here that he received his death wound. The interior of the work was covered with the dead of the enemy, among them Gen. Vasquez, Col. Palacio, and many of their officers, while the hill side down which they fled was strewn as well. Near 200 men were left dead, while the wounded would swell the number to at least 500—some even put it down as high as 760.

The regiments composing Col. Harney's command, and which successfully stormed the noted Cerro Gordo, were the 1st Artillery under Col. Childs, the 3d Infantry under Capt. E. B. Alexander, the 7th Infantry under Col. Plympton, and a portion of the rifles under Maj. Loring.[24] Many cases of individual bravery, performed by subaltern officers, have been mentioned; but as I cannot particularly notice such as I have heard of without perhaps doing injustice to others equally meritorious, I shall forbear writing until I have more full information. I had almost forgotten to state that four companies of the 2d Infantry, under Col. Riley, took an active part in the assault.

[G. W. K.]
*Daily Picayune*, May 7, 1847

Jalapa, Mexico, April 20, 1847

Here we are at last, in one of the most delightful places in all Mexico.[25] As we came in this morning, along a road fringed on either side with the

24. Not previously identified are Edmund B. Alexander, Joseph Plympton, and William W. Loring.

25. On April 19, 1847, Scott's army advanced to Jalapa, a town of about 10,000 inhabitants renowned for its mild climate and beautiful women. He established a base of operations there while sending an advance guard under General Worth westward some thirty miles, through difficult mountainous terrain, to Perote. The Mexicans had evacuated Perote on the nineteenth, considering it indefensible.

richest vegetation, the white crest of Orizaba, piercing the very vault of heaven, was plainly visible, and a busy hum of admiration ran along the line as the snow-clad mountain first broke upon the view. A spectacle of greater magnificence or grandeur is not to be seen the wide world over. Here were we, in a soft, bland air, and with verdure and flowers of rarest beauty and fragrance all around—above us, as it were, towering to the very skies, yet in plain view, was old Orizaba, clad in his eternal raiment of snow. But this place has been so often spoken of and written about that I shall not dwell upon it.

Santa Anna entirely disapproved of the surrender of Vera Cruz of course, in proof of which he sent Morales and Landero to Perote for trial. They stand a most excellent chance of being liberated in a few days by Gen. Worth.[26] What is to be done with Santa Anna himself? how is he to answer, after swearing he would shed the *last* drop of his blood at Cerro Gordo, for running off without shedding the *first* drop? There is a question for somebody to answer.

I send you files of *El Republicano.* I also forward several copies of papers published at this place (Jalapa), previous to the great battle of Cerro Gordo. The exulting tone of the editors, and the perfect confidence they express in the ability of Santa Anna to arrest the progress of the "vandals," read funny enough now that the sequel is known. I cannot recollect anything more amusing than Santa Anna's flowing proclamation announcing his victory over Gen. Scott on the 17th April, unless it was his disgraceful flight on a mule on the 18th.

In the number, published on the day of the great battle at Cerro Gordo, and under the head of "*Long Live the Mexican Nation!*" the following account of the skirmishing on the 17th is given. It reads as follows, and is most decidedly fat:

> Yesterday, between 11 and 12 o'clock, a column of the enemy, composed of 5 or 6000 men attacked our position at Cerro Gordo. They came commanded by Gen. Scott, who, inflated or puffed up (engreido)[27] with the assassinations he committed with impunity at Vera Cruz, hoped with the same impunity, to penetrate our camp here. At the commencement of the firing, Gen. Santa Anna ordered our troops to retire, in order to attract the enemy to a point nearer our batteries. It had the effect. Scott advanced, and

26. When Worth arrived in Perote on April 22, he found Juan Morales and José Juan Landero—first- and second-in-command, respectively, at Vera Cruz—imprisoned in Fort San Carlos de Perote.
27. Haughty, petulant behavior.

then our columns displayed in such manner as to facilitate the action of our cannon. Then commenced a vivid fire of both artillery and infantry, encircling the enemy, who was obliged to retire; and having twice afterwards attempted to force our positions, he was twice compelled to retire. These three charges have cost the enemy 1000 men in killed and wounded: we have lost 160, of whom we count 30 as killed and the rest wounded.

[G. W. K.]
*Daily Picayune*, May 7, 1847

Jalapa, Mexico, April 22, 1847

The city is full of rumors again today, all of which I will try and throw into some kind of shape, although I cannot be answerable for one of them.

In the first place, it is said that Gen. Taylor has arrived before San Luis Potosí.[28] They do not assert that he has taken the city, but simply that he has arrived in the neighborhood and close by. Again, it is confidently asserted that the Mexicans intend leaving the road entirely open from this to Puebla, but at that city they intend making a stand and entombing themselves beneath its ruins before Gen. Scott shall enter it. They *talk* so much about burying themselves beneath their ruined dwelling, and *do* so little in that way, that one can place no confidence in them. Another rumor is that in a day or two we shall hear of a revolution in the city of Mexico against Santa Anna. This looks reasonable. It is now near three weeks since they have had a *pronunciamento* in Mexico, and it is high time they should stir up a fresh outbreak. Has anyone ever attempted to count the cost of one of these Mexican revolutions? We are not so far advanced in civilization, and consequently, having been relieved of the luxury of overturning a government every three or six months, know not what the expense is.

Of Santa Anna we can hear nothing. Some say that he passed on towards Mexico by way of Orizaba; some that he has hid himself in the mountains.[29] The infantry that fled with him is dispersed in every direction, the larger portion throwing away their arms to accelerate their flight. The cavalry got off in better plight, although Gen. Guzmán,[30] who commanded 2000 of them, could not get them to face about when pursued by

28. Taylor remained at Saltillo with an army increasingly restless and unruly from inaction.

29. Santa Anna retreated south to Orizaba and gathered around him an assortment of raw recruits, irregulars, and stragglers from the defeat at Cerro Gordo before marching to Puebla in mid-May to defend once more the route to Mexico City.

30. Sebastián Guzmán.

Gen. Twiggs with only 150 Illinois and New York volunteers so badly were they frightened.

The weather here is lovely, and I do not hear of sickness of any kind among the troops stationed in the city and vicinity. I wish you could be here just to inhale one breath of really fresh and pure mountain air, and take one such bath as they offer you here. The bath-house is situated in a romantic garden, and the rooms are none of your little cooped-up places, redolent of steam and mildew, but large and airy, furnished with couches and all appropriate furniture, and neatly got up in every way. I have some idea of trying to hire one for a sleeping apartment.

The stage left here this morning for the city of Mexico, with Gen. Noriega and other officers, recently released on their paroles, as passengers. Tomorrow I believe that a stage starts for Vera Cruz.

I have seen, and shall endeavor to obtain a copy of *El Monitor Republicano*[31] of the 13th inst. It contains a long letter giving an account of the battle of Sacramento, near Chihuahua, on the 28th February, and the capture of the latter city by the Americans. Even the Mexican letter writers cannot turn or twist the affair into anything save a most inglorious defeat. The Mexicans numbered, according to his account, 2500 men, under Gens. Trías and García Condé—the latter commanding 1200 cavalry.[32] Their strength in artillery was 10 pieces of different calibres, placed in strong works, but so impetuously did the Americans charge that they were routed at once. The name of the American commander is not given, but he entered Chihuahua on the 2d of March. The letter mentions that Samuel Owens, the wealthy and well known trader, was killed; but I hope it may not be true. The American force only numbered 1200, including wagoners.[33] All the cannon, arms, baggage, provisions, ammunition, money—everything the Mexicans had—they left in even greater haste than their valorous countrymen did their effects the other day at Cerro Gordo. Trías and García Condé

31. *El Monitor Republicano* opposed the monarchist movement but was not closely allied with either the *puros* or the *moderados*.

32. The fiercely anti-American Angel Trías Alvarez, governor of Chihuahua, served as second-in-command to General José A. Heredia, who at Chihuahua commanded a force of approximately 3,000 regulars and 1,000 rancheros. Pedro García Condé, who selected the point on the Sacramento River where the Mexicans made their stand, commanded Heredia's cavalry force of 1,200.

33. Col. Alexander Doniphan, fresh from the conquest of El Paso late in December 1846, led the First Missouri Mounted Volunteers and a six-gun artillery battery (a force of approximately 1,000 men), along with a band of three hundred civilian traders and teamsters commanded by Samuel Owens, south to Chihuahua in February 1847. On February 28 at Rio Sacramento, the volunteers outmaneuvered and outfought Mexican defenders and forced Governor Trías to abandon Chihuahua. Samuel Owens was the only American killed in the battle for Chihuahua.

had gone on towards San Luis, pretending that they were desirous to see Santa Anna and obtain reinforcements to return and drive back the usurping invaders from Chihuahua. Neither one of them could be coaxed or driven back to Chihuahua as long as there is an American there. If I can contrive to get hold of the paper containing the account of the fight, you must publish it entire. It is one of the richest and most laughable things I have read in a twelvemonth.

Yours, &c.,

G. W. K.

P. S. There is no mistake that the Castle of Perote has been deserted by the Mexicans, and not having time to carry off their heavy guns they spiked them before they left. The talk now is, that the enemy is to adopt the guerrilla system of warfare, besides making a regular defence at Puebla; and in addition to this they say that their cavalry will give us a regular battle between Perote and Puebla. There will be rare fun if they attempt the latter. Another thing I have just heard reported, and that is that the Mexican Congress has granted Santa Anna full powers to treat with the United States for peace. I give the rumor precisely as it was given to me.

G. W. K.

*Daily Picayune*, May 6, 1847

Jalapa, Mexico, April 25, 1847

We have news which is thought to be reliable of Santa Anna. A report came in this morning to the effect that he is at or near Orizaba, in command of some 5000 troops, and that he intends opening a guerrilla war in person, by following in Gen. Scott's rear and attacking none save small parties. This course he should adopt, most certainly; but whether he will do it remains to be seen. The height of Santa Anna's ambition is probably to capture some detached and half unprotected wagon train; and by magnifying some such sneaking operation into a grand and magnificent action and victory—he understands the process better than even any Mexican alive—he hopes to reinstate himself in the affection and good opinion of his people.

The Mexicans here, one and all, denounce Santa Anna for a coward, a traitor, and everything else that is bad; and I verily believe that a majority of them would rejoice exceedingly had Gen. Scott captured him the other day and hung him upon the first limb strong enough to bear his weight. That he is playing them false you cannot beat out of their heads—that he has sold the battles of Buena Vista and Cerro Gordo for a consideration they are equally confident, and in proof they are eternally talking about the $3,000,000.[34] They do not understand why it was that President Polk allowed him to pass freely into Vera Cruz from Havana, unless there was bribery and corruption at the bottom—the idea that our troops are a whit better than theirs, or that they can whip them, even two to one, when posted behind batteries, has never entered their heads—and hence, as a better excuse than none, there are many of them who say that they have been sold by the "Hero of Tampico."[35] Again, there are doubtless many—perhaps the larger portion—who have lost all confidence, either in his honesty, or bravery; and although they may not desire a peace with us, they are still anxious to get rid of the tyrant on any terms. Such is the state of feeling here in Jalapa.

I informed you the other day that I had a story to tell of Santa Anna and his traveling carriage. In his great haste to leave it he went off without taking any of his effects—a small writing case only was found broken open, for he had no time to unlock it, from which he had evidently taken a few papers of great importance; but the majority of his effects—his silver plate, his papers, his money—all were there in good condition. Two of our officers entered the coach, and what did they find, after rummaging about, but a most excellent dinner, together with delicious wine and some highly flavored cigars. To say that they did not sit themselves comfortably down on his richly cushioned seats, partake of his sumptuous dinner, wash it down with his delicious wine, and finish it off with his highly flavored cigars, would be departing farther from the truth than I care about doing just now. The names of the officers were Capts. Williams and McKinstry,[36] and the dinner was a perfect windfall after a hard morning's work without eating, and with slim prospects ahead for food. A party of dragoon officers, some two or three weeks since, also had their own fun near Santa Anna's estate of Mango de Clavo. While hunting about the premises, they stumbled upon

34. In February 1847, a Congress deeply divided over David Wilmot's proposal to exclude slavery from any territory acquired from Mexico approved James Polk's request for a $3 million contingency fund to purchase territory from Mexico.

35. Santa Anna had earned this title for turning back a Spanish invasion at Tampico in September 1829. In March of the same year, the Mexican Congress formally expelled all Spaniards. Anxious to protect Spanish subjects and resist this affront to his authority, Ferdinand VII ordered soldiers barracked in Havana to retake the region for Spain. The force of 2,700 under General Isidro Barradas easily took Tampico on August 1. Meanwhile, Santa Anna raised an army and cavalry in the vicinity of Vera Cruz and sailed north to meet the Spanish invaders. Failing to execute a surprise attack, he laid siege to the Spanish force in Tampico, forcing its surrender on September 11. Santa Anna accomplished no great military feat—far from its base of supply, the Spanish force had little choice but to surrender—but he emerged from the siege a national hero. Jones, *Santa Anna*, 49–51.

36. Probably Sherrod Williams, Third Tennessee Volunteers, and Justus McKinstry, assistant quartermaster.

the building where he kept his fighting chickens. Those well informed upon the subject tell me there was a great deal of cock-fighting in that immediate section for a day or two, and that one particular fight created great excitement. A fierce looking rooster which they dubbed Gen. Taylor—not so large as some but with game sticking out all over him—was pitted against a long, gangling chicken that they gave his owner's name to—a heavy but clumsy bird, with little fight in him. Well, Gen. Taylor and Santa Anna, as represented by the chickens of the latter, were set upon one another, and after a few heavy hits from the former the latter "bamosed" out of the fight as fast as his two legs would carry him, leaving Gen. Taylor's representative upon the ground crowing right lustily. Such are some of the accidents that have befallen the "Hero of Tampico."

I send you a copy of *El Monitor Republicano* of the 17th inst. which is the latest paper received from the City of Mexico. It contains a few facts but a deal more fancy. You will see that at the capital, on the 16th inst., they had it that Gen. Scott had retreated from Plan del Rio to Vera Cruz, as fast as he could, and that the Mexicans were congratulating themselves thereat. It did not seem to me that Gen. Scott was retreating at the time.

Gen. Worth still remains at Perote, where he has nearly 2500 men. Col. Martin Scott, with the 5th Infantry, arrived last evening from Vera Cruz, and will proceed to join Gen. Worth.

The first number of the *American Star* is out today, and is completely running over with news and information.[37] The proprietors deserve all success for their public spirit, and I am glad to see that their edition of this morning is going off rapidly.

It is still uncertain when a main movement of the army is to be made. The want of transportation is severely felt, for with his present means Gen. Scott finds the greatest difficulty in extending his line of operations. In the meantime, small parties of ladrones[38] and rancheros are committing depredations in the rear, and such is the nature of the country that they can only be punished with the greatest difficulty.

Yours, etc.,

G. W. K.

P. S. *Important! 10 o'clock, A.M.*—The diligencia or stage-coach is just in from the city of Mexico, from whence they have received papers up to the 22d inst. The news of the terrible defeat at Cerro Gordo had reached

---

37. John Peoples and J. R. Barnard published this semiofficial camp newspaper until May 13, when they moved it with the army to Puebla. Copeland, *Kendall of the Picayune*, 194.

38. Robbers or highwaymen.

the capital, and while it astonished and overwhelmed all classes, the tone of the papers, of the public men, and of the Congress itself, would also show that it had served to inflame the people still more against the United States. Anaya has been appointed provisional President, I believe, and has been gifted with full powers on every point except that in relation to making peace with the United States—this no one thinks of. Congress, in extraordinary session, has even declared anyone a traitor who talks of peace.[39] The editor of *El Republicano* says that we may take Puebla, that we may even capture the city of Mexico, but that there must be no peace. The duty of the people is to see their cities sacked and destroyed, and themselves immolated, before they talk of peace. The guerrilla system of warfare appears to be recommended on all sides as their only salvation: by this means they drove out the Spaniards, and in the same way they say they must expel the iniquitous, usurping and grasping North Americans from their sacred soil. Better all die, and be blotted from the seals of nations, than come to any terms so long as a single hostile foot is on their soil or a hostile vessel on their coast—such is the language of the papers, of the civil bodies, and of the military.

From a passenger, a Spaniard, who arrived in the diligencia, we learn that as yet they have done little or nothing towards fortifying Mexico. He also says that there is a strong party in favor of peace, although the members hardly dare avow themselves. There are no regular troops of consequence on the route, and all those who escaped at Cerro Gordo, with the exception of a portion of the cavalry, have dispersed in every direction. On the 20th April, immediately after the receipt of the news of Santa Anna's defeat, Gen. Mariano Salas called a meeting of officers to devise some measures by which to preserve the nation from utter obliteration. No one here thinks that the Mexicans can ever make another stand and give another grand battle, but the impression is prevalent that small parties will be organized to annoy the roads, cut off supplies, and kill all stragglers. How great, in this case, is the necessity for two or three, or even one regiment of Texans.

---

39. On April 20, the Mexican Congress granted provisional president Pedro María Anaya broad authority to carry on the war and declared that anyone who sought to negotiate with the United States was a traitor. The legislation was in direct response to news of Santa Anna's defeat at Cerro Gordo. It was also in part a reaction to Gómez Farías's inaccurate claim that the United States sought territorial concessions south to the twenty-sixth parallel, a line that stretched from Matamoros on the Rio Grande across northern Mexico and intersected with the lower quarter of Baja California.

The papers, so far as I am able to learn, say nothing of the movements of Gen. Taylor. In haste, as I am told an express is about starting for Vera Cruz.

G. W. K.

*Daily Picayune*, May 6, 1847

Jalapa, Mexico, April 25, 1847—Afternoon

I have borrowed the copies of *El Republicano* for an hour. They are dated at the city of Mexico, April 21 and 22, and the latter gives a full account of the battle of Cerro Gordo.

The Mexican particulars of the combat, as usual, are peculiarly rich. They say that Santa Anna sustained the combat with 6000 men against 14,000, and fought valiantly to the very last. When, finally, he found himself entirely surrounded by enemies, he *forced a passage* through "los Yankees" with a column of the 4th Regiment of Infantry of the line! The fact, as everyone knows, is that Santa Anna left early—all the cutting he did was to cut the saddle mule from his coach, and then cut and run.

The Mexicans admit that they had two generals killed, but give no names save that of Vasquez. Cols. Cosio and Calatayud are also named as among the killed. Gen. Scott's loss, on the 17th and 18th, is put down at over 4000, while the loss of the Mexicans is admitted to be 2000 men in killed and wounded. They say that the Americans fought like hordes of savages, killing all that presented themselves, whether wagoners, old men or women.

Gen. Canalizo is openly accused of bad conduct at Cerro Gordo. They say that when he should have made a charge, which would have been decisive, he withdrew with his cavalry—in plain terms that he ran.

Don Pedro María Anaya has been appointed temporary President (presidente sustituto). One of his first acts was to concede full pardon to all prisoners who have been confined for political offenses since 1821, an entire forgetfulness of the past.

Gen. Salas, who was President *ad interim* before the arrival of Santa Anna from exile, has issued a proclamation announcing that he is empowered to raise a guerrilla corps, and calls upon all good Mexicans to join his standard. In his concluding sentence he says that "war to death, without pity, shall be the device of the guerrilla warfare of vengeance!"

President Anaya has issued a grand proclamation to the Mexican nation, calling upon one and all to turn out to the rescue. He dwells particularly upon the achievements of their fathers—the fathers of the present generation—and earnestly petitions their sons to do likewise.

*El Republicano* of the 22d inst. contains a long list of those persons who have contributed voluntarily towards establishing a foundry for the casting of cannon. The same paper mentions the arrival at Orizaba of Santa Anna; but says nothing of the number of troops he had with him.

One of the best jokes in the Mexican papers is contained in the last paragraph of Anaya's address to his countrymen. He says that he "has the satisfaction to announce that his Excellency, Señor Don Antonio Lopez de Santa Anna, President of the Republic and General of the Army, according to notices just received, although not official, has survived the catastrophe (defeat of Cerro Gordo,) from which it appears that Providence is not willing to fill the cup of our bitterness entirely to the brim!" This is entirely too good to be lost.

Above I have given everything of public interest contained in the Mexican journals of the 21st and 22d inst. If Gen. Taylor had arrived at San Luis the editors would most certainly make some mention of it.

Yours, &c.,

G. W. K.

*Daily Picayune*, May 6, 1847

Jalapa, Mexico, April 26, 1847

We have intelligence this morning to the effect that Gen. Worth has advanced one of his brigades, with a battery and a troop of dragoons, to a place called Tepe Agualca, twelve leagues beyond Perote, to enlarge his circuit of supplies. You may hear that a party of dragoons has been cut off by the enemy at the other side of Perote, but there is no truth in the rumor.

By way of Chagres and Havana you have doubtless received the intelligence of Gen. Kearny's three victories in California, and of the entire subjugation of that country by the force under his command. Gen. K. was himself badly wounded, and three of his officers, Capts. Moore and Johnston and Lieut. Hammond, were killed.[40]

40. Having peacefully brought New Mexico under American authority, General Stephen W. Kearny left Santa Fe for San Diego late in September 1846 to assist with the conquest of California. On December 6, 1846, Kearny's troops attempted to surprise a significant force of Californians under the command of Captain Andrés Pico near the village of San Pascual, not far from San Diego. The poorly executed attack left Benjamin D. Moore, Abraham R. Johnston, and Thomas C. Hammond dead, along with fifteen others, and Kearny and twelve others wounded. Having failed to strike a blow against the Californian resistance and open the route to the coast, the Americans were left to wait for Commodore Robert Stockton to send a relief party from San Diego to rescue them. Stockton broke the Californian resistance with victories at the battles of San Gabriel and La Mesa on January 8 and 9, suffering light casualties, and took Los Angeles on January 10, 1847. Kearny established control in California by March 1847, having resolved a dispute with Commodore Stockton over who controlled the civilian government.

We already hear of depredations committed by the Mexicans on the roads. Even Santa Anna's son-in-law, who has the appearance of an American, was set upon, robbed, and maltreated most shamefully by his own countrymen the other night. The stage-driver, who brings this news, says that all the young man's protestations that he was a true Mexican were of no effect—he had light hair, blue eyes, and must needs be a Yankee. We also have a report that a number of recruits for the army, coming up under charge of Capt. Winder,[41] have been killed by the rancheros or guerrillas between this place and Cerro Gordo. If the alcaldes and principal men were held fully accountable and responsible for the acts of the people in the vicinity of the roads, we should soon hear an end of these outrages.

If possible, I intend obtaining a full list of all the officers under Col. Harney who took part in the noted and successful storming of Cerro Gordo. The name of the hill should also be placed on the colors of each regiment engaged. Words cannot describe the strength of the place, nor the immense difficulty, to say nothing of the danger, attendant upon storming it. It is said that Santa Anna remarked, the evening before it was captured, *"If the Yankees can storm this place they can storm hell itself!"* The 3d and 7th Infantry, under Capt. Alexander and Lieut. Col. Plymptom, went side and side; the 1st Artillery, under Colonel Childs, although stationed a short distance in the rear as a reserve, could not be restrained and held back, while many of the Rifles even left the position assigned them, and were "in at the death," if I can be allowed such an expression. Not a man who looks at the natural and artificial obstacles these men had to encounter, but must think they would deter and dismay the stoutest hearts; yet every man under Col. Harney pressed onward, as if determined to be first at the breastworks. The history of war can hardly show a parallel to the storming of Cerro Gordo. Col. Martin Scott went on this morning with the 5th Infantry, to join the division of Gen. Worth. The general impression now is, that Gen. Scott, unable to keep up his communications regularly through the *tierra caliente*[42] for want of horses and transportation, will cut himself loose from Vera Cruz, push on towards the city of Mexico, and to a certain extent depend upon the natural resources of the country. To establish depots and guards between Plan del Rio and Vera Cruz would expose the lives of hundreds of men—I mean during the sickly season—and would, besides, give the acclimated rancheros living in that section continual opportunities to rob and destroy the trains, as well as kill the few men who could be spared to protect them. There is hardly a half mile on the road

41. John H. Winder, First Artillery.
42. Warm or hot countryside.

that does not possess the best of cover for an ambuscade, and the great difficulty is that those who perpetrate an outrage cannot be pursued and punished. As soon as Gen. Scott's intentions are made known in relation to his future movements you shall be made acquainted with them—at present I can only give you camp rumors.

Yours, &c.,

G. W. K.

*Daily Picayune*, May 6, 1847

Jalapa, Mexico, April 28, 1847

The diligencia came in this morning from Perote, but from no point on the other side, as the Governor of Puebla has ordered it to cease running this way. Passengers came through, however, bringing papers and verbal news, and in as concise a form as possible I will give you the amount of the intelligence.

Among other rumors brought by passengers, is one to the effect that Mr. Bankhead, the British Minister, has renewed his offers of mediation between Mexico and the United States, and that when the last diligencia left the city of Mexico the Congress was acting upon his propositions, whatever they may have been. Notwithstanding the fixed and denunciatory tones of the public press, there is certainly a peace party in Mexico, and there may be something in this report of English intervention in the distracted affairs of Mexico.[43]

Col. Garland's brigade left the Castle of Perote yesterday morning at day-light for Tepe Agualco, and will reach that place tonight. Major Smith's[44] light battalion, a troop of dragoons, and Col. Duncan's battery accompanied Col. G. We learn here that Gen. Worth has been very successful in collecting supplies.

An intelligent man with whom I have conversed, says that the Mexicans neither will nor can make any opposition at Puebla. The population is one of the worst in Mexico, and the most inimical to strangers; yet the dreadful

43. Late in April, the Mexican Congress considered and then rejected, amidst strong *puro* opposition, an old British mediation proposal. *Moderados* continued to look for ways to find a negotiated settlement. A number of unsuccessful efforts were made to dissolve Congress in order to neutralize *puro* opposition. In mid–April, Foreign Minister Manuel Baranda suggested that British Minister Charles Bankhead raise the possibility of a truce with General Scott. When Bankhead refused to act unilaterally, Baranda asked him to transmit confidential peace proposals to the American command. Baranda, however, soon left the government, and probably no contacts were made. Pletcher, *Diplomacy of Annexation*, 506.

44. John L. Smith, Engineers.

defeat at Cerro Gordo has completely paralyzed them. At the city of Mexico, a few light breastworks have been thrown up, not only as you enter the place by the Vera Cruz road but on the road leading to the convent of our Lady of Guadalupe; but nothing like a regular system of defence has been as yet undertaken. Not only the Government but the citizens appear, with all their vauntings, to have become stupefied at the succession of defeats which have befallen their country, and know not which way to turn nor what to do. Santa Anna has written to the Government from Orizaba, stating that he has 1500 men, and wants reinforcements and money; but his demands have been unheeded. At the city of Mexico, as well as in other places, the people appear to have lost much of their confidence in the "Hero of Tampico," and many have openly accused him of cowardice at Cerro Gordo, as well as of having sold the battle to the Americans. I am living at the Casa de Diligencias, or General Stage House, and at breakfast this morning some of the foreigners were speaking of a body of men, under Gen. León,[45] who were on the march from Oajaca to join Santa Anna, and they also said that León had shot two muleteers on the plea that they had aided the Americans.

The Mexican *ladrones* on the roads appear to be more at war with their own countrymen than with ours, probably because they can purchase easier victories. Two Mexican officers who left here a few days since for the capital, both of whom were wounded, were set upon by banditti on the road, and not only were they robbed but one of them was severely maltreated. The news has also come in, well authenticated, that Capt. Aranjo, a marine officer, who commanded both at Vera Cruz and Cerro Gordo, was killed by an Indian three days since. He had abused the alcalde of the village, when one of the bystanders shot him dead on the spot. Aranjo was a noisy, blustering fellow, and his own countrymen do not appear to shed any tears at his loss.

A paper published at Puebla on the 24th inst., *La Verdad Demonstrada*, came to hand today. I could only obtain the paper for a short time, but long enough to see that the fierce wrath of the editor was fairly boiling over. He denounces the Yankees, he denounces every body that will not turn to and help him to denounce them. He pretends that there is a party in Mexico, headed by Rejon and Gómez Farías, who are for selling the great Mexican Republic to the North American vandals. The following is a translation of a short article in *La Verdad Demonstrada*, which is given as a specimen of the editor's thunder:

45. Antonio León.

By private letters we learn that the iniquitous *Puros* (the party of Farías, who are the Republicans or ultra Democrats) are anxious to raise another pronunciamento, and proclaim a union with the abhorred Yankees. Farías is at Toluca, (a city 18 leagues west of Mexico,) with the traitor Alaquibel, preparing measures for the enslavement of his country. Rejon is equally hard at work at the city of Mexico. The valiant soldiers of the battalion of Hidalgo arrested him the other day, but the Government has placed him at liberty.

The cunning dissimulator Señor Ibarra,[46] venomous as a reptile, crawls forth obscurely from his lurking-place today, in order that tomorrow he may plant his malignant teeth in the vitals of the Republic. All those spurious Mexicans wish to assassinate their country. Impious ones! May the anger of God confound, and the popular indignation exterminate them!

Long live independence and liberty! Off with the heads of the vile traitors! May they die, to wash out with their blood the infamy they would bring upon this poor nation! and let us all prepare for a universal uprising, which, like an electric fire, will consume and devour the Yankees.

Whew! one has to take a long breath after reading this. What the editor is driving at it is difficult to divine; for the idea that either Farías or Rejon wish to sell their country is perfectly preposterous, at least to the Americans. Ibarra has been Governor of Puebla: Olaguibel,[47] I believe, is still Governor of Toluca, and there is not one of these men who holds other than the most cordial hatred to the United States, if their past acts are to go for anything.[48] It may be that the editor wants "something to tear," and is prudent enough to take hold of men who for the present are politically dead.

Majors Borland and Gaines, Capt. Clay, with the other prisoners taken at Encarnación some months since, are said to be at liberty in the city of Mexico.[49] No less than six of the party, as it is reported, have already been assassinated by the Mexicans.

Señor Atocha, who came out from the United States with some propositions of peace, or something of the kind—it turned out to be a species of fool's errand, at all events—catches it severely in *El Republicano* of the

---

46. Domingo Ibarra, governor of Puebla and the Mexican foreign minister in the summer of 1847.

47. Francisco M. de Olaguibel was governor of the state of Mexico.

48. Manuel Crescencio Rejon, Ibarra, Olaguibel, and Gómez Farías were all allied with the *puro* faction and had reputations as fervent Yankeephobes.

49. John P. Gaines and Cassius M. Clay, both of the Kentucky Cavalry Volunteers, were captured with Borland near Encarnación.

19th inst. The editor, in an article headed "Don Alejandro Atocha," goes on to say:

> This man has arrived at Vera Cruz. This circumstance is more aggravating than any misfortune that has befallen us in our war with the Americans. The losses which we have suffered, the affairs of Palo Alto, la Resaca, Matamoros, la Angosturas, fatalities or misfortunes occasioned by whatever cause, were occurrences to be found in the regular order of events; but the arrival of Atocha in Mexico, and his intervention as a negotiator of peace, confers upon us the greatest stain, the greatest contempt, and the greatest degradation. Atocha was here in certain times of pilfering and immorality; he made a rapid fortune, such as are made under cover or under the auspices of certain cabinets; he was exiled and proscribed, in the year 1844, as an enemy of the national representation, as a traitor, and as an exciter of revolt. He had the shamefacedness to return to Vera Cruz in February last to propose a peace, was despised, and now, after the loss of Vera Cruz, he presents himself again with the same object. This is the worst that can happen to Mexico! Atocha, the immoral pimp of the heartless leeches of times past, comes as the broker of a peace which Mexico is asked to make! Oh! God! this is the greatest sign that thou hast forgotten us! Send upon us bombs, rifles, grape shot, and every class of projectiles and misfortunes; burn us, reduce us to ashes, destroy us—these annihilate but do not dishonor us; send the entire North to subjugate and rule over us, but let not Atocha be the broker of a contract of peace, because that, involving upon us the greatest scorn and the greatest humiliation, would be, oh! God! thy greatest punishment!

Now, this is all very well. The sending of such a person as Atocha to this country—a man universally hated and despised by all save a few Government stock jobbers—was certainly most humiliating to the people here, and anything but calculated to open a door for a peaceful settlement of difficulties; and hence no one can blame the editor of *El Republicano*, or any other editor, for openly speaking their minds in relation to such an agent. But the writer in *El Republicano* has neglected to inform us on one important point. He speaks of "certain times" and "certain cabinets." Why did he not come out openly and say that Atocha's partners and friends were Santa Anna and some of his ministers? and why did he not come out at once and say that these men employed Atocha to do *their* dirty work, and help *them* out in their peculations to defraud the poor Government? No, they throw everything upon the shoulders of Atocha, because some of his former associates are still in power. All this, however, does not shield from blame those who sent Atocha here—the very last man who could bring about a reconciliation—unless the intention was still farther to exasperate the people of Mexico.[50]

*El Monitor Republicano* of the 21st inst. contains Gen. Taylor's address to the inhabitants of Tamaulipas, Nueva Leon and Coahuila, in relation to the outrages committed by Urrea. The editor contends that all Urrea's acts were honorable and legitimate, alludes to the bombardment of Vera Cruz as an offset to any acts of the Mexicans which may be construed into atrocities, and speaks openly of the barbarities of Scott and the despotism of Taylor.[51] (*Las barbaridades de Scott y el despotismo de Taylor.*) I have no time to send you a translation, for the article is very long, but cannot say that the editor handles his subject very ingeniously.

It is difficult sending to Vera Cruz since the outrages commenced upon the roads. I think I shall send you a package of letters and papers tomorrow by stage, however, although I may wait for a regular wagon train.

Yours, &c.,

G. W. K.
*Daily Picayune,* May 6, 1847

Jalapa, Mexico, April 29, 1847

At 12 o'clock today—it is now evening—I sent off a large package of letters and papers to Vera Cruz by the diligencia. It is thought there is great danger of its being attacked and robbed on the road; but as, if it gets through at all, it will arrive two or three days before the regular train, I conceived the better plan to be to run the risk. The news, although interesting, can be condensed into a few words: Santa Anna is no doubt at Orizaba with a small but ill-appointed force, and it is reported that Gen. León, with a body of fresh troops, is on his way to join him from Oajaca. "Old Santy," as the volunteers call him, has written to Mexico for money and reinforcements, but has been refused. He is now held in worse esteem than ever, many believing that the "three millions" are all going into his pockets, and that he sold the battle of Cerro Gordo for a portion of this sum. No resistance, everyone says, will be made at Puebla, and at the city of Mexico

50. The Polk administration had been divided over the merits of entrusting Atocha with an unofficial overture to the Mexican government. Santa Anna's absence from the capital upon Atocha's return doomed what was in any circumstance a risky venture.

51. General José Urrea had a reputation for brutality that he had earned during the war of Texas independence. Under orders from Santa Anna, he executed 350 Texans at Goliad in March 1836. During the winter of 1846–47, troops under his command regularly attacked American soldiers and teamsters in raids against Taylor's supply trains between Monterey and Camargo.

they have only thrown up slight breastworks and at last accounts were doing nothing. Their recent disastrous defeats, although they talk as vauntingly as ever, have completely paralyzed and stupefied all classes. Gen. Worth is at Perote, although he has thrown forward Col. Garland's brigade as far as Tepe Agualco. He is rapidly accumulating supplies at the former place. Such is the substance of the news I sent you this morning.

This evening another express has come in from Gen. Worth. He has received information, which comes from sources that may be looked upon as authentic, to the effect that Canalizo, with 3000 cavalry, has gone towards Orizaba with the intention of joining his old friend Santa Anna. An attempt upon one of Gen. Scott's depots or wagon trains everyone believes is intended, and every movement of the enemy in this quarter certainly gives color to this belief. In the meantime Gen. Worth is still further strengthening his supplies at Perote, and has made contracts for a large quantity of corn. An onward movement of the army will doubtless soon be made.

In the first paragraph of this letter I neglected to state that there is a rumor here that Mr. Bankhead, the English Minister at Mexico, has again offered his mediation to settle the differences between the United States and Mexico, and that at the last dates from the capital the Mexican Congress were acting upon his propositions. Some of the better informed inhabitants here certainly give credit to this report.

The greater portion of our wounded have been brought here and are doing well: there are also a large number of wounded Mexicans scattered about the city. The reported loss of the latter at Cerro Gordo is 1500—it was certainly immense. Gen. P. F. Smith is still confined to his bed, but is improving; the wound of Major Sumner is also getting better; although slowly. Gen. Shields continues in a favorable situation, notwithstanding it will be a miracle if he survives. I saw him but a few minutes after he was wounded, and at the time did not conceive it possible for him to live twenty-four hours.

The weather in this beautiful place continues delightful—nothing can exceed the delicious temperature of the climate. This afternoon we had a thundershower, serving to render the air more pure and balmy, if such a thing were possible. Col. Childs is governor of the city, and a New England village is hardly more orderly and quiet than is this same Jalapa.

Since this letter was commenced, a report has come in that Santa Anna has been made prisoner by his own men. The rumor is very vague and indefinite. He has enemies enough, to judge by their talking, to tear him in pieces if they could lay hold of him.

I have little doubt that an English influence is at work at the city of Mexico to bring about a peace, and it is equally probable that there is a party in the country disposed to listen to overtures. How peace is to be brought about is more than anyone can say—what terms we could offer that would be acceptable will be found a difficult matter by any commissioners that may undertake the job. To defeat the Mexicans in every encounter is easy enough—to settle all differences and disputes with them will be found an entirely different matter.

Yours, &c.,

G. W. K.

*Daily Picayune,* May 11, 1847

Jalapa, Mexico, May 1, 1847

I wrote a long letter this morning, which I shall send off by a regular train which leaves tomorrow under an escort; but learning that one of Col. Kinney's men is to run the gauntlet between this and Vera Cruz tonight, or at least that he is to attempt it, I scratch off a few lines to send by him. Enclosed you will also find the last orders issued by Gen. Scott. I might give you the exact time he is to move, the garrison he is to leave behind, and other intelligence; yet as it might all fall into the hands of the Mexicans I shall wait for some safe and certain opportunity.

A rumor was rife last evening which would be startling were any credit to be attached to it. A nephew of Santa Anna, residing here in Jalapa, has circulated a story to the effect that Urrea and Canales, by a forced march, have surprised and retaken Tampico from the Americans. The news, he says, came express to Gen. De Soto,[52] residing near here. It may be that the whole story has grown out of the capture of Tuxpán by Com. Perry.[53] The Mexicans make strange blunders sometimes.

Hart's theatrical company arrived last night and will open the neat theatre here tomorrow evening. This is another step civilization has taken westward.

At last accounts Santa Anna was near Orizaba, and with the force that had joined him under Gen. León had near 3000 men.[54] Some say that he is anxious to get out of the country, but the better informed believe that he intends making a descent upon Gen. Scott's rear, and by the capture of a

52. Juan De Soto Ramos.

53. Perry destroyed the fortress and captured the town at Tuxpán, the last Mexican fortification on the Gulf Coast, on April 17, 1847.

54. By the first of May, Santa Anna had drawn under his command at Oaxaca a force between 2,500 and 4,000, which included a brigade under the command of Antonio León, national guard forces, and an assortment of irregulars and conscripts.

wagon train, or some feat of the kind, attempt to reinstate himself in the affections of the people.

We have no later intelligence from the city of Mexico. Until the diligencias were ordered to cease running between Puebla and this place the papers came through regularly, but now, if any intelligence reaches Jalapa, it falls almost exclusive into the hands of the Mexicans, and there it lodges. Rumor has it that they are running their bells into cannon, both at Puebla and the city of Mexico, and farther that they will make a grand stand somewhere between the two cities, with a rabble of at least 100,000 men, collected any and every way. The more of this species of force Gen. Scott has to contend with the better.

I have been round this morning among some of the wounded officers. Lieut. Derby is improving, as is also Lieut. Maury. It was at first thought that the latter gallant young officer would lose one of his arms, but all fears have now subsided. Lieut. Ward[55] is mending rapidly, and will soon be up again. Visitors are not allowed to call upon Gen. Shields, yet strong hopes are still entertained that he will entirely recover.

The guerrillas are fairly at work, or you will doubtless have learned ere this direct from Vera Cruz. A party of French ladies who have arrived here, and who were along with the train attacked two days since, give a very animated account of the action. One man only was killed on our side, a volunteer, and he lost his life while charging the hill where the guerrillas had posted themselves. The French party is on its way to the city of Mexico, but it is in no particular hurry about starting just now. Never was there a time when the services of a regiment of well mounted Texans was as much needed as the present—were they here, on the road, the Mexicans would soon become even more sick of the guerrilla system than they now are of regular fighting.

I shall write you, "hit or miss," by every opportunity that offers, but fear that the chances of sending letters will be few and most precarious.

Yours, &c., &c.,

G. W. K.

P. S.—Since writing the above, the celebrated courier for the English merchants,[56] Rafael Beraza, has arrived from Mexico with letters for the British packet at Vera Cruz. He says but little, yet it has leaked out that

---

55. James N. Ward, Third Infantry.

56. The reference is probably to the English merchant house Manning and Mackintosh. Ewen C. Mackintosh was British consul general in Mexico City and closely allied with the Santa Anna government. See Chapter Six for more details concerning Mackintosh's role in the diplomatic maneuvering that coincided with Scott's military campaign.

they are organizing guerrillas rapidly in both Mexico and Puebla. All the robbers in the latter city, and their name is legion, have received regular licenses to rob and murder on the road. The beauty of the system has already manifested itself, for it is said they have already commenced plundering their own people on the roads.

In haste,

G. W. K.

*Daily Picayune*, May 11, 1847

Jalapa, May 2, 1847

By the diligencia, which leaves at 12 o'clock, noon, I send you a copy of the *American Eagle* of this morning. You will see that news has been received from the city of Mexico, brought by extraordinary courier. The slight fortifications should have been placed this side the capital instead of Puebla, as at the latter it has been determined upon not to make any resistance.

Gen. Bravo,[57] with the whole or a part of the garrison of Puebla, was met going up to the city of Mexico—Canalizo was met this side of Puebla by the courier. He had a cavalry force with him.

Some say that Santa Anna has fallen back upon Oajaca, but nothing certain of him is known.

Gen. Patterson's brigade, which is to march in a day or two, has been reduced to two brigades instead of three, the 1st under Col. Campbell of Tennessee, and the 2d under Gen. Quitman. Col. Haskell's regiment of Tennesseeans is to remain here as part of the garrison. The 3d and 4th Illinois Regiments, under Cols. Foreman and Baker, have been joined to Gen. Quitman's brigade.[58]

A surgeon dentist, named Kingsbury, was found this morning, most horribly cut to pieces on the road to Cerro Gordo. His groans first attracted the attention of some volunteers who were passing, and they found him with little life and completely fly-blown, although it is thought he may recover with proper attention. This is the commencement of the guerrilla system. He had been attacked by three Mexicans, and was robbed of $500. The appearance of the volunteers who brought him in did not indicate any great indulgence to such Mexicans as might fall in their power.

57. Nicolás Bravo, a hero of Mexican independence, served two brief terms as president, the second in 1846.

58. On April 30, Scott ordered these volunteer units to prepare to move toward Puebla on May 4 and 5. The orders were countermanded a few days later when few volunteers were willing to extend their enlistments for the duration of the war.

Col. Bohlen will leave for the United States, tomorrow, and by him I will send a large package of letters.

Yours in haste,

G. W. K.
*Daily Picayune*, May 11, 1847

Jalapa, Mexico, May 3, 1847–11 A.M.

I closed a letter to you early this morning, thinking the train was to start immediately; but Col. Bohlen having been delayed a few hours I have time to forward another.

We have no farther news from the city of Mexico, yet an intelligent Spaniard informs me that the most unparalleled distress prevails among all the poorer classes there. All the employees of the Government—the secretaries, clerks, and all who depended upon their salaries for support—are literally starving. They have received no pay for months, and are fairly obliged to beg the food with which to maintain life. Gaunt distress stalks through every street and thoroughfare, and even the better disposed are compelled to steal or call upon charity to save them from starvation.

Poor, and most unhappy Mexico! and what is to be the end of all this? Without an army, without military appointments, without resources of any kind, disorganized, disunited, every one of thy ports in the hands of the Americans, hemmed in on all sides and completely shut out from all communication with the fair world, there is nothing left to thy inordinate pride and a willful shutting of the eyes to thy utter incapacity farther to contend with a power morally and physically times innumerable thy superior. Of what avail are all thy vauntings and thy boastings? Why continually speak of thy Hidalgos, of thy past achievements, of the great prowess of thy chiefs? Will not the evidence of a dozen disastrous defeats convince thee of thy utter inability to continue a war which is daily sinking thee lower and lower in the scale of nations? Wilt thou blindly and perversely continue to shut thine ears against all proposals of an honorable peace?

If this war continues another year, and is prosecuted with that vigor which it becomes the United States to press it, there will be nothing left of Mexico but a name, and that not of the proudest. Torn by every species of intestine commotion—with a debt which it is impossible to pay—with a priesthood that still clings to the shadow of a power, and still draws sustenance from the starving mouths of its benighted and ignorant followers—with all her cannon and her military stores gone—with a horde of base and indolent officials still about her and preying upon her vitals—with all these, and many other evils, no one can see anything but the utter extinguishment of the Mexican power. How is she to begin the world again? Where is the virtue, the stern integrity, the true love of country, and that utter absence of self in her rulers that can raise her again even to the false position in which she stood before the war? These are questions left for the wise to answer.

Enclosed, in this hasty letter, you will find a sketch of Cerro Gordo, and of the position of the two armies previous to the battle. It was drawn by Lieut. J. P. McCown, of the 4th Artillery. It gives one a very correct idea of the Mexican batteries, and of the position of their different works.

Yours, &c.,

G. W. K.

*Daily Picayune*, May 23, 1847

Jalapa, May 4, 1847

Orders and counter-orders. This morning Gen. Quitman's brigade of volunteers was to take up the line of march towards Puebla, and tomorrow Col. Campbell was to move; but as the time for which many of the volunteers enlisted has nearly transpired, and as Gen. Scott has ascertained positively that but few of them will reenlist, he has determined upon disbanding them here, and will send them all home.[59] This will of course not only delay but alter his whole plan of operations, and the impression with many is that he will go no further than Puebla with his present force. You in the United States may think that he has an overwhelming power with him, and that he is fully able to run at will all over the country; but the truth is, that in the first place he did not have half men enough to advance upon the capital of Mexico, nor half transportation enough even for what he had.

The volunteers going home are the Georgia, Alabama, and 1st and 2d Tennessee Regiments. No one can blame them for this movement. Not only is their time out, but they are out of clothing and out of many of the comforts which make even a camp life bearable. They have seen service, too, enough to satisfy any body of men not intending to make military life a business, and now are retiring to their homes to see their wives, children, families and friends, and tell long tales of what they have seen and what they have suffered.

Had Gen. Scott a force sufficient to leave garrisons and keep up a regular communication with his rear, and then march directly upon Mexico

59. On May 6, 1847, General Patterson led back to the coast about 3,000 volunteers whose enlistments were due to expire during June, to prepare for their return to the United States. Having been unable to persuade these soldiers to extend their enlistments for the duration of the war, Scott was left with a force of just over 7,000 men.

with a fighting force even of 6 or 8000 men, the war would be ended in
one month's time, at least so far as this country would be able to make
farther resistance of any moment; but such a force he has not at his command just now. He may still go on to the capital, even with what he has,
for there are not Mexicans enough in arms to arrest him; yet whether such
a course would be prudent, or whether such are his intentions or not, is
more than anyone can say who is not thoroughly into his secrets. Had our
Government laid out a few extra dollars and called but a few more men in
the outset, this war would have been over by this time; but greatly to our
cost the "penny wise and pound foolish" system of economy must prevail,
and millions are added to the national debt as a consequence.

There is a rumor that Santa Anna with a large force intends attacking
the next upward train, which will have a heavy amount in specie. It will
be a costly experiment to him, for the wagons will be guarded by a force
sufficient to keep off every firelock in Mexico.

This letter goes by the diligencia, and I must tell you that it is considered anything but a safe conveyance.

Yours, &c.,

G. W. K.
*Daily Picayune*, May 11, 1847

Jalapa, Mexico, May 6, 1847

Many of the newspapers are finding fault with Gen. Scott for reducing
Gen. Taylor's strength so materially in the early part of last winter, but to
my thinking they do the former injustice. It may not be generally known;
yet I still believe it to be strictly true, that when President Polk decided to
change the base of operations from the Rio Grande to Vera Cruz, it was
arranged at Washington City that Gen. Scott should place Gen. Taylor on
the *defence*, and strictly so, until the new volunteers should reach him; and
I believe it to be equally true that Gen. Scott, in withdrawing troops from
Gen. Taylor, indicated the whole plan, and distinctly placed the latter on
the defensive, according to the plan arranged and approved at the seat of
Government.

Well, what was the result? Gen. Taylor, in his defensive position, was
assailed by Santa Anna, and with an immense force. Grant, now, what no
man denies, that Gen. T. gained a brilliant, a most glorious victory—bestow
upon him all the laudation that language can express, for richly does he
deserve it—yet still it must be admitted by everybody that the result fell
precisely *within* the plan arranged at Washington, so far as Gen. Taylor on
the Rio Grande frontier was concerned. Nothing has occurred on that line

to discredit the judgment, by whomsoever exercised, by which the hero of the Resaca and of Monterey was placed on the defensive, and by which he was enabled to add another glorious triumph to the American arms. The emergency was certainly greater than anyone anticipated when Gen. Worth's division was taken from him, yet the result shows how well he was able to cope with it.

On the other base, also, there has been the most complete and brilliant success. Vera Cruz and the noted castle of San Juan de Ulúa have been captured, through an application of the *science of war*, by which the most important results have been surely and securely accomplished. The stronghold, too, of Cerro Gordo has been stormed and taken, and Santa Anna has been twice discomfited and overthrown when he vainly hoped that victory was within his grasp. The whole plan has succeeded, then, both on the Rio Grande base and on the new base of Vera Cruz; and what ground there is of censure anywhere, either in the disposition or withdrawal of troops, is more than I can discover.

Let us examine a little, let anyone now go back and consider the probabilities when Gen. Taylor's force was weakened. It was then universally known that Gen. Scott was to assail Vera Cruz, an undertaking requiring veteran and tried troops. His communications to Gen. Taylor fully declared his object to be the reduction of Vera Cruz: those communications, by the murder of the unfortunate Lieut. Richey, fell into the hands of the enemy, and what then was naturally expected?[60] That Santa Anna would move up in full force to drive Gen. Taylor from an unimportant part of Mexico? Not at all. The universal, or the almost universal expectation was, that he would move a body of his best troops rapidly down to the protection of the principal jewel in the defences of the Mexican Republic. He had it in his power to move either way, and who could tell in what direction he would himself move? He chose, as the sequel shows, to leave Vera Cruz to its fate, fearing the regular troops drawn from the Rio Grande frontier by Gen. Scott, and to fall upon Gen. Taylor with the hope of obtaining a cheap victory. This contingency, though not probable, was still supposed possible from the first, and the result of the battle of Buena Vista, as before observed, was entirely within the calculations made at Washington in the fall of '46, which Gen.

60. Lieutenant John A. Richey of the Fifth Infantry had been ambushed and killed on January 13, 1847, while carrying a copy of Scott's orders to move Worth's regulars from Saltillo to Vera Cruz. This mission was necessary because Taylor, anticipating that Scott intended to deplete his command, avoided a direct meeting. Scott had summarized his entire strategy in writing, and it fell into Santa Anna's hands with Richey's ambush. Kendall was correct in concluding that Santa Anna's knowledge of the American strategy informed his attack on Taylor at Buena Vista.

Scott merely carried out with his best judgment. There is really, then, no ground of complaint in any quarter, but honor is due to all who have brought about the success which has crowned the whole plan.

It is a little singular, that while complaints like the above have been made in all quarters, we hear hardly a murmur about the great want of transportation that has been felt from the time when Gen. Taylor first crossed the Rio Grande. Any sensible and reflecting man in the army will tell you, without hesitation, that notwithstanding the brilliant achievements of our troops within the past twelve months—it will be one year next day after tomorrow since the battle of Palo Alto was fought—that twice as much towards the entire conquest of the country would have been effected had either Gen. Taylor or Gen. Scott been in a situation to pursue their successes. The latter, after the battle of Cerro Gordo, had not the means of subsisting his own troops, much less the prisoners taken; and no other course could be pursued than to turn all the latter loose upon the country. To follow up the fugitives who fled with arms was impossible, simply because he had no subsistence train. Everyone knows, who knows anything about the Mexicans, that a rout among them is like a *stampede* among cattle or horses. To attempt to rally the former would be as difficult as to turn or arrest the flight of the latter when the fright is upon them— neither stop this side of sheer exhaustion—and with the scare the illustrious descendants of the great Hidalgo[61] then labored under, they might have been driven all the way to Acapulco without once turning to fire a gun. The whole history of the retreat of those who fled at Cerro Gordo, the giving up of La Hoya and of the celebrated castle of Perote without resistance, proves this. By this time, too, had our army been in a situation to follow up its splendid victory, the American flag would have been flying from the palace in the city of Mexico, and the *morale* upon the country would have been tremendous. As it is, the Mexicans have time to collect their scattered senses; and although it is hardly probable they can ever make another such stand as they did at Cerro Gordo, they can still procrastinate and hold off, and involve our Government in millions of dollars of expense which might easily have been saved.

And where is blame to attach for all this? It will not hold with any of the agents of Government, for with them responsibilities are so easily shuffled off that all can clear themselves. Go to the lowest subordinate in any department of our Government, complain to him that this or that thing is wanting, and he will refer you to the next grade above him, the

61. Miguel Hidalgo y Costilla led a Mexican uprising against Spanish authority during the first decade of the nineteenth century. He was executed in 1811.

next to the next highest, the next to next, and so on until it reaches the President, who will very likely refer the whole thing back to the people. In this respect our Government is weak—the whole system reminds one, to use a rather homely comparison, of a dog chasing his tail—the end is never reached. A most niggardly economy—a continual counting of the almighty dollar—also creeps into every expenditure; months are consumed by Congress in raising new regiments when weeks should suffice, and millions after millions are lost in the procrastination which is sure to follow the attempt to save as many thousands. But enough of this for the present—to the little news stirring.

A move upon Puebla, an immediate move, is now contemplated. Gen. Quitman, leaving the 2d Pennsylvania Regiment here as part of the garrison, marches tomorrow with the New York, the South Carolina and the 1st Pennsylvania Regiments to Perote, where he will join the division of Gen. Worth. After placing a garrison in the castle of the latter place, composed probably of one of the volunteer regiments, Gen. Worth will then march at once upon the rich and beautiful city of Puebla, the second or third in size in the Republic. It is not thought there will be the least resistance made there, but some of the amiable inhabitants of the place have let out that they intend adopting a new plan. They say that they will open all the pulque and liquor shops in the city, and that when all the American soldiers get well scattered and well intoxicated, they intend falling upon them with knives and massacreing them to a man. This is certainly a most charming plan, and deserves just about as much credit as Capt. Bobadil's[62] did for destroying our army. The Poblanos will probably wait some little time before Gen. Worth gives them any chance of the kind, and it will go hard with them if they make any kind of resistance.

After Puebla is taken it is impossible for those not in his secrets to tell what Gen. Scott will do next. He may move towards the capital without waiting for reinforcements; but shorn as his army has been of all the older and better drilled volunteers, it is hardly probable that he will go this far unless it is well ascertained that the road is open and can be kept so. The latest accounts from the city of Mexico would induce the belief that they have no military force there except for guard purposes, and that all was anarchy and confusion. Some were for peace, others for war, while perhaps the larger portion, staggered by their reverses, did not know what they wanted. What a misfortune that Gen. Scott did not have 5000 addi-

---

62. The reference may be to a Colonel Badillo who commanded one of the artillery emplacements that defended the National Road on the right flank of the Mexican line.

tional troops immediately after the capture of Vera Cruz, with a sufficiency of transportation to move all directly upon the capital. At this very day, to all intents and purposes, the Republic of Mexico would not have been but a dependency of the United States, and any war she could have continued to wage would not have amounted to as much as did the Black Hawk campaign.[63] A deal of work does our Government cut out for its commanding generals, but it never gives them cloth enough to make it up.

The different volunteer regiments to be disbanded are starting off for Vera Cruz today, and all will be on the road by tomorrow. It is to be hoped they will be on board vessels before the *vomito* sets in, for, with what some of them suffered on the Rio Grande last summer, with hard marching, with exposure to all sorts of weather, and with fighting enough to satisfy any reasonable men, they have seen quite enough—quite their money's worth. The system of twelve months' volunteering is a most absurd one—of enlisting men for a term just long enough to make good soldiers of them, and then giving them their discharge very likely, as in the present instance, when their services are most needed; but the volunteers are not to blame for this.

They appear to be more quiet on the roads. Since the horrible attempt to murder Dr. Kingsbury no outrage has been committed that has been known. The wounds of Dr. K. are improving, and all say he will recover.

Yours, &tc.,

G. W. K.
*Daily Picayune*, May 19, 1847

Jalapa, Mexico, May 7, 1847

In a letter written yesterday, and which went off last night by private conveyance, I gave you all the news up to that time. The departure of the stage this morning gives me an opportunity of sending you another item.

A Mr. Gallagher, a man who has traded a good deal in this country, was missed by his friends about a week since, and the general supposition was that he had been murdered. Last night he came in, and gives a most interesting account of his capture and detention by the Mexicans. He was taken by a party of rancheros near Paso de Ovejas, and after narrowly escaping with his life, and after being robbed of nearly everything he had, was finally escorted to Orizaba. He did not see Santa Anna there, but says that he was reported as near by and with a force of 5000, which was

63. Between April and August 1832, the Sauk and Fox under Chief Black Hawk battled regulars and volunteers in Illinois and Wisconsin Territory over land that the Indians sought to reclaim, in what became known as the Black Hawk War.

rapidly increasing. Many of the soldiers he himself saw, and one of the officers to his sorrow; for the latter robbed him of everything the rancheros had left him. To make some amends for this, however, he connived at Gallagher's escape. The latter was near the spot where the Mexicans attacked the wagon train last week, a prisoner at that time. He says that the rancheros were very much disappointed because all our men did not run off immediately and leave the wagons.

Gen. Quitman, with three volunteer regiments, leaves this morning for Perote, and on Monday at farthest it is thought that Gen. Worth will take up the line of march for Puebla.

The weather here has been damp and showery for the past week, and colds and sore throats have followed. I cannot learn, however, that there is much sickness in the hospitals. The wounded continue to do well.

Yours, &c.,

G. W. K.
*Daily Picayune*, May 19, 1847

[Jalapa, Mexico, ca. May 7, 1847][64]

A Ruse de Guerre.[65]—With the Rifles, a portion of the 1st Artillery and one company of the 7th Infantry, this dashing officer had in the morning driven the Mexicans from two hills which were overlooked by their strong work on Cerro Gordo, but which were still important. This had been effected with great loss, and so many had been detailed to carry off the wounded and take care of the dead, that in the afternoon the colonel found himself with but a mere handful of men to protect and sustain the position he had won with so much difficulty. About 2 o'clock in the afternoon the Mexicans made a tremendous demonstration as if to retake the heights. Happening to be in a valley directly between Col. Harney and Cerro Gordo, whither a few of us had gone, under cover of the trees and brushwood, to obtain a good view of the Mexicans on the latter hill, we had a most excellent opportunity of seeing the whole movement. A furious clang of trumpets first announced that the enemy was in motion, and soon we could see a long line of infantry marching down the steep hill side and making directly for the height now occupied by Col. H. and his small but gallant band. With such tremendous fury did the trumpeters blow their instruments, that one unused to them would have thought that they alone

64. This dispatch has no dateline, but it follows one dated May 7, 1847, and is titled "Anecdotes of Cerro Gordo."

65. An account of Col. William Harney's role in the defense of the summit of Atalaya on April 17.

were sufficient to drive every Yankee completely from the heroic and sacred soil of Mexico. Onward still they came, and onward; louder came the blasts from the trumpets, as doubtless give themselves courage, as they neared the spot where they knew they would meet with war to the death. The position was all-important to them, and a host was on the way to attack it. Soon they reached a spot almost within musket range, and while they had halted a moment to form, to recover their wind, and collect and strengthen their nerves for the coming struggle, Col. Harney improved the occasion to play off a regular trick upon them. His men were partially concealed behind the brow of the hill, yet he himself was in plain view of the hostile host; and now he commenced a harangue which would have served for an army of 20,000 men, appointed every way with cannon, with cavalry, with mortars, and with all the appliances of war. "Don't shoot yet!" shouted he to his little band, and his lungs are none of the weakest; "wait till they come closer, and then give them h–ll! Don't draw a trigger, I tell you—double charge those cannons, there, with grape and canister, and wait till I give the word: I don't want one of them ever to get back alive!" In this strain he went on interlarding his battle speech with a few more of the strongest kind of adjectives than I care about repeating. The effect was glorious. Not a word of the harangue, which might have been heard a mile, was lost upon the Mexicans, not a quarter of that distance off; and as some one of them understood English, and at once interpreted the speech, especially about double loading the cannon with grape and canister, to the commanding officer, he very prudently wheeled his men and marched back the way he came without firing a gun! It is needless to say that Col. Harney had nothing in the shape of a cannon with him—it was the strongest kind of a "bluff game" he was playing and the sequel shows that he won at it.

Lieut. Reno.—During the same afternoon Lieut. Reno, with two of Talcott's mountain howitzers, did not a little execution by pitching grape and spherical case into the Mexicans. The latter are most destructive, and after one or two doses of them had burst upon the retiring column of the enemy, it was noticed that their pace improved materially.[66]

The 3d and 7th Infantry.[67]—On the following day, at the storming of Cerro Gordo, the leading men of the 3d and 7th Infantry reached opposite sides of the circular breastwork of brush the Mexicans had erected to protect their main fortification on the crest of the hill. The enemy had all

66. In their enthusiasm, Harney's forces rushed up the slopes of El Telégrafo after taking Atalaya. Jesse L. Reno's howitzers covered their retreat from the top of Atalaya.

67. An account of the storming of El Telégrafo on April 18.

been driven with loss from this outer work, and the victors had halted for a few moments to collect their breath and wait for those who were more exhausted to come up preparatory to the main attack upon the stronghold, when Lieut. Clitz, of the 3d, saw some of the men of the other regiment clambering over the breastwork. "Hurra! 3d!" he ejaculated; "over and at them or the 7th will be in first," and together the two gallant regiments went at the Mexicans. It is necessary to say that from his position Lieut. C. was the first to notice the movement of the 7th. It is said that Capt. Alexander of the 3d, killed two or three Mexicans himself with one of Colt's repeaters, and that Lieut. G. W. Smith, who commanded a company of engineers at the storming of the same place, signalized himself most gallantly, as did also Lieut. Buell of the 3d Infantry.[68] Well did both the 3d and 7th sustain their previous high reputation in this trying action, and I trust that all our readers may read the official reports of their daring deeds of valor.

A Fight After the Battle.—One more anecdote which is current about town, and I have done for today. In one of the religious establishments of this city, and in a portion of it from which it is said females are most scrupulously excluded, a number of our wounded have been taken, among them an Irishman, a Catholic, who has a wife of the same persuasion. The latter, anxious for her husband's well-being on her arrival after the regiment sought him out; and just as she had ascertained his quarters, and was about entering them, she was accidentally met by a priest. He at once, probably shocked at seeing a female entering prohibited ground, placed his hand gently upon her shoulder to arrest her progress, and pointing the other way ejaculated "bamos"—literally "let us go." The good woman not knowing him, and conceiving his intentions anything but honorable, fell to and gave the holy father a most unmerciful threshing upon the spot, using both hands and feet in the strange encounter; and the more he shouted the more she kicked and pummeled. Such is the story, but which is given without a voucher.

Yours, &tc., &tc.,

G. W. K.
*Daily Picayune*, May 19, 1847

---

68. Gustavus W. Smith, Engineers, and Don Carlos Buell.

# CHAPTER FIVE

# RUMORS OF PEACE AND POLITICS
## MAY 11 – JUNE 23, 1847

IN MAY 1847, THE AMERICAN ARMY advanced to Puebla, 186 miles west of Vera Cruz and about seventy-five miles short of the capital, Mexico City. In Puebla they waited for reinforcements and supplies. George Kendall arrived there with Winfield Scott late in the month, illness having prevented him from advancing earlier with William Worth's command.

In Mexico City, Santa Anna's defeat at Cerro Gordo produced an outburst of anti-Yankee sentiment that barely concealed the deep divisions within and among Mexico's political factions. Sentiment in favor of a negotiated peace existed across the political spectrum, although any discussion of negotiations with the United States was officially an act of treason. Conservatives saw negotiations as an alternative to the further confiscation of private property; ardent federalists, especially in the north, considered peace as an opportunity to advance secessionist schemes; *moderados* in the capital leaned toward negotiations and territorial concessions as the means to rid the country of Scott's invading army; and *puros* opposed territorial concessions and considered negotiations desirable only if the United States could be persuaded to support and protect a democratic government free from the influence of the Catholic Church and the army.

Prospects for British-assisted negotiations evaporated when Santa Anna returned to Mexico City and, inspired by military and political leaders who wanted the war to continue, took up the challenge of preparing the capital to resist an American assault. Hopes for a negotiated peace emanating from American circles also went nowhere in the early summer. After the news of Buena Vista and Vera Cruz convinced President James Polk that an opportunity to end the hostilities by diplomatic means might be at hand, he sent Nicholas Trist, chief clerk of the Department of State, to Mexico. The egotistical, Spanish-speaking former American consul in Havana arrived in Vera Cruz on May 6.

Upon hearing news of Cerro Gordo, Trist sensed an opportunity for peace. He arranged for the new American offer to negotiate with Mexican authorities to be forwarded to Scott at Jalapa by a platoon of dragoons capable of making the seventy-five-mile journey in just over twenty-four hours. Unfortunately, the accompanying instructions from Secretary of War William Marcy gave Scott the impression that Trist was empowered to order the suspension of hostilities. Secretary of State James Buchanan's full explanation of the diplomat's authority remained sealed. In fact, Trist had authority to declare the end of hostilities only with the ratification of a peace treaty by the Mexican government. The general's angry response to the diplomat's instructions provoked a heated reply from Trist clarifying the extent of his authority but also questioning whether Scott intended to interfere with the conduct of international relations by the Polk administration.

Relations worsened when Trist arrived in Jalapa. Ill from an attack of diarrhea, a complaint common in the army at the time, Trist chose not to meet with Scott. Nevertheless, he was eager to send word of his mission on to officials in Mexico City, so he wrote Scott informing him that he carried authority from the president to have his instructions taken to the capital under a flag of truce. Scott was enraged by what he considered to be an affront to his military authority. With each complaining bitterly to Washington about the conduct of the other, Trist and Scott followed the army to Puebla while refusing to have anything to do with each other. Trist now turned to Charles Bankhead, the British minister to Mexico (and an acquaintance since the early 1830s, when he had served as secretary of the British legation in Washington), to forward the administration's peace overture to the Mexican government. Scott still had no idea of the terms Polk had sent Trist to negotiate.

Jalapa, Mexico, May 11, 1847

Intelligent Spaniards here, men who have ample means of information, tell me that matters at the city of Mexico are daily getting worse and worse—all is anarchy and confusion. It cannot well be otherwise. Confidence is all gone, money is all gone, hope has vanished, and in their place poverty and despair reign supreme. The only chance left of opposing the Americans is to raise a frenzy or enthusiasm—call it which you will—similar to that planted in the early revolutionists by Hidalgo, and it is to be doubted whether there is even virtue enough left in the country to bring about such a consummation. At the celebrated battle of Las Cruces, fought near the city of Mexico, it may be recollected that Morelos and Hidalgo had an immense rabble to contend against the few royalists under Truxillo and that such was the frenzy of the former that in many instances, during the hottest of the fight, they ran up and stuffed their hats into the very mouths of the Spanish cannon.[1] They cannot get up such a feeling now.

Gen. Worth will probably enter the rich and populous city of Puebla on Friday next, Gen. Quitman accompanying him. No one anticipates opposition, but on the contrary it is said that the larger and better portion of the inhabitants are growing more and more anxious for the entrance of the Americans, for the protection they will afford them against the hordes of ladrones and leperos[2] which have always infested that city.[3] We hear nothing of the guerrillas of late—they are probably confining themselves to robbing their own countrymen.

The reports in relation to Santa Anna are still contradictory, but all agree that he is at or near Orizaba. He has certainly threatened an attack upon Vera Cruz, and also upon this place, and there are those who think, judging from his threats and actions, that he has become mad since his recent reverses. The probability is, that he keeps his force about him partly for his own protection, and partly to be ready to strike a blow should a favorable opportunity offer.

Gen. Scott will probably leave with Gen. Twiggs, in the course of a few days, for Puebla. His next movements will depend upon circumstances.

Gen. Quitman's appointment as major general meets with the full approval of the Army. The wound of Gen. Shields, which everyone at first thought would prove mortal beyond doubt, continues to improve, and the hopes of his recovery are stronger than ever.

I forward this by the diligencia. It is considered a very unsafe conveyance, and for fear my letters may be overhauled by the Mexicans I cannot say half I otherwise should.

Yours, &c.,

G. W. K.
*Daily Picayune*, May 18, 1847

---

1. José María Morelos had continued the struggle against Spanish authority after Hidalgo was executed in 1811. Torcuato Trujillo commanded the loyalist forces at Las Cruces that were overcome by Hidalgo's army in October 1810.

2. A pejorative term for those on the lowest levels of Mexican society.

3. On May 10, Worth's division and two of the three regiments under John A. Quitman, a force of about 4,000 men, advanced from Perote to Puebla. Puebla was Mexico's second largest city, with 80,000 residents, and was a center of proclerical and thus anti–Santa Anna sentiment. Its Catholic leaders, eager to stop Santa Anna's raids on the church's funds, worked behind the scenes to limit opposition to the American presence. While a small force maintained the American garrison in Perote, about half of the army remained under Scott's command in Jalapa.

Jalapa, Mexico, May 11, 1847—6 o'clock, P.M.

Since the diligencia went out at noon today for Vera Cruz, another diligencia has come in from the city of Mexico full of passengers, and bringing news of not a little importance. Among the passengers was Mr. Kennedy, who, after being badly treated here about the 1st of April, was driven to the city of Mexico.

All the passengers confirm what I wrote you this morning. They say that at the capital there was no Government, no order, no responsibility—all was anarchy. Anaya was still President *pro tem.*, but had neither influence nor authority. A new President is to be elected on the 15th of the present month—the tenth Chief Magistrate this distracted country has had within the last eighteen months. I cannot stop to count them all up, but such is the fact.

The ladrones—guerrillas I suppose they should be called now—are busy at work upon the roads, especially between Puebla and the city of Mexico. The same passengers were robbed the other day no less than seven times in one stage, and the inference is that the last robbers must have had rather poor picking if the first were very searching in their operations. The diligencia in which Mr. Kennedy came down was robbed twice on the road.

It is stated that the propositions made by England some months since, to offer her intervention in settling the difficulties between Mexico and the United States, have recently been taken up by the Mexican Congress, and after a warm discussion, in which one of the members said that the whole affair was but another attempt of the monarchists upon the sacred liberties of the Mexican Republic, the motion even to consider them was lost by a vote of 44 to 33. From this it would seem that the present Congress is determined to shut every door against all proposals of an honorable peace.

Santa Anna has sent a letter to Congress from Orizaba. He gives his own account of the battle of Cerro Gordo, and claims a great victory on the first day of the fight. On the second day Providence, according to his story, gave the advantage to the Yankees. He says nothing about the exertions of the latter. Santa Anna states that he now has seven thousand men, and that his force is rapidly increasing; and moreover that all are burning to encounter the Americans again. He wants money to carry on his operations, but Congress has not seen fit to vote him a copper—one reason probably being that it has not a copper to give. Santa Anna, so far as I can learn, is the only man who has been spoken of in Mexico as a candidate for the presidency, and he is in very bad odor with the mass.

The States north of Mexico—Guadalajara, Guanajuato, Querétaro, Zacatecas, Durango, San Luis, and others—talk openly of separating from Mexico, and letting her take care of herself. Not a dollar in the way of supplies are they sending on for the relief of the General Government in its emergency.

They were still doing a little in the way of fortifying in the city of Mexico, but a Spaniard informs me that all the obstructions they have erected so far could be kicked over with the foot. The city had been placed under martial law, and the direst excesses were anticipated. The citizens had all been called upon to take up arms in the common defence, but unfortunately nine-tenths of them had no arms to take up. Nor were there any cannon at the capital other than a few small and indifferent pieces.

There is certainly a party, and an influential one, in Mexico, which begins to talk of peace; and where four weeks since they did not dare breathe their sentiments, they now come out openly and avow themselves. Still the measure is far from popular. The peace party is composed of the more honest and intelligent property holders, the merchants, and perhaps the clergy—to these are opposed the military who have all disgraced themselves, and all the demagogues among the lawyers. If the priests could be made certain that they would continue to hold their rich benefices secure, they would probably be all in favor of peace.

On the approach of the Americans it is said that Congress, with all the archives of the Republic, will move to the city of Morelia. Of course all my news is verbal, not a paper having come through. I have dispatched a man to the capital for full files of the public journals, and if he gets back safe they shall be immediately forwarded to you.

Majors Borland and Gaines, Capt. C. M. Clay, and all the officers taken in the North, were at liberty in the city of Mexico, as was also Midshipman Rogers.[4] They are all said to be well and respectfully treated now, although the latter was infamously abused on the way up to Mexico from Perote.

Gen. Canalizo was at San Andres, a place north of Orizaba, at last accounts. The force with him is not stated, but is undoubtedly small. He is an old friend of Santa Anna, and is probably working at present for his master.

I write this in great haste, and have no time for comment. One thing I must say, and that is that there undoubtedly would be a very large peace party in Mexico were it not for the overweening pride of the majority of the inhabitants. It *is* hard to be thrashed into a peace, that's certain.

---

4. In December 1846, while military and naval officials were planning the assault on Vera Cruz, a plot was hatched to blow up a powder magazine near the city as part of the effort to neutralize the fortress on San Juan de Ulúa. Passed Midshipman R. Clay Rogers was taken prisoner in the unsuccessful effort. Naval officials had hoped to secure his release as part of the settlement following the surrender of Vera Cruz, but inadequate communications undercut that plan. K. Jack Bauer, *Surfboats and Horse Marines: U.S. Naval Operations in the Mexican War, 1846–48* (Annapolis, 1969), 60–61, 96.

I send this by a Mexican to Vera Cruz, who promises to ride through at his fastest speed. If it reaches you, well and good.

Yours, &c.,

G. W. K.

P.S.—*11 o'clock, night.*—Just as my express man was starting I was fortunate enough to get hold of the following hurried translation of a proclamation, which has been printed in Spanish, and addressed by Gen. Scott to the Mexicans. I have no time to peruse it, but those who have think it will have weight and influence with the Mexicans.[5]

In haste,

K.

New Orleans *Daily Picayune*, May 20, 1847

Jalapa, Mexico, May 14, 1847

For two or three days there has hardly been an item of news worth recording—not even a rumor of the least moment; but last evening and this morning reports have come in which are entitled to some little show of importance.

It is now confidently asserted that Santa Anna has moved from Orizaba, and in the direction of Puebla and the city of Mexico.[6] The *administrador de las diligencias*—general stage agent I suppose he might be called in the vernacular—left yesterday for the capital on business for the line, but this morning he returned with more speed than he went. He reports having met at Cerro de Leon, near Perote, with a force of seventy armed Mexicans, whose appearance he did not at all like. From stragglers he learned that Santa Anna, with a large force, had passed on towards Puebla; that the roads were filled with robbers and brigands, and that it would not be prudent for him to go on—so the *administrador de las diligencias* returned without effecting the objects of his mission.

Last night an intelligent Spaniard informed me that he had seen two letters from Orizaba, one dated the 6th and the other the 7th inst. On the first day the letter stated that the first brigade or division of Santa Anna's army started *en route* for Puebla, and on the 7th the other division marched

5. On May 11, 1847, Scott issued a proclamation he had written in consultation with representatives of the Catholic bishop of Puebla, Francisco Pablo Vázquez Vizcaíno. In it he claimed that the United States had been drawn into war despite a desire for peace, pledged fidelity with the people of Mexico, promised to assist in the fight for republican institutions, and guaranteed protection for those who remained neutral.

6. Santa Anna arrived in Puebla on May 11, 1847, with an army he claimed to number 4,500 men.

in the same direction. His entire force was put down at 2500, the most of them indifferently armed and under little or no discipline.

If Santa Anna has moved towards the capital, and there certainly is good reason to believe that he has, his intentions are doubtless to control the election for President, which takes place tomorrow. He cannot certainly have the temerity to even think of attacking Gen. Worth, whose division could put to flight 10,000 of the best Mexican troops that ever bore arms; so that the conviction is irresistible that he intends having a hand in the coming election. One would naturally think that after his many disgraceful reverses he would either attempt to leave the country, or else hide himself in some obscure part of it; but the cowardly tyrant loves power and place too well, and will cling to them as long as there is a dollar, a musket, and an open road on which to run left in the Republic.

Mr. Downie, sutler of the 2d Pennsylvania Regiment, arrived here yesterday. It may be recollected that he had a large sum of money stolen from him at Vera Cruz by a Mexican a short time since, that he pursued the rascal to Cordova, and that he succeeded in recovering the most of his money. So far so good; but the worse of it has yet to be told. Mr. D. came out with the permission of the alcalde and authorities of Vera Cruz in search of the robber of his money, found him, and succeeded, as is said above, in recovering the most of his treasure; but just at this moment a worse robber got hold of him in the shape of Santa Anna; poor D. was cast into prison as a spy, all his money again taken from him, and the only way by which he could obtain his liberty was to acknowledge himself a spy in writing! This Santa Anna insisted upon, as an excuse for robbing him of his money; but, on the other hand, Downie insisted as well in putting a protest at the bottom of his confession, stating that all he had said above was false! Did ever one hear of such a rascally farce? The way in which Downie now speaks of Santa Anna is anything but complimentary.

The long wagon train is now coming into the city from Vera Cruz, and has met with no opposition on the way. There are between three and four hundred wagons and between eleven and twelve hundred pack mules in the train—quite a string you would think were you to see them all together. Capt. Grayson, the stirring and most popular commissary, is along with the train, and I am pleased to learn is going on towards certain halls named after the elder Montezuma.

The foreigners in the city of Mexico are all extremely anxious for the arrival of Gen. Scott. It is said that a heavy sum has already been subscribed for a grand Fourth of July dinner, one individual, an Irishman, having put down his name for no less than $800. The war has been most disastrous to all the foreigners, breaking up the business of many entirely. The only advantage it has been to any has been the depreciation it has caused in the value of real estate. Houses in the city of Mexico belonging to the church, and which have been sold under the hammer, have been bought in by the English and other merchants at prices far below their real value.

You will doubtless learn with pleasure, as will doubtless his numerous friends in New Orleans, that Gen. P. F. Smith has again reported for duty. For no less than a month he was unable to put his foot to the ground, to such a degree was his ankle inflamed. I am also happy at being able to state that Gen. Shields is still mending, although slowly. The saving of his life may be put down almost as a miracle. I saw him but a short time after he received his dreadful wound, and no one then thought that he could then live twenty-four hours.

Gen. Scott's proclamations, which I sent off to you two or three nights since by an express rider, has been read with excellent effect. It is a most able document, and goes home to the feelings of the people. By this time it has been circulated at Puebla and the city of Mexico, and will doubtless turn the minds, at least of the honest and reflecting, toward peace.

I have been much amused at reading accounts in some of our papers at home of the road between Vera Cruz and the city of Mexico. One writer, who "talks like a book," says that there is a stream ten miles from the former city which is crossed *in scows*! We did not come that road. Again, the same writer says that the Puente Nacional is a *wooden bridge*! Wooden! whew! It is the best imitation of stone I have ever seen, and as durable as the rock of ages at that.

Mr. Trist arrived here this morning from Vera Cruz.[7] His business I do not know, but I suppose he goes on with the army. Gen. Scott, owing to the non-arrival of all the train, will not be able to move for two or three days to come. Capt. Walker, with his Rifles, is on the way up, guarding another smaller train. I trust there may be wagons enough to carry on the little baggage our officers now possess. For want of sufficient transportation heretofore they have been compelled to leave carpet bags here, trunks there, and boxes elsewhere, until nearly everything has been lost. The

7. After arriving in Vera Cruz on May 6, Trist left for Jalapa on May 8, traveling with 1,000 reinforcements and a slow wagon train carrying supplies for the army. The next day at San Juan del Rio, he received word of Scott's displeasure with his apparent instructions. That night he began what became a thirty-page denunciation of the general's conduct. On May 22, Scott read that letter and Trist's directive to forward his instructions to Mexican authorities as he was preparing to move forward to Puebla, 116 miles further inland. Trist received word of Scott's now even greater displeasure when he arrived in Puebla on May 29.

Government most certainly should make allowances for sacrifices which have been unavoidable on the part of its officers.

Yours, &c.,

G. W. K.

P.S.—With not a little trouble and expense I have been enabled to procure the very latest dates from the city of Mexico, and also from Puebla. You will see that the freedom of the press has been suspended, but not until the editors had lied most lustily about us miserable Yankees. The letter about Gen. Scott's destroying Encero, and offering a reward for Santa Anna, it would puzzle the father of lies to beat. On the contrary, a safeguard was placed upon the house of Santa Anna, and not a stone of it has been moved.

The report that Santa Anna has gone towards the capital receives additional confirmation. We hear nothing of Gen. Worth, but everyone hopes he has fallen in with Santa Anna.

A Mexican officer, Capt. Velasquez, died yesterday from a wound received at Cerro Gordo, and was buried with military honors. Lieut. Shelby Johnson, of the 4th Illinois volunteers, also died yesterday, and was buried with appropriate ceremonies. Gen. Scott and staff, with many other officers of our army, attended both funerals.

A work has been thrown up near this place which completely commands the city. It was constructed under the superintendence of Capt. Beauregard, a native of Louisiana, who enjoys a high reputation in the army.

G. W. K.
*Daily Picayune*, May 25, 1847

Jalapa, Mexico, May 16, 1847

I regret to state that Capt. Mason, of the Rifles, died last night. He is to be buried this afternoon with military honors. He was a gallant and most promising young officer, beloved by all.

The order is out for the marching of Gen. Twiggs's division. It is to move on Tuesday towards Puebla, Gen. Scott accompanying it. A garrison remains behind under Col. Childs, composed of both regulars and volunteers, every way able to hold the position against any odds the enemy may bring.

There is no mistake that Gen. Scott's last proclamation, which went directly home to every reflecting Mexican, is doing a great deal of good.

Hart & Wells, the theatrical managers, have given a *grand funcion* at the *Plaza de Toros*—a regular bull fight—so you see that we are not entirely destitute of amusements, especially those of a refined nature. Today there is to be a grand cock fight and also another bull fight, and at night there is to be a theatrical performance at the theatre. This is a lively country. A Spanish *danseuse*, said to be pretty, has arrived from the city of Mexico, has been engaged by Hart & Wells, and makes her first appearance tomorrow night.

Yours, &c.,

G. W. K.

*Daily Picayune*, May 28, 1847

Jalapa, Mexico, May 18, 1847

Up to 9 o'clock this morning we have no intelligence of the advance of the army under Gen. Worth. He must be in Puebla ere this, and if he had a battle the Mexicans here would most certainly have known it, and the result would have been plainly pictured in their countenances. Bad news shows perhaps more plainly and palpably in their faces than in those of any people alive, and vice versa.

From Santa Anna we have more positive information. It is certain that he has passed through Puebla, and with a force variously estimated from 15,000 to 30,000 men—the former number is doubtless nearer the mark. Some of the Mexicans here say that he will make a stand somewhere between Puebla and the city of Mexico, and that he has three or four pieces of cannon. Others believe that there will be one grand struggle at the city of Mexico—a last effort for the liberty of the Republic.

Among the foreigners, again, there are those who believe that Santa Anna is only pushing on towards the capital to control the elections and help himself, by force, to the highest office; and that then he will come out in favor of peace with the United States. Others, and among them those who pretend to great knowledge of the country and its public men, say that Santa Anna will never give up so long as he can draw around him a force sufficient to make any kind of a show against "los Yankees," he himself always taking care to be in a position where he can save his own precious body in case of a reverse.

I have thus given you all the various opinions afloat, and must leave it to wiser heads to pick out which is the most reasonable. Santa Anna's whole life has been one of ups and downs—has been a riddle. After his disastrous defeat at Buena Vista all thought his power completely broken up; yet he was found again in full force at Cerro Gordo. There he met with the worst reverse of all, and everyone supposed him completely annihilated; yet we now know that he has collected another force around him, that he is pushing for the capital, and it is fairly to be presumed that a man so full of expedients may yet give the American arms some trouble. Had Gen. Scott been in possession of the proper means on the eve of the battle of Cerro Gordo, the city of Mexico would at this moment have been under the American flag, and very likely without the loss of a man—he had not the proper means, and the road may not now be found an open way.

As yet I have received no further papers from the city of Mexico—nothing later than the 8th inst.—but I am in hopes daily of obtaining full files. They shall be forwarded immediately, by private express if no other opportunity offers.

Gen. Scott, owing to the non-arrival of a train expected this morning, will not move for two or three days to come.

Yours, &c.,

G. W. K.

P.S.—A Spaniard has just told me that Gen. Worth entered Puebla on Saturday last, without opposition. At that time he says, Santa Anna was encamped at San Martin Tesmelucan, ten leagues on the other side.

There is a report that Gen. Worth is in hard pursuit of him beyond Puebla, and I think very likely such is the case. Santa Anna will find very little rest to the sole of his foot if Gen. W. gets in pursuit of him. We must have definite intelligence before tomorrow of all that has occurred in the direction of Puebla.

*Daily Picayune*, May 28, 1847

Jalapa, Mexico, May 19, 1847—Forenoon

We have some further reports in relation to Gen. Worth's entrance into Puebla, although as yet there is no official or positive information. A German who arrived from the city of Mexico last night, and who appears to be an intelligent man, says that when the advance of Gen. Worth had reached a point a few miles this side of Puebla, on the 15th inst., Santa Anna was in the city distributing shoes to his soldiers; that to delay the advance of the Americans he sent out a party to skirmish with them; that this party was attacked by Gen. W., driven into the city with the loss of several killed and wounded, besides many horses, and that so hotly were they pressed, that Santa Anna was obliged to retire without having time to shoe all his men. Such is the report, and it looks reasonable enough, of the German. Gen. Worth entered the city at 5 o'clock in the afternoon of Saturday, the 15th. As the gentleman left

Puebla about that time, he could not say whether Santa Anna was pursued or not.[8]

Other accounts say that Santa Anna fell back as far as San Martin Tesmelucan, which he intended to fortify; while others again will have it that a grand stand is to be made at or near Rio Frio. The former is situated on a plain, and there nature has given little or no strength of position; while at the latter there are several very strong points, one in particular, which may be fortified. If Santa Anna, too, can get up another excitement at the capital—and he can do almost anything with his countrymen—he can obtain immense assistance in the way of throwing up works. Rio Frio, if my memory serves me right,[9] is but ten or twelve leagues this side of the city of Mexico; yet it is said there is a road which turns it completely. Be this as it may, there are certainly indications that the Mexicans are determined upon making another struggle, although it must again result in their utter discomfiture. After the successful storming of Cerro Gordo by Col. Harney, from which he drove a well fortified force of more than double his own number, there is nothing the American arms cannot do.

Some fears are manifested that an express from Gen. Worth has been cut off by the rascally guerrillas. He most certainly would have dispatched a messenger, unless he had received direct orders to the contrary; yet no person has arrived. The first thing the guerrillas know, a lot of them will be strung up one of these mornings.

The difficulty between Santa Anna and Gen. Miñon is a very pretty quarrel, as it stands. The former ordered Gen. M., at the battle of Buena Vista, to go in the rear of Gen. Taylor, and when he, Santa Anna, drove old "Rough and Ready" from the Angostura or Narrows, Gen. M. was to fall upon him and cut him and his army entirely in pieces. This was perfectly understood between them. Well, after Santa Anna was forced to fall back, for the very good and most excellent reason that he could not induce Gen. Taylor to budge an inch, he accuses Gen. Miñon openly of not obeying his orders. The latter says in justification, that if Santa Anna had

8. Santa Anna, having already sent his artillery and infantry marching toward Mexico City, hoped to stop the American advance by sending a cavalry force of more than 2,000 men to attack from the rear the American forces approaching Puebla. Mexican scouts considered Quitman's small brigade and cumbersome wagon train, which traveled a day's march behind the larger force under Worth's command, especially vulnerable. Worth anticipated Santa Anna's tactics, however, and slowed his division's advance so that by May 14, when it arrived in Amozoc (about ten miles from Puebla), Quitman's command was only two or three miles to the rear. Worth's forces spotted Santa Anna's cavalry on May 14; they fired artillery at the Mexicans and sent reinforcements to Quitman. Realizing that the opportunity for a surprise attack had been lost, the Mexicans retreated to Puebla and joined the march to Mexico City before sunrise the next day.

9. Kendall had traveled through Rio Frio in 1842, after his release from prison in Mexico City.

driven Gen. Taylor from his position, as he had agreed to do, that he was ready at the mouth of the Narrows to make an end of "los Yankees" with his cavalry. I do not know how the matter will end, but so far Santa Anna has the worst of it most decidedly.

There are occasional deaths among our wounded men, but the most of those injured at Cerro Gordo are doing well. Speaking of wounded men, I will relate one little incident. When Gen. Shields was brought out from the spot where he was wounded, to a place where several others had already been taken, I happened to be present. After the wound of the gallant general had been dressed, the wants of the others—perhaps there were some ten or fifteen of them—were attended to. Among them was one stout Illinois man, named Ford, the half of whose head at least appeared to have been carried away by a heavy cannon ball. One of our best surgeons, Dr. Wright,[10] went up to the poor fellow when his turn came and to my astonishment commenced clipping the shattered portions of his face, jaw, and ear which still hung to him, and afterwards dressed the wound as well as circumstances would admit. I say wound; it was worse than a wound, and a description of it would be too horrible. The battle was now over, and every moment they were bringing in some fresh victim of the result of the recent strife. It seemed to me that others needed the services of the good surgeon more than did the unfortunate individual in question—his case was certainly hopeless. There were arms and legs to amputate, balls to extract, and the writhings of the wounded showed how much they needed the surgeon's offices; yet he continued with the Illinois man until he had patched his shattered head and bound it up as well as he was able. This was on the 18th of April.

Two or three days since, when nearly a month had passed away, I met Dr. Wright here in the streets of Jalapa, and asked him how long the man in question lived. If I was ever astonished in my life, it was when he told me that he was still alive, and what was more, that he was well and hearty! A portion of his face, his jaws on one side, and his ear are gone, but the man will soon be strong enough to shoulder his musket again, and is said to be more anxious than ever to have another turn with the Mexicans.

Four men belonging to the army are to undergo most severe punishment this afternoon: they are to receive thirty-nine lashes each, in the Plaza, are to have their heads shaved, and after the word "*robber*" is pasted on each of their backs they are to be drummed out of camp. This thing of publicly whipping a man is most degrading; but their crime was the pre-

10. Joseph J. B. Wright.

meditated robbery of the house of a Mexican, and under circumstances deserving of the most severe punishment.[11] Three of them belonged to the 4th Artillery and one to the 2d Pennsylvania regiment.

Yours, &c.,

G. W. K.
*Daily Picayune*, May 28, 1847

Jalapa, Mexico, May 20, 1847

We are still without farther positive news from Gen. Worth, and it is now almost certain that his dispatches have been cut off. He would hardly enter so rich and populous a city as is Puebla without sending an official account of it to Gen. Scott—at least such is the impression.

The Mexicans here have news from the city of Mexico which we cannot get hold of, their own couriers doubtless running regularly. One of them told me last night that fifteen battalions of the National Guard have been thoroughly organized at the capital, that fortifications are already in process of construction at or near Rio Frio, that the bells have been run up into cannon, and that the owners of an iron foundry at the city of Mexico, Englishmen, have been compelled to cast balls on the promise of remuneration hereafter. Understand, distinctly, that I get all this from a Mexican, and that it must be taken with allowances; but that there is now a prospect of another fight, and a hard one, is considered certain by many. To my thinking it will depend much upon the result of the election of President, news of which has not as yet reached the Americans here. If Herrera has been chosen, and there certainly was a party in his favor, it may be put down as a guaranty that peace measures will prevail.[12] On the other hand, if Santa Anna has been elected, or a friend of his, the struggle may be protracted and another stand made this side of the capital. It is now certain that Santa Anna was not at the city of Mexico to control the late election in person, although his approach with an armed force may have had some effect upon the States of Puebla and Mexico.

The four individuals I spoke of yesterday as having been guilty of robbery, received a portion of their sentence last evening and the rest this morning. A most disgraceful figure did they cut, marching through the

11. Scott maintained tight control over the American army in Mexico, insisting that Mexicans and their property be respected.

12. Speculation about José Joaquín Herrera's election to the presidency reflected a general hope in the American camp that the proponents of peace negotiations would emerge preeminent from the political chaos that swept the Mexican capital after Santa Anna's defeat at Cerro Gordo. Herrera was one of four candidates, including Santa Anna, to receive votes from the state legislatures vested with the power to elect the president.

streets with their heads shaved, the word "*robber*" pinned upon their backs, and a band of music playing the "Rogue's March" immediately in their rear. Their names were Henry Reed, Hugh Duane and Benj. Potter, of the 4th Artillery, and D. F. Revalon, of the 2d Pennsylvania Volunteers. The latter was found guilty of horse-stealing; the three former of breaking twice into the house of the same Mexican, and with threats and violence robbing him of everything he possessed. Hard and degrading as was their punishment, everyone says it was deserved.

Yours, &c., &c.,

G. W. K.
*Daily Picayune*, May 28, 1847

Jalapa, Mexico, May 21, 1847

There is a good deal of doubt and uncertainty in relation to the election of President in Mexico; a good deal of surmise as to the manner of choosing this high functionary, in the present instance. By the constitution, the plan of electing the President is somewhat similar to that of our own country: each State in Mexico, through its *Assemblea Departmental* or State Legislature elects its candidate for Chief Magistrate from among the different names offered by the members. This vote is carefully sealed and sent on to the capital, and when all are counted the individual who has the vote of the greatest number of States is declared duly elected. Such is about the amount of the law in relation to the matter; yet it is known that in September last the Congress of the Republic, in an extraordinary session, chose Santa Anna President and Gómez Farías Vice President, and the same Congress, in the present distracted state of the country, may do the same again. If the high functionaries are chosen according to the constitution there are several States—Vera Cruz, Tamaulipas, Nueva Leon, Coahuila, Chihuahua, Nueva Mexico, Upper California, and perhaps one or two others—which can take no part in the election from the fact that they are occupied by our troops.[13] We shall know all about this matter in the course of a few days, and in the meantime I can inform you that there are many intelligent and thinking Mexicans here who believe that Herrera will be elected, but perhaps with them the wish is father to the hope.

13. Kendall accurately described the electoral arrangement. Santa Anna's opportunity to stay in power depended on the failure of the election to take place in all the states. He received only the vote of Chihuahua. Besides those states mentioned (excepting Chihuahua and Tamaulipas), Jalisco, Tabasco, and Yucatan did not cast ballots, leaving Santa Anna in a position to retain the presidency.

The advent of the American troops in any part of this country gives the population of the towns and cities two separate and distinct frights: the first is when they hear of the approach of "los Yankees," for such have been the reports circulated by the Government that they honestly believe that their houses are to be robbed, their wives and daughters violated, and every species of outrage committed; the second fright is when they hear that the Americans are to leave them, for they soon learn that their trade is better, that they have greater protection, and that the laws of the strangers are more wholesome, liberal and give greater safety than they have ever enjoyed under their own. They have been buying and selling, too, have been trafficking with the Americans, contrary to the express injunctions of their rulers, and now it is their own people, their own lawless and half fed soldiery, that they really fear the most. A day of sorrow will that be for Mexico when the Americans leave it, although for one I believe that that day is far distant. As long as the military hold supremacy in the country our armies certainly cannot evacuate it.

Mr. Trist is still here, although the object of his mission is kept a secret. In what capacity he comes—whether as a commissioner of peace, as an agent to settle terms, or with whatever authority clothed—the million are certainly none the wiser. In the language of Count Montalban in the "Honey Moon," they look upon the whole affair as

> "—— a riddle,
> Which he who solve'd the Sphynx's might die guessing."

I might give you a column of speculation upon this mission, and very likely hit upon many truths in so doing, but have neither the time nor inclination at present to say more than that I believe that the hard blows of 10,000 regulars will have more effect in bringing these people to their senses than all the soft words an equal number of diplomats could shower upon them.

The train which started up under escort of Capts. Walker and Ruff[14] arrived yesterday, and it is now said that an onward movement tomorrow has been decided upon. A great excitement has been caused here on its being ascertained that no less than twelve wagon loads of sutler's stores had been found scattered through the train, to the great detriment of the service. Arrests are talked of, and I suppose that several will take place. Many essentials for the use of the army were absolutely left behind to make room for the goods and baggage of private individuals.

14. Charles Ruff.

Besides Herrera, it is said that Elloriaga is talked of as a candidate for the presidency. It may be recollected that the latter made a close run with Santa Anna for the same office at the last election. He bears an excellent character among the foreigners, and it is thought is in favor of peace with the United States. He is not a military man, and that is saying a good deal for him.[15]

Gen. Shields has had a bad attack of the pleurisy, and strong fears for his recovery were at first entertained; but yesterday he improved, and today I am pleased to learn that he is decidedly better.

No news as yet from Gen. Worth, at least nothing positive.

Yours, &c.,

G. W. K.

P.S.—*11 o'clock, A.M.*—The stage is just in from Puebla, but I have little time to collect and write off the news. All was quiet at Puebla, and the people appear to be well enough satisfied under Gen. Worth.

Santa Anna, it is said, did not stop at San Martin, but kept on towards the capital after his lancers had been defeated this side of Puebla by Gen. Worth. There is a report that Gen. Valencia, with 14,000 men, is to meet our army this side of Mexico, but there are so many reports that we can make little out of them.[16]

Elloriaga is certainly talked of for the presidency.

*Daily Picayune*, May 28, 1847

Jalapa, Mexico, May 22, 1847

A statement is made in many of the papers of the United States, I believe in the *Union*[17] among others, to the effect that Gen. Scott will shortly have 20,000 men with which to march upon the city of Mexico. The assertion may not be positively made, but it is given in such a way that the public may really think that he has this overwhelming force. Now, what is the real state of the case? I will give it, formed upon the last data.

There are not, on this line of operations—including the garrisons of Vera Cruz, Jalapa and Perote—there are not, I say, more than 9000 effective men,

15. Francisco de Elloriaga, a *moderado*, probably received the vote of his home state of Durango. Besides Santa Anna, those receiving more than one vote were Juan N. Almonte (four), Herrera (three), and Angel Frís (three). In December 1846, the *moderados* sought to lessen the *puros'* influence in national affairs by persuading Gómez Farías to abandon Santa Anna and back the presidential candidacy of Elloriaga. The effort failed. Santoni, *Mexicans at War*, 161, 288.

16. Gabriel Valencia, one of Santa Anna's military rivals, commanded the veteran-laden Army of the North, based at San Luis Potosí. Santa Anna kept Valencia's army at a distance until the threat of an attack on Mexico City arose in July.

17. The Washington *Union* was a Democratic newspaper supportive of the Polk administration.

all told; nor are more than 1000 recruits at the present time on the way to swell the number. After leaving Perote Gen. Scott will not have more than 6000—at least not more than 6500—to move upon the city of Mexico— infantry, artillery, dragoons, sappers, ordnance men and volunteers, all told. To be sure they are all good men and true, and in a body can fight their way into or out of the country; but all will see that this force is not half as large as the public may think it is, judging from the erroneous statements made in some of the journals of the country. Whether the army should meet with new successes, or whether a reverse should overtake it, in either case the number of men should be known—if successful, the greater will be the credit due to the few who achieve new laurels; if the contrary, the exact number of men sent so far into the heart of an enemy's country should be known and published. "England expects every man to do his duty"—from the small number of men sent on an emprise which is extremely perilous, it would seem that the United States expects every man to do more. Gen. Scott has not half the men the public in the United States think he has.

Yours, &tc.,

G. W. K.
*Daily Picayune*, June 8, 1847

Jalapa, Mexico, May 22, 1847

There is nothing new of importance to communicate, although after my hurried postscript to the letter I wrote yesterday additional particulars in relation to Gen. Worth's movements were received.

It seems that the affair with Santa Anna's lancers took place at Amozoque, a small place about three leagues this side of Puebla. The number of the enemy was variously estimated at from 1500 to 2000. They charged up within cannon range with great apparent resolution, so much so that a regular movement was made to receive them; but the three first discharges of our artillery set them all scampering off as fast as their animals would carry them, leaving ten men and seven horses dead on the field. What a pity we have not a cavalry force sufficient to attach a command to each division of the army. Col. Harney has been compelled to remain here with the 2d Dragoons up to this time, to give the horses rest; had he been at Amosoque with only 500 men a great many of the 2000 Mexicans would not have answered to their next roll-call.

The better classes of Puebla appear to be well enough disposed towards the Americans, although they perhaps do not altogether like the idea that a force of 3000 men should enter a city of near 100,000 souls and without resistance. The lower orders—the *ladrones* and *leperos* with which Puebla abounds—are evidently but ill-disposed towards us. One of Gen. Worth's men has already been assassinated, but fortunately the murderers were immediately arrested. On the alcalde's telling Gen. W. that according to their laws, *a year and a half* would elapse before the case of the assassins could be settled in the courts of Puebla, he was informed that an American tribunal would render them full justice in *a day and a half*! The miscreants are now where they never will commit another murder.[18]

It is said that supplies of all kinds can be readily obtained at Puebla. The wheat crop has just ripened and is most abundant.

The news now is that the Mexicans have abandoned the idea of fortifying at the Rio Frio, but intend constructing a line of works at El Peñol, a position about nine miles this side of the city of Mexico. Perhaps they only intend this as a show of resistance, for the sake of saving their credit; again, they may hope to raise men enough to give a regular battle to the Americans. They can collect nothing, however, but an undisciplined rabble, and these our regulars can dispense like chaff. The more they have to contend with of this class the better—the quicker a panic can be created among them.

Santa Anna, after the dispersion of his cavalry, did not stop even at San Martin or Rio Frio, but kept on with all speed to the city of Mexico. Our knowledge of the state of affairs at the capital, since Santa Anna's arrival, is limited, but it was currently reported at Puebla on Wednesday last that on the previous day the two parties—the Polkas and the Puros[19]—were fighting like cats and dogs. Some new revolution has without doubt broken out, but the leaders at present are unknown.

Gen. Scott's last proclamation has been generally circulated at Puebla, and it is said with most excellent effect.[20] No less than three editions of it had been printed, and still the inhabitants were calling for more. The demand for it alone would show that its effects have been salutary. The numberless horde of military drones, and all the employees and hangers-on of the Government, are doubtless doing all they can to put down its

18. Under Scott's command, the martial law governing American troops extended to their assailants.

19. Opposed to Santa Anna and friendly to the Catholic Church, the moderate *polkas* were organized, along with other volunteer national guard units, in the winter of 1846–47. Drawn from the ranks of Mexico City's aristocrats, they took their name from the new dance that was popular at their social gatherings. They, conservatives, and *moderados* rebelled against the anticlerical *puro* leadership of Gómez Farías in the early months of 1847. *Puros* and their moderate counterparts found Santa Anna both a help and a hindrance to their political aims.

20. The reference is to Scott's proclamation of May 11, 1847, which denounced the weakness of the Mexican government, warned that guerrilla warfare would be unsuccessful, and called on the Mexican people to join the United States in the fight against European influence and for republican government in the Americas.

circulation and deaden its influence upon the masses; but they cannot keep it out of the hands of the middle and better class of citizens, the laborious and thinking artisans, nor prevent them from perusing and pondering upon its contents.

In a letter I sent you yesterday by the diligencia I believe that I stated that Gen. Valencia was coming out with 14,000 men to meet the Americans. The report is, that of this number 4000 are Pintos, or Indians of the South, under Gen. Alvarez.[21] They are called Pintos from the fact that after they come to manhood their faces, from some cause or other which I have not heard explained, become spotted—yellow and red. They are of little account as soldiers, and it is probable that Valencia's men, if he has the number given him by rumor, are nothing but raw recruits. If they stop to be fired at once they will not do it a second time.

There is much speculation in the army as to what is to be the result—as to what is to be the winding up of this war with Mexico. I can see no other result than the subjugation of the country entirely,—or at least in bringing it under the protection of the United States. As a nation Mexico is blotted out of the list—the candle of her independence is burnt down to the socket. If left to herself she would in a few months, from her utter inability to govern herself, be torn and divided by intestine commotions. No protection whatever could be given either to life or property, there are no men in the country who could make headway against the torrent of abuses that would at once creep into every department, there is no money or means with which to establish a new and stable government. What then is she to do? This is a question for wise heads to answer. Too utterly helpless to be left to herself, I repeat that the better plan would be to take her at once under our protection. Let some honest and well meaning man—there may be a few of them left—let some one of them be chosen or selected as President, and give them the assistance of a few thousand men to keep down revolutions, and awe the hungry horde of leeches, who have so long preyed upon the country. If they raise a *grito* or *pronunciamento*, put them down by the bayonet—pronunciamentos would soon become unfashionable if the precious blood of those who started them was brought in jeopardy. Give but one of their revolutions a tragic turn—they have been costly farces heretofore—and the people would soon become sick of them.

These remarks have been hastily thrown together, but they may possibly be as good as any speculations that can be offered. He who thinks that a lasting and beneficial peace can be made with Mexico, or believes that the

21. Juan Alvarez.

American troops are soon to be withdrawn, is some one who has not been over the country—he starts in his belief from false premises, and judges a race of people by the ordinary rules which govern human nature, while it is notoriously a fact that they have long since thrown all ordinary rules at defiance. The Chinese, when they painted hideous faces upon their walls to frighten off the English invaders, were not a whit behind these people when they get up their tremendous proclamations, and flatter themselves into the belief that what they say in them is all true—that they really are a great people, and able to contend with those whom they profess to despise.

Yours, &c.,

G. W. K.
*Weekly Picayune*, June 21, 1847

Jalapa, May 23, 1847

The division of Gen. Twiggs marched en route for Puebla yesterday afternoon—Gen. Scott starts this morning and will overtake him tonight. The 1st Artillery and 2d Pennsylvania Regiment remain behind to garrison Jalapa, all under command of Col. Childs.

We have news one day later from Puebla. Report has it that all was quiet there, and that Gen. Worth and his officers were very popular with all classes. A gentleman who reached here today says that he saw several of our officers riding out with some of the first ladies of the place, and in their own carriages—all very comfortable, is it not? Gen. Worth has taken up his quarters at the palace, and his troops are located at different strong points in and around the city.

Mr. Trenwitt, who was taken prisoner by Gen. Urrea in February last, and who has since been confined at the city of Mexico, came down yesterday. I believe that he recovered his liberty through the instrumentality of Mr. Bankhead, the British Minister. He states that all the American officers have the liberty of the city on their parole, but that the men are still confined, and are allowed but 18 cents a day upon which to support themselves. He will tell you his story when he reaches New Orleans, and you will find it interesting. The treatment of the prisoners has been most severe.[22]

I am fearful that an express man, who must have left Puebla with newspapers and letters for the *Picayune* has been cut off. It is known that there are several small guerrilla parties between Perote and Puebla, acting in gangs of between ten and thirty, and the last diligencia which went up was

22. Trenwitt is not identifiable, but he seems to have been taken prisoner during Urrea's murderous raids on American supply lines between Monterey and Camargo in February 1847. The officers and men mentioned were those captured at Encarnación in January 1847.

robbed by a set of these marauders. There were two pretty Spanish girls from Biscay, who had been here some time waiting for a passage, in the coach at the time. I trust the robbers treated them with some show of politeness and circumspection.

The friends of Gen. Shields will be pleased to learn that he has almost entirely recovered from his late severe attack of pleurisy. His wound is almost entirely healed.

We have no further accounts in relation to the election of President of Mexico. The revolution which is now going on at the capital has doubtless grown out of the canvass.[23] Mr. Trist is going on with the army, but in what capacity it is best known to himself. He has certainly had no personal communication with Gen. Scott.

G. W. K.
*Daily Picayune*, June 8, 1847

Puebla, Mexico, May 28, 1847[24]

Gen. Scott arrived here this afternoon with an escort of some 200 dragoons and 50 rifles under Col. Harney. He left Acajete this morning at half past 7 o'clock, and from all the information received there it was almost certain that the small command would be attacked by a body of 2 or 3000 Mexican cavalry under Gen. Canalizo, but not one was seen. Gen. S. came into the city at 3 o'clock and has taken up his quarters at the palace.

At last accounts it is asserted that the Mexican army is at El Peñon, a few miles this side the capital, and that it is under command of Generals Bravo, Valencia, León, Cortazar and Alvarez, the latter having several thousand Indians from the South. Reports are rife that they are fortifying El Peñon, and also near the city.

In the affair of Amozoque, where Gen. Worth was advancing upon Puebla, Santa Anna commanded his cavalry—supposed to be near 3000 in number—in person. Col. Duncan gave them something like seventy round shot from his battery; and Major Bonneville,[25] with a detachment, was

---

23. The political situation in Mexico City was increasingly complex. *Moderados*, including substitute president Anaya, maneuvered to prevent a presidential election that would likely unseat Santa Anna; at the same time, they sought to suspend Congress in order to open a way for the administration to accept the British offer of mediation. Finally, Santa Anna was expected back in the capital, and *puros* were anxious to use his return to reassert their political influence and prevent negotiations with the United States. Santoni, *Mexicans at Arms*, 203–7.

24. Kendall arrived in Puebla on May 27, 1847. His friend and occasional correspondent for the *Picayune*, Captain Forbes Britton, reported that the American command numbered "about 6000 men, 600 wagons and near 5000 horses and mules." Copeland, *Kendall of the Picayune*, 196.

25. Benjamin L. E. Bonneville, Second Infantry.

enabled to reach a position from which he gave them a severe fire of musketry. Near 70 Mexicans were killed or wounded, and the scampering of the rest is represented as amusing in the extreme. Santa Anna, it is thought, was endeavoring to get between the commands of Gens. Worth and Quitman, with the intention of having a brush with the latter, but, if this was his intention, he was most signally foiled.

The command here has been annoyed by continued rumors of an attack by troops from Mexico, aided by a rising of the inhabitants of the city; but the most active measures have been taken to guard against surprise. I enclose a proclamation issued by Gen. Worth today.[26]

As regards the next movement of the army, I can give no information. Gen. Twiggs's division will be up tomorrow or next day, and then a more definite plan of operations will be adopted.

I send this off haphazard by the diligencia to Jalapa, but it is doubtful whether it will reach New Orleans.

G. W. K.
*Daily Picayune*, June 22, 1847

Puebla, Mexico, May 29, 1847

The division of Gen. Twiggs entered this city today, as well. There were rumors in the morning that Gens. Bustamente[27] and León were advancing to attack Gen. Scott with an immense force, but so far we have heard nothing confirming the reports. Almost everyone thinks that the Americans are to have another grand battle, but where no one can divine.

The diligencia does not run between this and the city of Mexico, and so far I have found it impossible to lay hands upon any papers.

No one as yet knows what Gen. Scott's intentions are as regards his future movements, yet small as his force is many think he will advance upon the capital. We shall know in a day or two.

G. W. K.
*Daily Picayune*, June 8, 1847

Puebla, May 30, 1847

Intelligence was received yesterday from the city of Mexico up to the day before the 28th. Santa Anna on that day submitted to the Congress a

---

26. Worth, while establishing cordial relations with civil and religious authorities in Puebla, constantly feared attack during his early days in the city. The proclamation referred to here probably placed his division on alert against such an attack.

27. Anastasio Bustamente commanded the Army of the West.

formal resignation of his office as president *interino*, and the members of both houses went at once into session, to deliberate upon the matter.[28]

The result of the new election for President is not yet known, but the opinion gains ground that Herrera will be the successful candidate.

There are no troops between this and the city of Mexico, nor are there any fortifications in process of construction either at Rio Frio or El Peñon. What with the National Guard, the Indians under Alvarez, the Guanajuato troops under Cortazar, and the odds and ends under Valencia and other generals there may be some 25,000 badly armed and equipped at the capital. All was doubt, hesitation and confusion among the officers and no one knew what to do. This is the latest and most reliable intelligence.

In haste,

G. W. K.
*Daily Picayune*, June 22, 1847

Puebla, June 3, 1847

I send you a file of the *Courrier François* of the city of Mexico, as also a number of orders and other documents. The *Courrier* contains nearly all the news of importance. Do read and publish an account of Santa Anna's affair at Amozoque, as it is peculiarly rich. It is said that Almonte has been sentenced to be shot at the capital for holding treasonable correspondence with one of our generals.[29] He is certainly in prison, but I hardly believe he will be shot. There was another revolution at the city of Mexico two or three days since, at least such is the report, but it was put down by Gen. Bustamente almost immediately. The originators of it

---

28. Santa Anna returned to Mexico City to find the Anaya administration paralyzed by political intrigue aimed at removing Santa Anna from power, the city's defenses in disarray, and Congress awaiting the return of presidential ballots from the states. After agreeing initially to yield his political authority to Anaya, Santa Anna took up full executive authority on May 19, 1847, encouraged by General José María Tornel and *puro* leaders determined to continue the war. Maneuvering through a sea of political intrigue, supported by his army, and aided by the failure of his opponents to mount a unified opposition, Santa Anna promoted his followers while arresting or banishing his political rivals and reassigning competing military commanders outside the capital. On May 28, in the midst of this maneuvering, he resigned the presidency only to withdraw his resignation on June 2, promising to save Mexico from General Scott and anarchy. In the weeks that followed, Santa Anna's power grew while Congress, unable to gather a quorum, exerted little influence on events. These events marked the end of Santa Anna's ties with the *moderados* and the reemergence of the *puros* in national affairs.

29. Juan N. Almonte, rumored to have strong support in the outlying Mexican states for the presidency, was arrested and charged with conspiring with the Americans during the tumultuous period following Santa Anna's return to Mexico City.

are friends of Gen. Farías, and, as is supposed, of peace with the United States, and one of their cries was "death to Santa Anna." By the way, the story now is that the Mexican Congress will not accept the resignation of Santa Anna. Of course there was some trick in his resignation.

Yours, &c.,

G. W. K.

*Daily Picayune*, June 22, 1847

Puebla, Mexico, June 5, 1847

Some excuse may be necessary to account for my not writing you for the last five or six days, and as I have a tolerably good one I offer it. A rascally cold, caught at Jalapa in the early part of May, stuck to me, spite of every effort to get rid of it, until I reached this place, and here it wound up with a regular attack of chills and fevers or intermitting fever, with a neuralgic accompaniment all but severe enough to take one's life. Thanks, however, to starvation, to hot mustard foot baths, and to quinine—especially to quinine—I have been enabled to weather the attack, and am now so that I can "set up and be about" as the saying is. There is a good deal of fever and ague, intermitting fever, and other diseases of kindred nature in the army; but I believe that nearly every case yields readily enough to medicine. Bowel complaints, brought on by partaking too freely of the different fruits which abound, are also common; but they too, are brought under by proper remedies.

The news from the city of Mexico is of considerable importance. The report is, that Congress will not accept Santa Anna's resignation, all which he probably knew when he sent it in, and that he now intends to carry his schemes in a more high-handed manner than ever. To defend the capital he appears determined upon; but instead of adopting a conciliatory policy, and bringing about a union of the different parties and factions, he has sent a number of the most noted officers either to prison or into exile, and by threats and abuse is endeavoring to bring over their friends to his cause.[30] Officers who gave their paroles at Vera

30. Santa Anna's decision in May to take up the presidency and fortify the city destroyed the *moderados* coalition that had unseated Gómez Farías. In April, Congress had vested the government with extraordinary powers to carry on the war, and now many feared that a Santa Anna dictatorship would misuse those powers. The prospect of an American siege of the Mexican capital raised fears among clergy, property owners, and supporters of a negotiated settlement. Mariano Arista and Almonte were arrested; Pedro de Ampudia was exiled to Cuernavaca. All three had taken advantage of the chaos of mid-May to plot against Santa Anna. Santoni, *Mexicans at Arms*, 207.

Cruz or Cerro Gordo are forced into the army, or else are threatened with violence and driven from the city. All the American citizens in the capital were ordered, on the 1st inst., to leave at the expiration of twenty-four hours, either for Jalisco or Morelia, and many were obliged to pack up and be off without a moment's time to attend to their business. This tyrannical decree will of course be ruinous to the interests of all, but more especially to the heavy commercial houses. In the meantime, every citizen has been called upon to take up arms for the common defence, and the *leperos* are driven to work at the fortifications at the point of the bayonet. Cannon are being cast at a foundry in the city—balls and shells at iron works near San Rafael—and other establishments are busy turning out munitions of war. Defences are in process of construction at Chalco, Ayotla, Guadalupe, Chapultepec, and other points, and the war party would fain believe that they can resist the advance of the "infamous and cowardly" North Americans. Great hopes are entertained of the prowess of the Guardia Nacional—composed of the young men of the capital, merchants' clerks, law students, the better class of mechanics, &c.—but as it is known that many of them hire servants to carry their muskets to and from the parade ground, no great harm can be anticipated from their force. It is further thought that the Indians from the South, the Pintos under Alvarez, will strike perfect terror into the hearts of "los Yankees," in as much as they cast their arrows with great accuracy, and when charged upon throw themselves on their backs and fight vigorously with their *machetes* or short swords. It is fairly presumable, if they undertake this latter game, that but few of those who throw themselves upon their backs will ever arise to their feet in this world.

It is a very old saying, that those whom the gods intend to destroy they first make mad. If the Mexicans are not mad then their actions must go for naught. The pertinacity with which they cling to Santa Anna is one evidence of their being demented, and their absurd hope of defeating the Americans and preserving their nationality is another. Were a man gifted with forty different lives, and were he to lose thirty-nine of them by drowning while clutching at the self-same straw, the fortieth he would probably sacrifice in the same vain effort. So with the Mexicans: with the evidence of a long list of reverses and mal-practices staring them in the face, they still cling to the tyrant and his fortunes. He may be the best man among them—he is certainly the worst.

I know not how I shall send this, but will embrace the first opportunity. Our information from below is, that the guerrillas are at work between Jalapa and Vera Cruz, and that nearly all communication has been cut off.[31]

Yours, &tc.,

G. W. K.
*Weekly Picayune*, July 5, 1847

Puebla, June 6, 1847

I have obtained a file of *El Republicano* from the city of Mexico, as also several copies of *El Nacional*, published at Atlixco where the Legislature of the State is now in session. Some of the articles in the latter are decidedly rich. The editor has a correspondent in this city who pretends to keep him regularly informed of every circumstance that transpires; and the way he throws facts aside and walks into fancy, shows him to be an apt disciple of the Munchausen school. The most outrageous falsehoods he utters with an effrontery that is really amusing. I shall forward the papers whenever an opportunity offers.

From *El Republicano* we learn that Santa Anna has either imprisoned or sent out of the way Generals Ampudia, Almonte, Bravo, Arista, and some say Rejon. Arista has been ordered to Acapulco, and the editor thinks most unjustly. Ampudia refused to be banished to Cuernavaca unless they used force, and force was used. Report has it that Bravo and Rejon were ordered off because they refused to accept commands in the army offered them, alleging, it is said, that all attempts to arrest the progress of the Americans must end in defeat.[32] Such views do not suit Santa Anna, who, like every desperate gambler, still determines to play on against every semblance of hope. Almonte is in prison, and is charged with holding communication with the Americans. It is even asserted that he is accused of holding a treasonable correspondence with Gen. Worth. I am informed that every line which has passed between them was a simple letter of compliments, written by Gen. Worth at Saltillo last fall, and to which he has never even received an answer.

31. When Scott moved forward to Puebla, he ordered the garrisons at Jalapa, under the command of Thomas Childs, and at Perote, under the command of Francis M. Wynkoop, to join the main body of the army. This decision cut Scott's ties to Vera Cruz, making travel to and from the coast extremely hazardous. The *Niles' National Register* reported on August 21 that Kendall's effort to get news from the front had left one courier killed and three captured.

32. Nicolá Bravo and other officers, including Manuel Rincón, who commanded the Army of the East, resigned their posts as an expression of their dissatisfaction with Santa Anna. Rejon, allied with the *puros*, was named minister of foreign relations in June. He did not accept the position, although his influence and that of the *puros* continued to grow. Santoni, *Mexicans at Arms*, 207–8.

The editor of *El Republicano* puts down the entire force organised for the defence of the capital at 17,500, including Indians, irregulars, and all. Santa Anna is known to have compelled those who gave their parole at Cerro Gordo and Vera Cruz again to take up arms, both men and officers; and those of the latter who have refused have been most grossly abused and insulted. As regards arms, the infantry are probably but indifferently provided; but it is known that new cannon are constantly being turned out at the foundry established for that purpose, and in this arm Santa Anna may be enabled to oppose no inconsiderable strength to Gen. Scott.

Here in Puebla there appears to be no lack of amusements. A circus company, under the management of Bensley, is to give a performance this afternoon—Sunday—at the Plaza de Toros, and in addition there is to be a regular bull fight at the same place, the *picadores*, *matadores* and other operatives in this refined pastime being all Mexicans. Hart's theatrical company has also arrived, and fandangoes are common enough at the *Jardin del Tivoli*. In this connection, although it may not be an appropriate one, it should perhaps be stated that divine service is to be performed at the palace this afternoon by a Protestant clergyman—I believe he is a chaplain of the New York regiment.[33]

Yours, &c.,

G. W. K.
*Weekly Picayune*, July 5, 1847

Puebla, Mexico, June 7, 1847

We have had an arrival and a mail from the United States. Lieut. Daniels,[34] with a number of recruits for the 7th and other regiments, arrived last evening from Vera Cruz, bringing dates from New Orleans up to the 14th May. The gratifying intelligence has also been brought that large reinforcements for Gen. Scott are on the way, although it is a great pity they were not sent sooner.[35] But so it has always been ever since this

33. The reference is to John McCarty, an Episcopalian from Syracuse. McCarty had served as a navy chaplain in the 1820s. He was now chaplain to a New York regiment, and the only commissioned army chaplain in the Mexican War. Miller, ed., *Journal of Ralph Kirkham*, xx, and Alan Peskin, ed., *Volunteers: The Mexican War Journals of Private Richard Coulter and Sergeant Thomas Barclay, Company E, Second Pennsylvania Infantry* (Kent, Ohio, 1991), 193.

34. Charles B. Daniels, Second Artillery.

35. After the victory at Cerro Gordo, Secretary of War William Marcy promised Scott 20,000 additional men by the end of June, although discussions continued in Washington about how best to meet the general's needs. Troops diverted from the Rio Grande began arriving in Vera Cruz in early June. Transportation difficulties and harassment from guerrilla bands slowed the advance to the interior, however. Not until early August would Scott's command at Puebla exceed 10,000 soldiers.

war with Mexico commenced—every movement has been too tardy, and procrastination has given the Mexicans, after every defeat, an opportunity to recover from the shock and prepare for fresh resistance. Who will deny that Gen. Scott, had he had ever 12,000 available men and a sufficiency of transportation, would not at this moment have been in the city of Mexico, and very likely without even a skirmish? No one in his senses can dispute it. The fault lies not at the door, either of Gen. Scott or Gen. Taylor, that they have not been in a situation to follow up their successes. I have heard Gen. Taylor censured in New Orleans for not pursuing and annihilating the army of Arista immediately after the battle of the Resaca. He did pursue him to the Rio Grande and *into* the Rio Grande; but it would be asking too much even of American soldiers to order them to throw away their muskets, strip off their coats, and swim after a retreating foe with no other arms than their fists to fight them with in case they caught them. The pontoon train to finish the battle of the 9th of May[36] arrived, I believe, late in October at Point Isabel, which is about as near as the authorities at Washington have usually come in having all things in readiness. This Mexican war is a necessary and most just one—our Government, to my thinking, was perfectly justifiable in every act which brought it on; but its conduction by the proper department at Washington has been most weak, and calculated to spin it out until doomsday. Our generals are cramped for want of men, their hands are tied for want of means—this is notorious. In a letter I wrote from Jalapa, and which I am fearful fell into the hands of guerrillas, the quotation "England expects every man to do his duty" was used, with the addition that the United States expects every man to *do more*. Does it not seem so? The march of 5000 or 6000 men hundreds of miles into the heart of the country occupied by 8,000,000 people, will read like a romance in after times. The entrance of Gen. Worth into this noted and populous city, with his mere handful of men, has had no parallel since the days of Cortes.[37] But to such news as I have to offer.

Every arrival from the city of Mexico but confirms the previous reports that the war party is determined to defend the capital. One rumor has it that they have already ninety cannon of different calibres; but this is doubtless an exaggeration. A Frenchman who arrived today says that Chapultepec, Mexicalsingo, Guadalupe and Peñon Viejo are fortified, and

36. The Americans drove the Mexican army across the Rio Grande at the battle of Resaca de la Palma on May 9, 1846.

37. While it was not a preoccupation for Kendall, other commentators frequently noted the parallels between Scott's march and that of Hernando Cortes from Vera Cruz into the Valley of Mexico in 1519.

that at the different points they have sixty cannon. The generals in command at these places are Ignacio Gutierriez, Gaona,[38] Mariana Martinez and Gregorio G. Palomino. That they are not only casting cannon, but shells and balls, and with great activity, is certain. It is to be hoped that they may run up all the bells in the city into cannon, for their continual clatter is excessively annoying.

When a movement is to be made upon the city of Mexico is uncertain, but I presume as soon as a sufficient number of new recruits have arrived. Gen. Scott lays all his plans with the most consummate adroitness, and will make the most of the force the Government has given him. A heavy stock of provisions has been laid in here, for which the army is mainly indebted to Mr. L. S. Hargous. When Gen. Worth's division arrived at Puebla it had neither provisions nor money nor credit with which to purchase; but, thanks to the indefatigable exertions and known probity of Mr. H., he has been enabled to overcome obstacles that on the face seem insurmountable. The policy of the United States government is to pay good prices for everything purchased of the Mexicans, but unfortunately it does not send on the money, and its credit does not stand at the highest in this region.

Yours,

G. W. K.
*Weekly Picayune*, July 5, 1847

Puebla, Mexico, June 8, 1847

The rain it raineth every day, and the wet season appears to have fairly set in. The rains, which come mostly in the afternoon, will doubtless offer great obstacles to the operations of the army in the neighborhood of Mexico, especially on the direct road leading to the city; but like all other obstacles the Americans have to encounter, they will be overcome in some way.

The result of the election for President of this so-called Republic is not known, nor will it be until January. Congress has passed a decree to the effect that on the first day of the coming year the new Congress shall be installed, and that on the 15th of the same month the votes for the President shall be counted.[39] This may be some new trick of Santa Anna's getting up, as until the time he can have everything his own way. The refusal of the present Congress to accept his resignation as President *interino*, gives him

38. Antonio Gaona.
39. Santa Anna was able to legitimately retain his office of president *interino* because only fifteen out of twenty-three state legislatures held presidential elections.

unlimited sway, and he will not be slow to exercise all the powers of a dictator. That there will be *gritos* and *pronunciamentos* against him before January is as certain as that the intervening months will come and go; but he may be cat enough to fall upon his feet–(qu. foot?)–with every new revolution. An anarchist himself, his very element is anarchy, and the only peaceful moments he probably spends are passed amidst confusion.

Report now has it–we can learn nothing positive–report now has it that Santa Anna has between 30,000 and 40,000 men of all classes under arms at and near the city, and that this force is rapidly augmenting. The peace party dare do nothing, for the moment a man is even suspected he is sent off or thrown into prison. The American residents have all left, many of them in such haste that their business must suffer to a most ruinous extent, while it is reported that all the American prisoners, contrary to the laws of nations as well as of humanity, have been cast into a more loathsome prison and treated more rigorously than ever. Such are the verbal reports we receive from the capital.

Yours, &c.,

G. W. K.

P.S.–I have just learned that a delegate from each State in the Republic has been appointed, all to hold a meeting at some given point, for the purpose of taking measures to establish a peace with the United States. This I give as one of the rumors afloat, but cannot ascertain that it is entitled to the least credit or importance.

*Weekly Picayune*, July 5, 1847

Puebla, Mexico, June 9, 1847

The division of Gen. Twiggs has been out drilling today, and made a most beautiful display. The 3d and the 7th Infantry, which so nobly sustained themselves both at Monterey and Cerro Gordo, were attached to his command. Gen. Worth's division is to be reviewed on Saturday–a sight worth seeing.

We have a verbal report today that the Mexicans intend giving Gen. Scott battle at or near Tlascala, some eight or ten leagues from this, and a little off the direct road to the city of Mexico. The story is, that the alcalde of the place wrote to Gen. Canalizo for orders how to act, and was told to collect all the militia he could, and that he would be supported in the course of a few days by troops from Mexico. Such is the report.

From Mexico we have news of some considerable importance. I have seen a copy of *El Iris Española* of the 5th inst., which contains Santa Anna's withdrawal of his resignation as President. It is dated on the 2d inst., and is

Santa Anna all over. He goes on by stating that in the first place he had good and substantial reasons for renouncing the presidency, and had waited anxiously for six days for some one to be appointed in his stead; that he well knew, when he sent in his resignation, that the enemy was not approaching, and that, therefore, there was full and sufficient time for his successor to adopt such measures as he might deem necessary for the public defence. He next goes on to say that he has just heard that the enemy, *taking advantage of his withdrawal from power*, (modest!) was about to move upon the capital—an occurrence which he deems of such great importance that he has at once waived all other considerations and determined upon holding on to the supreme command, for the sole purpose of saving the country. (This was certainly very kind and very patriotic in him.) He next pretends that he has received innumerable assurances, from all classes, of their entire confidence in him, as well as prayers and entreaties that he may not renounce power—they all look to him, according to his showing, as the rock of their salvation—as the only person who can save their great and populous city! He sees, he says, that Gen. Scott has taken advantage of his resignation to create disorders in the capital, as well as distrust and discontent among the people—that he is farther endeavoring to stir up revolutionary movements, as well as give confidence to the friends of peace—and taking all these things into consideration, he, Santa Anna, has finally determined upon sacrificing all to the good of the great Mexican nation, and again to resume the reins of Government; in short, that his people shall not say of him that he has deserted them in their day of trial and tribulation. And when their difficulties are passed, he still holds firm in his resolution to retire from all place and power, unless his life should be lost in his endeavors to extricate them from their great strait—a life which he is completely willing to offer as a last sacrifice to his countrymen![40]

Such is about the amount of this last movement of Santa Anna. In a hurried way I have given you the substance of his letter to Congress. As regards his losing his life, I do not think that any insurance company which may have a risk upon it need give themselves much uneasiness.

Verbally we learn that Santa Anna has formed a new Cabinet, composed of Tornel, Rejon, Ibarra, and Baranda. Tornel, although nothing certain is

40. Santa Anna's decision to resign in late May was part of an effort to regain control of a deteriorating political situation. His aim was to portray himself as a victim of his own determination to fight the Americans, thus casting Congress in the role of wanting peace if it endorsed his resignation. He hoped that his departure would provoke public demonstrations that would enable him to return to power with even more authority. Santa Anna withdrew his resignation when he learned that Congress planned to accept it. Santoni, *Mexicans at War*, 207–8.

known, is probably Minister of War, Rejon of Foreign Relations.[41] Both are well known in the United States—both have previously held the positions given them above. Trigueros[42] has resigned his office as Governor of the District of Mexico, and Gen. Ignacio Gutierrez takes his place—all probably the work of Santa Anna.

Yours, &c.,

G. W. K.
*Weekly Picayune*, July 5, 1847

Puebla, Mexico, June 10, 1847

Some of the papers are rating the clergy of the place right roundly for the favor they show the Americans. One of the editors, among other things, says: "The holy fraternity, which in other times produced the chiefs and captains of our independence, are now deeply immersed in commercial projects or plans to preserve their treasures. They remain cold spectators of the evils which have befallen their unhappy country, and with a culpable remissness, or else with hidden treason, assist the triumphs of the invaders." A pretty hard blow, this, for a Mexican to strike at the priesthood.

Verbal rumors still would induce us to believe that Santa Anna is constructing fortifications around the capital with vigor, and that he has at least sixty pieces of cannon already cast. Among the generals noticed as having command of the different battalions, I see the names of Perez, León, Ramirez, Gorostiza, Cortina, and the late President *sustituto*, Anaya.[43]

From the reports from every point it would appear that Santa Anna intends striking one more heavy blow for victory—else his actions greatly belie him.

No news of importance today. The troops are being regularly inspected and drilled, and present truly a most soldierly appearance, as new clothing has been distributed to those who stood in most need.

Yours, &c.,

G. W. K.
*Weekly Picayune*, July 5, 1847

Puebla, Mexico, June 11, 1847

Full files of papers from the city of Mexico, up to the 8th inst., inclusive, have been received here. I have only had time to skim over their

41. Ibarra became minister of foreign relations when Rejon declined to take the post.
42. Ignacio Trigueros had been among those who had sought to persuade Santa Anna to give up his presidential powers in mid-May.
43. The Mexican leaders not previously identified are Francisco Perez, Simeon Ramirez, Manuel Eduardo de Gorostiza, and Juan Nepomucano Cortina.

contents, and send you an abstract of such intelligence as may be interesting.

The *Monitor Republicano* of the 8th inst. says that Alvarez, with his Indians, was to march on that day for Puebla, and was to be followed up by the regular cavalry. The same paper intimates that the rest of the army is also to immediately take up the line of march for Puebla, and the inference is that the enemy intends fighting the great battle in this neighborhood. In fact, the editor openly comes out and says that by this course they will avoid having the beautiful city of Mexico the scene of a grand battle. He hopes that by a well combined effort the glory of the Republic may be preserved, and that Santa Anna may wipe off some of the stain which at present sticks to his character. The editor does not exactly say this, but he means it. Everyone here in Puebla hopes that *the* battle or a battle may be fought in this neighborhood—the Mexicans will not make another stand this side the capital in that case.

The papers are filled with accounts of the approach of the Americans towards Durango and Sonora. The editors say that the "infamous Yankees" have joined with the Apaches, Comanches, and other "barbaros;" but this no one believes.

Chihuahua has given its vote for Gen. Santa Anna for the next constitutional President, Zacatecas for Lafragua, Durango for Elloriaga, and Sinaloa and Sonora for Almonte.[44]

Santa Anna, according to *El Monitor Republicano*, has fallen out with the following extensive list of general officers: Bravo, Rincon, Canalizo, Arista, Miñon, Urrea, García Condé, Requena, Morales, Almonte and Ampudia.[45] Fortunate it is for Mexico—perhaps I should say unfortunate—that it has "a few more left." The editor says that all the above are either in retirement or else in prison, and further gives it as his solemn conviction that the country now has great need of their services.

Among those whom Santa Anna still counted upon as friends there was the greatest discord. Baranda, who was appointed Minister of Foreign Relations, only remained in office twenty-four hours—he resigned on the second day in disgust.[46] Cortina had also thrown up the command of the battalion of Victoria.

---

44. This is an accurate accounting of the presidential votes in these states. José María Lafragua was an important *moderado* and a rival of the now-dominant *puro* faction around Santa Anna.

45. Not previously identified is Tomás Requena.

46. Baranda had *moderado* ties and, along with Trigueros, had been involved in the effort to persuade Santa Anna to leave the presidency in mid-May. His brief tenure reflected the mounting influence of *puro* leaders.

The editor of *El Monitor* is raving, perfectly outrageous, because our army was not cut up and destroyed in detail while on its march to this city, and in fact after its arrival. He thinks it a burning disgrace that small parties of the enemy are permitted to prowl with impunity about the country, when they have thousands of troops laying idle about the capital. Instead of attacking our troops they have been allowed to concentrate, until they are finally enabled to show a bold and combined front. He winds up his terrible tirade as follows: "It appears as though there were a desire that everything should go to the devil." (No parece sino que hay empeño, en que todo se lolleve et diablo.)

The papers in the city of Mexico are publishing the American correspondence which has been intercepted by the *guerrillas* between Jalapa and Vera Cruz. So far, with the exception of a letter from Mr. Marcy to Gen. Scott, dated 30th April, it is of little consequence to the enemy.[47] I owe the editors or authorities a thousand thanks for giving to the light several letters addressed to my humble self, else I should never have known their contents. Our latest dates from New Orleans we have received through the Mexican papers—singular enough, is it not?

There is a rumor in Mexico, at last dates, to the effect that some of the officers of the regular troops were about to raise a *pronunciamento* in favor of a dictatorship. The editor of *El Monitor* ridicules the report—believes that there is no foundation for it. Santa Anna may be at the bottom of a movement of the kind. *Quien sabe?*

Yours, &c.,

G. W. K.

P.S. Since writing the above, I have seen a letter from Col. Hunt,[48] the quartermaster in New Orleans, and which has been intercepted by the guerrillas, and published in *El Monitor* and other papers. It was directed to Capt. Hetzel,[49] and speaks of the great difficulty he, Col. H., has in raising funds to meet the pressing demands of the army. The Mexican editors jump at this. They say that their government has now only to remain quiet, and that the Yankees will soon be driven to straits, and disbanded and dispersed for want of the means of sustenance. Mr. Secretary Marcy's letter they set down as a tissue of falsehoods.

*Weekly Picayune*, July 5, 1847

47. This letter outlined the Department of War's plans to reinforce Scott's army by 20,000 men by the end of June 1847.

48. Thomas F. Hunt.

49. Abner R. Hetzel, quartermaster.

Puebla, Mexico, June 12, 1847

The city is today full of rumors and reports, some of these of most startling nature if they could be relied upon. The story is that the Mexican army is to advance upon and surround this place entirely. Even the names of the leaders—Valencia, Gubero, Lombardini,[50] and Alvarez—are given. That Alvarez has started with his command there can be little doubt, but the impression is that he has gone in the rear of Puebla—somewhere in the neighborhood of Nopalucam or Acajete—with the hope that he may be enabled to cut off some of the wagon trains known to be on their way up. The Mexicans are known to have seven or eight thousand cavalry, and their true policy would be to fight Gen. Scott in the open field; but he who judges of the Mexicans by the ordinary rules which govern mankind will find himself mistaken nine times out of ten—so there is no knowing what they will do.

A Frenchman who left the city of Mexico yesterday reports that he saw two thousand men busily at work upon the fortifications at El Piñon. This is a hill of no great size or elevation, about nine miles this side of the city and on the direct road, with a lake immediately in the rear of it and at its base. Another Frenchman, and one who appears to be intelligent, says that the Mexicans intend to make three or four stands—one between this city and San Martin or Tlascala, where they can use their cavalry, another this side of Guadalupe, and the last at Guadalupe itself. Amid such a multiplicity of reports it is hard coming at the truth, and perhaps the only way to ascertain the real intentions of the Mexicans at the capital is to pay them a visit with the army.

Gen. Worth's division was reviewed today, was afterwards drilled, and certainly made a most imposing display. A large number of Mexicans, including some ladies in coaches, were present. The division of Gen. Twiggs is equally well prepared for any emergency; and for one I have an abiding faith in these portions of the army.

Yours, &c.,

G. W. K.
*Weekly Picayune*, July 5, 1847

Puebla, Mexico, June 14, 1847

For a wonder, yesterday we did not have anything even in the shape of a rumor from the city of Mexico, nor could we learn anything positive of the movements of the enemy in this neighborhood. I saw a man, who arrived

50. Manuel María Lombardini.

from Atlixco in the morning, who said that 600 of the Indians of Alvarez were expected there immediately—this was the only report received. Atlixco is eighteen or twenty miles from Puebla, and not on the road to the capital.

I send you files of papers, from both Atlixco and from Mexico—the latest date for the latter being to the 7th June. I have found it impossible to lay hands upon later papers, although I have seen them. All their contents of any importance I have given.

As yet no one knows when the army is to make a forward movement. Gen. Scott certainly will not march until reinforcements arrive, which are now without question on the way.[51] A delay is certainly of more importance to our army than to that of the Mexicans, for even if the latter are enabled to augment their forces they will not be beaten—that is certain: and then there is a strong probability that so straitened are the Mexicans for means that a delay of a month will find them dispersing over the country for the very means of subsistence, or else cut up by internal discords.

As regards the prospects of a peace, they appear just as distant as ever. A peace patched up at the city of Mexico at this time will hardly last until the ink is dry with which it is signed; certainly not until the Americans are out of the country. Without doubt there is a large and influential party in favor of it, but they dare not avow themselves for fear of after consequences. I know not how it may turn up, but as I said in a former letter I do not at present see any other course than for the United States to hold and retain possession of the country—aye, and to govern it, too.

Yours, &c.,

G. W. K.
*Weekly Picayune,* July 5, 1847

Puebla, Mexico, June 15, 1847

If the Mexicans knew what they were doing or what they were about to do themselves, then we might make some calculations and form some opinions as to their intentions; but every recent act of theirs appears to have been made up of indecision, and the wisest are left in ignorance of their real designs. One hour we learn that large bodies of the enemy are marching this way, the next hour report has it that they are marching back again; one arrival brings the intelligence that they have given up all idea

51. Approximately 1,200 volunteers and regulars under the command of George Cadwalader, volunteer brigadier general from Pennsylvania, and Col. James S. McIntosh, Fifth Infantry, left Vera Cruz on June 4, escorting a wagon train that was carrying ammunition and cash to Puebla. Gideon J. Pillow followed on June 8 with 2,000 men. He had returned to Washington briefly after having suffered minor wounds during the fighting at Cerro Gordo. United into a single column at Perote, this mix of new recruits and new regiments did not reach Puebla until August 8.

of fortifying in the neighborhood of the city, the next comer asserts that he has seen thousands busily at work at El Peñol, at Rio Frio, and at other points; and so the rumors run. One thing is certain: large bodies of troops have been moving in this direction of late, and there is no doubt that a part or the whole of the command of Alvarez advanced as far as Atlixco; but the opinion is that they have all, or nearly all, marched back again. It may be, however, that the Pintos are on the way to some point between this and Peroté, but of this we shall know more in a day or two.

Santa Anna is now doubtless driven to greater straits than ever to preserve his position and power, notwithstanding Congress refused to accept his resignation, and some of the papers still speak of him as the rock of Mexican salvation. Nine-tenths nearly of the population look upon him as an evil, but as a lesser one perhaps than any of their other great men; and hence they cling to him. He, in the meantime, is beset with difficulties and surrounded by dangers—means to sustain his army are denied him, and he sees the premonitory symptoms of a new revolution in every movement. The recent marching and counter marching of his troops in the neighborhood of the capital must have been caused either by his inability to procure them supplies, or else from a fear of their becoming disaffected through the exertions of the emissaries of the adverse factions. Rumors that a revolution, headed by Gómez Farías, had already broken out in Jalisco, have reached this place, and it is well known that there is no unity among the leading men at the capital as regards a system of defence. The party which is known to be in favor of peace is prevented by its pride and its fear from openly avowing itself; the party most rabid for a continuance of the war knows not how to act. To be sure, the papers still talk, in their usual gasconading style, of the great things the illustrious descendants of Iturbide are yet to do, and of the terrible deeds the valiant sons of Morelos, Matamoros and Hidalgo are still to perform;[52] yet anyone can see with half an eye that they only talk to give themselves confidence, and that discord, distrust and dismay reign in nearly every breast.

Here in Puebla all is quiet among the Americans; the reports of the advance of the Mexicans disturb neither the sleep nor the digestion of anyone. The Mexicans, or at least many families, are moving out of town,

52. Mariano Matamoros, a principal lieutenant of Hidalgo and Morelos, was executed after a Royalist force of 360 men led by Agustín de Iturbide surprised Morelos's insurgent army of 20,000 at Valladolid in December 1813. Royalists captured and executed Morelos in the last months of 1815. Iturbide took up the cause of Mexican liberation in 1820 and established himself as the first emperor of Mexico in May 1822. Forced into exile in March 1823 by republican forces that included Santa Anna, he was executed when he returned to Mexico in July 1824.

frightened by rumors which they do not understand and which they are ignorant enough to believe. The bull fights have ceased as all the *matadores, picadores,* and others are in prison for stealing; but we have a theatre and a circus still open, to say nothing of ice cream gardens, coffee-houses, billiard rooms and other places where a pleasant hour can be whiled away. Puebla is one of the best built and handsomest cities in the world, renowned for the richness and beauty of its cathedral, and for the magnificence of its churches and other religious establishments generally.

Handbills, in German as well as English, have been freely circulated among our men, offering them the most flattering inducements to desert. Two only have been fooled by these lying promises—a couple of simple Germans, who will heartily wish themselves back again in their company before a week is over their heads.

Yours, &c.,

G. W. K.
*Daily Picayune,* August 8, 1847

Puebla, Mexico, June 18, 1847

I cannot see that there is either utility or amusement in writing a parcel of rumors as it were today, only to have the work of contradicting them on the morrow; and thus feeling, I did not write you a line yesterday. I might have told you that Alvarez was close by here with any number of men from 1 to 6000, for such a story was afloat; I might have told you that a commissioner or commissioners had arrived in Puebla to talk over peace matters with Mr. Trist, for so I was informed; I might have told you how we were all to be poisoned, for such stories have been afloat; I might have told you that the town was full of armed Mexicans, and that an attack from within and without was hourly anticipated, for such was the common report; in short, I might have told you many things besides and spun out a long if not an interesting letter, but as I did not happen to believe anything, I said nothing.

Great numbers of Mexican families continued to leave Puebla, frightened at the thousand and one reports that the city is to be attacked. One old fellow who started out this morning in his coach is probably now sorry he did not remain, for he was robbed of $10,000 by the guerrillas near Amosoque. A party of Americans started out this afternoon in pursuit of the robbers, but were unable to find them on account of a heavy rain which set in.

I have seen a man this afternoon, a Mexican who enjoys the singular reputation of being honest, who says that he left the capital two days since.

He states that the Mexicans are fortifying at Rio Frio, where they have cut down an immense number of trees, and that the works at El Peñon are also still going on. At Vienta de Cordova the Mexicans also intend making a stand—many think that at this place the main battle will be fought. Almonte was a close prisoner at Santiago—the old convent where the Texans were so long confined—and the above Mexican brings a rumor that he had been tried and sentenced to be shot.

Yours, &c.,

G. W. K.
*Daily Picayune*, August 8, 1847

Puebla, Mexico, June 19, 1847

The night passed off without a disturbance or outbreak of any kind, and this morning all are alive. The story now is that Canalizo is to enter Atlixco today, while Alvarez is to proceed towards Nopalucane with the hope of cutting off one of our upward trains. It would be a good joke if he himself should be cut off while making the attempt. That a large number of the enemy are scattered about at different points near Puebla is certain, but what the intention of their chiefs may be no one knows with certainty.

The Mexican papers I have obtained are copies of *El Monitor Republicano* of the 13th, 14th and 15th of the present month. In an article which appears in the number of the 14th the editor handles Santa Anna severely for renouncing power and a few days afterwards retracting his resignation. The article is five columns long, and I give the concluding paragraph as a specimen of the whole:

> Let us finish. The man who tells us in his renunciation, "I have the pride to terminate today and forever my public career," is the same who now (after a short week) offers us, with a light *quid pro quo*, the assistance which Jesus Christ promised to his church: "*Mexicans, I shall be with you always until the consummation of your ruin!*"

The same editor, in another number of his paper, rates Santa Anna's Ministry soundly for their supineness and want of either honesty or ability to take care of their distracted country. At the same time he manifests no love for "los Yankees," but it is certainly a marvel that Santa Anna allows himself and his friends to be treated with so little consideration.

We learn verbally that Santa Anna is emphatically between Scylla and Charybdis in plain English, that he is in "a fix." For the hundredth time, he has recently said that he intends to sacrifice his life for his country—that the usurping Americans shall shed the last drop of his blood before they enter the capital. On the other hand, a party of young men, not having that entire confidence in his protestations they might have, have asserted that if the Yankees do not take his life in the coming struggle that *they will!* A decided case of "between hawk and buzzard" this, or I am no judge.

The editor of *El Monitor Republicano* speaks in the strongest terms of reprobation of the inhuman manner in which Gen. Arista was arrested and dragged off to Acapulco. He was taken from his bed in the night, where he was confined by severe illness, and without being allowed to take even a change of clothing, was hurried by a guard of dragoons. No reason or motive is given for this outrage. In the meantime the editor of *El Monitor* recommends to the public consideration the claims of Gen. Bustamente, deeming him a man who should take a leading part in the defence of the country.

The anniversary of Santa Anna's birthday, the 12th June, was celebrated in various ways at the capital. A grand *función* was given by a circus company on the occasion, a grand banquet was given by his friends, and rich presents flowed in to the dictator from his adulators. At the banquet the wines and bouquets were of the most costly description, while the presents consisted of gold-headed canes, set with diamonds, gold snuff-boxes, rich chains, breast-pins, &c. Where will he be on his next birthday, and who will be present to do him honor? There is a question he cannot himself answer.

The Mexican Congress appears to be doing little or nothing, and one-half the time a quorum even is not in attendance. The members know not what to do, and hence absent themselves altogether. In any other country the times—such times as Mexico now sees—would bring forth great men—men of talent, worth and energy—but no such good fortune appears to be in store for the distracted Republic. Strange that the only man of talent Mexico has produced is Santa Anna himself, and almost the only capital *he* has to work with is a superior cunning to any of his fellow scoundrels.

At the banquet given to Santa Anna on his birthday, according to *El Monitor Republicano*, only three or four toasts were given. One was given by his Excellency himself, as follows: "To the internal peace and final triumph of the Mexican arms." Gen. Rangel[53] offered the following sentiment, a sentiment which did not go down altogether as well as it might: "When Santa Anna dies, I hope that his enemies will do him the justice that his

---

53. Joaquin Rangel played a pivotal role in the *polkas* rebellion, first backing Gómez Farías and then aligning himself with Santa Anna when the latter abandoned his *puro* ally.

virtue and his military valor merit!" Decidedly equivocal, and the editor of *El Monitor* says that no one knows why many of those present washed down the sentiment with cold water only.

On the morning of the 14th inst. several pieces of cannon, recently cast at the foundry at Chapultepec, were tried at El Peñon de los Baños in presence of a large crowd. They are said to be cast on the model of the French Paixhans guns. The entire number of pieces now in possession of the Mexicans is said to be seventy of different calibres, and the editors recommend unceasing drilling in this particular branch.

The editor of *El Monitor Republicano*, in his paper of the 15th inst. supplicates and implores Santa Anna not to place the smallest confidence, nor even to give a place in the army, to any of the officers who have run in any of the previous conflicts which have taken place with the enemy. This is the unkindest cut of all. Not an officer in the Mexican army but has had a little active exercise in the way of running, and Santa Anna himself, after his escapes at Cerro Gordo and Amosoque, may be said to be in tolerably fair training for a fresh race. Run, forsooth! Why it is a part of "their system," as the celebrated Dr. O'Toole says when caught brushing the coat of his pretended pupil.

On the 12th June the Minister of War and Marine, by order of Santa Anna, issued a species of proclamation filled with sage advice to the Mexican army generally, and to those who have given their paroles particularly. As the speculations in this precious document are new, and may benefit the civilized world, we give three or four paragraphs in relation to the matter of paroles. Read and learn:

> The Mexican nation, relying on military persons of decided character and who have a knowledge of their noble profession, cannot permit their unjust enemies to debase them; and to avoid this opprobrium appeals to its defenders, because she has never so much required their valor and sacrifices as at present. And since the valor and sacrifices which have been made up to the present time have proved useless, they must be continued with increased energy until the welfare of our unfortunate country be restored.
>
> As in what has passed up to the present time, in regard to the giving oaths to the enemy not to take up arms, there have been some examples of bad tendency. His Excellency the President has ordered that some observations be made concerning the subject of paroles, in order that they may reach the knowledge of all the individuals composing the Mexican army.
>
> The want of practice in the established usages of foreign war has caused it to be thought legal and proper for prisoners to give their parole to the

enemy, by which their liberty is granted them—an error of as great magnitude as is the evil which the tolerance of such vice would produce. A military person cannot deprive himself of the only title which confers on him the advantages and considerations he enjoys—cannot, by an oath, incapacitate himself from defending his country. If an accident deprives him of it, on account of his being taken prisoner, he ought to abide by his fate; but he ought never to render himself incapable of returning to his country's defence, either by ransom or exchange. It is prohibited, therefore, in future, for any individual of the Mexican army to give his parole.

His Excellency the President hopes that on an occasion so serious for the Republic the army will faithfully correspond to his noble views; and he is persuaded that with its valor and decision it will save the nation from the danger in which it is placed, each individual composing it being of course convinced that a regular service, and even one well performed, is not sufficient, but that it is necessary to have a noble enthusiasm caused by a glorious ambition.

This is the weakest invention of the enemy we have yet seen. By a species of sophistry particularly Mexican, Santa Anna perhaps hopes to draw into his ranks some of those who have already given their parole, while at the same time he would deprive his officers of a right which has been accorded to all military men from the feudal ages down to the present day. There will be hanging, I trust, before this business is over, and Santa Anna's own neck appears to be *benemerito de la cuerda*. His own people style him the *benemerito de la patria*—the well-deserving of his country. He is equally as well deserving of a rope, if not better.[54]

The papers from all parts of the country—from Aguas Calientes, from Leon, from Querétaro, from Zacatezas, from Guanajuato, from Guadalajara, and from San Luis—speak in the strongest terms of reprehension of the unfortunate citizens of Puebla. They call them traitors, cowards, vile slaves, phenomenons of iniquity, hypocrites, and other names equally complimentary. It is really amusing to hear these swashbucklers abuse their poor countrymen of Puebla, for everyone knows that they will be as quiet and as docile as lambs when their turns come to get a glimpse of the Yankees.

Not a line do the files of papers I have seen say of the fortifications around the capital—the recent decree enjoining silence has completely closed their columns against all information. Puebla is full of rumors in

---

54. The Mexican Congress had conferred the title *Benemerito de la Patria* (Benefactor of the Country) on Santa Anna after his victory over the Spanish at Tampico in September 1829. *La cuerda* means "the rope."

relation to bodies of the enemy seen in the neighborhood, and of move-ments to cut off our trains and small parties. Were I to give them all I should have room for little else.

The report now is, that Gen. Cadwalader and Col. Childs will be up tomorrow or next day, and that in the wagon train there is a considerable amount of money.[55] Everyone hopes it may be so, for the army here has been sadly straitened for want of it. To be sure, a large depot of provisions has been formed, sufficient to last for weeks and weeks; but no thanks to our Government for this. As I said in a former letter, it has been mainly owing to the exertions and the confidence the people here have in Mr. Hargous that the army has got along at all, for the credit of Uncle Sam would not buy a pound of beef or a pound of flour to satisfy the hunger of those who are fighting his battles hereaway in the heart of the Mexican Republic.

Two or three men who were out scouting today in the neighborhood of Cholula, report the enemy in considerable force in that direction. Report has it that Canalizo is at Atlixco, but report here is such an unconscion-able liar that no one can place the least reliance in anything told him. Alvarez, all reports true, has been in front and in the rear, on the right and on the left of Gen. Scott within the last twenty-four hours. There are some who begin to think there is no such man as Alvarez.

Yours, &c.,

G. W. K.
*Daily Picayune*, August 8, 1847

Puebla, Mexico, June 23, 1847

Arrests continue, and the way they are going on now every carcel will soon be full. Duran, a judge of one of the courts here, was arrested yesterday for contumacious conduct and neglect of duty. He will be kept in prison until he has apologized for what he has already done, and promises to behave better in future. A noted captain of guerrillas, named Vilas, has also been captured, and is now safe under guard. He was caught acting the spy. On the roads the guerrillas harm their own people infinitely more than they do ours, and the better policy may be to let the scoundrels entirely alone. I have previously stated that some of the Mexican papers are loud in their complaints against the system.

A foreigner arrived here last night with dates from the capital up to the 20th inst. He reports verbally that there are few troops on the road, and

55. The wagon train carried $350,000 to meet Scott's supply needs. Since moving to Puebla, Scott's army had depended entirely on supplies that could be purchased or seized in the area.

that although the fortifications are still going on they have taken up but one bridge on the main route. Santa Anna was expecting from some point on the Pacific no less than 20,000 muskets—a most important thing if he obtains them.

Our latest dates from the United States are got through papers published in the city of Mexico, and as they obtain their intelligence entirely from the columns of *La Patria*[56] we are but little wiser as to what is going on in our own country. So lined are the roads at the present time with ladrones and guerrillas that we cannot get a paper from Vera Cruz, and until we establish relations as friendly with the Mexican Government those which the editors of *La Patria* had been enabled to form, which will probably not be in the course of the ensuing twelvemonth, we have but little hope of either sending you Mexican papers in safety or receiving those from the United States in return. I have already forwarded you several files by private expresses, but doubt much whether they will ever fall into your hands. By the way, speaking of *La Patria*, I see that the Mexican editors, thankful for the smallest favors, are eagerly publishing all the articles upon the war which the former paper contains in their respective journals.

Yours, &c.,

G. W. K.
*Daily Picayune*, August 8, 1847

---

56. *La Patria* was a Spanish-language newspaper in New Orleans.

# CHAPTER SIX

# PROSPECTS FOR WAR
## JUNE 24 – AUGUST 6, 1847

THE HOPE FOR PEACE AND THE NEED for reinforcements stalled Winfield Scott's advance on Mexico City at Puebla through July 1847. Disease, combat, and the return home of twelve-month volunteers had reduced the army of 10,000 that Scott had landed at Vera Cruz to an effective force half that size. More than 3,000 men were scattered in military hospitals at Vera Cruz, Jalapa, Perote, and Puebla, all too sick to take up arms.

British diplomats, their efforts to mediate a settlement having been rejected by the Mexican Congress in April, remained eager to prevent an American attack on the Mexican capital. Great Britain no longer contested the acquisition of Texas and California, but its officials were anxious to prevent further territorial losses and to protect British business interests in the country. At Nicholas Trist's request, the British legation opened communications with Mexican officials and advised Scott and Trist—the two men reconciled late in June—of the financial inducements necessary to secure a majority for peace in the Mexican Congress. Although Santa Anna was encouraged by British diplomats in the Mexican capital, by the promise of financial inducements, and by the clear willingness of the Polk administration to reach a negotiated settlement, he found that the political consensus necessary for treaty negotiations was beyond his reach.

Scott, meanwhile, rebuilt his army with new recruits and new regiments. By early August, the arrival of soldiers under the command of General Gideon Pillow and General Franklin Pierce brought Scott's effective force to about 11,000 men. Reports from the capital indicated that Santa Anna had about 30,000 men under his command. George Kendall, impatient for action, busied himself reporting on the diplomatic maneuvering, political intrigue, and military preparations swirling around him.

By the end of July, Santa Anna's attention was on the defense of the Mexican capital. Determined to meet Scott as far from the gates of Mexico City as possible and eager to use the landscape's lakes and limited roadways to his advantage, he focused his efforts on the fortification of El

Peñon, a small hill about ten miles southeast of the city, next to the National Road that led to Puebla. Scott, with nearly 3,000 fresh troops in camp, renewed his march on Mexico City on August 7. Three days later, Santa Anna moved the first elements of his ill-trained but enthusiastic national guard troops to El Peñon to block the expected American advance.

### Puebla, Mexico, June 24, 1847

All the talk this morning was of the arrival of a member of the British Legation in Mexico on a visit to Mr. Trist. That such an individual arrived, and that he called on Mr. T., I will take my oath; but what the object of his visit, is more than I can divine. This is the second or third time the same gentleman has come down from Mexico to see Mr. T., and each time rumor has been very busy in accounting for his movements.[1] I can say one thing for Mr. Trist: if the Government of the United States instructed him to keep the objects of his mission secret, he has preserved a most commendable silence in all matters thereunto relating.[2]

Verbal reports continue to pour in from the capital, all which would go to prove that the enemy is fortifying every point—altogether too many points to defend with any hope of success. In the meantime the Governor of this State, from his retreat at Atlixco, is calling upon every man to arm himself for the defence of the country. Nine-tenths of those he calls upon are probably contriving means to sell their produce to the Americans, and defraud the State if they can gain anything by it; but this makes no difference—they are still called upon to arm.

Many will have it that Santa Anna, with all his protestations about war to the last, is still in favor of an immediate peace—that he is only prevented by his fear from openly avowing himself. Very likely this is all true.

1. Edward Thornton, secretary to the British legation in Mexico City, first arrived in Puebla on June 11. He came at the direction of Charles Bankhead, British minister to Mexico, after Trist wrote to Bankhead asking him to transmit word to Mexican officials of the American willingness to negotiate. Thornton met with Trist and Scott—separately, since the two continued not to speak—and brought the first news that a settlement might be negotiated. The Mexican foreign minister, Domingo Ibarra, received Trist's message through Bankhead when Thornton returned from Puebla, but the inability to convene Congress to consider a negotiated settlement left the ministry unable to do more than acknowledge Trist's communication. Thornton made a second, probably unofficial, trip to Puebla on June 24 accompanied by British Consul Ewen C. Mackintosh, who was both well connected to high Mexican officials and a supporter of peace. In this second visit, Trist, and possibly Scott, were advised that Santa Anna would need both time and money ($10,000 immediately and $1 million at the conclusion of negotiations) to secure support for a negotiated peace. Pletcher, *Diplomacy of Annexation,* 507–10.

2. The continuing feud between Scott and Trist left even the general still uninformed about the extent of the diplomat's authority and the terms upon which the Polk administration was willing to end hostilities.

Of course he cares not a straw for the honor or welfare of his country—
such considerations never entered his selfish breast—and knowing full well
that he will lose the next battle he may hazard, and consequently the
slight hold he may still possess in the hearts of the citizens of the capital,
he is at loss how to act and may have secretly thrown out an anchor in
favor of coming to terms with the United States. The passage to and fro of
a member of the English Legation must have come to his knowledge, perhaps by his advice and consent: and while he is blinding the eyes of the
more belligerent of his countrymen with high-sounding war-talks, he is
silently making overtures for peace. *Quien sabe?*

Yours, &tc.,

G. W. K.
*Daily Picayune,* August 8, 1847

Puebla, Mexico, June 27, 1847

Since my last letter nothing has occurred worthy a line. I might have
given you a ream of rumors, all about the movements of the enemy here
and the enemy there; but they have all turned out alike destitute of foundation, and I have saved myself much ink and trouble by not relating
them as they came.

A court of inquiry, called by Gen. Worth, has been in session for a day
or two. It seems that Gen. Scott has in some way expressed himself
dissatisfied with not only the terms of the capitulation entered into with
the Poblanos by Gen. W. but also with some of the acts of the latter while
in command of the city. Gen. Worth promptly called for an investigation,
and I trust that all may be satisfactorily settled.[3]

I must give you a rumor. It is said that Canalizo himself was in Puebla
last night, in disguise of course and that he went out this morning in the
direction of Amosoque and Napaluco. It is further said that he sent a force

---

3. Worth requested a court of inquiry after he and Scott differed over the terms of the
American occupation of Puebla. Tensions initially developed over the lenient terms of surrender
Worth had granted to Puebla's civil and religious officials, especially the concession that allowed
local authorities to retain jurisdiction over crimes committed by Mexicans against American
soldiers. Scott rescinded Worth's concessions and issued instead General Order no. 20, first proclaimed in Tampico in February 1847, which provided for martial law in the theater of American
operations. Under it, all law breakers—military, civilian, American, or Mexican—fell under the
jurisdiction of American military courts. Worth then claimed that his command was independent
of Scott's and requested a court of inquiry to vindicate his actions in Puebla. On June 30, the
court, consisting of John Quitman, David Twiggs, and P. F. Smith, upheld Scott, ruling that Worth
should be rebuked for his actions. The incident continued the deterioration of relations between
Worth and Scott that had begun when the latter chose General Twiggs to lead the march from
Vera Cruz into the interior.

of some considerable amount by a road north of this place, which he is to overtake, and then, after joining Alvarez at some given point, is to attack the upward train at the first favorable place that offers. This story is told with a plausibility and sincerity that would give it credit in any other country, but here one knows not what to believe.

I send this batch of letters off at a venture as it were—it is impossible to say whether the man will get through safe or not. I have already dispatched several private messengers, and have reason to believe that some of them at least have gone through safe.

Yours, &c.,

G. W. K.

P. S.—Mr. Thornton, the gentleman attached to the British Legation at Mexico, and who was here on Sunday, started back on the same afternoon. I believe he called on Gen. Scott, as well as Mr. Trist, but the result of either interview is a most profound mystery to the mass of inquisitive Yankees now quartered in Puebla. I would wager a good dinner—a thing, by the way, you cannot get here—that his visits have something to do with peace, and that Santa Anna is privy to the whole matter.[4] That they will amount to anything, is entirely a different matter. All accounts agree that the greatest discord exists at the capital, that a *pronunciamento* is daily expected, and that there is no unanimity in the councils of the nation. Anyone who reflects can well hazard the conjecture that Santa Anna, while holding out war to the more belligerent, may still be so working his cards as to induce some one in Congress, or elsewhere, to open the question of peace, and then go over himself if there is the least chance of success. This is mere speculation, but it would be like the "Hero of Tampico," at all events. By all this you must not understand that I think the war is over.

*Daily Picayune*, August 8, 1847

Puebla, Mexico, June 29, 1847

The ever-varying, ever-changing kaleidoscope of Mexican politics, which but a few days since presented a phase all red, sanguinary and belligerent, by the single turn which the rising and going down of the sun has given it presents a new and most pacific aspect this morning. As another revolution of the machine may bring another change, and that within the tolling of a few short hours on the city clock, I shall wait until the last moment before I give you what may be termed the prospects of a peace.

---

4. Santa Anna had close ties to Ewen C. Mackintosh, the British consul general and merchant banker who accompanied Thornton to Scott's camp.

Within the last two days some twelve or fifteen prisoners, Mexicans who have been confined for different periods from one to ten or more years, have been liberated by Gen. Scott. That some of them have been guilty of gross and most heinous crimes there can be no doubt, but that they are any worse than those who incarcerated them is questionable. So long have some of them been confined, that even the original charges against them have been lost—one of them says that all he ever did against the law was to strike an officer for insulting his wife. It was a study to watch the faces of the poor devils as they were brought from their dens to be questioned as to their past delinquencies, and again to see their eager looks as they once more stepped forth free and saw the face of the blessed sun of which they had been so long deprived. Their families, too, hearing that they were to be liberated, crowded around the threshold of the prison; and the different groupings formed a picture which will not soon be forgotten by those who witnessed it. The hair of one prisoner, although his face denoted that he had not even yet reached middle life, was perfectly white. Another prisoner, a Frenchman, was one of the most noble specimens of humanity I have ever seen. He had been incarcerated several years, charged with aiding in some robbery on the road, but had never been brought to trial.

Our latest papers from the capital are to the 22d inst.; from Atlixco we have *El Nacional* of the 26th. Santa Anna is striking boldly at the liberty of the press, and hence we are unable, through the papers, to come at the true state of affairs at the city of Mexico. Señor Sojo, the printer of the *Bulletin of Democracy*, (*Boletin de la Democracia*) has been sent to Acapulco, whilst Señor Eufemio Romero, the principal writer for *La Calavera*, has been packed off to San Luis at a moment's warning. Torres, the editor of *El Monitor Republicano* has been repeatedly threatened by the authorities with imprisonment, but notwithstanding these threats keeps up a constant fire at Santa Anna and his ministers. Why he, too, is not sent off, it is hard to say.

Ibarra has been appointed Minister of Foreign Relations, and Vicente Romero, of Justice. Both are said to be ultra *Puros*, and with little or no character. It is asserted that no honest man will take office under the present Government, and a dishonest one does not appear to retain it more than eight-and-forty hours.

The latest papers from the capital contain two orders purporting to come from Gen. Taylor, at Monterey, the first numbered 465, dated the 8th May, and directing the first division of his army to march on the 17th June for Catorce, the second numbered 466, without date, and directing the other division to march on the 22d June for San Luis. Many of our officers doubt whether these orders are genuine. The *Diario del Gobierno* of the 21st inst. pretends to have dates from Monterey up to the 6th inst., at which time it is said Gen. Taylor was confined from an injury or wound he had received in one of his feet. His disposable force was then put down at between 5 and 6000, and the impression was that he would move upon San Luis shortly.[5] Of course you know more of the movements of Gen. T. than we do.

The Mexican papers continue to brag about the successes of the guerrillas between Vera Cruz and Jalapa. We shall know with what reason when the train comes up.

A letter from Mazatlan, dated June 2, states that that neighborhood has been declared under martial law. The U. S. ship *Independence* sailed from Mazatlan on the 1st inst., destination not mentioned, leaving the *Cyane* only off the bar.[6]

The only article I have seen in any of the Mexican journals, relating particularly to the action of the Congress on the question of peace is the following in *El Monitor Republicano* of the 22d inst. The editor says:

> "A communication has been addressed to our Government from Gen. Scott, at Puebla, in which the arrival there of a commissioner from the United States, fully empowered for the adjustment of a peace, is announced; but it has been sent to the Congress for that body to deliberate on so important an affair. We think that a sufficient number of deputies will not assemble; and should this be the case, the absentees will appear in our columns, in order that the public being made acquainted with them may never return them again."[7]

This is the English of the entire article, but what the editor is driving at in the last clause it is difficult to make out. It may be that he threatens to expose the absent members because he wishes them to appear and vote against listening to any propositions of peace, and it may be exactly the

5. Taylor's army remained in a defensive posture around Saltillo after the battle at Buena Vista, although he held orders granting him discretionary authority to advance on San Luis Potosí. The departure of the twelve-month volunteers and the redirection of reinforcements to Scott's command made an advance impossible.

6. The American navy imposed blockades on the port of Mazatlan and other Pacific ports from time to time from the fall of 1846 through the summer of 1847.

7. The communication actually came from Trist through the British legation. On his visit to Puebla on June 24, Thornton informed Trist that Buchanan's note had been delivered on June 12. Santa Anna forwarded the offer of negotiations to Congress because in April it had acted to make negotiations with the United States an act of treason.

reverse. He must be a shrewd observer who can tell from what a Mexican editor says one day what his feelings will be the next.

I wrote you a few days since, giving you a small specimen of the ravings of one of the San Luis editors on the subject of coming to terms with the vile North American vandals. He said that his State would never listen to propositions of peace until Gen. Scott was on his knees kissing the hands of Santa Anna, and Gen. Taylor was chained in one of Gen. Valencia's stables! but the man was evidently excited when he said all this. A wag of an officer at my side says that if they do chain old "Rough and Ready" in a stable, they will find him standing up to the rack. The writer for the same paper—*El Extandarte de los Chinacates*—handles Gen. Scott severely for his Jalapa proclamation. I shall endeavor to forward you the paper, with the hope that you may read and translate his ravings for the benefit of those fond of the tomahawking and scalping style.

We have a thousand and one conflicting rumors in relation to the upward bound train under Gens. Pillow and Cadwalader, and as many reports about the movements of Canalizo, Alvarez and other Mexican generals, who are said to be leagued in the attempt to cut it off. The train, mangre all the attempts of the Pintos, guerrillas and others, will be along in the course of a day or two.

Yours,

G. W. K.
*Daily Picayune*, July 8, 1847

Puebla, Mexico, June 30, 1847

All the talk now is of peace, immediate peace, with the great Mexican nation, and those who talked but a short week since of reveling in the halls of the Montezumas, now appear to think they are just about as near the aforesaid halls as they ever will be. I hardly know what to think of the matter. The arrival of the heavy reinforcements known to be on the way for Gen. Scott, combined with the loss of confidence the Mexican leaders have in themselves and their followers, have turned their feelings to a degree, and the most belligerent among them may now really be in favor of coming to terms. Santa Anna himself, although he will be very far from starting the ball, will doubtless help to keep it in motion when it is once under way. His very salvation depends upon it. He knows that he will be defeated and lose all if he makes another stand; by making cat's-paws of some of the members of Congress, and getting them to look with an eye of favor upon propositions for peace, he thinks that he may be able to second their movements if everything looks favorable, and finally himself reap all the benefits that may grow out of it. What the propositions are that have been made to the Mexican Government few here know; but what with British inference, and the timidity of the Mexican leaders, they have evidently been listened to.

Three days since and hardly a man in Gen. Scott's army thought that there was a hope of coming to terms with the enemy; now, the tune has changed, and many of the officers are even talking of the chances of avoiding and escaping the *vomito* on their way home. With all the cry of peace, I am not one of those who think that our affairs with Mexico are yet settled. A great deal depends upon circumstances. Should the upper train, containing as is supposed a large sum of money, meet with a reverse, the Mexicans would be emboldened to offer fresh resistance; should Santa Anna find, on counting noses, that a majority are against him in any committee appointed by Congress, he will be found among the first to scoff at any idea of terms with the perfidious Yankees; should, in fact, anything turn up out of which the Dictator may make capital for himself, no matter whether for or against the best interests of his dearly beloved (?) country, he will embrace it for his own aggrandizement. He wants time, he wants to procrastinate, he wants to delay the approach of Gen. Scott upon the capital—in short, he wants to do anything which may aid and further his own ambitious schemes.[8]

There is some reason to suppose that Gen. Taylor is advancing upon San Luis, although there is no positive information to that effect. With the American flag flying at San Luis and Zacatecas, the inhabitants of the capital might be more disposed towards talking of peace—this, in case the inhabitants wish to save the seat of government from the disgrace of having it occupied by *los estrangeros*. But, as I have before said, these people cannot be judged by any rules which apply to other nations, and therefore the effect of seeing their foes upon every side, and knocking at every gate, cannot be counted upon.

I might run on for hours with speculations as to the present condition and future prospect of this war with Mexico; but as it would all end in speculation, I shall close with a few remarks which may be taken for what

8. Kendall's characterization of affairs in the Mexican capital was accurate. Not eager to take up the issue of negotiations, the Congress was slow to form a quorum. When it did convene, *puro* delegates carried the day, rejecting the call for negotiations by a 52 to 22 majority. In mid-July, the Santa Anna administration—led by the *moderado* José Ramon Pacheco, who was then serving as the minister of foreign relations—tried to repeal the April 20 decree preventing negotiations. This effort also failed. Neither Congress nor Santa Anna wanted to confront the matter of negotiations with the United States directly.

they are worth. Santa Anna, tired of fighting the Americans, is anxious to make peace with them, although fearful of openly avowing it. The peace party in the capital—the capitalists and property holders—are also anxious, unwilling to support the war longer and taxed already beyond what they consider their means. The military are anxious to see the war continued, as the only means by which they can support themselves; the *leperos*, the ragamuffins of the country, care but little, one way or the other, how affairs go, so that they can steal enough to supply themselves with blankets, chinguirito,[9] and frijoles and tortillas sufficient to support life. The Indians care for nothing, and they are the most numerous class, so that they can sell their produce for silver in which they have sufficient confidence to bury, and many of the other inhabitants of the country will follow their example. The priests—perhaps I should have placed them at the top of the list—are anxious to preserve their position and their riches, although they may look upon us as dogs and heretics: and thus you have a mere inkling of the feeling of the different parties. All these feelings and interests—after taking into consideration that all hate and despise us—you may mix up and then make out the chances for a peace.

I do not know that anyone has reflected much upon this subject, but to me it seems that this thing of making a peace is to be a more difficult matter than making war upon the Mexicans, and will be surrounded with greater perplexities. Texas has to be brought into question, other boundaries taken into consideration, California is to be a bone of contention, indemnifications and costs of war are to be called into account, and a thousand other matters will be found in the catalogue of stumbling blocks in the way of an amicable arrangement of difficulties. The "three millions," after Santa Anna has helped himself—for he must be thought of first—will not go far, in way of salve or cordial for the many wounds under which poor Mexico is suffering, and there will be other provisos than Wilmot's for increasing the sum.

Let me conclude this hasty scrawl. The talk, as I said at the outset, is now of peace; but it will all end in Santa Anna's advancement or his utter downfall. In all his diplomatic arrangements—whenever he has been allowed to argue his point—he has been invariably a winner; at this game, some how or other, he always turns everything to his own advantage, or at least always has so far. How he will succeed in his present scheme remains to be seen, but he should and probably will, be closely watched. A few days will bring us out of the doubt and uncertainty in which everything is

9. Rum made from the lees of sugar cane.

at present enveloped, and I shall make opportunities to keep you informed of everything that transpires.

G. W. K.
*Daily Picayune*, July 8, 1847

Puebla, Mexico, July 13, 1847

An order has at length been issued which looks as though an immediate movement was anticipated. Gen. Scott is to commence reviewing the different divisions on the 15th inst., after which it is thought there will be a general turn out and then an onward march. The general impression now is, that there will be a harder fight at the city of Mexico than any that has yet taken place in the country, but no one can tell anything with certainty.

In my last letter I intimated that a letter had been received from one of the American officers still unjustly retained in Mexico. It was dated on the 8th inst., and I give one or two extracts:

Since my last, the preparations for your reception here have gone on with great spirit. An army of not less than 23,000 men, well dressed and apparently well armed, are now in this city and neighborhood. Handsome pieces of artillery have lately been cast, while their fortifications are nearly completed. The artillery may reach 100 pieces—they certainly have not less than 60 in number. The display here is quite imposing and the nation is made to believe that the great anxiety of the United States for peace proceeds from an apprehension that our army dare not attempt to move upon the capital. The long delay of Gen. Scott at Puebla, the arrival of a minister of peace, and our repeated offers to treat, give color to the idea in the estimation of this people that Gen. Scott is fearful of attempting the reduction of the capital. We here know perfectly well the value of these speculations: but it is nevertheless true that they are rapidly becoming riveted on the public mind. * * * * * Be assured, there can be no peace made with Mexico at this time—Santa Anna *dare* not and Congress *will* not. Let our army but come here and the resources of the nation are cut off; and the people seeing the capital in our hands, peace must follow. * * * * * The strongest defence of the Mexicans is at El Peñon, three leagues from here and on the best road leading into the city; but the best approach is by Guadalupe or Chapultepec, and the position for throwing shells better from either. The road to Guadalupe branches about one and a half miles short of the Peñon, passes round the lake of Tescuco, and is thirty miles farther than the direct route. There is two or three leagues of soft ground on this road, made so by the recent rains, which may occasion some difficulty to heavy carriages; but good judges think it may be overcome. The road to Tacubaya and Chapultepec is good, and here is the supply of water for the city, which may be cut off. * * * * * I have written to the Minister of War here in relation to our detention, but can get no answer. I was asked a day or two since by Col. Moreno, a Mexican officer, why our government had not proposed to have us exchanged? I replied that I had no information on the subject, except that according to the official statements, both of Gen. Taylor and Santa Anna, we were exchanged the day after the battle of Buena Vista, but whether any steps had been taken to secure a compliance I was not informed. The health of our party is as good as could be expected under the circumstances.

I have given you all the more interesting extracts from this letter, and when I state that it is from an officer well informed and on the spot, his opinions should pass for something. His ideas in relation to peace are coincided in by almost everyone here. The dragoons under Kearny and Sibley,[10] accompanied by a white flag, which I mentioned in my last as about ready to start, went out yesterday morning towards the capital with a white flag. One object of this mission is to procure the liberty of the American officers now detained,[11] and it is hoped it will be successful, even if they are sent home by way of Tampico.

Speaking of prisoners, has it ever occurred to you that there are other Americans in Mexico besides those held in the capital, who are certainly so far confined as to be utterly unable to leave? I might give you a long list of names, and you would find that of your humble servant in the number, who have seen quite enough of Mexico and are anxious once more to breathe the free air of the United States; but to all intents and purposes we are prisoners here, and there is no such thing as telling when we are to be released. To be sure we are "on the limits"; that is, we can walk about inside the sentinels; but he who goes outside of the sound of "Who goes there?" does it at great peril. The largest liberty is here compressed into the smallest possible space, and that perfect freedom of coming and going we enjoy at home may be now quoted in Mexico as merely nominal.

A Spanish company of actors is giving a series of entertainments at *El Colisco*, one of the theatres of the place. The horrible drama of "Lucretia Borgia" was performed on Sunday night with startling effect.

10. Philip Kearny and Henry S. Sibley, First Dragoons.
11. The reference is to the officers captured at Encarnación in January 1847.

The rains continue. Hardly an afternoon passes without a drenching shower, and as the army has no tents the poor soldiers must suffer incredibly on the road to Mexico.

Alluding to the advance upon the capital, there are certainly individuals in the army, and those who should be well informed, who do not think we shall reach it—who are of the opinion that peace or an armistice will be settled or entered into this side. Negotiations of some kind are certainly going on, all probably relating to peace, but the mass know nothing of the nature of them.

Yours, &c.,

G. W. K.
*Daily Picayune,* August 8, 1847

Puebla, Mexico, July 14, 1847

This morning I was enabled, through the exertions of a Spanish priest, to obtain a look at a file of Mexican papers up to the 11th inst. I hastily give you a synopsis of such items as may be of the least moment, premising that the papers contain little matter of interest.

José Ramon Pacheco has been appointed Minister of Foreign Relations, in place of Señor Ibarra resigned. He entered upon the duties of his office on the 8th inst., and up to the 11th continued in office.

Under the head of "*Persecutions,*" *El Monitor Republicano,* of the 8th inst., says that an order had been issued for Gen. Almonte to march for Tulancingo within twenty-four hours, and that all aid and assistance had been refused him.

Dates from Mazatlan up to the 24th June have been received. At that time the British men of war *Constance* and *Carysfort* were lying in the harbor, but no American vessel was in sight. The writer says that they had all gone off to avoid the storms, but would return after the rainy season was over. They were expecting several merchant vessels from Europe, and appeared confident they would be able to run in and discharge their cargoes.

A letter from Chihuahua, dated on the 15th June, is published in *El Republicano.* It announces the arrival at Sante Fé of 2000 volunteers and 300 families, the latter coming out with the intention of colonizing. This may be true and may not.

On the 4th inst., says *El Republicano,* the holy sacrifice of mass was celebrated in the *plaza de armos,* in order that all the troops in the city might hear and witness the ceremonies. The concourse on the occasion was said to be great.

A Zacatecas correspondent of *El Republicano*, writing under date of the 30th June, says that at last accounts Gen. Taylor was busy preparing wagons and barrels to transport water, and that he was shortly to advance upon San Luis.

A letter has been received here in Puebla, dated at the city of Mexico on the 12th. I have not seen it, but am told that the writer expresses himself confident the Mexicans will make a hard struggle to preserve the capital—the hardest they have yet made. There is no telling what a few days may bring forth.

The papers continue to be most profoundly silent as regards the fortifications around the city, but we continue to receive reliable verbal information to the effect that the Mexicans are making every preparation to receive "los Yankees." Works in addition to those of El Peñon have been constructed at different points along the road, ditches and trenches have been cut, the streets have been barricaded, and cannon are mounted at every available point. These demonstrations certainly look as though war to the death was determined upon.[12]

We have a rumor received through Mexican channels, to the effect that Congress was to meet yesterday, or today, a quorum having been formed. If this be true, the first business before that body will probably be Mr. Buchanan's last propositions of peace, and a most stormy session may be anticipated.[13] There is no mistake that the friends of peace, especially among the rich property holders of the capital, are more in favor of coming to terms now as the danger approaches.

I send this letter off although it does not contain news enough to cover one-tenth part the postage. In the course of a week, if not sooner, I shall have something far more interesting to offer, unless my judgment belies me.

Yours, &c.,

G. W. K.

12. When Santa Anna took command of the defense of Mexico City in May, some of his generals pressed to block Scott's advance from Puebla. In the end, Santa Anna decided to fortify points where the raised roads through the swampy region around the city intersected with the rim of the basin that surrounded it. Successfully held, these defenses would protect Mexico City from American artillery fire, while allowing the cavalry under General Juan Alvarez to sweep behind Scott's advancing army and cut off its retreat to Puebla. El Peñon, a heavily fortified rocky hill about seven miles east of the city along the main road to Puebla, was Santa Anna's headquarters.

13. The instructions that Secretary of State James Buchanan prepared for Trist called for the recognition of the Rio Grande boundary and the acquisition of New Mexico and California by the United States. He hoped to obtain the right of transit across the Isthmus of Tehuantepec, too, but it was not a requirement for peace. Trist was authorized by the Polk administration to pay as much as $30 million for these concessions.

P. S.—Just as I was closing this letter, Capt. Kearny returned. He was not permitted to go farther than Rio Frio. At the bridge of Tesmelucan he encountered a body of the enemy, who fled at his approach although he had a white flag flying. Kearny pursued, with the hope of overtaking the runaways, but was finally compelled to send a Mexican ahead to tell them the objects of his mission. At Rio Frio he handed his letters to Gen. Portilla,[14] and finding he could proceed no farther set about returning at once. The great Canalizo was present, and as Kearny was starting he begged that officer to allow two of his aides to accompany him back as far as a hacienda where he had left his trunk and a young son of his in his flight! The scamper of the Mexicans, at the approach of our little body of dragoons, is represented as having been most ludicrous.

*Daily Picayune*, August 8, 1847

Puebla, Mexico, July 16, 1847

The division of Gen. Twiggs was reviewed yesterday by Gen. Scott, and made a most brilliant show. Gen. Quitman's division is to be reviewed today, the cavalry on Saturday, Gen. Pillow's division on Sunday, and Gen. Worth's division on Monday. Col. Garland's brigade, attached to the latter, is now absent in the direction of Perote—one reason why the division is not to be reviewed sooner. No one can say with certainty, but the impression prevails that the army will move onwards by the middle of the ensuing week.

I have had time to look over the last papers from the capital more at my leisure. The editors announce that Alvarez has recently had several long interviews with Santa Anna at the palace, but the result has not been made public.

Santa Anna appears to have had ill luck with his coaches. One he lost at Cerro Gordo, and on the 8th inst., while visiting the fortifications around the city, another in which he was riding broke flat down. He was moving in great state at the time—with an advance guard, a rear guard, and numerous generals and colonels galloping on either side—and the editor of *El Monitor* ridicules the whole affair from first to last.

The same editor announces that extensive preparations are being made at the palace for the reception of the youthful consort of Santa Anna, who was hourly expected. He intimates that her appearance will alleviate and distract the illustrious general from other cares, and further says that while she is by his side he probably will not be able to hold as frequent con-

14. Nicolás de la Portilla.

versations with other ladies as has been his wont of late, to the great prejudice of a third person, (the Señora Santa Anna he doubtless means.) Rather a hard hit, this, and as a guard of soldiers entered the *Monitor* office a short time afterwards in search of the editor, it was probably felt.

Almonte has been sent off to Tulancingo, to take command of the post there, but this here is considered as equivalent to a disgrace, and is noticed by the editor of *El Monitor* under the head of "*Persecutions.*" Almonte himself complains that he has no time to collect baggage appropriate for an officer of his rank, being hurried off at only twenty-four hours' notice.

A letter from Durango, dated on the 28th June, states that Gen. Filisola had started in the direction of Saltillo with 600 infantry, 400 cavalry, and 4 pieces of artillery. He was to be joined by Gen. Reyes, with the Zacatecas troops. This would go to confirm the truth of a recent letter from the latter city, but no one here believes that either of the above generals will ever venture within gunshot of Gen. Taylor.

Under the head of "*Very Important!*" the *Republicano* of the 9th inst. has the following:

> The *Diario* of yesterday announces that according to information which it can rely, the enemy will move from Puebla upon this capital on Monday next. If this be certain, and the rumor false which supposes that 6000 more men are about to disembark at Vera Cruz, we are persuaded, that Scott is about to make a hopeless although very imprudent attempt to force the gates of the capital of the Republic. The Mexicans, by only recalling to mind the brilliant feats of arms which made their struggle for independence memorable, (they must forget their recent shameless defeats of course,) will feel in their hearts the necessary impulse to repel an army such as that which threatens us, which is in truth sufficiently contemptible. Of what avail are 10 or 12,000 men, the greater part of them discontented, before an army of more than 20,000 and a population of 200,000? This consideration alone ought to keep the Americans back; but supposing that they dare defy Mexico under such a disadvantage, they will meet with, we believe, an exemplary chastisement!

The idea of the Americans being *very imprudent* is peculiarly rich. In the same paper we notice accounts of the departure of different small bodies to work on the fortifications at Chapultapec and at the gate of Nonoalco.

I have now given you everything of interest in the latest papers, at least a synopsis of everything. Of verbal reports we have a multiplicity, some of them carrying the evidence of their falsity on the face, while others would seem to be entitled to more credit. The rumor that Congress had formed a quorum and commenced its sessions receives additional confirmation, although I cannot yet learn that it is a well established fact. We shall know in a day or two.

And now let me finish with a few speculations of my own—mere speculations, mind you. All our accounts from the city of Mexico, both verbal and through the newspapers, would indicate that the enemy is determined upon making a stout resistance, and that they will do it is the general impression. No man can well believe otherwise with the lights now burning openly before him; but at the same time there may be secret influences at work, to bring about an adjustment of our differences with Mexico, which no man out of the circle of those engaged in the secret can know anything of. I should be far from surprised were I to learn positively that English influence and American gold were now at work at the capital, and that bribery was endeavoring to take from the bayonet its legitimate office.[15] Sincerely do I hope that such influences may not be at work, and that if they are they may prove unsuccessful. The idea of *purchasing* a peace of these people must be repugnant to every true lover of his country—it would be dishonorable on the very face of it, and would be far from proving lasting in the end. If Congress is really now in session there are doubtless many of the members ready to do anything for money—they have heard of the "three millions," and the honor and best interests of their country must stand aside if there is any chance of their pockets being replenished. Santa Anna, too, will aid and abet any movement, so that he can come in for the lion's share; and such are the men bribery and corruption have to work upon. I repeat, that I hope that neither English influence nor American gold may be able to effect anything in bringing about a peace. It is impossible for me to say with certainty that these agents are at work, but I believe they are; and I further think it anything but creditable to our country to make use of them. With the American flag flying at the palace in the capital perhaps we might hear something in the shape of a

15. Kendall may have been aware that Scott, urged by Trist and encouraged by British reports from the capital, had agreed to offer a $10,000 bribe to initiate negotiations while guaranteeing $1 million with the signing of a peace treaty. The money came from a fund Scott had at his disposal to support secret military activity. Scott discussed the plan with his generals on July 17; they largely opposed the idea. The scheme ended when the Mexican Congress refused to authorize negotiations. Santa Anna kept the $10,000. The effort to "purchase a peace" was later leaked to the press and became the subject of a court of inquiry in 1848. Scott denied that he had paid money directly to Santa Anna. That was likely true. It appears that the money was transferred through Ewen Mackintosh. Dean B. Mahin, *Olive Branch and Sword: The United States and Mexico, 1845-1848* (Jefferson, N.C., 1997), 98–104.

proposition—the first one—from Mexico. At all events, while we are thus far in the country, the experiment were preferable to hiring a beaten enemy to accept our terms.

Yours, &c.,

G. W. K.

P. S.—*5 o'clock, evening*—The rumors of peace are again prevalent, and the talk now is that the army will not move for two weeks—some think not at all. Every hour puts a new phase upon matters, but something unusual is now in the wind. You shall learn all about it in my next.

*Daily Picayune*, August 8, 1847

Puebla, Mexico, July 25, 1847

Since dispatching my last courier, three days ago, I have not written you, for the simple reason that I had nothing to say. Even rumors have not been as abundant as they were a week since, the jade who circulated them with so prolific a hand on our first arrival having either tired herself down or worn herself out. Not ten days since, and we had twenty different stories in relation to Santa Anna in as many different hours—his stock, if I may be allowed to use the term, was purely of a fancy description, rising and falling with every puff of wind from the capital. Now, we simply hear occasionally that he continues to lead Congress and the people by the nose—in short, that he is having everything his own way. Dictator he was, at last accounts, to all intents and purposes, and his measures, whatever they may have been, he was carrying out with a high and most unscrupulous hand. The law of one day, if it stood the least in his way, was abolished the next, and he who raised a word of opposition or dissent was placed where his voice could not be heard, let him shout at his loudest. Such was the state of affairs at the capital four days ago—they may have altered since then.

In my last, I mentioned the capture of a Mexican mail by a party of dragoons. Since then another package has been taken, and the contents of one of the letters was outrageous beyond belief. The writer, a young man half crazy and two-third knave, spoke of women being daily outraged by not only our men, but the higher grades of officers; said that the most gross excesses were perpetrated in open day; that females were not safe even in their own houses; that many good citizens of Puebla had already died of rage, and that he himself could not possibly live much longer and witness such horrible crimes as were hourly committed by the savage and perfidious Yankees—he must die from an excess of choler. He winds up his letter by swearing to the truth of all he has written, and then asks his friend in the city of Mexico to read and circulate the precious document. He is now safely lodged in prison, and gives as an excuse that he only wrote the letter in joke! As he has been told that he must remain in prison until he proves one of the statements he has so solemnly sworn to, his incarceration is likely to be a long one.

I have seen an order, issued at the city of Mexico on the 19th inst. by Gen. Lombardini, in which, after stating that it is now time for the great Mexican nation to show the world that her sons have not degenerated, the commander-in-chief goes on to decree as follows: That on the Americans' first appearance in sight of the capital a gun shall be fired in the plaza; that instantly, all the bands shall strike up the alarm; that all the military shall at once hurry to their appropriate stations; that all the stores, save those where charcoal and provisions are sold, shall be immediately closed; that no carriage shall be allowed in the streets, and that there shall be no assemblage of persons in any part of the city. Such is the plan of giving the first alarm, and of the after government of the city. The idea of showing to the world that her sons have not degenerated is purely Mexican, but what a pity they should not have thought of this before. It will take a deal of hard fighting and bloodshed to place them where they stood previous to the battle of Palo Alto.

In one of my last letters I noticed the death of Lieut. Tipton, of the Rifles— a son of Senator Tipton, of Indiana. Since then a son of Senator Sturgeon, of Pennsylvania, a lieutenant in one of the regiments from that State, has died, and he, too, I have been told, was a young man of much promise.[16] I cannot learn that any of our officers are now seriously indisposed, and the health of the army generally is improving. To be sure there are 1500 or 2000 men still on the sick list, but a larger portion of them are convalescing.

I wrote you a short time since that I had dispatched a man to Vera Cruz with letters, and that after his departure I was obliged, in virtue of a verbal contract, to pay all the expenses of his family during his absence, to keep a candle continually burning and have a *funcion* performed in one of the churches for his safety and *buen viaje*. I have just learned that the fellow was captured on the road by the guerrilleros, stripped, beat most unmercifully, his horse—I paid for the animal—taken from him, and was then turned loose to make the best of his way back to Puebla. The story of his adventures and capture is most amusing, and I will give it if ever I live to get home; at present I will only say that I thought the family made too much fuss from the first.

16. Mentioned are Spear S. Tipton, Rifles, and John Sturgeon, Pennsylvania Second Volunteers. They were the sons of Senators John Tipton and Daniel Sturgeon.

Last evening, on the strength of a letter said to have been received from the Spanish Minister in Mexico,[17] peace stock went up. It was rumored that the contents of his communication made peace inevitable—that the Congress and Santa Anna were disposed to agree to anything in order to insure it; now, while I am writing, intelligence has come in from which it would appear that there is no earthly chance for an amicable adjustment of our difficulties. From all accounts, it would appear that Santa Anna and Congress are at sword's points, and that the former has all the advantage over the constituent wisdom of the great and magnanimous Mexican nation. It may be recollected that some two months since Congress passed an act declaring anyone a traitor who would even entertain the idea of a peace with the North Americans. So far so good. When Santa Anna received Mr. Buchanan's last propositions, a few weeks since, he at once submitted them to Congress for that body to act upon the matter in the premises; but what did Congress do but send the papers back with an answer that the initiatory steps belonged exclusively to the Executive. At this Santa Anna became enraged—said that he did not send the papers before Congress to ascertain what his prerogatives were—he knew their full extent well—but he had laid the matter before that body in order that the members might rescind their former decree declaring anyone a traitor, &c., if they saw fit. That he thought they would do this, and thus give him all and every power, is highly probable; but Congress took a stubborn fit, and here the whole affair rests for the present. I do not even see who is to deign offer an answer to Mr. Buchanan's propositions, which seem to have been transferred into a species of foot-ball to be kicked backwards and forwards by Santa Anna and the Congress—neither party, in the present distracted state of the country, daring to lay hands upon the unfortunate document. Bold and unscrupulous as even the tyrant is in all matters of state policy, he dare not take a responsibility so heavy upon his shoulders as to come out alone and advocate a peace.[18] The impression now is, that he has determined to hazard the defence of the capital, and this impression gains strength when it is known that he has Congress to lay the blame upon in case he suffers another defeat. Another battle, in my humble opinion, will be of immense advantage to the United States; for if Gen.

17. Salvador Bermúdez de Castro.

18. The Mexican Congress had met on July 13 and refused to authorize negotiations with the Americans, claiming that the responsibility for treaty-making under the revived constitution of 1824 rested solely with the executive branch. On July 27, Santa Anna sought the support of his generals for negotiations, but they argued for another opportunity to revive Mexican fortunes on the battlefield.

Scott moves upon the capital the Mexicans will certainly be defeated, and if he remains here, and there is no more fighting, the enemy will contrive to come out of the war conquerors. They will endeavor to make it appear that the Yankees, fearful of risking a battle at their principal city, sued for peace, and in the eyes of the world they will be able to make a tolerably clear case.

Santa Anna has recently levied a contribution—a forced loan it may be called—upon the inhabitants of the capital, in which he calls for $280,875 to carry on the war. The churches and convents, as well as private individuals are assessed, and it is hinted that the tyrant has left the names of some of his few friends off the tax list. The foreigners, who have been called upon without stint, have made regular protests it is said against the unjust exactier, but Santa Anna does not stand upon trifles in his money transactions.

From every indication, it would appear that Gen. Scott intends an immediate movement upon the city of Mexico—at least within a week or ten days.[19] Hard bread is being baked for the march, the quartermasters have been ordered to hold themselves in readiness, and in every department all is bustle and activity. It being found impossible to receive clothing from the United States, hundred of Mexicans are hard at work, putting our men in uniform. Some even think that the army will move before Gen. Pierce comes up, but it is hardly probable that Gen. Scott will march before that officer gets within one or two days' march.[20] At least 1500 of the sick will be left behind, but a majority of them will be in a situation to take up arms in case the garrison was attacked.

Speaking of sickness, the South Carolina regiment has suffered more than any other in the service. This was not expected. It was thought that

19. On July 21, Trist had received word from Thornton indicating that Santa Anna believed the American army would have to move closer to the capital before negotiations could take place. The message convinced Scott that a move into the Valley of Mexico was necessary to end the stalemate. By the end of July, Trist and other members of Scott's command were reporting news from the British legation that Santa Anna was prepared to allow the American army to advance unmolested to within ten miles of the capital. Santa Anna reportedly believed that the army's proximity would create an environment in which peace could be negotiated. Mahin, *Olive Branch and Sword*, 105–6.

20. Franklin Pierce, who had recently declined an appointment as attorney general in order to serve with the volunteers, arrived in Vera Cruz in mid-June, in command of 2,500 new recruits, fifty wagons filled with materiel, and $85,000 for purchasing supplies. His column of reinforcements did not leave the coast until July 14. They engaged Mexican forces six times before arriving in Puebla on August 6. Scott was worried enough about Pierce's progress that he sent Persifor F. Smith's brigade to Perote to escort Pierce to Puebla. Pierce was elected president of the United States in 1852.

the Northern regiments would suffer most hereaway in the tropics, but the New Yorkers and South Carolinians have been, as it were, side and side, and the former have had but few cases on the sick list comparatively. The South Carolinians, out of 900 strong when first mustered, now turn out but about 400. Of the other 500 some, 140 have died, 200 have been left sick in the rear, and the rest are now in hospital here. The health of the regiment is improving, however, and many are convalescing.

Yours, &c.,

G. W. K.

*Daily Picayune*, August 7, 1847

Puebla, Mexico, July 28, 1847

Rumors from the city of Mexico are at a discount, but reports from the direction of Vera Cruz are more eagerly sought after. Many think that the arrival of Gen. Pierce will be the signal for an immediate movement of the whole army, and hence the anxiety to learn his real whereabouts. A day or two since intelligence was received that he had taken the Orizaba road, and that he had been heard of even this side of that city; yesterday news came in that he had reached Jalapa with his command, and this story is more generally credited. On the strength of reports that a large guerrilla force was in front of Gen. P., and that some 2000 men with four pieces of artillery were on the way down from the neighborhood of the capital to aid in capturing the train, Gen. P. F. Smith's brigade was ordered to move in the direction of Perote. His regular command consists of the 1st Artillery, 3d Infantry, and Rifles, but in addition to this force a squadron of dragoons and Duncan's battery accompanies him. Woe to any Mexican force that may fall in the way of this command.

For the last week we have had but little rain, and it is certainly much to be regretted that Gen. Scott has been unable to improve it. The weather has been of that nature—cool and bracing—that the men could have performed their marches without fatigue—it has been one of those dry spells that usually come in the midst of the rainy season, and had Gen. Pierce been here the entire army might have marched to the capital dry shod. Old weather-wises, those who have lived here long, say that this pleasant weather will be followed by drenching rains. I trust their predictions may prove untrue, but am fearful that we have not yet seen the worst of the wet season.

I said above that rumors from the city of Mexico were at a discount—we have no other reports than that a portion of the city has been overflowed, that much sickness prevails, and that the Mexicans intend giving Gen.

Scott the hard battle at the Peñon. There are those in the army who think that before a gun is fired Santa Anna will send out a white flag and come to terms.[21] We shall see.

Gen. Worth, with Mr. Trist and a large party of officers and gentlemen, started out this morning on a visit to the noted pyramid of Cholula, and returned about dinner time highly delighted with the trip.[22] A party of Mexican guerrillas went out at the opposite side of the town as Gen. W. entered, scampering off as fast as their horses would carry them. They started in the direction of Atlixco, and in their fright probably reported that the whole American army was in motion.

The robbers and guerrillas made a fine haul last night, taking over one hundred mules from a single pen almost within the limits of the city. This will doubtless embolden them to more daring attempts.

Yours, &c.,

G. W. K.
*Daily Picayune*, August 7, 1847

Puebla, Mexico, July 30, 1847

We have a story, tolerably well authenticated, that over a million of dollars has recently arrived at Vera Cruz for the army. A day after the fair, again, for how is this money to find its way up in season to relieve the great necessities of those who have so long been suffering? The straits to which our commissaries and quartermasters have been driven, as well as the army agent, Mr. Hargous, to raise the means for the absolute support of the men, has beat the kite-flying and skinning days of '37 all to pieces. A dollar is a dollar, and more than a dollar, here in Puebla.

In relation to the movements of the army, I can give you no other than the impression that Gen. Scott will march immediately on the arrival of Gen. Pierce. The men composing the divisions of Gens. Worth and Twiggs are probably better soldiers than any at present in the world. In the first place, the material is equal if not superior to any; they are equally well drilled; have the best of officers to lead them; and, what is of the greatest importance, a great portion of them have been in the front rank of battle

---

21. Ethan Allen Hitchcock, Scott's inspector general, wrote in his diary on July 25 that "we must advance on the capital, [but] we will be met by a flag before we reach the Peñon." Quoted in Mahin, *Olive Branch and Sword*, 105.

22. The pyramid at Cholula was a popular attraction for American soldiers. A pre-Columbian structure over two hundred feet high, it is the largest pyramid of its kind in the Americas. At the time of the Mexican War, many Americans thought it was larger than the Egyptian pyramids. Even Winfield Scott made a visit, possibly inspired by Napoleon's famous tour of the Egyptian pyramids. Peskin, ed., *Volunteers*, 129.

in numerous fields. Nor is the division of Gen. Quitman, which will doubtless take an active part in any operations yet to take place, much behind
the others. The regiments composing it, the New York, South Carolina, and
1st and 2d Pennsylvania, have been long enough in the field to become
well drilled, while Steptoe's admirable battery is attached to it. The army
that will set down before Mexico will be the strongest and best appointed
we have yet had in the field, and let the Mexicans fight as they will the
result of any contest that may take place cannot be doubted.

I have seen a gentleman who left the capital two days since. He says
that the Mexicans were quietly awaiting the approach of Gen. Scott, have
all their works and fortifications completed. The story that the city was
partially overflowed is confirmed, but the report of the extent of the inundation, and of the sickness it had occasioned, have been exaggerated.
There was a strong belief among many of the foreigners that there was a
perfect understanding between Gen. Scott and Santa Anna, and that a
peace would grow out of it.[23] The Congress was still at loggerheads with
the President, all business was completely at a stand, and the only law
known was that of the military.

Copies of the *Diario del Gobierno* up to the 27th inst. have been
received here. It is the only paper now published at the capital, and contains little save Government orders and decrees, or articles published under
the express sanction of Santa Anna. In one of the latter the editor asks the
people not to forget their great and glorious victory over "los Yankees" on
the triumphant field of Buena Vista, nor the three pieces of cannon and
the standard then and there taken from Gen. Taylor! He himself has probably entirely forgotten the seven or eight hundred cannon captured from
his countrymen within the last eighteen months, as well as the flags
innumerable that have been sent on to Washington.

I must close this letter with a few speculations of my own. There is now
every indication that the army will move upon the capital in the course of
the coming six days, and it is more than probable that the hardest fight
yet will be at the city of Mexico—this is the opinion of the majority. Santa
Anna, however much he may be averse to it, can hardly avoid a battle,
although he will still creep out of it if possible. No one not in all the
secrets can know anything with certainty, but there are yet strong reasons
to believe that the English legation is exerting every influence to keep the
Americans out of the capital, and to effect this Santa Anna has been

23. Hitchcock recorded in his diary on July 29 that "the English minister, Mr. Bankhead, thinks
our advance to Chalco would bring peace." Quoted in Mahin, *Olive Branch and Sword*, 105–6.
Thornton reported a similar view to Trist on the same day.

tampered with, and golden showers, of American coinage, mind you, have been made to rise before him. The English do not want to see us in the city of Mexico—they have interests of their own to subserve, and are fearful the American hold upon this shattered Republic will soon be too strong to be shaken off except to their great detriment.[24] If an immediate peace is made, why then the United States can help herself to such portion of Northern Mexico as she may covet, while England will come in at the southern extremity and lay hold of territory to her heart's content.

The obstinacy of Congress, the deep hatred of the Mexicans to the Americans, and the slight hold Santa Anna has upon the people, may, and probably will, prevent his own schemes and those of the English from being carried out—the coming fortnight will tell the story. No wonder the English are anxious to see this war brought to a close, for it has already proved most disastrous to their heavy mercantile interests in the country, and its continuance must hasten its utter ruin in more ways than one.

Difficult as it now is to get letters off to the coast, I shall continue to attempt it, for the events of the coming month must be pregnant with interest.

Yours, &c.,

G. W. K.

P. S.—I might mention, as an item of interest to his numerous friends, that Gen. Shields is here and in good health. The health of the army continues to improve, and a large portion of the soldiers may now be said to be acclimated.

*Daily Picayune*, August 7, 1847

Puebla, Mexico, August 3, 1847

Intelligence has just been received that Capt. Ruff, with a squadron of cavalry, has given the guerrillas a severe drubbing at San Juan de los Llanos. Gen. P. F. Smith learning on his arrival at Ojo de Agua that a party of these gentlemen of the road had a rendezvous at the former place, dispatched Capt. R. with orders to surprise them if possible. The expedition was successful in every way—the guerrillas were surprised before they had time to reach their horses, and at once took refuge in a church and in two or three stone houses adjoining. Into these our men at once charged, the Mexicans recoiled in dismay, and after a short struggle were entirely defeated, with a loss of between 30 and 40 killed and some 50 wounded. A priest and curé said to have been in some way connected with the guer-

---

24. British officials were especially fearful that an attack on the city would lead to the destruction of British property.

rillas, were taken prisoners. Such is the report of the affair at present current—I shall probably learn more of it before I close this letter.

Midshipman Rogers, about whose imprisonment so much has been said, has taken the liberty of releasing himself—in plain English, he has escaped from the city of Mexico, and has arrived here in safety. He was not on parole at the time, but at large in the capital under a bond with a money penalty not to break his bounds. Learning that the American officers were to be removed to Toluca, and that there was no probability of his being exchanged, he started off in the night towards Chalco lake in a boat. Arriving there, he started on horseback through the mountains with a guide, and, as above stated, got through in safety. He reports that Santa Anna has not so many men as has been stated—that he has not more than 15,000 who are well armed and well organized. Perhaps he did not know that Valencia had arrived with reinforcements from San Luis. Both Rogers and Lieut. Semmes,[25] who was sent on by Com. Perry to attend to his case, will go on to the capital whenever the army moves, and take a part in any game that may be there played. In fact, the same may be said of all who are with the army and not immediately connected with it—there will be work for all of them and their greatest safety will be in the neighborhood of balls, shells, and kindred projectiles. In relation to young Rogers, it is said he came off with the knowledge and by permission of his surety.

We have a rumor this morning, and a startling one to the effect that Santa Anna is moving upon this city with his entire army and fifty pieces of cannon. The news is too good to be true and no one credits it.

I believe I have already mentioned the death of Lieut. Hill,[26] of the 2d Dragoons, and that he was buried with military honors. Dr. W. H. Hamuse, of the South Carolina volunteers, died this morning. Just before his death he embraced the Catholic religion and received the absolution of the church. I learn that a portion of his family in the United States are of the same faith. The health of the army is generally improving.

We have information today that Gen. Pierce is at Perote, and that he is awaiting there the arrival of 500 marines and 1000 of the new levies. This will be another detention—will probably cause another delay in the march of the army.

I wish you could see the *Jota Arragonse*, as danced here at the Spanish theatre by the Señoritas Ruperta and Moñoz and two masculines whose names are not given in the bills. It is full of life, action and castanets, and was loudly and warmly encored last night. The women folks who take a

25. Raphael Semmes, Navy, published a widely read history of the war in 1851.
26. John H. Hill.

part in the dance labor under no particular restraint that can be discovered, but throw themselves into attitudes that would be deemed unseemly by a committee of prudes in our own country. Here, however, the audience was composed almost entirely of officers, and the more voluptuous the postures of the *figurantes* the more rapturous the applause. We never see the *Bolero* and other Spanish dances given with proper effect in the United States.

Yours, &c.,

G. W. K.
*Daily Picayune*, August 20, 1847

Puebla, Mexico, August 5, 1847

Gen. Smith has returned with his brigade, and the report is that Gen. Pierce is to sleep tonight at Amosoque and will arrive here tomorrow. The account of Capt. Ruff's adventure with the guerrillas at San Juan de los Llanos is fully confirmed. No less than 43 of the enemy were killed, a great number were wounded, all their arms were destroyed, and their flag brought off. The two padres who were taken prisoners in the church, and who were supposed to have some connection with the guerrillas, have since been released by Gen. Smith.

The letter mail brought up by Gen. Pierce, with dates from New Orleans to about the 8th July, has come up—the main newspaper mail will arrive tomorrow. Many of the officers have told me that their anxious mothers, wives and sisters have done little but reprimand them for not writing to them oftener—they would not blame them so much if they knew the extreme difficulty of getting letters down to the coast.

I have already mentioned the successful escape of young Rogers from Mexico. Last night about 10 o'clock, Maj. Gaines came in passing safely through the entire Mexican lines. It seems that on Monday last all the American officers were ordered to the headquarters of Gen. Lombardini, and were there told that they must prepare, in twelve hours, to move to Toluca. All of them, save Majors Gaines and Borland, and Capt. Danley,[27] gave their paroles that they would proceed to that place; but Maj. G. distinctly told Lombardini that his parole was at an end—that he did not ask for its renewal, nor should he accept it. On Tuesday morning the officers, with three exceptions above named, started in the stage for Toluca, and on the same night Maj. Gaines, accompanied by a trusty Mexican guide, set out for this place, and after being once in the hands of the guerrillas, and

27. Christopher C. Danley, Arkansas Mounted Volunteers, was also among those captured at Encarnación.

running many narrow risks, besides, succeeded in coming through in safety. He informed Lombardini distinctly, through the interpreter, a brother of Almonte, that he should not give his parole for Toluca, and anticipated being arrested and put under guard at once; but not thinking probably he would attempt to escape, he was allowed to depart. The sequel is known.

Maj. Gaines thinks that Santa Anna has about 15,000 tolerably well uniformed and drilled men, to which number must be added a rabble of undisciplined recruits, caught and picked up every way, and giving little strength to the army.[28] The main defence of the Mexicans—that upon which they most rely—is at the Peñon, and at this point they have planted some of their best cannon. Santa Anna himself is described as being in a greater dilemma than ever. The jealousy and obstinacy of his enemies prevent his openly avowing himself in favor of peace, and he is shrewd enough to know that the next battle must result against him. Thus his own downfall is staring him in the face turn which way he will, and he is now awaiting some revolution of Fortune's wheel to extricate himself. His utter downfall would seem inevitable did not his past history afford abundant evidences that he has risen above every species of reverse, and so fruitful is he in expedients that he may still rise triumphantly from the whirlpool of difficulties by which he is surrounded.

Since I commenced this letter Gen. Scott's orders for the march of the army have been issued. The division of Gen. Twiggs is to move on Saturday, the 7th instant, that of Gen. Quitman's on the 8th, Gen. Worth's on the 9th, and Gen. Pillow's on the 10th. In the meantime Col. Childs remains in Puebla as military and civil governor, and Capt. De Hart[29] as lieutenant governor, while an efficient garrison, in addition to the sick and those who are convalescing, will be left behind.[30] Gen. Scott himself will probably accompany Gen. Quitman's division, and the entire army will concentrate at some point this side of the capital.

The order for a move has been received with rejoicing by all—by the heads of the commissary's and quartermaster's departments in particular, for at the capital it is almost certain that an abundance of money can be obtained. No man in the United States could believe for one moment the straits to which our army has been driven for want of cash, especially after reading the statements made in some of our papers. Here in Puebla it is given as a fact past all gainsaying, that since April last the commissary's

28. The Mexican army guarding the approaches to Mexico City numbered 36,000 soldiers.

29. William C. De Hart, Second Artillery.

30. Scott's army included approximately 14,000 men, of whom more than 3,000 were sick or otherwise unfit for duty.

department alone has sent to Washington for near $800,000 with which to meet current expenses, and of this amount not a cent has been received. The exertions of Capts. Irwin[31] and Grayson, combined with those of Mr. Hargous, have effected much, however, and through them a large depot of provisions has been got together here, sufficient for the army for months.

Yours, &c.,

G. W. K.
*Daily Picayune*, August 20, 1847

Puebla, Mexico, August 6, 1847

Gen. Pierce arrived his morning—his men, though much jaded and travel worn, making a most soldierly appearance. The 9th regiment in particular—the New England regiment commanded by Col. Ransom[32]—attracted much attention from the crowds assembled to see the new division levies enter.

Notwithstanding all the stories told in the Mexican papers, it seems that Gen. Pierce has brought his command through without losing a man, and with but three or four wounded. He was attacked several times by guerrilla parties, yet by prompt measures succeeded in routing them on every occasion. A good story is told of Capt. Bodfish,[33] who commands one of the New England companies—a regular lumber man and bridge-builder from "way down in the State of Maine." Arrived at Plan del Rio, what did they find but that the bridge had been destroyed; yet Capt. B. had his Yankee ingenuity about him, and in a few hours time the entire command was taken safely over by means of a new road which he himself cut. A Yankee will be a Yankee, transplant him as you will.

The officers with Capt. Ruff, at the time he routed the guerrillas at San Juan de los Llanos, were Lieut. Walker, of his own company, and Lieut. Hawes, with a company of the 2d Dragoons.[34] The defeat was complete.

We have a hundred conflicting rumors from the city of Mexico. One is to the effect that Valencia is coming out with 12,000 men to attack us in front, while Alvarez, with 5000 Pintos, makes a demonstration in the rear: another report has it that Santa Anna has disarmed 3000 of the Guardia Nacional, having discovered that they were hatching some plot against him; while still another report would have it that a regular revolution had broken out against the *benemerito* of his country, and that all was "confu-

31. James R. Irwin, Commissary.
32. Trueman B. Ransom, Ninth Infantry.
33. Charles N. Bodfish, Ninth Infantry.
34. John G. Walker, Rifles, and James M. Hawes, Second Dragoons.

sion worse confounded" at Mexico at last dates. Then, again, we have it that Puebla is to be attacked immediately after the army has left, the garrison put to the sword, and the citizens severely mulcted and robbed for the good treatment they have given the Yankees. For anyone of these rumors there is probably not the least shadow of foundation; yet as the Mexicans feed themselves upon the hopes of what they should do, they have given them circulation as facts, and very likely one half of the community believe them. There can be little doubt of one thing—that Santa Anna is compassed about with difficulties, and that although at present he "rides upon the whirlwind and directs the storm," the obstinacy of Congress and the jealousy and stubbornness of such men as Valencia hedge him in with a perfect wall of opposition. A long way the shrewdest and most far-seeing man among them, he may still be enabled to keep the upper hand and sustain himself in such power as a broken down and fallen Government may afford anyone. There is no such thing as foreseeing what such a man as Santa Anna can do—look at what he has done since his terrible defeat at Cerro Gordo for example. No one but he would have dared show his face at the capital after such a reverse; but with a miserable remnant of an army he boldly entered the city, and since, with an empty treasury and with obstacles that seemed insurmountable, he has collected and appointed a numerous force, inspired the hopes of a people he has a thousand times deceived, and for the time being at least rides rough shod over everything. What the next fortnight may turn up it is impossible to foresee, and in such a state of affairs it is idle to speculate.

Contrary to all expectations, the train which came up today did not bring any money, and hence the poor providers for the absolute wants of the army are worse off than ever. As high as *fifteen per cent.* has been paid today for money to defray the expense of the short march from this to Mexico, and some of the holders here are even chaffering for *eighteen!* Such are the straits to which our quartermasters and commissaries, abandoned as they have been by the Government at home, are driven. Nor is clothing brought, nor are any of the necessaries for the well-being of the army, to say nothing of the comfort, and hence all has to be purchased at rates which amount to ruinous extortion. I give you facts which every man here knows—comments may suggest themselves.

I finish this letter in haste, and late at night. Tomorrow morning Gen. Twiggs moves with his division, as I have already stated. Reports continue to come in that large bodies of the enemy are moving in the neighborhood, and just now we hear that from 800 to 1000 guerrilleros, who have been dogging Gen. Pierce, were seen this afternoon at El Pinal. The coming fortnight will come to us burthened with news, and whether it be of peace, or war to the knife, I shall give you the intelligence as early as possible.

Yours, &c.,

G. W. K.
*Daily Picayune,* August 20, 1847

# CHAPTER SEVEN

# THE BATTLE FOR MEXICO CITY
## AUGUST 22 – SEPTEMBER 17, 1847

BY AUGUST 14, 1847, WINFIELD SCOTT'S army of just under 11,000 men had advanced, largely unhindered, some fifty miles along the National Road to a crossroads within twenty miles of the Mexican capital and about ten miles from the fortifications at El Peñon. Scott paused to reconnoiter the Mexican defenses before ordering William Worth to lead his army to the south and west around Lake Chalco, toward San Agustín and the main road leading to the capital from the south. Santa Anna, leaving a reserve behind at El Peñon, deployed his army of 20,000 men to block Scott's impending approach along the road from Acapulco; he aligned his forces along a five-mile front from Churubusco to San Angel.

On August 18, Worth's division, with George Kendall along, was advancing along the Acapulco road northward, from San Agustín toward San Antonio, when it met heavy resistance about three miles south of Churubusco. Scott ordered Worth to hold his position rather than assault the well-fortified town; the next day he laid plans to flank the Mexican positions, expecting to meet little resistance by marching the main body of his army around a rugged lava bed, known as the Pedregal, and attacking Churubusco and San Antonio from the west. Unbeknownst to Scott, General Gabriel Valencia had moved his 5,500-man command some five miles past San Angel to the south, near the village of Contreras and directly in the path of Scott's turning maneuver.

On August 20, the Americans cut off and then destroyed Valencia's army before sweeping past San Angel and, now joined with Worth's division from the south, overrunning Mexican defenders at Churubusco. Scott might have marched into the capital, but his army was exhausted, and he yielded to British pressure to arrange a truce and negotiate an end to hostilities.

Negotiations went nowhere, however. On September 7, Scott ended the armistice, having received confirmation that Santa Anna had used the truce to rebuild the capital's defenses. While readying his army to take Mexico City, Scott on September 8 sent Worth's division to take Molino del Rey, a reputed weapons foundry on a main route into the city and a mile south of the strategically important Castle of Chapultepec. Expecting only a skirmish, Scott watched as Worth's command suffered heavy losses in hand-to-hand fighting against Mexican defenders who were well prepared for the American attack. Four days later, Scott directed his siege guns on Chapultepec, hoping artillery fire would eliminate the need for an assault. On September 13, however, he ordered his army to scale the walls of the fortress. Fierce fighting followed, but within hours the American flag flew above the castle's walls, and before the day had ended American soldiers held the northwest and southwest gates leading into the capital.

Kendall was with Worth throughout the fighting at Molino del Rey and Chapultepec and watched as Scott triumphantly entered the central square of Mexico City on September 14, 1847. Santa Anna had evacuated the city under cover of darkness the night before.

Tacubaya, (near Mexico,) August 22, 1847

The celebrated Archbishop's Palace of Tacubaya is now occupied by Gen. Scott; and a portion of the army, after twice defeating the enemy in two of the hardest fought battles of the war, are quartered immediately around him. I have already sent you off a hurried sketch of the glorious events of the 20th,[1] and even the present letter must be but a hurried synopsis of the battles, which have shed such additional glory upon the American arms.

On the 14th inst. a reconnaissance made by Col. Duncan having proved that a road for artillery and wagons could be cut from Chalco to San Agustín, Gen. Worth's division moved on the afternoon of the 15th in that direction.[2] Gen. Pillow followed the next morning; at the same hour Gen. Quitman broke up his encampment at Buena Vista, a small hacienda between Vienta de Cordova and Ayotla, and immediately Gen. Twiggs was in motion from the latter place. By this move a new line of

---

1. The dispatch to which Kendall refers, describing the fighting at Contreras and Churubusco, never reached New Orleans. The *Picayune* reported on September 8, 1847, that "a courier dispatched by him [Kendall] on the 20th with the first account of the battle fought on that day was cut off." The first news of the battles at Contreras and Churubusco arrived in New Orleans on September 3, having been forwarded by American newspapermen in Vera Cruz, who received the news on August 26 when a copy of *Diario Official del Gobierno* arrived from Mexico City.

2. Scott's topographical engineers, William Turnbull and Robert E. Lee, began studying the route into Mexico City while encamped at Puebla. Lee first proposed the route Kendall describes after determining that 7,000 Mexican defenders occupied El Peñon with thirty cannons.

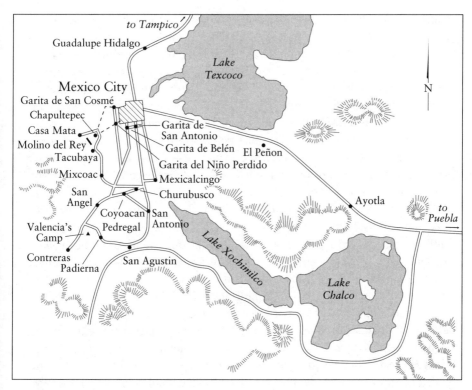

The Valley of Mexico.

operations was taken up on the southern and northwestern side of the city of Mexico, and the strong works of the Peñon and Mexicalzingo, upon which Santa Anna had bestowed such immense care and labor, were completely turned.

On the 16th of August Gen. Worth marched as far as the hacienda of San Gregorio, beyond which it was found that the enemy had cut up and ditched the miserable trail along which the artillery and wagons were obliged to pass. He would have gone to Santa Cruz, another hacienda a league farther on, had not an order come up from Gen. Scott for a halt. It seemed that Gen. Twiggs had met a large force of the enemy drawn up in front of him near Chalco, as if with the intention of disputing his advance, cutting him off from the main body of the army, and perhaps bringing on a general action. Gen. Twiggs promptly ordered some of his heavier guns to be unlimbered, and after a few discharges the enemy was dispersed, with the loss of five or six killed, but the demonstration made by the Mexicans, as I have before said, caused a halt of Gen. Worth's division before half a day's march was made.[3]

At 6 o'clock on the morning of the 17th Gen. Worth resumed his march, his route running through cornfields and narrow and rocky lanes, along which carriages had never passed before. The filling up of the ditches caused some little delay, but by 8 o'clock the advance was in sight of Santa Cruz, and the spires and domes of the noted capital of Mexico could be discerned in the distance. The obstructions in the road, of which I have spoken, were obviously of recent construction—evidence that the enemy had but just got wind of our approach, and that Gen. Scott had completely stolen a march upon Santa Anna.

Other than the ditches and rocks which had been rolled down from the precipitous hillside, no opposition was made to the advance of Gen. Worth until he had reached a point in the road not far from Santa Cruz—but now a scattering fire was opened upon the head of his column by a force stationed at advantageous positions above the road to the left. The enemy was quickly dispersed, however, by Col. C. F. Smith's light battalion and the 2d Artillery, under Maj. Galt.[4] As the division neared the hacienda of La Noqia the advance was again fired upon, but again the enemy's pickets were driven in, without loss. A turn of the road beyond La Novia brought the pleasant village of San Agustín in sight, and after two or three light skirmishes, in which the Mexicans had two or three lancers killed and wounded, our troops had quiet possession of San Agustín. Our only loss during the day was one man, a soldier of Smith's light battalion, who was wounded from a cornfield near Xochimilco.

At 7 o'clock on the morning of the 18th, Gen. Scott arrived at San Agustín, and at 10 o'clock Gen. Worth was in full march for the city of Mexico by the main road. Majors Smith and Turnbull, Capt. Mason[5] and other engineer officers, were sent in advance, supported by Capt. Blake's squadron of dragoons, to reconnoitre, as it was known the enemy was in force at or near San Antonio.[6] The party, when within a thousand yards, was fired upon from a battery, which was masked by trees, and the first ball

3. David Twiggs's troops were harassed by a cavalry unit under the command of Juan Alvarez. The Mexican unit was part of the Army of the North, under the command of Gabriel Valencia, which Santa Anna had ordered to take up positions between San Agustín and the capital after Scott turned his army away from El Peñon.

4. Patrick H. Galt.

5. Martin L. Smith, Engineers; James L. Mason, Engineers.

6. Scott initially hoped to approach Mexico City using the main road from Acapulco through San Antonio, but Worth quickly determined that the town of San Antonio could be taken only at great cost.

from a 12-pounder instantly killed Capt. Thornton, of the 2d Dragoons, besides severely wounding a guide, Jonathan Fitzwalters. Col. Garland's brigade was now ordered to occupy the hacienda of Carrera, within plain sight and range of the enemy's batteries at San Antonio, while Col. Clarke's[7] brigade and the battery under Col. Duncan took a station in the rear close by. The engineer officers were at once sent out to reconnoitre by Gen. Worth, to ascertain the practicability of turning the strong works of the enemy, and in the meantime Gen. Scott had dispatched Capt. Lee with a supporting party, composed of Capt. Kearny's squadron and a body of the 11th Infantry under Col. Graham,[8] to ascertain the practicability of finding a road by which the village of San Angel could be reached, and thus turn the stronghold at San Antonio.[9] This latter party had a sharp encounter with the advance of the enemy, the main body being found posted at a strong point not far from the factory of Contreras. In the skirmish some six or eight Mexicans were killed and as many more taken prisoners—on our side not a man was touched. The result of the reconnaissance proved favorable. It was ascertained that a road could be made which would enable the army to reach San Angel, and thus turn the strong batteries at San Antonio, and perhaps others the enemy might have upon the road between that and the city of Mexico. The Mexicans were plainly seen in force at a commanding position near Contreras, and it was evident that they had a number of cannon in position; but at a council held at night, it was determined upon to attack them the following day.

In the meantime, while this reconnaissance was in progress, Gen. Worth had established his headquarters at the hacienda of Curera, while from the windows countless numbers of the enemy could be seen at work upon the batteries of San Antonio. About noon they opened upon the hacienda with both round shot and shell, nearly everyone of which took effect, but without doing other injury than to the building. Late in the evening the batteries again opened, but with no other result than showing the position of the different guns. For a marvel the batteries were silent during the night. Had the fire been kept up, the hacienda might have been torn in pieces and the entire command compelled to retire. Before going further, it may be well to state that the city of Mexico lies about nine miles nearly

7. Newman S. Clarke, Sixth Infantry.
8. William M. Graham.
9. Lee's reconnaissance force traversed the Pedregal—an oval-shaped lava bed, five miles long and three miles wide, that stood between San Antonio and an open road leading to San Angel. Santa Anna's base, Churubusco, was on the north rim; Scott was encamped at San Agustín on the south rim.

north of San Agustín, that San Antonio is about three miles in the same direction, while the point occupied by Gen. Valencia, near Contreras, for he had command at that place, is at least three miles in a straight line and in a direction nearly west.[10] It was ten miles the way many of our troops had to march, for you cannot imagine a more rough, uneven and jagged surface.

At 3 o'clock on the morning of the 19th the batteries again opened on Gen. Worth's position at the hacienda near San Antonio, the balls crushing through the walls and filling the rooms with fragments of plaster and broken furniture. Shell also burst in the air over the building and the pieces dropped among the men stationed in the rear. So hot was the fire that the troops were obliged to gain shelter behind the building, but still did not give up the position. About 9 o'clock the divisions of Gens. Pillow and Twiggs were ordered to advance in the direction of Contreras,[11] and by 1 in the afternoon were in plain sight of the enemy's batteries, and within range of his heavier guns. The brigade of Gen. P. F. Smith was ordered to advance directly towards the enemy's works, while that of Col. Riley moved towards a small village to the right, with orders to gain the main road and thus be enabled to cut off any reinforcements which might be sent to Valencia from the city. An incessant firing of cannon was opened upon the advance of Gen. Smith, and soon the Rifles were engaged in skirmishing with the pickets of the enemy and driving them in. The 12-pounder battery of Capt. Magruder was pressed forward with all speed, as was also the rocket and mountain howitzer battery, now commanded by Lieut. Callender, of the Ordnance Department. As soon as they could gain a position they opened upon the enemy, but were so much exposed to a fire from heavier guns that they were soon silenced. Lt. Johnstone, of the 1st Artillery, but attached to Magruder's battery, was mortally wounded, while Lieut. Callender was severely wounded in both legs.[12] At 3 o'clock the brigade of Gen. Cadwalader was ordered out to support Col. Riley, heavy reinforcements being seen on their way out from the city, while Gen. Pierce's

10. Santa Anna had ordered Valencia's 4,000-man army to defend San Angel, a position on the western flank of the Mexican line and some distance from the point of the expected American attack. Valencia, however, moved his force five miles forward to a position near Contreras. Ignoring Santa Anna's repeated orders to return to San Angel, Valencia hoped to defeat the Americans in a battle independent of Santa Anna's direction and, as a result, to replace Santa Anna at the head of the Mexican army. Valencia's army was on the western edge of the Pedregal at San Geronimo, a location misidentified in both Scott's official reports and Kendall's dispatches as Contreras.

11. Scott, not realizing the strength of the Mexican force at Contreras, sent Pillow and Twiggs to open a road wide enough to carry artillery.

12. John B. Johnstone and Franklin D. Callender.

brigade was sent to sustain Gen. Smith.[13] The firing from the batteries of the enemy continued incessant, while from a hill just outside the range of their guns, the spectacle was most grand and imposing. At about 4 o'clock Gen. Scott arrived,[14] and seeing the immense strength of the Mexicans, at once ordered Gen. Shields's brigade from San Agustín—a part of Gen. Quitman's command—to the right to support Riley and Cadwalader, and prevent, if possible, a juncture of the forces coming out from the city with those of Valencia. But few of the movements of our own troops could be seen from the hill where we were posted, owing to the dense chaparral, sharp rocks and ravines, but not a motion of the enemy but was plainly visible. The order of battle of Valencia was certainly most imposing— infantry were seen drawn up to support the batteries, while long lines of the enemy's cavalry were stationed in the rear, as if awaiting the shock of battle. Two separate charges of the latter were distinctly seen repulsed by Col. Riley, who had moved his brigade at one time to a position partially in the rear of the enemy's work. Col. Harney was exceedingly anxious to march his cavalry to the scene of action, but it was deemed utterly imprac- ticable.[15] The nature of the ground was such that the infantry even had great difficulty in finding the way across the *pedregal*, as the Mexicans term it—ground covered with sharp, jagged rocks.

Until night had fairly closed in the fire from the enemy's batteries did not slacken—it had been a continuous roar for nearly six hours. Gen. Scott retired to San Agustín about 8 o'clock, and in the midst of a hard rain which had just commenced falling. Gens. Twiggs and Pillow came in about 11 o'clock, wet and completely exhausted. It was impossible to use horses on the rough and exceedingly broken ground on which they had been operating for nearly twelve hours. Not anticipating the immense strength of the works of the enemy, or the almost insurmountable difficulties of reaching them, it had been at first thought that the batteries would be taken at a dash, and that the troops would be all comfortably quartered in San Angel for the night; instead of this, a large portion of them were com- pelled to bivouac without blankets in the midst of a pitiless rain, and on ground where they could not even stretch themselves out. Add to this, the prospects of the morrow were far from flattering—were enough to dismay

13. Cadwalader's brigade was joined by the Fifteenth Infantry, under Colonel George W. Morgan, in a flanking movement that placed 3,500 Americans beyond the reach of reinforcements and between Valencia and the Mexican army to the north. Pierce's division joined in the support being provided the artillery.

14. Pillow was in command until Scott arrived.

15. Harney's cavalry remained at San Antonio.

any but the stoutest hearts—that the enemy would doubtless reinforce and strengthen his works during the night, having every superiority in knowledge of the ground—add again to this that the men were weakened by long exertions, want of food, and chilled by the continuous night rain, and it is not saying too much to assert that the bivouac of the 19th August was gloomy in the extreme.

Early on the morning of the 20th, Gen. Worth was ordered to move with a part of his division—Garland's brigade—towards the scene of action at Contreras, to aid in the attack upon Valencia, for to force this position was deemed indispensable. A few discharges of cannon were heard about 7 o'clock, and a heavy rattling of musketry, and some even said that in the distance they had seen large masses of Mexicans in full flight towards the city; yet few dreamed that the batteries at Contreras had been stormed and carried. Yet so it was. Gen. Scott himself, accompanied by Gen. Worth, started for the scene of action, when they were met by Capt. Mason with the joyful intelligence that Valencia had been completely routed after a short but terrible struggle. The attack upon his works was planned by Gen. Smith, and resulted in the capture of 15 pieces of artillery, some 1,500 prisoners—among them Gens. Blanco, Garcia, Mendoza, and the notorious Salas;[16] all the ammunition and camp equipage, while the road along which those who escaped fled was strewed with muskets. No less than 700 of the enemy, among them many officers, were left dead on the field—the number of wounded was undoubtedly far greater.[17] I have no time now to enlarge or comment upon this well-planned and brilliant achievement, but reserving a more full description for some other time, must pass on to other exciting events.[18] The works at Contreras completely in the power of

16. Salas was notorious among Americans for organizing the so-called Guerrillas of Vengeance.

17. Valencia's army was totally destroyed. Scott reported seven hundred Mexicans killed and 813 taken prisoner. Among the senior officers captured were Valencia's second-in-command, former president and brigadier general José Mariano Salas, as well as Miguel Blanco de Estrada, Manuel Garcia Pueblita, and N. Mendoza.

18. Recognizing the vulnerability of the troops near Contreras, Persifor F. Smith, without orders from Scott, Twiggs, or Pillow, joined Cadwalader, Morgan, and Riley late in the day, hoping to strike northward. Confusion among the American commanders prevented an attack before night fell, however. With heavy rain falling, Santa Anna abandoned plans to reinforce Valencia, who had wrongly concluded that the end of American artillery fire signaled an impending American withdrawal. Meanwhile, Smith, having taken command, turned his attention to Valencia's army. When Riley's engineers discovered a route around the Mexican camp, Smith positioned his men to attack from three sides. After sending Lee back to Scott's headquarters with word of his plan and a request for artillery cover, he prepared to attack from the Mexican rear at dawn on August 20. Smith's attack, which took the Mexican soldiers by complete surprise, routed Valencia's army in a matter of minutes and opened the way for Scott's army to march on Churubusco.

the American army, Gen. Scott at once ordered Gen. Worth to fall back upon San Antonio, to turn and capture that work and then to push on towards the capital by the main road, while the main body of the army under Gens. Twiggs, Pillow, Smith, Pierce, and Cadwalader, moved on towards San Angel and Coyoacán. Scarcely had the advance of Gen. Twiggs got half a mile beyond the latter village, before a rattling fire of musketry announced that it was actively engaged with the outposts of the enemy, and the heavy booming of cannon now gave token that the noted 2d division had fallen upon another strong work. But a few minutes more and a tremendous firing from the right, and immediately in the main road from San Agustín to the capital, made it evident that Gen. Worth's division was actively engaged. He had completely turned the strong works of San Antonio, but while doing so the enemy had abandoned the place with the loss of their heavy guns, and had fallen back upon his second and stronger line of works.[19] It was now at the commencement of the battle, about 1 o'clock in the afternoon, and sure such a rattling of firearms has seldom or never been heard on the continent of America, accompanied with such booming of artillery; and this was continued over two hours and until the enemy was fully routed from every point, and until those who were not killed or taken prisoners were in full flight for the city. Let me endeavor in words to give the reader an idea of the position and works of the enemy. As you come along the road leading from San Agustín to the capital, and immediately this side the Puente del Rosana, the Mexicans had thrown up a strong and exceedingly well-built battery, commanding the road completely. On the right as you faced the city, stretching for a long distance was a continuous ditch, behind the bank of which an immense number of Mexican infantry were posted. On the left of the *tete de pont*, or work at the bridge, and about three hundred yards distant, was the church of Churubusco, or San Pablo, strongly fortified with works for infantry, and also having a well constructed battery containing a number of guns of heavy calibre. This work was a little advanced from the *tete de pont*, and nearly in a line between it and the village of Coyocacán. Further on, on the other side of the work at the bridge, and about three hundred yards from the road, was a large building, well adapted for the protection of infantry, and in which the enemy had also posted an immense body. The ground in the vicinity of all these points was completely covered with corn, and other fields, cut up in every

19. Worth, impatient with Scott's orders to delay an assault on San Antonio until Pillow's troops arrived from the west, opened the route northward by sending Newman Clarke's brigade through the Pedregal to the rear of the town, causing its defenders to flee in panic. Churubusco was Santa Anna's second line of defense.

direction by wide and deep ditches, presented obstacles innumerable to the advance of our troops. No reconnaissance of the position of the enemy had been made, and consequently its strength could only be ascertained by hard blows and knocks.

The divisions of Gens. Twiggs and Worth were at once engaged, the former with the church and stronghold of Churubusco, and the latter with the batteries at the bridge; and in the meantime Gen. Shields's brigades—the New York and South Carolina volunteers—together with the 9th, 12th and 15th Regiments of Infantry under Gen. Pierce, were hurrying onward from Cohoycan to attack the hacienda. Soon they too were engaged, and now the battle became general. The enemy had over twenty pieces of cannon, all in admirable position, and served with more than ordinary skill, while but few of our guns could be brought to bear. The battery of Capt. Frank Taylor, it is true, opened a well-directed fire upon Churubusco, but so exposed was its situation that it suffered most terribly, both in officers and men.

To describe the fierce conflict, even now that two days have elapsed, or to give an account of the part taken by the different regiments, were impossible. From the opening of the strife up to the time the Mexicans were entirely routed and in full flight for the city, was one continuous roar of cannon and musketry, accompanied by the loud shouts of the victors as some new vantage ground was gained; and high above the din rose a dense column of smoke, at times completely shrouding the combatants. The strength of the enemy at this battle is known to have been 15,000 at least, many say 20,000, all fresh troops and in a position of uncommon strength. Opposed to them were about 6000 Americans, jaded and broken down by marches and counter marches, and by incessant toil before the stronghold of Contreras and San Antonio. At Churubusco, the Mexicans themselves say, Santa Anna commanded in person, but that he left early. The noted battalions of Hidalgo and Victoria, and of Independicia—the *Polkas*, or young men of the capital, from whom so much was expected—nearly all fled without firing a gun.[20]

In the different works (but mostly in the church) taken by Gen. Twiggs near 2000 troops were captured. Among them were Gen. Rincon, who

20. Santa Anna's army was devastated, with an estimated 4,000 killed or wounded and another 3,000 captured. Scott suffered heavy losses, too, largely because the rushed attacks on the two heavily fortified Mexican positions took place without adequate reconnaissance. With approximately 8,500 soldiers engaged, Scott reported casualties of 1,053, including 133 killed, over the two-day battle. The Mexican units mentioned were civilian militia units with *puro* political leanings.

Battle at Churubusco. Toned lithograph (hand-colored), 1851, by Adolphe-Jean-Baptiste Bayot, after Carl Nebel; reproduced from George Wilkins Kendall, *The War between the United States and Mexico Illustrated* (New York: D. Appleton and Company, 1851), plate 7; © Amon Carter Museum, Fort Worth, Texas (186.72/7).

commanded in person, Gen. Anaya, lately President *Sustituto,* and Gen. Arevallon, as also Col. Gorostiza, formerly Minister at Washington. Gen. Garay was captured near San Antonio by Gen. Worth, and several influential officers, among them Col. Miramon,[21] by Gen. Shields at the hacienda; but the most important capture of all was the entire Foreign Battalion, mostly made up of deserters from our own army, with their commander, the notorious Riley himself. They are all now under close guard, and I trust will be strictly dealt with.[22]

The loss on our side has fallen most heavily upon the South Carolina and New York volunteers, the 6th Infantry and Smith's light battalion, attached to Worth's division, and the batteries of Capts. Magruder and Taylor. The South Carolina regiment was nearly cut to pieces, losing 137 out of 272 men, with which it went into action. The 1st Artillery has suffered severely in officers.

The Mexican accounts acknowledge the loss, in killed, wounded and prisoners, of no less than thirteen generals (among them three ex-Presidents) and forty-five pieces of cannon. One of our officers says that we have captured more ammunition than Gen. Scott has used since he has been in the country.

Yours, &tc.,

G. W. K.
*Daily Picayune,* September 8, 1847[23]

Tacubaya, August 24, 1847

I have spent not a little time in endeavoring to collect a list of the killed and wounded officers in the great battles of the 20th, not a difficult matter inasmuch as the different divisions are quartered in villages several miles apart. The following will be found in the main correct:

U. S. Regulars.

Killed.—Major Mills, 15th Inf'y; Capt. Burke, 1st Art.; Capt. Hanson, 7th Infantry; Capt. Thornton, 2d Dragoons; Capt. Capron, 1st Artillery; Capt.

---

21. Miguel Miramón.

22. Called the San Patricio battalion in honor of its Irish-born members and the Irish harp on its unit flag, this unit contained a large number of American deserters, including its ranking American officer, John Riley, formerly a private in Company K, Fifth Infantry. Seventy-two soldiers were court-martialed in the weeks between the battle for Churubusco and the fall of Mexico City. Of the seventy soldiers found guilty, Scott pardoned five, sentenced fifty to be executed, and ordered lesser sentences for the remaining fifteen. The executions took place on September 10 and 13, 1847. Miller, *Shamrock and Sword,* 68–112.

23. This dispatch, along with those dated through August 28, arrived in New Orleans early on September 8, 1847. It was reprinted on September 9.

Quarles, 15th Infantry; Capt. Anderson, 2d Infantry; Lieut. Irons, 1st Artillery, but attached to Gen. Cadwalader's staff; Lieut. Preston Johnson, 1st Artillery, but attached to Magruder's battery; Lieut. Easley, 2d Infantry; Lieut. Goodman, 15th Infantry; Lieut. Hoffman, 1st Artillery.[24]

Wounded.—Col. Clark[e], 6th Inf'y, slightly; Col. Morgan, 15th Inf'y, severely; Maj. Wade, 3d Art., severely; Maj. Bonneville, 6th Infantry, slightly; Capt. Wessells, 2d Infantry, severely; Capt. Phil. Kearny, 1st Dragoons, left arm shot off; Capt. McReynolds, 3d Dragoons, severely; Capt. Craig, 3d Infantry, severely; Capt. Ross, 7th Infantry, severely; Capt. J. R. Smith, 2d Infantry, severely; Capt. Chapman, 5th Infantry, slightly; Capt. Johnson, 9th Infantry, slightly; Capt. Holden, 12th Infantry, slightly; Capt. Hathaway, 1st Artillery, slightly; Capt. Hoffman, 6th Infantry, slightly; Lieut. Schuyler Hamilton, 1st Infantry, but attached to Gen. Scott's staff, severely; Lieut. Halloway, 8th Infantry, but attached to Smith's Light Battalion, severely; Lieut. Bacon, 6th Infantry, severely. Lieut. Callender, of the Ordnance, but commanding howitzer battery, severely; Lieut. Arnold, 2d Artillery, severely; Lieut. Herman Thorn, 3d Dragoons, attached to Col. Garland's staff, slightly; Lieut. Hendrickson, 6th Infantry, severely; Lieut. Humber, 7th Infantry, severely; Lieut. Boynton, 1st Artillery, but attached to Taylor's battery, slightly; Lieut. Lorimer Graham, acting with 1st Dragoons, severely; Lieut. Van Buren, of the Rifles, slightly; Lieut. Martin, 1st Artillery, right arm shot off; Lieut. Goodloe, 15th Infantry, mortally; Lieut. Farrelly, 5th Infantry, but attached to Smith's Light Battalion, severely; Lieut. Lugenbeel, adjutant 5th Infantry, slightly; Lieut. Bee, 3d Infantry, slightly; Lieut. Lovell, 2d Infantry, slightly; Lieut. Chandler, 3d Infantry, slightly; Lieut. Collins, 4th Artillery, slightly; Lieut. Tilden, 2d Infantry, severely; Lieut. Newman, 9th Infantry, severely; Lieut. Gardner, 2d Infantry, severely; Lieut. Hayden, 2d Infantry, slightly; Lieut. Sprague, adjutant 9th Infantry, slightly; Lieut. Palmer, 9th Infantry, severely; Lieut. Buckner, 6th Infantry, slightly; Lieut. Cram, 9th Infantry, slightly; Lieut. Simpkins, 12th Infantry, slightly; Lieut. Peternell, 15th Infantry, slightly; Lieut. Bennet, 15th Infantry.[25]

24. Not previously identified are Frederick D. Mills, Martin J. Burke, Erastus A. Capron, Augustus Quarles, James W. Anderson, Thomas Easley, John B. Goodman, and Satterlee Hoffman.

25. Not previously identified are Richard D. A. Wade, Henry H. Wessells, Andrew T. McReynolds, Lewis S. Craig, Joseph R. Smith, Lorenzo Johnson, Nathaniel B. Holden, John S. Hathaway, William Hoffman, John D. Bacon, Thomas Hendrickson, Edward C. Boynton, Lorimer Graham, Michael E. Van Buren, James G. Martin, William H. H. Goodloe, Patrick Farrelly, Pinckney Lugenbeel, Barnard E. Bee, Charles S. Lovell, Daniel T. Chandler, Francis Collins, Bryant P. Tilden, Jr., William T. Newman, William M. Gardner, Julius Hayden, Charles J. Sprague, Alpheus T. Palmer, Simon B. Buckner, Daniel H. Cram, John C. Simpkins, Charles Peternell, and John R. Bennet.

The above may be considered as nearly a correct list of the killed and wounded officers in the regular divisions of Gens. Worth, Twiggs and Pillow; some few names may have been left out but their wounds are unimportant. The entire loss in the division of Gen. Twiggs was 266, in that of Gen. Worth 339, in that of Gen. Quitman (Shields's brigade,) 240, in that of Gen. Pillow 212.

## Volunteers.

The regiment of New York Volunteers lost 103 in killed and wounded. The following is a list of the casualties among the officers:

Killed.–Lieut. Chandler.[26]

Wi unded.–Col. Burnet, severely; Capt. Fairchild, slightly; Capt. Dykeman, severely; Lieut. Sweeney, severely; Lieut. Jenniss, slightly; Lieut. Cooper, severely; Lieut. McCabe, slightly; Lieut. Potter, severely; Lieut. Griffin, slightly; Lieut. Malachwoski, slightly.[27]

The 15th Infantry under Col. Morgan, (belonging to Gen. Pierce's brigade,) lost one-third of its disposable force; the 9th Infantry under Col. Ransom, (belonging as well to the brigade of Gen. P.,) suffered severely. Col. Morgan was wounded in the leg and badly. The limb will be saved, but it is feared it will be some time before he recovers entirely.

*List of the killed and wounded of the Palmetto Regiment, South Carolina Volunteers, during the Battles of the 20th August, near Mexico.*

FIELD AND STAFF.–Killed–Col. Pierce M. Butler. Wounded–Lt. Col. J. P. Dickinson, severely; Capt. Jas. D. Blanding, slightly; adj. Jas. Cantey, severely.

COMPANY A.–Killed–Corp. Wilder, Private Thos. Black. Wounded–Lieut. Sumter,[28] slightly; Corporal W. T. Norton, and Privates B. Caughman and J. M. Smith, severely; Privates C. H. Moody, E. Hunt and Jas. Dunn, slightly.

COMPANY B.–Killed–Priv. W. R. Davis. Wounded–Sergeant G. W. Curtis, slightly; Corporal Postell, severely; Corporal A. J. Hood, slightly; Privates Thos. Charles, D. McHenry and James Young, dangerously; Private Jas. Faucett, severely; Privates T. Cahill, J. Connor, T. C. Dallas, T. O. Estes, J. M. D. Hood, T. Robbins and S. Terrell, slightly.

COMPANY C.–Killed–Private Hilton. Wounded–Capt. K. S. Moffatt,[29] slightly; Lieut. K. G. Billings, Sergeants Gay and Geo. Waters, Corporals

26. Edgar Chandler.
27. Not previously identified are Morton Fairchild, Garret Dykeman, Thomas W. Sweeney, Charles [Innes?] Jenniss, Charles S. Cooper, James S. McCabe, James D. Potter, Jacob Griffin, and Morritz Van Malachwoski.
28. Sebastian Sumter.
29. Keith S. Moffatt.

Caston and Horton, Privates Bradley, Hunter, Meggs, Stratton, Tidwell and Villisaigue, severely; Privates Ballard, Wooten and Humphreys, slightly.

COMPANY D.—Killed—Lieut. David Adams, Private Thos. F. Tillman. Wounded—Lieut. Joseph Abney, severely; Corporal W. B. Brooks, dangerously; Privates Jas. Goff, J. Whittaker, J. Addison, F. Posey, R. J. Key and W. F. Unthank, severely; Privates J. Lank, E. Simkins and R. Sioman, slightly.

COMPANY F.—Killed—None. Wounded—Sergeants J. D. Walker and J. N. Hicks, severely; Corporal J. F. Quinn, slightly; Corporal J. McCollum, Privates Campron, Gilbert, Hartman, Mackey, Murken, Pratt, Valentine and Weatherby, severely; Privates Miott, Vannoy, Wright and Wagner, slightly.

COMPANY G.—Killed—None. Wounded—1st Lieut. J. R. Clark, dangerously; 2d Lieut. J. W. Stein and 3d Lieut. J. R. Davis, slightly;[30] Sergeant Rowe and Corp. McCreight, seriously; Corp. Myers, slightly; Privates M. Harper, T. H. Reynolds, J. McNeill and J. Cain, dangerously; Privates Wm. Nelson and W. B. McCreight, severely; Privates S. F. Bone, M. B. Travis, S. Camak, M. B. Stanley, S. Newman, R. J. Barber, W. J. Sanders, R. J. Gladney, W. M. Goodlet, S. Alexander and J. Romedy, slightly.

COMPANY H.—Killed—Privates Timothy Kelly and Shadrack Wiggins. Wounded—Capt. W. DeSaussure,[31] and Sergeants H. Beard, S. L. Percival, J. M. Miller and T. Beggs, slightly; Privates, J. Kennerly, Wm. Mooney, R. H. Corley, W. S. Johnson, W. F. Purse, W. Devlin, T. Price, J. P. Cantwell, R. Waddell, J. F. Watts and W. Barkelow; M. Brown, H. J. Caughman, J. Campbell, J. T. Lupo, E. C. Randolph, J. D. Standford and D. Polock, slightly.

COMPANY K.—Killed—Lieut. W. R. Williams[32] and Privates John Slattery and Bernard Creagan. Wounded—Corporal W. B. Eaves, slightly; Priv. J. Baughman, mortally.

COMPANY L.—Killed—Serg't Jas. Denson. Wounded—Corporal J. A. Speers, Privates, W. Shephard, C. Wood, M. B. O'Neale, G. H. Abney and M. Clopton, severely; V. R. Gary, B. H. Mattis and J. Warner, slightly.

Total, killed and wounded, 137.

The field strength of this regiment, before the action commenced, consisted of 1 Colonel, 1 Lieut. Colonel, 1 Major, 1 Adjutant, 1 Commissary, 7 Captains, 24 Subalterns, 22 Sergeants—273 rank and file, including 21 corporals.

The New York Volunteers also suffered severely, but not in proportion to the regiment from South Carolina. Col. Butler, who commanded the latter,

30. James R. Clark, James W. Stein, and Jonathan R. Davis.
31. William D. DeSaussure.
32. Wilson R. Williams.

behaved in the most gallant manner. In advancing upon the hacienda attacked by Gen. Shields, at the head of his regiment, his horse was shot dead. He then advanced on foot until he received a severe wound in the leg, which caused him to fall. In a fainting condition he was carried to the rear, but soon rallying he again advanced to the head of his regiment, when a musket ball struck him in the head and he died almost instantly. South Carolina lost one of her bravest and most generous spirits when Col. Butler fell.

I have not had time to obtain a full list of all the killed and wounded in the different divisions of the army, but shall endeavor to do it at the earliest opportunity. A great proportion of our loss—perhaps nine-tenths—was in the attack upon the strong works at Churubusco—Santa Anna's second line as he called it. As I have previously stated, no reconnaissance whatever of this strong position had been made. The brilliant success of the morning had inspired both officers and men with the highest enthusiasm, and they rushed pell-mell into the positions the most exposed, and where they were mowed down by hundreds.

It will be seen that our own loss falls a little short of *eleven hundred*— about 6,000 men were actively engaged. When the works of the enemy are examined, one naturally wonders that Gen. Scott's entire force was not swept away. Put his army in the same position and since the days of the viceroys there have not been Mexicans enough born to drive them out.

White flags are now constantly passing and repassing between the Palace here and the Palace in Mexico.[33] At this game the Mexicans can beat us.

Yours, &c.,

G. W. K.
*Daily Picayune*, September 9, 1847

---

33. Late in the afternoon of August 20, Ewen C. Mackintosh and Edward Thornton rode from Mexico City to Scott's headquarters to seek protection for British citizens in the city and assurances that the Americans would consider negotiations. Scott's reply was inconclusive, leading Santa Anna's foreign minister, General José Ramón Pacheco, to inform the British embassy that the Mexican government was now prepared to listen to Trist's long-standing proposals to end the war. The Mexican government did not officially request an armistice, however; instead, General Ignacio Mora y Villamil, chief of military engineers, delivered copies of the communications between the Mexican and British governments to Scott's headquarters on August 21 and unofficially appealed for an end to hostilities. Encouraged by Mora y Villamil's appeal, Scott put aside a call for the city's surrender and instead sent Santa Anna a proposal to begin negotiations to end what he called "this unnatural war." As Kendall expected, Mexican officials quickly took advantage of the situation, claiming that the Americans had sought the armistice to end a scandalous war. Nevertheless, a truce was signed on August 23, providing for the exchange of prisoners, an end to military activity within ninety miles of the capital, the free flow of goods in and out of the city, and American access to supplies purchased in the markets of Mexico City. Pletcher, *Diplomacy of Annexation*, 513–14.

Tacubaya, August 24, 1847[34]

Peace stock rises and falls oftener and more suddenly here than any of the New York fancy stocks. One hour it is just as certain that a treaty will be signed as that the sun will rise tomorrow, and the next there is no more chance of an amicable adjustment than when Gen. Taylor first crossed the Rio Grande. The opinion still holds good at headquarters, where they should certainly know best, that it will be brought about. The commissioners meet again today, and it is said that the deliberations have been brought to a point when something decisive must turn up.[35]

I am one of those who, without censuring Gen. Scott for not entering the capital at once, believe it would certainly have been more satisfactory to the country, if not the wiser policy. He doubtless has instructions in his pocket from his Government, and has obeyed them; and if any disadvantage should now grow out of his not pursuing a panic-stricken enemy to their utter discomfiture, the fault must not lie at his door.[36] It has always seemed to me that the authorities at Washington wish all their generals to fight their battles with their gloves on, after the manner of pugilists who do not wish to hurt each other—they are fearful of thrashing the enemy too soundly, lest the smarting of defeat might render them deaf to fresh propositions of peace, which are always sure to be at hand. Magnanimity is entirely lost upon this people, conciliation has heretofore been scoffed at or taken advantage of to our hurt. The present soothing system, thanks to Santa Anna's desire for peace, may effect something; but if a peace is signed it will not be with the majority of the nation, and the larger States, it is more than probable, will pronounce against the President at once. This, however, will make no difference with us—Mr. Bankhead's endorsement that Santa Anna is the Government of Mexico will be all sufficient for Gen. Scott.[37]

34. The *Picayune* printed this dispatch with the dateline September 24, 1847. Both the place of dispatch and the contents indicate that the month should be August instead of September.

35. John A. Quitman, Persifor F. Smith, Franklin Pierce, Ignacio Mora y Villamil, and Benito Quijano negotiated the armistice.

36. Nothing in Trist's instructions prohibited Scott from assaulting the city, although the American emissary had been seeking a peaceful resolution to the war since his arrival in Mexico early in the summer. The American army's own situation likely contributed to Scott's willingness to secure a truce. Santa Anna was believed to have as many as 20,000 men in the capital, and little was known about the quality of its defenses. Moreover, Scott's army had suffered heavy losses in the previous forty-eight hours. Sick and wounded soldiers were scattered at four sites along with military materiel and a large number of prisoners. Food was in short supply. Had an assault on the city failed, the army might have faced starvation, whereas disorder and confusion would have accompanied a successful assault.

37. This and subsequent critical statements concerning Scott's failure to advance immediately into Mexico City and the armistice that followed generated considerable criticism of Kendall in the Washington *Union* and other newspapers sympathetic to the Polk administration and the Democratic Party.

For two or three days no provisions have been brought out of the city, and this morning three hundred pack mules, ordered in for supplies, were sent back from the garita[38] unladen. Two nights since a large store-house, belonging to Mr. Hargous and containing provisions, was broken into and robbed in the face of the authorities. At 3 o'clock in the morning, just as our pack animals were approaching the building to be loaded, some eight or ten of the robbers were arrested, Santa Anna has apologized for the outrage, I am told; and I suppose has promised to refund everything stolen—and so the matter will be dropped. The fact that our wagons are not allowed to enter the city cannot be construed into anything but an infringement of the armistice;[39] yet as Santa Anna says he is fearful of a mob, and Gen. Scott has been instructed to tax his patience and long-suffering to the last, I suppose it will be overlooked.

Last night three Americans, one of them Mr. Peoples of the *American Star*, were confined all night in the guard house of the National Palace. They were told they were only placed there for protection, that they were not prisoners; but as a sentinel was put over them, and they were counted every fifteen minutes, they certainly did not enjoy the largest liberty. At 11 o'clock this morning they were set free, after again being told that they had not been prisoners. They say that everything in the city indicates a most war-like feeling—that from the general tone of conversation the inhabitants have no desire for peace. Expect in the matter of cannon, Santa Anna is still strong and growing stronger, say the Mexicans, while we are constantly becoming weaker; and some of them openly say, moreover, that they are only humbugging us with false hopes of peace, with the intention of thinning off our force by sickness or starvation and then destroying us entirely.

The headquarters of Gen. Scott are here in Tacubaya, where Gen. Worth's division is also quartered. Gen. Pillow is at Mixcoac, two miles south, Gen. Twiggs at San Angel, about four miles further south, and Gen. Quitman at San Agustín. Some sickness prevails in the army, but the health of the troops may be put down as generally good.

The wounded officers are all doing well. A day or two since both Lieuts. Hamilton and Halloway were reported as in a dangerous condition, but I believe that all danger is now considered as over.

I have written out a full diary of the occurrences of the past week, as also several anecdotes of the great battles of the 20th August; but I dare not send the letters off, fearful they may be taken. You shall have copy enough by the first safe conveyance that goes down.

38. Sentry box.
39. This was the first indication that Santa Anna would not live up to the terms of the armistice.

Yours, &c.,

G. W. K.

P. S. I have learned, just as I was about closing this hasty scrawl, that the peace commissioners do not meet until Monday next, the 6th. By that time I trust we may know something definite as regards the chances of peace, for we are now most profoundly in the dark. One thing is certain: Santa Anna at this very hour is making every exertion to strengthen his army in every way, and he attempts to persuade his own countrymen that he is doing it to defend the honor of the nation. The high-handed workings of the mob, the robbing of the store, &c., has evidently been winked at, and he tells the Americans quietly that he has been obliged to do it to preserve appearances with his own countrymen. If he is not playing a strong game never did man undertake one, and he will be found prepared either for peace or war. Report has it that there was to be a meeting of the wealthy proprietors and moneyed men of the capital this morning to talk over the affairs of the nation. Santa Anna wants to hear what they have to say about his own governance.

*Daily Picayune*, September 26, 1847

Tacubaya, August 25, 1847

The armistice has finally been settled and signed, and I do not tell half the story when I say that it has produced universal dissatisfaction in the army—in the entire army. In the first place let me give you, from recollection, its main provisions, and then I will give you an idea as to the mode by which it was brought about.

The articles of the armistice first go on to say, that hostilities between the two armies are at once to cease, in order that the peace propositions of the United States may be listened to, and that they, the hostilities, are not to be renewed until either commander shall give the other forty-eight hours notice; that in the meantime all work on fortifications on both sides shall cease, and that no further reinforcements for either party shall be allowed to approach nearer than twenty-eight leagues of the capital; that no persons other than citizens shall be allowed to enter the city, and they only with passports from the Mexican authorities; that certain persons of the American army shall be allowed to enter the city to borrow money and purchase supplies, but no officers are allowed to pass in except upon special business and under a flag. Such are about the amount of the different articles of the armistice, signed on our part by Gens. Quitman, Smith and Pierce, and on the part of the Mexicans by Gens. Mora and Quijano.

Let me now give my speculations as to the mode by which this armistice was brought about. On the night of the 20th inst. after the great Mexican army was thoroughly beaten, broken to pieces and routed, Mr. Thornton, of the English legation, accompanied by the British Consul, Mr. Mackintosh—a man who regards Santa Anna, hates the Yankees and never moves unless his own ends are to be gained[40]—came out of the city post haste on a visit to Gen. Scott. The next morning Gen. Mora, accompanied by Mr. Arrangoiz[41] who was formerly Mexican consul in New Orleans, came out, also on a visit to Gen. Scott, and on the same day the latter wrote a letter to the Mexican authorities, hinting at an armistice between the two armies with a view of opening negotiations for a peace. This proposition was eagerly jumped at by the Mexican Minister of War,[42] at the instigation of Santa Anna of course, and the result has been a treaty of armistice in which, according to rumor, nearly everything the Mexicans asked for was conceded. I know nothing of the proceedings of this commission except from hearsay. There are many who believe that Gen. Scott has been compelled to adopt this policy, at the threshold of the Mexican capital, by Mr. Trist and his instructions, but there are few, and I must acknowledge myself among the number, who think that a peace honorable and satisfactory to the United States is to grow out of this matter. The whole affair, on the face of it, looks like one of Santa Anna's old tricks to gain time and plan some new scheme of trickery and dissimulation, and as he has British influence to back him he will be likely to carry out what he undertakes. I have always said and always believed that Santa Anna was favorable to peace—to peace from policy only—and still believe he may endeavor to bring it about; but great as is his power, like a sail vessel he can only go with the wind and current, and has too many and too powerful enemies to carry out his present schemes, at least without strong assistance from the United States.[43]

40. Mackintosh seems to have sought to protect his business interests by supporting Santa Anna's military preparations as well as the American diplomatic initiative. Ethan Allen Hitchcock wrote in his diary in September 1847 that the British consul general had advanced money to Santa Anna for the defense of Mexico City while urging Scott to remain in Puebla and allow diplomatic efforts to run their course. The *North American* reported from the capital in March 1848 that Mackintosh's firm provided $600,000 in July 1847 for the construction of fortifications in and around Mexico City. Mahin, *Olive Branch and Sword*, 104–5.

41. Francisco de Paula Arrangoiz y Berzábal.

42. Lino José Alcorta.

43. Trist reported to Secretary of State James Buchanan that the terms of the truce were designed to protect Santa Anna from the pressures of nationalist political leaders who retained hopes for a military settlement. From the Mexican general's perspective, he faced military defeat if Scott attacked, and political defeat if he yielded to the pressures to negotiate with the Americans.

Santa Anna accuses Valencia of having lost the capital by not obeying his orders to abandon Contreras on the 19th, and has ordered him to be shot wherever found; on the other hand, Valencia accuses Santa Anna of having lost everything by not coming to his assistance, and it is now said that he has pronounced against him and peace with the Yankees at Toluca.[44] Thus matters stand between these great Mexican leaders. Again, it is reported that Paredes is advancing from Orizaba, which place he successfully reached from Vera Cruz, breathing nothing but death and utter annihilation to the infamous North Americans, while it is further stated that Bustamente is at or near the capital with 6000 men, breathing the same amiable sentiments.[45] The papers of the capital are almost silent about everything—they do not even give an account of their recent terrible defeat.

The number of deserters and other foreigners found fighting against us the other day, and who are now prisoners, is 72. A court martial, with Col. Garland as president, is now in session here, for the trial of a portion of this precious set of scoundrels, and it is to be hoped they may have full justice done them. Riley, the Irishman who commanded the battalion of San Patricio as it is called, openly makes his brags of what he has done, and says he expects no mercy.[46]

Gen. Scott was himself wounded on the 20th inst. by a grape shot. It struck him on the outside of the leg below the knee, and gave so little pain at the time that he said nothing about it; but it has since caused him more uneasiness.

Our own loss, in killed, wounded and missing, is put down in round numbers at 1000—it may possibly range a little under. The Mexican loss in killed alone amounted to nearly that number, their prisoners to about 3000, while their wounded we have no means of computing. Among the

44. Valencia and Santa Anna had long been political rivals. Although the two had worked together to oust President Anastasio Bustamante in 1841, Valencia had helped to depose Santa Anna late in 1844. Throughout the war with the United States, Santa Anna kept his rival as far from Mexico City as possible, even leaving his veteran Army of the North in San Luis Potosí when it could have played a part in the defense of Cerro Gordo. Santa Anna was within striking distance of the American forces that took up positions on Valencia's right flank on September 19. His troops could have come to Valencia's aid but instead withdrew to San Angel when the weather turned rainy that night. Santa Anna's army was not a threat when the brigades under P. F. Smith's command struck Valencia's army early on September 20.

45. Exiled since Santa Anna's return the summer before, Paredes arrived in Vera Cruz aboard a British mail steamer on August 15. His presence gave rise to fears of a British-backed effort to establish a monarchy in Mexico.

46. Two courts-martial were convened to try the deserters. John Garland convened the court at Tacubaya, and Bennet Riley conducted the proceedings at San Angel.

officers taken prisoners were three members of Congress, and I believe they are to be liberated to take part in the proceedings of that body in relation to peace.

Yours, &c.,

G. W. K.
*Daily Picayune*, September 9, 1847

Tacubaya, August 26, 1847

We now have certain intelligence that Valencia arrived at Toluca with only two men, his aide-de-camps, and they were thankful for their good horses or else they could not have kept up. It is asserted positively that he was drunk on the night of the 19th inst., and promoted all his officers for their extraordinary gallantry in standing firmly to their guns during the afternoon when no one was returning their fire.[47] The account that he has pronounced against Santa Anna is not fully confirmed, but there is no doubt that Santa Anna has denounced him in a public decree, and accuses him of all blame in bringing about the recent disasters to the country. He must accuse somebody, and Valencia, by his disobedience of a cowardly order, has made himself amenable—offers a fair target for his master's wrath.

The prospects for a peace look brighter, although the treaty is far from being signed. Our accounts from the city would certainly indicate that a strong peace feeling pervades the better class of citizens, as well as those of the middling order—they have evidently lost all confidence in their own vaunting soldiers, and are anxious to get rid of future taxes for their support. For a wonder, such places as Saguntum, Numantia and Saragoza,[48] whose examples they were to follow and even excel in the matter of defending themselves to the last, have not been mentioned nor alluded to for a week past. The Mexicans are certainly becoming rational. No more do the Polkas, the "upper ten thousand" of Mexico, parade the streets petitioning like, so many Claude Melnottes,[49] to be placed where their country most needed soldiers: their shameless conduct before Churubusco, in running without even firing a gun, has taken all the conceit out of them. No more do even the noisy military demagogues talk of a future; no more

47. When the American artillery forces at his front ceased to fire late in the day on September 19, Valencia celebrated the occasion with promotions and drink, thinking that the silence of the American guns marked their impending withdrawal.

48. Sites of important battles in Spanish history.

49. The reference may be to the musical arranger of the same name, who was to publish a piano arrangement of Verdi's *Il Trovatore* late in the nineteenth century.

do they fume, and brag, and vaunt of what they are going to do, and of how the rapacious North Americans are to find a common grave under the walls of their beleaguered city; the blow has been too great for them. The capital was their jumping-off-place—there, by an extraordinary prowess they supposed themselves to possess even against the evidence of a dozen disgraceful defeats, the infamous Yankees were to be taught their utter inferiority when compared with the valiant descendants of the illustrious Hidalgo—there they have been routed by a force not one-third as large as their own; driven from strong vantage grounds without what would be deemed a struggle by the real nations of the earth; so shamefully defeated that even all the Mexican ingenuity of lies and excuses can find no palliation for their discomfiture. Divide all the self-sufficiency and overweening pride in the world at the commencement of this war into two parts, and the Mexicans possessed one half; and if they had only clung to their batteries with the same tenacity they did to their paper valor they might have retained their credit even although they lost their guns. Now, all is gone—means, material, name, and standing in the world—and there certainly is a portion of the proud people of the Mexican capital disposed to listen to peace and sheath their useless swords.

The policy of Gen. Scott or of Mr. Trist—I do not know which is responsible for the measure—in effecting an armistice and consequently an opportunity to negotiate—this policy, I say, although not very flattering to the pride of those who fought the sanguinary battles of Contreras and Churubusco, may still have a tendency to soften that of the Mexicans, and lead to some kind of a peace. So perfect was the panic among the sons of Iturbide on the 20th that one of our weakest regiments could have entered the Grand Plaza with but little opposition—in fact could have driven every soldier either out of the city or to some hiding-place within its walls. Santa Anna and the miserable semblance of a Government would also have fled, and there would have been no power with which to open negotiations, with which to treat. Perhaps it is better, then, that the army did not at once enter and occupy the capital, at least in view of a peace—this is a question yet to be solved. I must acknowledge, however, even as matters now look that I am one of a large majority who feel anything but rejoiced that the army did not enter the city at first, and that peace negotiations are not to be entertained at the National Palace.

Yours, &tc., &tc.,

G. W. K.

P. S. Since the above was written, we have received a thousand and one rumors from the city. The report that Bustamente is approaching with some 6000 troops is renewed, as well as the account of the advance of Paredes upon the capital. All the shops in the city are closed, and consternation still reigns. Many will have it, the evidence being their own proper eyes, that the Mexicans are throwing up breast works and constructing batteries at different points, and they say too, that Santa Anna either is desirous of gaining time, or else to make one of the main conditions of peace that he is to be supported by American arms against any faction that may rise against him. In this they are probably more than half right. A train of wagons, which was going in this morning headed by Capt. Wayne[50] and an escort of dragoons, were turned back by the Mexicans on the pretense that there were regular soldiers with the convoy. I don't known how the matter will be settled, but Santa Anna will probably have his own way. Our own officers are many of them outrageous at the occurrence.

*Daily Picayune*, September 9, 1847

Tacubaya, August 27, 1847

The official report of Gen. Salas, who was second in command at Contreras and who is now a prisoner, has been published in Mexico. He admits that his defeat was total, but as usual lays the blame on some of his brother officers. He says that on the afternoon of the 19th—(*this was while no one was returning their fire*)—the Mexicans fought with uncommon valor and enthusiasm, but that early on the morning of the 20th August they were suddenly surrounded and at once thrown into confusion, and in the end utterly routed. Salas says that at the outset of the disorder he shouted "Victory for Mexico," ordered the trumpets to sound, and directed Gen. Torrejón to charge with his lancers; but according to the same account that officer fled in the most cowardly manner, the infantry got mixed up with the cavalry and also fled, and the rout of all was complete and most disastrous. Salas says that Gen. Valencia ran off at the commencement of the fight, that he does not know what has become of him, and for this reason has felt himself called upon to make a report. Such is the account given by his Excellency Gen. Sr. Don I. Mariano de Salas of the defeat at Contreras—one of the most brilliant victories achieved by our arms since the commencement of the war—brilliant and most important for the great results produced with so little loss on our side, and for which Gen. Smith, as well as Col. Riley and the other officers engaged in it, are receiving the unqualified approbation of the entire army.

50. Henry C. Wayne, Quartermaster.

Gen. Salas himself acknowledges that in this battle Gen. Frontera[51] was killed, that besides himself Gens. Mendoza, Blanco and Garcia were wounded and taken prisoners, in addition to a list of over 100 other officers—colonels, captains, &c.,—who were either killed, wounded or are now in our hands. And here let me mention one fact in relation to the after battle of Churubusco, which will show how near Gen. Scott was capturing the entire Mexican army. At the time Gen. Worth was pressing upon the *téte de pont*, Gen. Twiggs upon the church, and Gens. Shields and Pierce upon the hacienda farther on, the commander-in-chief ordered Maj. Sumner to take command of the Rifles, and by a circuitous march to reach the road between the enemy and the city. Nothing but the daring impetuosity of our own men in front prevented this plan from succeeding—had the Mexicans held out or our own soldiers held off ten minutes longer, the enemy would have been in a bag as it were, and killed or captured to a man. Santa Anna might perhaps have escaped, as he has a peculiar way of his own; but he would not have taken even the remnant of an army with him.

A Mexican mail was captured by a party of our dragoons on the 22d inst. on its way from the city to Morelia. It contained a multitude of letters dated on the 21st, the day after the great battles, and they give vivid and at the same time most doleful accounts of their terrible and utter defeat. Some of the writers lay the blame on Santa Anna alone, some on Valencia, some on Santa Anna and Valencia, some on Santa Anna, Valencia, and all the officers, while others say that Santa Anna, Valencia, and all the officers *and soldiers* are utterly worthless. The latter writers are more comprehensive and probably nearer the mark. Many of the letters are exceedingly rich. One loving husband writes to his wife, whom he calls "angel," and "idol," and his "adored *Chulita*," and tells her not to occasion herself any uneasiness about his safety, as he does not intend to expose himself! Another officer comes out even plainer: he tells his beloved Rosa that he thought of her when the balls were flying, *and ran*! The capture of these letters is valuable in more ways than one—they give much information as regards the strength and plans of the enemy, and freely and frankly acknowledge that they have been defeated and utterly disorganized. The number of Santa Anna's grand army is put down at from 30 to 35,000, and nearly all of them took a part in the battles of the 20th.

Santa Anna has come out in a long manifesto to the Mexican nation. He begins by saying that he shall speak openly and candidly to his fellow-citizens, as frankness has always been a characteristic of his administration! He next speaks of what he has lately done in the way of collecting an

---

51. José Frontera.

army and munitions for the defence of the capital, and then goes on to lay all the blame of his reverse upon Valencia, who would not obey his orders on the 19th, evacuate Contreras, and fall back upon the second line of defence at Churubusco. He intimates that he continued with his soldiers until the last moment, and after they were routed and driven from Churubusco he says that he was enabled to rally his troops at the Garita—the third line—*and thus save the capital!* On the following day, he says, while occupied in reorganizing his forces, strengthening his batteries, and placing himself once more at the head of a column to defend the capital until the last extreme, he received a letter from Gen. Scott proposing an armistice, &c., (Santa Anna says nothing about his talking this matter over the previous evening with Mackintosh and Thornton and their immediate departure for the American lines, but absolutely harangues his countrymen as though the first propositions came from Gen. Scott.) In the concluding paragraphs of his manifesto Santa Anna says that he has granted an armistice to the Americans to listen to what their peace commissioner has to say. He gives it as his opinion that a suspension of hostilities is always beneficial, that war is always an evil—in fact that a perpetual war is an absurdity![52] He intimates that he has competent authority to listen to overtures of peace, and then goes on to tell his people that he has a sufficient number of troops to sustain the rights and vindicate the honor of the nation. He considers himself as free as though he had obtained a signal victory, and that his fellow-citizens need have no fear of his being deceived or imposed upon by the negotiators of the enemy, inasmuch as he does not dread their men or cannon! If peace can be brought about without losing the honor of the nation, well and good; if not, Santa Anna intimates that he will return to the sword as an arbitrator. Such is a mere outline of a document which makes nearly three columns in the *Diario del Gobierno.*

The commissioners upon the part of the Mexican Government to listen to our overtures of peace are Gens. Mora y Villamil and José Joachin de Herrera, the latter formerly President and now military commandant of Mexico.[53] His

---

52. Santa Anna's misrepresentation of events arrived in Washington ahead of American accounts of the truce and the subsequent negotiations, causing the Polk administration to believe that Scott and Trist had been duped by Mexican officials. This view would be instrumental in Polk's decision to order Trist's recall.

53. Mora y Villamil's experience as a topographical engineer prepared him to deal with the boundary questions at hand. Herrera headed the *moderados* who were willing to consider an end to hostilities. Joining these men were José Bernardo Couto, a leading moderate in Congress and an authority on civil and constitutional law, and Miguel Atristain, formally an agent for Manning and Mackintosh and reportedly placed on the commission at Mackintosh's insistence. Mahin, *Olive Branch and Sword,* 116.

character, as all our readers know, is that of an honest but weak man. Don Antonio Garay, a well-known capitalist and formerly Minister of Finance, was also appointed on the commission, but refused to serve. He is known to be warmly in favor of peace, probably from interest. The commissioners on the part of Mexico, with Mr. Trist, it is said are to hold their first meeting this afternoon, at some place near this.

I may be mistaken, but my humble opinion is that there are *three influences* now at work in the city of Mexico to bring about a peace. The first and foremost is Santa Anna himself, sick and tired of the war, and seeing nothing in its continuance but his own utter and irretrievable ruin. The second is Mackintosh, Thornton & Co., the latter gentleman secretary of legation or *attaché* to the English minister, and both representing English interests. The third, and an all-powerful interest it is, is American gold, of which Santa Anna and some of his friends are known to be exceedingly fond, and to handle which they will stop at nothing. Thornton, during the illness of Mr. Bankhead, does the talking on the English side—Mackintosh acts as banker and general agent.[54] Not one of these men care any more for the honor or credit of the Government of Mexico than they do for that of the Tongo Islands—self is at the bottom of all, and Santa Anna is the most selfish man of the lot. On our own side we have *two influences* at work: the first is Gen. Scott, hampered and hand-bound by his own Government, and anxious to bring about a peace, because he believes a majority of his countrymen are warmly in favor of it; and the second is Mr. Trist, covetous, as any man in his position would be, of the distinction so important a deed as the making a peace must give him. Opposed to these influences is a proud but cowardly set of Mexican military demagogues—a band of leeches who have lost all cast but still retain a species of hold upon the people—and then there is the great body of the people themselves, who know not themselves what they want, but who are hoodwinked and led by the demagogues. Santa Anna has no friends; but he has power, and that suits him just as well—perhaps better. Now all the influences enumerated above are to be used to bring about a peace, but how they will succeed is a matter of conjecture. I suppose that the means should not be rejected so that the ends are gained.

The trial of the deserters—the celebrated battalion of St. Patrick—is still going on, but how the affair will terminate no one but those on the court

---

54. Mackintosh had close business ties with the Mexican government. As consul general and a principal in the merchant banking firm Manning and Mackintosh, he had played a major role in the consolidation of Mexico's foreign debt in 1845. He also had profited in the Mexican bond market and was a member of a group of investors holding the rights to develop a trade route across the Isthmus of Tehuantepec. He had, as Trist reported, "immense interests . . . at stake upon the restoration of peace." Mahin, *Olive Branch and Sword*, 103–5.

martial can say. A strong influence is at work in favor of the prisoners. In the first place, all the Mexican ladies in this town, La Señora Cayetano Rubio among the number, have signed a warm petition in their favor, which has been sent to Gen. Scott. The lady whose name I have given is the wife of the rich Rubio, who has a country house here in Tacubaya. The English, and perhaps some of the other foreign ministers, have also interested themselves in behalf of the scoundrels.[55] I might here state that the celebrated flag of the foreign battalion was captured by the 14th Infantry, attached to Gen. Pillow's division.

The banner is of green silk, and on one side is a harp, surmounted by the Mexican coat of arms, with a scroll on which is painted "*Libertad por la Republica Mexicana.*" Under the harp is the motto of "*Erin go Bragh!*" On the other side is a painting of a badly executed figure, made to represent St. Patrick, in his left hand a key and in his right a crook or staff resting upon a serpent. Underneath is painted "San Patricio." To their credit be it spoken, the Irish in our own army are loudest in denouncing the miserable wretches who fought and killed so many under this flag. I know not what disposition will be made of them, but as hardly a person has been punished for an offence committed against our own army since it first crossed the Rio Grande, the rascals may get off easily.

*Two o'clock, afternoon.*–News has just come in from the capital which has caused great excitement. At an early hour a train of wagons, under charge of Capt. Wayne, dressed in citizens' clothes, started for the city. Scarcely had they reached the Plaza before the wagons were surrounded by an immense concourse of *leperos*, who at first commenced cursing and jeering the wagon-masters and wagoners. Soon, however, they began to pelt the poor fellows with stones and other missiles, and notwithstanding the pretended exertions of a squad of Mexican soldiers, who acted as a guard, the entire train was driven out of the city. Several of the wagoners received severe bruises and contusions from the showers of stones thrown at them, and foremost in the mob were said to be the women of the town. One Mexican was shot by one of the wagon-masters, and another by a Mexican officer, but not until they had half killed an American.[56] In the crowd of loafers or leperos were seen many men, apparently of the better class from their dress, who excited the mob to acts of violence, while in the balconies were ladies looking on and evidently enjoying the sport.

55. A number of San Patricio soldiers were British subjects and had corresponded with British officials in Mexico City in the year before their capture.
56. This incident, which occurred on August 26, left two teamsters dead. The American army received no supplies from the city during the armistice.

Even the Mexican cavalry guard, or many of them, sat upon their horses—not indifferent spectators, for they fairly laughed to see the unfortunate and unarmed teamsters beset in a manner so cowardly. I suppose that Santa Anna will apologize for the outrage, and that thus the matter will be settled; but this does not prevent many from thinking that the tyrant instigated the whole affair. He is up to all sorts of trickery. There are others who think, and probably with good show of reason, that the mob was set on by the enemies of Santa Anna and peace, with the intention of involving the whole party and breaking off all negotiations. Be this as it may, the Mexicans have won a great battle in driving our wagons from the city, and will not fail to exult over it. I know not what measures Gen. Scott will now resort to in order to obtain his money and supplies from the city.

The Mexican Government has added two additional members to the Board of Commission to listen to the question of peace—Señores Atristain and Bernardo Couto. Both are *licenciados* or lawyers, and the latter enjoys a high reputation, not only as regards talents, but for the probity of his character. The commissioners held their first meeting this afternoon, at a place called Atzcapuzalco, about two leagues from here, and I learn that Mr. Trist manifests himself as highly pleased with the proceedings thus far, and of the continued flattering prospects of peace.[57] They may not look quite so flattering when he comes to talk of slices of territory, but of this we shall know all in good time.

Yours, &c.,

G. W. K.
*Daily Picayune*, September 9, 1847

Tacubaya, August 28, 1847

Capt. Beauregard, of the engineers, has been kind enough to furnish me with a sketch of the battle grounds of the 20th inst. Of course it was executed in great haste, but still gives one a complete idea of the scene of operations, and of the strong positions held by the Mexican army at the outset. Capt. B. conducted Gen. Smith's brigade to the attack upon Contreras, and thus knows the ground full well. Lieut. Tower,[58] also of the engineer

---

57. Negotiations did not begin well. The Mexican commissioners represented a government willing to recognize an independent Texas north of the Nueces only in exchange for a promise of an indemnity. They were empowered only to receive Trist's proposal. He provided them with a copy of Buchanan's draft treaty that called for the recognition of the Rio Grande as the boundary of Texas and for the cession of New Mexico and California. Several days later, Trist passed the word that the United States was willing to pay up to $30 million for this agreement.

58. Zealous B. Tower.

corps, conducted Col. Riley to the attack of Valencia in the rear, while Capt. Lee, with portions of the 9th and the 12th Regiments, made a diversion in front. Why some of our engineer officers were not killed in the different reconnaissances and actions is a miracle, for they were always foremost.

The accounts this morning from the city would go to show that the Mexicans are chuckling over the *defeat* of the wagon train yesterday, and its expulsion without the walls—they absolutely term it a victory! The authorities pretend they did everything in their power to suppress the row, but no one who understands Mexican character believes them. If anything in this world can be driven easier than Mexicans *with* arms in their hands; (vide Churubusco and Contreras,) it is Mexicans *without* arms. A Mexican mob can be likened to nothing save a flock of sheep—as easily routed and dispersed—and now the authorities pretend that they did everything in their power to suppress the one which was raised yesterday. A single squadron of our dragoons could have ridden over the rioters as easily as they could over a lawn. I suppose now that the wagons will not be allowed to enter the city—another point gained by the enemy. They certainly have not been in today.

The *Diario del Gobierno* of yesterday is almost entirely filled with documents and letters, all undertaking to prove that Valencia was the sole cause of the defeat of the great Mexican army. Santa Anna's friends are at the bottom of all this of course. Several of Valencia's letters are logged into the document, in one of which, dated at 8 o'clock on the evening of the 19th, at Contreras, he speaks of having routed the entire American army at all points, and that the liberty and honor of his country had been saved by the glorious victory. He further discloses the fact that Gen. Frontera was killed while heading a charge of cavalry, and that Gen. Parrodi[59] was wounded. This is news: we shall get all the truth out of them after a while. The last we hear of Valencia he was at Toluca, whither he had gone, according to his own published proclamation, to collect forces to vindicate the honor of his country!

The same number of the *Diario* contains an account of the attack upon the wagon train. It makes light of the whole affair, says that a few persons were slightly injured, that Gens. Tornel,[60] Herrera and Quijano soon dispersed the rioters, and that the fact of the wagons going as far as the Plaza Principal was an error or oversight. Among those who received a shower

---

59. Anastasio Parrodi.

60. José Maria Tornel, long a supporter of the continuation of the war against the United States, was probably instrumental in shaping the Mexican government's approach to the peace negotiations. He was not a likely foe of the rioters that had encircled the American supply train.

of stones on the occasion was Mr. Hargous, the gentleman who has mainly fed and clothed the army since it marched from Jalapa. He was in the city after supplies at the time.

I believe that up to this time I have neglected to mention that Major Gaines, who recently escaped from Mexico, was on the staff of Gen. Scott during the recent battles, and that Midshipman Rogers was on that of Gen. Pillow. After the rout at Contreras, and while our troops were on the way to Churubusco, a house where Capt. Danley and Major Borland were secreted was passed. The former was quite unwell at the time, but the latter came out, shouldered a musket, and was in at the defeat of Churubusco. I hear that Clay and all the other prisoners will now soon be released.

Yours, &c.,

G. W. K.
*Daily Picayune*, September 9, 1847

Tacubaya, August 29, 1847

The peace commissioners met again yesterday, and at a point nearer this place. Nothing positive in relation to the proceedings of this second meeting has transpired—some say that everything went on smoothly, others say not, which is tolerably strong proof that but little is known one way or the other in relation to the deliberations.[61] The new commissioner, Bernardo Couto, was present, as was also Atristain. The latter is represented as a tool of Mackintosh's; but if he can do anything towards bringing about a peace this makes no difference. They say that in the city they indulge the hope that the commissioners will agree upon the Nueces as a boundary. This is carrying the stakes and stones a little too far. "Give them an inch and they'll take an ell" is applied to many people in the world—give a Mexican an inch and he'll take at least seven miles and a half.[62]

I must close this letter in haste, as a messenger has just come in to say that the express man is about to start. You shall be kept informed of everything.

Yours, &c.,

G. W. K.
*Daily Picayune*, September 9, 1847

61. The meeting took place about two miles from Tacubaya in the home of a Señor Alfaro. The Mexican commissioners reported that they were considering the American proposals and that they expected to come to the next meeting fully empowered to negotiate. The next meeting was scheduled for August 30 but was delayed until September 1. Mahin, *Olive Branch and Sword*, 116.

62. Mexican hopes that the Nueces might be established as the boundary between Mexico and Texas were encouraged by the erroneous report conveyed by a British merchant visiting Puebla that Trist's demands were not as harsh as the Mexicans might fear. Mahin, *Olive Branch and Sword*, 116.

Tacubaya, August 30, 1847

Since I wrote you yesterday we have a thousand conflicting rumors from the city. Santa Anna certainly has some 15,000 troops under arms, but is as much in favor of peace as ever. He has opponents in every party and every quarter, many of them, too, warmly in favor of peace. They perhaps may overcome their scruples to the man for the sake of the measure, but of this we shall know more anon.

The Congress of the State of Mexico, in session at Toluca, has come out against peace measures, and the Governor, Olaguibel,[63] has also issued a manifesto on the same side.

The peace commissioners, after being in session two or three days, have adjourned until the 1st September, Wednesday next. Of their proceedings no one knows anything, but it is rumored that both Gen. Scott and Mr. Trist express hopes that a treaty of peace will be signed.

Valencia is at Toluca, endeavoring to write himself out of the scrape his great lack of fighting propensities got him into at Contreras. Santa Anna, meanwhile, loads all the blame upon Valencia—his insubordination, he says, lost everything. With this I send you one of the intercepted letters, captured on the 22d inst. by our dragoons. It is rich, and probably as true as it is rich. "Maria" speaks her mind freely, and if the valiant *Polkas* can find anything complimentary in what she says it is more than I can. I have the promise, in company with another correspondent, of being allowed to copy all the best of the letters.

Yours, &c.,

G. W. K.

### (*Copy.*)

Mexico, August 21, 1847

*My Much Loved Uncle*—Considering that you would be uneasy on our account under present circumstances, I write to relieve your mind. Everything is lost, and I believe there is no hope for us. Day before yesterday Valencia had a fight with the enemy near Contreras, and it was supposed he was victorious; but the next morning he lost everything. Yesterday some National Guards that were at San Antonio had a small fight and the battalions of Hidalgo and Victoria (*Polka troops—Gentleman soldiers*) ran like cowards—as also did the cavalry of the 11th and the 3d Light Infantry. This is a strange fatality, and it

---

63. Olaguibel was an ally of General Valencia. Together they had gathered the support of several key military and political leaders, including Juan Alvarez, Mariano Paredes, Juan Almonte, and Valentín Canalizo. This group represented a spectrum of Mexican political positions and was united by a mutual distrust of Santa Anna.

seems our troops are good for nothing but to boast. I only heard them cry, there come the Yankees, overcome with terror—and running a whole league without stopping, from which fact I have no hope that resistance can be made at the gates, as is intended; you will see what will happen if a defence is attempted. They will all run and their history will end. Ruperto saved himself, as he had the luck to run away in company with the "Victorias," and he is *now safe with his dear aunt and quite tranquil.* It appears quite impossible that 12,000 men under the command of Scott should have put to flight and entirely cowed 32,000 of our men. It confounds reason—the fact is opposed to reason and almost incredible; yet, strange to say, it is true. This misfortune has no remedy, and the affair must soon end and we can do nothing. Do not believe the thousand lies our troops may tell you, and of which they boast. You know that here (in Mexico) a thousand lies are told from our next door neighbors—therefore how much more exaggerated they will be when traveling to you. Do not be afflicted, but hold all you hear at quarantine. Recommend yourself in God and trust in him and he will take care of us.

Maria

P. S.—*My Dear Uncle*—I refer you to my sister's letter for the news. I can add nothing to it but that we the Mexicans are * * * * *

(This postscript, although not signed, was probably written by the brave and chivalrous Ruperto, who left tranquility and his dear aunt for a moment in order to prove to his uncle that he was really quite safe.)

*Daily Picayune*, September 26, 1847

Tacubaya, August 30, 1847[64]

The funeral of poor Irons, Gen. Cadwalader's aide, who was mortally wounded at Churubusco, yet who lingered until the 28th, was most numerously attended by his brother officers yesterday. The chances of war have so ordained it that some of the most gallant and popular spirits of the army should fall victims. Of Col. Butler I have already spoken, and the memory of such men as Burke, Willoughby, Anderson, Hanson, Capron, Thornton, Preston,[65] Johnstone, Hoffman, Easley and others will live in the minds of those who knew them as long as recollection lasts.

64. This dispatch was introduced with the following comment: "The letters which we have already published from our associate in Mexico, received by the *Fashion*, were written subsequently to the renewal of hostilities. Those written immediately prior to the rupture of the armistice necessarily possess less stirring interest, but they throw great light upon the state of parties in Mexico and are more instructive than those sketching the course of military events. We resume today the publications of the letters."

65. William Preston.

Since I sent off my letters yesterday, our reports from the city are so conflicting and so contradictory that we can make little out of them. It is certain that Santa Anna yesterday reviewed no less than 14,000 troops, and those who saw them say that they made truly an imposing appearance; it is also certain that breastworks have been thrown up in the vicinity of many of the entrances to the capital, yet the friends of Santa Anna and of peace say that they have only been constructed to overawe the enemies of pacific arrangements, both within and without the walls. As regards the probabilities of peace, no one not immediately in all the secrets can form a conjecture. One hour everything looks favorable; the next comes, and not a man in the army but will tell you we are even farther from an amicable adjustment than when Gen. Taylor crossed the Rio Grande, and raised the stars and stripes at Matamoros. All is doubt and confusion, and no one knows at night, when he lays himself upon his bed, what the early morrow will bring forth. In the city, save the coffee-houses, billiard-rooms and grocery stores, all places of business continued closed, while hordes of hungry *leperos* are prowling about, robbing and inciting to every species of outlawry. No property is safe, and I hear it hinted that millions of dollars, belonging to wealthy Mexican families, have been placed under a foreign flag for protection, and that the immense amount is claimed as the property of the citizens owing allegiance to that banner.

From eye-witnesses I have received a full account of the recent outrageous attack upon our wagon train in the city. A more wanton or cowardly outrage was never committed. A little French woman, who lived in a house near the scene, is said to have come out and openly harangued the rabble which assailed the unfortunate teamsters. Calling the rioters all sorts of hard names, she told them they had just found a calling for which they were fitted—that they had finally encountered a set of men without arms in their hands, and it was a fit occasion for them to show their great valor by attacking them a hundred to one. It is also said that a knot of foreigners—Frenchmen and others—who saw the outrage, were so much incensed that they proceeded to arm themselves in order to attack the miscreants; but the wagons were moved from the scene before they could be organized. Santa Anna, from a balcony of the Palace, was a cool spectator of the whole affair, and had a thousand men all drawn up in front that were not ordered to move. His apologists say that he kept them there for his own safety, as amid the shouts of the crowd were cries of "Death to the wooden-legged tyrant!—Down with the traitor who wants to sell us!"

Let me give you as correct an idea as I am able of the state of parties and feeling in the city of Mexico yesterday—as everything changes here with the sun, I cannot be responsible for the correctness of the picture today. In the first place, then, there is the rabble, by far the larger part of the population, who attribute the fact that the American army did not enter the city to fear. Their own manifestoes and documents all go to prove this, the opponents of Santa Anna and peace do all they can to spread the belief, and the fact that the wagon train was driven from the city and no steps to obtain redress for the outrage or punish the offenders taken, gives coloring to the belief. These people know no more about the Nueces or the Sabine than they do about the Wabash or Salt river—care no more about the one or the other, or about any point in dispute between the two Governments—but they have been nurtured amid broil and disturbance, see no pleasure except in revolution and turmoil, expect no change in their condition from peace, and look upon the Americans as their common enemy. They have no master mind among them to point out the evil and direct the right—they move on without rudder or compass, one day glorifying Santa Anna as a god and the next kicking his mutilated limb about the gutters and dung-hills—they have all the blood-thirstiness and depravity of the French *canaille*[66] in the worst days of the revolution, but not one tithe of the courage of the amiable co-laborers of Marat.[67] Even up to this time it has never struck the majority of all classes that they are the most arrant cowards that Christendom has ever produced, that they have neither valor nor prowess. Adversity furnishes them no teaching— defeat exposes not their weakness and utter worthlessness. Ten of our men may chase one hundred of them until they drop from sheer exhaustion, and the moment they recover their breath they are just as valiant as ever— talk of what they are *going to do*, of how they are to expose their lives to the last gasp, and against all odds, to vindicate the honor of their country! Forgetful entirely that there are such places as Palo Alto, Buena Vista or Cerro Gordo, they talk of the deeds of Hidalgo and Morelos, and claim to be their valiant descendants. Take from them a province, a castle, an important stronghold, and not a whit are they the wiser as to their true merits—they shrug their shoulders, articulate "*aguarde un poco*" (wait a little) and still believe that they are the greatest people and the greatest nation on earth, and that they are yet to come out of the war conquerors. They rely not upon Providence, much less upon their own arms; but look into the glass darkly and hope against every semblance of hope. Idle words with them stand in the relation of facts among any other people, and empty boastings pass for deeds actually performed—they imagine victories upon

66. Rabble, the lowest level of society.
67. French revolutionary Jean-Paul Marat.

paper, yet do not realize defeats while yet wounded and panting on stricken fields. Such is a feeble portrait of the rabble of Mexico—of nine-tenths nearly of the population—useless, worthless, abandoned, yet with a happy self-sufficiency that renders them blind to every disgrace and indifferent to every disaster. With this population we have to make peace.

The thinking portion of the liberal classes again, the *Puros* or ultra-democrats in part, however much they may desire peace to protect their property, are perfectly outrageous that Santa Anna should have anything to do with the making of it. Much rather would they see an American government established at once in the capital, great as is their hate for us, than see a peace patched up with the tyrant who has so long ruled and ridden rough-shod over them. This is the party who would do away with every shadow of a standing army, who would reduce the power and revenue of the clergy, who would do away with all monopolies, and who would cut down the offices and expenses of the Government to the lowest figure. With such a people their schemes must prove Utopian, but they hate Santa Anna, and many of them will oppose every obstacle in their power to his making a peace.

Then there are the *Moderados*—those who oppose alike the agrarian notions of the *Puros* as well as the absolutism of the *Monarquistas*—and this party embraces a large portion of the wealthy proprietors, followers of the church, and better class of society generally—they may be in favor of peace, but they are alike opposed to Santa Anna.[68] Many of this party, notwithstanding their pride, would be rejoiced to see the United States establish a secure and safe government over them—some of them even go in for annexation at once. Santa Anna has a few friends in this party— friends only from interest; but the larger portion mistrust him, and there is everywhere a portion who will throw every obstacle in the way of his making peace. A fraction of all these parties have been mixed up in the late riot, but the majority of the malcontents have been *Puros.*

Opposed to all his enemies, Santa Anna has a large portion of the officers of the army immediately around him, together with some 15,000 troops still under arms. No doubt he is anxious for peace, and will exert every means to bring it about; but time has been given him to look about him and feel the national pulse, and he will undoubtedly act as may best further his own ambitious schemes. If he finds that he can make peace and still preserve his ascendancy, which I much doubt, well and good; if not, he will probably make another show of resistance, and contrive to humbug

68. Santa Anna's opponents—*puros* and *moderados* alike—feared that he might use a financial settlement for the ceded territories in order to consolidate his political base.

his countrymen into the belief that he has done everything for their honor and glory. If ever man was placed in an extremity it is Santa Anna; if ever man was capable of extricating himself, he is the one. A ruler who has deceived and cheated everyone with whom he has had dealings thus far has still wit enough to overcome all his enemies.

In the meantime, the Congress of the State of Mexico, in session at Toluca, the capital, has protested against making peace with the United States, or coming to any terms until the blockade of all the ports is raised and all our troops are withdrawn from the territory. The Governor of the State, too, Don Francisco M. de Olaguibel, has come out with a strong manifesto against peace. He is a Puro, but a man of character and standing, a friend of Gómez Farías, who is now living at Toluca. Valencia is also there, and has recently come out with a strong paper vindicating his own conduct while in command at Contreras. To read it, one would think that on the 19th of August he had completely annihilated the entire American army—the document is Mexican all over.

I have perused a manifesto issued at Toluca, which breathes nothing but war to the very last against the United States—war without rest and war without quarter—and the writer makes it out that our future annihilation is inevitable. If there were any meaning in Mexican threats, I presume that Gen. Scott would either capitulate or evacuate the country with his army forthwith; but these furious paper proclamations of the Mexicans, like the fierce heads and figures the Chinese paint outside their walls, frighten no one. Has it ever struck you that the Chinese and the Mexicans resemble each other? Some of the foreigners here even call the latter the Chinese of America.

The peace commissioners have adjourned their meetings until Wednesday next, the 1st September. Rumor has it that Mr. Trist has given them their ultimatum, but this I doubt. The talk is, that both Gen. Scott and Mr. T. are sanguine that peace will be brought about. They of course have the best chances of knowing everything, but my humble opinion is that all their hopes will prove groundless.

To get provisions out of the city, since the wagons are not permitted to enter it, our commissaries and quartermasters are compelled to steal supplies out as best they may. For this purpose pack mules are sent to the suburbs every morning before daylight, loaded, and driven out before the mob has time to collect, while money is also clandestinely smuggled out in coaches. It is rather humiliating to be compelled to resort to such trickery in the presence of an enemy so contemptible; but as concession is the order of the day, with the hope that a speedy peace is to be brought about,

I suppose it is best to put up and bear with every indignity offered. The terms of the armistice have certainly been broken in more ways than one by the Mexicans.

Yours, &c.,

G. W. K.
*Daily Picayune*, October 16, 1847

Tacubaya, August 31, 1847

A party under Capt. Wood,[69] escorted by a squadron of Dragoons under Capt. Hardee, went out a day or two since in the direction of Toluca after grain, and reports are current that it has been cut off by the Mexicans. At all events another party has been sent out to gain information on the subject. In the city, where there is such an immense rabble, it is a different matter; but in the country I hardly think the Mexicans will offer great molestation to any foraging party that may be sent out. We shall see.

I have conversed with several gentlemen from the city today, and they tell me that the general impression among the foreigners is that there can be no peace. They say that Santa Anna, much as he desires it, does not give it his consent. Congress will, of course, oppose the measure to the last, or perhaps will not meet to approve of it, which is all the same thing; but then if Mr. Bankhead gives Santa Anna a receipt that he is the Government of Mexico, and is willing to acknowledge him as having full power, it makes but little difference to us what course Congress may take.

There are doubtless a great many Mexicans, perhaps a large majority, who think that a few weeks or months inaction or delay of the Americans outside the capital will destroy their army, and hence the opposition they evince to the removal of provisions and supplies from the city. They may perhaps flatter themselves into the belief that Gen. Scott will be either forced to retire upon Puebla for want of food, or else starved into a surrender here in Tacubaya. In the meantime, they are digging intrenchments in different quarters, throwing up breastworks, and reviewing their troops. The friends of Santa Anna say that all these preparations are made to put down anticipated revolution against himself—they are certainly in progress.

A large portion of our wounded officers are doing well—the two most difficult and dangerous cases are perhaps Lieuts. Halloway and Hamilton, and the strongest hopes are entertained that they will recover. Capt. Kearny is improving, so too is Capt. McReynolds and Lieut. Graham. The charge of these gallant officers, upon the garita of Mexico after the glorious

---

69. George W. F. Wood, Commissary.

battle of Churubusco was over, was most daring.[70] Had they been supported by a single column of infantry the Mexicans would not have made a struggle to defend the city, so great was the panic among them; but Gen. Worth, who was in advance, had no orders on the subject, and thus the opportunity was lost.

The intercepted letters, mention of which I have already made, say that the Polkas scattered each man to his house on entering the city, and changed their uniforms with the greatest haste. No band of music playing martial airs preceded them, nor did the ladies throw bouquets and flowers upon the heads of these valiant descendants of Iturbide as was the case when they went out to defend their capital to the last—the stampede was perfect, and we have the evidence of their own letter writers in proof.

Yours,

G. W. K.

P. S. *Nine o'clock, night.*—Major Palacios, the joint commissioner with Col. Bolton[71] to see that the terms of the armistice are carried out, has just sent word advising that the pack mules be not sent out tomorrow morning, as the authorities anticipate a mob and further acts of riot. So the war wages—humbug has the day.

*Daily Picayune*, October 16, 1847

Tacubaya, September 1, 1847

The expedition under Capt. Wood, about which some fears were entertained, returned today in safety. At Lerma, about midway between this and Toluca, they were met by the Governor of the State, Olaguibel, and were told that they could proceed no farther, while the pickets of his force were seen plainly a short distance in advance. He, however, treated our officers very politely, directed them to a hacienda where they could obtain everything they wanted, and then retired. He did not leave, however, until he told Capts. Wood and Hardee that he had no respect for the armistice lately signed.

Santa Anna has issued a bando or decree prohibiting all foreigners and others from leaving the city and visiting the lines of the Americans, unless they have a passport signed by himself. What his motives are for this obnoxious measure no one knows, but he doubtless has good reasons of his own. In the first place he issued an order, about a week since, for all families to return to the city within three days, and now he wishes to keep

70. As the fighting at Churubusco came to an end, Philip Kearny's dragoons dashed forward to the gates of Mexico City. Kearny's injuries led to the amputation of his left hand.

71. Possibly Francis S. Belton, Third Artillery.

them there. Everyone who comes out will have it—and they assert it upon the evidence of their own proper eye-sight—that the Mexicans are fortifying at different points, and especially at San Cosmé.[72] If this all be true, it is a direct violation of the armistice.

Among the guns captured at Contreras on the 20th ult. those which attract the most attention are the two taken from Lieut. O'Brien at the battle of Buena Vista, and over which the Mexicans made such a rejoicing. Is it not strange that the same company of the 4th Artillery which lost the guns should have had the proud gratification of retaking them. The company was commanded by Capt. Drum at Contreras,[73] and I learn that it is Gen. Scott's intention, after suitable inscriptions are engraved upon them, to present the guns to the company or regiment. The Mexicans will not get them back in a hurry.

A great many anecdotes of the individual gallantry of our officers are told, in connection with the glorious battles of the 20th August, but until I have more time and obtain more full particulars I must forbear recording them. I cannot avoid noticing, however, the personal gallantry of Chaplain McCarty, the only chaplain I believe who has followed the army, and whose conduct at Churubusco in particular, was noticed by all. Ever foremost, and where the balls were flying thickest, he was not only ready to give consolation to the dying but spur on the living to fresh deeds. He not only sought the best places for crossing the ditches with which the ground was cut up, but helped our advancing soldiers across as well; and as some of the voltigeurs were wading a ditch more than waist deep, where their flasks were touching the water, the worthy parson pointed out the circumstance and told them to be careful and *keep their powder dry!* Such a chaplain is worth having in a small army like ours. On Sundays he gives us a sound and sensible Episcopalian sermon, and his praise is in every mouth.

The peace commissioners met again today, Major Van Buren[74] accompanying Mr. Trist, and report has it that *the dinner on the occasion was most excellent!* I believe it was furnished by the Mexicans, and the army wags will have it that the richness of the viands and the flavor of the wine induced a fall of one parallel of latitude in our demands. But to speak seriously, it is said that both Gen. Scott and Mr. Trist express themselves highly gratified with the prospects of an amicable adjustment, at the flattering

---

72. San Cosmé was the gate that guarded the northwestern approach to Mexico City.

73. Mentioned are John P. J. O'Brien and Simon H. Drum.

74. Abraham Van Buren, son of the former president, accompanied Trist at these early meetings at the suggestion of General Scott.

chances that a peace between the two countries will be ratified. I must acknowledge that for one I shall be much astonished when I learn that a satisfactory peace to our country is signed with Santa Anna, or even any kind. The man who has cheated and humbugged everyone with whom he has had diplomatic dealings thus far has not yet lost his trickery and cunning, and we are altogether too frank and honest in our transactions even to hope to make a fair bargain where nothing but dissimulation and deceit are pitted against us.

Yours, &c.,

G. W. K.
*Daily Picayune*, October 16, 1847

Tacubaya, September 2, 1847

The mules, or a great part of them, sent into the city at an early hour this morning after supplies, came back unloaded, and the story is that a large building, occupied as a depot of provisions by Mr. Hargous, was broken into during the night and robbed of nearly everything—rice, flour, sugar and bacon. As bright a moon as ever shone was looking down upon the scene, patrols were in every street, and it would be deemed too great an insult upon the watchfulness of the Mexican authorities to say that the outrage was committed without their knowledge; but as a few of the robbers were arrested just as our own men arrived at the place, they may make it appear that it was without their connivance or consent. I suppose that the matter will be amicably settled, for long-suffering and forbearance, thanks probably to instructions from Washington, are virtues which are possessed here in an eminent degree. I wish Gen. Jackson was alive and President.

Scarcely an hour passes that Santa Anna is not issuing some new bando or order. Yesterday a decree was published, prohibiting all private foreigners from hoisting the flags of their nation upon their houses—why or wherefore the deponent knoweth not. Another order was promulgated to prevent all strangers from leaving the city, and still another commanding all members of the National Guard to appear immediately at the quarters of his regiment: if he does not comply he is to be declared a deserter in front of the enemy, sentenced besides to serve ten years in the ranks of the regular army, and if he is in the Government employ to lose his place forever. Santa Anna says, that in moments so critical Mexico expects everyone of her sons to defend her, and that now the honor of the country is at stake no one can refuse his services without shame. This talk is all very fine, but the regimental quarters of the National Guard will not be crowded to any particular state of suffocation in consequence. The valiant Polkas have not yet forgotten Churubusco.

But the richest thing which has appeared as yet is an editorial in the *Diario del Gobierno*, announcing a meeting of Santa Anna and his principal officers to talk over the affairs of the nation. Not in Don Quixote, nor in Hudibras, nor in Pickwick even, do we find recorded a scene so exceedingly ludicrous.[75] In the first place came forward Bravo and the renowned Alvarez, who, after congratulating the country upon the possession of so great a treasure as was he, Santa Anna, next went on to inform his excellency, the "well-merited," that they had the utmost confidence in his wisdom, valor, integrity, and all that sort of thing to carry them safely through all the perils with which the nation was surrounded, and that they would faithfully stick by him forever and ever—which in Mexican means until they can do better. Gen. Tornel next came up, and he too beplastered Santa Anna with any quantity of soap of such exceeding softness, that our wonder is how even the great man could withstand the application. The President had told his officers that he would resign; but with one accord they all said no—there was a unanimity about it that would almost make one believe they had been drilled before hand not to listen for one moment to the thought of his giving up the helm of state. Santa Anna, full of emotion at seeing such extraordinary unanimity, and enthusiasm, reluctantly told all his officers that, as it was *their* will, he would hold on and do his utmost, as he always had done— including risking his life ever since 1821—to steer his vessel safely through. They then all said something coinciding with Santa Anna's views as regards the question of peace, and hoping that an honorable one might be concluded, but, if the war was to be continued, they each of them begged it as a special and very particular favor to be placed in the most dangerous position that could by any possibility be found—on this point they were all clamorous. Can anyone imagine a scene more supremely ridiculous. Tornel and Alvarez beseeching to be placed in positions where the danger might happen to be the greatest! There were excellent openings of this kind at Churubusco, but we do not learn that one of these *valientes* improved them.

Peace stock rather fell this evening, it somehow coming to the ears of the public that at the meeting of the commissioners this afternoon the prospects were not so flattering as they were the day previous. No fancy stock in New York ever rose and fell as rapidly as does this peace or war stock here—it goes up or down ten times where the sun does once. Santa

75. The references are to Cervantes's *The Adventures of Don Quixote*, Dickens's *Pickwick Papers*, and Samuel Butler's *Hudibras*, a long narrative poem first published in 1663 and widely read in the eighteenth and nineteenth centuries.

Anna, with all the opposition his own demented countrymen may make against it, probably remains as firm in his purpose to bring it about as ever, while he has the full influence of the English and some of the other foreign Ministers to back him. The Prussian Minister has come out with a letter, very flattering to Santa Anna, in which he trusts that he may be able to consummate a peace with his enemies and relieve his downtrodden country. He sees Mackintosh busying himself in the matter, and he also wishes to have a finger in the pie. In the meantime, there is certainly evidence abroad that some of the more thinking minds, both among the puros and moderados—notwithstanding their hatred and distrust of Santa Anna—are coming over to the peace party and advocating the measure. They want some protection and quiet, see none in a continuance of the war, and are even willing to assist the tyrant in his schemes as the lesser evil. We hear not a word as to the terms of the treaty, at least not a word that can be relied upon; and in case a peace is concluded we know not whether we are to have New Mexico and California, or one of them, or not a foot of either—all is doubt and most perplexing uncertainty.[76] The commissioners, I believe, do not meet again until Saturday, the 4th inst.

Perhaps it might interest you to know the present location of the forces under Gen. Scott. He has his headquarters here in Tacubaya, with the division under Gen. Worth. Gen. Pillow's division is at Mixcoac, about two miles south of this; that of Gen. Twiggs, about four miles further south, while Gen. Quitman's is at San Agustín. The health of the army is in the main good, although there are many on the sick report.

Yours, &c.,

G. W. K.
*Daily Picayune*, October 17, 1847

Tacubaya, September 4, 1847

Notwithstanding the bandos to the contrary, several foreigners made their way out of the city yesterday. They state that peace prospects were

76. The meetings on September 1 and 2 yielded at least the promise of a peace. Trist, persuaded that the Mexican Congress would not accept the Rio Grande as the country's eastern boundary, agreed to recommend to the Polk administration that the treaty name the Nueces as the Texas frontier. In exchange, the Mexican commissioners agreed to cede most of what is today New Mexico, Arizona, and southern California for $30 million. The deal gave the United States the access it wanted to the Pacific coast, but in giving up the Rio Grande as the boundary it raised questions about the territorial claim that had been used to justify the war in the first place. Trist warned his fellow peace commissioners that little likelihood existed that the American government would accept the Nueces; he did not anticipate, however, that merely proposing the new boundary would contribute to President Polk's decision to order his recall. Mahin, *Olive Branch and Sword*, 116–19.

absolutely brightening apace in the capital—that many influential persons, albeit opposed to Santa Anna, were advocating the necessity of coming to terms with "los Yankees." A *junta des notables,* or convention of great men, has been called to meet today and talk over the affairs of the nation, and it is thought and hoped that something may grow out of it. The heavier property holders and moneyed men of the city are the ones whom Santa Anna has called upon, and their interests are for peace of course, although their feelings are against it. The commissioners are also to meet today, and rumor has it that their deliberations have reached that point when something decisive must transpire. We shall see.

If peace be made, it will be the most singular that has ever been patched up since the Crusades. From the time the war broke out our Government has been an humble suitor at the feet of Mexico for peace—a degraded suitor would hardly be too harsh a phrase—while she has not *even* taken the *trouble* to coquette with us, at least not until now. The boasted magnanimity of our rulers has either been attributed to fear by the Mexicans in their ignorance, or scoffed at as insulting to them in their pride. Olive branches sufficient to turn the whole world into a vast community of Quakers have been worn out, yet with every scornful rejection a fresh twig has been cut and a fresh offer made. By these means victories have been robbed of their results; the Mexicans have been allowed what Napoleon never gave his enemies—*time.* Like the man importuned to purchase of another what he knew he was obliged to sell, they have hung off for a better bargain; and now, when driven to the corner as it were, it is certainly problematical whether any offer we can make them will be accepted. I have said that if peace was made it would be a most singular consummation. Look at it for a moment. In the first place there is Santa Anna, ambitious and most avaricious, anxious for peace and ready to sell it for a price, yet fearful of losing power and place in his own country and all claim to standing as a patriot or a ruler in the eyes of the world. Watched with wary eyes by his enemies, he sees that he cannot accept bribes and be the sole master of the secret—his fears and not his honesty hold him halting as to what course to pursue. Time has been given him, and no man can work greater wonders with it than he—he has an opportunity to feel the public pulse at his leisure, and will make the most of the extension. If he finds that he can drive, coax or frighten the master-spirits around him into his own views, can gain their support and cooperation, he will pocket any money offered and sanction a peace—he wants accomplices in the crime, but no sharers in the spoils. If he ascertains that he cannot sustain himself against his enemies, he will make a virtue of being the best patriot among them, and bide the issue of another battle. So much for Santa Anna and the chances of making peace with them, but there are elements at work which will go far to obstruct his effecting its consummation. To nine-tenths of the inhabitants the war, as carried on, has been a pastime—to many a harvest. While those immediately on the lines occupied by our troops have made themselves rich by it, it still has not estranged them from their own idols or made them our friends. They, from policy and a species of patriotism, wish to see the war continued. The people remote from the scenes of actual strife, in their blind pride and over-weening self-confidence, have no desire for peace, because they think that any peace would be ignominious. This idea is in their heads, and cannot be driven out. I have now spoken of the poorer classes, of the mass; let us look at the rich proprietors and moneyed men. A portion of them, from selfish interest alone, are in favor of peace—their hate for the Americans is every bit as cordial and as strong as that of the mass. Perhaps even a majority of this class would rejoice if peace were made, yet not one in a hundred of this majority could be induced openly to come out and advocate it. Very few friends can Santa Anna count upon among this part of the population, while he has long since made deadly enemies of such men as Arista, Ampudia, Requena, Almonte, and a host of other officers, many of them the best Mexico has ever produced. Among those immediately around him he doubtless has many friends who will aid and stick to him—men whom he has raised to the army not from any talent they possess but for their influence—while at the same time it is strongly suspected that two of his Ministers, Tornel and Pacheco, are opposed to his schemes, and have been mainly instrumental in getting up the recent rows and preventing our army from obtaining money and supplies from the city. It is hinted at by those who have some inkling of state secrets that Mackintosh, the broker and disbursing agent of all the moneys appropriated towards purchasing a peace, has overlooked these worthies in making his distributions, and as they have hands open to receive the smallest favors they may have become nettled at the slight. The leperos of the city, the gentlemen armed with knives, having nothing to gain from peace and much to hope for in the way of plunder from a continuance of the war—they are all decidedly belligerent. Not one in a hundred, perhaps not one in a thousand of the entire community, allows reason or good sense to have any part in the controversy, or thinks of the future welfare of the country—and thus stand matters at the present writing. If peace be made, it will be purchased of Santa Anna—regularly bought—and this against the wishes of nine-tenths of the population. It will be purchased, too, of a weak and imbecile enemy, the vendor really the worst enemy they have, while the National Congress, a body that I had almost overlooked, is opposed to the bargain. Santa Anna has the army and its leaders immediately around him, and his avarice may induce him to sign a peace with the hope that he will be able to put down the revolution which must immediately be raised against him; but I doubt whether he will do it. His fears of after consequences will overcome his avarice, his enemies will lend all their endeavors to thwart him, the time he has had to listen to peace propositions he has improved in strengthening his defences, and another battle must ensue.

I have thus hurriedly given you my opinions of today—circumstances may compel me to alter them tomorrow, but I have thought it best to put them in writing at all events. From the first I thought that no peace would grow out of the armistice—I think so still: but if a treaty is signed it will stand out, as I have already remarked, the most singular document of the kind on record—brought about by agencies most strange, and effected through means which reflect little credit on either party concerned.

Yours, &c.,

G. W. K.

P. S. I was wrong in saying that the commissioners were to meet this afternoon—their next meeting is to take place on Monday next, and it will probably be the last. Report has it that the Mexicans are willing to give up what they consider the cause of the war, Texas, but only to the Nueces— New Mexico and California they say must be subjects of after stipulation. Look out for a break up and perhaps a row at the next meeting of the commissioners.

*Daily Picayune*, October 17, 1847

Tacubaya, Sunday Morning, September 5, 1847

I have time only to write a few lines before the express rider starts. The *Diario* of last evening contains an account of the breaking open the store of Mr. Hargous, and says that some 400 men, armed with knives, took a hand in the transaction. The author does not try to palliate the outrage in any way, but goes on to comment upon it as follows: "This act, and the excitement manifested when the wagons of the enemy were seen coming into our city to be laden with provisions, make us believe that, in case hostilities recommence, the people will rise in mass for the defence of the capital, and with the same patriotic ardor of which they have given proofs in times past. And who can vanquish 40,000 or 50,000 valiant men (*valientes*) armed with knives or daggers, or even with sticks and stones, decided to die defending the rights most dear to them—their independence, their religion, their families and their home?" However patriotic this language may appear, it certainly sounds neither amiable nor pacific, especially when it is known that there is an armistice between the two countries, and that the editor grounds his article upon a palpable and gross violation of it on the part of his own countrymen.

It is said that at the *junta des notables* yesterday, which was attended by some of the richest men in the capital, Santa Anna told them plainly that he must have money. They pled exceeding poverty, which was probably what the President expected. In case he succeeds in making peace he will be sure to use as an excuse that money to continue the war was denied him.

There is a strange story afloat, to the effect that the Mexican commissioners have offered to give up Texas to the United States—Texas as far as the Nueces only—and also to allow us the privilege of constructing a cotton factory in California! They cannot think of making any further concessions. I know not how the report got about, but it is certainly quite current.

In the course of the present week we shall know whether the war is to be continued or a peace is to be made—now all is speculation, doubt and uncertainty. If we could place credit in one tenth part of what is told him in relation to Santa Anna's movements, it would seem almost impossible that peace could be made. A man comes in from the city and asserts most positively that he has seen breastworks in process of construction; that large numbers of sand bags are being contracted for and made; that bodies of troops are daily drilled, reviewed and inspected, and that even Santa Anna employed himself all day yesterday in inspecting the fortifications and other means of defence of the city. All this, the actions of the inhabitants, the tone of the press, &tc., certainly look most belligerent; but then one is told that Santa Anna is compelled to act as he does, in order to work out his ends. If peace is made with the Mexicans it will be a strange one, will stand alone, will have neither precedent nor parallel, and all the credit the government at Washington will get for its agency in the matter I am fearful will not elevate us much among the nations of the earth.

Yours, &tc.,

G. W. K.
*Daily Picayune*, September 26, 1847

Tacubaya, September 6, 1847

I did not write a line yesterday for the very good reason that there was nothing to write about. Proofs accumulated that Santa Anna was hourly breaking the armistice, by preventing supplies from coming out and by erecting breastworks within and near the city. In the evening, a *simulacro* or sham fight came off in the city, and the firing was quite brisk for a space and plainly heard out here at Tacubaya. Some thought it was a *pronunciamento* or revolution against Santa Anna, but it turned out that he was only exercising his troops. Peace stock is decidedly down, but I shall make no comment until I hear what has been done by the commissioners.

*Afternoon, 6 o'clock.*–The farce is over, and now comes the tragedy. Gen. Scott has sent in to Santa Anna announcing that the armistice is broken, and that at 12 o'clock tomorrow–I believe that is the hour–hostilities are to recommence. He would not give the forty-eight hours it is said, as he had abundant evidence the Mexicans had broken the armistice over and over again.[77]

Mr. Trist has returned from the conference, and although we cannot learn what transpired we know that nothing was effected.[78] From a Mexican of standing I learn that one of the commissioners on the other side handed Mr. Trist a letter of instructions from Mr. Buchanan, dated in July last and which had been intercepted. The letter went on to say that a line running near the parallel of 32 might be accepted, at which point it would leave the Rio Grande and branch off to California, following nearly the course of the Rio Gila.[79] As I have said, I get this story from hearsay; if it is true, it will show that the Mexicans knew every card in Mr. Trist's hand, to use an uncommon but apt expression, before he had a chance to play them.

*Night, 12 o'clock.*–A white flag came in from Santa Anna half an hour since with a message. Gen. Scott was informed that the Mexican President regretted very much the delays in getting out provisions, &c., to the Americans, that no fortifications or other works had been made, and that

77. Santa Anna had begun active efforts to defend the city on September 3–banning the sale of provisions to American forces, recalling soldiers in the vicinity of the capital, and warning the governors of the states that the American terms were unacceptable. Efforts to strengthen the city's fortifications began with the rejection of the American proposals on September 4.

78. The Mexican cabinet debated the proposal negotiated by Trist and the Mexican commissioners at a prolonged and stormy meeting on September 4 and 5. The commissioners urged that Trist's proposals be accepted. Most of the cabinet concurred, but Foreign Minister Pacheco and General Tornel argued for the continuation of the war and ultimately won Santa Anna to their side. On September 6, the Mexican commissioners informed Trist that their government would cede Texas. They had been instructed, however, to insist that the Mexico–United States boundary extend northwest from the Nueces to Santa Fe. That boundary would have left the United States no part of New Mexico or California south of a line that stretched westward along the thirty-seventh parallel to San Francisco. Trist broke off negotiations on September 7.

79. The letter also scolded Trist for his failure to work with Scott.

by tomorrow at noon the supplies could all be got out. The report is, that Gen. S. sent back word that if the provisions were furnished it would be an evidence of Santa Anna's desire to bring about an amicable understanding. So much for so much. A wag says that Santa Anna only wants to humbug us until he gets two cannon, cast a day or two since near Chapultepec, finished and ready for use!

Yours, &c.,

G. W. K.
*Daily Picayune*, October 17, 1847

Tacubaya, September 7, 1847

This morning the enemy is making preparations for our reception in real earnest. At any early hour long lines of infantry were seen emerging from the city, filing past Chapultepec, and taking up positions at the Molino del Rey, at a strong work known as the Powder Magazine, and as is supposed at the foundry where the Mexicans cast all their cannon.[80] I might here mention that Chapultepec is about three miles directly west of the city, that the Molino is about one thousand yards farther west, and that the other positions occupied by the Mexicans stretch along at intervals in the same direction. Chapultepec itself is on a steep hill or mound, noted as the residence of Montezuma, is fortified, and is also said to be mined. From the archbishop's palace to this work is but little over or under one mile; from the former to the Molino about twelve hundred yards. The palace is nearly south of Chapultepec, which brings the new positions of the enemy directly to the left as our army faces them. Close reconnaissances of their works have been made this morning by Capt. Mason, and as the destruction of the foundry is considered of paramount importance, it has been determined upon to attack the enemy tonight.[81] A hard resistance is anticipated, as large bodies, both of cavalry and infantry, are in plain view. Four pieces of cannon have been discovered in position, and it is thought the enemy has several others so masked that they cannot be seen.

In the meantime the greatest enthusiasm exists in the army—all appear anxious again to attack an enemy whose cowardice has no parallel, and whose treachery and duplicity would shame the veriest barbarians. Unpop-

---

80. Although no weapons foundry existed at Molino del Rey, Santa Anna, anticipating the American attack, hurriedly reinforced the complex with strong infantry, artillery, and cavalry units probably numbering less than the 12,000 to 15,000 men reported by Kendall and others at the time.

81. Worth, who commanded 3,500 men, persuaded Scott to delay the attack until dawn.

ular as was the armistice from the first with all, and uncalled for as they deemed it, its shameful violation by the Mexicans has served but to inflame, while the infamous intentions of the Mexican leaders in signing it, now rendered so palpable, has incensed both our officers and men to a degree that the enemy will feel in any encounter that may now take place.

*Night, 9 o'clock.*—The plan of attack has just been settled upon at a council of officers held at Gen. Worth's. Col. Garland's brigade is to move on the right in the direction of the Molino, watching Chapultepec and to be governed by circumstances. A storming party of 500 picked men under Maj. Wright,[82] and conducted by Capt. Mason, is to attack the work supposed to be the foundry. Capt. Huger,[83] with two 24-pounders, is to open upon the building as soon as it is light enough to see. Col. McIntosh, now that Col. Clarke is disabled, commands the 2d brigade of Worth's division, and will attack the enemy's right, Duncan's light battery and a large dragoon force under Maj. Sumner will act according to circumstances. To strengthen the movement, Gen. Cadwalader's brigade is also to take a part, and will probably attack in the centre. There are many who do not approve of the attack. They think that Chapultepec should be included in the programme of the performances, but of this Gen. Scott should be the best judge.

Yours, &c.,

G. W. K.
*Daily Picayune*, October 17, 1847

Tacubaya, September 8, 1847

*Forenoon, 10 o'clock.*—I have just returned from another battlefield—one on which the victory of the American arms was complete, and on which our troops contended against an enemy immensely superior in number and strongly posted. Gen. Worth commenced the attack at early daylight, and in less than two hours every point was carried, all the cannon of the enemy were in our possession, an immense quantity of ammunition captured, and nearly 1000 men, among them fifty-three officers, taken prisoners.

For more than an hour the battle raged with a violence not surpassed since the Mexican war commenced, and so great the odds opposed that for some time the result was doubtful. The force of the enemy has been estimated at from 12,000 to 15,000, strongly posted behind breastworks, and to attack them our small force of scarcely 3000 was obliged to approach on an open plain and without the least cover; but their dauntless courage carried

82. George Wright, Eight Infantry.
83. Benjamin Huger, Ordnance.

Storming of Chapultepec—Pillow's attack. Toned lithograph (hand-colored), 1851, by Adolphe-Jean-Baptiste Bayot, after Carl Nebel; reproduced from George Wilkins Kendall, *The War between the United States and Mexico Illustrated* (New York: D. Appleton and Company, 1851), plate 10; © Amon Carter Museum, Fort Worth, Texas (1972.186.7).

them over every obstacle, and notwithstanding the Mexicans fought with a valor rare for them, they were finally routed from one point or another until all were driven and dispersed. The defeat was total.

But to gain this victory our own loss has been uncommonly severe—it has been purchased with the blood of some of the most gallant spirits of the army. The 5th Infantry has suffered the most.[84] This regiment along with the 6th and 8th, was engaged in the attack upon a strong work on the enemy's right, and was opposed to such superior numbers that it was compelled to retire along with the others. The celebrated Col. Martin Scott was killed in this attack, along with Lieuts. Burwell[85] and Strong, while Col. McIntosh and many other officers were badly wounded. The worse than savage miscreants in the fort, after our men retired, set up a yell and came out and massacred such of our wounded as were unable to get off. In this way poor Burwell lost his life. Fully were they avenged, however; for within half an hour Duncan's battery, aided by the fall of another of their works, drove the dastardly wretches in full flight across the fields. No one knew or even surmised the strength of the place: it was an old fort, constructed long since, and was one of the main defences of the line of works.

On the enemy's left, and nearer Chapultepec, our loss was also great, although not as severe. It was here that Col. Wm. M. Graham, as brave a spirit as ever lived, was killed: Capts. Merrill and Ayers also fell in this part of the field. The wonder now is how anyone could come out safe under such a terrible fire as the enemy poured from his entire line of works.[86] Nothing but the daring and impetuosity of our men, who rushed onward while their comrades were falling thick around them, gained the victory— had they once faltered all would have been lost.

The broken ground on the right of the enemy, cut up by deep ravines, saved many of Santa Anna's troops in their flight: yet as it was our dragoons killed and captured many of the fugitives. Large bodies of the Mexican cavalry approached the scene of strife several times, but they were driven like sheep by Duncan's battery.[87]

84. The Fifth Infantry lost more than a third of its effective strength in the series of charges and retreats needed to overwhelm Casa Mata, a reinforced stone structure five hundred yards from Molina del Rey, defended by troops under the command of Francisco Perez.

85. William T. Burwell, Fifth Infantry.

86. The American units advanced believing the Mexican lines were only lightly defended. Surprised by heavy artillery fire and hit from the right by a Mexican counterattack launched from Chapultepec, the Americans suffered heavy losses before reinforcements supported by artillery fire drove the Mexicans from Molino del Rey.

87. Juan Alvarez commanded 4,000 cavalry located on the American far-left flank.

The Mexican loss has been even more severe than our own. Gen. Balderas, Gen. León,[88] and many other officers are numbered among the dead, while the interior of their works, the tops of the houses from which they fought, and the ground over which they fled are strewn with lifeless bodies. Such was the panic that many of our officers say that a few fresh troops might have taken Chapultepec itself almost without a struggle; but other than a few shots fired at that point from some of the captured cannon, no demonstration was made.

After the battle was over Gen. Scott came out, accompanied by his staff, and also by Mr. Trist. The Mexicans at the time were throwing shells at some of the wagons Gen. Worth had sent out to pick up the dead and wounded. They had placed a howitzer in position on Chapultepec at the close of the action, and now, seeing no enemy within reach, the cowardly wretches opened upon the ambulances and those who were gathering the bodies of their wounded and lifeless comrades. On seeing this worse than savage outrage, one of our officers, with a sarcastic expression of countenance, asked whether Mr. Trist had any new peace propositions in his pockets. Mackintosh did not come out after the battle to gain more time for his friend Santa Anna, nor worm out fresh intelligence of the strength and movements of our army, in order that he might be of service to the Mexicans by communicating it.

The Mexican prisoners say that Santa Anna himself was on the ground in the rear of their works, but left at the commencement of the rout. They admit that their entire force was 15,000; it is certain that including killed, wounded, prisoners and dispersed their loss has been near 5,000. Many of them were regulars, the 11th and 12th Infantry Regiments suffering most. The commander of the latter, Col. Tenorio, is a prisoner in our hands; some fourteen officers belonging to the former are also prisoners, but the commander, Gen. Perez, escaped.

The foundry, in which several moulds for casting cannon and other apparatus were found, was entirely demolished, and after ascertaining this, Gen. Scott, not wishing to hold the position, ordered all the forces to retire. The whole affair, as a military movement, is severely criticized by many of our officers. They contend that no result has been gained commensurate with the immense loss we have sustained in the battle. This is a matter I do not feel myself qualified to discuss, but it must be certain that the *morale* upon the Mexicans, of a defeat so disgraceful and so disastrous, must be important. They have now, (it is 5 o'clock in the afternoon,) returned to

88. Lucas Balderas and Antonio León commanded troops in Molino del Rey.

their positions; and if Santa Anna was on the ground as is stated, and can find no one to lay the blame upon, he may twist the whole affair into a victory—*on paper*. It will not be the first time he has done this thing.

Since I commenced this letter I have been out endeavoring to obtain a full list of the killed and wounded officers, but so far have been unable. Knowing the deep anxiety felt in the United States by the families of all, this shall be my first care. The entire loss in Gen. Worth's division, out of some 1,800 or 2,000 that went into action, will not fall much short of 600.[89] The Dragoons and Gen. Cadwalader's brigade did not suffer so severely in comparison. What the next movement is to be no one knows, but it is thought the city will be attacked immediately.

Yours, &c.,

G. W. K.
*Daily Picayune*, October 14, 1847

Tacubaya, September 9, 1847

I have been enabled to gather a full list of all the killed and wounded officers in Gen. Worth's division in the great battle of Molino del Rey, as also of those in Maj. Sumner's command of Dragoons. Gen. Cadwalader's loss I will obtain before I close this letter. The list which follows may be relied upon.

### GEN. WORTH'S DIVISION.

KILLED.—Col. Martin Scott, 5th Inf.; Capt. Merrill, 5th Inf.; Capt. G. W. Ayers, 3d Art.; Lieut. E. B. Strong, 5th Inf.; Lieut. W. Armstrong,[90] 2d Art.; Lieut. W. T. Burwell, 5th Inf.; Lieut. Farry, 3d Art.

WOUNDED.—Col. McIntosh, 5th Inf., severely; Maj. C. A. Waite, 8th Inf., badly; Maj. G. Wright, 8th Inf., slightly; Capt. E. K. Smith, 5th Inf., severely; Capt. Cady, 6th Inf., slightly; Capt. Larkin Smith, 8th Inf., severely; Capt. Walker, 6th Inf., severely; Capt. R. Anderson, 3d Art., severely; Asst. Surgeon W. Roberts, dangerously; Capt. J. L. Mason, corps of engineers, severely; Lieut. M. L. Shackleford, 2d Art., severely; Lieut. C. S. Hamilton, 5th Inf., severely; Lieut. C. B. Daniels, 2d Art., severely; Lieut. Ernst, 6th Inf., severely—lost right hand; Lieut. J. G. Burbank, 8th Inf., mortally; Lieut. J. D. Clark, 8th Inf., badly; Lieut. C. F. Morris, 8th Inf., severely—lost right foot; Lieut. J. Beardsley, 8th Inf., badly; Lieut. G. Wainwright, 8th Inf.,

---

89. American losses amounted to nearly a quarter of Worth's command, with nearly eight hundred casualties, including 116 men killed. These losses exceeded Taylor's at Monterey, and they were suffered by a force half the size of Taylor's command. Mexican casualties approached 2,000 killed or wounded. Scott took 685 prisoners, including fifty-three officers.

90. William Armstrong.

severely; Lieut. H. J. Hunt, 2d Art., slightly; Lieut. J. G. S. Snelling, 8th Inf., severely; Lieut. H. F. Clark, 2d Art., slightly; Lieut. W. Hayes, 2d Art., slightly; Lieut. J. G. Foster, corps of engineers, severely; Asst. Surgeon J. Simons, slightly; Lieut. Dent, 5th Inf., severely; Lieut. H. Prince, 4th Inf., severely; Lieut. A. B. Lincoln, 4th Inf., severely; Lieut. Hermann Thorn, 3d Dragoons— aide to Col. Garland, severely; Lieut. Montgomery, 8th Inf., slightly; Lieut. Andrews, 3d Art., slightly.[91]

## MAJOR SUMNER'S COMMAND.

Capt. Croghan Ker, 2d Dragoons, severely; Lieut. Tree, 2d Dragoons, severely; Lieut. Walker, Mounted Rifles, slightly; Lieut. Williams, 3d Dragoons, slightly.[92]

The above list is complete and perfect. There has been much difficulty in obtaining it, as nearly all the orderly sergeants and executive officers have been killed or wounded. The conduct of all the non-commissioned officers has been gallant and most conspicuous, while several of them behaved so nobly that they have been recommended for immediate pro- motion to Gen. Scott. Their names are Sergeants Benson, Wilson and Robinson of the 2d Artillery; Sergeant Heck of the 3d Artillery; Sergeants Updegraff, Farmer, Archer and Daily of the 5th Infantry; Sergeant Major Thompson of the 6th Infantry; Sergeant Major Fink of the 8th Infantry.[93] I trust and hope that Gen. Scott will at once promote these brave fellows. More than half the officers in Gen. Worth's division have been struck down, either killed or wounded, in the actions of Churubusco and El Molino del Rey, and many of the companies have absolutely no one to command them.

Of our wounded officers, I cannot learn that one of them has received mortal injury, although three or four are in a dangerous situation. The wound of Major Waite, although severe, will not keep him long from duty. The same may be said of Capt. Mason and Lieut. Foster of the engineers. Major Wright was struck in the stomach by a partially spent ball, while gallantly leading the storming party of 500 picked men, but is now recov- ering from the effect. I shall make further enquiries in relation to the wounded officers before I close this letter.

91. Not previously identified are Carlos A. Waite, Ephraim Kirby Smith, Albemarle Cady, William H. T. Walker, Robert Anderson, William Roberts, Charles S. Hamilton, Rudolph F. Ernst, John G. Burbank, John D. Clark, Charles F. Morris, John Beardsley, Henry J. Hunt, James G. S. Snelling, John G. Foster, James Simons, Frederick Dent, Henry Prince, Abram B. Lincoln, and George P. Andrews.

92. Not previously identified are Arthur Tree and James C. D. Williams.

93. Those who are identifiable are John H. Heck, Joseph Updegraff, Henry Farmer, Edward Thompson, and Theodore Fink.

No less than *nineteen* of the deserters, captured by Gens. Twiggs and Shields at Churubusco, have been found fully guilty, and are to be hung tomorrow morning. The miscreant Riley, who commanded them, escapes the punishment of death, as he proved that he deserted before the war. He has been sentenced, however, to be severely whipped, to be branded as well, and to wear a ball and chain in front of the army during the war![94] A deserter taken among the prisoners at the Molino, on the 8th, was summarily dealt with. It seems that he deserted from Monterey last fall, and a comrade who recognized him, to save the trouble of a court martial, at once pitched him into the mill frame and he was crushed to pieces by the wheel! Another batch of deserters, who have been undergoing a trial here in Tacubaya, will be hung in a day or two it is said. Most richly do they deserve their fate.

The following list of the officers killed and wounded in Gen. Cadwalader's brigade I believe to be nearly correct. If there is any inaccuracy in it I will correct it. It so happened in the order of the battle that the 11th Regiment was immediately engaged. The brigade of Gen. Pierce was called into action towards the close of the battle. He lost a few men, but I learn that no officers were killed. Both Gens. Cadwalader and Pierce behaved with the greatest alacrity and gallantry on the occasion. Here is the list of the killed and wounded in the brigade of the former:

GEN. CADWALADER'S BRIGADE.

KILLED—Col. Wm. M. Graham, 11th Infantry; Lieut. Dick Johnson, 11th Inf.

WOUNDED—Major Savage, 14th Inf., slightly; Major Talcott, Voltigeurs, slightly; Capt. Guthrie, 11th Inf., slightly; Capt. Irvin, 11 Inf., slightly; Lieut. Lee, 11th Inf., slightly; Lieut. Kintzing, Voltigeurs, slightly; Lieut. Thos. Shields, 14th Inf., slightly; Lieut. Swan, Voltigeurs, slightly.[95]

The loss of the non-commissioned officers and privates in this brigade I have not yet ascertained; it will not exceed 100. The loss in Major Sumner's command, which consisted of 280 men, was 6 killed and 33 wounded. Of horses he had 27 killed and 78 wounded. Nearly every officer had a horse shot under him.

---

94. The executions took place at San Angel on September 10. Six men, including Riley, escaped the death penalty because they had deserted before Congress had declared war. Nine others escaped hanging due to the circumstances surrounding their capture and impressment into the Mexican army. All fifteen were branded with the letter D, given 50 lashes, and imprisoned until the war ended. Miller, *Shamrock and Sword,* 102.

95. Not previously identified are John H. Savage, Presley N. Guthrie, William H. Irvin, David S. Lee, Gustavus S. Kintzing, Thomas Shields, and Robert Swan.

I may possibly send this letter off tonight by a Mexican, but it will depend upon whether there is a prospect of another battle tomorrow or next day. Matters are approaching a crisis, while the great mistake in not entering the capital on the night of the 20th, when the Mexicans were perfectly panic stricken and in total flight, is hourly developing itself. The great sacrifice of life yesterday—the loss of so many gallant spirits—has all been owing to the cessation of hostilities and the armistice which followed, and an awful responsibility rests either with the Government or with Gen. Scott and Mr. Trist. The instructions will show, but I am of the opinion that the former is mostly to blame. The latter are censurable for placing faith in Mackintosh, in giving Santa Anna so much time, or even in having any reliance upon his power and ability to make peace under all the circumstances, however much he might have desired it personally. I will say nothing of the bribery—that dark side of the picture is undoubtedly the work of the exceedingly wise men at Washington. Bad advisers have been busy, both here and at home, in recommending measures to bring about a peace, and their counsels have prevailed to the exclusion of the opinions of men who might have been listened to with profit. I trust the experience of the past may prove a lesson for the future, and that by this time our rulers must see and feel that in order to bring about a peace with the Mexicans they must use hard blows instead of soft words.

Yours, &tc.,

G. W. K.
*Daily Picayune*, October 14, 1847

Tacubaya, September 10, 1847

We have accounts from Mexico, brought in by Frenchmen and other foreigners, to the effect that Santa Anna's loss at El Molino was much more severe than anyone here had anticipated. They say that during the afternoon of the 8th no less than 1500 wounded men came into the city, while the number of killed was over 600. The slaughter from the batteries of Col. Duncan and Capt. Drum must have been terrific. Santa Anna, it is said, would have laid all the blame of the defeat upon Gen. León, but that officer, unfortunately for him, died. He has since torn epaulets from the shoulders of Col. Miguel Andrade, commander of the celebrated regiment of Hussars, accuses him of everything, has thrown him into prison, and denied him all communication. He must have some one to break out upon.

Everything looks quiet today, but the Mexicans are busily employed in fortifying at every point. At Chapultepec they can be seen at work, while they are also repairing the damage done at El Molino and other points on that line. On the Piedad road they have strong works, while at the Niño Perdido and San Antonio Abad entrances to the city they are also fortifying with the greatest vigor.[96] Gen. Pillow's division, as also Col. Riley's brigade, attached to that of Gen. Twiggs, occupy the village of La Piedad and neighborhood, in plain sight and in fact under the guns of the enemy. Gen. Worth remains here in Tacubaya, but he is sending all his sick and wounded to Mixcoac, out of the range of the guns of Chapultepec. No one knows what point will be first attacked, but this question will soon be determined. The next blow struck will be hard, and all hope decisive. It must read strange, the story that some 7 or 8000 men have set themselves down before a strongly fortified city of over 200,000 inhabitants, with an army of at least 25,000 men to defend it; but the tale is a true one and the proud capital of Mexico must fall.

Yours, &c.,

G. W. K.
*Daily Picayune*, October 14, 1847

Tacubaya, September 11, 1847

A small party of us have just returned from a ride over to La Piedad, the headquarters of Gen. Pillow. Gen. Scott was there, as also were some of his principal officers, holding a council as to the best mode and point of attack.[97] The result of their deliberations is not known, but it is thought that the infantry will have some respite after their hard labors, and that all the heavier cannon recently captured from the Mexicans will be employed in sending their own balls back at them. With their own guns, and those brought up by Gen. Scott, at least fifty pieces of heavy calibre can be opened at any one point—enough to demolish any work the Mexicans have constructed in time incredibly short, and give them a lesson they will not soon forget.

From the Puente del Hermita, which has been destroyed by the Mexicans, they can plainly be seen at work on several fortifications between the roads of San Angel and San Antonio de Abad. These works are but little more than a half a mile from the city, which is also in plain view. Shortly

96. These gates defended the southern entrances to the city.

97. This meeting followed several days of reconnoitering by Scott's engineers to determine which routes through the marshy land around the city were most suitable for maneuvering artillery and infantry units. Discussions focused on the approach to San Antonio Garita on the capital's south side and a route from the west to the Belén and San Cosmé gates. After hearing presentations that featured the views of Lee and Beauregard, Scott chose the latter approach, which required the taking of Chapultepec and which he had probably favored from the outset.

after we left, the enemy opened with two of their heavy guns upon our pickets or engineers, and continued the fire for near an hour. I cannot learn that they did any injury. On our return to Tacubaya we found that Maj. Sumner and Col. Duncan had had a little brush with the enemy's lancers near the battle ground of El Molino. Capt. Ruff, with his company of Mounted Riflemen, drew a large party of the Mexican cavalry immediately within the range of one of Duncan's guns, when one or two discharges sent them scampering off in every direction. Only one man was wounded on our side, but it is known that the enemy lost several in the skirmish. They opened with one heavy gun from Chapultepec on our men, but did no harm other than frightening the inhabitants of this place half out of their wits.

Lieut. Burbank, who was mortally wounded at El Molino, died yesterday, and Capt. E. Kirby Smith this afternoon of wounds received at the same time. Lieut. Col. Dickenson, shot badly in the ankle at Churubusco, is also dead. All were gallant officers, and their loss is much regretted.

I have already mentioned the execution of nineteen of the deserters captured on the 20th August at Churubusco. Gen. Scott has just signed the death warrant of thirty others, taken at the same time, and they will suffer the same fate in the course of a day or two.

From various movements, there is certainly strong reasons to believe that Gen. Scott will open a heavy fire upon Chapultepec tomorrow morning, from not only his own siege guns but from those captured from the enemy. Whether it is a feint to draw the Mexicans to that point and weaken other defences, is not known.

Yours, &c.,

G. W. K.
*Daily Picayune*, October 14, 1847

Tacubaya, September 12, 1847

At early daylight this morning a heavy cannonade was opened upon the stronghold of Chapultepec, which was increased during the day as additional siege guns were placed in position. The Mexicans returned the fire with great spirit at intervals during the day, but with little effect other than dismounting one of our guns—I cannot learn that a man has been killed at any of the batteries. Several of the Voltigeurs, while skirmishing with the enemy's sharpshooters at the foot of Chapultepec, were wounded, but none of them severely. A 10 1/2-inch mortar was opened upon the place during the afternoon, and as several shells have been seen to fall and explode directly within the enemy's works it is certain that great damage has been caused. A firing of heavy guns has also been heard in the direction of La Piedad, showing that the Mexicans have been diverted in that quarter.[98]

At dusk this evening several loads of scaling ladders were sent down towards the foot of Chapultepec, and the movements of our infantry and other light corps would indicate that the strong works upon the crest are to be stormed early tomorrow. A large portion of the entire army will be brought to the struggle, and it is thought the contest will be terrible. I have little time to write.

Yours, &c.,

G. W. K.
*Daily Picayune*, October 14, 1847

City of Mexico, September 14, 1847[99]

Another victory, glorious in its results and which has thrown additional lustre upon the American arms, has been achieved today by the army under Gen. Scott—the proud capital of Mexico has fallen into the power of a mere handful of men compared with the immense odds arrayed against them, and Santa Anna, instead of shedding his blood as he had promised, is wandering with the remnant of his army no one knows whither.

The apparently impregnable works on Chapultepec, after a desperate struggle, were triumphantly carried—Gens. Bravo and Monterde, besides a host of officers of different grades, taken prisoners; over 1000 non-commissioned officers and privates, all their cannon and ammunition, are in our hands; the fugitives soon were in full flight towards the different works which command the entrance to the city, and our men at once were in hot pursuit.[100]

Gen. Quitman, supported by Gen. Smith's brigade, took the road by the Chapultepec aqueduct towards the Belén gate and the Ciudadela; Gen. Worth, supported by Gen. Cadwalader's brigade, advanced by the San Cosmé aqueduct towards the garita of that name. Both routes were cut up by ditches and defended by breastworks, barricades, and strong works of every descrip-

98. Scott sent Quitman's division toward La Piedad on the city's southwest corner to prevent Santa Anna from strengthening Chapultepec and at the same time to direct heavy artillery fire on the castle in hopes of forcing the Mexican defenders to evacuate. By nightfall on September 12, the Mexicans had lost the use of two cannons but still held their ground. Meanwhile, Scott prepared for an infantry assault.

99. The *Picayune* published the first news of Scott's victory on September 25, 1847, having received sketchy reports of the fall of Mexico City from the American customs official F. M. Dimond in Vera Cruz. This dispatch by Kendall, along with one authored by the *Delta*'s Freaner, arrived in New Orleans on October 13, providing the first confirmation of the American victory.

100. With heavy artillery fire and hand-to-hand fighting, the Americans overwhelmed the less than 1,000 men commanded by Nicolá Bravo in the undermanned fortification. Mentioned is José Mariano Monterde.

tion known to military science; yet the daring and impetuosity of our men overcame one defence after another, and by nightfall every work to the city's edge was carried. Gen. Quitman's command, after the rout at Chapultepec, was the first to encounter the enemy in force. Midway between the former and the Belén gate, Santa Anna had constructed a strong work; but this was at once vigorously assaulted by Gen. Quitman, and aided by a flank fire from two of Duncan's guns, which Gen. Worth had ordered to approach as near as possible from the San Cosmé road, the enemy was again routed and in full flight.[101] They again made a stand from their strong fortifications at and near the Belén garita, opening a tremendous fire not only of round shot, grape and shell, but of musketry; yet boldly Gen. Quitman advanced, stormed and carried the works, although at great loss, and then every point on this side the city was in our possession. In this onslaught two of our bravest officers were killed—Capt. Drum and Lieut. Benjamin.

Meanwhile Gen. Worth was rapidly advancing upon San Cosmé. At the English burying ground the enemy had constructed a strong work. It was defended by infantry for a short time, but could not resist the assault of our men—the affrighted Mexicans soon fled to another line of works nearer the city, and thus Gen. Worth was in possession of the entrance to San Cosmé. As his men advanced towards the garita, the enemy opened a heavy fire of musketry from the house tops, as well as of grape, canister and shell from their batteries, thus sweeping the street completely. At this juncture the old Monterey game, of burrowing and digging through the houses, was adopted. On the right, as our men faced the enemy, the aqueduct afforded a partial shelter; on the left, the houses gave some protection; but many were still killed or wounded by the grape which swept every part, as well as by the shells which were continually bursting in every direction. About 3 o'clock the work of the pick-axe and the crow-bar, under the direction of Lieut. G. W. Smith, of the Sappers and Miners, had fairly commenced, and every minute brought our men nearer the enemy's last stronghold. In the meantime two mountain howitzers were fairly lifted to the top of one of the houses and into the cupalo of the church, from which they opened a plunging and most effective fire, while one of Duncan's guns, in charge of Lieut. Hunt, was run up under a galling fire to a deserted breastwork, and at once opened upon the garita. In this latter daring feat, four men out of eight were either killed or wounded, but still the piece was most effectively served. The work of the Miners was still going on. In one house which they had entered, by the pick-axe, a favorite aide of Santa Anna's was

101. Kendall was slightly wounded during this action.

found. The great man had just fled, but had left his friend and his supper! Both were well cared for—the latter was devoured by our hungry officers; the former, after doing the honors of the table, was made a close prisoner. Just as dark was setting in, our men had dug and mined their way almost up to the very guns of the enemy, and now, after a short struggle, they were completely routed and driven with the loss of everything. The command of the city by the San Cosmé route was attained.

During the night, Gen. Quitman commenced the work of throwing up breastworks and erecting batteries, with the intention of opening a heavy cannonade upon the Ciudadela with the first light this morning. At 10 o'clock at night Gen. Worth ordered Capt. Huger to bring up a 24-pounder and a 10-inch mortar to the garita or gate of San Cosmé, and having ascertained the bearings and distance of the grand plaza and palace, at once opened upon those points. The heavy shells were heard to explode in the very heart of the city. At a little after midnight Major Palacios, accompanied by two or three members of the municipal council of the city, arrived at Gen. Worth's headquarters, and in great trepidation informed him that Santa Anna and his grand army had fled, and that they wished at once to surrender the capital! They were referred to the commander-in-chief, and immediately started for Tacubaya; but in the meantime the firing upon the town ceased.[102]

At 7 o'clock this morning Gen. Scott, with his staff, rode in and took quarters in the national palace, on the top of which the regimental flag of the gallant Rifles and the stars and stripes were already flying. An immense crowd of blanketed leperos, the scum of the capital, were congregated in the plaza as the commander-in-chief entered it. They pressed upon our soldiers, and eyed them as though they were beings of another world. So much were they in the way, and with such eagerness did they press around, that Gen. Scott was compelled to order our Dragoons to clear the plaza. They were told, however, not to injure or harm a man in the mob—they were all our friends!

About five minutes after this, and while Gen. Worth was returning to his division near the Alameda, he was fired upon from a house near the Convent of San Francisco. Some of the cowardly Polkas, who had fled the day previous without discharging their guns, now commenced the assassin game of shooting at every one of our men they saw, from windows, as

102. At the urging of city officials, Santa Anna withdrew some 12,000 troops from the city to Guadalupe Hidalgo shortly after midnight. A delegation of city officials were at Scott's headquarters near Chapultepec by 4 a.m., requesting terms of capitulation; Scott refused to grant any concessions.

well as from behind the parapets on the azoteas or tops of the houses. In half an hour's time our good friends, the leperos, in the neighborhood of the hospital of San Andres and the church of Santa Clara, also commenced discharging muskets and throwing bottles and rocks from the azoteas. I have neglected to mention that just previous to this Col. Garland had been severely wounded by a musket, fired by some miscreant from a window.

For several hours this cowardly war upon our men continued, and during this time many were killed or wounded. It was in this species of fighting that Lieut. Sidney Smith received his death wound. The division of Gen. Twiggs in one part of the city, and Gen. Worth in another, were soon actively engaged in putting down the insurrection. Orders were given to shoot every man in all the houses from which the firing came, while the guns of the different light batteries swept the streets in all directions. As the assassins were driven from one house they would take refuge on another; but by the middle of the afternoon they were all forced back to the barriers and suburbs. Many innocent persons have doubtless been killed during the day, but this could not be avoided. Had orders been given at the outset to blow up and demolish every house or church from which one man was fired upon, the disturbances would have been at once quelled. At it is, I trust that the lesson the rabble and their mischievous leaders have received today may deter them from future outrages.

On entering the palace Gen. Scott at once named Gen. Quitman governor of Mexico—a most excellent appointment. Some wag immediately proclaimed aloud in the plaza as follows: "Gen. John A. Quitman of Mississippi, has been appointed governor of Mexico, vice Gen. Jose Maria Tornel, resigned—*very suddenly!*" It seems that the valiant Tornel ran off at an early hour, and his magnificent house has been converted into a hospital for our wounded officers.

Yours, &c.,

G. W. K.
*Daily Picayune*, October 14, 1847


City of Mexico, September 17, 1847

The capital is now quiet enough, and although the inhabitants say but little they are probably not altogether contented with their new masters. They say that the Lord and Santa Anna are to blame for all their misfortunes—their own lack of prowess and courage is not thought of. They say that Providence withheld the rains and gave the Yankees fair weather for their operations, while Santa Anna deserted them in their extremity, and gave up the city without even making terms for them. The latter has gone no one knows whither. Some contend that he is on his way to the coast, with the intention of leaving the country; others say that he has gone towards Querétaro; while many think that he is lurking about Guadalupe or San Christobal, within a few miles of this, yet with only a small force of cavalry at his command. His wife, who has been living all the while at the house of his particular friend Mackintosh, has gone out in the direction of San Christobal in search of him. Santa Anna just before he left the city grossly insulted Gen. Torres, who commanded at the Belén gate, for deserting his post. It is also said that he has quarreled with Lombardini. These are old tricks of the tyrant—throwing the blame upon others to cover his own shameless conduct.

Lieut. Morris, of the 8th Infantry, has died of the wound he received at the hard-fought battle of El Molino, and it is thought extremely doubtful whether Lieut. Ernst, of the 6th, wounded at the same time, can recover. I do not learn that any other officers are considered as in a dangerous condition.

The following is a list of the killed and wounded officers in the taking of Chapultepec and the capture of the city.[103] It will be seen that some of the brightest ornaments of the service have fallen:

KILLED.—Col. Ransom, 9th Inf.; Lieut. Col. Baxter, N. Y. Vols.; Major Twiggs, U. S. Marines; Capt. Drum, 4th Art.; Capt. Van O'Linde, N. Y. Vols.; Lieut. Gantt, 7th Inft.; Lieut. Calvin Benjamin, 6th Inft.; Lieut. J. B. Monague, S. C. Vols.; Lieut. A. P. Rodgers, 4th Inft.; Lieut. J. Willis Cantey, S. C. Vols.; Lieut. J. P. Smith, 5th Inft.; Lieut. Sidney Smith, 4th Inft.[104]

WOUNDED.—Maj. Gen. Pillow, severely; Brig. Gen. Shields, severely; Col. Garland, com'g 1st brigade, Worth's division, severely; Col. Trousdale, 14th Infantry, severely; Lieut. Col. Johnston, Voltigeurs, slightly; Lieut. Col. Geary, 2d Penn. Vols., slightly; Maj. Gladden, S. C. Vols., severely; Maj. Loring, Rifles, severely; Capt. Pearson, N. Y. Vols., severely; Capt. Gates, 8th Inf., slightly; Capt. C. C. Danley, volunteer aide to Gen. Quitman, severely; Capt. Jas. Barclay, N. Y. Vols., slightly; Capt. J. B. Backenstoss, Rifles, slightly; Capt. McPhail, 5th Inf., slightly; Capt. E. C. Williams, 2d Penn. Vols., slightly; Capt. J. S. Simonson, Rifles, slightly; Capt. Barnard, Voltigeurs, severely; Capt. Beauregard, Corps Engineers, slightly; Capt. Magrader, 1st Artillery, slightly; Capt. Silas Casey, 2d Inf., slightly; Capt. Jas. Miller, 2d Penn. Vols., severely; Capt. M. Fairchild, N. Y. Vols., slightly; Capt. Jas. Caldwell, 2d Penn. Vols., severely; Capt. George Nauman, 1st Artillery, slightly; Capt. S. S. Tucker, Rifles, slightly; Capt. Mackall, A. A. Gen.

---

103. American casualties included 130 killed, 703 wounded, and twenty-nine missing.

104. Not previously identified are Charles Baxter; Levi Twiggs, the brother of Gen. David Twiggs; Abram Van O'Linde; John B. Monague; Alexander P. Rodgers; and Joseph P. Smith.

Worth's division, slightly; Capt. F. N. Page, Gen. Quitman's aide, slightly; Capt. Marshall, S. C. Vols., slightly; Capt. Williams, S. C. Vols., slightly; Lieut. Earl Van Dorn, aide to Gen. Smith, slightly; Lieut. J. M. Brannan, Adj. 1st Artillery, severely; Lieut. Nat. Lyon, 2d Inf., slightly; Lieut. Jas. Longstreet, 8th Inf., severely; Lieut. Tilton, Voltigeurs, slightly; Lieut. Sprague, Adj. 9th Inf., slightly; Lieut. M. Clark, Adj., S. C. Vols., severely; Lieut. J. A. Henderson, U. S. Marines, slightly; Lieut. Bell, S. C. Vols., slightly; Lieut. Reno, Voltigeurs, severely; Lieut. John Keefe, 2d Penn. Vols., severely; Lieut. Martin, Voltigeurs, slightly; Lieut. Maurice Melsney, 4th Inf., slightly; Lieut. M. Lovell, on Gen. Quitman's staff, slightly; Lieut. J. Selden, 8th Inf., severely; Lieut. Stevens, Corps of Engineers, severely; Lieut. J. W. Green, N. Y. Vols., slightly; Lieut. A. S. Touison, 2d Penn. Vols., severely; Lieut. Armistead, 6th Inf., slightly; Lieut. Mayne Reid, N. Y. Vols., severely; Lieut. Selleck, S. C. Vols., severely; Lieut. F. S. K. Russell, Rifles, slightly; Lieut. J. A. Haskin, 1st Artillery, severely; Lieut. D. D. Baker, and Lieut. J. W. Stein, S. C. Vols., severely; Lieut. J. S. Delvin, U. S. Marines, slightly; Lieut. A. H. Bannon, S. C. Vols., slightly; Lieut. Robertson, S. C. Vols., severely; Lieut. C. S. Kirkland, S. C. Vols., slightly; Lieut. J. R. Davis, S. C. Vols., slightly; Capt. J. M. Scantland, 14th Inf., slightly; Capt. King, 15th Inf., slightly; Lieut. H. C. Longnecker, Voltigeurs, slightly; Capt. R. G. Beale, 14th Inf., slightly; Lieut. Richard Steele, 14th Inf., slightly; Lieut. Robert Bedford, 14th Inf., slightly; Lieut. I. N. Palmer, Rifles, slightly.[105]

[G. W. K.]
*Daily Picayune*, October 14, 1847

Mexico, September 17, 1847[106]

The Mexican loss it is impossible to ascertain, but it has been immense.[107] Among the killed at Chapultepec were Gen. Juan Nepomecuno Perez, Col. Juan Cano, a distinguished officer of engineers, and Lieut. Lucian Calvo, one of Gen. Bravo's aides. Gen. Saldaña was badly wounded, as were many

105. Not previously identified are William Trousdale, John W. Geary, Adley H. Gladden, Charles H. Pearson, Collinson Gates, James Barclay, Jacob B. Backenstoss, Daniel H. McPhail, Edward C. Williams, John S. Simonson, Moses J. Barnard, Silas Casey, James Miller, James Caldwell, Stephen S. Tucker, J. F. Marshall, John M. Brannan, Nathaniel Lyon, Michael R. Clark, Ralph Bell, William J. Martin, Joseph Selden, Isaac I. Stevens, Ashton S. Touison, Lewis A. Armistead, Frederick W. Selleck, Francis S. K. Russell, Joseph A. Haskin, Lewis F. Robertson, Charles S. Kirkland, James M. Scantland, Edward A. King, Henry C. Longnecker, Robert G. Beale, and Innis N. Palmer.

106. This dispatch begins with the following editorial note: "We now resume the narrative from his [Kendall's] letter of the 17th, which was abruptly broken off after giving the killed and wounded in the army in the battle of the 13th."

107. Estimates of Mexican casualties ranged from 2,000 to 3,000. Scott took 823 men prisoner.

other distinguished officers. Five generals, three colonels, seven lieutenant colonels, and near one hundred majors, captains and lieutenants, were taken prisoners, together with 800 or more rank and file. At the garitas of Belén and San Cosmé many officers were killed or wounded, but their names are not known.

The total number of deserters hung at San Angel and Mixcoac was *fifty*, and well did they deserve their fate. Thirty of them were hung at Mixcoac on the morning of the 13th. They were compelled to stand upon the gallows until the flag they had deserted was flying from Chapultepec, and were then all swung off at the same time. Not one of them complained that his fate was undeserved.[108]

It is no time now to mention the hundreds of cases of individual gallantry noticed at the different battles, but I cannot help paying a passing compliment to the noted chaplain, Parson McCarty, as he is called by all. The worthy man was seen in all parts, and where the danger was greatest, comforting the wounded and exhorting the wavering to press forward, and all the time regardless of his own safety. No man exerted himself more to ensure a victory, no man is more entitled to special commendation.

We are still without any positive or definite information as regards Santa Anna's great army, but all agree that it is disorganized and broken up. There is a report that Gen. Herrera has reached Querétaro with 4000 men in a body, but it requires confirmation.

Yours, &c.,

G. W. K.
*Daily Picayune,* October 15, 1847

---

108. The executions were directed by William S. Harney, a man with a reputation according to his obituary, as "'a right hard hater always; somewhat ferocious, too in the award of punishment!'" Besides coordinating the hanging of the deserters with the fall of Chapultepec, Harney insisted that a deserter lying near death in a field hospital after losing both legs during the battle of Churubusco be brought to the gallows and executed with the rest of the San Patricios. Miller, *Shamrock and Sword,* 105–8.

# CHAPTER EIGHT

# IN THE HALLS OF THE MONTEZUMAS
## SEPTEMBER 20 – OCTOBER 29, 1847

WITHIN DAYS OF HIS EVACUATION OF Mexico City, Santa Anna resigned the presidency. Still in command of the army, he tried unsuccessfully first to capture the small American garrison at Puebla and then, at Huamantla, to ambush reinforcements who were marching to join Scott. Ordered by temporary president Manuel de la Peña y Peña to abandon his command and await court-martial, Santa Anna moved around the country for a time before finding his way into exile, first in Jamaica and then in Venezuela.

Scott's soldiers settled into the role of an occupying army. By mid-October, communications with Vera Cruz had been reestablished, and plans were laid to expand the American presence into the outlying regions. Winfield Scott's old adversaries, Generals Gideon Pillow and William Worth, busied themselves with plots to enhance their reputations at the expense of their commanding officer.

Meanwhile, the Mexican government, now temporarily located 140 miles to the north in Querétaro, scrambled to reconstitute itself. Peña y Peña had temporarily assumed the office of president, and Congress was called to meet on October 5. A quorum was slow to gather, and when it did, factional disputes hampered decision making. Nevertheless, by mid-November the Mexican Congress had elected a provisional president and committed itself to securing a negotiated peace. Nicholas Trist watched these developments and waited patiently for new instructions from Washington, unaware that Polk had ordered his recall.

Kendall observed all of this through the end of October, complaining along the way about the failure of the Polk administration to send reinforcements, gossiping about the machinations of Mexican politics, describing a destructive earthquake, and reflecting on the advantages of life in New Orleans. He also prepared both for his own departure for New Orleans and for continued coverage of events in Mexico City. He left Mexico City on November 1, 1847, with the first military train bound for Vera Cruz.

City of Mexico, September 20, 1847

All our wounded have been brought in from Mixcoac and other places and have been made as comfortable as circumstances would admit. Chapultepec is still held by our troops, but all the other points have been deserted, and the main body of the men are quartered within the limits of the city.

Gen. Bravo's official report of the loss of Chapultepec has been published in a Toluca paper. He blames Santa Anna for not sending him reinforcements as he requested, materially underrates his own force, and accuses one of his engineer officers, Aleman, who had charge of the different mines on the hill sides, with being absent at the critical moment when by springing them the fate of the day might have been changed. If possible, I will send on his report.

In the same paper, we see it stated that Santa Anna has renounced the Presidency of the Republic, and in this juncture names Don Manuel Peña y Peña, Chief Justice of the Supreme Court of Mexico, as his constitutional successor.[1] Peña y Peña is at a hacienda of his close by, is a lawyer of great standing, and may possibly assume the reins of power in the present crisis. It is hardly probable that he will retain them, however. In the present distracted state of the country no one can expect to hold them long.

We hear but little, one way or the other, as to what the Mexicans intend to do in future: whether they are for peace or a continuance of the war. In fact, it is hardly time for them, after their recent disastrous discomfitures, to think of anything. Everything will now depend upon our own Government. If the nonsensical soothing system is continued, if another dose of magnanimity is to follow the hard blows which have lost us so many lives—the war will be spun out until doomsday. On the contrary, if a rigorous system is at once adopted, if men and means are poured into the country, and the rulers of Mexico are for once made to believe that we are in earnest, six months will suffice to make *them* sue for peace. Heretofore, the propositions, with a stretch of magnanimity positively ridiculous, have all come from our side, and we all know with what contumely and insult they have been treated.

1. Santa Anna resigned on September 16, 1847. The constitution of 1824 called upon the president of the Supreme Court to assume the presidency in the event of a resignation, but that post was vacant. Thus, Santa Anna named Peña y Peña, the senior judge on the Supreme Court as well as a prominent lawyer and law professor, to head the government. Peña y Peña took the post on September 27, serving briefly as a caretaker president between Santa Anna's departure and the election of Pedro María Anaya as interim president on November 11, 1847. *Moderados* looked to Peña y Peña to chart a path toward a negotiated settlement. He returned to the presidency in January 1848 when Anaya's two-month term ended. During Anaya's brief presidency, Peña y Peña served as foreign minister.

General Scott's entrance into Mexico. Toned lithograph (hand-colored), 1851, by Adolphe-Jean-Baptiste Bayot, after Carl Nebel; reproduced from George Wilkins Kendall, *The War between the United States and Mexico Illustrated* (New York: D. Appleton and Company, 1851), plate 12. © Amon Carter Museum, Fort Worth, Texas (1972.186.12).

Speaking of sending men and means to Mexico, do the people of the United States know the real force which has achieved the recent glorious triumphs here in the valley of this proud Republic? I have not seen the paper, but I have been told that a recent number of the *Union* states that when Gen. Scott would reach the vicinity of Mexico his army would number 22,000 effective men. If such a statement has been made, one more false or ungenerous could not have been promulgated. Gen. Scott arrived on this side the mountains with a fraction over 10,000 men, of which number at least 1,000 were new recruits. Of this force, so insignificant when compared with the magnitude of the enterprise, at least 1,000 were on the sick list before a blow was struck. With a disposable army, then, of 9,000—not a man more—the bold attempt was made to reduce a populous and well fortified city, and after a succession of hard fought battles the result is known. The 12,000 paper men, then, manufactured at Washington by Gens. Marcy, Jones[2] & Co., must remain where they have been during all the recent struggles—either unenlisted, in hospitals, in camp, or *in transitu*—and not detract from such merit as has been gained by the 10,000 true men, who have borne the battle's brunt and won such laurels for their country. To them all honor and credit is due, and I will procure the muster roll of every regiment that passed the Vente de Córdova[3] if it should be necessary to prove my statement as to their actual number.

Gen. Terrés,[4] who commanded at the Belén gate, has come out with a report of the part taken by himself and command on the 13th. It is pretty much the same old story. He complains that he had not men enough; says that those he did have fought with determination, bravery and enthusiasm; intimates that he sent for reinforcements, at a juncture when the tide of battle might have been turned against Gen. Quitman, which were refused, and finally openly accuses Gen. Pedrigón Garay,[5] who commanded his reserve, with running off without firing a gun or rendering him the least assistance. He himself speaks of the gross insult bestowed upon him by Santa Anna after the battle—an insult, he says, that he could not resent. We now have the reports of Bravo, who commanded at Chapultepec, and of Terrés, who commanded at the Belén gate: Santa Anna and Gen. Rangel were both of them at the San Cosmé gate, and it remains to be seen what frivolous excuse they will make for their disgraceful defeat. Of course the blame will not rest on their illustrious shoulders.

2. Roger Jones, adjutant general of the army.
3. The Vente de Córdova is on the National Road at the eastern edge of the Valley of Mexico.
4. Andrés Terrés.
5. José Guadalupe Pedrigón Garay.

The *American Star,* published by Peoples & Barnard, made its appearance today in neat form, and the talk is that another new paper, the *North American,* is to come out in the course of the week.[6] Meanwhile, the city is rapidly becoming Americanized. From every quarter, stating in the largest capitals, we see such announcements as "Union Hotel," "Mash and Milk at all Hours," "American Dry Goods," "United States Restaurant," "St. Charles Exchange," "Egg-Nogg and Mince Pies for Sale Here," and other kindred notices to the passer-by as to where he can be served on home principles. Nor is there to be any lack of amusements, for already the posters announce a bull fight, a circus, a theatre, and even an Italian opera as shortly to be produced. We are a great people.

Yours, &c.,

G. W. K.

*Daily Picayune,* October 15, 1847

City of Mexico, September 24, 1847

Among other rumors, we hear today that there has been a coalition of some of the States north of this, that Señor Cosío[7] has been appointed President, that 12,000 men are immediately to be raised and organized to carry on the war with vigor, and to make them effective $1,000,000 is to be levied. Bustamente and Paredes are to command the army, as the story goes, while Santa Anna has leave to retire from public service and from the country if he sees fit. Another report current would make us believe that the Mexican Congress is shortly to assemble at Querétaro, and that the peace question is to be talked over with Mr. Trist in real earnest. These are all but mere rumors.[8]

6. The *North American* was published in Mexico City from September 29, 1847, to March 31, 1848, with the editorial agenda of annexing Mexico to the United States. Its publisher, William C. Tobey, devoted much of his efforts before arriving in Mexico City to covering the activities of the Pennsylvania volunteers for the Philadelphia *North American.* He wrote under the pseudonym "John of York." The pro-Whig *Star* and the pro-Democratic *North American* carried on a lively editorial battle during the months in which they competed for readers in the Mexican capital. Reilly, "American Reporters and the Mexican War," 354–55, and Eisenhower, *So Far from God,* 346–47.

7. Probably Manuel González Cosío. Associated with the *puro* faction, he was governor of Zacatecas. During the fall and winter of 1847, he was involved with Gómez Farías and others in an effort to organize a number of states into what was called the Lagos coalition. The coalition, which never became a viable political force, was dedicated to resisting centralism and "shameful" treaties or agreements with the United States. Santoni, *Mexicans at Arms,* 219.

8. Mexico was awash in conspiracy. Almonte maneuvered among the *puros* to gain the presidency; Paredes returned to Mexico with hopes of reviving his plans to establish a monarchy; *puros* looked to Gómez Farías to continue the war; and *santanistas,* led by Tornel, plotted to establish a dictatorship. It was the latter effort that caused Peña y Peña to dismiss Santa Anna from his position as commander in chief on October 7.

Speaking of Mr. Trist reminds me of a story current on the 13th. It is said that shortly after Chapultepec was carried that gentleman rode up the height, and on being recognized by a gallant Irish soldier the latter accosted him with "I say, sir, it's a beautiful thraty we've made wid'em today, sir." The story is worth relating at all events.

Although all appears quiet on the face of the city, assassinations are still frequent. Our men are led off to drinking-houses in the by-streets and in the suburbs, are plied with liquor until they become intoxicated, and are then stabbed. Nor will this cowardly system be put down until each house where a murder is committed is razed, and exemplary justice dealt out to all its inmates. It has come to the knowledge of the authorities that knives and dirks have been recently distributed to the horde of thieves and murderers liberated by Santa Anna on the night he fled from the capital, and with no other intention than that they might do the work in the dark he had not the courage to perform in open day. By an order issued by Gen. Scott it would seem that active measures have been taken to ferret out the assassins, and also the miscreants who have set them on to murder.[9]

Among the papers captured at the palace—for in his haste to run Santa Anna left almost everything—were many rich and at the same time most valuable documents. Among them are two letters, one written by Rejon to Santa Anna, and dated at Querétaro on the 29th August, with the answer of the latter, dated here in Mexico on the 31st. In brief, Rejon informs his friend that he has learned with pain that negotiations for a peace have been entered into, an act offensive to the army and humiliating to the Republic. He contends that the war ought to be prosecuted, and that if the capital cannot be saved, like Puebla it must be abandoned, while the withdrawn troops must contend with the enemy as best they can. Resources, he says, will not be wanting, as the States, with the slightest encouragement, will supply them. He contends that peace will destroy Santa Anna, while war will ever crown him with honor and glory if he but carries it on without truce and with energy. In Querétaro, Rejon continues, the disgust was general when they first heard of the said negotiations (*furestas negociaciones,*) and on the morning previous to the date of his letter a courier passed through from Toluca with communications arousing the States against any authority that should make peace at the capital. Rejon finishes his letter as follows: "With the frankness of a friend I inform you

9. For more than a month, civil order was maintained only with difficulty in Mexico City. Upon entering the city, Scott issued orders reminding American soldiers that the war had not ended and directing them to maintain orderly and peaceful relations with the civilian population. On September 17, he established martial law in the city, applying it to soldiers and civilians alike.

that I am committed to this course. Continue the war and I will perish by your side."

In answer to all this Santa Anna says that he learns with bitter regret the charges which have been made against the Government for the course it has pursued. He urges that Gen. Scott solicited an armistice, (he does not say what Mackintosh came out for after the battle of Churubusco,) in order that Mr. Trist might be heard, which solicitation he granted, "*because the suspension of hostilities would give his troops rest, reestablish their morale, and give him an opportunity to collect the dispersed and enable him to adopt other measures to ensure a reaction!*" These are Santa Anna's own words. I have not time or space at present to give you the whole of his answer to Rejon, but will procure it for some future period. I have thought all along the "well-merited" of his country really desired peace, reasoning the while that he was to be well paid for it, and that he knew he must be defeated again, in the event of another battle; but I now begin to have some misgivings that he was humbugging us all the time. If he really had Mr. Buchanan's ultimatum to Mr. Trist in his pocket, as has been stated, he well knew that there was no earthly chance for an amicable result to the negotiations. Let his real intentions, however, have been what they may, self was at the bottom and his poor country unthought of. To show the man's avarice, I have been told by those who know Mexican affairs well, that since Mr. Polk allowed him to return from Havana he has contrived to pick and steal nearly a million of dollars, which is all safely placed in the hands of his foreign agents or friends.

Yours, &tc.,

G. W. K.

*Daily Picayune*, October 15, 1847

City of Mexico, September 24, 1847

Not a little joy has been manifested by all at the arrival here of the American prisoners—Capts. Clay, Heady and Smith, Lieuts. Churchill, Davidson and Barbour, and sixteen privates—who have recently been confined at Toluca.[10] It seems that they were released by the Governor, Olaguibel, on his own responsibility, they promising that the same number of Mexican prisoners, and of equal rank, should be delivered up to him. Those officers who refused to give their parole when all were ordered to Toluca,

---

10. William J. Heady was taken prisoner while leading a detachment of Kentucky cavalry in search of the troops who had been captured at Encarnación on January 23, 1847. Thomas J. Churchill, William T. Barbour, George R. Davidson, and Green Clay Smith, all Kentucky volunteers, were captured along with him.

and who afterwards escaped, have performed active service here in the different battles. Major Gaines has been serving on the staff of Gen. Scott, Midshipman Rogers on that of Gen. Pillow, Major Borland on that of Gen. Worth, and Capt. Danley on that of Gen. Quitman. The latter was severely wounded on the 13th, but will recover.

Yours, &c.,

G. W. K.
*Daily Picayune*, October 14, 1847

City of Mexico, September 26, 1847

Assassinations continue. No less than ten murdered soldiers were found this morning in the vicinity of the quarter of San Peblo, and eight on the previous day. The fault lies partially with our own men, who straggle from their quarters and get intoxicated at the first *pulqueria* or grog shop; yet the fact that even in this state they are set upon by gangs of armed ruffians shows that a feeling of revenge and deep hatred obtains against us; and the frequency of the murders would prove that a regular system of assassination has been organized, the wire workers very likely some of the priests and leading men.

One great reason for this is the almost insignificant force under the command of Gen. Scott.[11] True, he has had enough to achieve victories and capture the city of Mexico, and for this reason many may think that he has sufficient men. But such is not the case. The very smallness of our army is more degrading to the pride of the Mexicans than any defeat that has befallen them. Had an army respectable in numbers, compared with the enterprise undertaken and accomplished, entered the valley of Mexico, the smartings of discomfiture would have been alleviated by the evidence that they had not been beaten so shamefully by a body of men so inferior in numbers to their own grand army. Nor will they think of peace until forced to it by an army so large that there will at least be some merit in succumbing in the eyes of the world. Rigorous measures, too, must be adopted, for anyone who runs may read, that if the *quasi* war heretofore carried on is continued, it will be prolonged until the causes which brought it on are forgotten.

Bring the matter home for a moment. Supposing that an army composed of 9,000 of the picked men of Christendom should set themselves down before New Orleans, a city of but little over half the size of Mexico,

11. By year's end Scott had only about 8,000 soldiers available to hold the city; early in January 1848, however, reinforcements brought the occupying American army to approximately 15,000 men.

and that we had 25,000 soldiers and strong fortifications to defend it—how could we reconcile the entrance of the former into our streets and squares as conquerors? Of course I am supposing an impossibility, but there is not a citizen between Faubourg Marigny and Carrollton but will at once see and feel the degrading position in which the Mexicans are placed, and will hardly blame them for continuing a contest even against every semblance of hope. But let an army of 50,000 men be placed upon the line between this city and Vera Cruz, let the communications be kept thoroughly open, and let the inhabitants here be made to know and feel that our intention is to compel them to sue for terms, and there will then be an excuse for them, which in their eyes will hold with the nations of the earth, to come to an amicable arrangement. At present all the territory we possess in Mexico is comprised within the range of our guns. This we can have and can hold, against any force the enemy can bring; but until our army is increased to a size sufficient to command the territory on our line of operations, we can have no peace. The Mexicans are now bewildered, not subjected; they think there has been some grand mistake in all that has occurred. Their own inferiority and lack of military skill they do not take into the scale—they believe that for a space Providence has forsaken them—and thus believing, they will continue to preach war without truce against the North Americans, and honestly think they will in the end come out victorious. Nor can their eyes be opened until they see that we have men and means at our hands sufficient to overrun their country at will. Hastily I have scratched off a few speculations as regards the future conduct of the war; they may be of no service, but still are my honest convictions. We must either hold this line with a force sufficient to awe the enemy, or else retire from it altogether; and the sooner our Government bestirs itself the better.

In my last I stated that Col. McIntosh was sinking under his wounds—that brave officer died last night and is to be buried tomorrow with all military honors. He fell pierced by two balls, while gallantly leading his men to attack the Casa Mata on the 8th September, and his system, suffering under wounds received in former battles, was not able to overcome the shock.

Yours, &c.,

G. W. K.
*Daily Picayune*, October 15, 1847[12]

---

12. This dispatch appeared in the *Picayune* on October 14, 1847, without the first and last paragraphs.

City of Mexico, September 28, 1847

We have rumors without number from Puebla today. One is that Santa Anna has been killed in an encounter with Col. Childs in the vicinity of that city, another story would make us believe that he has been taken prisoner, after defending himself for sometime at the paper mill called La Constancia, in the neighborhood of Puebla. The accounts say that Col. Childs was reinforced by Maj. Lally, and that he immediately entered the city, drove out the guerrilleros and surrounded the mill above named.[13] What credit to place in these rumors I know not; but if Santa Anna is really a prisoner, it has been intentional—he has given himself up. If he has been killed, it has been what the Mexicans would term one *casualidad*, a sheer accident, for no such intention ever entered his head.

As a prisoner, Santa Anna knows perfectly well that he can humbug Mr. Polk with ease, and all his friends besides. We shall know the whole truth of the matter in the course of a day or two.

It is said that the Mexican Congress is to assemble at Querétaro, on the 5th of October—next week—and that Peña y Peña has gone out to be installed as the acting President. I have heard Mexicans say that the body has many members who will deliberate manfully and seriously in favor of peace; but my opinion is, that a majority of them will talk of little save honor and ditches and glory, and last extremities and ruins, and of being buried under them, and kindred nonsense. Some of them may be bribed, or hired, to espouse the peace side. We shall see.

Rejon, in his letters to Santa Anna, told him that if he would continue the war, he would perish by his side; but they say, that when the armistice was broken, he remained at Querétaro and forgot all about fighting. Valiant man is Manuel Cresceneis Rejon! but he has a prudent way of manifesting it in the hour of peril.

Paredes was here in the city a few days since, without followers, and has gone North, perhaps towards Guadalajara, his old and favorite ground, to stir and influence the minds of the people against the Yankees, and try his hand against them. He is, no doubt, one of the bravest and best generals Mexico has ever produced.

13. After the defeat at Mexico City, Santa Anna led a portion of his army to Puebla, where he sought to cut the American line leading back to Vera Cruz by capturing the American garrison under the command of Thomas Childs. When the Americans refused to surrender, Santa Anna laid siege during the last week of September. Folliot T. Lally, Ninth Infantry, and General Joseph Lane (who had separately led reinforcements to Jalapa in August and September) marched to Childs's assistance in early October. Santa Anna, learning of the approaching reinforcements, moved east along the highway toward El Pinal and hid his army at Huamantla. From there he hoped to attack the rear of the American force as it passed by.

Gómez Farías is at Querétaro, but we do not hear what he is doing. Gen. Herrera is also there, and if any leading man in Mexico is in favor of peace, he is the one. His influence, however, is confined almost entirely to the *moderados.*

Mr. Wells, the partner of Hart in the Army theatre, died here a day or two since. He may be recollected in the United States, not only as a pantomimist but as a dancer and actor of some distinction. Capt. Pemberton Waddell, of one of the new regiments of infantry,[14] is also dead. The wound of Gen. Shields, although painful, is improving. A musket ball struck him in the left arm at the storming of Chapultepec, but binding a handkerchief round it he continued with his men until everything was calmed. Gen. Pillow has almost entirely recovered. Since commencing this I have heard another rumor to the effect that Alvarez and the Congress of Puebla have risen upon Santa Anna and put him to death. This can hardly be credited. Alvarez is doubtless in that direction. He took especial good care to keep himself and his pintos out of harm's way during the recent struggles in this vicinity.

The loss in the different divisions in the storming of Chapultepec and capture of the city on the 13th is as follows: In that of Gen. Quitman about 300, in that of Gen. Twiggs 268, in that of Gen. Pillow 142, in that of Gen. Worth 138. Owing to his previous heavy loss the latter only had about 1000 men engaged in the last battles. As I know it will be of great interest to their friends, before closing this letter I will state that the wounds of almost all the officers are doing well. I can speak positively of Col. Garland, Majors Wade, Waite, Loring, and Gladden, of Capts. Mason, Walker, Danley, and of Lieuts. Foster, Shackelford, Selden and Lugenbeel, and I mention them as being some of the most severely wounded.

I send you a few papers and documents of interest, which, I trust, will reach safely. Had I an opportunity, I could furnish you with a volume of letters, papers, &tc., all found in the palace and other places, which would be a rare treat to our readers. You shall have them all in good time. I send you a species of glory from the 30th August up to this date in the shape of letters, written from day to day. In the main, I believe I was correct in my surmises, although not always right. I write in great haste, as the courier is just starting.

Yours, &tc.,

G. W. K.

*Daily Picayune*, October 14, 1847

---

14. The Eleventh Infantry.

City of Mexico, October 3, 1847

An earthquake! we have had an earthquake! Between the hours of 7 and 8 yesterday morning, and when all nature was hushed in a stillness most profound, suddenly the earth began to rock with a strange and most fearful motion. I am living at the house of Peña y Peña, the headquarters of Gen. Worth, immediately in front of the beautiful alameda, and the first indication we had of the dread convulsion was the violent slamming of the doors, accompanied by a furious jingling of the glass pendants attached to a chandelier hanging and swinging from the ceiling of the room. Soon our beds commenced rocking, something after the manner of a ship becalmed at the close of a storm, and then came the shrieks of innumerable women and children, driven, half-dressed, affrighted into the streets—the dreaded *temblor*, as the Mexicans call it, was upon us. Most strange and impressive was the scene disclosed from the front windows, as reeling and staggering we approached and opened them—to walk steady was impossible, so violent were the upheavings and oscillations of the mighty earth. The tops of the large trees in the alameda were swaying, the water in the reservoirs was billowing to and fro, the walls around us were cracking and gaping asunder, the wide street in front was crowded with women and children as well as men, screaming and praying, and crossing themselves in the extremity of their fright, while our own soldiers were reeling unsteadily in their midst, astonished and awe-stricken at the strange commotion. The sentinels halted upon their rounds, uncertain and not knowing what to do—the *callejons*, or narrow lanes, continued to pour forth their hundreds of affrighted inhabitants, all seeking the refuge of the wider streets and open squares, lest their own houses might totter and tumble upon their heads, while on bended knees they confessed their sins aloud, and earnestly petitioned forgiveness ere it was yet too late. A wounded officer in our house, bedridden and apparently unable to move since the hard-fought battle of El Molino, came hobbling hurriedly from his room, driven thence by the cracking of the walls and the strange tumult from without. The stillness of the morning, so profound had been the repose of nature, but added to the general feeling of wonder and of awe—of consternation perhaps I should term it, a fear caught from the actions and countenances of those "native here and to the manner born," those cradled and rocked amid commotions of a kindred nature. The domes and steeples of the innumerable churches and convents reeled like drunken men—the lakes hard by rolled their sluggish waters as though moved by an elemental strife from above instead of the earth in which they are nestled in her sore travail. An officer in the street, about to mount his horse at the commencement of the commotion, suddenly found the animal receding from him. Astonished, he inquired of a soldier close by the cause; but the man was as ignorant as himself. The puddles in the streets—for there had been a severe shower the night before—spread themselves and disappeared upon the pavement, so great was the motion, while the trees in the alameda continued to lash their huge tops as if swayed by unseen yet all-powerful hands. The shock lasted over two minutes—perhaps I should say succession of shocks, for the oscillatory motion of the earth at short intervals became calm—while the whole scene impressed everyone anew with the might, the majesty, and the manifold power of the Most High.

But if the streets and open ways presented a spectacle most impressive, doubly awful was the effect produced among the wounded men in the different hospitals. Unconscious of the cause of the strange commotion, filled with apprehensions which ever attack with ten-fold force the disabled and the infirm, and dreading results from a phenomenon they must have deemed akin to the supernatural, the poor fellows rose and hobbled from their cots—trembling and stricken by deep awe, yet not knowing whither to fly. The armless hurried hither and thither, the legless hobbled about in all directions, while the bedridden, the prostrate, and the utterly helpless, panic-stricken and desponding, earnestly prayed and petitioned not to be left unprotected—not to be deserted in an extremity which their ignorance made painfully terrifying. But by and by the earth became relieved of her mighty throes, the staggering steeples resumed their quiet, the affrighted inhabitants rose thankful from their knees, the sentinels recommenced their rounds—the fury of the dreaded *temblor* was spent.

Innumerable anecdotes, and some of them amusing enough, are told of the earthquake and its effects. An Irish soldier says that the Mexicans, unable to fight us fair, are adopting a new system—that there is no such thing as getting at the bottom of an earthquake, and no particular fear in being on top. Another says that this is a very *unsettled* country, and that he is anxious to leave, while a Yankee from "way down East" contends that the whole affair is a species of "clearing-up shower" to the war, and that peace must soon follow. A knot of officers were discussing the movement of the earth; one said it was vibratory, another contended that it was oscillatory. In joke the matter was referred to a mulatto servant—a fellow whose yellow face had turned to a color between a blue black and an invisible green during the "quake," as he termed it—and he decided the question by saying that the motion was *wabbleatory.* And wabbleatory it was—too much so for comfort if not for safety. For one, I have always desired to see, or rather to *feel* the effects of an earthquake. A single convulsion has sufficed to cure all curiosity—I never wish to be present at a repetition. The same Providence that has power to shake a large city to its foundation, has the power also to lay every dome and steeple, tunnel and tower, level with the ground.

But to leave, for the present, this subject, and to offer a few remarks upon the army and its past deeds. It is still difficult to account for the fact that we are here, here in the great capital of Mexico—not the 22,000 paper men of the *Union,* but what is left of the 10,000 real men by whom the work of subjugation has been accomplished. The whole seems like a dream, even to those who have taken part in the hard conflicts—yet here in Mexico we are, and masters. After a succession of battles, each one of which may be counted a forlorn hope—after a succession of victories, each one of which was obtained over an immensely superior force—after formidable works, each one of which seemed impregnable, have been stormed and successfully carried—here, amid the "Halls of the Montezumas," the numerically insignificant band of Anglo-Saxons has found a partial rest from its toils and its dangers, a breathing place after its innumerable trials and perils. Not the chronicles of ancient wars, nor the prowess of modern achievements, furnish a parallel to the second conquest of Mexico, while the lustre which hung around the name of Cortes and his hardy adventurers, burnished by the glowing descriptions of Prescott,[15] becomes dimmed by the deeds of these latter days.

You in the United States cannot be made to feel and appreciate all that stern and unflinching courage has effected in the beautiful valley of Mexico since our little army first entered it—words are inadequate to give even a faint picture of the brilliant succession of events which have ended in the subjection of this proud capital. The deeds of Cortes, brave and vigorous as they were, must suffer by a comparison. The hardy and adventurous Spaniard, surrounded by his host of Tlascalan and other allies, brought agencies then deemed supernatural to the work, had all the engines and appliances of modern war at his disposal, and fought against an enemy superstitious and awe-stricken, and provided only with the ruder implements of battle. Grant that they were brave—but their bravery was of a piece with that of the Hindoo widow, who fearlessly and unresistingly chants her own death song on the grave of her lifeless husband. The followers of the Aztec monarchs, of Montezuma and of Guatemozin, offered themselves as sacrifices to their idols. The mass, when all hopes of victory had banished, still continued the fight, it is true; but in their onslaughts

15. William H. Prescott, *History of the Conquest of Mexico and History of the Conquest of Peru* (New York, 1843). Prescott's history was widely read by American soldiers during the war.

upon the iron ranks of the Christians they were but fulfilling their own destiny, and rushing upon a doom that was inevitable. The altars of their gods demanded yearly and even daily sacrifices long before the advent of the strangers—the demands were now increased, yet the victims were ever ready. True, a follower of the cross occasionally fell, borne down by some avalanche of pagan warriors; but for every drop of Christian blood a river would flow, and well did Cortes know that in the end he must conquer. His calculations were based upon mathematics, and in the problem of life and death he foresaw that the result would be in his favor. Science, severe discipline, strange animals bestrode by powerful men, invulnerable armor, all the appliances which make war terrible, love of gold, and blind religious zeal—these, all these, were pitted against undisciplined, unmailed, and comparatively unarmed masses—and the results of such encounters were known even before the eyes of the shrewd and calculating Castillian rested upon the rich vallies of Anahuac.

But widely different was it when, a short two months since, the second conquerors first came in sight of the domes and turrets of Mexico. In some respects the cases may have been parallel. The Anglo-Saxons were cut off from all succor and support from home, and had naught but their own stout hearts and strong arms to depend upon: but they had not coats of mail and fire-arms, in the days of the first conquerors so terrible, with which to oppose cotton shirts and bows and arrows. On the contrary, they had to contend with a proud and implacable enemy, an enemy provided with the same means of attack and resistance as themselves, strongly fortified, immensely superior in numbers, pretending to the highest advancement of civilization, chivalry and valor, fighting for home and fireside, and insolent in his fancied strength and security. Breastwork and barricade were to be assailed from causeway and open field, and auxiliaries the Americans had none as was the case with the early Spaniards.[16] The Yankee invaders found the valley bristling with bayonets, against which bayonets were to be opposed; at every avenue they found heavy cannon in position to check their advance, and at disadvantageous points only could they plant their guns for the attack. They had before them a city of 200,000 inhabitants—a city in which every house was a fortress: they had a population incited against them by a thousand and one idle tales and calumnies—by stores of brutalities and excesses they were said to have committed, and which they were advancing to repeat; a population which

16. I trust I am not insulting *our* Tlascalan allies, the forty odd thieves liberated from Puebla, and who rode about under the protection our guns afforded them, headed by the greatest robber of all, Chato Dominguez. —*Kendall.*

had learned the sieges of Saguntum and Saragoza by heart, and in their exceeding pride of valor doubtless thought they were to rival if not excel the deeds enacted by the defenders of those valiant cities. With the least reverse it was understood that all the Americans were to be massacred—the brutal murder of our wounded men at El Molino proves the savage intention—and thus our army had emphatically nothing but "victory or death" before it. The result, as everyone knows, was victory—victory most complete—the entire prostration of an enemy all powerful in numbers and position, if not in prowess. The evidence is that we are here, and that Santa Anna's proud army is scattered and destroyed; yet still all appears like a dream. The long roll may sound for an hour, and scarce 7000 able-bodied men will flock to the alarm call; yet they are masters of the heart of the Republic. The page that records the history of this campaign will be deemed a doubtful one in after times: it will be difficult to credit that a handful of men numbering only 10,000, with not thirty pieces of artillery all told, discomfited and drove 30,000 men protected by all the subtleties of engineering, and with three times their number of heavy guns: yet the proofs of Holy Writ are not stronger. The result of the two campaigns against Mexico—that of the early Spaniards and the Yankees—has been the same—the subjugation and occupation of the capital: it now remains to be seen how the world will compare the two achievements.

Yours, &c.,

G. W. K.
*Daily Picayune*, November 7, 1847

City of Mexico, October 10, 1847

For the past week all has been quiet in the capital. To be sure, there was a slight shock of an earthquake on the 3d inst., and a more severe convulsion on the 5th, but neither were "any great shakes" compared to that which emphatically made everything tremble on the morning of the 2d October. Those pretending to knowledge in these matters say we shall not have another visitation before April next, and long previous to that time I hope to be well out of the country. They say, farther, that earthquakes are affairs one can never become used to, a matter I do not feel the least inclined to dispute.

Up to this time we do not learn that the Mexican Congress has done anything at Querétaro, or that even a quorum has been formed. A decree or order has been issued by the Provisional President, Peña y Peña, dated at Toluca on the 7th inst. depriving Santa Anna of the command of the Mexican army, and appointing Gen. Rincon in his stead. The latter together with Gen. Bravo, I believe have been exchanged for Capts. Clay, Heady, and the other prisoners. In the meantime, until Rincon can join the main body of the army, Gen. Alvarez is to take command. The Provisional President says, that in every well organized country the generals must answer before the proper tribunal for the faults they have committed, and even for the misfortunes which they have suffered in their campaigns, and he furthermore orders that a competent military court be organized at some suitable place, to try Santa Anna for the loss of the actions he directed as general-in-chief, but principally for the loss of the capital. It has got to be a received opinion among the Mexicans that any officer taken prisoner, no matter under what circumstances, must necessarily be both brave and efficient. Were it not so, how could Rincon, after losing the battle of Churubusco and being himself captured, be now placed in command without a hearing, and furthermore be ordered to form a court martial to try Santa Anna, and perhaps others who had opportunities denied them—those of running away? Rincon himself would not have been taken had he not been so hard pressed on one side by the division of Gen. Twiggs, while his retreat on the other side had been cut off by the capture of the strong work at the bridge-head by the division of Gen. Worth.

An intelligent Spaniard, with whom I have conversed today, thinks it extremely doubtful whether a quorum of the Congress will assemble at Querétaro. He further says, that a majority of the States north and west—in fact all of them—although entirely without resources, are still in favor of a continuance of the war. They can form no plan nor raise any means for carrying it on, but still are not disposed to listen to any propositions of peace. The party most hostile to the United States, paradoxical as it may appear, is the one most favorable to peace. Santa Anna, he thinks, instead of taking the route towards Oajaca as many suppose, will make the best of his way to Tuspan, and will there embark for Jamaica or some other English West India island. Cuba he will not revisit, he says, as while residing there he was strongly suspected of being engaged in some plot to overturn the Spanish Government. My informant even goes so far as to hint that a vessel is at this time in readiness at or near Tuspan, on which the great man is to embark, and that his old and constant friend Mackintosh is an active agent in the business. I give his speculations for what they are worth, believing them entitled to as much credit as one-half that are afloat. Of all the reverses Santa Anna has ever met with—and he has risen above them all—the last has been the most severe; and how he can recover in the present instance no one can divine. For anyone but him there would be no hope.

We have news from Alvarez, to the effect that after Santa Anna dispersed his officers at El Pinal, giving such of them leave to retire to their homes as desired it, he, Alvarez, fell back upon Puebla with about 2000 ragamuffins, plundering their subsistence as they went along. Before he left, the army was without provisions or resources of any kind, disorganized and dispirited, and Santa Anna found it utterly impossible to keep it together any longer. It now remains to be seen what Alvarez is to do. Until Rincon is installed he is to be commander-in-chief, but where is his army? Even if he is reinforced by Reyes and Bustamente, he still will not have more than 6000 men. If Gen. Scott had even 4000 additional troops at this time—just enough to hold the capital and fit out a small expedition besides—he might break up and scatter the Mexican army with ease.[17] But he does not hold a foot of land between this and Vera Cruz outside the range of a 24-pounder, nor will he until reinforced.

What *is* to be the policy of our Government in relation to the conduct of this war? I hear it agitated that we are to take up some line as a boundary, fall back upon it, cease all active operations, and merely hold and sustain the boundary that may be adopted. This course, although preferable to our past milk-and-water policy, will never do to my humble thinking—we shall be at war with the Mexicans for all time. The simple withdrawal of our troops will be looked upon as proof positive of our inability to sustain ourselves here in the heart of the Republic, while a long line of military defences will be harassed by a proud but ignorant people until Montezuma is forgotten or his history incorporated with heathen mythology. No kind of warfare, if warfare it could be called, would suit the Mexicans as well—we should be placing a species of wall between them and the murderous inroads of the dreaded Apaches and Comanches, and while they would laugh at us for our pains they would annoy us for our presumption. Relieved from immediate danger, the thousands of worthless military demagogues would bestir themselves in forming new armies and in raising new means, and what could they not effect against the slight curtain of defences on a line extending from the Gulf to the Pacific, or from the Rio Grande to the California coast? It will help the matter some, perhaps, if a strict blockade of all the seaports of the country is put down on the programme of the new system, but all will fail in bringing about a peace with a nation utterly blind to its own interests, and brave to a degree when danger is afar off.

17. Scott resisted pressure to send expeditions to San Luis Potosí, Zacatecas, and Mazatlán, recognizing that his command was barely adequate to hold Mexico City.

You may ask, then, how is peace to be obtained? The safest, wisest, most expeditious and cheapest plan would be, to reinforce this line at once with 50,000 men. This should be the first step. Then real war should be declared against Mexico, not a quasi, half-and-half state of hostilities as at present—keep all that we have got and let it be understood that we are to get and hold all that we can—send every officer captured a close prisoner to the United States, and provide strong places in which to keep all the privates—*have no talk with the people or their leaders save that our intention is to overrun, destroy and conquer*—let all the inhabitants be made to know that we are at war with them—follow up blows *with blows*, not with soft words—leave peace commissioners and peace propositions at home, instead of sending them to a market where there is no demand for such absurdities—in short, and to repeat what I have already urged, have a force in the country sufficient to give the enemy no respites nor time to recover their *morale*; but let every hard fought battle have a result, which has never yet been the case, and we shall soon have a peace. I hear that Gen. Scott is blamed in some of the papers of the United States for delaying his march upon the capital as long as he did. How could he do otherwise with the force he had on first entering Puebla? With the scanty means afforded him he adopted altogether the wiser policy. Supposing that he had pushed upon this city in the early part of June, he might have driven Santa Anna and the army out it is true, and with comparatively little loss; but at that time he would have had a large and hostile population within the gates with not more than sufficient numbers to keep them in subjection, while Santa Anna would have surrounded the capital with the force then at his hands, occupied every avenue, cut off all supplies, and finally compelled Gen. Scott to fight the battle of Mexico at every disadvantage. It had to be fought somewhere, and our commander-in-chief only waited until he had a sufficient force to ensure success. I may revert to this subject again.

Yours, &c.,

G. W. K.
*Daily Picayune*, November 7, 1847

City of Mexico, October 14, 1847

We still receive the intelligence that nothing is doing at Querétaro. No quorum has as yet been formed, and some of the most intelligent minds are of the opinion that it will be impossible to assemble a sufficient number of the members of Congress for the legal transaction of business. An attempt has been made, started by the military, to keep Peña y Peña from the Presidential chair, the malcontents even going so far as to contend, in the very teeth of the constitution, that he is not entitled to it; but disorganized as the country now is, they probably will not succeed.[18] Meanwhile, Querétaro is crowded with hungry officers, clamoring for their pay, and not a cent of money is there to give them. In this city, to such straits are the members of the late Mexican army driven, that there are not only colonels but generals without a sign of support for their families; and some of them are fain compelled to call upon our officers for the means to furnish their daily meals. Still no one thinks of peace!

Stories are afloat that there have been disturbances in the State of Jalisco. As the reports go, it would seem that the civil authorities had called upon the ecclesiastical—the usual resource—for money, and on its being refused the parties of either resorted to arms. The name of Gómez Farías is mixed up in the business.[19]

It is now exactly a month since the American flag was hoisted on the National Palace of Mexico, and during that time the occurrences one day tell the story of all. The men have been paid off, and with the money in their pockets many of them have visited the innumerable dram shops. Drunkenness would follow, and in many instances while in this state they have been assassinated. Gen. Quitman, the Governor, has taken every means granted him to ferret out the murderers, but in too many cases without success. The inhabitants of the city look humble and crest-fallen, but sullen. Had their streets been entered by 50,000 men, instead of by the insignificant number composing Gen. Scott's entire force, on the morning of the capitulation, they could have borne the infliction with better grace. Day by day we have rumors of the movements of the enemy in this direction and in that, but all come in such questionable shape that no reliance can be placed on them.

Of amusements we cannot complain, either as regards the number or the quality. First and foremost, we have a most excellent Spanish company at El Teatro Nacional,[20] giving us a series of entertainments than which we have seldom witnessed anything better, if as good, at home. The principal actor is Señor Viñolas, a finished artist, but the most charming feature in

18. *Puros* questioned Santa Anna's power to issue a decree naming his successor, in part because the recently amended constitution of 1824, although formally adopted, was not yet operative. Ultimately, the *moderado* political leadership prevailed, setting aside constitutional technicalities and vesting Peña y Peña with executive authority until a president could be chosen.

19. Gómez Farías left for Lagos, Jalisco, when Peña y Peña assumed the presidency, to avoid association with the new *moderado* government and to seek support for efforts to resist concessions to the United States.

20. The theatre had recently changed its name from Grand Teatro Santa Anna. Peskin, ed., *Volunteers*, 196.

the company is the Señora Cañete, an actress of versatile talents—chaste and polished in her style to a degree, while her voice is most musical, her eye bright and joyous, her smile irresistible, and the whole expression of her face sunny as a bright day in May. She has seen some thirty-odd summers—begging her pardon for speaking upon a point so tender—yet still is a handsome, a beautiful woman, with whom time has dealt most leniently. To a charming *naïveté* she unites a thorough conception of character and an exhaustless flow of spirits, and at the same time is just as much at home while enacting the lisping and sentimental victim of love as while portraying the boisterous hoyden. I cannot call to mind the equal to La Cañete on the American stage. In all their appointments and accessories the Spanish are infinitely ahead of us—even at our own French theatre in New Orleans they are behind these Castilian comedians in the richness and appropriateness of costume. Attached to the company is an excellent *corps de ballet*, composed of some six or eight male and female dancers. The principal is La Gozze, a pretty and sprightly little woman, with a Jewish cast of countenance lighting up so well on the stage, while her limbs would serve as models. Nor is she at all chary in the display of them, but vaults, whirls, and—and—cavorts is a good word—about the stage in a style highly gratifying to "los Yankees." Not a particle of prudery is there in her pirouettes—quite the contrary. There appears to be a joyous *abandon* about all the dances given by these Spanish *artistes*, and if a New York or New Orleans audience could see one of their Boleros, or "La Jota Arragonesa" for instance, as given here at the National theatre, there would be some little attempt at shouting. There is only one word that has ever fallen upon my ears that can truly define this style of the pretty Señorita Gozze, and I doubt whether that word can be found in Webster—her style is *high falutin.*

The Spanish company perform three nights in each week at El Nacional—Tuesday, Thursday and Sunday. On the other evenings Hart gives an American performance with his company, pieced out with tolerably fair singing from the Italian opera troupe. The principal cantatrice is the Señora Lopez, a Mexican by birth, who has a voice of good compass with a fair execution. While Borghese was here in Mexico she appeared with her on several occasions, both taking principal parts in the same operas. The theatre is one of the largest in America and one of the finest in the world—larger even than the old St. Charles, and perfect in all its appointments. The orchestra is a very good one, and nightly they give "Yankee Doodle" and "Hail Columbia" in a style which wakes up the patriotism of the Anglo-Saxons, nine-tenths of the audience being composed of this particular class of the human family.

The *Teatro del Progreso,* another fine theatre in the same street as the National, is nightly opened by Bensley with his equestrian company. The pit has been taken out to make room for the ring and the accompanying sawdust, and good audiences are in constant attendance. The principal attraction at this establishment is the Señora Armand, a little Habanera married to a French Hercules. She is not as graceful as Blangy, but is as bold as Joan of Arc—a well formed woman enough, turns somersets, rides on one leg, jumps through hoops, dances the Cachuca, and makes up in strength and agility for what she lacks in polish. Another attraction at this establishment is Hamblin, the India Rubber man, who shuts himself up like a jack-knife and performs various games of that sort, while two of the equestrians, Kelly and Kincade, would pass muster under Stickney's management. Then they have an Ethiopian extravaganza singer, with a banjo, who gives "Lucy Neal" and "Old Dan Tucker" between the acts. Who would have thought, a twelve month since, that such atrocities would have been introduced into one of the first theatres in Mexico? but I am chronicling the truth. In addition to all I have so far mentioned, we have a panorama of some sort, performances at the Diorama, regular bull-fights at the Plaza de Toros, and a promise of sport in the way of cricket playing and horse racing, so you will see that such of the American people as are sojourning in the neighborhood of the "Halls of the Montezumas" have no great lack in the way of amusements.

[G. W. K.][21]
*Daily Picayune,* November 10, 1847

Mexico, October 14, 1847 [An extract.]

Up to this time I have written out no detailed account of the great battle of Contreras, of Churubusco, of El Molino, and of Chapultepec—all ending with the capture of the city. In the first place, I have not been able to see the official reports, from which, coupled with personal observation, a full and impartial narrative could only be made out; and secondly, the means of sending such a mass of manuscript to the coast, at least with safety, are questionable. The maps I forwarded to you, from the great haste in copying them, I know were imperfect, and in the hurried synopsis of the events which I sent off for publication I am confident many omissions were made. The important part taken by the batteries of Steptoe and Taylor, in diverting the enemy in the direction of La Piedad and Niño Perdido I am fearful were not even alluded to. If I live to get home, full and most complete justice

21. This dispatch has no identifying initials, but it is introduced with the heading "Mr. Kendall's Letter from the Army."

shall be done to all who took part in the glorious achievements—in the hard and most sanguinary battles which ended in the conquest of Mexico.

I regret to state that two more officers—Lieut. Shackleford, of the 2d Artillery and Lieut. Bacon, of the 6th Infantry—have died since my last of their wounds. They were most deserving and popular officers, and were buried this morning with all honors in the English cemetery of San Cosmé. At this last resting-place of the dead, a quiet and beautiful spot just as you enter San Cosmé from the north or west, all our officers have been interred.

Mr. Bankhead, the English Minister, whose health is still bad, has advertised all his furniture, wines, &tc. for sale, and, accompanied by his lady, is to leave the country in the course of a week or ten days. I believe Mr. Doyle[22] is expected out in the next packet from England, to take the place of Mr. Bankhead.

I send this letter off without knowing whether it will get through. By the same conveyance I also forward a file of the latest newspapers published here. As yet Gen. Scott has not determined upon sending down a train to Vera Cruz, so there is no ascertaining when we can get away.

Yours, &tc.,

G. W. K.

P. S.—Since commencing this letter I learn that Dr. Roberts, surgeon of the 5th Infantry, died yesterday from a wound received at El Molino. His gallant conduct on that occasion was noticed by all, and his loss is much regretted. Both Gens. Shields and Pillow are out. The wound of the latter is stated not to have been as severe as was first represented. It was a bruise rather than a wound, and was received in the grove at the foot of Chapultepec.

*Daily Picayune*, November 7, 1847

City of Mexico, October 15, 1847

I see that some of the journals of the United States, the *N. Y. Sun* among others, are attacking Gen. Scott for his dilatoriness in advancing upon this city—contending that his long delay at Puebla was unnecessary, and that instead of remaining there to "suck oranges" he should have advanced at once. Without being the apologist for all the acts of Gen. S., a sense of justice induces me to say that he chose the right time to march from Puebla, and that had he moved directly on his arrival there upon this place, the consequences would have been most disastrous. Grant that in the early part of June he might have marched upon and captured the city

22. A British career diplomat, Percy W. Doyle had served in the United States during the 1820s.

of Mexico with comparatively little loss, what would have been Santa Anna's course? It requires but very little foresight to say, that with the force he then had he would have left the capital to its fate, taken up positions in the neighborhood, shut up every avenue of communication, and leaving a hostile population to take charge of the 4000 Americans—for Gen. Scott could not at that time have brought more—he would have fallen back upon Puebla, or else upon the brigades of Gens. Cadwalader and Pierce on their way up, and have crushed them in detail from the very superiority of the numbers he could have brought to act upon them. It should be recollected that Gen. Scott had scarce 6000 men all told on his arrival at Puebla, and that many of them were recruits, while Santa Anna already had no inconsiderable force organized, although perhaps the capital was not fortified at all points. Alvarez, with 4 or 5000 men, was at that time within striking distance of Puebla, ready at all times to pounce upon any small force; the guerrilla parties, even then on the road below Peroté, were sufficiently strong to annoy if not check the advance of the reinforcements; and the signal of Gen. Scott's advance upon the capital could not but have induced Santa Anna to concentrate his forces with those already in the rear, and by a succession of easy blows, for at the time he would have had none but new recruits to contend with, his victories would have been cheaply won and complete. Gen. Scott would have been shut up in the capital, with his insignificant force, and the past action of our Government, in the way of affording ample succor, shows what he might have expected from home in the way of assistance. Exulting under the influence of victory, Santa Anna himself would have been the attacking party—would have assaulted the capital already filled with our enemies—and it would be asking too much of the valor even of the American arms to suppose that they could do more than cut their way to the coast. A succession of events, resembling those above enumerated, must have followed a movement upon the capital in the early part of summer, and another "noche triste," another disastrous evacuation of the capital, would have been added to the annals of Mexican history.

But what did Gen. Scott do? Chafing under the delay in sending reinforcements, he still waited their arrival. Nor was he idle the while. The divisions of Gens. Worth, Twiggs and Quitman were being constantly drilled on the plains bordering Puebla, until their discipline was complete, while the hundreds of sick were allowed time to recover and the well to become hardened and inured to a climate new to them. The brigade of Gen. Pierce, the last of the reinforcements expected, arrived at Puebla on the 5th August, and on the 7th Gen. Twiggs commenced the march upon the capital, the other divisions following in succession. The battle of Mexico had to be fought somewhere: and although Gen. Scott's force even in August was too weak for the dangerous enterprise, still his own skill and that of his officers, combined with the obstinate valor of his soldiers, overcame all obstacles. The proud capital of Mexico was heroically entered, her army dispersed and demoralized, and all fears of a successful descent upon a weak and partially unprotected rear thus done away with. Any other course than that pursued by Gen. Scott, with the exceedingly limited means at his disposal, would have brought ruin and defeat, and it ill becomes writers at home, snugly and safely ensconced in their sanctums, to criticize and censure movements they have no means of understanding.

Some of the Mexican writers, too, are abusing Gen. Scott, singling out for their special animadversion the hanging of the deserters at Mixcoac. They call the act inhuman, savage, worse than barbarous—an indelible stain upon the name of Gen. S. and upon the fair escutcheon of his country. If ever men deserved hanging, those men did: and in carrying out their sentence in the face of the entreaties, perhaps not personal, of the English embassy, of the importuning of the Irish Jesuit priest, Macnamara, and of the hundreds of native and foreign ladies who signed petitions in their behalf, the American commander but evinced a stern determination to let Justice have her way. It was a bold act, but one imperiously demanded, and while we cannot but feel sad at seeing fifty human beings launched into eternity, it affords consolation that even the erring unfortunates themselves acknowledged their sentence just.[23]

Assassinations continue in the streets after night, no less than seven or eight soldiers having been murdered within the last three days. As yet I cannot learn that a single offender has been brought to justice. The weapon used in most cases by the assassins is a slim but exceedingly sharp sword-cane, and so expert are the cowardly miscreants in their murderous office that but one stab is necessary to take life. The smallness of our force emboldens the assassins, and unless prompt measures of retaliation are adopted—upon the innocent, if they will not bestir themselves in ferreting out the guilty—no one can tell when a stop is to be put to those acts. If the priests do not instigate, they at least do not exert themselves to arrest

23. Our own soldiers were to a man eager to see the full sentence of the law carried out against their former comrades. They contend, and with good show of reason, that the battalion of San Patricio killed and wounded more than ten times their number of the Mexican troops. I send you an appeal, made by the miscreant Reilly to his countrymen, which was found at the Palace after the city was entered. —*Kendall.*

these assassinations; and if a few of them are imprisoned and threatened with punishment more severe, the effect will be most salutary.

The papers which I send you will give all the news from the interior States. No movement in favor of peace has been made in any quarter, but they talk of continuing the war as fiercely as ever, especially those who are out of the way of its immediate effects—in plain English, out of all danger. At Querétaro all is "confusion worse confounded," if reports be true. What can induce any man to seek office under a prostrate and demoralized Government it is difficult to divine, but it would seem that the candidates for place are as numerous as ever. Perhaps a desire for the plunder of office may actuate many, although it would seem that poor Mexico had already been drained to the last extremity. No one can say who is to be chosen President. The principal candidates are Almonte, Angel Trias, Olaguibel, and Herrera. A force of one thousand men, with six light pieces of cannon, has recently arrived at Querétaro from Guadalajara, under the command of Gen. Heredia. One of the letter writers says that they—the new arrival of troops—are "full of enthusiasm," and then goes on to account for it by saying that they are *Nacionales.* Their enthusiasm will evaporate very fast if ever they get within range of the muskets of "los Yankees." Has it ever occurred to you how wonderfully full of valor and enthusiasm the Mexicans are just previous to a fight, but how soon it all subsides at the first onslaught of battle?

Gen. Rangel, who commanded at the San Cosmé gate, and who fled leaving his own supper and that of Santa Anna hot and smoking upon the table, announced to the nation that he is wounded and that he has taken up his residence at Toluca. It remains to be seen how this formal announcement will affect the price of Mexican stock, or operate upon the question of peace or war. The government at Querétaro has fixed upon Teloloapan as the residence of Gen. Paredes, he to give his word of honor not to leave it, considering it as necessary to the public tranquillity. Gen. Lombardini has been appointed military commandant of Querétaro, while it is stated that the reception of Peña y Peña by the authorities of that city was cordial and most gratifying. The next we will hear, in all likelihood, is that they have driven him off with contumely and reproach.

I have already informed you that Gen. Rincon—who, together with Bravo, have been given in exchange for Capts. Heady and Clay, and the other American prisoners taken at Encarnación—has received the command of the Mexican army, and that until he is in readiness Alvarez is to be chief—all this by an order from Peña y Peña in a decree dated at Toluca. Santa Anna has been ordered to answer, before a military court martial, for the recent disasters which have befallen the Mexican army, and particularly for the loss of the capital.[24] It is not probable that he will manifest his goodly person before any such tribunal in a hurry, unless he has a force with him of sufficient strength to have everything his own way.

I have already several times alluded to our places of amusement here in Mexico. The popular Cañete, of the Spanish troupe, grows in favor apace. Her style, especially in farce, may be set down as a little broad—rather Fanny Fitzwilliamish, an actress whom she somewhat resembles—but then she is all life and spirits, and keeps the audience in good humor from the rising of the curtain to its going down. A new candidate for equestrian honors, a certain Señora Turin, recently appeared for "one night only," at the Teatro del Progreso. She appeared with one foot on one side of her horse and one on the other, and indulged in sundry masculine extravagances of like nature. It was too much for the audience. Men who walked cheerfully and fearlessly up to the ditches and walls of Churubusco and Chapultepec were taken aback by Señora Turin, and she has not appeared since.

G. W. K.
*Daily Picayune*, November 14, 1847

City of Mexico, October 15, 1847 [An extract.]

Capt. Pearson, of the New York volunteers, who was wounded at Chapultepec, has since died of his wounds; so, too, has Lieut. Stein, of the South Carolina Regiment. Capt. Huddlestone,[25] of the 14th Infantry, died a day or two since of bowel complaint. The climate of Mexico, so dry and checking all perspiration, is represented as extremely unfavorable to gunshot wounds, and hence the impossibility of saving many who were not at first thought to be hurt seriously.

[G. W. K.]
*Daily Picayune*, November 7, 1847

City of Mexico, October 17, 1847

There can be little doubt of two things: first, that Santa Anna has been defeated by someone below Puebla; and second, that there has been some kind of a revolution in Guadalajara, and it is more than probable that Gómez Farías is either at the bottom or has had some hand in getting it up. He is an ultra, a perfect enthusiast on one point—he attributes the principal part of the disasters which have befallen the country to the fact that the priests have locked up and hoarded a large portion of her treasures,

---

24. The order was issued on October 7, 1847. At the same time, Herrera was named commander of the Mexican Army.

25. Creed T. Huddlestone.

without which every limb of the body politic must necessarily be paralyzed. To get hold of the immense estates and revenues of the clergy, and to appropriate them honestly to the welfare of his country, has long been a darling object of his, and this may have been the foundation of the pronunciamento in Guadalajara.

From the different States North and West of this our reliable news is meagre enough. All would indicate, however, that no movement in favor of peace has been made. No means or resources for continuing the war noted, yet the different leaders *talk* as fiercely of what they intend doing as ever, and thus they will continue to talk until they see that we have some show of force in the country, until war is declared in earnest, and until all their cities are brought under subjection with a strong hand.

I must close this letter in haste, as I am told the gentleman who takes it to Vera Cruz is about packing up preparatory to a start. Of late I have had but indifferent luck with my expresses, two that I have dispatched since the capture of the city having been cut off. They both escaped with their lives, however, and I shall continue to send off others whenever anything of importance turns up.

Yours, &c.,

G. W. K.

*Daily Picayune*, November 14, 1847

City of Mexico, October 21, 1847

They may say what they will about the climate of Mexico—its clear skies, delightful temperature, &c., &c.—but give me the regions of the lower Mississippi after all that has been said and sung. If one has the least tendency to complaints of a rheumatic nature, this climate, so dry and so closing to every pore, will be sure to bring them out. I say bring them out; but in this I am really all wrong. They all develop themselves hereaway with forty-horse power, but as for bringing or driving them out that is another matter. I have been a sufferer to an extent that has almost banished sleep for a fortnight, and were my right arm in the same fix as my left I should be compelled to hire an amanuensis, or one of the *escribientes*[26] with which the city abounds, to let you into the secrets. A dull, sluggish, but continual pain in the right knee and ankle it would seem would be sufficient, but as if this were not enough a nerve leading from the left elbow to the tip of the little finger, keeps up a running neuralgic accompaniment, so severe that to sleep is impossible. The thermometer at 100

26. Clerks or writers.

would be a luxury indeed, while any countless number of mosquitoes, with a climate to match, would be bearable and a positive relief. I should not mention my own individual case were it not that hundreds are afflicted in the same way. An officer told me yesterday that he would give two months' pay for the mere privilege of being permitted to help "wood" and "fire up" on a Mississippi steamer—the exercise and attendant opening of the pores he thought would be a relief to him.

The latest advice from Querétaro would make it appear that there are not enough members of Congress to form a quorum in attendance. There has been ample time for a sufficient number to assemble, but they do not come forward. Many of them evidently have no confidence in themselves nor in each other—no hope for their country—no thought of being able to restore her lost honor or even preserve her nationality—and hence they keep aloof. They see that no front can be opposed to the Americans, and hence do not care about being in at the death. Meanwhile, to make matters worse for poor Mexico, it is said that Santa Anna has promulgated another manifesto announcing his intention to hold on to the office of President in defiance of his recent renunciation, and in the same document he denies Peña y Peña the privilege of seating himself quietly in the executive chair—in plain terms, refuses to recognize him, and with the intention of reassuring himself the power of Chief Magistrate. Some even go so far as to say that Santa Anna has passed this city in the direction of Querétaro to assume his former station. I cannot credit all these reports, although there is no such thing as prophesying what such a man as this tyrant may do.

The most gratifying intelligence brought by the last arrivals from the United States, is that our Government is to reinforce this line of operations strongly, and prosecute the war with vigor. This is as it should be, and every true lover of his country should rejoice at the cheering intelligence. Quarter 15,000 men here in the capital, employ 10,000 more in keeping open the line to Vera Cruz, occupy Orizaba and other flank positions with 5,000 or whatever forces may be necessary, and you then put down the guerrilleros entirely—one great step towards bringing about a peace. The next step should be to have a force sufficient to march to Querétaro, Guanajuato and San Luis Potosí, and even to Guadalajara, giving the inhabitants a taste of the full vigors of war as practiced by other nations, and many will be much mistaken if a speedy settlement of difficulties is not brought about. I have said before, that the insignificance of our present force was a great drawback in the way of an amicable settlement. Who's there that does not know that if Gen. Scott had set down before the city of Mexico with 40,000 men—and the number would not have been deemed too large for the magnitude of the enterprise—who is there that does not know, I say, that with such a force there would hardly have been a gun fired, and that the enemy would have had a fair excuse before the world for listening in earnest to proposals of peace? But the smallness of our force was but an incentive to fresh exertions on the part of the Mexicans, and the complete victories achieved by that force have but added to the false pride of their leaders in so far as the matter of coming to amicable terms is concerned. Even the party in favor of peace before the capitulation of the city—for it is notorious that there was such a party—is now scattered and broken up. To be sure, no one proposes any scheme or offers any aid for carrying on the war; on the other hand, we hear of no one coming out and advocating peace. Cut off all the taxes; destroy all the public resources of revenue; shut up every avenue through which a dollar finds its way into the Mexican treasury; make the war felt, and seriously felt, by the rich; tell them that our objects are peace or a conquest, and prove to them our ability to achieve the latter, and we shall soon have a peace, or I am much mistaken. The world cannot say but that we have exercised the full measure of forbearance in our past efforts to bring about an amicable adjustment, and cannot blame us if in future we prosecute the war with the utmost rigor permitted by the laws of nations. But enough of this for the present.

The news that Santa Anna was defeated at Huamantla a few days since, and that he lost his cannon, is confirmed. Gen. Lane commanded, and it is too true that Capt. Walker, of the Rifles, lost his life in the attack.[27] I hear it rumored that Augustín Iturbide, son of the former Emperor, and who is well known in the United States, where he was educated, was taken prisoner on the occasion. They say that he has a captain's commission, and that he has been serving in Santa Anna's staff as aide.

One word about the Spanish company of El Nacional—the great Santa Anna theatre. They have produced a grand scenic drama, "The Tyrant of Astracan, or the Magician of Servan," and in a style we have never seen approached. It is full of tricks, magic, enchantment, processions, oriental dancing, sudden changes, blue fire, deviltry, and what not; the costumes are rich and most appropriate, and there is a clock-work nicety of arrangement in all the stage appointments and arrangements such as have rarely been equaled. The immense size of the establishment gives them ample

27. Samuel H. Walker was killed leading an advance party of Lane's command against Santa Anna's forces near Huamantla on October 9, 1847. The Mexican general had hoped to ambush the American army as it moved to support the garrison under siege at Puebla. After the Mexicans withdrew, Lane allowed his army to ransack the town.

scope for the production of spectacles of this description, and well has the empresario or manager improved every means at his hands. The cañete has won additional laurels and gained new admirers by her admirable personation of a character in this piece.

Yours, &c.,

G. W. K.

*Daily Picayune*, November 20, 1847

City of Mexico, October 21, 1847 [An extract.]

Our army here has to mourn the death of another distinguished and most meritorious officer—Capt. S. Mackenzie,[28] of the 2d Artillery. On the memorable 13th September it may be recollected that two storming parties, of 250 men each, were selected from the divisions of Gens. Worth and Twiggs. Capt. Casey commanded the latter, while Capt. Mackenzie gallantly led the former to the assault. Again, at the attack upon the San Cosmé *garita*, he headed his little band, and his brave and noble conduct was the theme of universal praise. Day before yesterday, while sitting up, he suddenly expired. His health had been feeble for some time. The excitement of battle buoyed him up with a strength unnatural; but when all was over and the victory won he gradually sunk, and death finally stepped in to cut off his career in the prime of life. His body rests quietly with the comrades who have gone before him, in the English cemetery of San Cosmé, and many friends mourn his early loss.

[G. W. K.]

*Daily Picayune*, November 7, 1847

City of Mexico, October 22, 1847

Affairs do not seem to go on altogether as smoothly as they might in Querétaro. Señor Don José Guadalupe Perdigón Garay,[29] member of the Congress, colonel of the battalion of Lagos and brigadier general by brevet—if I have omitted any of his titles, I beg his pardon—has come out with a document denying that Peña y Peña is entitled to his seat as President. He contends, in the first place, that by some omission on the part of the sovereign constituent Congress he is not legally the Chief Justice of the Supreme Court of the Republic, and hence has no constitutional right to the Presidency; and secondly, he argues that from his lack of energy and character he is positively disqualified from holding the office of Chief Magistrate in the present sorrowful and troublous state of the country. As a political writer, Garay has

28. Samuel Mackenzie.
29. Perdigón Garay was among the leaders of the *puros* in the Mexican Congress.

some standing—as a military man he is beneath all contempt. He commanded at San Antonio on the memorable 20th of August, and was captured in his attempt to escape by the division of Gen. Worth. Report has it that his aide-de-camp, finding that the tide of battle was going against them, stole his general's horse and made good his own escape, a story entitled to some credit inasmuch as the illustrious commander of the valiant Lagos battalion was caught running for dear life, and a sorry figure he cut in his flight, for he is of a Falstaffian size—fat, greasy, and most filthy withal, a mountain of ungainly flesh unused to any such luxuries as a bath, while his habiliments had long been strangers to the wash tub. When finally caught he feigned sickness, and for the time some grains of pity were bestowed upon him. A few days afterwards, when the English friends of peace were mustering all the members of Congress they could lay their hands upon, Perdigón Garay was released, unconditionally I believe, although it was at the time understood that no honorable man would again take up arms. The history of the armistice, and the futile attempt at making peace, are old stories, but the after part taken by Garay may not be so generally understood. At the Belén gate, while Gen. Terrés was manfully battling with Gen. Quitman, he commanded the reserve, and his prudence entirely overcoming his valor he withdrew his command at double quick time, himself leading the retreat and long before the strife of the contest had reached him. When he was first released, it was shrewdly remarked by Gen. Worth that if he could do no good in a civil capacity he at least could do no harm in a military—that even in case he again took up arms he would be sure to start the first in the retreat and take others along with him—and the sequel proves that he was correct. What influence he may now have remains to be seen, but he has certainly made out a pretty strong case against the legal claims of Peña y Peña to the presidential chair—he admits that he is the eldest judge of the Supreme Court, but contends that some important form has been neglected in the premises.

By letters received from Guadalajara, we learn that the earthquake of the 2d inst. was severely felt in that vicinity. The town of Ocotlan was almost entirely destroyed, and Cojima also suffered great damage. A letter sent to the bishop of Guadalajara, written by the curate of one of the villages, says that while some two thousand persons had gathered about the ruins they looked up and beheld the crucified Savior in a cloud, his image remaining plainly visible for full half an hour, and that during that time the awe stricken fell upon their knees and worshipped. Such is one of the nonsensical impositions palmed off upon the superstitious and benighted inhabitants of this unfortunate land.

Torres, the proprietor of *El Monitor Republicano*, has got himself into a scrape from which he will hardly escape without a severe threshing. Pursuing his meddling propensities, he a day or two since came out with a short article, in the Polyanthus style, something like the following:

> A certain young Mexican lady, of a frolicsome disposition and romantic inclinations—a good singer, and who, since the arrival of the Americans at San Angel, has become *familiar* with an officer of that army, will soon be annexed, like Texas, and passed over to American dominion. The censure of the fair sex among her own people has fallen heavily upon her.

This is nothing more than a sneaking and most contemptible fling at a highly respectable and most talented young lady, the daughter of a Mexican officer—against whom there is not the least breath of suspicion. The object of Torres is, to prevent all intercourse between the first families of the city and our officers, and for his pains he will get most severely punished.

It is now certain that a train is to be sent down to Vera Cruz in the course of the coming week, and it is also certain that Gen. Shields, and many other wounded and disabled officers, besides Major Gaines and party, will accompany it on their way home. Many of the "outsiders," who have been with the army all summer unable to get away, are in perfect ecstacies at the idea of once more revisiting the United States, and, what is more, you will not catch them back here in any hurry.

Yours, &c.,

G. W. K.
*Daily Picayune*, November 20, 1847

City of Mexico, October 24, 1847

As everyone anticipated, and as he most richly deserved, Torres yesterday received a terrible cowhiding at the hands of one of our officers, and this, too, in the Plateros, the Broadway of Mexico. He skulked and hid for a day or two, but was finally caught by Lieut. Brooks,[30] one of the aides of Gen. Twiggs, and handled as aforesaid. Lieut. B. was acquainted with the young lady insulted, and has thus dealt summary and most just punishment upon the traducer. Torres is said to have been most instrumental in getting up the cowardly wagon row, and there are some who think that he may now endeavor to inflame the *léperos* to acts of violence in revenge for his own personal injuries. He has used every means, the

30. William T. H. Brooks.

most insidious, to prevent the Mexican ladies from visiting the theatres and other places of public amusement. Hereafter he may busy himself as he has done heretofore, but he will work secretly and covertly, not openly and aboveboard.

Santa Anna has taken another farewell of the Mexican army and nation. The document is dated on the 16th inst. at Huamantla, and is the same story over and over. Inconsistency does not affect one's political standing in the least in this country, and therefore Santa Anna can resign and reassume power with every revolution of the sun and not a whit does he lose by it in the estimation of his people. In our country there is no *credit* in being consistent, honest and virtuous—here in Mexico there is no *discredit* in lacking all these essentials to honorable advancement, else how could a large portion of her ruling men retain place and power as they do. Santa Anna has some scheme in his head, all for his own advancement, which he will divulge only when everything is matured. His friends are busy at work at Querétaro without doubt—secretly yet industriously—and it certainly would not be strange if ere another month is over we should find him at the new seat of government vested with all his former power. Peña y Peña is in no way qualified as a leader in the present crisis of the country— Santa Anna, with all his faults, is still the best man they have. There is a rumor afloat—a mere rumor—to the effect that some of the leading men, both in this and other principal cities, are determined to take hold of the peace question in earnest with the determination of carrying it through. If there happens to be the least truth in this report, it may be put down as more than probable that the news of heavy reinforcements on the way, combined with the fate which has already befallen Puebla, have opened the eyes of the nation to the absolute necessity of coming to terms at once.

Yours, &c.,

G. W. K.
*Daily Picayune*, November 20, 1847

City of Mexico, October 27, 1847

Through the Mexican papers we learn that a portion of the force recently under Santa Anna in the neighborhood of Puebla has reached Tula, on the way to Querétaro. The whole line of march of this force has been one of robbery and rapine. The soldiers have literally stolen everything they coveted in the smaller towns and haciendas, the unfortunate inhabitants dreading their approach far more than they would the advance of a division of the very Yankees they have decried so much. One great reason why the Mexican army is kept together at all is the fact that singly the soldiers know they must starve, whilst in a body they can rob their own countrymen of at least enough to satisfy the cravings of hunger. Never was there a nation so utterly bankrupt, in money, means and credit, as is this miserable Mexico, and still many of her citizens vapor and fume as though they were of a country as rich in all resources as the fabled lands of antiquity, yet it is doubtful at this very time whether there is money enough in the treasury at Querétaro to pay the doorkeeper his last week's salary. Gen. Quitman had hardly taken possession of the National Palace here before he was beset by crowds of upholsterers, furniture dealers, and other artisans, with requests for permission to remove the different articles with which the apartments were furnished. They proved incontestably that they had received no pay for them. It seems that Santa Anna and his officers, so certain were they of defending the city and defeating the Americans, set to work refurnishing the palace in most gorgeous style in the early part of July, anticipating the pleasure of celebrating their new victories and also their national independence all on the same day—the 16th of September, their Fourth of July.[31] On that day our own people were in full possession, as conquerors, of the Halls of Montezumas, and all the hopes of a proud but weak and cowardly enemy were dashed to the ground. Still they will not talk of peace, but go on vaunting of what they are to do the same as ever. There is not a man among them who has got the courage or the character to come out for peace, or to collect and head an army for the national defence.

Yours, &c.,

G. W. K.

*Daily Picayune*, November 20, 1847

City of Mexico, October 27, 1847

There is now more probability that a quorum of Congress will soon assemble at Querétaro, although there is no certainty of it. The city is overrun with candidates for different offices, but more especially for President. The principal candidates of the Moderados are Pedraza,[32] Peña y Peña, Anaya and Herrera, the latter probably standing the best chance of being elected. The Puros talk of Almonte and Cumplido.[33] Why anyone should

---

31. September 16, 1810, marked the beginning of Miguel Hidalgo's revolt against Spanish authority.

32. Manuel Gómez Pedraza.

33. A quorum was not in place until November 2. The *moderados* settled on Anaya as their presidential candidate, and he prevailed in balloting held on November 11. Juan Cumplido was the leading *puro* candidate. Almonte sought *puro* support, too, but his well-known hatred of Santa Anna made it impossible for him to attract the *santanista* element within the *puros*.

covet the office at this present time is singular enough, unless the successful man hopes to realize something from the stealings of place—rather poor picking one would think.

A duel was fought this afternoon between Capt. Porter of the Rifles, and Capt. Archer of the Voltigeurs[34]—the weapons pistols. On the first fire the pistol of Capt. A. missed, when the other party threw away his ball into the ground. On the second fire, Capt. A. did not discharge his pistol at all, but received the ball of his adversary in the abdomen—a severe but I am told not a dangerous wound. The cause of the difficulty grew out of some remarks made by Capt. Porter in relation to the Pillow controversy, the Voltigeur officer espousing in some way the course of his superior.[35]

The weather is damp, dreary and most disagreeable, a heavy norther probably blowing at Vera Cruz, while the roads between this and the Peñon are in a condition so bad that the departure of the train has been postponed for a few days—probably until the first of the coming month.

Gen. Quitman is going home with the train—as is said to take command of Gen. Taylor's division of the army. Gen. P. F. Smith has been appointed military and civil Governor of Mexico in his stead and was duly installed this afternoon. The ceremonies at the Palace on the occasion were neat and most impressive. I am told they are to be published in the *American Star*, in which case I will send you on a copy. Gen. Quitman leaves this line of operations with the best wishes of the entire army, his gallant conduct in the field and gentlemanly deportment in private life having endeared

---

34. Andrew Porter and James J. Archer.

35. Gideon Pillow and William Worth had conspired in the last weeks of the Mexico City campaign to discredit Winfield Scott. James Duncan was also involved. Pillow's motives reflected his own inflated political and military ambitions; Worth, on the other hand, had grown increasingly disillusioned with Scott since being denied the opportunity to lead the army out of Vera Cruz. Duncan felt underappreciated for his role in the maneuvering before Mexico City. After the battle of Contreras and Chapultepec, Pillow and Worth wrote reports that discredited the general-in-chief. Scott's request that Pillow's account of the battle be corrected generated further insulting correspondence. About the same time, Pillow wrote a letter, over the signature "Leonidas," extolling his own accomplishments and belittling Scott. The letter found its way into the New Orleans *Delta* on September 10, 1847. Scott responded with a general order republishing President Polk's prohibition against the publication of private accounts describing military operations. Worth, Duncan, and Pillow were later formally charged with insubordination. In the midst of this controversy, charges surfaced that Scott and Trist had bribed Santa Anna in an effort to end hostilities. The turmoil in the army's command gave Polk the opportunity he needed to relieve Scott. The general left his command on February 19, 1848. He remained in Mexico to participate in the court of inquiry that investigated the charges of insubordination and bribery. The court concluded that Scott's operations had not been influenced by bribery; it also cleared Pillow of having written the "Leonidas" letter but upheld the charges of insubordination. The charges against Worth were later dropped, as were the charges of unprofessional behavior that the two generals had leveled against Scott.

him to all. The appointment of Gen. Smith to the office of Governor is one of the most popular that could have been.

Among the list of wounded officers at the battle of Molino del Rey, did I mention Capt. Glenn[36] and Lieut. Davis of our city? I know that I alluded to Lieut. Shields, but think that I may have omitted the others. They were slightly wounded, it is true, and were able to take a part in the after combats at Chapultepec and the Garitas.

According to *El Monitor*, Peña y Peña has appointed Gen. Mora y Villamil as Minister of War—the best choice he could have made without doubt. The editor says that this officer is warm in favor of peace, but this remains to be seen.

The latest accounts we have of Santa Anna—or one of the latest accounts—he had gone to Tehuacan with a small escort only, as is said in obedience to an order from the Supreme Government. Others say that he has gone to Oajaca; others, again, toward Tuspan. Wherever he may be he is up to some scheme or other for his own good.

Another gallant and most deserving officer—Lieut. C. B. Daniels, of the 2d Artillery—has died of the wound he received at El Molino. Not an officer in the army had more friends than Lieut. D.—not an officer more richly merited general esteem.

The diligencias are running regularly between this place and both Querétaro and Cuernavaca—the latter city in the direction of Acapulco. The passengers are always robbed, going and coming. The editor of one of the Mexican papers says that there is an entire brigade and *thirteen generals* at Cuernavaca, and still the stage is robbed daily within plain sight of them.

You shall hear from me again before the train starts.

Yours truly,

G. W. K.

*Daily Picayune*, November 7, 1847

City of Mexico, October 29, 1847

An important rumor is in circulation—at least one that would be important in any country where rumors do not so much abound as in this—to the following effect. It is stated that there are letters in town, directed to influential Mexicans, communicating as a fact that at a meeting of the leading men of the country at Querétaro, it has been determined upon to move every element to raise four grand divisions, and all the necessary munitions, for the purpose of attacking and wresting this city from the Americans, the

---

36. Thomas Glenn, First Regiment Smith's Brigade. Davis is not identifiable.

leaders looking for great assistance within the walls for the successful carrying out of the plan. One of the divisions is to be commanded by Anaya, another by Herrera, the third by Filisola, and the last by Almonte—Gen. Bustamente to be commander-in-chief. There may be something in this, at least the leading men of the country may have some grand project of the kind on foot. It is known that there are many Mexican officers of rank hid away here in the capital, and that they hold nightly meetings in some secret place; more than this, it is highly probable that their deliberations may have some connection with a grand project similar to that mentioned above; but whether it will be carried out is another matter. We have no evidence in the past history of the Mexicans—at least in the history of the past ten years—that as a nation they will step forward as one man, and freely risk life, property, *all,* for the good standing and defence of the common country, and unless this is done nothing can be effected. Heretofore all has been as it were *talk,* mere idle *talk*—self-sacrifice, a giving up of everything, *action* is wanting—and are the Mexicans equal to this? An officer in their army will spend his money freely enough in the procuring gold lace for his coat, and in furnishing his outward man with gaudy trappings until he is bedizened from head to foot; but we have few instances where they have forborne the show for the substance of man—where they have given up the ornamental tinsel for the useful powder and ball and other appliances of real combat. The innumerable clergy should give up all their temporal goods, but *will* they? The rich proprietors should at once throw their plentiful substance into the common purse; yet will *they* do this? The past tells us that they will not. They want confidence in themselves and in one another—some man must rise among them on whom all can unite—all must flock to his standard without money and without price; and then they can at least command the respect of the world in their misfortune if they do not come out of the combat victorious. That the present leading men, as I have already said, may have some project for uniting another grand army is probable, that they have some scheme on foot to retake the capital is reasonable enough to suppose; but that all will put their shoulders to the wheel and work like true men is more than can be anticipated of the degenerate race. Men may be raised and means procured for the enterprise; but the former will be rendered ineffective by the wranglings, the petty jealousies, and the inexperience and cowardice of their officers, while the money will be squandered in corruption and idle shows instead of for the real interest and well-being of the army and country. But all speculation in this matter may be deemed futile. A Mexican future in many respects is the darkest of all, and he who can look into and fathom it must read other stars than those that now shine in her firmament.

The weather continues cold and cheerless, and up to this morning I believe that no time has been set for the departure of the train. To move many of the disabled and infirm officers at this time from their warm rooms, and expose them to the cold and discomforts of camp, would doubtless endanger their lives, and this is one cause for the delay. There is also a story in circulation that the Mexicans have no inconsiderable force at Rio Frio—some even put it down at 7000—ready to attack, and destroy our wagons on the march. There may be something in this story, although it needs confirmation.

G. W. K.<br>
*Daily Picayune*, November 20, 1847

City of Mexico, October 29, 1847

The "Leonidas" letter continues to be the subject of remark and speculation. Gen. Pillow has denied all knowledge of the letter or its author, and says distinctly that he had no hand in the precious document, but at the same time he does not provoke inquiry into the matter. If it could be brought before a court you would read some rich testimony—testimony which would prove that the substance of the letter, personal encounter and all, was the common talk at Mixcoac three weeks or a month before it returned to this place in print. As it is, I am much mistaken if you do not ere long read letters in some of our journals at home that will cause a sensation and open the eyes of the people to their utmost width.[37]

Let me ask one or two questions. How is it that Gens. Quitman, Shields and Smith, all appointed about the same time with Gen. Pillow, get along smoothly, to use a homely phrase, whilst he, Pillow, is eternally involving himself in difficulties? How is it that the first mentioned officers are popular with the entire army and country, and that their conduct has been made the subject of public and general approval, whilst the reputation of the latter is but equivocal even among his best friends, and he has lost all cast with nine-tenths of the army if not the country? How is it that Gens. Pierce and Cadwalader have won the good opinions of all, whilst the great Gen. Pillow has made himself as it were the laughing-stock of the army? I repeat, why is all this? It is because the latter has the vanity to believe himself a great and most astounding military genius and the impudence to

---

37. Pillow seems to have slipped the "Leonidas" letter into James Freaner's mail packet after the correspondent had rejected a similar letter as inaccurate. The editors at the *Delta* printed the letter assuming that it had been endorsed by their correspondent.

trumpet his own exploits; it is because he has a grasping ambition and a dishonest one—an ambition which diligently seeketh to build a reputation for himself, even at the expense of others; it is because he has had the effrontery, time and again, to pester not only his own officers but editors with stories of his prowess, and with bold requests that they might assist in spreading his deeds before the world; in short, it is because he has a restless and feverish desire and craving after all the honors of a campaign which has shed such lustre upon our arms, with the insufferable weakness to believe that he is deserving of them. I must acknowledge that for one I thought that the man was used a little harshly for his conduct in the Cerro Gordo business, but his antics here in the face of the army have done away with all favorable and mitigating impressions. I will now close by repeating that you will see letters in some of our papers at home, or I am much mistaken, which will expose the whole matter in a way that will astonish all.

In my hurried letters I have given you all the various and contradictory Mexican rumors afloat—not that I believe them, but to let you know, as the saying is, what was going on. Whatever a few rational and sensible minds among the Mexicans may wish, I do not believe that the mass desire peace—many would even prefer that we should hold the entire country, and perhaps to this complexion it must come at last. But to be prepared for everything, men should be sent forward without stint. Enough has already been performed by forlorn hopes[38]—we now want soldiers in sufficient numbers to overrun, conquer and *hold* the entire country, at least if the Mexican leaders will not listen to the voice of reason. The plan which obtains with some, of falling back upon a boundary and sustaining it by a military force, will never do. The work of conquest, if conquest it is to be, is now almost done—50,000 men will settle the business in six months' time, and if our troops are withdrawn from this line all the work will have to be done over again.

I close this letter in great haste, as the courier is on the point of starting. Yours, &c.,

G. W. K.
*Daily Picayune*, November 7, 1847

---

38. "Forlorn hope" was the nickname for the storming parties used in numerous assaults during the Mexican War.

# INDEX